CONSUMER BEHAVIOUR IN AUSTRALIA & NEW ZEALAND

CONSUMER BEHAVIOUR IN AUSTRALIA & NEW ZEALAND

Robert Lawson
University of Otago

Paula Tidwell
University of Southern Queensland

Paul Rainbird
Central Queensland University

David Loudon
Northeast Louisiana University

Albert Della Bitta
University of Rhode Island

The McGraw-Hill Companies, Inc.

Sydney New York San Francisco Auckland Bogotá
Caracas Lisbon London Madrid Mexico City
Milan New Delhi San Juan Singapore
Toronto Kuala Lumpur

McGraw·Hill Australia

A Division of The McGraw·Hill Companies

Reprinted 1996, 1997

Text and design © 1996 McGraw-Hill Book Company Australia Pty Limited

Published by arrangement with McGraw-Hill, Inc.

National Library of Australia Cataloguing-in-Publication data:
Loudon, David L.
Consumer behaviour in Australia and New Zealand.

Includes index.
ISBN 0 07 470259 9.

1. Consumer behaviour—Australia. 2. Consumer behaviour—New Zealand. 3. Consumer behaviour—Australia—Case studies. 4. Consumer behaviour—New Zealand—Case studies. I. Tidwell, Paula. II. Lawson, Rob (Robert) III. Loudon, David L. Consumer behaviour. IV. Title. V. Title: Consumer behaviour.

658.8342

Published in Australia by
McGraw Hill Book Company Australia Pty Limited
4 Barcoo Street, Roseville NSW 2069, Australia
Typeset in Australia by Post Typesetters, Brisbane
Printed in Singapore by Kyodo Printing Company Pty Ltd

Acquisitions Editor: Jae Chung
Production Editors: Elizabeth Neate and Caroline Hunter
Designer: Pamela Horsnell
Permissions Editors: Natalie Muir and Judy Greer

PUBLISHER'S NOTE
At the time of his death, Paul Rainbird had not fully referenced Chapters 8, 13 and 14. An attempt has been made to finish this work. However, some references still remain incomplete.

CONTENTS

PREFACE

AS WITH PREVIOUS US editions of this book, it is intended that the book is appropriate for a first course in consumer behaviour, either at an undergraduate or graduate level.

No special assumptions have been made regarding student preparation, although it is assumed that most students will be following other marketing courses. Familiarity with basic terms from an introductory paper in marketing will also help in following some examples and case studies. Although some students may be familiar with some of the behavioural concepts discussed, all students can benefit from a review and an examination of applications from a managerial perspective.

We are pleased to have had the opportunity to be involved with the preparation of this Australasian edition because the philosophy and approach of the previous US editions set high standards and good guidelines. We have made every effort to produce a highly readable book that does not shirk from tackling this complex area at an appropriate conceptual level while including lots of illustrations and examples to make the subject relevant for all students. For example, students following a more theoretical program should be able to develop discussion around the conceptual material and also follow up the many references that are included to support all the chapters. Other students, perhaps studying a graduate MBA program, will want to focus on the applications, so the instructor can develop the examples in the book and pursue the discussion questions included with each chapter.

The book is arranged in five major sections, working generally from a macro to a micro perspective. This sequence provides for the logical development of an understanding of consumer behaviour since dealing with the broad cultural issues first allows the development of the schema required for the full understanding of the psychological elements of consumer behaviour.

Part 1 comprises the first two chapters. The reader is introduced to the discipline of consumer behaviour by defining and describing its scope and importance, discussing the market function and providing numerous examples of consumer behaviour relevance in the managerial decision making. Chapter 2 builds on this introductory framework by developing consumer behaviour applications to marketing activities like segmentation and positioning. Chapter 2 also provides a review of major demographic changes in Australia and New Zealand which are provided as foundation knowledge.

Part 2 examines socio-cultural influences on consumer behaviour and presents them in a hierarchical order ranging from the broadest to the most immediate. The roles of culture, social class, social groups, the family and interpersonal influences are examined.

Part 3 considers individual determinants of consumer behaviour. These are internal variables that influence the way a consumer proceeds with the different stages of the decision process. Successive chapters consider the topics of personality and self-concept, motivation and involvement, information processing, learning and memory, and attitudes.

Part 4 considers the consumer decision process arranged over four chapters—problem recognition, search and evaluation, purchasing processes, and postpurchase activity. Placed at this stage in the book, study of the decision process helps to integrate all the different influences considered in Parts 2 and 3.

Part 5 looks at three additional dimensions to consumer behaviour. Chapter 17 reviews some of the models of consumer behaviour and ways of researching the behaviour of consumers in the market place. The subject of consumerism is considered in Chapter 18, including a review of some of the most important aspects of consumer protection in Australia and New Zealand. The final chapter considers the buying behaviour of organisations as a special topic and highlights the similarities and differences between organisations and consumers.

Instructors may prefer to use the material in a different order and the book is flexible enough to allow many different approaches. For example, one popular approach to teaching consumer behaviour considers individual before socio-cultural determinants. The chapters are cross referenced so that the instructor will find that it is an easy matter to reverse Parts 2 and 3 of the book if this approach is preferred. Another method considers the consumer decision-making process at an early stage of the course and then develops the roles of the influencing variables. In this case, the instructor may bring Part 4 forward to an early stage of study.

The text is accompanied by a range of support materials including an instructor's manual, providing hints for teaching as well as guidance on discussion questions included in the book. McGraw-Hill representatives will be able to provide information on all supplementary materials.

We are indebted to a large team of people who have helped with the preparation of this Australasian edition. Grateful thanks go to the original American authors, David Loudon and Albert Della Bitta for their support for the venture. Hume Winzar, Murdoch University, provided many helpful suggestions and particularly contributed to the development of Chapter 2. Anne Crossman, Otago University, advised on the legal aspects of Chapter 18 and Lisa McCullough and Emma Woodward, Otago University, provided a great deal of help with illustrations and figures.

Also, we would like to express our appreciation for the helpful comments from the following reviewers: Mammy Helou, University of Western Sydney; Ian Walker, Monash University; Beth Goodwin, Waikato University; and Charles Lamb, Lincoln University.

A particular debt is due to Jae Chung, our acquisitions editor at McGraw-Hill. Jae was simply magnificent in her support and her ability to be able to organise us. The final vote of thanks goes to our respective families for their support, patience and understanding for the many times a work like this intrudes upon their activities. Our one regret is that Paul did not live to be able to write this preface with us. His shocking and untimely death just as the book was about to go to production was a very sad event. With his death, Australian marketing education lost a very important contributor and a person of absolute integrity. This book is dedicated to his memory.

Robert Lawson
Paula Tidwell

PART **1**

STUDYING CONSUMER BEHAVIOUR

CHAPTER 1

INTRODUCTION

LEARNING OBJECTIVES

AFTER STUDYING THIS CHAPTER YOU SHOULD UNDERSTAND:

➡ what is meant by the terms 'ultimate consumer', 'industrial buyer', 'customer', and 'consumer behaviour'.

➡ how knowledge of consumer behaviour can be useful to marketing managers, administrators of not-for-profit and social organisations, and those involved in consumer protection or educational activities.

➡ that consumer behaviour is subtle, complex and often unobservable in nature.

➡ some of the physical and mental activities that consumers engage in before, during and after making purchases.

This book deals with the fascinating subject of the behaviour of consumers. Many who have seriously studied consumers find their behaviour to be intricate, difficult to influence and often mystifying. This is probably what motivates so many to learn more about the topic.

Consumer behaviour is an exciting field, but for two reasons it is also one that requires serious study. First, the behaviour of consumers can be quite subtle in nature, making it difficult to understand fully. Secondly, because consumer behaviour is so prevalent, it significantly affects all aspects of our lives through either our own actions or the actions of other consumers. Therefore, it has a great deal of practical relevance to our daily lives.

To help you to better appreciate the nature and scope of consumer behaviour, the remaining sections of this chapter focus on four very basic issues:

1. defining the nature of consumer behaviour;

2. appreciating why we should study consumer behaviour;

3. developing a framework for studying consumer behaviour;

4. applying consumer-behaviour knowledge.

This material will provide a basis on which we can build in subsequent chapters.

DEFINING CONSUMER BEHAVIOUR

Before continuing, it is appropriate to offer a definition in order to clarify the focus of our study. Consumer behaviour may be defined as:

> . . . *the decision process and physical activity individuals engage in when evaluating, acquiring, using or disposing of goods and services.*

Several aspects of consumer behaviour need emphasis and elaboration so that their meanings can be more fully appreciated.

Customers and consumers

The term 'customer' is typically used to refer to someone who regularly purchases from a particular store or company. Thus, a person who shops at Woolworths or who uses Caltex petrol is viewed as a customer of these firms. The term 'consumer' more generally refers to anyone engaging in any of the activities used in our definition of consumer behaviour. Therefore, a customer is defined in terms of a specific firm while a consumer is not.

The traditional viewpoint has been to define consumers strictly in terms of *economic* goods and services. This position holds that consumers are potential *purchasers* of products and services offered for sale. This view has been broadened over time so that at least some scholars now do not consider a monetary exchange essential to the definition of consumers. This change implies that potential adopters of free services or even philosophies or ideas can also be encompassed by the definition. Consequently, organisations such as Auckland WaterCare Services, Save the Children and the Family Planning Association, as well as religious and political groups, can view their various publics as 'consumers'. The rationale for this position is that many of the activities that people engage in regarding free services, ideas and philosophies are quite similar to those they engage in regarding commercial products and services. Later sections of this and other chapters will expand on this idea.

Quality, from source to tap.

Water quality testing on Lower Huia Reservoir.
Auckland

From our bushland catchments, through our extensive

reticulation network, we meticulously monitor and

control Auckland's water supply.

Aucklanders can be sure that their water consistently

meets New Zealand's drinking water standards as our

scientists carry out over 56,000 analyses every year.

We, in partnership with our local councils, are

committed to providing quality, service and value to

our customers.

water Care
services limited

Auckland WaterCare advertisement promoting quality control of water to the New Zealand public
COURTESY OF WATERCARE NEW ZEALAND

The ultimate consumer

Our primary attention will be directed toward *ultimate consumers*—individuals who purchase for the purpose of individual or household consumption. Some have argued that studying ultimate consumers also reveals much about industrial and intermediate buyers and others involved in purchasing for business firms and institutions.[1] While not denying this, we must recognise that much industrial purchasing behaviour is unique because it often involves different buying motives and the influence of a large variety of people.[2] Organisational-buyer behaviour is covered in the final chapter but, for the sake of simplicity, all the preceding chapters will focus only on ultimate consumer behaviour and will not become involved in drawing comparisons with industrial purchasing situations.

The individual buyer

The most commonly thought of consumer situation is that of an individual making a purchase with little or no influence from others. However, a number of people can be jointly involved in a purchase decision. For example, planning a vacation or deciding on a new car can involve an entire family, or the purchaser may be acquiring a product for someone else who has asked for a certain item. These situations suggest that people can take on different roles in what we have defined as consumer behaviour. Table 1.1 presents one way of classifying these roles.

Some purchase situations involve at least one person in each of these roles, while in other circumstances a single individual can take on several roles at the same time. For example, a wife (initiator and influencer) may ask her husband (buyer) to pick up a box of Weet-Bix cereal on his shopping trip because their child (user) said she wanted it. At another time the husband could act as the initiator, buyer and user by purchasing a fitness club membership for himself.

Any study of consumer behaviour would be incomplete if it treated only one consumer role. However, emphasising one role, while still devoting adequate treatment to the others, can simplify our study in many cases. When it becomes useful to consider only one role, we will tend to choose the *buyer*—the individual who actually makes the purchase. This approach is useful because even when told what to purchase, the buyer often makes decisions regarding purchase timing, store choice, package size and other factors. Therefore, focusing on the buyer, but allowing for the influence of others on the purchase decision, still gives considerable flexibility while concentrating on one consumer role.

TABLE 1.1 Some consumer behaviour roles

Role	Description
Initiator	The individual who determines that some need or want is not being met and authorises a purchase to rectify the situation
Influencer	A person who by some intentional or unintentional word or action influences the purchase decision, the actual purchase, and/or the use of the product or service
Buyer	The individual who actually makes the purchase transaction
User	The person most directly involved in the consumption or use of the purchase

Source: Gerald Zaltman & Philip C. Burger, *Marketing Research: Fundamentals and Dynamics*, 1975, p. 142. Adapted with permission of the authors.

The decision process

The way in which our definition characterises behaviour also deserves special attention. That is, consumer behaviour is seen to involve a *mental decision process* as well as *physical activity*. The act of purchase is just one stage in a series of mental and physical activities that occur during a period of time. Some of these activities precede the actual buying, while others follow it. However, as all are capable of influencing the adoption of products or services, they will be considered as part of the behaviour in which we are interested.

An example will illustrate the benefits of this viewpoint. Suppose a photographer who regularly purchases one brand of film suddenly switches to a competing brand even though there has been no change in either the films or their prices. What has caused this shift in loyalty? Just noting that the individual's purchase behaviour has changed does little to help our understanding of the situation. Perhaps the competing film received a strong recommendation by a friend, or possibly the photographer switched because of a belief that the competing brand best captures the colours of some subject matter of interest. On the other hand, the decision may have been generated by general dissatisfaction with results from the regular film or by recent exposure to an advertisement for the competing brand.

This example suggests the complexity of decision processes and demonstrates the limitations of viewing consumer behaviour as just the act of purchasing. Therefore, to understand consumers adequately, we should stress that, in addition to physical activities, their purchasing behaviour involves a mental decision process that takes place over time. This time period can be very short, or it can be quite long—for example, making a decision regarding which university to attend or where to go on a major overseas vacation may take a year or more.

A subset of human behaviour

Viewing consumer behaviour in such a broad context suggests it is a subset of human behaviour. In other words, factors affecting individuals in their daily lives also influence their purchase activities. Internal influences, such as learning and motives, as well as external factors, such as social expectations and constraints, affect us in our role as consumers as well as in our other capacities. In fact, because most consumer behaviour is instrumental to performing other behaviours, it is often difficult to draw a distinct line between consumer-related behaviour and other aspects of human behaviour. To illustrate, a casual conversation with your neighbours on lawn care may quickly lead to discussion of the merits of Masport versus Flymo cutters, because their relative performances may be critical to how good your lawn looks.

The fact that consumer behaviour is a subset of human behaviour is to our advantage. Several disciplines collectively referred to as the *behavioural sciences* have studied human behaviour for some time, and we can draw upon their contributions for understanding consumer behaviour. This borrowing has been quite extensive and includes theories used in explaining behaviour as well as methods useful in investigating it. In fact, this borrowing is so extensive that consumer behaviour is often said to be *multidisciplinary* in nature. The behavioural science disciplines that have most contributed to our understanding of consumers are:

1. *Psychology*. Study of the behaviour and mental processes of individuals.

2. *Sociology*. Study of the collective behaviour of people in groups.

3. *Social psychology*. Study of how individuals influence and are influenced by groups.

4. *Economics*. Study of people's production, exchange and consumption of goods and services.

5. *Anthropology*. Study of people in relation to their culture.

WHY STUDY CONSUMER BEHAVIOUR?

Understanding the reasons for studying a discipline enables a better appreciation of its contributions; therefore, this section presents a justification for the time and effort that the reader will expend in learning about consumers.

Significance in daily lives

In a general sense, the most important reason for studying consumer behaviour is the significant role it plays in our lives. Much of our time is spent directly in the marketplace, shopping or engaging in other activities. A large amount of additional time is spent thinking about products and services, talking to friends about them, and seeing or hearing advertisements about them. In addition, the goods we purchase and the manner in which we use them significantly influence how we live our daily lives. These general concerns alone are enough to justify our study. However, many seek to understand the behaviour of consumers for what are thought to be more immediate and tangible reasons.

Application to decision making

Consumers are often studied because certain decisions are significantly affected by their behaviour or expected actions. For this reason, consumer behaviour is said to be an *applied discipline*. Such applications can exist at two different levels of analysis:

1. The *micro* perspective seeks application of this knowledge to problems faced by the individual firm or organisation.

2. The *societal* perspective applies knowledge of consumers to aggregate-level problems faced by large groups or by society as a whole.

MICRO PERSPECTIVE

The micro perspective involves understanding consumers for the purpose of helping a firm or organisation accomplish its objectives. Advertising managers, product designers and many others in profit-oriented businesses are interested in understanding consumers in order to be more effective at their tasks. In addition, managers of various non-profit organisations have benefited from the same knowledge. For example, the New Zealand Department of Conservation have been effective in applying an understanding of consumer behaviour concepts to their activities, including the use by tourists and trampers of their facilities and New Zealand's natural resources.[3]

SOCIETAL PERSPECTIVE

On the macro, or aggregate, level we know that consumers collectively influence economic and social conditions within an entire society. In market systems based on individual choice, consumers strongly influence what will be produced, for whom it will be produced and what resources will be used to produce it. Consequently, the collective behaviour of consumers has a significant influence on the quality and level of our standard of living.[3]

Consider the overall impact of Australian consumers' strong desire for private cars for transportation. Vast amounts of resources have been earmarked to produce cars, highway systems and petroleum products used in their operation. It has also strongly influenced where many of us live (e.g. the development of sprawling suburbs around our major cities) and how we run our daily lives (e.g. what we eat, where we shop, and how we are entertained). Furthermore, this collective desire not only has led to the development of a strong transportation network but also has significantly contributed to our pollution problems, energy needs and international relations. (Many business and trade links with countries such as Japan and Korea hinge around the motor vehicle industry.) At another level our expectations regarding mobility in Australia and New Zealand, coupled with dispersed populations over wide geographic areas, have led to the development of internal aviation networks that are unparalleled in the world in relation to the population bases of the two countries.

As this illustrates, understanding consumer behaviour from a macro perspective can provide insight into aggregate economic and social trends and perhaps even predict such trends. In addition, this understanding may suggest ways to increase the efficiency of the market system and improve the well-being of people in society.

APPLYING CONSUMER BEHAVIOUR KNOWLEDGE

The following selections have been made from a variety of practical applications in the field of consumer behaviour. Some involve a societal perspective while others illustrate a micro viewpoint. Together they underscore the importance of understanding consumers in order to solve a variety of contemporary problems.

Consumer behaviour and marketing management

Effective business managers realise the importance of marketing to the success of their firm. *Marketing* may be defined as:

> . . . *the process of planning and executing the conception, pricing, promotion and distribution of ideas, goods and services to create exchanges that satisfy individual and organisational objectives.*[4]

Notice that the definition encompasses services and ideas as well as products. A sound understanding of consumer behaviour is essential to the long-term success of any marketing program. In fact, it is seen as a cornerstone of the *marketing concept*, an important orientation of philosophy of many marketing managers. The essence of the marketing concept is captured in three interrelated orientations:

1. *Consumers' wants and needs*. When the focus is on identifying and satisfying the wants and needs of consumers, the intention of the firm is not seen as merely providing goods and services. Instead, want and need satisfaction is viewed as the purpose, and providing products and services is the means to achieve that end. The advertisement for Rectinol, below, illustrates this.

2. *Company objectives*. Consumers' wants and needs are numerous. Therefore, a firm that concentrates on satisfying a small proportion of all desires will most effectively utilise its resources. Company objectives and any of the firm's special advantages are used as criteria to select the specific wants and needs to be addressed.

3. *Integrated strategy* An integrated effort is most effective in achieving a firm's objective through consumer satisfaction. For maximum impact this requires that marketing efforts be closely co-ordinated and compatible with each other and with other activities of the firm.

An advertisement relating use of a product to need satisfaction   COURTESY OF PFIZER PTY LTD

Several limitations of the marketing concept have been noted, especially in regard to the degree to which attempting to satisfy consumers' wants and needs can generate negative consequences for society.[5] To illustrate, convenience packaging has contributed to a solid waste-disposal problem for society, and the propellant formerly used in many aerosol sprays has been linked to depletion of the ozone layer of our atmosphere. Adjustments to the marketing concept that incorporate societal objectives have been made to alleviate such shortcomings.[6] Some fast-food chains have reduced the volume of their packaging and have undertaken information campaigns to raise consumer awareness of environmentally friendly products. However, the basic need to understand consumers is still fundamental to these revised schemes.

Several major activities can be undertaken by an organisation that is marketing-oriented. These include market-opportunity analysis, target-market selection and marketing-mix determination, which includes decisions on the proper combination of marketing variables to offer consumers. Each of these is briefly discussed below with examples to illustrate the relevance of consumer behaviour to their accomplishment.

MARKET-OPPORTUNITY ANALYSIS

This activity involves examining trends and conditions in the marketplace to identify consumers' needs and wants that are not being fully satisfied. The analysis begins with a study of general market trends, such as consumers' lifestyles and income levels, which may suggest unsatisfied wants and needs. More specific examination involves assessing any unique abilities the company might have in satisfying identified consumer desires.

A variety of recent trends have resulted in many new product offerings for consumer satisfaction. Companies attuned to the fitness interests of Australians have been quick to offer such new products as exercise equipment for step-ups or sit-ups. In the tourism area, companies sensing consumers' growing environmental awareness have offered a range of products under the label of 'ecotourism'.

TARGET-MARKET SELECTION

The process of reviewing market opportunities often results in the identification of distinct groupings of consumers who have unique wants and needs. This can result in a decision to approach each market segment with a unique marketing offering. Consider the soft-drink market. Here, major segments of ultimate consumers are distinguished by the type of purchase situation: the food-store segment, the 'cold bottle' or vending-machine segment, and the catering/restaurant market, including public houses and bars. Unique packaging arrangements (container type and size), point-of-purchase promotions and other variations are made for each segment.

In other cases, the marketer may decide to concentrate company efforts on serving only one or a few of the identified target markets. An excellent example of this is the way in which Nike have concentrated upon particular market segments rather than the mass market for shoes. Their advertising is well attuned to trendy kids who want fashion sports shoes. By segmenting consumers appropriately Nike claim that their market share in New Zealand rose by 30 per cent in the 12 months ending June 1993.[7]

MARKETING-MIX DETERMINATION

This stage involves developing and implementing a strategy for delivering an effective combination of want-satisfying features to consumers within target markets. A series of decisions are made on four major ingredients frequently referred to as the marketing-mix variables: product, price, place and promotion. The following characterises each area and provides a small sampling of how knowledge of consumer behaviour is relevant for decision making.

PRODUCT   The nature of the physical product and service features are of concern here. Among decisions that are influenced by consumer behaviour are:

➡ What size, shape and features should the product have?

➡ How should it be packaged?

➡ What aspects of service are most important to consumers?

➡ What types of warranties and service programs should be provided?

➡ What types of accessories and associated products should be offered?

Underwear and socks are traditionally regarded as basic commodities. They are low-interest products. Few people ever go into stores with the specific aim of buying underwear or socks, and brand loyalty is low with a plethora of cheap imported products and much discounting.

Yet the launch of Hanes products by the Sara Lee Corporation in March 1993 in Australia has changed all that. Extensive consumer advertising to support the Hanes launch brought an equally strong advertising response from Pacific Dunlop's two divisions, Bond Industries and Holeproof. In the six months following the Hanes launch, the market for these products grew by between 3 per cent and 4 per cent and retailers confirm that Hanes and Bonds are now successfully building brand loyalty for their products. Marketers have created consumer interest in basic and largely inconspicuous small-value clothing items.[8]

PRICE   Marketers must make decisions regarding the prices to charge for the company's products or services and any modification to those prices. These decisions will determine the amount of revenues the firm will generate. A few of the factors involving consumer behaviour are:

➡ How price-aware are consumers in the relevant product category?

➡ How sensitive are consumers to price differences among brands?

➡ How large a price reduction is needed to encourage purchases during new product introductions and sales promotions?

➡ What size discount should be given to consumers who pay with cash?

➡ How important is price relative to quality for consumers?

There has been much doom and despair in the Australian clothing industry for the last three years. One company that has defied the trend and maintained its turnover is Spinelli Clothing, based in Adelaide. It is known in some fashion circles as the Escada label of Australian clothing. It manufactures a mix-and-match range of tailored suits and blazers and superfine knitted wool garments in a top-of-the-market niche, where a tailored jacket can cost more than $1000. Ten per cent of turnover is exported to New Zealand.

Frank Spinelli admits that in a recession you have to have steady nerves and the courage of your convictions.

There will always be a point in tough economic times when you think you could use some less expensive materials, for example, and take prices down to compensate, but we didn't and we wouldn't. Customers see our garments as an investment whatever the depth of the recession. To have changed what we gave them would have broken trust.[9]

PLACE The place variable involves consideration of where and how to offer products and services for sale. It also is concerned with the mechanisms for transferring goods and their ownership to consumers. Decisions influenced by consumer behaviour include:

➡ What type of retail outlet should sell the firm's offering?

➡ Where should the outlets be located, and how many should there be?

➡ What arrangements are needed to distribute products to retailers?

➡ To what extent is it necessary for the company to own or maintain tight control over activities of firms in the channel of distribution?

➡ What image and clientele should the retailer seek to cultivate?

One way in which New Zealand differs from Australia is in its emphasis on pharmacies rather than department stores for prestige cosmetic sales. Many department stores have not fared well in New Zealand and several have closed their doors in recent years.

The key to the success of cosmetics sales through pharmacies in New Zealand lies in the image of the pharmacies, which differs from that of their Australian counterparts. According to the manager of sales and marketing for Shiseido, 'In

Australia pharmacy doesn't have a good image. They sell shoes, sugar and the works'. Conversely, department-store business for cosmetics is very strong in Australia. In New Zealand the image of the pharmacist is that of a health-care professional, which links in well with the trend towards technologically more advanced products, especially in skin care. The industry has even coined the term 'cosmeceuticals' for these products, which they view as a cross between cosmetics and therapeutic treatments.[10]

PROMOTION Of concern here are the goals and methods of communicating aspects of the firm and its offerings to target consumers. Consumer-related decisions include:

➡ What methods of promotion are best for each specific situation?

➡ What are the most effective means for gaining consumers' attention?

➡ What methods best convey the intended message?

➡ How often should a given advertisement be repeated?

Such questions had to be addressed when the managers of Fujifilm decided on a rather novel advertisement for their product.

Careful examination of this ad will reveal many communication goals set by the advertisers of Fujifilm   COURTESY OF HANIMEX PTY LTD (AUSTRALIAN DISTRIBUTOR OF FUJIFILM)

'Take babies, animals and a dash of humour, mix together or use alone, and it seems you are well on the way to having a sure-to-rise recipe for a successful commercial.' This is the interpretation of the results from the aggregated 1993 Ad-Pulse surveys. These are based on telephone interviews with a total of 8609 New Zealanders aged 15 years and over who were asked which television advertisement was their favourite at the present time.

Most of the ads in the top 20 were part of a successful series rather than one-offs and three advertisements in one series from Ansett New Zealand all made the top 20. The most popular of these three featured drenched cat Fluffy going AWOL to the air-port in its owner's car boot. The cat is taken over by Ansett staff, dried off and sent home in a taxi, all as part of the Ansett service. Ansett believe the treatment of the cat makes the ad particularly appealing and they have had overwhelming and unexpected feedback both directly from cat lovers and indirectly through the Society for the Protection of Animals. The ad is designed to show the small but significant ways in which service can exceed customer expectations and uses wry, gentle humour. The general manager of the Campaign Palace who created the series says, 'There's no question that one of the roles advertising must play is to entertain. The trick to it is creating the relevant humour'.[11]

Meet Fluffy. (He's the one on the right.)

If you'd like to meet 'Fluffy', the star of the Ansett New Zealand 'Puss in Boot' TV commercial, he'll be guest of honour at the Whiskas National Cat Show at Auckland's Alexandra Park Raceway on Sunday May 31. Let's hope it doesn't rain...

Humour is evident in the Ansett campaign   COURTESY OF ANSETT NEW ZEALAND

Consumer behaviour and non-profit and social marketing

Can crime prevention, charitable contributions or the concept of family planning be sold to people in much the same way that some business firms sell soap? A number of writers have suggested that various social and non-profit organisations can be viewed as having services or ideas that they are attempting to market to target groups of 'consumers' or constituents. Such organisations include government agencies, religious orders, universities, schools and charitable institutions.[12] In New Zealand alone, leaving aside major international and national charities, it is estimated that there are 25 000 groups chasing disposable gift dollars. Often these groups must appeal to the public for support as well as attempting to satisfy some want or need in society. Clearly, a sound understanding of consumer decision processes can assist their efforts.

Consider, for example, the benefits such knowledge has to administrators of the Cancer Society or Red Cross. Both organisations have developed donor bases using selective methods to increase the efficiency of their appeals, rather than undertaking general mailing to 'cold lists' of people. Increased competition for donations has rendered untargeted appeals uneconomic. Fundamental information, such as the characteristics of potential contributors, what motivates their generosity and how these motives can be most effectively appealed to, is highly useful. It means that the Red Cross and the Cancer Society are able to mail their lists two or three times a year and achieve a 25–30 per cent response rate with average donations of around $25.[13]

Many other examples demonstrate the fundamental role a consumer orientation plays in non-profit and social-marketing endeavours. The following serves as an additional illustration.

In Africa, as in many other regions, the incidence of AIDS has reached alarming proportions. Consequently, many pioneering efforts have been mounted in African countries to curb the spread of the disease. A unique blend of government aid (African monies as well as American funds via the Agency for International Development) and capitalistic motives has fostered a variety of social-marketing programs that are showing promise of success.

In many cases program goals are to make people aware of the disease, how it is transmitted and what precautions can be taken to avoid it. In Zambia one educational program features newspaper advertisements and comic books showing an ugly AIDS virus that says, 'I am dangerous'. Many anti-AIDS clubs have also been formed at high schools. The Ivory Coast uses posters with a stark skeletal man saying, 'Don't Die of Ignorance', and in Uganda the softer 'Love Carefully' posters are used along with anti-AIDS postage stamps to send the message out.

Some believe that action is required that is more aggressive than basic advertising. In Zaire this belief resulted in a program to distribute condoms along with informative ads and instructions on how to use the devices properly. However, in something of a new twist, even though it was possible to distribute condoms for free, it was decided to sell them to the population at a low cost. Why not give them away if the goal is to stop the progress of AIDS? The argument was that more people would be persuaded to use the product if it were made available through local retailers who would have the profit motive to encourage distribution. Also, it was believed that the population would perceive more value in the product if it were not free for the taking.

Are these attempts at using consumer-behaviour and marketing concepts meeting with any success? While it still may be too early to tell, there are some encouraging signs that condom sales are increasing, especially in areas where advertisements and aspects of social-marketing programs have been employed. In Zambia the reported incidence of sexually transmitted disease has declined 15 per cent per year for the last three years. If these pioneering programs prove sufficiently successful, they could be employed in other areas of the world.[14]

Consumer behaviour and governmental decision making

In recent years the relevance of consumer-behaviour principles to governmental decision making has become quite evident. Two major areas of activity have been affected:

1. government policies that provide services to the public or result in decisions that influence consumer behaviour;

2. the design of legislation to protect consumers or to assist them in evaluating products and services.

GOVERNMENT SERVICES

It is increasingly evident that government providers of public services can benefit significantly from an understanding of the consumers, or users, of these services. Analysts have noted that our frequently failing public transportation systems will not be viable alternatives to private automobile travel until government planners fully understand how to appeal to the wants and needs of the public. In other cases, state and municipal planners must make a variety of decisions, including where to locate highways, what areas to consider for future commercial growth and the type of public services (such as health care and libraries) to offer. The effectiveness of these decisions will be influenced by the extent to which they are based on an adequate understanding of consumers. This understanding requires knowledge of people's attitudes, beliefs, perceptions and habits, as well as how they tend to behave under a variety of circumstances.

The Government Advertising Service had its 50th birthday in August 1991. In the early days of World War II it was realised that the amount of advertising being generated by the Commonwealth government needed to be co-ordinated. Instead of various government departments competing against one another for space and time, these departments would be presented to the media as a single advertiser. In 1941, therefore, the War Effort Publicity Board was created, which has evolved into the Government Advertising Service (or 'GAS' for short). GAS is Australia's biggest advertiser, spending $47.5 million in the 1991/1992 financial year across a variety of projects.

The government advertises in order to:

- convey information (e.g. changes to Social Security entitlements);
- influence attitudes ('Don't drink before you drive');
- influence behaviour (persuade voters to enrol)
- recruit people ('Join the Navy and see the world')

The government regards advertising as an effective method of communication. Press releases can be distorted by media, while advertising can achieve high impact and can be accurately targeted to the audience.[15]

CONSUMER PROTECTION

A number of agencies at different levels of government are involved with regulating business practices for the purpose of protecting consumers' welfare. Some government programs are also designed to influence certain consumer actions directly (such as the use of car seat belts and bicycle helmets) and discourage others (speeding, drug abuse and so on). In addition, several industries, such as banking, insurance and parts of the tourism industry, have developed their own codes of practice to control the business practices of some of their members for the benefit of consumers. Codes of practice developed by the market research and advertising industries in both Australia and New Zealand are particularly relevant to consumer behaviour. Though legal controls also exist, these codes provide the most widely applied guidance for ensuring that high ethical standards are maintained in research, and that claims presented to consumers are fair and reasonable. The following serves to illustrate the nature of some of the issues the advertising decision makers confront in their consumer-protection efforts.

Budget Screens and Awnings objected to an advertisement placed by a competitor, Atlas Awnings, in the *Northern Star* newspaper. The Atlas advertisement read '50% OFF VERTICALS PLUS 10 TO 30% OFF OTHER ATLAS PRODUCTS', with no reference to the full prices. Four other products as well as the vertical screens were depicted in the advertisement and the complainant argued that it was not clear which discounts applied to what products, and indeed what price was being discounted—a normal selling price or an inflated list price.

The Advertising Standards Council upheld the complaint and requested that the advertisement be withdrawn from publication. They determined that the missing information, which would have allowed consumers to make an accurate assessment of the offer, could have been easily included in the advertisement, and that in its current form the advertisement was potentially misleading. Thus they determined it was in breach of clause 7 of the Code of Advertising Ethics, which states: 'Advertisements shall be truthful and shall not be misleading or deceptive'.[16]

Consumer behaviour and demarketing

The history of private enterprise in Australia and New Zealand has long been characterised by intensive efforts to stimulate the public to greater levels of consumption. Various government policies have supported such efforts because of their favourable effect on economic development. Recently, however, it has become increasingly clear that we are entering an era of scarcity in some natural resources such as oil, natural gas and even water. This scarcity has led to promotions stressing conservation rather than consumption. The efforts of electric power companies to encourage reduction of electrical use serves as one illustration. In other circumstances, consumers have been encouraged to decrease or stop their use of particular goods believed to have harmful effects. Programs designed to reduce drug abuse, gambling and similar types of consumption are examples. These actions have been undertaken by government agencies, nonprofit organisations and other private groups.

The term 'demarketing' refers to all such efforts to encourage consumers to reduce their consumption of a particular product or service. The following example illustrates a demarketing program:

In 1992 New Zealand suffered under a prolonged drought that reduced levels of hydro lakes to extremely low elevations. As a consequence most of the country experienced significant power cuts during the winter as the Electricity Commission attempted to come to grips with the situation.

One pocket of warmth was in Dunedin Electricity's distribution region. Dunedin Electricity is a fully corporatised, wholly owned City Council enterprise responsible for distribution of electricity to 70 per cent of the supply area. Dunedin's success in maintaining an uninterrupted supply was due to the effects of an award-winning demarketing scheme. Dunedin Electricity put an immediate scheme in place aimed at reducing consumption by offering households rebates on power charges based on savings achieved over normal consumption rates for that time of year. Extensive promotional support for the scheme presented the problem as a 'hydro shortage' rather than an 'electricity crisis' to dissociate the company from the causes of the supply problem. During the critical winter period 68 per cent of Dunedin Electricity's customers made savings amounting to 18 per cent of total normal consumption. Elsewhere in New Zealand the Electricity Industry Committee was asking for a 15 per cent reduction in consumption. Dunedin exceeded the target figure by voluntary savings with a successful demarketing program. The pooled savings from the scheme available for rebates reached $3.1 million by the end of July 1992.[17]

Some demarketing efforts have met with considerable success while many others have made hardly any impact on changing long-established consumption patterns. An analysis of the successes and failures of various efforts strongly suggests that demarketing programs must be based on a sound understanding of consumers' motives, attitudes and historically established consumption behaviour.

Consumer behaviour and consumer education

Consumers also stand to benefit directly from orderly investigations of their own behaviour. This can occur on an individual basis or as part of more formal educational programs. As we study what has been discovered about the behaviour of others, we can gain insight into our own interactions with the marketplace. For example, when we learn that a large proportion of the billions spent annually on grocery products is used for impulse purchases, and not spent according to pre-planned shopping lists, we may be more willing to plan our purchases in an effort to save money. In general, as we discover the many variables that can influence consumers' purchases, we have the opportunity to understand better how they affect our own behaviour.

What is learned about consumer behaviour can also directly benefit consumers in a more formal sense. The knowledge can serve as data for the development of educational programs designed to improve consumers' decision making regarding products and services. Such courses are now available at the high-school and university level and are becoming increasingly popular. To be most effective, these educational programs should be based on a clear understanding of the important variables influencing consumers.

STUDYING CONSUMER BEHAVIOUR

The study of any subject is made easier by examining it in an organised fashion. Therefore, we should determine the general classes of variables influencing consumers' behaviour, understand the nature of these variables, and learn how to make inferences based on this knowledge.

Three classes of variables are involved in understanding consumer behaviour: stimulus, response, and intervening variables.

Stimulus variables, such as advertisements, products and hunger pangs, exist in both the individual's external and internal environment. These generate the sensory inputs to consumers.

Response variables are the resulting mental and/or physical reactions of individuals who are influenced by stimulus variables. Purchasing a product or forming attitudes about it could be viewed as a response variable.

Stimulus variables often do not influence responses directly. Instead, they influence a third class of variables, called 'intervening variables' because these variables literally intervene between the stimulus and response variables. That is, they act to influence (magnify, reduce or otherwise modify) the effect of stimulus variables on response variables. For example, an advertisement featuring a movie star to influence consumers positively towards a brand may actually be perceived negatively by some consumers who happen to hold an unfavourable attitude towards that particular movie star. Here the intervening variable of attitude modifies the effect of the advertising stimulus. Intervening variables are internal to the individual and can include values, mood, knowledge and so on, as well as attitudes.

Many of the variables affecting consumers (such as personality, learning, perceptions of external situations, motives and so forth) cannot be directly observed. Therefore, if researchers want to learn about the variables affecting consumers, they must often make inferences to determine the extent to which a given variable is having an influence. Like the scientist who cannot see oxygen and must infer its properties by looking for its effects on other variables, a consumer researcher must look for the influence of unobservable variables on the activities of consumers that can be observed. The problem is that these variables have different aspects and can change over time. If we observe the effects of the variable at two different points in time, we might draw different inferences about its characteristics. We must be ready to accept this ambiguity because of the difficulty of studying unobservable behaviour. We should also read about more than one investigation of the same variable, because such studies will help us to home in on the specific nature of the variables that are of interest to us in achieving our goal of understanding the behaviour of consumers.

Modelling behaviour

The study of consumer behaviour can be quite complex, because of the many variables involved and their tendency to interact with and influence each other. Models of consumer behaviour have been developed as a means of dealing with this complexity. They can help organise our thinking about consumers into a coherent whole by identifying relevant variables, describing their basic characteristics and specifying how the variables relate to each other. A number of models of consumer behaviour have been offered, and a review of them would be beyond the scope of this chapter. (See Ch. 17 for an illustration of these models and perspectives on consumer behaviour.) Therefore, we have adopted a simplified approach to guide our discussion. A diagram of this approach is presented in Figure 1.1. The diagram is an organised picture of the factors that have been identified as the most important general influences on consumer behaviour.

Figure 1.1 is made up of three major sections: external environmental variables influencing behaviour; individual determinants of behaviour; and the consumer's decision process. These major sections are treated in Parts 2, 3 and 4, respectively, of the text.

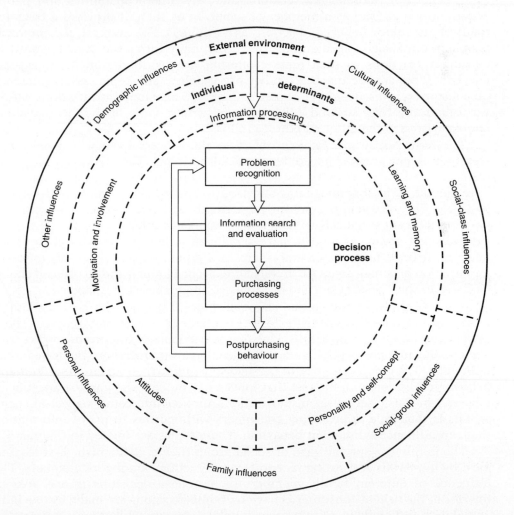

FIG. 1.1 A simplified decision-process framework for studying consumer behaviour

EXTERNAL VARIABLES

The external environment depicted in the outer circle is made up of six specific influences and one catch-all grouping for all other factors. The six specific influences are demographics, culture, social class, social group, family and personal. The open partitions (dotted lines) denote the influence of these variables on individual determinants and on each other. These environmental influences are discussed in Part 2 of the text.

The first of these sections relates to demographic influences. Major demographic trends are reviewed in Chapter 2. We consider issues in population growth, distribution and structure. In many ways these are the most general of all influences and impact on all the other external variables in Figure 1.1.

Culture has been characterised as 'that complex whole that includes knowledge, belief, art, morals, law, custom, and any other capabilities and habits acquired by man [sic] as a member of society'.[18] As such, it provides a basis for many of our values, beliefs and actions as consumers. For example, the emphasis people in our society place on time and punctuality forms the basis for positive consumer reactions to such market offerings as fast-food franchises, express checkout lanes at supermarkets, and quartz watches. This topic and its influence on consumers is discussed in Chapter 3. Chapter 3 also looks at variations within Australian and New Zealand cultures, in particular some of the distinguishing characteristics of the different ethnic groups.

The term 'social stratification' refers to the process by which people in a society rank one another into different social positions. The result is a hierarchy often referred to as a set of social classes. People within a given social class have similar socioeconomic status and tend to share beliefs, values and ways of behaving. They also tend to associate more closely with one another than with people from different social classes. The values, wants and interactions that develop in these distinct groupings tend to have significant influences on consumers. They affect such basic factors as membership in a group, choice of neighbourhoods, appreciation of certain styles (of architecture, decor, clothing and so on) and choice of places to shop. Social class and its influence are discussed in Chapter 4.

A social group can be viewed as a collection of people who have a sense of relatedness resulting from some form of interaction with one another. These groups can have many functions. One that is particularly important from a consumer-behaviour perspective is the influence that group members can have on the individual. The group can serve to persuade and guide the individual's values and behaviour. The common interest that university students show in the latest fashions and in music serves as an illustration. Another interesting aspect of social groups is their role in providing consumers with various forms of information that can influence subsequent behaviour. These topics are treated in Chapter 5.

The family is a special form of social group that is distinguished, at least in part, by numerous and strong face-to-face interactions among its members. The influence of different family members on purchase decisions is one area of interest in the field of consumer behaviour. Some decisions are made by one individual with little influence from other family members, while at other times the interaction is so strong that it is said to yield a joint decision rather than just an influence of one member on another. Of course, the nature and degree of influence in these decision-making patterns are quite important to marketers attempting to inform and persuade consumers regarding their offerings. Another aspect of family influence on consumer behaviour is the way in which the stage of a family's life cycle (newly married, young children and so on) influences the need for products and services. In a similar vein, the changing patterns of family and household structures, including families with both parents working and those made up solely of singles, have significant implications for consumer behaviour. These and related topics are considered in Chapter 6.

The process of personal influence, which can be described as the effects on an individual of communications with others, has long been of interest to marketers. Interest in this subject is strong because personal influence has an important effect on the amount and type of information that consumers obtain about products. It is also considered to be a significant force acting on a consumer's values, attitudes, brand evaluations and interest in a product. In fact, personal influence is an important function of opinion leaders. People look to opinion leaders for advice, opinions and suggestions regarding purchase decisions. Personal influence also strongly affects the process of diffusion by which new product and service innovations spread in the marketplace. Personal influence, diffusion of innovations and other closely related topics are examined in Chapter 7.

The last category of environmental influences in Figure 1.1 is labelled 'other influences', and encompasses influences on consumers that are not specifically treated in chapters dealing with the topics just reviewed. An example might be the effects of media that are not incorporated into one of the other categories. The editorial content of newspapers, magazines and television programs may affect people's moods and subsequently affect their evaluation of advertising and their consumer behaviour. Many of these influences, including physical surroundings, the interpersonal setting, national events and the consumer's available cash, can be summarised by the term 'situational variables'. The influence of these situational variables is treated at a number of points in later chapters.

INDIVIDUAL DETERMINANTS

Major individual determinants of consumer behaviour are portrayed in the inner ring of Figure 1.1. These variables influence how the consumer proceeds through a decision process regarding products and services. The decision process itself is shown in the centre of the figure. An arrow leading from the external environment into individual determinants demonstrates that environmental stimuli do not directly influence consumers. Instead, the stimuli are modified by internal influences such as learning, personality, attitudes, information processing and motives. The opened circle between the decision process and these variables denotes the great influence they have on the decision process. The opened partitions between the individual determinants themselves represent the influence they have on each other.

The five major groups of individual determinants to be discussed further in Part 3 of the text are personality and self-concept, motivation and involvement, information processing, learning and memory, and attitudes.

Personality and self-concept provide the consumer with a central theme. They provide a structure for the individual so that a consistent pattern of behaviour can be developed. In Chapter 8, several major personality theories are examined for their usefulness in understanding consumers. The chapter then discusses the importance of self-concept in understanding consumer behaviour. How the self-concept develops, its role in influencing purchase decisions and the practical relevance of the subject to the marketer are reviewed.

Motives are internal factors that energise behaviour and provide guidance to direct the activated behaviour. Involvement describes the personal relevance or importance that the consumer perceives in a given purchase situation. High involvement will lead to a motivated state. Various types of involvement and motive situations, factors that influence them and their influence on the behaviour of consumers are subjects treated in Chapter 9.

The term 'information processing' refers to the activities that consumers engage in when acquiring, integrating and evaluating information. These activities involve actively seeking information or passively receiving it, attending to only certain parts of the information, integrating information that has been attended to with information from other sources, and evaluating the information for the purpose of making decisions. Such activities are varied and occur at all stages of the decision process. They also strongly involve some individual factors, including motivation, learning and attitudes. Chapter 10, on information processing, introduces these issues and also discusses several marketing-strategy areas in which an understanding of the process can be of considerable benefit to the marketer. However, because of their importance, treatment of these issues is not confined to just one chapter or section of the text. Several chapters in Part 3 elaborate further on the subject. Additional discussion is contained in Part 4, where the critical role that information processing plays in the consumer's decision process is examined.

The important roles of learning and memory are discussed in Chapter 11. What consumers learn, how they learn and what factors govern the retention of learned material in memory are all issues of considerable importance for understanding consumers. Not only do consumers acquire and remember product names and characteristics, but they also learn standards for judging products, places to shop, problem-solving abilities, behaviour patterns and tastes. Such learned material stored in memory significantly influences how consumers react to each situation that they confront.

The topics of attitude and attitude change are examined in Chapter 12. Attitudes guide our basic orientation toward objects, people, events and our activities. As such, attitudes strongly influence how consumers will act and react to products and services, and how they will respond to communications that marketers develop to convince them to purchase their products. After a review of the nature and function of attitudes, attention is turned to how attitudes are formed and how they are related to purchase behaviour. We then discuss attitude-change strategies and marketing communications, and how various aspects of a message, its source and characteristics of the consumer can have a significant effect in modifying the consumer's attitudes.

THE DECISION PROCESS

The inner portion of Figure 1.1 details the consumer decision process regarding products and services. The major steps in this process are shown as problem recognition, information search and evaluation, purchasing processes, and post-purchase behaviour.[19]

The process may be viewed as starting when consumers engage in problem recognition, a topic covered in Chapter 13. *Problem recognition* occurs when consumers are activated by awareness of a sufficient difference between their actual state of affairs and their concept of the ideal situation. This can occur through internal activation of a motive such as hunger, by confronting some external stimulus such as an advertisement, or by being affected by additional variables such as social or situational influences. In any case, action occurs only when consumers perceive a sufficiently large discrepancy between their actual and ideal states.

Given that the consumer is aroused to action, the next stage, addressed in Chapter 14, is to undertake an information search. This usually starts with an *internal search*—a quick and largely unconscious review of memory for stored information and experiences regarding the problem. This information is in the form of beliefs and attitudes that have influenced the consumer's preferences toward brands. Often such a review results in recognising a strong brand preference, and a routine purchase occurs. However, if an internal search does not provide sufficient information about products, or how to evaluate them, the consumer continues with a more involved *external search* for information. This results in exposure to numerous informational inputs called *stimuli*, which can arise from a variety of sources, including advertisements, printed product reviews and comments from friends.

Any informational stimuli are subjected to *information-processing* activities, which the consumer uses to derive meaning from stimuli. This process involves allocating attention to available stimuli, deriving meaning from these stimuli and holding this meaning in what is termed 'short-term memory', where it can be retained briefly to allow further processing.

The alternative-evaluation phase, also treated in Chapter 14, involves comparing the information gained in the search process for alternative products and brands with the product-judging criteria or standards the consumer has developed. When such a comparison leads to favourable evaluations, the consumer is likely to develop a purchase intention toward the alternative receiving the most favourable evaluation.

A purchasing process usually follows strong purchase intentions. This process, addressed in Chapter 15, involves a series of selections, including the type of retail outlet as well as the specific brand or service to use.

The consumer's purchase then leads to various outcomes. One such outcome is satisfaction as a result of direct experience in using the brand. Satisfaction will affect the consumer's beliefs about the brand. Other outcomes are dissatisfaction and post-sale doubt. These can generate a heightened desire for additional information and influence subsequent problem recognition. In both cases, post-purchase experiences result in feedback to the problem-recognition stage. Postpurchase behaviour is covered in Chapter 16.

The above is a brief synopsis of most of the text but the final part deals with additional dimensions that do not fit directly within the scheme outlined in Figure 1.1. Chapter 17 deals with some of the issues involved in modelling and researching consumer behaviour, and Chapter 18 looks at the macro element of consumerism and associated issues of consumer protection. The final chapter gives an overview of organisational buying. It points out the many similarities with consumer buying but also shows the fundamental differences.

SUMMARY

This chapter serves as an introduction to the field of consumer behaviour. After several orienting examples, discussion centres on defining consumer behaviour and describing the focus the text uses for studying it—to view consumer behaviour as the decision process and physical activity of individuals purchasing for the purpose of individual or household consumption. Therefore, we recognise that in certain situations consumers will purchase products and services for use by other individuals. Also, we must realise that other individuals can have an influence on the consumer's decision process.

Discussion then turns to considering various reasons for studying consumer behaviour. Most attention is focused on the applied nature of the discipline. The relevance of consumer behaviour to a variety of practical applications, including marketing management, social marketing, governmental decision making, demarketing and consumer education, is discussed.

The chapter ends with a review of the benefits and uses of consumer-behaviour models. A simplified decision-process diagram is offered to assist students in their reading about consumer behaviour. A general preview of the remainder of the book is also provided. These should prove useful to students as they progress through their reading.

MANAGERIAL REFLECTIONS

For our product or service situation:

1. Who is likely to take on the roles described in Table 1.1? Do different purchase situations change this answer?

2. What are my target market's wants and needs?

3. Are there target markets that are sufficiently viable for our marketing effort?

4. What are the more critical decisions regarding the product?

5. How price-aware are consumers?

6. Are we selling in the proper retail outlets?

7. Are the promotional methods and advertising claims having an adverse effect on consumers?

8. What consumer motivations and problem-recognition situations may serve as sources for new product or service ideas?

9. Are there any typical consumer information-search patterns we expect or assume for our products and services?

10. What evaluative criteria do consumers appear to have for our products or services and how are they developed?

11. What postpurchase processes are important?

12. Can we develop a general model of consumer behaviour?

DISCUSSION TOPICS

1. An American marketer in the cosmetics industry once remarked: 'In the factory, we make cosmetics; in the drugstore we sell hope'. How does this relate to the marketing concept and the need for marketers to understand consumer behaviour?

2. 'Every consumer is unique, and any study that concentrates on the "average" consumer is meaningless.' Comment on this statement.

3. In terms of understanding consumers, what are the advantages and disadvantages of viewing behaviour as both a decision process and a physical activity, as opposed to just a physical activity?

4. In what ways is the study of consumer behaviour useful to consumer-advocate groups concerned with designing laws to assist and protect consumers?

5. Choose an existing non-profit organisation and suggest areas where knowledge of its 'consumers' might improve the services it provides.

6. A hard-nosed marketing manager was heard to remark, 'All of this talk about consumers' decision process still just boils down to the same old fact — it's what the consumer buys, and how much of it, that's really important to the practising marketer'. What is your response?

7. Relate one of your experiences where postpurchase outcomes significantly influenced your future purchase behaviour.

8. Observe a consumer engaged in a shopping activity. Attempt to infer the variables involved in the situation and the nature of their influence. Be prepared to describe:
   (a) the behaviour you observed;
   (b) the inferences you drew from these actions.

REFERENCES

1. John A. Howard & Jagdish N. Sheth, *The Theory of Buyer Behavior*, Wiley, New York, 1969.
2. Jagdish N. Sheth, 'A Model of Industrial Buyer Behavior', *Journal of Marketing* 37, October 1973, pp. 50–6.
3. W. T. Tucker, *Foundations for a Theory of Consumer Behavior*, Holt, New York, 1967, pp. 1–2.
4. 'AMA Board Approves New Marketing Definition', *Marketing News*, 1985 March 1, p. 1.
5. Martin L. Bell & C. William Emery, 'The Faltering Marketing Concept', *Journal of Marketing* 35, October 1971, pp. 37–42; and Lawrence P. Feldman, 'Societal Adaptation: A New Challenge for Marketing', *Journal of Marketing* 35, July 1971, pp. 54–60.
6. See James T. Rothe & Lissa Benson, 'Intelligent Consumption: An Attractive Alternative to the Marketing Concept', *MSU Business Topics* 22, Winter 1974, pp. 29–34; George Fisk, 'Criteria for a Theory of Responsible Consumption', *Journal of Marketing* 37, April 1973, pp. 24–31; and Philip Kotler, *Marketing Management: Analysis, Planning and Control*, 3rd edn, Prentice-Hall, Englewood Cliffs, NJ, 1976, pp. 16–18.
7. 'Sharp Shoe Shuffle', *Marketing Magazine*, June 1993, p. 28.
8. Based on Neil Shoebridge, 'Hanes, Bonds Puff Up Their Chests', *Business Review Weekly*, 3 September 1993, pp. 69–70.
9. Based on Alex Kennedy, 'Classic Italian Flair Defies Recession', *Business Review Weekly*, 3 December 1993, p. 44.
10. Based on 'More than Lip Service', *Marketing Magazine*, December 1993, pp. 26–29.
11. Based on 'Ad Pulse '93—New Zealand's Favourite Ads for 1993', *Marketing Magazine*, February 1994, pp. 23–28.
12. Philip Kotler & Gerald Zaltman, 'Social Marketing: An Approach to Planned Social Change', *Journal of Marketing* 35, July 1971, pp. 3–12; and F. Kelly Shuptrine & Frank A. Osmanski, 'Marketing's Changing Role: Expanding or Contracting?', *Journal of Marketing* 39, April 1975, pp. 58–66.
13. Peter Hull, 'Forging a Donor Relationship', *Marketing Magazine*, May 1993, pp. 39–40. See Karen F. A. Fox & Philip Kotler, 'The Marketing of Social Causes: The First Ten Years', *Journal of Marketing* 44, Fall 1980, pp. 24–33, for an evaluation of social-marketing programs in the United States.
14. Based on John Tierney, 'With "Social Marketing", Condoms Combat AIDS', *New York Times*, 18 September 1990, pp. Al, A10.
15. Based on Phil Rutledge, 'How Australia's Biggest Advertiser Spends Your Money', *Marketing*, August 1993, pp. 40–1.
16. Based on Australian Advertising Standards Council, *Case Report*, No. 8239, October–December 1990, AASC, Sydney, 1991, pp. 24–5.
17. Based on 'Winning Scheme to Cut Back Sales', *Marketing Magazine*, October 1993, pp. 36–7.
18. Edward B. Tylor, *Primitive Culture*, Murray, London, 1891, p. 1.
19. These steps are based on a more detailed series of activities proposed in James F. Engel, Roger D. Blackwell & Paul E. Miniard, *Consumer Behaviour*, 6th edn, The Dryden Press, Chicago, 1990.

CHAPTER 2

UNDERSTANDING CONSUMERS AND MARKET SEGMENTS

LEARNING OBJECTIVES

AFTER STUDYING THIS CHAPTER YOU SHOULD UNDERSTAND:

➡ how market aggregation compares with market segmentation in terms of marketing strategies, benefits, costs, usage and performance;

➡ demographic characteristics of the Australian and New Zealand markets and how specific facets may be used as bases for segmentation;

➡ how use of lifestyle and psychographic information increases understanding of market segments and leads to effective marketing-strategy decisions;

➡ the various facets of consumer usage that are relevant to the marketer and how these may be used as bases for segmentation;

➡ the role of benefit segmentation in helping to analyse why consumers purchase different brands;

➡ why product-positioning decisions are important in the segmentation process, and which positioning bases are frequently used.

One of the most profound realisations to strike any marketer is that there is a great diversity among consumers. Close inspection of the total market shows that smaller groups of individuals have more homogeneity than the group as a whole in certain characteristics, especially their consumer behaviour. This chapter introduces the concept of identifying and selectively marketing to homogeneous

29

groups of consumers. The associated topic of product positioning is also discussed and is related to market segmentation.

Marketers may approach target markets in their aggregate and heterogeneous form or as smaller, more homogeneous segments. The following sections will discuss these two alternatives.

MARKET AGGREGATION

A market-aggregation strategy means that little if any subdivision of the market is applied. With this approach, a firm would produce a single product and offer it to all consumers with a single marketing program. Although the marketer recognises that not everyone will buy the product, numbers sufficient for profitable operations are expected to be attracted. This approach has also been described as *mass marketing, undifferentiated marketing* and *product differentiation*.

The reasoning behind market aggregation is that, although consumers may differ, they are sufficiently alike to be approached as a homogeneous grouping for the product under consideration. Market aggregation, therefore, presents a standard product that may differ little from its competition, which can make the selling task much more difficult.

MARKET SEGMENTATION

It is difficult to see the market for any product category as a single, homogeneous group of customers, all buying for the same motives, in the same circumstances and in the same way. Typically, firms employ a strategy of segmentation, viewing the market as being made up of small segments, each more homogeneous than the total in important characteristics. Market segmentation is the process of partitioning the heterogeneous market into segments. The various segments identified should be homogeneous within themselves, but heterogeneous in total (i.e. different from other segments). The goal is to facilitate development of unique marketing programs that will be most effective for these specific segments.[1]

Market segmentation and targeting should not be confused with product differentiation. Product differentiation is a product-focused strategy designed to make one company's offering appear different from its competitors—a differentiated product may, or may not, appeal to a different group of people. In practice, it is often difficult to tell the difference between the two approaches without knowing the thinking behind the strategy. Product differentiation may be a useful strategy for producers of frequently purchased consumer goods where consumers are motivated by their need for variety. Product differentiation also is a function of the nature of the organisation. Your university, for example, probably sees itself as competing for the same group of high-school graduates in your state. Your department is differentiated from similar ones in other universities according to the resources available and the philosophy of the university. Segmentation and targeting, on the other hand, form a customer-focused strategy in which an offering is designated expressly for the needs of an identified group.[2]

Companies employing market segmentation typically select, or target, several market segments to appeal to with different products, using different promotional efforts and prices, and perhaps selling through different distribution outlets. Many companies fit this description, such as Procter & Gamble, which produce several brands of detergents to meet different consumers' needs (at least as they are perceived by purchasers of these brands).

BENEFITS AND COSTS OF MARKET SEGMENTATION

The process of market segmentation and targeting is consistent with the marketing concept. This customer-orientated philosophy means that the marketer first identifies the needs of the customers within a submarket (segment) and attempts to satisfy those needs.[3] With a better understanding of customers, marketers are better able to design and distribute products to suit customers' needs, price them profitably, and communicate better with their customers. Marketing efforts are more focused and resources are used more efficiently. Obvious examples of segmentation come from large companies that develop a range of different product forms for different segments. More interesting examples are small firms that compete very effectively by catering to the specialised needs of one or two market segments, such as a printing company that specialises in business cards or a computer firm that handles the unique requirements of law firms.

The result of understanding and relating to an increasingly fragmented marketplace is termed 'micromarketing'.[4] Mass media offer an illustration of micromarketing. Among magazines, a marketer could select one for a region, a city, a hobby, an age group or a combination, making the choices as diverse as the customers they serve.

Although market segmentation products benefits for the firm, it also boosts costs. Typically, manufacturing costs can be higher because of shorter production runs; research costs are higher because of the need to investigate more segments; promotion costs are higher when quantity media discounts are lost; and overlapping market coverage may result in some 'cannibalisation' as one product steals sales from another in the same company's line. Thus, market segmentation can result in greater sales for a company, but at higher costs. Of course, the goal is to increase revenue more than costs, and so raise profits.[5] Therefore, the decision to develop separate products for different markets should be the result of a careful balance between benefits gained and costs incurred.

Some industry experts insist that segmentation is frequently unnecessary or uneconomical in the Australian and New Zealand marketplaces. With a relatively small combined population of less than 21 million people spread over a very large section of the globe, the costs of developing truly differentiated marketing programs frequently outweigh the benefits.[6]

DEFINING MARKET SEGMENTS

It is often said that a market consists of people with purchasing power and the willingness to buy. That is:

Market = people × purchasing power × willingness to buy

If we examine these three elements of the consumer market, we will obtain useful insights on which to base segmentation decisions. Criteria for defining and then describing effective market segments should cover these elements.

A decision to use a market segmentation strategy should rest on consideration of four important criteria that affect its profitability. In order for segmentation to be viable, the market must be identifiable and measurable, accessible, substantial and responsive.

1. *Identifiable and measurable.* Segments must be identifiable so that the marketer can determine which consumers belong to a segment and which do not. However, there may be a problem with the segment's measurability (the amount of information available on specific buyer characteristics) because numerous variables (e.g. psychological factors) are difficult, if not impossible, to measure. For example, if a marketer discovered that consumers who perspire profusely favoured a particular brand, very little could be done with this information as such a group would be difficult to measure and identify for segmentation purposes.

2. *Accessible.* This criterion refers to the ease of effectively and economically reaching chosen segments with marketing efforts. Some desired segments may be inaccessible because of legal reasons; for example, alcohol and tobacco products are not available to people below certain ages. More often segments may be inaccessible because the marketer is unable to reach them at a reasonable cost and with minimum waste via existing promotional media and distribution systems.

3. *Substantial.* This criterion refers to the degree to which a chosen segment is large enough to support profitably a separate marketing program.[7] A strategy of market segmentation and targeting can be costly, and so a marketer must carefully consider not only the number of customers available in a segment but also the amount of their purchasing power.

4. *Responsive.* There is little to justify the development of a separate and unique marketing program for a target segment unless it responds uniquely to these efforts. Therefore, the problem is to identify market segments that will respond favourably to marketing programs designed specifically for them.[8] Conversely, if all identified groups will respond favourably to the one marketing effort, it only makes sense to treat them as one unit.

If the four criteria are fulfilled, segmentation will be an attractive marketing strategy. The question remains, however: by which variables or bases may the market be segmented? Before exploring these bases in detail, we will first describe the process of performing market-segmentation studies.

Performing market segmentation studies

This section reviews the steps involved in a typical market-segmentation study in order to illustrate a successful approach that may often be taken.[9] The eight steps are as follows:

1. *Define the problem or determine the use to be made of the research.* Market segmentation can be used to answer a wide range of questions about the response of market segments to the firm's marketing strategies (such as price or product changes, new product offerings and advertising themes), and can aid in the selection of target market segments for the firm's offerings.

2. *Select a segmentation basis.* Segmentation studies are usually conducted by marketing practitioners using one of two general alternatives for choosing a segmentation basis: *a priori* and *clustering methods.* For purposes of illustration, the a priori approach will be described here. The clustering method will also be addressed briefly at the end of this section.

   In the a priori segmentation approach, management decides *in advance* what basis to use for segmentation. If, for example, concern is with the likely impact of a price increase, consumer-income or price-sensitivity measures may be chosen as the segmentation basis. With this type of market-segmentation approach, therefore, the marketer must begin by selecting some basis for it.

   Generally, segmentation bases used by marketers can be categorised as falling into one of two major groupings: general consumer characteristics and situation-specific consumer characteristics. General consumer characteristics to be discussed in this chapter include demographic, geographic, socioeconomic and lifestyle characteristics. Situation-specific consumer characteristics to be examined include product usage, purchase patterns and benefits sought in a product. Used as a basis, each of these groupings offers advantages as well as disadvantages, depending on the situation faced by the marketer. The relevant considerations for making a selection in the segmentation process are management's specific needs and the state of knowledge about each variable's relevance as a market-segmentation basis.

3. *Choose a set of descriptors that defines, characterises or relates to the segmentation basis.* These descriptors of segments can include virtually any variable (sex, social class and so on). To illustrate, the degree to which a person may respond to price deals may be linked to such demographic descriptors as age, income and location. In fact, the enormous number of possible variables from which to select makes the decision process complex for the marketer.

4. *Select a sample of consumers that is representative of the larger population of interest.* Here, the idea is to research and identify segments on a low-cost basis. Instead of gathering data from the entire population, a less costly sample of consumers is selected. It is then determined if

segments are identifiable within this sample. If so, the next step is to project sample results to the relevant population in order to segment the entire market.

5. *Collect data on segment descriptors from the sample of consumers.* When obtaining these data, the marketer may rely on primary data-collection efforts or on available secondary sources (e.g. several market research companies offer clients a variety of measures on a national panel of consumers).

6. *Form segments based on chosen consumer descriptors.* Here the marketer must define and use a dividing line to determine to which segment each sample consumer will be assigned.[10] For example, if the marketer were segmenting consumers into heavy-use and light-use soft-drink users, the decision might be to classify heavy users as those who purchase more than 4 litres of soft drinks per week.

7. *Establish profiles of segments.* Once respondents have been classified into segments, profiles of these segments can be established on the basis of their key discriminating characteristics. For example, a segment of television viewers who may be frequent watchers of television movies may be profiled as having the following characteristics: lower income and education, and traditional, conservative values; compulsive television viewing; pride in a clean home; unwillingness to take risks; concerned with security; content with being homebodies; and price consciousness. Several analytical techniques exist for accomplishing this process, but discussion of their use is beyond the scope of this text.[11]

8. *Translate the results into a marketing strategy.* This is the most difficult aspect of any segmentation project. During this stage the marketer uses findings about the segments' estimated sizes and profiles to select target market groups and design appropriate marketing mixes for the chosen segments. Thus, the key to a successful segmentation study is the ability to interpret results and use them as guidelines for the design, execution and evaluation of and appropriate marketing strategy. The selection of target segments is a complex 'art' in which the marketer considers such factors as the segments' expected responses to marketing variables, their reachability, the nature of competitive activity within each segment, and the company's resources and ability to implement a segmented strategy. Information from the segment profile should help generate diverse ideas and creative strategies for appealing to chosen segments.

The a priori approach has been the traditional method of selecting a basis for segmentation. However, it has the serious potential limitation that the marketer may not have sufficient information in advance to select the best segmentation basis. Unless the marketer is fortunate enough to begin the process by correctly identifying the most useful basis for segmentation, a less-than-optimum segmentation of the market is likely to occur.

The clustering method presents an alternative that addresses this potential limitation of the a priori method. In this approach, rather than selecting a basis for segmentation in advance, the researcher first attempts to see how a sample group of consumers may form their own groupings based on a variety of descriptor variables, such as needs, attitudes, benefits sought and lifestyle characteristics. This procedure typically starts with measuring consumers on a wide variety of descriptors. Then, usually with computer-based grouping methods, the researcher attempts to find how consumers may cluster together on the basis of these measures. Such an approach is said to allow consumers to form 'natural' groupings, instead of forming only those pre-established by the researcher when the a priori method is used. If such natural groupings are identified, the next step will be to determine what descriptor or set of descriptors may be associated with, or explain, these groupings. This information will then be used to form the basis or bases for segmentation.[12]

Marketers have increasingly adopted database marketing techniques to reach a fragmented marketplace.[13] Table 2.1 offers advice on building an effective marketing database. Database marketing involves the development of huge lists of names and addresses of potential customers who are then courted directly.

TABLE 2.1 How to build a database for marketing

1. Compile a computerised list of your individual customers, including the information you already have about each customer. How long has a person been a customer? How much does he or she spend? Does this person pay with a cheque or credit card? What type of product or service does this person buy?

2. Review the data items to determine which ones can help you improve the efficiency of your marketing efforts and which ones don't matter. The details of the purchasing behaviour of your customers is important, for example. So is knowing a person's age and sex. But if everyone who buys your product is university-educated, maybe you don't need to collect information about educational attainment.

3. Figure out what's missing. It's unlikely you already have all the information you need to target your customers more precisely. To find out more about the demographics, psychographics and media habits of your customers, you may need to survey a sample of your database. If you can't afford that, many firms can take a list of your customers' addresses, assign each one to its census block, and supply you with the typical demographic characteristics of the households in that block.

4. Determine who your best customers are. Segment your database by the dollar value of your customers. By knowing the characteristics of your best customers, you can target potential customers who share those characteristics.

5. Keep your database up-to-date. A customer database is a long-term relationship, not a one-night stand. Keeping it up-to-date will require money and constant maintenance, but it should pay off in bigger profits.

Source: Joe Schwortz, 'Databases Deliver the Goods', *American Demographics*, September 1989, p. 25.

Information about existing customers is used to develop lists of similar people who may be regarded as potential customers. After they become customers, their buying patterns are tracked and their brand loyalty is strengthened with special offers, ultimately converting the buyer to an enthusiastic salesperson for the company.[14] The strategy's success, however, is dependent on the development of large, detailed, sophisticated databases containing market-by-market information that can be used to understand consumers and their purchases.

The remainder of this chapter will examine a number of popular segmentation bases in more detail. It should be noted again, however, that no one basis will be appropriate for all marketing decisions; in fact, a combination of approaches may lead to much better information for decision making.

Demographic segmentation

Demography is the study of human population statistics, including size, age, sex, race, location, occupation, income and other characteristics. This section discusses the major demographic characteristics of the Australian and New Zealand populations with which the reader should be familiar.

At last, pure moisturisation.

OIL of ULAN
Hydro-Gel

We keep our promise to young skin.

What age group does Oil of Ulan target? What age group should Oil of Ulan target?

COURTESY OF PROCTER & GAMBLE AUSTRALIA PTY LTD

POPULATION GROWTH

It is helpful first to examine the overall size and growth patterns of populations in the region, even though the population as a whole does not represent a 'segment' of interest to most firms.

In 1991 the Australian population stood at 17.3 million. The New Zealand population was 3.4 million. Population growth is affected by two major causes: birth rates and migration. Changes in birth rate have been evidenced by the postwar 'baby boom' and recent declines in the number of children born to families. In addition, Australia has always been a country with a large proportion of migrants, especially since World War II. At the 1991 census, over 3.8 million Australians were born in 224 countries. That is, nearly a quarter (23 per cent) of Australians were born overseas. A further 3.3 million born in Australia had at least one parent born overseas. New Zealand has a proportionally smaller migrant population with 16 per cent born overseas, about half of whom were born in the British Isles.

The 'cohort' approach to analysing a population works on the notion that people differ according to the time when they grew up. Three major cohorts have been identified: 'the mature' cohort, the 'baby boomers' and the 'post-boomers'.

The mature cohort are Australians aged over 50. They grew into adulthood having experienced the Great Depression and World War II. Having seen hardship and upheaval, they were concerned that the prosperity for their families might not last. They were cautious—investing in homes, staying in jobs and building security.

The baby boom began in 1946 and lasted to the early 1960s. Children born during this period were raised in a time of rapid economic growth, expansion, new ideas and opportunity. 'This was the generation that moved from 1960s protest movements to 1980s "yuppiedom". Their essential belief was that good times (with occasional hiccoughs) would last forever.'[15] Material possessions, purchased by hard work and easy credit, were the measures of success. These attitudes have changed somewhat in the last decade due, in part, to the stock market crash of 1987, recession and economic restructuring.

Children of boomers, the post-boomers, often called 'Generation X', are growing up in quite a different world.[16] As they grow into adulthood, the youngest of the postboomers have many worries. Most frustrating is the realisation that, in a changing economic climate, many are unlikely to achieve the same levels of economic security of earlier generations. The areas where there are employment opportunities are shifting. Manufacturing is contracting and becoming less labour intensive. Job growth is in service and information-based industries. Jobs are harder and harder to get for those without the education to cope with the new work structures. Even established jobs require literacy and numeracy skills that were never needed in the past. Postboomers are staying in educational institutions longer, staying in parental homes longer, marrying later and starting families later—keeping their options open. In this environment it might be expected that the postboomers would be pessimistic about their prospects and resentful of their parents' generation. On the contrary, research by AMR: Quantum Monitor Services suggests that these young adults generally are confident about their futures and are prepared to take a pragmatic view of their lives.[17]

What differentiates the postboomers most from their parents, says the research, is their different focus on education and employment. Education is seen far more as the means to a job than as something of value in its own right. The postboomers are more prepared to invest time and effort into education in order to compete for scarce jobs. When they get a job, they are likely to be prepared to work long hours to achieve higher pay, at least until they face marriage commitments. In other respects, postboomers, those under 35, are much like the boomers, those aged from 35 to 50, in the 1990s. They desire access to what are seen as luxuries, but their materialism is tempered by a need for self-fulfilment and satisfaction with what can be afforded.

The Quantum research also noted the effect of life commitments. Being a full-time student, being 'adrift' (unemployed and not studying full time), being a single worker, or being 'settled' (married and working or 'home-making') are more powerful indicators of attitudes and behaviours than age as such.

THE CHANGING AGE MIX OF THE AUSTRALIAN AND NEW ZEALAND POPULATION

We are living longer and having fewer children than ever before. Australia and New Zealand, therefore, have ageing populations. The proportion of children is decreasing and the proportion of older people is increasing. In the two decades to 1991 the median age in Australia rose five years to 32.4 years. Changes in age structure will have major implications for marketers as well as on economic and social planning.

A useful measure is known as the 'dependency ratio', which is taken as the ratio of dependent persons (those aged under 16 and over 65) to the working-aged population (those aged between 16 and 65 years). It can be further divided into the youth dependency ratio, which is the ratio of dependent persons aged under 16 to the working-aged population, and the aged dependent ratio, the proportion aged over 65 to the working-aged population. In New Zealand, where the dependency ratio is defined by the ages 15–59, it is expected to rise from 0.620 in 1988 to 0.799 in 2031. This reflects the sharp upturn in the aged dependency ratio, which will almost double from 0.247 to about 0.478 in that time. In 1991 for every person aged 65 years and over there were 5.7 persons of working age (16–65), but by about the time today's university students retire in 2031 there is expected to be only 3.1 persons of working age for each elderly person.

Although cohort factors are difficult to predict, the following are observable trends compared with earlier decades. First, there are more women working. The growth is important because it has occurred largely among women who have small children. Hence, there have been demands for more day care and paid maternity leave. Overall the proportion of women in the labour force has risen to over 60 per cent. Seventy-five per cent of all two-parent families have both parents employed.

Secondly, there will continue to be few children per family. However, because a very large number of women are entering prime child-bearing years, total births may jump in spite of a low overall birthrate.[18] Also, a large share of these births will be of first children—an estimated 40 per cent of births in 1985 were of first children, versus only 25 per cent in 1960. This is significant as it has been estimated that an additional $700 is spent by parents 'tooling up' for the first child. In fact, a leading consulting firm estimates that during the first three years, a first-born child accounts for over $2000 in retail sales. Thus, this expected baby 'boomlet' could account for an incremental $1 billion in retail sales each year.[19] Parents' changing spending patterns are also causing a significant growth in the children's market. For instance, today's parents have more money to spend on kids because they have waited to have children about two years longer than their parents did. The further along they are in their careers, the more money they have to spend. When parents decide their child must have something, cost may not matter.[20]

A third cohort factor is the growth in the number of households (which are composed of those related and unrelated individuals who occupy a housing unit). Although the total population is an important factor, for many companies it is not nearly as critical as the total number of households. One of the reasons for the rapid growth in households is the high rate of divorce. The divorce rate for all marriages is currently 50 per cent, and census experts estimate that approximately half of all children born in 1980 will spend a large part of their childhood with only one parent. At current rates, 60 per cent of American women now in their 30s will go through at least one divorce. Among the 70 per cent who remarry, 52 per cent will go through a second divorce.[21]

REGIONAL DISTRIBUTION OF THE POPULATION

Population is not distributed evenly across Australia and New Zealand but instead is concentrated in certain states and regions. The south-eastern corner of Australia and the top half of New Zealand's North Island, respectively, account for more than half of each country's population.

A NATION OF URBAN DWELLERS

Despite its vast land mass, Australia is the most urbanised country on earth. About 86 per cent of the population live in urban centres. Six out of 10 Australians live in a capital city. Table 2.2 shows that 71 per cent of the population live in just 13 cities of more than 100 000 people.

TABLE 2.2 Australian cities with populations greater than 100 000

Cities over 100 000	Population at 30 June 1991	Proportion of population	Average annual growth rate 1981–91
	'000	%	%
Sydney	3672.9	21.2	1.1
Melbourne	3156.7	18.3	1.2
Brisbane	1358.0	7.9	2.2
Perth	1188.8	6.9	2.6
Adelaide	1057.2	6.1	1.0
Newcastle	444.9	2.6	1.0
Canberra—Queanbeyan	313.4	1.8	2.4
Gold Coast—Tweed Heads	279.6	1.6	5.6
Wollongong	244.9	1.4	0.6
Hobart	186.9	1.1	0.9
Geelong	151.6	0.9	0.7
Sunshine Coast	119.3	0.7	6.2
Townsville	116.2	0.7	1.9
Total	12290.4	71.1	1.5
Rest of Australia	4993.7	28.9	1.4
Total	17284.0	100.0	1.5

Source: Ian Castles, 'Australia in Profile', *Census of Population and Housing 6 August 1991*, Australian Bureau of Statistics, Canberra, Cat. no. 2821.0.

INTERNAL MIGRATION

Recent ABS figures show a declining population in Victoria and South Australia accompanied by rapid growth in south-eastern Queensland (Brisbane and the Gold Coast) and the Northern Rivers region of New South Wales, and Perth in Western Australia. Reasons for internal migration in Australia include a decline or low growth in heavy industries of the southern states and economic growth in Queensland and Western Australia, with accompanying improvements in opportunities for employment.

NON-METROPOLITAN POPULATION

Australia and New Zealand have witnessed a steady change in the structure of the rural population. Small towns are declining in importance and in population as people move to larger rural towns. Mechanisation and increased scale of operation have reduced the need for labour on farms and properties. Advances in communications and transport have diminished the need for many of the services for which some towns were established. Lastly, a recession in agricultural and mineral prices, static world demand for commodities and, in some cases, overambitious financing by property owners and banks have led to a decline in the ability to employ people in some rural sectors. However, the total proportion of people not living in urban centres has changed little in the past 20 years, and is not expected to change in the next few years.

Marketers are increasingly learning that there are important regional differences and for many products the shotgun approach of a single national advertising campaign is less effective than more precisely targeted regional strategies.

National brands are spending less, proportionately, on national media and more on regional television, radio and newspapers. This marketing approach emphasises local colour, appeals to regional tastes, problems and styles, uses local celebrities for testimonials, ties in with local events and sometimes offers a regionalised product. For example, all of the commercial television networks in Australia, and the ABC, produce a national news service that is presented in different regions by local newsreaders and augmented with local stories. National current affairs programs also have regional editions.

GEOGRAPHIC MOBILITY

People move home for a variety of reasons. Research in the United States suggests that about 43 per cent of people move for a job change or job transfer, about 24 per cent move for a larger house or better location, and 10 per cent in order to own a home. The remainder move to be closer to relatives, for retirement or for health.[22] In Australia and New Zealand the reasons are likely to be similar, but we tend to be less inclined to move outside of our home cities or home states.

The mobile segment has been found to be a potentially superior market for such products as furniture, clothing and drapes, and consumer durables such as cars and appliances.[23] Once relocated, mobiles must rebuild shopping patterns in their new community.[24] They learn about new suppliers primarily from talking with friends, neighbours and co-workers. However, mass-media sources such as newspapers and the Yellow Pages are also important, as is personal observation while driving around. Mobiles tend to rebuild shopping patterns rapidly, in part because of holding charge accounts with national retailers, which allows them to transfer their store and brand loyalty to the new community.

Because of the value of this segment, successful retailers and suppliers servicing regions with rapidly growing populations are cognisant of the efforts necessary to attract the geographically mobile market. For example, a retailer could benefit from setting up a newcomer program to identify new arrivals and make contact with these families before their shopping habits have been rebuilt. One retail chain, based in Brisbane and the Gold Coast, checks government records of residential sales each week and delivers an introductory gift, accompanied by a brochure and discount voucher, to new residents. Such promotions are designed to build awareness and loyalty.

GEODEMOGRAPHIC CLUSTERING OF MARKETS

By using computer geomapping software in conjunction with sophisticated demographic databases, marketers are able to better understand market diversity and target potentially attractive segments. The combination of geographic and demographic consumer information is known as *geodemographics* and is an important segmenting tool. Applications of this technique have included improving media plans, choosing retail sites and predicting sales at new locations, introducing new products, planning merchandise mixes and segmenting customer

Consumers in country areas tend to share the same values and attitudes. Their media habits are quite different from those of consumers in the cities
COURTESY OF AUSTRALIAN TOURIST COMMISSION

lists. For example, each of the petrol companies in Australia uses geodemographic analysis by coding its credit-card customer base to find its best customers and identify growth segments for targeting. Other retailers can also analyse which merchandise is best suited to an area's needs.

A number of Australian vendors offer geographic clustering services. The Salmat Group sells Marketfind, which incorporates computer-based maps and the results of a cluster analysis of key components of the 1991 census. Twelve population segments are identified in the Marketfind database, identified according to census collectors' districts. These are explained in Table 2.3. A marketer can overlay the residential locations of existing customers on a map to discover the types of homes in which they live. Based on the logic that potential new customers are likely to be similar to existing customers, the results can help to develop direct-marketing programs, and to profile customers' lifestyles for promotions.

TABLE 2.3 Marketfind profiles

Established Prestige 6%
Suburbs of very wealthy, well-educated and professional families, larger houses. High home ownership. Children in private secondary schools. Two-income families. High levels of employment in finance, property and business.

Affluent Estates 10.7%
Suburbs with better-off, two-income families, often with adolescent children and middle-aged parents. Living in large houses, many with mortgages, in newer suburban areas. Many households have three motor vehicles.

Urban Young 11.3%
Areas of younger white-collar workers and professionals, living in flats and other high-density accommodation. Many rent, as singles, couples or group households. Work in finance, property and business services and travel to work by public transport.

Desirable Suburbia 11.9%
Established better-off suburbs with many qualified and professional persons. Dual households, with high levels of home ownership. Many persons 65+ years.

Elderly Enclaves 3.1%
Enclaves of older people. Mainly widows and retirees. Not necessarily poor. Households with welfare incomes. Low vehicle ownership. Found in small clusters within larger suburban areas.

New Estates 8.4%
New estates with young families, vocational skills, dual incomes, three bedrooms, two cars and a mortgage.

Middle Australia 11.6%
Working-class families, middle-aged with teenage children. Homes generally three bedroom and mortgaged. Work in manufacturing. Low levels of higher education and professional qualifications. Few migrants.

Multicultural Suburbia 9.8%
Established and stable suburban areas. High home ownership. Married couples 55+ years, and single persons 65+ years. Many born in Europe and speak a European language. Work in manufacturing and clerical occupations.
Continues

TABLE 2.3 Marketfind profiles *continued*

Senior Citizen 14%
Older, industrial and poorer retirement suburbs. Many married persons 55+ years and single persons 65+ years. Low incomes. Few migrants.

Urban Low Income 3.8%
Low-status urban areas. Many work in manufacturing, as plant operators, labourers. Rent flats and other high-density accommodation. Use trains and other public transport. Low levels of higher education. Many migrants, particularly of Asian origin.

Suburban Battler 4.6%
Low-status suburban areas. Two-parent families, three-bedroom homes. Many plant and machine operators and labourers. High proportion of Asian and European migrants with lower education and employment status.

Suburban Welfare 4.7%
Very poor areas. One-parent families, welfare incomes, housing-commission rentals and low levels of higher education.

Source: Courtesy of Salmat.

A number of other geodemographic mapping companies, such as GEOSMART offered by Robert Dommet & Associates, provide corporations with customised segmentation and clustering services designed to link individual brand and product potential with specific regions, and calculate the probability of successful sales.

Geographic segmentation is rarely based on clusters of people. Segmentation based on the census data involves clustering of small geographic regions based on the average scores for all the households within each region. To simplify an otherwise nearly impossible task, and one that may also risk an invasion of privacy, all households living within a region are assumed to be similar to the average of the region. There are some obvious dangers to this approach—it's a bit like saying, for example, that on average commerce students are different from science students; therefore, *all* commerce students are different from *all* science students, which of course is not true. On the other hand, if we know that a particular student is enrolled in commerce, it's a safe bet that he or she will behave more like a commerce student than a science student.

INCOME (PURCHASING POWER)

The marketer is very interested in the second part of our equation concerning what constitutes a market: what people have available to spend. But just what is income? Economists point out that there are three different concepts involved:

1. *Personal income.* The income from wages, salaries, dividends, rent, interest, social security, farming and so on.

2. *Disposable income.* The amount left over for personal-consumption expenditures and saving, after deducting taxes.

3. *Discretionary income.* The amount available for spending after taking care of fixed expenditures on necessities such as housing, transport, utilities, food and clothing.

Determining what is meant by discretionary income can be difficult because of the word 'necessities'. Specifying this amount requires an arbitrary decision as to exactly what is necessary. For example, how much of your money spent on food is 'necessary' and how much is 'luxurious'? Other important influences on discretionary income include the number of income earners in a household, family life stage and area of residence. Consider the discretionary income of a worker living in Sydney's western suburbs, travelling into the city each day, paying a mortgage and supporting a young family. Consider the discretionary income of a similar worker earning the same personal income but living in Brisbane's southern suburbs. The Sydney worker is likely to be paying a much higher mortgage and spending more time and money travelling between home and work and, as a result, is likely to have a much lower level of discretionary income.

Researchers may define discretionary income as any income that is more than one standard deviation higher than the average for households of similar size, location and age. To get a better handle on the individual tastes and preferences that decide whether expenditures are necessities or luxuries, the researcher must understand the types of expenditures to which consumers are committed and how they feel about their income. Consumers may be financially committed to paying for an expensive car, or for a home in a prestige part of the city. These commitments certainly reduce consumers' ability to make purchases of other goods they may desire. For a marketer of consumer products, and for the consumers themselves, discretionary income may be low.

A useful concept may be subjective discretionary income (SDI), which incorporates the idea of how satisfied people are with their life and with their perceived economic well-being.[25] People who score high on an SDI scale say they have enough money to buy what they think they need. Those scoring low are indicating they have difficulty making ends meet. Depending on such factors as expectations, goals and family situation, a person may have a high or low SDI at any level of personal income.

WILLINGNESS TO BUY   The last portion of our equation regarding what constitutes a market is the consumers' willingness to buy. Consumers' discretionary demand is a function of both ability to buy—primarily income—and willingness to buy.[26] Thus, it is the combination of these two elements that holds the key to future buying. One indication of willingness to buy is the consumer's plans for future spending and is typically measured by the level of confidence of the consumer. If consumers are confident of their financial security in the immediate future, they may be more willing to make major purchasing decisions, such as buying a car or home appliance or taking out a mortgage on a house.

The Department of Economics at Monash University publishes its index of consumer confidence every six months. It is closely watched by major companies and by banks and government. The surveys not only help organisations to anticipate trends in the economy, but also help in understanding the past.[77] Another special form of confidence indicator is the Australian Chamber of Commerce's Index of Business Confidence, which is used to measure business's willingness to invest in expansion and create jobs.

Consumer confidence surveys attempt to blend psychology and economics to achieve an accurate estimate of consumers' willingness to buy. Questions covering personal finances, business conditions and buying conditions are not intended to establish the absolute level of consumer sentiment at any given time, but to measure the direction and degree of change. One can also analyse why these changes in consumer attitudes and expectations occur and how they relate to later shifts in consumer behaviour.[78]

LIMITATIONS OF DEMOGRAPHICS IN PREDICTING CONSUMER BEHAVIOUR[29]

There has been much discussion in recent years about the role of demographic factors as correlates or even determinants of the consumption behaviour of people. A number of researchers have expressed scepticism that such factors can be effectively used. For example, there are some undeniable demographic patterns to purchasing, such as that razor blades are purchased mainly for men. However, except for specific products aimed directly at specific demographic groups, evidence indicates that demographic measures, outside of education, are not an accurate predictor of consumer behaviour.[30]

One potential limitation of demographics in explaining consumer behaviour is based on the claim that while demographic factors may have been very relevant in the past (even up until World War II), they are now obsolete because of the narrowing differences in income, education and occupational status. Nevertheless, there is much evidence showing that group differences among *categories* of income, education and occupation are large and statistically significant in spite of a large number of within-group differences. It should also be noted that demographic factors include numerous other variables (such as age, sex, race and religion) that are much less subject to influence from environmental change. For example, older people tend not to listen to rock music, men drink more beer than do women, and Catholics still tend to use contraceptives much less than the rest of the population.

A second and more basic argument against using demographics is that they have generally failed to explain and predict consumption behaviour. However, although demographics have failed to explain brand-choice behaviour, they seem to succeed in explaining buying behaviour at the broad product-class level of such items as durable appliances, automobiles and housing. Thus, it has been suggested that before demographics are abandoned because of their lacklustre performance, several past problems with demographic research should be subjected to further study. These problems are mainly associated with techniques for measuring demographic variables, assumptions underlying their relationship to consumer behaviour, inclusion of a small group of people in such studies who do not have a consistent pattern of behaviour, and techniques of statistical analysis that are performed on the data.

Important reasons exist for the continued use of demographics in segmenting markets. First, they are easier to collect, easier to communicate to others and often more reliable in measurement than many of the competing approaches to segmentation. Moreover, only through demographic factors is the researcher able to project results to the country's population, because the Australian Bureau of Statistics and Statistics New Zealand collect and update only demographic profiles.

For these reasons, discarding demographics would seem to be premature. Instead, they should continue to be used as one element along with numerous other variables in approaching the puzzle of explaining consumer behaviour. Improvements in demographic measurement, variables and techniques used by marketers are likely to improve the quality of demographic contributions to marketing.[31] In any event, demographics will continue to be used for projection, identification and segmentation of markets as long as our census data are limited to a socioeconomic–demographic profile of citizens.

Lifestyle segmentation

One of the major problems of demographic segmentation is its lack of 'richness' in describing consumers for market segmentation and strategy development. If a demographic difference is found in preferences or consumption, that difference rarely gives us any indication of why. Consequently, many firms look for a better way to define markets or to fill in the gaps left by demographics. One of the most promising approaches to selecting target markets is *lifestyle and psychographic segmentation*.[32] Although the concepts of lifestyle and psychographics are often used interchangeably, they are complementary rather than equivalent.

The term 'lifestyle' is not new, but its application to marketing is recent. Alfred Adler coined the phrase 'style of life' over 50 years ago to refer to the goals people shape for themselves and the ways they use to reach them. From our perspective, lifestyle can be viewed as a unique pattern of living that influences and is reflected by a person's consumption behaviour.[33] Therefore, the way in which marketers facilitate the expression of an individual's lifestyle is by 'providing customers with parts of a potential mosaic from which they, as artists of their own lifestyles, can pick and choose to develop the composition that for the time seems best'.[34] Many products today are 'lifestyle' products; that is, they portray a style of life sought by potential users.

How does the concept of psychographics relate to lifestyle? Unfortunately, it is not an easy matter to define psychographics because there is no general agreement as to exactly what it is. It has to do with mental ('psycho') profiles ('graphics'), or the profiling of customers in psychological terms.[35] One of the more precise statements about its nature is the following: Psychographics is the systematic use of relevant activity, interest and opinion constructs to quantitatively explore and explain the communicating, purchasing and consuming behaviours of persons for brands, products and clusters of products.[36]

Psychographics may be viewed as the method of defining lifestyle in measurable terms. It should be noted, however, that there is some question about the use of psychographic instruments as a precise measure of the lifestyle of the individual consumer.[37] Nevertheless, the basic premise underlying lifestyle research is that the more marketers understand their customers, the more effectively they can communicate and market to them.[38] In many cases the primary targets of such marketing efforts are heavy users. Heavy users have traditionally been looked at demographically, but by incorporating lifestyle characteristics the marketer obtains a better, more true-to-life picture of such customers.[39]

The 'Look at Me' segment   COURTESY OF ROY MORGAN RESEARCH CENTRE PTY LTD

THE TECHNIQUES OF LIFESTYLE SEGMENTATION

Lifestyle-segmentation research measures:

1. how people spend their times engaging in activities;

2. what is of most interest or importance to them in their immediate surroundings;

3. their opinions and views about themselves and the world around them.

The 'Socially Aware' segment   COURTESY OF ROY MORGAN RESEARCH CENTRE PTY LTD

Together, these three areas are generally referred to as *Activities, Interests and Opinions*, or simply *AIOs*. Table 2.4 indicates the lifestyle dimensions (particularly AIOs) that may be investigated among consumers.

In a typical large-scale, lifestyle research project, questionnaires are mailed to members of a nationwide consumer panel. The questionnaires solicit traditional demographic information, average usage rates for as many as 100 different products, media habits, and respondents' activities, interests and opinions. Approximately 300 AIO statements may be included, to which respondents indicate the extent of their agreement or disagreement on 6-point Likert scales ranging from 'definitely disagree' to 'definitely agree'. The following are typical of the AIO statements employed:

➡ I have more self-confidence than most of my friends.

➡ Our family is too heavily in debt today.

➡ I am a homebody.

➡ I like to be considered a leader.

➡ I would be willing to pay more for a product with all-natural ingredients.

➡ I am an impulse buyer.

➡ My family is the most important thing to me.

Where do AIO items originate? They may come from intuition, hunches, conversations, research, reading, and group or individual in-depth interviews.

TABLE 2.4 Lifestyle dimensions

Activities	Interests	Opinions	Demographics
Work	Family	Themselves	Age
Hobbies	Home	Social issues	Education
Social events	Job	Politics	Income
Vacation	Community	Business	Occupation
Entertainment	Recreation	Economics	Family size
Club membership	Fashion	Education	Dwelling
Community	Food	Products	Geography
Shopping	Media	Future	City size
Sports	Achievements	Culture	Stage in life cycle

Source: Joseph T. Plummer, 'The Concept and Application of Life Style Segmentation', *Journal of Marketing* 38, January 1974, p. 34, published by the American Marketing Association.

Armed with three sets of data—AIOs, demographics and product usage—the marketer constructs user profiles. The analysis involves relating levels of agreement on all AIO items with the levels of usage of a product and with demographic characteristics. Typically, a pattern emerges in which AIO statements cluster together; that is, similar respondents are grouped together from a lifestyle perspective.

Generally, then, the process of lifestyle segmentation involves two steps. First, a determination is made of which lifestyle segments will efficiently produce the greatest number of profitable customers. Often heavy users are sought but, as we have seen, other segments also have potential. The second step involves defining and describing the selected target customers in more depth to understand how they may be attracted and communicated with more efficiently and relevantly.

One danger of relying on psychographic models, even when they are appropriate, is that marketers may risk alienating groups with a low index of usage, who make up a much larger proportion of the population. For example, yogurt consumption by one psychographic segment may be 20 per cent better than average, but if this segment comprises only say, 3 per cent of the market, this usage really doesn't compare to that of another psychographic group representing 40 per cent of the market, which although only consuming an average amount of yogurt, may account for one-third of all the yogurt sold. How to appeal successfully to each different psychographic group is an extremely challenging issue for marketers.[40]

APPLICATION OF LIFESTYLE SEGMENTATION

Lifestyle may be used as a basis for segmentation in several ways.[41] In one approach the marketer seeks to classify the consumer population into groups based on general lifestyle characteristics so that consumers within the groups have similar lifestyles. Using the research approach described above, a representative sample of consumers responds to a questionnaire containing AIOs, product usage, media consumption and demographic items. Through statistical routines (clustering and others) the marketer attempts to find out if people can be grouped together into distinct groups. Each group represents a different pattern of needs for and consumption of products and services. Once these groups are identified, the marketer is able to direct the product to appeal to one or several segments.[42]

More on lifestyle segmentation pertaining to cultural values will be discussed in Chapter 3.

Usage segmentation

Another segmentation approach often used by marketers is based on product or brand usage by consumers. Usage segmentation can take a number of directions. The marketer may want to identify various segments of users for a particular product category or users of the company's brand. In other cases, the marketer may want to segment users into those who buy frequently versus those who buy only occasionally (either product or brand), or into users who usually purchase just one brand versus users who switch from brand to brand. It may also be useful for the marketer to understand how segments arise based on different product usage situations. For example, some people may regularly buy Moccona instant coffee for everyday use, while others will have it on the shelf only to serve to guests. Any usage segmentation approach needs to specify the relevant dimensions of interest.

VOLUME SEGMENTATION

Volume segmentation attempts to identify frequent users of a product category or brand. Marketers often refer to the '20:80' thesis; that is, that 20 per cent of the market accounts for 80 per cent of sales of their product. Although the exact proportions may vary and the rule may not universally apply, it does indicate the importance of a relatively small group of consumers to the health of a firm's product or service.

THE TECHNIQUE OF VOLUME SEGMENTATION Frequently, buyers are segmented by dividing the market into heavy users, light users and non-users of the product, then examining their distinguishing characteristics. At one time this was an extremely difficult process for most companies, but today several marketing research organisations are able to provide such data. For example, Morgan Research conducts periodic national studies of product usage, personal characteristics and media habits of a large sample of adults in order to assist the marketer in identifying potential audiences.

APPLICATION OF VOLUME SEGMENTATION Marketers of a broad range of goods and services utilise volume as a fundamental segmentation criterion.

Research on packaged consumer goods indicates that the best way to increase sales of a product is to persuade present users to use more of that product, rather than to attract new users. This suggests that marketing efforts should generally be aimed at light to heavy users rather than at non-users.[43]

One of the real attractions of the usage approach to market segmentation is the ease with which the technique can be employed by so many firms. Most companies are able to segment consumers by usage rates because of access to marketing-research services and data-processing systems that can quickly categorise and analyse consumers by purchase activity. Department stores are able to analyse charge-account customers' purchases with regularity; banks can assess their customers' banking usage; and many packaged-consumer-goods firms can subscribe to syndicated services that provide usage information. Many firms have established programs to reward high-frequency customers for their loyalty. For instance, Ansett and Qantas offer 'Frequent Flyers' bonus travel when they meet certain minimum usage conditions. Myer department stores offer bonus purchases to charge-card customers who spend more than a certain amount during the Christmas period.

BRAND-USER SEGMENTATION

The marketer is generally most interested in determining whether those who purchase the company's brand are different, either demographically or psychologically, from those buying competitors' brands. If characteristics can be distinguished, then marketing programs can perhaps be developed to attract more buyers who resemble the preferred buyer.

PRODUCT-USER SEGMENTATION

Even if buyers of different *brands* may not be found to have different characteristics, the marketer will be interested in segmenting *product* users on the basis of any such distinguishing demographic or psychographic characteristics in order to reach them effectively. Within a product category such as soft drinks, for example, it may be found that those who consume low-calorie drinks differ demographically and psychographically from regular soft-drink users, although perhaps Diet Pepsi and Diet Coke drinkers are virtually the same. Of course, for many products, non-users may represent a significant marketing opportunity. Also, public-goods and non-profit-organisation specialists are continually confronted with the reality of the need to convert non-users to users. Consider the following marketing problems:

➡ Convincing non-using men and women to avail themselves of cancer checkups.

➡ Attracting non-riders to mass transportation.

➡ Attracting non-subscribers to symphonies, lectures and other cultural events.

Each of these problems represents a marketing opportunity to convert non-users to users. Obviously, the past rate of success for such projects has not been great, but with increased application of marketing research to understanding the motivations of different segments, greater success should occur in the future.

LOYALTY SEGMENTATION

Marketers are often interested in attracting not just brand users but, perhaps more importantly, those who consistently purchase the company's brand. When these brand-loyal buyers are identified (assuming they differ on certain characteristics from non-loyal buyers), appropriate marketing strategies may be developed to attract competitors' buyers who have similar characteristics or to increase the loyalty rate among current less loyal buyers.

Loyalty segmentation can also be successfully applied to retail-store customers.[44] Efforts to establish stronger bonds with buyers, known as *relationship marketing*, have great potential. By using database programs to identify and reach customers with relevant rewards, companies can cement the buyer–seller relationship. For example, both Myer and David Jones retail emporiums distribute brochures to credit-card holders with their monthly accounts. The selection of brochure frequently is based on a computer analysis of the types of products that person or household buys regularly. Customers receive information about products in which they are interested, and much less about products with which they are not concerned.

SITUATION SEGMENTATION

Marketers often become complacent after identifying their market by demographics and psychographics ('who' buys) and may go no further to understand 'how' the product is used and enjoyed, whether the consumer is at work, play or home. Actually, a manufacturer's or retailer's product line can be seen as a range of items appealing to the needs of diverse person-situation market segments.[45] This segmentation approach divides the market by groups of consumers within usage situations.

Benefit segmentation

The approaches to market segmentation discussed so far are all helpful to the marketer. However, they suffer from an underlying disadvantage—all are based on an ex post analysis of the kinds of people who make up specific segments of a market. That is, emphasis is on *describing* the characteristics of different segments rather than on learning what *causes* these segments to develop. However, proponents of benefit segmentation claim that the *benefits* that people are seeking are the basic reasons for purchase and therefore the proper basis for market segmentation.[46]

THE TECHNIQUE OF BENEFIT SEGMENTATION

The technique of benefit segmentation typically involves a three-step process:

1. Exploratory research to develop a complete listing of benefits of possible value in segmenting the relevant market.

2. Development of sensitive and reliable scales to measure major attitude dimensions.

3. Quantitative measurement of the market, usually involving a national sample, resulting in clustering of respondents by their attitudes. Individual clusters (or segments) are described in terms of their behaviour, lifestyles, demographics and other relevant characteristics. Segments, therefore, are discriminated by their attitudes, and differences in their behaviour are analysed through cross tabulations.[47]

Although the concept appears simple, its implementation is very complex, often requiring computers and sophisticated multivariate attitude-measurement techniques. The statistical methods employed relate the responses of each consumer to those of every other respondent and then develop clusters (typically three to seven segments) of consumers with similar rating patterns. Each of these segments represents a potentially profitable and different opportunity for marketing effort.

PRODUCT POSITIONING

Effective product positioning is a key ingredient of successful marketing today. This section discusses the importance of positioning as it relates to the segmentation process, and discusses several approaches to the process.

The interrelationship of market segmentation and product positioning

Segmentation is essentially the accommodation of different consumer groupings in a marketing plan or strategy. Knowing that different consumers respond differently to products, promotions, prices and channels means that the marketer should not consider just the overall population's reaction to, say, a product, but also the reaction among different market segments. Market segmentation, therefore, is both the process of defining the characteristics of various segments in the marketplace and the allocation of marketing resources among these segments.

Product positioning is closely linked with market segmentation. A product's position is the place that it occupies relative to competitors in a given market as perceived by the relevant group of customers, that is, by the target-market segment. Positioning involves determining how consumers *perceive* the marketer's product and also developing and implementing marketing strategies to achieve the desired position in the market. Product, price, distribution and promotional ingredients should all be viewed as potential tools for positioning a company and its offerings. Positioning, therefore, has no value in itself, only in its effect on the target-market segment. Marketers must look at segmentation and positioning in tandem. The process may start either by selecting a target-market segment and then trying to develop a suitable position, or by selecting an attractive product position and then identifying an appropriate market segment. Whether the product is new or old, positioning is a key ingredient for achieving successful market results.

Although business people have long been positioning their products to appeal to target-market segments, these decisions have not always been made consciously or successfully. To increase the chances of success, a systematic approach to the decision is needed. The remainder of this chapter will discuss various strategies and techniques used in a systematic approach to positioning.

Strategies to position products

Many ways exist for positioning a product or service (or even an organisation). The following illustrate some of these approaches. It should be noted that combinations of these approaches are also possible.[48]

POSITION ON PRODUCT FEATURES

The product may be positioned on the basis of product features. For example, an advertisement may attempt to position the product by reference to its specific features. Although this may be a successful way to indicate product superiority, consumers are generally more interested in what such features mean to them; that is, how they can benefit by the product.

POSITION ON BENEFITS

This approach is closely related to the previous method. Toothpaste advertising often features the benefit approach, as the examples of Crest (decay prevention), Close-Up (sex appeal through white teeth and fresh breath), and Aqua-Fresh (a combination of these benefits) illustrate. The difference between this and the features approach is illustrated by the adage, 'Don't sell the steak, sell the sizzle'.

POSITION ON USAGE

This technique is related to benefit positioning. Many products are sold on the basis of their consumer-usage situation. Companies have sometimes sought to broaden their brand's association with a particular usage or situation. Campbell's Soup for many years was positioned for use at lunchtime and advertised extensively over noontime radio. It now stresses a variety of uses for soup (recipes are on labels) and a broader time for consumption, with the more general theme 'Soup is good food'. Gatorade was originally a summer beverage for athletes who needed to replace body fluids, but it has also tried to develop a positioning strategy during the cold or flu season as the beverage to drink when the doctor recommends consuming plenty of fluids. Arm & Hammer very successfully added a position to their baking soda—as an odour-destroying agent in refrigerators—and sales jumped tremendously.

POSITION ON USER

This approach associates the product with a user or a class of users. Some cosmetics companies seek a successful, highly visible model as their spokesperson (Christie Brinkley for Cover Girl) as the association for their brand. Other brands may pick a lesser-known model to portray a certain lifestyle in their ads (e.g. Revlon's Charlie cosmetics line). With its humorous sports personalities Miller Lite beer has been very successful in positioning itself as a beer for the heavy user who dislikes that filled-up feeling. A company may sometimes need to appeal to new users as it shifts markets. Johnson & Johnson now present adult users as well as babies in its ads for baby shampoo. Because users and usage situations are related, they may often be linked in an ad.

POSITION AGAINST COMPETITION

Often success for a company involves looking for weak points in the positions of its competitors and then launching marketing attacks against those weak points.[49] In this approach, the marketer may either directly or indirectly make comparisons with competing products. For example, the famous 'Uncola' campaign successfully positioned 7-Up as an alternative to Coke, Pepsi and other colas (almost two-thirds of soft drinks consumed in the United States are colas). Notice, too, how this brand confronted a situation of special-usage positioning. For instance 7-Up was originally thought of as a hangover cure, and it is still viewed as a special-occasion beverage, for an occasion other than a cola time.[50]

Positioning analysis

The marketer may use several techniques for determining the appropriate positioning for a brand. Whether the brand is new or old, focus groups and in-depth interviews may be helpful in providing insights from consumers. In addition, survey and experimental research approaches such as those discussed in Chapter 17 may provide useful positioning data. Lifestyle information and a technique known as perceptual mapping can also be helpful in positioning decisions.

LIFESTYLE POSITIONING

Consumer AIOs can be used in designing a marketing strategy for potential markets. This approach is illustrated by positioning for the volunteer army. The army found dramatic differences between young men favouring and those not favouring the army as a career. Data suggest that it may be a mistake to position the army as a continuous party in which discipline is relaxed and nobody is required to stand in line, clean rooms, follow orders or shoot guns. Young men and women who agree that the army is a good career appear to be unusually patriotic and conservative, and are willing to accept hard work, discipline and direction.[51]

PERCEPTUAL MAPPING

The above discussion suggests that consumers' perceptions of products are developed in a complex way and are not easily determined by the marketer. However, a technique known as perceptual mapping may be used in exploring consumers' product perceptions. As products can be perceived on many dimensions (such as quality, price and strength), the technique is multidimensional in nature. That is, it allows for the influence of more than one stimulus characteristic on product perceptions. Typically, consumers fill out measuring scales to indicate their perceptions of the many characteristics and similarities of competing brands. Computer programs analyse the resulting data to determine those product characteristics or combination of characteristics that are most important to consumers in distinguishing between competing brands. Results of this analysis can be plotted in terms of perceptual 'maps', which display how consumers perceive the brands, and their differences, on a co-ordinate system.

Figure 2.1 presents a brand-image map created to understand New Zealanders' actual perception of different countries as tourist destinations. Surveys to generate such perceptual maps ask consumers to rate products on a series of attributes. In this case, 18 attributes were used, including such features as climate, landscape, entertainment, culture, safety and value for money. The answers ultimately result in a mathematical score for each destination, which is plotted on a graph showing broad criteria for evaluating buyer appeal.

By plotting strong areas of consumer demand on the map, a tourism analyst can determine whether its products are aimed at the right target. And from the concentration of dots representing competitive destinations, a marketer can tell how much competition will be met in a particular segment on the map. Such a map can also be used to position individual products (both current and future). Changing the marketing mix can move a model into an unoccupied space on the map, thus carving out a distinctive market niche.[52]

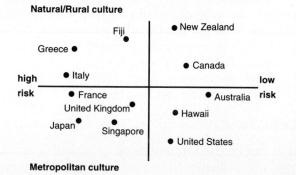

FIG. 2.1 Perceptual map of countries as tourist destinations   Source: Angie Driscoll & Rob Lawson, 'New Zealand's Position as a Destination for New Zealanders: A Multidimensional Scaling Approach', *New Zealand Journal of Business* 12, 1990, pp.105–18.

THE FUTURE OF SEGMENTATION AND POSITIONING

The various bases for segmenting markets discussed in this and the previous chapter have underscored the need to understand consumers. Each segmentation approach has merit, and although not all have exhibited the ability to predict consumers' purchasing habits, they do enable marketers to understand better their target markets. When combinations of approaches are used in aiming at the total marketing problem, segmentation research can be very meaningful.[53] With enhanced understanding comes the ability to develop more tailored marketing programs. The need to segment markets and position products effectively is increasingly being recognised by marketing managers. For instance, a recent survey of top marketing executives showed that developing market-segmentation strategies was one of the key pressure points they had to deal with in a recent year.[54]

The great deal of attention and interest generated by the concept of market segmentation is sure to become even more significant in the future. Three environmental factors are expected to lead to this growth. First, the advance of the consumerism movement will foster market segmentation, as critics have pointed to segments they believe are neglected in our present system. The result of these critic pressures is that managers become more attentive to previously unrecognised consumer needs. A second factor encouraging market segmentation is intensified competition. With increasingly competitive markets (domestic and worldwide) in the future, business people will seek untapped segments to gain an advantage over rivals. The third factor stimulating market segmentation is the growing awareness of non-business applications of the technique. It will be increasingly utilised for marketing in non-traditional areas such as politics, religion and public issues.[55]

SUMMARY

In this chapter many consumer characteristics were presented. All of these consumer attributes were discussed within the framework of market segmentation; that is, an approach to selecting groups of homogenous consumers as targets for marketing activity. Whereas market segmentation seeks to carve a large, heterogeneous market into smaller, more uniform subdivisions, at the other end of the strategy spectrum—market aggregation—no subdivision of the market is applied. Most firms today follow a market-segmentation approach. Furthermore, it was shown that in order for market segmentation to be effective, the target group must be identifiable and measurable; accessible; substantial; and responsive.

With these criteria in mind, four alternative bases for segmentation were discussed: demographic, lifestyle, usage and benefit. First, major demographic characteristics of Australasian consumers were described. In addition, a number of marketing implications were suggested based upon these variables' influence on consumers' behaviour.

Although the use of demographic variables is intuitively appealing and widely available to marketers, their record as predictors of consumer behaviour is not very strong. However, the problems in their use seem to be the result of a state-of-the-art limitation in analysis rather than a fundamental defect in the technique. Consequently, they should continue to play an important role in segmentation efforts by marketers.

Some newer approaches to market segmentation were also presented. Traditional approaches, however, are still incorporated in these techniques because marketers must have demographic, geographic and socioeconomic information about any segments chosen if they are to market effectively to them.

This chapter suggested techniques that may provide a richer portrait of potential customers, through lifestyle, usage or benefit segmentation. All of the techniques suggested as well as others not discussed overlap and are complementary. Therefore, choices have to be made regarding the best combination of methods to employ for each product or service.

The close interrelationship between market segmentation and product positioning was also discussed. Several approaches to product and company positioning were described along with analytical methods for making such decisions.

Finally, from this discussion of market segmentation, a clearer understanding should be gained about the *who* of consumer behaviour—that consumers are people of widely varying characteristics. Appreciation of this fact and an understanding of the ways in which clusters of consumers with more homogeneous characteristics may be carved out of the heterogeneous marketplace should establish a firm foundation for further exploration into the factors that influence consumer behaviour.

MANAGERIAL REFLECTIONS

For our product or service situation:

1. Is market aggregation or market segmentation more appropriate?

2. Is segmentation effective? That is, does one or more market groups appear to be identifiable and measurable, accessible, substantial and responsive?

3. How does the growth in total population affect our sales prospects?

4. What are the implications of the changing age mix of potential consumers?

5. Are there regional trends in consumption that can be effectively used for geographic segmentation?

6. Are there differences in terms of metropolitan and non-metropolitan buyers?

7. How does geographic mobility influence market segments and sales?

8. What education levels have potential buyers achieved and how may this influence our marketing?

9. What occupational categories are represented by buyers?

10. How do income and expenditure patterns of our market affect demand?

11. To what extent can consumers' buying intentions or willingness to buy be forecasted?

12. Can customer groups be segmented by lifestyle?

13. How may relevant segments' lifestyles be characterised in terms of their activities, interests and opinions?

14. What differences exist between users of different brands or product types that may lead to effective segmentation?

15. Who are the loyal and heavy-user consumers in this product category, and how may they be attracted?

16. Are there differences in usage situations among consumers that may be identified and used as the basis for appeals?

17. What benefits are consumers seeking and/or what problems are they trying to avoid with this purchase?

18. What product position is most appropriate among chosen market segments, and what strategy will be used to secure it?

DISCUSSION TOPICS

1. How does the concept of market aggregation differ from market segmentation?

2. What are the benefits and costs of market segmentation?

3. Why are the following segmentation approaches or groups not very effective?
   (a) segmenting a market on the basis of personality
   (b) advertising to triathletes in *Time*
   (c) developing an insurance plan for all quadruplets born in Australia.

4. What are the major population changes taking place in Australia and New Zealand? What implications are there for the marketer of:
   (a) baby furniture?
   (b) insurance?
   (c) electronic products?
   (d) sporting goods?
   (e) food?

5. What products might effectively segment their market on the basis of:
(a) education?
(b) occupation?
(c) income?

6. Find a recent article from your local newspaper and report on the current mood of consumers and their willingness to buy.

7. Suggest a marketing strategy to convert non-users of the following goods and services into users:
(a) cancer detection checkups for women aged 40–50;
(b) bus for getting to work;
(c) unit price information in a supermarket;
(d) a symphony series;
(e) paper towels.

8. Determine the primary benefits that might be sought by consumers of the following products:
(a) hair colouring;
(b) mouthwash;
(c) barbecue grill;
(d) small car;
(e) bread.

9. How is lifestyle segmentation useful in developing promotion campaigns?

10. For the following goods and services, suggest an appropriate segmentation strategy:
(a) a dinner theatre in a medium-sized city;
(b) a church on campus;
(c) your university;
(d) sailboats;
(e) coffee;
(f) *Cosmopolitan* magazine.
How would you determine the size and behavioural attributes of the segments? What marketing strategy might be appropriate?

11. Attempt to determine how each of the following products is positioned:
(a) Apple personal computer;
(b) Ford Falcon car;
(c) Kodak films;
(d) Levi jeans;
(e) Slaam jeans;
(f) Sony radios and televisions.

REFERENCES

1. A. R. Morden, 'Market Segmentation and Practical Policy Formulation', *Quarterly Review of Marketing*, Winter 1985, pp. 1–12.
2. Malcolm Wright & Don Esslemont, 'The Logical Limitations of Target Marketing', *Marketing Bulletin*, 5, 1994, pp. 13–20.
3. William J. Stanton et al., *Fundamentals of Marketing*, McGraw-Hill, Sydney, 1991.
4. Danny L. Moore, 'What is Micromarketing?', *AIM*, 11 (2), 1990.
5. Frederick W. Winter, 'A Cost-Benefit Approach to Market Segmentation', *Journal of Marketing* 43, pp. 103–11. Fall 1979.
6. Michael Kiely, 'Singleton Slams Dills and Wankers in Adland', *Marketing Magazine*, August 1989. See also Michael Kiely, 'Ten Years of Marketing', *Marketing Magazine*, April 1994.
7. Shirley Young, Leland Ott & Barbara Feigin, 'Some Practical Considerations in Market Segmentation', *Journal of Marketing Research* 15, August 1978, pp. 405–12.
8. James F. Engel, Henry F. Fiorillo & Murray A. Cayley, *Market Segmentation: Concepts and Applications*, Holt, New York, 1972, p. 8.
9. This section is based on Yoram Wind, 'Issues and Advances in Segmentation Research', *Journal of Marketing Research* 15, 1978, pp. 321–2; and Art Weinstein, 'Ten-point Program Customizes Segmentation Analysis', *Marketing News*, 23 May 1986, p. 22.
10. See Douglas MacLachlan & Johny K. Johansson, 'Market Segmentation with Multivariate AID', *Journal of Marketing* 45, 1981, pp. 74–84; and Henry Assael and A. Marvin Roscoe Jr, 'Approaches to Market Segmentation Analysis', *Journal of Marketing* 40, October 1976, pp. 67–76.
11. Wind, op cit, Ref 9, pp. 330–2.
12. Thomas C. Kinnear et al., *Australian Marketing Research*, McGraw-Hill, Sydney, 1993.
13. Paula A. Francese & Leo M. Renaghan, 'Finding the Customer', *American Demographics*, January 1991, pp. 48–51.
14. Joe Schwartz, 'Databases Deliver the Goods', *American Demographics*, September 1989, pp. 23–5, 68.
15. Don Porrit, 'Market Segments or Market Myths?', *Australian Professional Marketing*, February 1994, pp. 20–1.
16. Mark Miller, 'The Age of Neglect', *Australian Professional Marketing*, November 1993, pp. 10–13; Don Porrit, 'Market Segments or Market Myths', *Australian Professional Marketing*, February 1994, pp. 20–21 and p. 34; Don Porrit, 'Generation X—The Moving Target', *Australian Professional Marketing*, May 1994, pp. 37, 41; Sue Williams, 'Livin' Large', *The Australian Magazine*, July 1994, pp. 12–21.
17. Don Porrit, 'Generation X—The Moving Target', *Australian Professional Marketing*, May 1994, pp. 37, 41.
18. Richard Kern, 'The Mommy Boom', *Sales and Marketing Management*, 1 April 1985, p. 14.
19. Thayer C. Taylor, 'We the People: Older, Smarter, Liberated, Richer', *Sales and Marketing Management*, The Marketer's Complete Guide to the 1980s/A Special Report, 10 December 1979.
20. Paul B. Brown et al., 'Bringing Up Baby: A New Kind of Marketing Boom', *Business Week*, 22 April 1985, pp. 58–65; and Leo J. Shapiro & Dwight Bohmbach, 'Outlook Brightened by Boomers' Babies', *Advertising Age*, 13 May 1985, p. 96.
21. 'The Divorced Generation', *American Demographics*, July 1986, p. 11.
22. William Dunn, 'Americans on the Move', *American Demographics*, October 1986, pp. 49–51.
23. 'Movers Could Be Shakers', *Chain Store Age, General Merchandise Trends*, June 1986, p. 9.

24. See Alan R. Andreasen, 'Geographic Mobility and Market Segmentation', *Journal of Marketing Research*, 1966, pp. 341–8; and James E. Bell Jr, 'Mobiles—A Neglected Market Segment', *Journal of Marketing* 33, April 1969, pp. 37–44.
25. William D. Wells, Thomas C. O'Guinn & Martin L. Horn, 'The Micawber Connection: Subjective Discretionary Income', in Richard J. Lutz (ed.), *Advances in Consumer Research*, Vol. 13, Association for Consumer Research, Provo, UT, 1986, pp. 349–53.
26. 'How Good Are Consumer Pollsters?', *Business Week*, 8 November 1969, p. 108.
27. Fabian Linden, 'The Consumer as Fortune Teller', *Across the Board*, June 1981, p. 62; and Edward Meadows, 'The Unhealthy Glow on Retail Sales', *Fortune*, 3 July 1978, pp. 46–8.
28. Richard T. Curtin, 'Indicators of Consumer Behaviour: The University of Michigan Surveys of Consumers', *Public Opinion Quarterly* 46, 1982, pp. 340–52.
29. Much of this section is based on Jagdish N. Sheth, 'Demographics in Consumer Behaviour', *Journal of Business Research* 5, June 1977, pp. 129–38.
30. John C. Bieda & Harold W. Kassarjian, 'An Overview of Market Segmentation', in Bernard A. Morin (ed.), *Marketing in a Changing World*, American Marketing Association, Chicago, 1969, p. 250.
31. Louis G. Pol, 'Demographic Contributions to Marketing: An Assessment', *Journal of the Academy of Marketing Science* 19, Winter 1991, pp. 53–9.
32. Jeanie L. Wasson, 'Psychographics: An Aid to Demographics', *Adweek's Marketing Week*, 21 September, 1987, p. 48.
33. William Lazer, 'Life Style Concepts and Marketing', in Stephen Greyser (ed.), *Toward Scientific Marketing*, American Marketing Association, Chicago, 1963, p. 130.
34. Harper W. Boyd Jr & Sidney J. Levy, *Promotion: A Behavioural View*, Prentice-Hall, Englewood Cliffs, NJ, 1967, p. 38.
35. W. Thomas Anderson Jr & Linda L. Golden, 'Lifestyle and Psychographics: A Critical Review and Recommendation', in Thomas Kinnear (ed.), *Advances in Consumer Research*, vol. 11, Association for Consumer Research, Provo, UT, 1984, pp. 405–11.
36. Fred D. Reynolds & William R. Darden, 'An Operational Construction of Life Style', in M. Venkatesan (ed.), *Proceedings of the Annual Conference of the Association for Consumer Research*, 1972 p. 482.
37. Alvin C. Burns & Mary Carolyn Harrison, 'A Test of the Reliability of Psychographics', *Journal of Marketing Research* 16, February 1979, pp. 32–8.
38. Emanuel H. Demby, 'Psychographics Revisited: The Birth of a Technique', *Marketing News*, 2 January 1989, p. 21; Joseph T. Plummer, 'The Concept and Application of Life Style Segmentation', *Journal of Marketing*, 38, January 1974; and Phillip Meyer, 'The ABCs of Psychographics', *American Demographics*, November 1983, p. 25.
39. Tim Bowles, 'Does Classifying People by Lifestyle Really Help the Advertiser?', *European Research*, February 1988, pp. 17–24.
40. Aimee Stern, 'Tired of Playing Mind Games', *Adweek's Marketing Week*, 13 July 1987, p. 6.
41. Sunil Mehrotra & William D. Wells, 'Psychographics and Buyer Behaviour. Theory and Recent Empirical Findings', in Arch G. Woodside, Jagdish N. Sheth & Peter D. Bennett (eds.), *Consumer and Industrial Buying Behaviour*, Elsevier North-Holland, New York, 1977, pp. 49–65; and William D. Wells, 'Psychographics: A Critical Review', *Journal of Marketing Research* 12, 1975, pp. 196–213.
42. Peter W. Bernstein, 'Psychographics Is Still an Issue on Madison Avenue', *Fortune* 97, January 16, 1978, pp. 78–80.
43. Bernice Finkleman, 'Ads Should Reinforce Current Users, Not Necessarily Convert Nonusers of Products', *Marketing News*, 15 January 1974, p. 1.
44. Kenneth E. Miller & Kent L. Granzin, 'Simultaneous Loyalty and Benefit Segmentation of Retail Store Customers', *Journal of Retailing* 55, Spring 1979, pp. 47–60.
45. Peter Dickson, 'Person-Situation: Segmentation's Missing Link', *Journal of Marketing* 46, Fall 1982, pp. 56–64.

46. Russel I. Haley, 'Benefit Segmentation: A Decision Oriented Research Tool', *Journal of Marketing* 32, July 1968, p. 31.
47. Russel I. Haley, 'Benefit Segments: Backwards and Forwards', *Journal of Advertising Research* 24, February/March 1984, p. 21.
48. This section is based on Yoram Wind, 'Going to Market: New Twists for Some Old Tricks', *Wharton Magazine* 4(3), 1980; and David A. Aaker & J. Gary Shansby, Positioning Your Product', *Business Horizons*, May–June 1982, pp. 56–62.
49. Paul Brown, 'Forget Satisfying the Consumer—Just Outfox the Other Guy', *Business Week*, 7 October 1985, p. 55.
50. Jack Trout & Al Ries, 'The Positioning Era: A View Ten Years Later', *Advertising Age*, 16 July 1979, p. 40.
51. William D. Wells, 'Life Style and Psychographics: Definitions, Uses and Problems', in William D. Wells (ed.), *Life Style and Psychographics*, American Marketing Association, Chicago, 1974, pp. 322–5.
52. John Koten, 'Car Makers Use Image Map as Tool to Position Products', *Wall Street Journal*, 22 March 1984, p. 33.
53. Nariman K. Dhalla & Winston H. Mahatoo, 'Expanding the Scope of Segmentation Research', *Journal of Marketing* 40, April 1976, pp. 34–41.
54. 'Segmentation Strategies Create New Pressure Among Marketers', *Marketing News*, 28 March 1986, p. 1.
55. James F. Engel, Henry Fiorillo & Murray A. Cayley (eds), *Market Segmentation: Concepts and Applications*, Holt, New York, 1972, pp. 459–65.

CASE STUDIES

CASE 1   THE LIONS CLUB

Lions Clubs International is a worldwide community service organisation formed in the United States in 1917. Clubs raise funds for international and national projects including blindness, medical research and drug awareness, as well as for local community projects. Last year Aussies munched on 542 540 Lions Christmas cakes, giving a $1.25 million fundraising boost to Lions projects. Australia and Papua New Guinea have 32 000 Lions Club members. The Lions Clubs International objectives are:

- to create and foster a spirit of understanding among the peoples of the world;
- to promote the principles of good government and good citizenship;
- to fund and otherwise serve the civic, cultural, social and moral welfare of the community;
- to assist financially, culturally, socially and morally the handicapped, disadvantaged and infirm of the community both directly and indirectly;
- to unite the clubs in the bonds of friendship, good fellowship and mutual understanding;
- to provide a forum for the open discussion of all matters of public interest, provided, however, that partisan politics and sectarian religion shall not be debated by club members;
- to encourage service-minded people to serve their community without personal financial reward, and to encourage efficiency and promote high ethical standards in commerce, industry, professions, public works and private endeavours.

Several members of the Lions Club of Bathurst, New South Wales, were interested in increasing membership in their club. In addition, they wanted to know if members of the public were aware of the Lions Club, and what their perceptions were of the many things Lions do for the community. They decided to take a marketing approach to these issues and found a market research consultant to conduct the research.

To determine public awareness, a survey was conducted on the residences of Bathurst. The age of the respondents ranged from 15 to 77 years. Occupations and socioeconomic groups varied widely. Results showed a very low awareness of the Lions Club and for service clubs in general. Only 7.7 per cent of those surveyed were members of a service club. In addition, 17 per cent of those surveyed did not even know what a service club was. Despite this, 32 per cent of those surveyed knew about the Lions Club.

A well-known fact in marketing is that it is very difficult to change the status quo of consumer knowledge and/or behaviour. Therefore, if we view the public as potential consumers (members) of the Lions Club, it would be easier to attract those who are already aware of service clubs to membership in Lions. It is also a well-known fact that promotions are more effective at maintaining current customers than attracting new customers. In other words, if the Lions Club spent much time, money and effort on promoting the Lions Club in an attempt to increase awareness, given these survey results and past research on consumer behaviour, the promotion would have very little impact on membership.

This is not to say that increasing awareness would not help Lions—it would. Eventually increased awareness may result in a membership increase; however, this method is more difficult and may take years to make an impact on membership. Therefore, it would be better to target the 32 per cent who already know about Lions for membership.

Public perceptions

Any time a target market is established, it is important to understand the perceptions of this market regarding the product.

So what kinds of things *do* service clubs do? When asked this question, those surveyed said the following.

%
33 Community service
32 Raise funds for charities
11 Provide public facilities, such as parks
6 Exchange programs

When asked what these clubs had done for the local community, 38 per cent had no idea, while 15 per cent said 'nothing' or answered incorrectly. Of those who knew of some way a service club had helped the local community, only 6 per cent mentioned the Lions Club and cited their local park. It is important to note that this was an unbiased, unprompted open-ended question. This means that only 6 per cent of those surveyed have a high brand awareness for the Lions Club compared with other brands of service clubs.

When asked what kinds of things services clubs *should do* in *general*, those surveyed said:

	%
Community service	25
Raise funds for charity	15
Continue as they are	12
Help the elderly	9
Help the poor and unemployed	8
Raise money and organise activities for youth	6
Build parks	3
Help in educational services	3
Organise self-defence classes	2
Promote business	2
Advertise	2
Don't know	19

When asked what service clubs *should do specifically* for the local community those surveyed said:

	%
Don't know	31
Help provide facilities for aged, poor, disabled, or homeless	18
Promote/support local industry/keep money in community	11
General community service	9
Raise funds for charities	9
Continue as they are	8
Provide community facilities such as parks	6
Provide support/facilities for youth	6
Advertise/promote themselves	5
Nothing	3
Increase female membership	2
Encourage interaction between young and old	2
Provide sporting equipment	2
Increase environmental awareness	2

Only after the unprompted unbiased questions were asked could the prompted questions about the Lions Club be used. When asked what they knew about Lions Club, responses varied:

	%
Nothing	56
Fundraising/charity work	14
Community service	11
Help people	9
Sell lollies and Christmas cakes	6
Run food van	5
It's a service club	5
Organise student exchanges	3
Help/maintain facilities for aged	3
Only make memberships (negative)	3
Have meetings	3
Built park	2
Have raffles	2
'Youth of the Year' quest	2
Entertainment/social activities	2
Raise money for sports	2
Promote the town	2

When asked what Lions *had done specifically* for the local community, those surveyed said:

	%
Don't know	71
Raise funds for charity	11
Lions Park	8
Help community	6
Help disadvantaged groups	6
Lions food van	3
Provide hospital equipment for terminally ill	3
Make city a better place	3
Raise money for sport	2
Support groups for the needy	2
Driver reviver program	2

When asked what the Lions Club *should do* for the local community, responses also varied:

	%
Don't know	31
Help disadvantaged groups such as the elderly and disabled	20
Continue with what they're doing	14
Raise funds for charity	11
Raise funds for hospital and terminally ill	8
Work with and organise activities for youth	8
Raise awareness of the Club	7
Promote the city	6
Community service projects, such as parks	6
Raise money for eyes and cancer research	5
Provide baby change rooms and facilities for out-of-town people	2
'Youth of the Year' Quest	2
Keep city tidy	2
Provide home for homeless children	2
Provide meals	2
Organise self-defence classes	2

Defining the target market

Now that we know that 32 per cent of those surveyed were aware of the Lions Club, but only 6 per cent were aware of something Lions has done for the community, it was critical to figure out what motivated a person to purchase this particular brand compared with other brands of service clubs. In other words, what makes a person become a Lion? To answer this question, another research methodology was required. A consumer psychologist trained in qualitative research methods, and specialising in one-on-one in-depth interviewing techniques, interviewed members of the local Lions Club using this method. Members were selected over a broad spectrum—in terms of age, the number of years in the Lions Club, the year of joining Lions, and the number of positions held in Lions. A few members who had transferred from other Lions Clubs were also included in the sample.

Several important themes and relationships emerged from these interviews. They provided a full understanding of the target market and their members' underlying psychological motivations for joining Lions. The interviews also provided insight into the relationships between the motives for becoming a Lion.

The first and most important thing is that *all* of the members interviewed were aware of Lions before they considered joining . . . an awareness comparable to the 32 per cent found in the quantitative survey previously mentioned. Although the time lapse between awareness and joining varied, all but one of the members interviewed became involved in Lions activities through close friends or work mates within a few months of becoming a member. The one person who did *not* was evidently part of a membership campaign by the Lions and was invited to a meeting by someone he did not know, but who had identified him as the type of person who would make a good Lion. Once this person came to the meeting (out of curiosity) he recognised a friend at the meeting. The point here is *You have to know a Lion before you decide to become a Lion*. These findings indicate several significant opportunities for Lions to increase membership:

1. *Word-of-mouth advertising is the best way to increase membership*: Invite people in your workplace, church and other clubs, your neighbours or friends to a meeting.

You will be surprised at how many will decide to become a member if they are invited to do so!

2. *Inviting people you don't know well in a membership campaign can work if the person knows someone in the club.* In smaller towns it would be difficult for this not to be the case. Make a list of people in the community who are recognised as having the qualities of a Lion and invite them to a meeting. Then, make sure they are welcome when they come.

This describes how to get people to a meeting. However, not everyone you invite will decide to join. What is the difference between those who decide to join Lions and those who do not? Members of Lions have three psychological needs underlying their membership:

1. *Altruism*. The need to give to others.
2. *Affiliation*. The need to associate with others.
3. *Status*. The need to feel better than others and be recognised for it.

Each person who decides to join Lions may have one, two or all three of these underlying needs operating, but each person has different strengths of each. For example, a person may have a strong need for affiliation, but no need for status and a medium level of altruism. A strong need for altruism may approach 'true' altruism, which was defined in a recent conference paper 'as giving to others when there is no benefit to self'.[1] However, being an altruistic Lion means that on occasion some will thank you for helping them. Whether or not this gratitude is expected, all of those interviewed derived some benefit (happiness, a good feeling, a warm glow, and so on) from giving to others. The act of giving to others ultimately reassures the Lion that there is hope in an otherwise seemingly hopeless world. As one Lion said:

> It feels good when I am around people who give their time. With all the terrible things in the world, there are still those who'll do good. It restores my faith in human nature.

In fact, all the Lions interviewed operate on a very old heurism, or rule—'Give and thou shalt receive'. Having been in many service clubs myself, I am aware of a saying used by the Lions, which is common to most service clubs, 'You get out of Lions what you put into it'. In business we call this reciprocity; however, because different people have different needs and different strengths of those needs, different Lions have different expectations about reciprocity. These expectations come from the values inculcated by their parents and their culture, which Lions have no control over, but awareness of these differences can increase member (consumer) satisfaction over time.

Maintaining membership

This brings us to customer satisfaction. Once a person becomes a Lion, the amount of satisfaction the person receives from consuming the product over time, through membership, depends on the initial expectation of reciprocity. How much and what kinds of benefits a member receives in return for donations of time, money and hard work depend on the individual's motivations for joining. For example, one person was motivated to join by a high need for affiliation. This person expected nothing in return from the formal Lions organisation, but expected that the friendships he made in the Club would endure in both good times and bad. He spent many hours helping on Lions projects and developed many friends. The friends were there for the good times, but when bad times hit they were not there for him. His expectations were not met, and his satisfaction with Lions dropped, as did his attendance.

Those who have joined Lions with a high need for altruism expect to have more direct contact helping others (to get the warm glow) compared with those with a low need for altruism. Therefore, to keep these customers happy, Lions should not limit their activities to fundraising. Helping the elderly, say, where there is direct contact with those being helped, is essential for the altruistic Lion.

The extent to which the needs and expectation levels are represented in the population will require further research. In order for the Lions Club to keep its customers (members) satisfied, further research also needs to be done.

QUESTIONS

1. Which segments in the Bathurst population were identified in the initial quantitative survey? How do these segments relate to the Lions Club goal of increasing membership?

2. In the qualitative research conducted with Lions Club members, which segmentation variables were identified for interview purposes? Speculate why these segmentation variables were selected by the researcher. What other segmentation variables could have been used and why?

3. How should Lions use the three emotional segments identified in current members to increase their membership?

This case study was prepared by Dr P. M. Tidwell, trading as Market Research Services of Bathurst.

For more information on this case, please ring 015 259 964.

REFERENCE

1. Association for Consumer Research, Paper presented to Asia Pacific Conference, Singapore, 1994.

CASE 2 SBS TELEVISION SERVICE

The special purpose SBS Television service has a quite specific role among the five Australian networks. Its charter obligations require it to demonstrate the cultures, philosophies, lifestyles and backgrounds of the many different language groups that have settled in Australia. It is also required to present programs that portray the issues and way of life of contemporary Australia.

As a consequence of its charter obligations, much of the program content within its weekly schedules is not directly targeted to the light entertainment, mass-audience markets sought by the other networks, but tends to be more special interest in nature.

While this can lead to quite selective viewing of individual SBS programs, it has its rewards in attracting highly active and involved viewers, who derive well-above-average satisfaction from SBS programs in which they have a strong interest, and which they have specifically sought out in preference to the other networks.

Early impressions of the SBS network were summed up by such descriptions as 'elitist' and 'mainly for ethnics', but it is clear from recent qualitative research that such impressions have undergone a radical change. Audiences have broadened their perspective of the network and now see it as offering new forms of alternative programming. This is illustrated by a range of phrases emanating from respondents participating in recent research studies. Asked to described the present day SBS service, the following descriptions were among those offered:

For contemporary Australians

Serving all Australians

A fresh look at the world

Covering all interests

For people who want to know more

Leading the way

Looking outward

One step ahead

Quality

Broad ranging

Stimulating

Thought provoking

Diverse

Entertaining

Intelligent

Alternative

Pluralist

Unexpected

The following tables detail the performance of 'core' SBS programs in Sydney, Melbourne, Adelaide, Brisbane and Perth. The A. C. Neilsen meter measurement service operates only in these five cities.

TABLE 1   Success of programs

Program		Homes %	Homes '000s	People '000s	People viewing per home
SBS World News	(7 days)	12.9	500	887	1.77
Dataline	(6 days)	9.5	368	604	1.64
World Sports	(5 days)	3.9	151	233	1.54
The Cutting Edge	(1 day)	6.0	232	333	1.43
Connections	(1 day)	3.8	146	203	1.39
Masterpiece	(1 day)	3.9	152	211	1.39
People	(1 day)	3.5	137	195	1.42
Telling Tales	(1 day)	2.4	93	118	1.27
Detective	(1 day)	3.5	134	182	1.36
Cooking	(1 day)	3.3	127	199	1.57
The Movie Show	(1 day)	4.5	173	248	1.43
Face The Press	(1 day)	2.3	91	127	1.40
Vox Populi	(1 day)	2.1	80	119	1.49
The Bookshow	(1 day)	2.0	78	100	1.28
Hotline	(1 day)	1.9	74	94	1.27
Eat Carpet	(1 day)	2.6	102	120	1.18
Nomad	(1 day)	2.1	82	97	1.18
9.30 pm movies					
Sunday night		5.2	200	271	1.36
Monday night		6.3	244	333	1.36
Tuesday night		5.9	230	309	1.34
Wednesday night		6.0	234	338	1.44
Thursday night		5.8	224	313	1.40
Friday night		5.7	223	315	1.41
Saturday night		5.2	203	276	1.36
Saturday night late movie		3.0	117	150	1.28

TABLE 2   Weekly reach of audiences

	Total Potential Audience	World news	Dateline	Face the Press	Vox Populi	Hotline	Cutting Edge	Connections	Telling Tales	People	Masterpiece	SBS Audience
Total People reached	'000s 11 614	'000s 887	'000s 604	'000s 127	'000s 119	'000s 94	'000s 333	'000s 203	'000s 118	'000s 195	'000s 211	'000s 2 862
	%	%	%	%	%	%	%	%	%	%	%	%
Children 5–12	**11.2**	6.3	6.8	1.6	3.4	2.1	3.0	3.4	3.4	4.1	1.9	**5.9**
Teens 13–17	**7.0**	3.0	2.6	1.6	2.5	4.2	3.3	2.5	4.2	3.1	1.9	**4.9**
Men 18–24	**5.8**	3.6	3.5	3.1	2.5	3.2	3.6	3.4	4.2	4.1	5.2	**6.3**
Men 25–39	**12.0**	11.9	12.6	13.4	13.4	9.6	13.5	11.8	16.1	14.4	13.3	**14.7**
Men 40–54	**9.7**	14.0	15.9	15.7	13.4	23.4	19.8	18.7	17.8	16.9	14.2	**13.9**
Men 55+	**9.1**	18.0	16.4	15.0	18.5	20.2	18.6	18.2	18.6	14.4	20.4	**13.5**
Women 18–24	**5.7**	2.4	2.5	1.6	2.5	2.1	2.7	2.0	2.5	3.1	2.8	**3.4**
Women 25–39	**12.2**	8.9	9.1	10.2	9.2	7.4	10.2	9.4	8.5	11.8	9.9	**11.4**
Women 40–54	**9.5**	10.7	11.1	12.6	12.6	11.7	11.1	12.3	8.5	11.3	10.9	**9.4**
Women 55+	**10.8**	18.0	16.2	24.4	22.7	16.0	12.9	16.3	14.4	14.4	19.4	**12.8**
Australian-born	**74.0**	52.4	54.5	58.3	47.1	57.4	60.1	56.2	58.5	62.0	62.1	**62.9**
Overseas-born (ES)	**11.6**	16.9	16.2	24.4	18.5	16.0	16.8	18.2	16.9	15.9	20.4	**16.1**
Born in Europe	**3.5**	10.8	11.3	9.4	12.6	9.6	7.2	10.8	9.3	8.7	6.2	**5.9**
Born in Asia	**3.6**	6.4	5.6	3.1	7.6	3.2	4.5	5.4	4.2	4.6	3.3	**4.7**
Born in other (NESC)	**7.3**	20.6	19.0	11.0	21.8	24.5	17.1	15.8	16.9	13.3	11.8	**15.1**
SE/AB	**9.3**	13.4	13.1	17.3	11.8	12.8	14.4	13.8	11.9	15.4	18.0	**12.8**
SE C1	**17.5**	16.0	16.6	25.2	19.3	21.3	19.8	19.2	16.9	21.0	20.8	**19.5**
SE C2/D/E	**15.3**	17.5	18.9	15.0	18.5	22.3	22.5	20.2	22.0	18.5	18.0	**17.7**
Grocery buyers	**33.4**	41.3	42.2	49.6	50.4	47.9	43.8	45.3	40.7	43.6	46.4	**37.5**

QUESTIONS

1. Discuss how SBS could use these findings in understanding consumers and developing marketing strategies.

2. What additional dimensions of consumer behaviour would you recommend SBS investigate?

3. How might the television audience market be segmented?

4. What suggestions can you make for the role of SBS as a medium for advertisers promoting other products and services?

This case study was prepared by Professor Rob Lawson, from material kindly supplied by SBS Ltd.

ENVIRONMENTAL INFLUENCES ON CONSUMER BEHAVIOUR

COURTESY OF AUSTRALIAN TOURIST COMMISSION

CHAPTER  3

CULTURE AND VALUES

LEARNING OBJECTIVES

AFTER STUDYING THIS CHAPTER YOU SHOULD UNDERSTAND:

➡ the meaning of 'culture' and its most important characteristics;

➡ the nature of cultural values in general, as well as the core values held by Australian and New Zealand consumers;

➡ the nature of cultural variation in Australia and New Zealand;

➡ that cultural values do influence consumer behaviour;

➡ that because culture changes, marketers must monitor and be prepared to take advantage of these shifts;

➡ the importance of cross-cultural knowledge of consumer behaviour in developing effective marketing programs internationally.

Now that we have considered many of the basic demographic features of Australia and New Zealand, we turn our attention to the very broad, basic and enduring factor of culture. In this chapter we shall investigate the role and usefulness of cultural analysis in the development of marketing strategies. After defining and characterising culture, the basic cultural values of Australian and New Zealand consumers will be outlined.

Much of the chapter will be devoted to the discussion of values in preference to following other approaches to cultural analysis such as language or material aspects. We see this approach as reflecting many of the more important recent developments in consumer behaviour research and it provides a rich supply of information of real practical value to marketers.

The material in this chapter also recognises that much cultural variation exists, and we examine some aspects of the different ethnic subcultures in the two countries. In fact, both countries recognise themselves as multicultural societies and we regard this as a more appropriate description than the use of the term 'subculture', which may carry slightly derogatory associations when improperly used and defined. The recognition of this variation leads to an examination of cultural change and its effect on consumer behaviour. Finally, cross-cultural consumer behaviour and its implications for international marketing will be discussed.

CULTURE DEFINED

It is difficult to present only one definition of culture and expect it to portray the richness of the field and its relevance to understanding consumers. However, the following two are representative:

> . . . that complex whole that includes knowledge, belief, art, morals, law, custom and any other capabilities and habits acquired by man [sic] as a member of society.[1]

> . . . the distinctive way of life of a group of people, their complete design for living.[2]

Therefore, culture is everything that is socially learned and shared by the members of a society. Culture consists of material and non-material components. Non-material culture includes the words people use; the ideas, customs and beliefs they share; and the habits they pursue. Material culture consists of all the physical substances that have been changed and used by people, such as tools, automobiles, roads and farms. In a marketing and consumer-behaviour context, artefacts of the material culture would include all the products and services that are produced and consumed; marketing institutions such as Woolworth supermarkets, Kmart discount houses and advertisements. Non-material culture would include the way in which consumers shop in supermarkets, their desire for newer and better products and their responses to the word 'sale'.

The significance of culture in understanding human behaviour (of which consumer behaviour is a part) is that it extends our understanding of the extent to which people are more than just chemistry, physiology, or a set of biological drives and instincts.[3] The implication is that although all customers may be biologically similar, their views of the world, what they value and how they act differ according to their cultural backgrounds.

THE CHARACTERISTICS OF CULTURE

Although the definitions of culture presented earlier are excellent, they seek to characterise culture in only a few words. It is evident that the concept is difficult to convey clearly in any definition. As one writer notes, 'It's like putting your hand in a cloud'.[4] This section, therefore, will expand on these definitions by discussing the significant characteristics, or features, of culture. Many characteristics of culture may be cited to illustrate its nature, but most social scientists agree that the following features are essential.

Culture is invented

Culture does not simply 'exist' somewhere waiting to be discovered. People invent their culture. This invention consists of three interdependent systems or elements:

1. an *ideological system*, or mental component, that consists of the ideas, beliefs, values and ways of reasoning that human beings learn to accept in defining what is desirable and undesirable;

2. a *technological system* that consists of the skills, crafts and arts that enable humans to produce material goods derived from the natural environment;

3. an *organisational system* (such as the family system and social class) that makes it possible for humans to co-ordinate their behaviour effectively with the actions of others.[5]

Culture is learned

Culture is not innate or instinctive, but is learned early in life, and is charged with a good deal of emotion. The great strength of this cultural stamp handed down from one generation to another is such that, at an early age, children are firmly imbued with their culture's ways of acting, thinking and feeling.

Culture is socially shared

Culture is a group phenomenon, shared by human beings living in organised societies and kept relatively uniform by social pressure. The group that is involved in this sharing may range from a whole society to a smaller unit such as a family. Important parts of Australian and New Zealand culture are shared with foreign countries, especially aspects that Australia and New Zealand have imported from the United States. In common with many other countries, we have imported a massive amount of American popular culture, broadly defined as ranging from movies, music, television programming and home video, to licensed consumer products (such as Mickey Mouse and Power Rangers), McDonald's hamburgers, Levi's jeans, and Coca-Cola soft drinks. The extent of the sharing can be realised by considering that worldwide exports of American pop culture make it the United States' second largest export earner after aerospace products.[6]

Cultures are similar but different

All cultures exhibit certain similarities. For example, each of the following elements is found in all societies: athletic sports, bodily adornment, a calendar, cooking, courtship, dancing, education, family, gestures, government, housing, language, law, music and religious ritual. There is, however, great variation from society to society in the nature of each of these elements, which may result in important consumer behaviour differences around the world.

Culture is gratifying and persistent

Culture satisfies basic biological needs as well as learned needs. It consists of habits that will be maintained and reinforced as long as those who practise them are gratified. Because of this gratification, cultural elements are handed down from generation to generation. Thus, people are comfortable doing things in the customary way.

Our culture is so thoroughly inculcated in us that it persists even when we are exposed to other cultures. No matter where we go or what we do, we cannot escape our cultural heritage. Its persistence means that change, although not impossible, is often quite difficult as resistance to it may be strong.

Culture is adaptive

In spite of our resistance to change, cultures do continually change. Some societies are quite static, with a very slow rate of change, while others are more dynamic, with very rapid changes taking place.

Culture is organised and integrated

A culture 'hangs together'; that is, its parts fit together. Although every culture has some inconsistent elements, overall each culture tends to form a consistent and integrated whole.

Culture is prescriptive

Culture includes ideal standards or patterns of behaviour so that members of society have a common understanding of the right and proper way to think, feel and act. *Norms* are society's rules or guidelines specifying what behaviour is appropriate or inappropriate in given situations. For example, Australians and New Zealanders generally take for granted the norm of 'first come, first served'. This rule affects our shopping patterns as we line up waiting to be served in a bank or restaurant. This type of norm is an example of a *folkway*, which is a customary and habitual way of acting. If someone 'broke in' at the head of the line, thus violating the norm, other people in the queue would likely respond negatively. *Sanctions* are pressures brought to bear on deviant individuals so that they conform in their behaviour to what society expects. *Mores* are norms (which have been generally codified into laws) that are vital to society's survival and well-being. They prohibit such things as murder, robbery and treason. Violators of mores are often sanctioned severely, being punished by fines or imprisonment.

Although folkways and mores appear to be relatively stable and slow to change, our desire for novelty and variety as consumers must also be met. This occurs through the process of short-term conformity. *Fashions* are folkways that are widely accepted within society and last for only a short time. Styles of clothing, automobiles and home design illustrate how looks that are popular one year may be unpopular within a few years. *Fads* are folkways that are even shorter lived and accepted by only a narrow segment of the culture.

CULTURAL RELEVANCE TO MARKETING DECISIONS

It has long been recognised that culture influences consumers. For example, Ducsenberry observed in 1949 that all of the activities in which people engage are culturally determined, and that nearly all purchases of goods are made either to provide physical comfort or to implement the activities that make up the life of a culture.[7] Thus, an understanding of culture enables the marketer to interpret the reaction of consumers to alternative marketing strategies.

Sometimes guidance from *cultural anthropologists* (social scientists who study people and their culture) is sought in order to gain a better understanding of the market. Anthropologists are able to assist the marketer in understanding how culture is reflected in individuals and in society. The following are such manifestations of culture:

➡ *National character*, or the differences that distinguish one national group from another.

➡ *Differences within* the multicultural societies such as Aboriginal, Maori, Italian and Pacific Islander cultures.

➡ The *silent language* of gesture, posture, food and drink preferences, and other nonverbal clues to behaviour.

➡ The significance of *symbols* in a society. The science of *semiotics* provides a structure for studying and analysing how signs (anything that conveys meaning) function within a culture. Advertising is a prime example of using semiotics to invest products with meaning for a culture whose dominant focus is consumption.[8]

➡ *Taboos*, or prohibitions, in a culture, relating to various things such as the use of a given colour, phrase or symbol.[9]

➡ *Ritualised activities* in which people participate at home, work or play, both as individuals and as members of a group. Such behaviour is expressive and symbolic, occurs in a fixed episodic sequence and tends to be repeated over time.[10] *Rites of passage* are ritual events marking significant points in a person's life as that person passes from one status to another, as in graduation, marriage, retirement and death.

Anthropologists have also helped marketers recognise that consumer goods have a significant ability to carry and communicate cultural meaning. This occurs through a process in which meaning is drawn from a particular cultural world, transferred to a consumer good through advertising and the fashion system, and then transferred from these goods into the life of the individual consumer through certain consumption rituals. This allows individuals to use goods and services as symbols to communicate information about themselves and their groups to other people in society and to other societies.[11]

In Figure 3.1, the culturally constituted world is essentially defined as comprising two components: cultural categories and cultural principles. Cultural categories represent the basic distinctions with which a culture divides up the phenomenal world. Some of these are fairly objective, such as time, but others are much less so. McCracken identifies categories associated with time, space, nature and the person. For consumer behaviour we are most interested in the latter and typical of these categories are distinctions in terms of class, status, gender, age and occupation. Recognition that cultures work at a broad level by ascribing different meanings to persons based on these categories is fundamental to understanding why patterns of behaviour vary across them, and hence why they are applicable for market segmentation as described in other chapters.

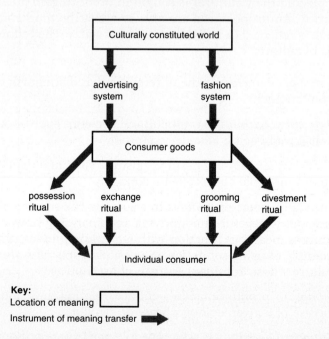

FIG. 3.1 The movement of meaning in consumption Source: Grant McCracken, *Culture and Consumption*, Indiana University Press, Bloomington and Indianapolis, IN, 1988, p. 72.

The other component of the culturally constituted world in McCracken's scheme are what he terms 'cultural principles'. These are the ideas, or values, according to which the categories are organised. As an example, our societies have values that are related to achievement. These help us, with other ideas as discussed in Chapter 4, organise a set of personal categories related to class and status. Other values relate to politeness and humanity and over time they have become associated with gender-based categories. Discussion of cultural change in Australia and New Zealand, like the development of the SNAG (sensitive new age man), is based on a redefinition of the relationship between the principles, or values, and the categories. The place of values in the McCracken scheme emphasises why it has become such a fruitful area for consumer research, as detailed later in the chapter.

The two main instruments of transfer of meaning from culture to goods are the advertising and the fashion systems. In advertising, the creative director seeks to find ways of linking elements of the cultural world with the product, and when this is successful the consumer recognises those properties as part of the product to be consumed. In the fashion industry, goods are also systematically invested and divested of their meaningful properties with the help of the media and opinion leaders. The fashion industry also acts as a mechanism for cultural reform. It may be possible to identify other channels in society—for example, educational systems—that also have some impact on the transfer of meaning from culture to goods, but the essence of McCracken's view is that advertising and fashion are most important because it is their primary purpose and they perform it in a more or less systematic way.

That goods possess cultural meaning is without doubt. Clothing, cars, food, housing interiors and exteriors, jewellery and other adornments all convey information we can associate with categories and values in society. Meaning is transferred to the individual consumer by what anthropologists describe as a 'ritual'. A ritual is a prescribed order of behaviour that covers required or usual sets of actions. The *possession ritual* is the most obvious of these. Acquisition of a Porsche by one individual consumer and a Lada by a second conveys different meanings into the lives of the two individuals. Evidently possession rituals are very strong in Australia and New Zealand, and their existence and relative strength reflect the degree of materialism present in a culture.

Exchange rituals are characterised by gift-giving behaviour. Some consumer behaviour research has been conducted in the United States on this dimension of culture but specific studies are not available for Australia and New Zealand.[12] Gift giving is evidently related to family and friendship categories and is used to express love, affection and obligations. For example, the association of gift giving with birthdays is a ritual that links consumption with cultural classifications based on age. Ages such as 18, 21 or 65 take on special significance in different cultures, as they symbolise the passage of an individual from one cultural category to another. Obviously more research is required into exchange rituals and consumer behaviour, but it is accepted that both the choice of gift and of the amount of money spent on the gift convey meaning. It is also apparent that approaches to exchange rituals vary across different ethnic groups in both Australia and New Zealand. It is believed that Anglo-Celtic Australians and New Zealanders place a heavier emphasis on a tangible gift, and the monetary value of that gift, than do other groups who may exchange time in preference to actual goods. Thus Italians, Greeks, Chinese, Maoris and others may all place a higher value on being present at a birthday celebration within the family, rather than on giving a physical gift to the person.

Grooming rituals refer to repeated actions that are necessary to draw the meaning out of some goods. Clear examples of grooming rituals are those associated with perishable services such as the arts. In order to adequately draw the meaning out of such products, it is necessary to repeat the behaviour. In Sydney there is clear status associated with attending the Opera House. However, a one-off attendance is insufficient to transfer the meaning. To convey meaning successfully from the service to the individual consumer, the ritual must be repeated and maintained over time.

McCracken uses the term 'divestment ritual' to cover two sorts of behaviours. In the first instance it characterises behaviours such as cleaning out and redecorating previously owned products such as cars or houses. These rituals allow the new owner to purge the product of meanings associated with previous owners. It is the existence of such rituals as these that allow for substantial second-hand markets in many goods in Australia and New Zealand. Other cultures, for example Germany and Japan, do not facilitate the acquisition of second-hand items. In the second sense, an individual who is about to dispose of a good will go through a process of emptying the meaning from the product before it is surrendered. Children may remove all the stickers from their old bicycle before it is sold to a new owner, despite the fact that the stickers cannot be reused. Divestment rituals are in themselves the least relevant to most marketing situations but they do emphasise an important consideration. As goods may be emptied of their meaning by such rituals, it should also be evident that meanings ascribed to goods have a movable quality and are not fixed indefinitely. Hence, marketers must continuously work to maintain brand images or they may seek to change the meanings ascribed to their products through repositioning strategies.

The following scenario illustrates the pervasiveness in modern life of ritual behaviour as an important part of our culture:

From the house we step outside, into the 'outdoor living' area. This is possibly the most ritualised of spaces in our homes, dominated by codes of behaviour and gradually being converted with technology into a place of real complexity. The Australian male has turned the outdoor living area into an essential and central feature of the suburban home. Here Ted Bullpit reigns, surrounded by his range of insect sprays, barbecue 'tools', lighting fixtures, garden furniture and plants in a variety of rustic pots. In a 'Rembrandt'-style home, typically, the outdoor living area is semi-covered, paved, with a table and chairs. Here nature and culture are brought into a different balance—the covering reflecting distrust of the weather, the table and chairs indicating a comfortable reassurance of its docility.

At one end of the outdoor living area is a space to be filled by a barbecue, the high altar in the ritual of outdoor living that signifies more than any other item ... The barbecue is the most 'natural' way of cooking: culture is closest to nature here. There are no utensils intervening in the process, a minimum of fats and oils, just the natural elements of fire and meat. There is a significant reversal of sex roles in barbecue cooking that may only be explicable in terms of this nature–culture relationship. Outdoor cooking is typically performed by the male, seeking an analogy for his definitively masculine role as a hunter in 'natural' societies. The hunter male proudly cooks the meat which he has symbolically caught and, in the barbecue enactment of 'natural' social relations, brings it to the salad which his wife (the gatherer or cultivator) has prepared indoors in the sphere of culture. The barbecue meal celebrates the transformation of nature into culture.[13]

The activities described above are associated with various types of rituals and demonstrate how consumer behaviour and culture are inextricably linked through the symbolism that is imbued into consumer goods.

CULTURAL VALUES

Cultural values are important to the organised and integrated nature of culture. A cultural value can be defined in a sociological perspective as 'a widely held belief or sentiment that some activities, relationships, feelings, or goals are important to the community's identity or well-being'.[14] In a psychological vein, Milton Rokeach defines values as centrally held and enduring beliefs that guide actions and judgments across specific situations and beyond immediate goals to more ultimate end-states of existence. Values, therefore, produce inclinations to respond to specific stimuli in standard ways.[15] That is, a specific behaviour is expected either to help or to hinder the attainment of some value or group of values. Consumers, then, are motivated to engage in behaviours designed to enhance the achievement of certain values and to avoid those behaviours perceived to hinder the attainment of certain value states.[16]

Chapter 12 will discuss the concept of attitudes and their relationship to consumer behaviour. Because there often is confusion over the concepts of attitudes and values, it may be useful at this point to clarify these terms. Attitudes can be viewed as the individual's positive or negative evaluations of objects, situations or behaviours, which predispose the individual to respond in some manner. Values, on the other hand, transcend specific objects and situations. They deal with modes of conduct (*instrumental values*) and end-states of existence (*terminal values*). That is, an individual who has a 'value' has an enduring belief that a particular mode of conduct or end-state of existence is preferable to some other mode of conduct or end-state of existence. Values serve as standards or criteria that tell us how to act, what to want and what attitudes to hold, and they allow us to judge and compare ourselves with others. Compared with attitudes, which focus directly on specific objects, situations or actions, values transcend specific circumstances. Whereas individuals may possess thousands of attitudes, they are likely to possess fewer than 100 values.[17] In other words, values work at a higher level of abstraction and are deeper seated, more pervasive influences on behaviour. Schwartz sums human values up very simply as 'desirable goals, varying in importance, that serve as guiding principles in people's lives'.[18]

Values are culturally determined; this means that they are learned from social interaction, largely with our families and friends, in settings such as schools and churches. Values strongly influence consumer behaviour. Even though specific situations may dictate slightly different actions, overall there is much similarity in consumer behaviour within a given culture, such as in tastes, methods of shopping and so forth.

It is crucial for the marketer to understand society's basic value structure so that strategy decisions do not fly in the face of ingrained cultural patterns. It is much easier to harmonise with the culture than to attempt to change fundamental cultural values. Values, either singly or in combination, may also be used by the marketer as a basis for market segmentation, and the different types of appeal made in marketing communications often relate to basic cultural values such as patriotism, achievement or efficiency. For example, Australian ownership was a key feature of the Telecom campaign in the 1994 ballot with Optus.

In the next sections we will look first at some of the internationally important studies on values, then we will examine some research pertinent to Australia and New Zealand.

An appeal to the consumers' value of patriotism   COURTESY OF LION BREWERIES

Values and the study of consumer behaviour

Intuitively we can see that culture is a strong force in consumers' milieus affecting their choice of behaviour, and marketers have long recognised the importance of appealing to consumers' values. Perhaps the most influential of all authors on the subject of values has been Milton Rokeach.[19] Rokeach believes that values guide actions, attitudes and judgments, and that the consequences of people's values are evident in practically any phenomenon that social scientists may think worthy of study and understanding.

In order to create a meaningful objective research instrument to improve the value measurement process, Rokeach created the Rokeach Value Survey (RVS), consisting of two sets of values—18 instrumental values and 18 terminal values—each of which is ranked by subjects in order of the value's importance or is responded to on an agree–disagree scale.[20] As we have seen, instrumental values relate to modes of conduct and terminal values relate to end-states of existence. Rokeach also breaks up each of these two categories into two further groups. Instrumental values may be either *moral* values or *competence* values. Moral values have an interpersonal focus and, when violated, arouse pangs of conscience or feelings of guilt. Honesty, obedience and politeness are all examples of moral instrumental values. Competence values have a personal rather than interpersonal focus. Behaving logically, intelligently or imaginatively may lead to fulfilment of competence values. When violated, these values lead to feelings of personal inadequacy rather than guilt about wrongdoing. Terminal values may be considered to be either *personal* or *social*. End-states such as salvation and peace of mind are personal while world peace is social. Table 3.1 presents these 36 values.

TABLE 3.1 Cultural values

Terminal values (end-states of existence)
A comfortable life (a prosperous life)
An exciting life (a stimulating, active life)
A sense of accomplishment (lasting contribution)
A world at peace (free of war and conflict)
A world of beauty (nature and the arts)
Equality (brotherhood, equal opportunity)
Family security (taking care of loved ones)
Freedom (independence, free choice)
Happiness (contentment)
Inner harmony (freedom from inner conflict)
Mature love (sexual and spiritual intimacy)
National security (protection from attack)
Pleasure (an enjoyable, leisurely life)
Salvation (saved, eternal life)
Self-respect (self-esteem)
Social recognition (respect, admiration)
True friendship (close companionship)
Wisdom (a mature understanding of life)

Continues

TABLE 3.1 Cultural values *continued*

Instrumental values (modes of conduct)
Ambitious (hard working, aspiring)
Broad-minded (open-minded)
Capable (competent, effective)
Cheerful (light-hearted, joyful)
Clean (neat, tidy)
Courageous (standing up for your beliefs)
Forgiving (willing to pardon others)
Helpful (working for others' welfare)
Honest (sincere, truthful)
Imaginative (daring, creative)
Independent (self-reliant, self-sufficient)
Intellectual (intelligent, reflective)
Logical (consistent, rational)
Loving (affectionate, tender)
Obedient (dutiful, respectful)
Polite (courteous, well mannered)
Responsible (dependable, reliable)
Self-controlled (restrained, self-disciplined)

Source: Reprinted from Milton Rokeach, 'The Role of Values in Public Opinion Research', *Public Opinion Quarterly* 32, Winter 1968–69, p. 554. Copyright 1969 by the Trustees of Columbia University.

One criticism of the Rokeach approach to values and explaining consumer behaviour is that it is too general and includes some values that have little to do with consumption. These may obfuscate the results of research using the Rokeach method, and response researchers at the University of Michigan have created an alternative value-measurement scale and procedure. Their List of Values (LOV) may be better for establishing important relationships between values and consumption and may relate more closely to the values of life's major roles (such as marriage, parenting, work, leisure and daily consumption). Table 3.2 defines these values and reports the percentage of Americans who selected each value as most important in their lives. One study showed that LOV explains a higher percentage than RVS of terms that people say influence their daily lives.[21]

TABLE 3.2 LOV segments

1. Self-respect is the 'all-American' value in that it was selected by the largest number of Americans and it has the least distinctive endorsers. People from all age and income groups selected this value as most important. About 21.1% of Americans selected it in 1976, 23.0% in 1986.

2. Security is a deficit value, endorsed by people who lack economic and psychological security. People who endorse it tend to report anxiety, trouble sleeping, dizziness and shortness of breath. Blacks, southerners and retired people also select this value frequently. It was selected by 20.6% of Americans in 1976, 16.5% in 1986.

3. Warm relationships with others is an excess value, endorsed by people, especially women, who have a lot of friends and who are friendly. Midwesterners rate this value highly. Endorsers include divorced men, Lutherans, frequent churchgoers, housewives and clerical workers. People in this segment usually have supportive families and good social support networks. The percentage has risen from 16.2% to 19.9%.

4. Likewise, people who endorse a sense of accomplishment have accomplished a lot. These people tend to be successful middle-aged men. They often have good jobs and high incomes. They tend to be well-educated managers and professionals. They may be Jewish or Methodist, but they often do not go to synagogue or church. These people like conspicuous consumption but dislike any television watching that interferes with accomplishment. Earlier, about 11.4% endorsed this value, but more recently endorsement grew to 15.9%. The percentage is higher in the north-east.

5. People—mostly 'young urban professionals'—who endorse self-fulfilment are relatively well fulfilled economically, educationally and emotionally. They are healthy and self-confident. They resent excessive demands from their families that distract from self-fulfilment. They like movies more than television. Overall 9.6% of Americans subscribed to this value earlier, but the rate fell more recently to 6.5%. The percentage is higher in the Pacific states.

6. Being well respected is selected by the Rodney Dangerfields of the world. They are often over 50 and have little occupational prestige, yet they love their jobs. This value is endorsed by farmers, craftspeople, operators, divorced women and retired people. They have low incomes and lack formal education. It is interesting to contrast self-respect, which one can achieve alone, with being well respected, which requires the co-operation of others. People who value self-respect are much better adjusted, according to our measures. Psychologically, people who value being well respected tend to be external, depressed, unhappy, pessimistic and unhealthy. For fun they like to bowl. The 1976 and 1986 percentages are, respectively, 8.8% and 5.9%.

7. Sense of belonging also requires the help of others. Like warm relationships with others, it is a social value selected by women. However, it is less reciprocal and seems to result in greater dependency. It is a home- and family-oriented value particularly popular in the mountain states. Endorsers tend to be housewives and clerical workers. Although they tend to have only a high-school education, they tend to be middle-income. They are happy in family roles, although physically they experience dizziness, anxiety, nervousness and headaches. They go to church weekly, usually as Presbyterians, Lutherans, or Catholics. They like to read *TV Guide* and *Reader's Digest*. The endorsement rate was 7.9% and has fallen to 5.1%.

8. You might think that fun and enjoyment in life would isolate the hedonists in America, but the cliché that best describes these people is 'Stop and smell the roses'. Young people who appreciate life especially like this value. They are often unemployed or work in sales or

Continues

TABLE 3.2 LOV segments *continued*

labour, but they are optimistic and well adjusted. They dislike family roles, religion and children, however. They do like sports and entertainment, and they read *Playboy, Rolling Stone* and *Cosmopolitan*. About 4.5% of Americans endorsed this value in 1976, and the percentage has risen to 7.2%. The rise has been especially dramatic among young males.

Source: Lynn R. Kahle & Patricia Kennedy, 'Using the List of Values (LOV) to Understand Consumers', *Journal of Services Marketing* 2 (4), 1988, p. 51.

The security of knowing it works.

No matter how large or small the animal. No matter whether it is an important pet or part of a farm income, the need for proper care remains the same. That kind of animal health care which both pet owners and farmers rely on, can only come with the kind of research a company like Bayer is prepared to make. Last year alone Bayer spent more than $1,200 million on research. Bayer Research. In a hundred different ways it helps New Zealanders make, grow and care for things.

Bayer New Zealand Ltd, Marine Parade, Petone.

Making over 10,000 different veterinary products, agricultural chemicals, plastics, dyestuffs, pigments, textile fibres, pharmaceuticals.

This advertisement emphasises values associated with security and care of loved ones
COURTESY OF BAYER NEW ZEALAND LTD

Rokeach and LOV scales are both fundamentally important approaches that have furthered our understanding of the nature of values and the way they impact on consumer behaviour. However, from our perspective in Australasia, they are potentially limited by their American origin. It may be that neither adequately captures the full multicultural nature of our societies. They may either include values that are not relevant or exclude values that may be important within our cultures. Recently Schwartz has conducted a major study that attempts to look at the structure and content of values in 20 different countries using samples of teachers and students in each country.[22] While not absolutely representative of the general populations, these samples are still useful because teachers have a major role in influencing and transmitting values in a society and students are probably indicative of future changes in value strengths. American college graduates, for example, are considered to be about five years ahead of their non-college contemporaries in describing value changes in the United States. In any event there are high levels of consistency in Schwartz's results, which suggests we may be able to identify a number of core values with a common structure that can be measured across very different cultures. These have not yet been tested with general populations or in the specific context of consumer behaviour, but it is a potentially exciting development for marketers and consumer researchers interested in international studies. It may provide a more relevant structure for examining local markets than either Rokeach or LOV methods.

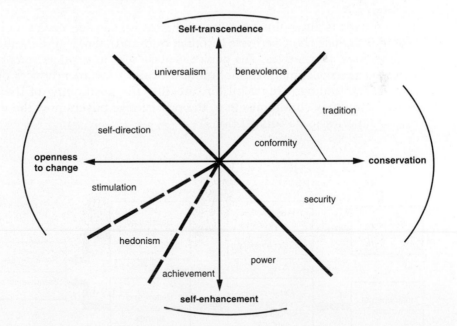

FIG 3.2   Individual value structures   Source: Shalom H. Schwartz, 'Universals in the Content and Structure of Values', *Advances in Experimental Social Psychology* 25, 1992, pp. 1–61.

Schwartz summarises 10 primary values noted around the outside of Figure 3.2. These primary values are derived from the individual value questions noted in each space, and are arranged so that values correlating highly with each other are positioned adjacent to each other and opposite from values that are inversely correlated. For example, self-direction is a personal terminal value that is highly correlated with stimulation and opposite from security, which in Schwartz's results is both an individual and a collective terminal value. This graphical portrayal is very useful, as it gives a quick intuitive understanding of the relationships between different values and the structure of value systems. The primary values identified by Schwartz cover personal, social, moral and competence values.

The effects of values on consumer behaviour vary according to the value type. For example, an investigation of homemakers' purchases of household appliances has used terminal and instrumental value lists to discover an important relationship between purchases and values. Women were interviewed who planned to make a purchase of one or more of eight major household appliances. Terminal values were found to be related much more strongly to the product-class level of choice than were instrumental values (e.g. when deciding between washing machines such as full-sized automatics, 'mini' automatics and compact portables). At the brand-choice decision level (such as deciding between Simpson and Fisher & Paykel) instrumental values were found to be related, while terminal values were not related at all. Thus, terminal values would seem to guide choice among product classes, while instrumental values would seem to guide choice among brands.[23]

This concept is diagrammed in Figure 3.3. As we can see, each set of values is thought to influence choice criteria (product or brand); that is, the standards used to judge various alternatives. The choice criteria are, in turn, seen as having an influence on the consumer's formation of attitudes toward products or brands. These research findings are useful for directing the positioning of the brand so that advertising may communicate to the prospective buyers how the marketer's offering is superior to its competition.[24]

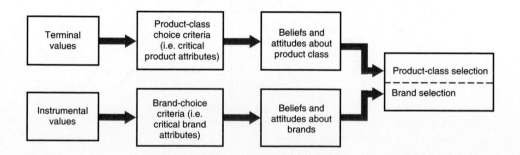

FIG 3.3   How cultural values influence purchase decisions

Researchers using both the LOV and RVS have examined several consumption questions and found that differences exist based on values held by consumers. For example, people more highly endorsing a sense of belonging tend to be heavily involved in individual and group leisure activities with others. In other words, they search for activities that enable them to fulfil their important values or needs. Consumers endorsing fun and excitement in life apparently desire more exciting media, such as police dramas, and engage in more exciting activities, such as jogging and skiing. Conversely, those who more heavily stress security seem to prefer passive activities, such as watching sporting events and having hobbies, and they have different media preferences.

All these approaches to values can prove helpful to the marketer in understanding important consumption facets. Knowing that consumers who endorse certain values more highly than other values have different lifestyles may be extremely useful in determining promotion appeals, product positioning and design, channels of distribution and pricing approaches. In market segmentation decisions, knowledge of personal values can significantly enhance demographic understanding.[25] For example, one American study involving a national chain of family restaurants and its leading competitor found that brand preference was not differentiated with respect to demographic characteristics of consumers who ate at both chains and had a stated preference for one or the other. However, market segments based on value orientations of these fast-food restaurant customers did reveal differences that related to consumers' brand preferences. This kind of information is useful in designing effective advertising campaigns and developing products with salient product attributes, thereby enhancing the competitive posture of the brand. Values have also been found to relate to contributions to charitable causes, to help explain preferences for different types of cars, to predict mass-media usage, and to relate mass-media vehicles to promotional messages.

However, more research is needed on the subject of values as they relate to purchasing behaviour. There is still much disagreement on how widely and how intensely values must be held among consumers. A greater understanding is also needed on the origins and consequences of values. In addition, more research is necessary to understand cultural value influences on consumer behaviour across a broader range of products than has so far been investigated.[26]

Several companies are pursuing such a goal of broadening the application of consumer values to understanding the behaviour of users of a wide range of products. Internationally, SRI International are the most prominent of these and combine value and lifestyle (termed VALS) information with available demographic data.[27] The purpose is to create a general psychographic framework that can be used to understand consumers of a variety of products, from deodorants to television sets. Because SRI developed the psychographic approach and because of the company's prominent and influential position, we will briefly review their work on the United States before considering equivalent work in Australia and New Zealand.

After over a decade of research into consumer values and lifestyles, SRI has created VALS 2, which identifies eight types of consumers, each so distinctive in its behaviour and emotional make-up that it is held to constitute a specific market segment. The eight types—the five major categories and their subcategories—are identified in Figure 3.4 and described in Table 3.3. The table summarises representative demographics of these consumer segments.

The typology is built on two dimensions. The first, self-orientation, pertains to the patterns of attitudes and activities that help people to reinforce, sustain or even modify their social self-image. Principle-oriented consumers are guided in their choices by their beliefs or principles, rather than by feelings, events or desire for approval. Status-oriented consumers are heavily influenced by the actions, approval and opinions of others. Action-oriented consumers are guided by a desire for social or physical activity, variety and risk taking.

The second dimension, resources, involves the capacities and means that enable people to act on their desires and decisions. This dimension is a continuum ranging from minimal to abundant. It encompasses education, income, health, self-confidence, eagerness to buy, intelligence and energy level. Resources generally increase from adolescence through middle age, while they decrease with extreme age, depression, financial reverses, and physical or psychological impairment.

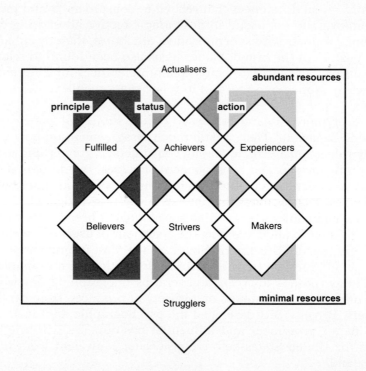

FIG 3.4 The VALS 2 network   Source: SRI International.

TABLE 3.3   VALS 2 segments

Actualisers
Actualisers are successful, sophisticated, active, 'take-charge' people with high self-esteem and abundant resources. They are interested in growth and seek to develop, explore, and express themselves in a variety of ways—sometimes guided by principle and sometimes by a desire to have an effect, to make a change. Image is important to Actualisers, not as evidence of status or power, but as an expression of their taste, independence and character. Actualisers are among the established and emerging leaders in business and government, yet they continue to seek challenges. They have a wide range of interests, are concerned with social issues and are open to change. Their lives are characterised by richness and diversity. Their possessions and recreation reflect a cultivated taste for the finer things in life.

Fulfilled and Believers: principle-oriented
Fulfilled are mature, satisfied, comfortable, reflective people who value order, knowledge and responsibility. Most are well educated and in (or recently retired from) professional occupations. They are well informed about world and national events and are alert to opportunities to broaden their knowledge. Content with their careers, families and station in life, they tend to centre their leisure activities around the home. Fulfilled have a moderate respect for the status quo institutions of authority and social decorum, but are open-minded about new ideas and social change. Fulfilled tend to base their decisions on strongly held principles and consequently appear calm and self-assured. While their incomes allow them many choices, Fulfilled are conservative, practical consumers; they look for functionality, value and durability in the products they buy.

Believers are conservative, conventional people with concrete beliefs based on traditionally established codes: family, church, community and the nation. Many Believers express moral codes that are deeply rooted and literally interpreted. They follow established routines, organised in large part around their homes, their families, and the social or religious organisations to which they belong. As consumers, they are conservative and predictable, favouring American products and established brands. Their education, income and energy are modest but sufficient to meet their needs.

Achievers and Strivers: status-oriented
Achievers are successful career and work-oriented people who like to, and generally do, feel in control of their lives. They value consensus, predictability and stability over risk, intimacy and self-discovery. They are deeply committed to work and family. Work provides them with a sense of duty, material rewards and prestige. Their social lives reflect this focus and are structured around family, church and career. Achievers live conventional lives, are politically conservative, and respect authority and the status quo. Image is important to them; they favour established, prestige products and services that demonstrate success to their peers.

Strivers seek motivation, self-definition and approval from the world around them. They are striving to find a secure place in life. Unsure of themselves and low on economic, social and psychological resources, strivers are concerned about the opinions and approval of others. Money defines success for Strivers, who don't have enough of it and often feel that life has given them a raw deal. Strivers are easily bored and impulsive. Many of them seek to be stylish. They emulate those who own more impressive possessions, but what they wish to obtain is generally beyond their reach.

Experiencers and Makers: action-oriented2
Experiencers are young, vital, enthusiastic, impulsive and rebellious. They seek variety and excitement, savouring the new, the off-beat and the risky. Still in the process of formulating life values and patterns of behaviour, they quickly become enthusiastic about new possibilities but are equally quick to cool. At this stage in their lives, they are politically uncommitted, uninformed

Continues

TABLE 3.3 VALS 2 segments *continued*

and highly ambivalent about what they believe. Experiencers combine an abstract disdain for conformity with an outsider's awe of others' wealth, prestige and power. Their energy finds an outlet in exercise, sports, outdoor recreation and social activities. Experiencers are avid consumers and spend much of their income on clothing, fast food, music, movies and video.

Makers are practical people who have constructive skills and value self-sufficiency. They live within a traditional context of family, practical work and physical recreation and have little interest in what lies outside that context. Makers experience the world by working on it—building a house, raising children, fixing a car or canning vegetables—and have sufficient skill, income and energy to carry out their projects successfully. Makers are politically conservative, suspicious of new ideas and respectful of government authority and organised labour, but resentful of government intrusion on individual rights. They are unimpressed by material possessions other than those with a practical or functional purpose (e.g. tools, pick-up trucks and fishing equipment).

Strugglers

Strugglers' lives are constricted. Chronically poor, ill-educated, low-skilled, without strong social bonds, elderly and concerned about their health, they are often resigned and passive. Because they are limited by the need to meet the urgent needs of the present moment, they do not show strong self-orientation. Their chief concerns are for security and safety. Strugglers are cautious consumers. They represent a very modest market for most products and services, but are loyal to favourite brands.

Source: SRI International.

TABLE 3.4 Representative VALS 2 consumer demographics

Segment	Percentage of population	Male sex	Median age	Median income	College education	White-collar occupation	Married
	%	%	yrs	$	%	%	%
Actualisers	8	59	43	58 000	95	68	72
Fulfilled	11	47	48	38 000	81	50	73
Believers	16	46	58	21 000	6	11	70
Achievers	13	39	36	50 000	77	43	73
Strivers	13	41	34	25 000	23	19	60
Experiencers	12	53	26	19 000	41	21	34
Makers	13	61	30	23 000	24	19	65
Strugglers	14	37	61	9 000	3	2	47

Source: SRI International.

Based on information gathered by SRI on dozens of products, the VALS 2 program appears to have much usefulness for understanding the activities, product purchases and media habits of each category of consumer. Researchers involved with the LOV system claim that it works better than does VALS,[28] while VALS researchers claim that their system is preferred over LOV as a segmentation basis.[29] Nevertheless, SRI's pioneering work on the values and lifestyles of consumers has achieved much notice and success within the business community.

In Australia and New Zealand the major research equivalent to VALS is that completed by the Roy Morgan Research Centre.[30] Based on samples of 32 860 Australians and 13 370 New Zealanders, Roy Morgan have developed a comprehensive values segmentation that distinguishes the 10 different segments shown in Table 3.5. A key point is the obvious similarity in the composition of the two populations, which is the result of the many shared aspects of culture experienced by Australians and New Zealanders.

TABLE 3.5   Roy Morgan values segments in Australia and New Zealand

Segment	Proportion of population Australia	New Zealand
	%	%
Basic Needs	4	3
Fairer Deal	7	7
Traditional Family Life	18	19
Conventional Family Life	11	11
Look At Me	14	15
Something Better	9	8
Real Conservatism	5	5
Young Optimism	7	6
Visible Achievement	15	18
Socially Aware	10	8
Total	100	100

Source: *The Roy Morgan Values Segments*, Roy Morgan Research Centre Pty Ltd, Sydney, 1994.

1. *Basic Needs*. These people seek a life of security and focus on their daily basic requirements. They are older, often retired and widowed with government pensions as the main source of income. Members of this group hold very traditional social, moral and religious views. They enjoy passive activities and are fairly satisfied with their lives. In terms of their consumer behaviour, they are least likely to own major household items, or to be considering such purchases. They are also least likely to have credit cards, use air travel or entertainments such as cinemas. In terms of media, they are heavy viewers of commercial television and above-average commercial-radio listeners. There is an above-average readership of *New Idea*, *Woman's Day* and *Your Garden*.

2. *Fairer Deal*. Members of this group have a low economic position and are typically under 35 years of age. Money worries and employment insecurity create high levels of pessimism and cynicism. This group contains the highest proportion of unskilled and semi-skilled workers, many of the incomes are below $15,000 (AUS) and the typical educational achievement is less than four years of secondary schooling. A distinguishing characteristic of these people is that they believe society is giving them a raw deal and that other people always tend to get the breaks in life. Their consumer behaviour has several distinctive features, including the highest proportion of smokers, above average consumption of fast food and ownership of hi-fi systems, VCRs and colour televisions. It is suggested that all these behaviours, which are regarded by many as discretionary, can be interpreted as a form of compensation for the insecurities perceived by the Fairer Deal group. Media consumption is characterised by above average readership of *TV Week*, *Woman's Day*, *People*, *Australian Playboy* and *Penthouse*.

3.   *Traditional Family Life*. Members of this segment are mainly over 50 and few have children living at home. They retain a strong commitment to traditional family roles and values and are very religious. They have below-average education levels and consider themselves to the right politically. They are cautious, concerned about health but generally satisfied with their standard of living and home life. Most own their own home. They are above-average viewers of commercial television but below-average radio listeners. This group contains the highest readership of *Reader's Digest*, *Your Garden* and *Prime Time*. (Readership of *New Idea* and *Woman's Day* is almost as high as for the Basic Needs group.) This group also has above-average readership of publications such as *Open Road* and *Royal Auto*.

4.   *Conventional Family Life*. These people are typically aged between 30 and 50, on average incomes and working to improve themselves and the position of their children. They are generally satisfied with life and place a higher value on time spent with family and friends and have less work ambition than their more success-orientated counterparts in society. They are committed to marriage as an institution and see making money as instrumental to a better lifestyle for the future. They are concerned about long-term security and are prepared to reduce current expenditure to take out insurance for later in life. In other aspects of consumer behaviour, Conventional Family Lifers are likely to possess Bankcard and Myer cards rather than other credit and charge cards, and are less likely to consume alcohol. Pet ownership is high and they are above-average readers of *Australian Woman's Weekly*, *New Idea*, *TV Week*, *Woman's Day*, and other home and gardening magazines.

5.   *Look at Me*. This phrase refers to the pattern of responses that characterises young people (under 30 years) who seek an active, exciting prosperous life. They are typically unmarried and when married have no children. They enjoy freedom and demand a lot from friends, employers and society. Look at Mes are unsophisticated, outer-directed people who are very fashion and trend conscious. They have the highest patronage of fast-food and take-away outlets and are at the stage of life where they are busy equipping themselves with colour televisions, VCRs, hi-fi systems and cars. They are heavy commercial-radio listeners and slightly above-average commercial-television viewers. They have above-average readership of *Cleo*, *Cosmopolitan*, *Vogue*, *Elle*, *Dolly*, *Wheels*, *Street Machine* and sports magazines.

6.   *Something Better*. These are the younger, more modern families who seek the freedom to achieve. They are well-educated people in responsible jobs and on above-average incomes. They tend to be strongly individualist, confident people, who see themselves as progressive. They strongly support free enterprise and oppose government regulation and intervention. They emphasise all aspects of individual freedom, except the belief that military service should be required for all young men. Something Betters show high intentions to buy major household appliances and make extensive use of Bankcard, Mastercard and Visa. Cars are likely to be luxurious imported or exotic models. In media behaviour, this group are heavy listeners to commercial radio and have the highest readership of *Better Homes and Gardens*. They are generally orientated towards home-maker magazines and general women's magazines, except those specifically associated with fashion and youth.

7. *Real Conservatives*. Members of this group are over 35 years and not tertiary educated. They are characterised by a cautious approach to life and hold traditional social, moral and ethical values. This group observes society rather than actively participates. Real Conservatives watch little commercial television and patronise fast-food and take-away outlets infrequently. They have a high ownership of major credit cards and look for secure investments such as government bonds, debentures or real estate. They have above-average readership of *New Idea* and some motor-club magazines.

8. *Young Optimism*. The people in this group are today's student generation, generally of upper socio-economic background and interested in image, style, new technology and career opportunities. They believe that people control their own destiny and are optimistic about the future. They are heavy viewers of commercial television, very socially active and also likely to travel a lot. They are likely to own entertainment items like CD players and may be beginning to acquire items like microwaves.

9. *Visible Achievement*. Careers and success are important to this group. They enjoy high incomes and retain 'middle-of-the-road' values about home, work and society. Many have achieved success without the benefits of tertiary education. They are confident, competent and seek recognition of personal achievement. This group dines out regularly, attends cultural activities, is likely to be involved in sports and travel extensively, though often for business. They are likely to own expensive household items and up-market cars. They are the highest users of all credit cards and have higher readership of business, finance and home and gardening magazines.

10. *Socially Aware*. This group sees itself as socially responsible, middle class and progressive. The 'Socially Aware' are most likely to be involved in environmental movements and are least likely to support traditional family roles. They are likely to have a tertiary education and to be involved in a professional vocation. They have relatively high incomes but are not consumption-orientated, buying on practicality and not for brand or image. They attend cultural activities often, are low users of commercial television but do read home and garden magazines and some business or finance publications.

It is clear that many of the same values that underlie the VALS scheme from the United States also underlie the Morgan classification, though the proportions of the populations holding those ideals vary. All four aspects underlying Figure 3.5 showing the VALS network are identifiable in the Morgan segments. The abundance of resources is a clear factor delimiting some segments, and principle, status and action values are also clearly discernible. It is difficult to place Conventional Family Life on the two-dimensional classification, as it shows characteristics of both the Makers and Fulfilled groups from VALS. The Socially Aware show characteristics of both the Actualisers and the Fulfilled. Other Morgan groups fit more readily on the single dimensions defined in VALS, though they may fit between VALS groups on the basis of resources. In particular, the Fairer Deal and Look at Me groups parallel the Strivers and show the same tendencies to indulge in *compensatory consumption* because of their status orientation. Compensatory consumption was first identified in studies of consumption behaviour among African American groups, but the results of values-based research show it to be more clearly identified with low resources and a search for status than any particular ethnic characteristic.

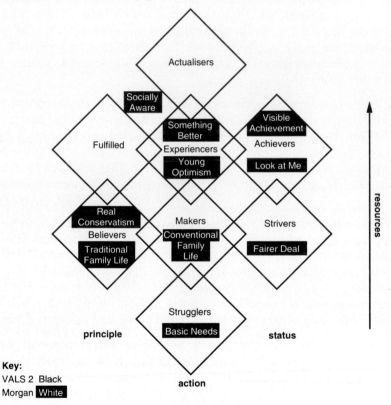

FIG. 3.5 A comparison between VALS 2 and Morgan segments

(Note that the principle, status and action columns have been changed to provide a better fit. It is our contention from evaluating the Morgan results and the Otago study detailed in the following section that there is less overlap between the status and belief groups than between the action and belief and the action and status. Hence the action groups are positioned in the centre of Figure 3.5 and not the status groups as in the original VALS 2 diagram in Figure 3.4.)

From an applied marketing point of view it may well be necessary to combine some of the more similar groups in the Morgan values classification in order to produce segments that are of sufficient size and potential profitability to warrant a marketer's interest. Even in Australia, a segment comprising 4 per cent of the population is very limited and in New Zealand the situation is obviously more extreme. A major 1989 study of New Zealand consumer values conducted by the University of Otago produced six segments, which have many parallels to the Morgan groups:[31]

1. *Success-driven Extroverts (8.9 per cent).* Career and social players—living it up and socialising—excitement and pleasure focus—free enterprise—impressing people—money and modernity.

2. *Educated Greens (12.4 per cent).* Societal reformers—support topical causes—intellect and education focus, culture, fashion, sophistication—secure well-off future.

3. *Active Family People (21.9 per cent).* Family life enthusiasm—active warm togetherness—children and development focus—protective of family health environment and heritage—family activities and outings.

4. *Traditional Values Family People (20.3 per cent).* Orderly family life—discipline and obedience, parental roles focus—traditional institutions—spiritual values and trust—local community activities.

5. *Envious Strivers (21.1 per cent).* Give me a break—life's a struggle—achieving ambitions focus—cautious and conformist—wanting life's 'essentials'—escapist activities.

6. *Friendly Quiet Lifers (15.4 per cent).* Neighbourly chat enjoyment—familiar hassle-free life—friendly close-to-home focus—elderly and nostalgic—companionship and good health.

In this classification:

➡ Envious Strivers mainly parallel the Fairer Deal and Look at Me Morgan groups.

➡ Quiet Family Lifers represent Basic Needs and part of the Traditional Family Life group.

➡ Traditional Values Family People parallel Traditional Family Lifers and Real Conservatives.

➡ Active Family People are closest to the Conventional Families and Something Betters.

➡ Success-driven Extroverts mainly represent the Young Optimists and Visible Achievers.

➡ Educated Greens parallel the Socially Aware.

The description of the Morgan segments showed how consumer behaviour varies across value segments in some aspects such as media behaviour. Table 3.6 gives further insight into variations by value segments in other aspects of consumer behaviour.

TABLE 3.6 Representative New Zealand values consumer indicators

	Base[a]	Quiet Family Lifers	Envious Strivers	Active Family People	Traditional Values Family People	Success-driven Extroverts	Educated Greens
Activities							
Gardening	0.317	134	112	109	69	72	94
Attended church	0.184	95	76	82	217	18	45
Bought lottery ticket	0.332	116	116	111	79	77	85
Visited library	0.154	134	70	98	90	76	145
Did art or craft work	0.132	60	86	130	117	42	135
Visited restaurant	0.227	65	100	104	68	197	124
Visited gymnasium	0.086	47	98	110	87	152	138
Played bowls	0.060	178	102	107	80	67	41
Products owned							
Loan (except housing)	0.218	78	67	86	102	149	168
Visa or Bankcard	0.479	81	88	115	76	130	136
Camera over $100	0.508	74	97	108	85	142	120
Automatic dishwasher	0.257	64	82	120	93	126	133
Microwave oven	0.496	76	95	116	95	107	113
Trampoline	0.099	44	61	157	130	72	105
Media							
Time Magazine	0.110	70	84	87	98	144	153
Woman's Day	0.163	59	127	132	105	48	73
Reader's Digest	0.178	104	98	115	121	53	72
TV Guide	0.181	76	124	113	118	64	63

(a) Figures in the base rate column are the proportion of the survey population using the product or service. Figures under each segment are the index for each segment (100 = base rate usage). Activities are based on a weekly period, except restaurants, which is fortnightly. Media is based on readership of over half the issues published.

CULTURAL CHANGE AND COUNTERCULTURES

The core values of a culture are not fixed or static, but instead are dynamic, changing elements. A culture may change slowly in an evolutionary manner, or it may change rapidly, which tends to place more stress on the system. The marketer needs to understand that cultures do change and to appreciate the implications this may have for consumer behaviour. It should also be clear that, by definition, cultural values as held by individuals are enduring and long-lasting phenomena. Therefore, although an individual's values may be modified over a lifetime, the major differences in values that exist between generations are cohort differences rather than the result of the ageing process. When marketers and other social commentators refer to 'older subcultures' and 'younger subcultures', they are referring to cohorts of the population whose values have been modified by particular experiences that affected their generation. The most notorious illustration of such cohorts are the 'baby boomers', who were discussed in Chapter 2. In his book *Reinventing Australia*, Hugh Mackay talks about this group as the 'Me Generation'. He argues that this generation (like similar groups in other Western societies) became obsessed with personal gratification, personal freedom and personal power. This was the generation that challenged many postwar values in society and redefined standards of behaviour. The Me Generation saw itself as idealistic but in the end only settled for one ideal—self-fulfilment. Many uncertainties and changes in values and norms of behaviour in Australia and New Zealand in the 1990s are attributed to members of the Me Generation searching for a redefinition of their place in society as they collectively approach their 'mid-life crises'.[32]

As the world around us is transformed politically, environmentally and economically, values in Australia and New Zealand are undergoing some major shifts. As indicated, these differences show up in different cohorts within the population. What makes the particular situation of both Australia and New Zealand unique is the multicultural focus of both societies. While the basic demographic statistics as presented in Chapter 2 are readily understood, it is much more difficult to assess the impacts on values across both countries. What must be accepted is that both societies are pluralistic, and the marketer faces a situation in which new value trends coexist with long-standing values still deeply rooted in the country.

The evolution of cultures is affected by many global trends in demographics, economics, politics, the natural environment and technology. Everything from ozone depletion to the General Agreement on Tariffs and Trade (GATT) and developments in multimedia technologies impact on, and are impacted by, our systems of values. Mackay believes that many of these trends have had the effect of fragmenting social groups and breaking down the sense of social cohesion in society. He describes seven aspects to support this assertion, and reviews of studies in New Zealand imply that they are equally appropriate there.[33]

1. The struggle between men and women over the redefinition of gender roles has led, for the time being, to a cautious, more adversarial approach to relationships between the sexes, replacing our traditional acceptance of pair bonding as the basis of our social structure with greater emphasis on the individual.

2. The rising divorce rate has fragmented family life to an extent that has forced many Australians to search—often fruitlessly—outside a family for a group, a herd, a tribe to which they might belong.

3. The 'personal growth' movement, which gained so much momentum during the 1970s and 1980s, encouraged egocentricity and, for many people, led to an obsession with personal gratification to the exclusion of traditional concepts of social cohesion.

4. Multiculturalism has seemed, in the short term, to place more emphasis on diversity than unity.

5. Politics has become virtually synonymous with economics and, in the process, has seemed to many Australians to have retreated from a concern for human values and social justice.

6. In corporate life, information technology has become so sophisticated that data transfer is often confused with communication, and personal relationships within organisations have suffered directly as a result. Sending and receiving disembodied information is increasingly allowed to occupy time that used to be spent in keeping closely in touch with each other.

7. On the domestic front, technology has played its part in fragmenting the herd: the dishwasher replaces an episode of personal interaction during washing up; the microwave oven reduces the need for the family to eat at the same time.

As a consequence of this fragmentation, the major change in the 1990s in both Australia and New Zealand is a wish to incorporate what people see as traditional values into contemporary life, often referred to as 'getting back to basics'. It should be clear that, except for small numbers of very strong traditionalists, this is not a general yearning to return to the past but a search for a way of stabilising and improving the present and the future. According to Hugh Mackay's research this translates into value words such as:

Responsibility	Balance
Restraint	Safety
Moderation	Purity
Heritage·	Loyalty
Conservation	Decency
Morality	Discipline
Integrity	Motherhood
Simplicity	Domesticity
Nature	The family

Source: Hugh Mackay, *Reinventing Australia*, Angus & Robertson, Sydney, 1993, p. 240.

These words emphasise values associated with belief, tradition and security, rather than the status and action values that have supposedly characterised the postwar years, and particularly the decades from the 1960s through to the 1980s. It should be stressed that this does not mean that all Australians are gazing inwardly in deep contemplation of the meaning of life. The Australian Social Monitor indicates that 62 per cent of Australians are not concerned with understanding their reasons for doing the things they do.[34] The values that drive our behaviour as a culture are not the result of long periods of conscious evaluation by individuals.

To emphasise the pluralism and the idea of counterculture Mackay describes a group of Australians who do not follow this trend and whom he describes as 'compulsive futurists'. These can obviously be associated with the action-based groups of Young Optimists and Something Betters from the Morgan classification. For this group, the search for enduring values is a fruitless quest. They focus on science and technology and accept the turbulence of the modern world. Their philosophy to life is dictated by an acceptance of change and the need to react and adapt, believing that everything will come right—there *will* be a vaccine for AIDS, and we *will* find a way to close the ozone hole and combat global warming! The consumer behaviour of such a group is obviously driven by quite different forces from those that drive the 'back to basics' Believers group and emphasises how potentially important an understanding of values can be for market segmentation.

Implications of cultural change for the marketer

Changes in norms such as those cited above signal the emergence of a new pattern of values for Australia and New Zealand. A few examples of how they will impact on marketers are cited below:

⇒ There will be a new emphasis on the home. Technology may enable more individuals to work from home and this will add a further dimension to its importance. In the 1980s the home became a focal point of social activities, long-term investment and personal expression.[35] Inflation caused people to evolve a new economic logic, and the home increasingly became seen as an investment. Coupled with changing lifestyles, there is, consequently, more of a focus on obtaining items for the home and spending time in the home. The stay-at-home urge, also known as 'cocooning', has helped to spur the do-it-yourself market and the sales of home-technology items such as VCRs and computers, as well as recreational or leisure assets such as exercise machines, swimming pools and spa baths.

⇒ There is a concern to introduce order and discipline into our lives. This results in a shift in people's notions about individual rights and responsibilities. Increasingly consumers feel that they are entitled to such things as adequate retirement income, comprehensive health care, and decent housing and education. Consumerism may be expected to expand. This entitlement psychology will lead to an escalation in people's insistence on having their 'rights' to safe, proven, non-polluting products and packaging. More informative and truthful labelling and advertising may also be expected. In both Australia and New Zealand large majorities of consumers favour more government regulation and control of the economy and environment.[36] This is not to be confused with support for public expenditure or ownership.

⇒ Finally, the back-to-basics or 'simple is better' trend has been influential in the rejection of the artificial and the acceptance of the natural. This has found expression in many product areas, including apparel (natural fabrics), toiletries (natural make-up and herbal-fragrance shampoos), pharmaceutical (stressing simple ingredients with no harmful side-effects), food (natural ingredients, health foods and home preserving) and housing (earth tones and indoor plants). It is even translated into preferences for car colours. Rich green colours are seen as the emerging option of the 1990s. They are seen to symbolise harmony and counteract stress. Car colours in the 1980s were dominated by reds and whites, colours associated with status and aggression. Red in particular is seen as the colour choice of the career climber.[37]

Tired of trendiness and materialism, some Australians and New Zealanders are rediscovering the joys of home life, basic values and things that last. This change has carried over into business strategies where 'value marketing' is becoming the watchword for the 1990s. Customers are demanding the right combination of product quality, fair price and good service. As a result, value marketers are hotly pursuing the following approaches:

1. offering products that truly perform;

2. giving more than consumers expect;

3. giving enhanced guarantees;

4. avoiding unrealistic premium pricing;

5. giving customers the facts;

6. building relationships with buyers.[38]

AUSTRALIA AND NEW ZEALAND AS MULTICULTURAL SOCIETIES

With changes in migration patterns to both countries and variations in demographics (such as the difference between Maori and pakeha[76] birthrates in New Zealand) understanding the ethnic variations within our cultures is becoming increasingly important for marketers. By knowing the characteristics and behavioural patterns of the segment they are trying to reach, they are in a better position to refine the marketing mix required to satisfy that target segment properly.

As we saw from the discussion of cultural change and countercultures, not all segments of a society have the same cultural patterns. Some of the most important differences in cultural patterns are reflected in the different ethnic groupings within Australia and New Zealand. These groups are often referred to as *subcultures* because, along with older and younger groupings (e.g. students) in society, religious groups and other sectors, they have values, customs, traditions and other ways of behaving that are peculiar to a particular group within a culture.

Though the term 'subculture' is an accepted label in anthropology, sociology and consumer behaviour research, it is one we prefer to avoid. We find that its use can be patronising and often assumes normative rather than descriptive properties; that is, it is taken to mean that one group may be inferior in some respect. It is also misleading because it emphasises diversity and distinctions. Quite clearly there are large overlaps in values and behaviour between different groups and, in using the concept of subcultures, it is often forgotten that people will be a member of more than one group. Following from these problems there are at least two important practical mistakes that marketers may make. First, there is a tendency to produce unnecessarily simple stereotypes to depict different groups, which say that all Aborigines, Italians, Pacific Islanders, students or homosexuals are the same. Secondly, because the groups that are traditionally considered subcultures are not mutually exclusive, there may be some double counting when segmentation strategies are employed.

In this section our focus is on ethnic variations within Australia and New Zealand. 'Ethnic' is the generic term used to describe groups characterised by a distinctive origin. Ethnic identification is based on what a person is when he or she is born, and it is largely unchangeable after that.[39] Members of a given ethnic group:

1. generally descend from common forebears;

2. tend to reside in the same locale—and one that is distinct from another ethnic group—over generations;

3. tend to marry within their own group;

4. give certain objects meanings unique to their ethnic group over generations;

5. share a common sense of peoplehood—of kindredness.[40]

Consumers may be subdivided into the following three types of ethnic dimensions, only the first two of which will be considered further in the discussion in this chapter:

1. *Race*. Racial groups are made up of people with a common biological heritage involving certain physical distinctions. In our context, the three most significant are the two indigenous populations of Australia and New Zealand and Asian immigrants.

2. *Nationality*. People with a common national origin constitute another type of ethnic group. The nationality grouping is usually characterised by a distinctive language or accent. Italians and Greeks in Australia are two examples of this category.

3. *Religion*. Religious subcultures are composed of people with a common and unique system of worship. Two important minority religious segments are Jews and Catholics. However, useful knowledge about the consumer behaviour of these and other religious groups is extremely limited, even outside Australasia, and we are not able to consider these segments further.

Both Australia and New Zealand have welcomed migrants over most of their recent history. Underlying this attitude has always been a presumption that people had chosen to move to the two countries because of a wish to be an 'Australian' or 'New Zealander' and they would adopt the dominant values of the countries. The situation, of course, has never been so simple as this. In 1985 *The Mackay Report on Multiculture* showed that some migrants to Australia took great pride in their original cultural heritage, their close family ties, their educational qualifications, their capacity for hard work and the quality of their parenting. In these respects, together with their enhanced commitment to the extended family, they always considered themselves different from 'British' Australians.[41] In recent years there have been at least two important changes that have precipitated the adoption of a multicultural perspective in both countries. The first is the growing numbers of Asian migrants to both countries, and we may add also Pacific Islanders to New Zealand. Asians appear not only physically different but also more distinctive in terms of their cultural heritage and religious beliefs. As the two countries have both developed more commercial ties with the Asian region there has been more recognition in politics, business and the media of the need to understand many of the basic cultural differences. The second, and probably even more fundamental, change precipitating a multicultural view in both countries is the resurgence of Aboriginal identity in Australia and Maori identity in New Zealand. The latter would seem to be further developed, and coincides with the growth in the proportion of the New Zealand population who now *view* themselves as Maori as opposed to wishing to identify with the pakeha majority.

Multicultural marketing in Australia

Instant lottery products specifically designed to capture the Chinese and Vietnamese markets by timing their release with the Lunar New Year have proved a marketing coup for the NSW State Lotteries. When NSW State Lotteries reviewed its marketing approach several years ago research highlighted the significance of ethnic groups within the state. Different marketing opportunities were then discussed including a promotional 'scratchie' ticket to coincide with the Chinese New Year.

As the game was first released in the Chinese Year of the Monkey, it was called 'Lucky Monkeys'. The $2 card featured traditional Chinese good-luck symbols such as firecrackers, blossom and lanterns. To maintain the link between the name of the game and the year, the main prize symbol winning

$100 000 was a monkey. The game was advertised in the ethnic media and through a number of special agency-based promotions in those areas where there was a predominance of Asian customers. As 'scratchie' tickets are usually a spontaneous purchase, the point-of-sale material had to be attractive and appropriate. To encourage Chinese people to buy the lottery tickets, small red packets, in which Chinese traditionally put money for gifts, were provided at the point of sale.

So successful was the first release of 'Lucky Monkeys' that the initial order of 2.8 million tickets was increased to 4.8 million. Since 1992 the NSW State Lotteries has continued the strategy, with 'Lucky Rooster' in 1993 and 'Lucky Dog' in 1994.[42]

This is one example that illustrates the recent developments in multicultural marketing in Australia. In general, the trends in multicultural marketing are being set by a limited range of industries where there is clearly scope to take advantage of the diversity, and where the ethnic groups in Australia may be linked to advantages for international business. The major companies that employ multicultural marketing strategies are in telecommunications (it has been a strong feature of the Optus/Telstra marketing battle), hotels, specialised foods and banking.

The development of multicultural marketing has been given strong impetus by SBS introducing advertising in 1992.* Some estimates suggest that SBS achieved as much as a 5 per cent share of the $1.6 billion commercial television advertising market in its first year. This would be well ahead of its market share of audience, which averages around 2.5 per cent across the country. SBS is regarded as the major player in advertising to ethic groups in Australia, but it should be recognised that its audience profile also includes some affluent, well-educated non-ethnics who have switched from the ABC, and that these target audiences are also important for advertisers on the channel. Audience measurements show that 42 per cent of SBS viewers each week come from non-English speaking countries. This gives SBS the second highest level of penetration to ethnic markets after specialist radio stations, which enjoy as much as 60 per cent penetration in major markets in Sydney and Melbourne. Companies as diverse as Legal & General and Citibank through to Coca-Cola currently commit major parts of their advertising budgets to use through SBS.[43]

Further important developments in multicultural marketing in Australia include the evolution of pay-TV channels, which are emerging for the ethnic markets well ahead of supply to the English-speaking population. Three companies are involved with the supply of specialist services carrying much of their material in languages other than English. The Jade Network are a new-to-the-market Chinese-language broadcaster; Australis own Chinese, Italian and Greek channels and also operate ALB in Arabic and Lebanese; and Multilingual Subscription TV (a subsidiary of SBS) joined the market in 1995 using the main pay-TV satellite highways.[44]

CONSUMER BEHAVIOUR ACROSS ETHNIC COMMUNITIES

There is little systematic work detailing variations in consumer behaviour across different ethnic communities, but some important trends can be stated.[45]

LANGUAGE According to the 1991 census the number of Australians speaking a language other than English in their home rose to 2.48 million, of which the single largest group is 418 000 people who speak Italian. There are 285 700 who use Greek at home, and a further 162 900 use each of Cantonese and Arabic. Further, even though many members of some ethnic communities use English to speak, they can also be accessed through other languages. Chinese script is read by most literate Chinese whatever their country of origin and whatever language they usually speak. Assessments of the efficiency of translating English-language text into other tongues varies. Not only can poor translations confuse concepts and result in misunderstandings, but obvious translations may also be regarded as evidence of insufficient commitment on the part of the marketer to the interests of the audience. However, it is now recognised by business in Australia that 'multicultural marketing' goes beyond providing a translation service and starts with people *within* the ethnic communities doing appropriate market research.

---

* For New Zealand readers, SBS is a television network primarily founded by the Australian federal government with a distinctive charter to provide broadcasting services for ethnic communities in Australia.

DEMOGRAPHICS There are huge variations in the demographic characteristics of different ethnic groups in Australia. Middle and southern European communities tend be older, while the Vietnamese are much younger. Within different communities it is also recognised that behaviour varies significantly by age. One example suggests that many older Chinese are from rural backgrounds and are suspicious of services such as banks. Younger Chinese are likely to be of urban origin and totally familiar with such institutions—though they may have a different perspective on service from that of the average Australian. For example, in Hong Kong it is common to receive a statement with every transaction whereas in Australia (and New Zealand) not every paying-in book even allows for a receipt to be issued.

FAMILY DECISION MAKING The influence of the extended family varies across different ethnic groups, but intergenerational links are assumed to be stronger than in average Australian families. Further, the best English-language skills are often exhibited by the children, who then may act as translators and information brokers for their parents and grandparents. As an example, an investigation of sources used by non-English-speaking Australians for information about government services showed that they were over twice as likely to rely on family and friends as were English-speaking residents—59 per cent of instances compared with 27 per cent. Not surprisingly, English-speaking residents were able to draw much more on television and newspapers.[46]

EMPLOYMENT AND EDUCATION Migrants fall into very different categories. There are some who arrive with few skills, especially language, and find initial education and employment very difficult. Others are well qualified, with financial security and a strong understanding of business. Whatever the community, it is worth reiterating the conclusions from the Mackay report outlined earlier about the great value migrants place on educational qualifications and hard work.

HOME OWNERSHIP Australian-born people rank fifth in home ownership behind migrants from Europe, Asia, the Middle East and Africa. For example, 69 per cent of people born in Australia own or are buying their own home, compared with 86 per cent of Italians, 82.6 per cent of Greeks and 78.1 per cent of Yugoslavs. These differences are further exaggerated if outright home ownership is considered—80 per cent of Greeks and Italians compared with 53 per cent Australians. The consequence for marketers is that some ethnic communities have more discretionary dollars available for expenditure than Australian-born people.

DIFFERENCES IN VALUES Little published information is available here that relates to consumer behaviour, but one illustration demonstrating fundamental differences between ethnic groups comes from research conducted for anti-smoking campaigns. The 'Quit for Life' campaign, which focuses on individual health issues, was found to have no effect on either Greek or Lebanese men. For Greeks, defiance of danger can be very important, therefore a campaign based on exposing physical risks was seen to have no effect. The focus of the campaign was switched to quitting cigarettes to protect their health for the sake of their children, and thus appealing to another strong Greek value associated with family security. The Lebanese tend to offer cigarettes as gifts to guests, so in their case the campaign was adjusted to appeal to their values associated with hospitality and concern for damaging their guests' health rather than their own.

It is conspicuous that all the discussion of multicultural marketing in Australia excludes information on Aborigines. This is probably a sad reflection of their place in Australian society as a community with limited spending power and hence of low special-interest value to most commercial organisations. Also, there are only 45 200 people who speak Aboriginal languages at home, less than three times the number who speak Arabic or Cantonese. One illustration of consumption differences between Aborigines and white Australians is in attitudes to alcohol consumption.[47] In part because Aboriginal drinkers have not been welcomed into 'white' pubs, but also because they are prepared to drink in the open, in parks and streets, there is a different view of their behaviour, which runs counter to the norms established by white Australians. In this scenario the whites are labelled as the 'Good Boozers' and the Aborigines as the 'Dirty Drunks', and the punitive treatment accorded Aboriginal drinkers serves to separate them from full membership of white Australian society. Clearly, there is a need for systematic research into Aboriginal affairs, which embraces consumer behaviour and goes beyond strategic issues such as health and housing.

Multicultural marketing in New Zealand

In New Zealand the major ethnic groupings are defined around white New Zealanders, born either in New Zealand or overseas, and Maori and Pacific Island peoples. In the last few years there have been significant numbers of Asian immigrants, particularly from Hong Kong and they now form significant groups in some localities of Auckland. Auckland is overwhelmingly the largest centre for migrant settlement in New Zealand, and carries the title as the largest Polynesian City in the world because of the Pacific Island people who have moved there.

Table 3.7 summarises some of the important differences in consumer behaviour between some ethnic groups in New Zealand. The differences are described using indices that show the variations from the white New Zealand population born in New Zealand, who comprised the majority—over 70 per cent of the survey. Figures for this largest group were indexed to a score of 100, so the table can be interpreted as saying that Pacific Islanders are 63.7 per cent less likely to have fixed-term deposits and 70.9 per cent less likely to hold credit cards than the majority white population born in New Zealand. Migrants to New Zealand who were born in the United Kingdom showed very few differences from the main group and were therefore excluded from the table. Also, because of the small numbers in some of the groups, all Pacific Islanders and all Europeans from other than the United Kingdom and Ireland (i.e. non-English native language) have been combined into two groups. There are no figures for Asian migrants as the survey predates the major growth that has taken place in the 1990s.

TABLE 3.7   Selected differences in consumer behaviour in New Zealand

Consumer Behaviour	Europeans	Maoris	Pacific Islanders
Ownership			
Savings accounts	103.7	89.5	94.6
Fixed term deposits	94.1	50.3	63.7
Credit cards (Visa etc.)	97.1	32.8	70.9
Medical insurance	100.0	63.7	79.2
Life insurance	86.7	83.9	68.3
House:			
With mortgage	98.6	73.6	103.0
No mortgage	86.7	39.2	53.1
Rental	127.7	270.1	180.3
VCRs	75.0	103.7	111.3
Camera (value over $100)	114.6	70.4	83.2
Microwave oven	91.6	52.9	65.5
Dishwasher	116.1	34.6	58.6
Gas barbecue	46.0	73.8	79.6
Behaviour			
Drive a motor vehicle	100.0	78.3	74.0
Use mail-order shopping	65.0	106.1	107.9
Overseas holiday in the last 12 months	111.3	33.2	67.5
Holiday in NZ in the last 12 months	97.2	82.9	85.3
Buy lottery tickets weekly or more	113.4	112.5	138.0
Bet on horses at least once a month	100.0	192.2	106.0
Bought at lease one book in last year	92.7	62.5	110.2

Source: Extracted from *NZ into the 1990s*, Department of Marketing, University of Otago, Dunedin, 1989.

Attitudinal differences between the different ethnic groups showed Maoris to be less in favour of change and more protective of New Zealand in terms of such aspects as continued immigration and foreign investment in the country. Both Maoris and Polynesians attached more importance to family relationships than white New Zealanders, and the Pacific Island respondents emphasised stronger beliefs regarding both the authority of the father and the importance of the church. European-born New Zealanders tend to be critical of the emphasis placed on sport in the country and, as is to be expected, show a greater interest in overseas affairs and ways of behaving. The differences described in this section are also reflected in the placement of the groups in the New Zealand survey shown in Table 3.7. Maoris are over-represented in the Envious Strivers groups while

Pacific Islanders are spread across all the less affluent groups, including the Traditional Family. Our feeling is that most of the differences recorded in Table 3.7 are determined by the economic resources and social characteristics, such as education and the status of the relative groups, rather than intrinsic variations caused by ethnically derived differences in values between the communities. Even possession of VCRs, like televisions in the 1960s, may be regarded as a logical feature for low-income households to adopt because the ongoing cost of the entertainment is very low compared with many other options. Some of the behaviours best defined by values relate to features in the comparison of other Europeans with the majority of white New Zealanders—noticeably the low ownership of gas barbeques or even the use of mail order for shopping. Continental-born Europeans are much less likely to be involved in the outdoor barbeque, beer-swilling and rugby-watching aspects of New Zealand culture.

We share this country of diverse heritage
We live in this land of many cultures
We enjoy the language of two voices, Māori and English
We are New Zealand

KO TE REO TE TAIKURA O TE WHAKAAO MĀRAMA

For further information contact the Māori Language Commission
P.O. Box 411 Wellington. Telephone (04) 710 244

Te Taura Whiri i te Reo Māori

This advertisement illustrates the growing importance of Māori language in New Zealand, which will gradually have an impact on marketing activity COURTESY OF MAORI LANGUAGE COMMISSION

Multicultural marketing is not nearly so developed in New Zealand as in Australia, because the size of segments is small and the spending power of the two largest groups is also relatively low. The need to find better ways to communicate than in English seems to have been a spur to the development of multicultural approaches in Australia. Though use of other languages in the home is growing in New Zealand, and there is a particular revival in Maori, English is generally well understood and it will be some time before there is enough diversity and sufficient numbers to warrant equivalent developments to Australia. Currently radio stands as the medium offering most direct access to ethnic communities in languages other than English.

Multicultural marketing — a warning

There is no doubt that marketers will continue to give more attention to ethnic marketing programs in both New Zealand and Australia. One feature that must always be borne in mind in considering ethnic segmentation strategies (or ones based on personal characteristics such as gender or sexuality) is the possibility of contravening either laws or norms on discrimination. After research was published early in 1994 on the characteristics of the 'Pink' market in Sydney, which revealed both high levels of education and discretionary income, the New Zealand Tourism Board announced that it considered the 'Pink' market as being a viable niche market and provided a holiday for a Sydney same-sex couple as the first part of a campaign aimed at that segment. The Tourism Board have not been supported by many of the regional tourism promotion associations, such as the Queenstown Promotion Board in the South Island of New Zealand. The Queenstown Board followed the objections of the local district council, who have taken a stand against any promotions based on 'ethnicity, race, religion or sexual orientation'. If marketing strategies based around these characteristics are seen to result in more favourable treatment of some groups than others (e.g. differential pricing), the marketer is likely to run foul of the law and other organisations such as the Advertising Standards Council, whose work is reviewed in Chapter 18.

CROSS-CULTURAL UNDERSTANDING OF CONSUMER BEHAVIOUR

In this section we will briefly look at some of the major differences that exist in cultures internationally. Both Australia and New Zealand are heavily dependent on overseas trade for the vitality of many of their businesses and their general economy. Much has been made of the 'global marketplace' in the last 15 years and, with new agreements on GATT and other trade developments, we may expect this trend to continue. Indeed, in a historical context, it is possible to see current globalisation phenomena as simply part of a long-term trend, which established itself in the early 15th century with the beginning of modern geography and the spread of the Gregorian calendar. Robertson describes five phases of globalisation to date:[48]

1. *The germinal phase*. Lasting in Europe from the early 15th century until the mid-18th century, growth of national communities and the down playing of medieval 'transnational' systems (e.g. the Church and aspects of feudalism).

2. *The incipient phase*. This lasted from the mid-18th century until about 1870, and was characterised by the formation of formalised systems of international relations and increased numbers of organisations dealing with transnational regulation and communication.

3. *The take-off phase*. From the 1870s to the 1920s, increasingly global conceptions for a 'correct outline' of an 'acceptable' national society together with ideas about humanity arose. There was a sharp increase in global forms of communication and global competitions such as the Olympics and Nobel Prizes were developed. There was almost universal adoption of the Gregorian calendar and the implementation of World Time. World War I occurred and the League of Nations was formed.

4. *The struggle-for-hegemony phase*. From the 1920s to the 1960s, there were global conflicts concerning forms of life. The nature and prospects of humanity were brought into focus by the Holocaust and the atomic bomb. The United Nations was formed.

5. *The uncertainty phase*. The period from the 1960s to the present has been marked by the inclusion of the developing world in international decision making, the end of the Cold War and the spread of nuclear weapons; the economic rise of Asia; the moon landing; increasing multiculturalism and polyethnicity in national societies; more global institutions, including business but also other pressure groups such as Greenpeace, Amnesty International and global charities, which apply pressure for common worldwide standards regarding the environment and human rights and conditions; and, finally, the consolidation of a global media system.

In this context it is possible to see globalisation as not just a business and marketing phenomenon; rather, it is the result of a long history of evolutionary forces that shaped our societies and values. A full analysis of this topic is properly the subject of a text on international marketing, so in this section we will consider some of the more important differences in value systems, with some examples of differences in behaviour between different countries, including between Australia and New Zealand.

The need for cross-cultural understanding

A recent study of almost 12 000 managers around the world found that although changes were occurring in every country, culture and corporation, there is still no common culture of management. Moreover, managers' views tend to correspond more to their country's cultural heritage and less to its geographic location.[49] The diversity among cultures is reflected not only in management but also in marketing and consumer behaviour, and it can be difficult to adjust to. Thus, when managers venture abroad, they experience what anthropologists call *culture shock*; that is, a series of psychological jolts when they encounter new customs, value systems, attitudes and work habits. This shock reduces their effectiveness in foreign commercial environments.[50] Therefore, it is crucial to effective operations that managers be well schooled in the host cultures. A lack of understanding of the host cultures will lead managers to think and act as they would in their home culture. Such a *self-reference criterion*—that is, the unconscious reference to one's own cultural values—has been nominated as the root cause of most international business problems abroad. The goal should be to eliminate this cultural myopia.[51] The following effectively expresses the pay-off from understanding how culture may influence cross-cultural executives:

> *A general comparative analysis of cultures may help marketing executives to anticipate the responses of their rivals, understand more accurately their customs in business transactions, and deal with colleagues of different nationalities in joint decision making. Culture makes a difference in problem identification and in the objectives motivating choice. Culture also may make a difference in the communication of problems and recommendations, and particularly in the decisiveness of recommendations. Failure to understand these differences may lead to 'noisy' communication, misinformation, and misunderstanding. Culture also makes a difference in individual strategies to adjust decision situations to facilitate choice and mitigate undesirable consequences for the organisation and the decision maker.*[52]

VALUE ORIENTATIONS

The marketer needs a frame of reference within which to understand and evaluate the range of cultural values that may be encountered. A useful conceptualisation of the possible range of variations in values found in different cultures is offered in Table 3.8, which presents a classification of value orientations that might be encountered by the international marketer. This model suggests five basic orientations, which are thought to be common to all human groups. These relate to human nature, relationship of people to nature, sense of time, activity and social relations. The marketer's task then becomes one of seeking to understand what type of value system predominates in a given culture and relating effectively to that system through marketing activities.[53] Generally Australians and New Zealanders fall on the right-hand side of this value range.

Major sources of misunderstanding among cultures are the differences in values and priorities indicated in Table 3.8. Consider how differences in the cultural factors cited in Table 3.8 might play havoc with cross-cultural management and communication.[54]

TABLE 3.8   Variations in value systems

Orientation	Range		
Human nature	Evil (changeable or unchangeable): most people are basically evil and can't be trusted	Mixture of good and evil (changeable or unchangeable): there are evil and good people in the world	Good (changeable or unchangeable): most people are basically good and can be trusted
People–nature relationship	Subjugation to nature: life is largely controlled by outside forces	Harmony with nature: live in harmony with nature	Mastery over nature: people should challenge and control nature
Time sense	Past-oriented (tradition-bound): people should learn from and emulate the glorious past	Present-oriented (situational): make the most of the present moment; live for today	Future-oriented (goal-oriented): plan for the future in order to make it better than the past
Activity	Being: spontaneously express impulses and desires; stress who you are	Being-in-becoming: emphasise self-realisation; development of all aspects of the self as an integrated whole	Doing: stress action and accomplishment
Social relations	Lineal (authoritarian): lines of authority are clearly established, with dominant–subordinate relationships clearly defined and respected	Collateral (group oriented): a person is an individual as well as a group member participating in collective decisions	Individualistic: each person is autonomous and has equal rights and control over his or her own destiny

Source: Adapted from Florence R. Kluckhohn, 'Dominant and Variant Value Orientations', in Clyde Kluckhohn, *Personality in Nature, Society, and Culture*, 2nd edn, Alfred A. Knopf, New York, 1953, p. 346.

TIME   There are two recognised approaches to considering time: monochronic and polychronic. It is recognised that many problems in international business relate to differing concepts of time between business people and consumers.[55] Monochronic time (or M-time) is best typified by the approach of most American managers, who want to get right to the point and the 'bottom line'. This directness contrasts with those cultures typified by polychronic time (or P-time), which is characterised by a much looser notion of time and schedules. Many Pacific Islanders would, therefore, view interruptions and delays as routine, as human activities are not expected to proceed like clockwork. In reality, M-time and P-time describe opposite ends of a continuum rather than two simple groups. Australians and New Zealanders have been much more relaxed in their approach to considering time than many European and North American countries, and this impacts on business productivity and other features such as shop opening hours. Recent changes in both countries have moved towards M-time values, with the placement of a much higher priority on time and a belief that efficiently conserving time is a significant asset.

THOUGHT AND COMMUNICATION PATTERNS As in the United States, the speech and thought behaviour in Australia and New Zealand is direct, or linear, whereas in some other cultures it is more circuitous. In 'low-context' cultures such as ours, communication depends mostly on explicit expressions—oral, and through reports, contracts and other written messages. In contrast, 'high-context' cultures do business more slowly because communication depends more heavily on the verbal and nonverbal aspects of the situation. Thus, in Japan it may take considerably longer to transact business, because the people need to know more about each other before a business relationship develops.[56]

RELIGION While there are significant variations within Australia and New Zealand, neither society is characterised by strong active involvement in religion. The 1990 New Zealand values study showed less than 20 per cent of the population were involved in religion, making it one of the most secularised societies in the world.[57] In Australia 10 per cent of the population profess to having no religion at all, and of those who do only one-quarter attend church more than once a month.[58] In many other cultures religion dominates the routine of daily lives. For example, Islam is an inextricable part of many Arab cultures. Arab daily routines revolve around prayer times and religious holidays and events. 'It was Allah's will' is given as the explanation for major disasters. In an environment where religion governs business and social practices, foreign business people must respect their hosts' customs, such as those pertaining to prayer and diet. Moreover, any changes threatening religious and cultural patterns will encounter resistance from religious and government leaders.

COMPETITIVENESS AND INDIVIDUALITY Cultures vary in their encouragement and reward for individual ambition. Some cultures see it as a natural and desirable trait, while other cultures value modesty, team spirit, collectivity and patience more.

SOCIAL BEHAVIOUR The use and interpretation of many non-verbal signs is different from culture to culture. Noisy eating and belching are viewed as unacceptable behaviour in many 'English cultures', while in some other cultures they are expected as evidence of satisfaction. Conversely, other behaviour that Australians and New Zealanders accept as innocuous, such as showing the sole of one's foot, using the left hand to deliver an object or speaking first, may be deemed inappropriate in other cultures. When a company is marketing products internationally, a thorough understanding of cultural practices is useful in determining whether a single strategy can be effective in different national environments, or whether several strategies must be adopted, with each geared to the distinctive cultural setting. Global marketing with a single approach has its champions.[59] Some companies have been successful with a single marketing strategy or have at least reduced some of the duplication that existed in their efforts. For example:

Playtex developed a global advertising approach to sell their new Wow bra in 12 countries—a departure from the 43 different versions of advertisements they had running throughout the world a few years ago.

But there were difficulties in accomplishing the task. The company came up with appropriate names for the product in each language (such as *Traumbugel* in German and *Alas* in Spanish). Dozens of models were screened before the final selection of a woman with blonde hair and two women with dark hair (which is said to have universal appeal). One hundred and fifty popular-style bras were used to film the commercials, because, for example, the French like lacy bras while Americans prefer plain, opaque styles. Television standards at the time in the United States and South Africa didn't allow women to be shown modelling bras, and so models held the bra on a hanger; but in other countries models wore the bras. In all commercials, though, a single Wow feature having universal appeal was stressed: underwire support and shape achieved without the uncomfortable wires, because of a new plastic.

A monumental editing job was necessary to produce the commercials to each country's requirements. Nevertheless, the campaign allowed Playtex to present one unified message and save money at the same time.[60]

Companies attempt to deal with the wide variations encountered by identifying any 'universals' that may be involved in the buying process and then incorporating these factors into the segmentation and marketing programs wherever the company operates. For example:

Goodyear Tyre & Rubber have developed a decision-based segmentation system that can be applied anywhere in the world. Finding that consumers make three key decisions when buying tyres—outlet, brand and price—Goodyear learned that the sequence of pairing these dimensions was even more critical. Goodyear initially identified six consumer profiles, but combined them into four groups for global marketing purposes: quality buyers, value buyers, price buyers and commodity buyers. Although segment sizes vary from country to country, the elements in each segment's profile remain largely the same. The extent to which these elements change determines how much Goodyear must customise their marketing programs.[61]

ANOTHER APPROACH TO VALUE DIFFERENCES

An alternative approach to considering differences in values across countries is given by Schwartz.[62] Analysis of data from Schwartz samples at the aggregate (country) level as opposed to the individual level produced seven cultural-level value types, which are plotted in two dimensions on Figure 3.6. This figure gives a spatial representation of the values, their interrelationships and the countries most associated with each value. The two overall dimensions on which the values are placed are concerned with individualism versus collectivism and control (hierarchy and mastery) versus balance and consensus (harmony and social concern).

COLLECTIVISM This represents values where the interests of the person are not viewed as distinct from the group; the values emphasise the maintenance of the status quo, propriety and avoidance of actions that might disturb the traditional order. Eastern European and some Asian countries are most associated with collectivism.

INTELLECTUAL AND AFFECTIVE INDIVIDUALISM These values view the person as an autonomous entity entitled to pursue his or her own goal. There are two distinguishable types of individualism. Intellectual individualism emphasises self direction, with flexibility of thought and feelings, and is most closely associated with Holland, Germany, Japan and New Zealand. Affective individualism is concerned with stimulation and hedonism and may be a polar opposite to collectivism. No particular countries are positioned more strongly than others on this dimension, but it is associated with Spain, Greece, New Zealand, the United States, Zimbabwe, Japan and Israeli Jews.

HIERARCHY This value type represents individual values associated with humility and power that emphasise the legitimacy of hierarchical roles in society. It is mostly highly correlated with mastery among the other values, and is most importantly represented in the People's Republic of China and Zimbabwe.

MASTERY Mastery is concerned with control over the social environment through self assertion. It represents active efforts to modify one's surroundings and get ahead of others. Like affective individualism, mastery emphasises stimulating activity and changing social behaviour. The United States and Japan are both positioned very strongly on this value type.

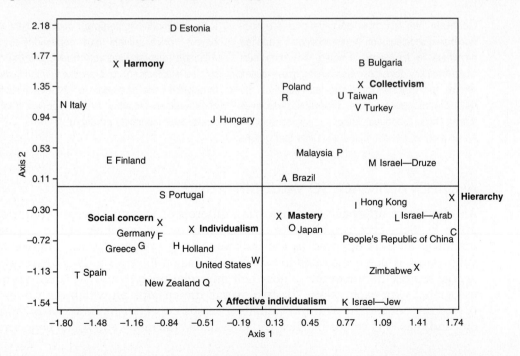

FIG. 3.6 Differences in values across 24 nation-cultures

Adapted from S. H. Schwartz 'Cultural Dimensions of Values: Toward an Understanding of National Differences', in U. Kim, H. C. Triandis & G. Yoon, *Individualism and Collectivism: Theoretical and Methodological Issues*, Sage Publications, London, forthcoming.

SOCIAL CONCERN These values express concern for the welfare of others and oppose the hierarchy and mastery types of values. Social concern includes ideas such as benevolence, universalism and freedom. It is a characteristic most associated with Western European countries.

HARMONY This set of values emphasises harmony with nature together with other aspects such as the 'world at peace' and 'social justice'. Italy, Estonia and Finland are most associated with the harmony values.

Readers should remember that Schwartz's results are not based on random samples from each country, but the work is important because it is the most advanced attempt to develop and validate the measurement of values cross-culturally. Furthermore, the results do make good intuitive sense and fit our general understanding of different cultures. This is a fundamental requirement when assessing both the approach and the findings.

Decision areas for the international marketer

The outline presented in Table 3.9 is suggested for use by the international marketer in conducting cultural analysis. It should also be noted that this outline is perhaps just as helpful a framework to the domestic marketer.

Gaining a better understanding of the host culture is made difficult, however, by problems confronting consumer research abroad. Researchers in developing foreign markets encounter numerous difficulties in obtaining satisfactory consumer interviews, because of a general mistrust of strangers asking questions. Moreover, certain subjects may be taboo and thus are not to be discussed, especially with strangers. In a number of countries even the subject of consumption habits is considered inappropriate.[63] In such an environment, it is clear that the marketer will have a difficult time piecing together information on which to base the company's strategies. One of the most effective research approaches, particularly in developing economies where language and cultural differences hinder people's understanding of survey questions, is simply to observe behaviour in order to assess what influences people's purchasing decisions. Although this approach can be tricky, because it needs to be undertaken by a trained observer—usually an anthropologist—it can help companies learn how to market more effectively in different parts of the globe, as well as improve understanding of age and ethnic groups in their home markets. The research method is called *ethnology*, and it involves studying through observation how customs motivate consumers to use and buy products differently in different cultures.[64]

The approach can be expensive because of its high labour intensity, but its insights are often very meaningful and practicable. This technique helped Colgate-Palmolive create a profitable new product category in Latin America. By watching Venezuelan women wash their clothes, the company learned that instead of detergent women used slivers of bar soap mashed together to form a paste. As a result, Colgate developed Axion soap paste, which is sold in a plastic bowl, and is the leading laundry cleaner in many of the 10 countries where it is marketed.

TABLE 3.9   Elements of consumer-behaviour analysis in a cross-cultural setting

1. Determine underlying values and their rate of change within the relevant market: What values are generally held strongly within the general market and the intended market segment? What is the rate and direction of value changes taking place within the relevant culture?

2. Evaluate the product concept as it relates to this culture: Is this product concept one that harmonises with current and evolving values? If there are value conflicts with ownership of this product, can the product be changed to fit these values? How can the product be effectively identified with positive values? What needs does this product satisfy for members of the culture? Are these needs important? How are competitive products and brands currently satisfying these needs?

3. Determine characteristic purchase decision-making patterns: How do consumers make decisions about this product? Which family members are involved in purchase decision making and use of this product? What role does each member typically play in the process? What purchase criteria and sources of information do consumers use in making buying decisions for this product? What is the cultural attitude toward acceptance of innovations? What cultural values might be congruent with or conflict with purchase and use of this product?

4. Determine appropriate promotion methods: What means of communication exist for advertising to consumers? How is advertising perceived among those in the culture? Must different languages be used to reach various cultural groups? What are the most relevant appeals for this product among the culture? What taboos (such as words, themes, colours or pictures) exist that may impinge on our sales or advertising strategy? What is the role of the salesperson in this culture?

5. Determine appropriate distribution channels: What are the characteristic distribution channels for this product? Are capable institutions available for handling this product? Might new channel opportunities exist that would be readily accepted by consumers? What is the nature of the shopping process for this product?

6. Determine appropriate pricing approaches: Are consumers aware of prices in the product category? Are they sensitive to differences in prices between brands? How important is price in consumers' purchasing decisions?

The following discussion of several marketing decision areas reveals some of the cultural barriers that may be present.

MARKET SEGMENTS

It is critical to recognise that just as in domestic marketing, there will be market segments that must be identified and understood in order to develop successful marketing programs internationally. Marketers should be aware that segments may be identified globally as well as within individual countries or regions. For example, one study surveyed over 15 000 adults in 14 countries on five continents to identify five distinct global consumer segments that share attitudes, values and actual purchasing patterns, uniting them across national boundaries and different cultures:

1. *Strivers* are young—their median age is 31—and lead active lives. They are under stress most of the time and prefer products and services that are sources of instant gratification.

2. *Achievers* are about the same age as Strivers, but they have already found the success they seek. They are affluent, assertive, and society's opinion and style leaders. Achievers value status and quality in the brands they buy, and are largely responsible for setting trends.

3. *Pressureds* are mainly women, in every age group, who find it extremely difficult to manage all the problems in their lives. They have little time for enjoyment.

4. *Adapters* are older consumers who live comfortably. They are content with themselves and their lives, and they recognise and respect new ideas without losing sight of their own values. They are willing to try new products that enrich their lives.

5. *Traditionals* embody the oldest values of their countries and cultures. They are resistant to change, and they are content with the familiar products.[65]

The survey showed that, during the next decade, consumer tastes will grow increasingly materialistic and divisions between consumer classes will widen, and marketers should emphasise products and services that help consumers to control their lives.

A further example of cross-cultural segmentation is a large European study by Homma and Ueltzhoffer.[66] They profiled consumers from Great Britain, France, Germany and Italy, and used similar dimensions to those outlined for VALS—and which were evident in the Morgan and Otago studies outlined earlier—to explain their results. Homma and Ueltzhoffer identified eight common cross-cultural trends all operating in the same direction in each country:

1. consumer hedonism

2. individualism

3. nostalgia—the search for roots, security and order

4. environmentalism

5. opening-up and outward looking

6. anomie and social aggressiveness

7. focus on the body

8. irrationalism.

Consumer hedonism was identified as the strongest of these trends and this fits well with other interpretations of trends in Western societies in the 1980s. Figures 3.7(a) to 3.7(d) show how each of the countries is broken down across the values and social-class dimensions. From the comparisons, eight multinational target groups were identified that showed essentially common characteristics across all four countries. One major group is identified in Italy—the *Cultura Rurale Tradizionale*—that has no counterpart in any other country. Homma and Ueltzhoffer also identify distinctions between some of the equivalent groups that would require marketers to make local adjustments to their strategies to gain maximum benefit from the segmentation. For example, the major trendsetting groups are the *Progressive Middle Class* in the United Kingdom, *Les Managers Modernes* in France, the *Borghesia Illuminata* in Italy and the *Technokratisch Liberales Milieu* in Germany. All these share important values in tolerance, career success, education and culture, pro-European, hedonistic luxury consumption and individualism. One value on which they are distinctly different is environmental concern. This was not identified as at all salient to the French group but was extremely important to the German Technokratisch Liberales and also to a lesser extent to the British Progressive Middle Class. The Germans try to harmonise their hedonistic impulses with environmental issues while the French do not. This results in differences in food preferences and car choices, for example. The health attributes of foods and features such as petrol consumption, pollution and recycling of car parts play a more important role in product selection for the German trendsetters.

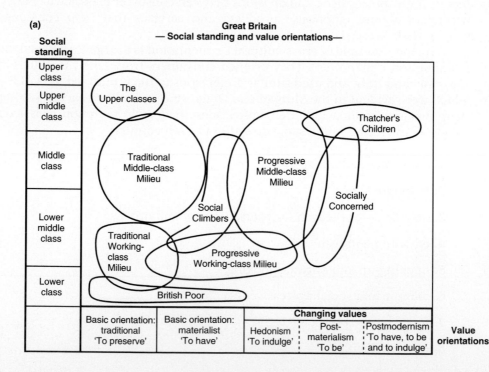

(b)

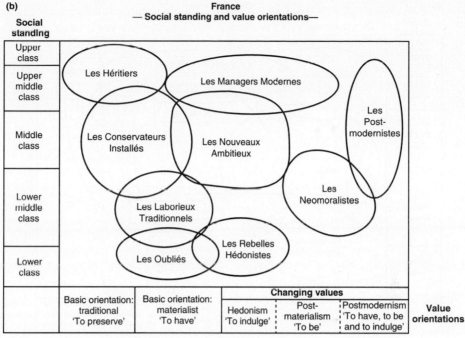

France
— Social standing and value orientations—

Social standing

	Value orientations

Upper class / Upper middle class / Middle class / Lower middle class / Lower class

Les Héritiers

Les Managers Modernes

Les Post-modernistes

Les Conservateurs Installés

Les Nouveaux Ambitieux

Les Neomoralistes

Les Laborieux Traditionnels

Les Oubliés

Les Rebelles Hédonistes

Basic orientation: traditional 'To preserve'	Basic orientation: materialist 'To have'	Changing values		
		Hedonism 'To indulge'	Post-materialism 'To be'	Postmodernism 'To have, to be and to indulge'

(c)

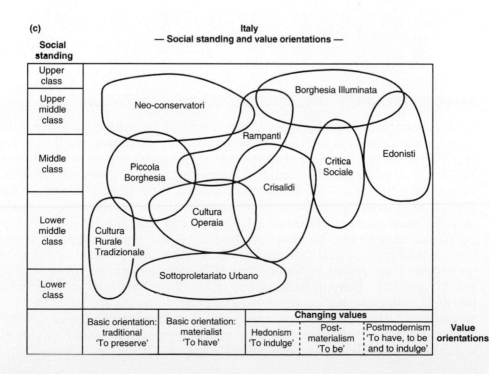

Italy
— Social standing and value orientations —

Social standing

Upper class / Upper middle class / Middle class / Lower middle class / Lower class

Neo-conservatori

Borghesia Illuminata

Rampanti

Piccola Borghesia

Critica Sociale

Edonisti

Crisalidi

Cultura Operaia

Cultura Rurale Tradizionale

Sottoproletariato Urbano

Basic orientation: traditional 'To preserve'	Basic orientation: materialist 'To have'	Changing values		
		Hedonism 'To indulge'	Post-materialism 'To be'	Postmodernism 'To have, to be and to indulge'

Value orientations

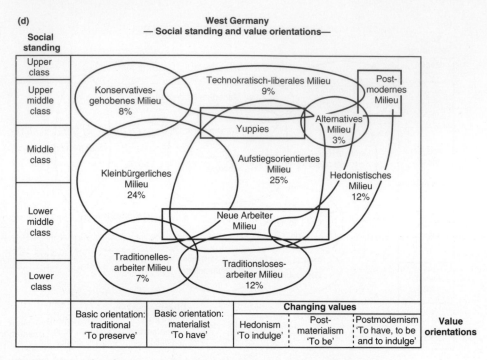

FIG. 3.7   Social milieus in Great Britain, France, Italy and Germany

Source: Norbert Homma & Jorg Ueltzhoffer, 'The Internationalisation of Everyday-life-research: Markets and Milieus', *Marketing and Research Today*, November 1990, pp. 197–207.

RANKING PRODUCTS ON CULTURALLY BOUND CONTINUUM

Each country has a different mix of consumption. Therefore, the types of products that are saleable in each culture vary. Table 3.11 illustrates how the per-capita spending index for a variety of consumption categories differs markedly among 12 European countries. For example, household appliance ownership data for several neighbouring Western European nations show quite differing consumption patterns, even though these countries are at similar levels of economic development. Such a pattern of consumer behaviour can be attributed more to cultural differences and to the different distributions of the types of market segments identified by Homma and Ueltzhoffer within each country. Other European studies support these results by finding that differences among the young people are subsiding as their tastes in music, sports and cultural activities become more similar, and confirming that wealthier, highly educated Europeans share cross-border similarities.[67] The importance of cross-cultural differences is seen to vary by the type of product or service. Products can be categorised and ranked on a most-to-least culturally bound continuum, as follows:

➡ Consumer products are most culture bound; industrial products the least.

➡ Established product categories are most culture bound; new product categories the least.

➡ Simple technology is most culture bound; complex technology the least.

➡ Kitchen-based items are most culture bound, followed in descending order by such item categories as bath and bedroom, living room, garden and garage, and items for use away from the home.[68]

TABLE 3.10   Multinational target groups in Great Britain, France, Italy and Germany

Great Britain	France	Italy	Germany	General Milieu
The Upper Classes	Les Héritiers	Neo-conservatori	Konservatives-gehobenes Milieu	Upper Conservative Milieu
Traditional Middle-class Milieu	Les Conservateurs Installés	Piccola Borghesia	Kleinbürger-liches Milieu	Traditional Working-class Milieu
Traditional Working-class Milieu	Les Laborieux Traditionnels	Cultura Operaia	Traditionelles-arbeiter Milieu	Traditional Working-class Milieu
Social Climbers Progressive Working-class Milieu	Les Nouveaux Ambitieux	Rampanti Crisalidi	Aufstiegs-orientiertes Milieu	Modern Mainstream Milieu
Progressive Middle-class Milieu	Les Managers Modernes	Borghesia Illuminata	Technokratisch-liberales Milieu	Trendsetter Milieu
Thatcher's Children	Les Post-modernistes	Edonisti	Hedonistisches Milieu	Avantgarde Milieu
Socially Concerned	Les Neo-moralistes	Critica Sociale	Alternatives Milieu	Sociocritical Milieu
British Poor	Les Oubliés Les Rebelles Hédonistes	Sotto-proletariato Urbano	Traditionsloses-arbeiter Milieu	Underprivileged Milieu

Source: Norbert Homma & Jorg Ueltzhoffer, 'The Internationalisation of Everyday-life-research: Markets and Milieus', *Marketing and Research Today*, November 1990, pp. 197–207.

TABLE 3.11 European differences: Index of per-capita spending in Europe by product and country (100 equals the average for Europe)

	Luxembourg	Denmark	West Germany [a]	France	Great Britain	Belgium	Italy	Netherlands	Spain	Ireland	Greece	Portugal
Total spending	116.4	114.6	111.8	109.8	105.8	105.7	104.2	101.5	74.4	59.9	59.7	52.1
Food	105.3	92.7	91.3	114.9	83.8	102.4	121.4	89.2	94.2	85.0	105.0	79.6
Drinks	111.5	126.0	155.9	115.6	79.8	74.6	75.2	105.7	66.2	200.8	61.4	64.2
Tobacco	258.8	124.4	98.2	101.8	100.0	125.8	103.8	112.5	89.9	96.0	154.1	0.6
Apparel and footwear	89.8	89.7	128.4	93.7	109.7	86.3	118.6	101.4	54.2	55.0	59.5	49.4
Housing	87.4	126.7	79.7	94.0	117.5	83.8	112.2	80.0	131.2	51.6	38.2	78.0
Heat and light	222.7	141.3	139.3	101.5	119.6	142.0	78.4	133.6	44.2	68.4	40.0	32.9
Furniture	180.2	110.6	171.8	120.7	72.4	100.7	87.9	112.1	50.7	30.9	23.6	35.0
Household textiles	82.7	119.7	128.8	111.5	73.7	93.5	98.3	71.8	100.1	60.5	105.5	63.3
Home appliances	168.2	101.7	128.5	100.3	132.7	117.3	93.9	81.4	54.0	39.1	48.9	28.7
Other household	98.6	79.7	108.9	117.7	74.5	174.1	118.9	101.5	73.2	50.1	76.1	62.8
Health and medical	88.4	83.3	130.8	146.8	93.4	128.4	83.7	114.7	45.6	53.2	36.4	31.7
Transportation, vehicles	244.1	133.6	150.4	100.4	113.1	132.4	96.6	99.6	39.3	37.5	17.6	17.2
Transportation, maintenance	190.0	109.3	130.3	123.9	97.6	99.1	84.3	62.3	88.8	50.2	30.7	63.5
Public transportation	25.9	104.9	75.4	88.9	139.2	46.0	105.4	68.8	93.7	41.8	264.6	34.8
Communications	246.3	155.6	124.7	114.5	81.1	52.6	100.8	185.0	45.0	35.8	178.6	15.1
Entertainment, education, and legal	87.9	152.3	116.7	99.5	112.0	107.5	112.8	114.8	51.5	74.6	42.9	56.3
Restaurants and hotels	83.7	52.4	68.1	100.7	138.4	89.8	105.1	63.7	139.7	8.7	76.8	31.5
Other	155.8	187.3	93.8	109.2	123.0	107.5	115.8	127.5	56.7	45.8	27.2	30.2

(a) Prior to reunification.
Note: Low indices, in some cases, reflect sales to foreign nationals.
Source: Blayne Cutler, 'Reaching the Real Europe', *American Demographics*, October 1990, pp. 42–3.

PACKAGING AND DESIGN

Many of the examples of failed products in international markets are the result of a failure to understand differences in signs and symbols between different cultures. These affect the product itself, its packaging and its promotion. Even such seemingly simple elements as product package design and colour have played havoc with many international marketers. For example, colour preferences are very culture bound. Black is the colour for mourning in some countries, while in others it is white. Green is a popular colour in Muslim countries because it is the colour of Islam. Benetton's label is a deep, cool forest green that is said to convey a sense of global togetherness, a fortuitous choice in association with the world environmental movement. Package symbols can be effective or a hindrance. For example, Mercedes' three-point star logo is 'an archetypal symbol of integrity and strength'.[69] However, a soft-drink marketer got in trouble in Arab markets because the label of one of its products featured a series of six-pointed stars that were felt to be too suggestive of Israel's Star of David.[70]

The following examples are representative of some of the problems encountered by companies:

A Japanese toy-maker selling Barbie dolls had near-zero sales for decades until he persuaded Mattel Inc. to allow a change in the Westernised look of the doll. When the toy-maker reduced the doll's bosom, changed her blue eyes to brown and darkened her blonde hair, sales zoomed.[71]

Colgate-Palmolive's 'Cue' toothpaste is a pornographic word in French.

Standard Oil's Enco brand meant 'stalled car' in Japanese—a good reason for changing to Exxon, which is meaningless in any language.

Avon Products had to reshape their personal selling program for Hong Kong. In countries such as Australia, New Zealand, the United States and the United Kingdom, the Avon saleswoman is accustomed to being greeted at the door by the woman of the house and led into the living room where she could sell over a cup of coffee or tea. In Hong Kong, however, it was likely to be a servant peering through a metal gate who met the visitor and announced that the mistress of the household wasn't home. Because of this difference, Avon began recruiting special saleswomen for Hong Kong. They tended to be well-to-do housewives or women at a certain professional level, such as travel consultants or executive secretaries, who were thought to be able to sell to their acquaintances or gain access to women in their neighbourhoods who would invite them to stop by.[72]

Coca-Cola's first attempt to translate their trademark into Chinese characters resulted in something that sounded like 'Coca-Cola' but meant 'bite the wax tadpole'. It was later changed to 'happiness in the mouth'.

'Body by Fisher' became 'Corpse by Fisher' in Flemish.

De Beers, the raw-diamond suppliers, ran ads for years in Japan that depicted Western couples in evening dress, reflecting the standard mentality that equates diamonds with grandeur. After only small marketing gains, the company finally learned that Japanese women don't smile and kiss their husbands when they receive diamonds as presents. Instead they shed a few tears and pretend they're angry at their husbands for spending so much money. De Beers' subsequent Christmas campaign showed a tired wage-earner and his hard-working wife in their tiny apartment. Upon receiving the sparkling present, she snaps at her extravagant spouse, 'Oh, you stupid!' The ad was a marketing success, boosting the popularity of diamonds in Japan.[73]

An Australian exporter experienced great difficulty selling condoms to Pakistan before the condom colour was changed from white to orange. In Muslim countries white is associated with purity but no such inhibitions are associated with orange.[74]

Of course, orange condoms are not likely be acceptable in a Buddhist country where orange is a sacred colour. These examples—and there are many others in the international marketing literature—emphasise cultural differences in consumption. Nevertheless, it is evident that there are more and more universally applicable products. McDonald's, Coca-Cola and Levi Strauss are much-quoted and obvious examples but the list extends well beyond this to computers, and even petrol service stations. A Shell garage with its distinctive red and yellow colours is an internationally standard icon. As outlined at the beginning of this section, there are many forces that are contributing to the continued globalisation of world markets. Besides trading agreements and global communication systems, consumers themselves contribute greatly through the impact of migration and through participating in international tourism. Since World War II, tourism has grown to become the world's largest industry. Tourism has undoubtedly contributed to the spread of universal products, as tourists take both ideas and products from the cultures they visit back to their home and they also demand the presence of some of their familiar comforts in their destinations. These products are then available for adoption by local people. This is primarily how Japanese food has become accepted in Australia and New Zealand.

AUSTRALIA AND NEW ZEALAND AS ONE MARKET[75]

With the development of ANZCERTA (the Australia and New Zealand Closer Economic Relationship) many marketing practices have been harmonised on both sides of the Tasman. Some of these are referred to in Chapter 18 on consumerism, but there are also many advertisements common to the two countries and a large overlap in popular magazines; for example, *Australian Woman's Weekly* is a top-selling magazine in its category in New Zealand. There are evidently many similarities between consumers in Australia and New Zealand but there are also recognised differences. New Zealand is recognised as retaining more of its British heritage than Australia, which has responded to the Mediterranean influences. Therefore, in matters of food, New Zealanders are supposed to prefer sweeter items including cream cakes and high teas, while Australians are more accepting of foods such as olives, anchovies and feta cheese. Even so, some obvious products do not follow this pattern. Cadbury acknowledge that they make chocolate in New Zealand more bitter to suit local taste. Other differences in foods between the two countries reflect differences in climate, particularly Australians' preference for saltier snack foods such as chips. Some are less explicable, like New Zealanders' preferences for hard, crisp cookies, whereas Australians favour soft, moister biscuits. Arnotts' launch of 'Fruitables' in New Zealand in 1993 positioned it as a softbake fruit snack in order to avoid the impression of a stale cookie.

Climate differences are also used to explain differential reactions to fragrances such as eucalyptus. In Australia it evokes memories of days in the country, freshness and the great outdoors. In New Zealand, the connotations are completely different. It represents colds and winter because of childhood memories associated with Vicks VapoRub. Such differences in association with fragrances become very important for products such as toiletries and air fresheners, where the scent is often regarded as the most important attribute in differentiating the product.

As well as many common bonds between the two countries there are some intense rivalries, especially in sport. This element of competition also impacts on promotions in Australia and New Zealand that use sport. Lion Breweries, for example, have to be very careful to develop independent campaigns for XXXX, Tooheys and Steinlager with their different Australian and New Zealand connections. The major danger that is perceived in dealing with Australia and New Zealand as a single market is resistance from New Zealanders who feel that they may be being taken for granted by their larger Australian cousins. This reaction has been noted to some Australian advertising in New Zealand though many campaigns are successfully used in both countries. The independence of the smaller country is reflected in New Zealand's tendency to support the underdog. This reaction has definite impact on marketing strategies that use comparative advertising. Advertising agencies regard comparative campaigns as being much less successful in New Zealand than in Australia. In New Zealand the consumer tends to feel that comparative advertising diminishes the product that is 'throwing the mud'.

'Inga the Winger' talks about his favourite things.

"The thing I like best in life is devouring the opposition on the rugby field.

Especially if they're Australian.

My next favourite thing is eating. Knowing my taste for cheese, the cheese people invented a big delicious, nutritious roll and said they'd name it after me.

It's called a Hero Roll and I can't resist them. Before the game, during the game, after the game, half-time, anytime!

If I had my way I'd have one in each hand when I played - but then of course, I wouldn't be able to catch the ball.

But there's one thing I don't understand. If they were going to name it after me how come they called it Hero. When my name's Va'aiga Tuigamala?

Still I suppose Tuigamala rolls would be a bit of a mouthful..."

HERO ROLLS

Crusty rolls filled with Gruyere, ham, salad and grainy mustard. Preparation: 10 minutes. Serves 4.

4 large crusty whole-grain bread rolls.
1/2 cup mayonnaise.
8 lettuce leaves.
1/2 cucumber, sliced.
8 slices ham, folded in half.
2 tomatoes, sliced.
4 slices New Zealand Gruyere Cheese.
1 tablespoon grainy mustard.

1. Split rolls in half and spread with mayonnaise.
2. Place 2 lettuce leaves on the bottom half of each roll. Top with sliced cucumber, 2 slices folded ham, sliced tomato and Gruyere Cheese.
3. Spread the top half of the roll with mustard.

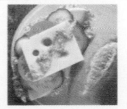

Part of the appeal of this advertisement is based on rivalry between Australia and New Zealand COURTESY OF NEW ZEALAND CHEESE PROMOTIONS LIMITED

One other facet that can be important in distinguishing between Australia and New Zealand is that New Zealand, because of its compact size and broad socio-economic profile, is often used as a test market for new products—particularly electronic items. Bar codes and EFTPOS (electronic funds transfer at point of sale) are two such examples that have had major impacts on consumer behaviour. In consequence, New Zealand is often slightly ahead of Australia in the adoption of these technologies.

In summary, there are sufficient differences between Australia and New Zealand for companies not to be blasé about treating the two markets identically, even though many of the value systems are shared, as evidenced by the Morgan research. Arnotts and Johnson & Johnson are examples of two companies that recently pulled out of New Zealand and decided to control all operations from Australia. Both found that they were losing touch with the New Zealand market, which was following different trends from Australia, and both companies have found it worthwhile to reinstate local marketing operations in New Zealand. This examination of Australia and New Zealand carries lessons for marketing and the globalisation debate. It further emphasises the Playtex and Goodyear examples discussed previously, which showed that thinking globally is easier at a strategic level. At the tactical level, where detailed consideration of the product and its pricing, promotion and distribution is concerned, adjustments are always likely to fit the idiosyncrasies of each culture.

SUMMARY

In this chapter we examined one of the most basic factors influencing the behaviour of consumers—their cultural heritage. We described the nature of culture, its functions and its components. The core approaches to values were presented and the changing orientation of these values was discussed. This shift in values may have great marketing significance, especially as it presents untapped market opportunities. It can be seen, therefore, that the concept of culture offers many general and specific insights into the behaviour of consumers. This, then, is a starting point for the marketer who wishes to understand a market better. It is imperative for the marketer to appreciate cultural nuances governing the relevant marketplace, whether it be in Australia and New Zealand or elsewhere.

MANAGERIAL REFLECTIONS

For our product or service situation:

1. Which core cultural values (using the RVS or LOV approaches) are of greatest importance to our chosen market in this purchase?

2. Which VALS 2 segments appear to be appropriate target markets?

3. Are changes occurring in the cultural values of the market that will have an effect on its purchase?

4. If foreign marketing exists or is planned, how do these various markets differ in cultural values and systems that might affect our success?

5. What significant market segments may be distinguished within the foreign culture?

6. Can our marketing mix be transplanted or must it be adapted or a new mix developed to satisfy target cultural segments?

DISCUSSION TOPICS

1. Define culture. What are the most important characteristics of culture that reflect its nature?

2. Why is the study of culture important to the marketer?

3. What is the function of culture?

4. What are the core cultural values held by members of the Australian and New Zealand cultures?

5. How have core cultural values changed in Australia and New Zealand over the past generation? What shifts do you expect in these core values over your own generation? What effects are there likely to be on consumer behaviour and marketing?

6. Cite examples of marketing practices that either conform to or actively take advantage of core cultural values.

7. Name three products that are presently culturally unacceptable. What marketing strategies would you use to overcome cultural resistance to these products?

8. Why is an understanding of the foreign cultural environment especially important to the international marketer?

9. Locate two articles on marketing failures by companies operating in a foreign market. Could an improved cultural understanding have prevented these failures? How?

REFERENCES

1. Edward B. Tylor, *Primitive Culture*, Murray, London, 1891, p. 1.
2. Clyde Kluckhohn, 'The Study of Culture', in Daniel Lewer & Harold D. Lasswell (eds), *The Policy Sciences*, Stanford University Press, Stanford, CA, 1951, p. 86.
3. R. P. Cuzzort, *Humanity and Modern Sociological Thought*, Holt, New York, 1969, p. 356.
4. 'Corporate Culture', *Business Week*, 27 October 1980, p. 149.
5. Richard T. LaPiere, *Sociology*, McGraw-Hill, New York, 1946.
6. John Huey, 'America's Hottest Export: Pop Culture', *Fortune*, 31 December 1990, pp. 50–60.
7. James S. Duesenberry, *Income, Saving and the Theory of Consumer Behavior*, Harvard University Press, Cambridge, MA, 1949, p. 19.
8. Richard D. Zakia & Mihai Nadin, 'Semiotics, Advertising and Marketing', *Journal of Consumer Marketing* 4, 1987, pp. 5–12.
9. Charles Winick, 'Anthropology's Contributions to Marketing', *Journal of Marketing* 25, 1961, pp. 55–6.
10. Dennis W. Rook, 'The Ritual Dimension of Consumer Behavior', *Journal of Consumer Research* 12, 1985, p. 251.
11. This section is based on Grant McCracken, 'Culture and Consumption: A Theoretical Account of the Structure and Movement of the Cultural Meaning of Consumer Goods', *Journal of Consumer Research* 13, 1986, pp. 71–84; and Grant McCracken, *Culture and Consumption*, Indiana University Press, Bloomington and Indianopolis, 1988.
12. R. W. Belk, M. Wallendorf & J. F. Sherry, 'The Sacred and the Profane in Consumer Behaviour', *Journal of Consumer Research* 16, June 1989, pp. 1–38.
13. John Fiske, Bob Hodge & Graeme Turner, *Myths of Oz: Readings in Australian Popular Culture*, Allen & Unwin, Sydney, 1987.
14. Leonard Broom & Philip Selznick, *Sociology: A Text with Adapted Readings*, 4th edn, Harper & Row, New York, 1968, p. 54.
15. Milton J. Rokeach, *Beliefs, Attitudes and Values*, Jossey Bass, San Francisco, 1968, p. 161.
16. Jonathan Gutman & Donald E. Vinson, 'Value Structures and Consumer Behavior', in William L. Wilkie (ed.), *Advances in Consumer Research*, vol. 6, Association for Consumer Research, Ann Arbor, MI, 1979, pp. 335–6.
17. Milton J. Rokeach, 'The Role of Values in Public Opinion Research', *Public Opinion Quarterly* 32, 1969–70, pp. 550–1.
18. Shalom H. Schwartz, 'Cultural Dimensions of Human Values', in U. Kim, H. C. Triandis & G. Yoon (eds), *Individualism and Collectivism: Theoretical and Methodological Issues*, Sage Publications, forthcoming.
19. Milton J. Rokeach, '*The Nature of Human Values*, Free Press, New York, 1973.
20. Sharon Beatty, Lynn Kahle, Pamela Homer & Shekhar Misra, 'Alternative Measurement Approaches to the Rokeach Value Survey', *Psychology & Marketing* 2, Fall 1985, p. 199.
21. Sharon Beatty, Lynn Kahle, Pamela Homer & Shekhar Misra, 'Alternative Measurement Approaches to Consumer Values: The List of Values and the Rokeach Value Survey', *Psychology & Marketing* 2, Fall 1985, p. 192.
22. Shalom H. Schwartz, 'Universals in the Content and Structure of Values: Theoretical Advances and Empirical Tests in 20 Countries', *Advances in Experimental Social Psychology* 25, 1992, pp. 1–61.
23. R. E. Pitts & A. G. Woodside, 'Personal Value Influences on Consumer Product Class and Brand Preferences', *Journal of Social Psychology* 119, 1983, pp. 37–53; and Alfred S. Boote, 'Psychographics: Mind Over Matter', *American Demographics*, April 1980.

24. Alfred S. Boote, An Exploratory Investigation of the Roles of Needs and Personal Values in the Theory of Buyer Behavior, PhD thesis, Columbia University, 1975.
25. Wagner A. Kamakura & Jose A. Mazzon, 'Value Segmentation: A Model for the Measurement of Values and Value Systems', *Journal of Consumer Research* 18, September 1991, pp. 208–18.
26. See, for example, Alfred S. Boote, 'Market Segmentation by Personal Values and Salient Product Attributes', *Journal of Advertising Research* 21, February 1981, pp. 29–35; and Kenneth D. Bahn & Kent L. Granzin, 'Alternative Means of Marketing Segmentation in the Restaurant Industry', in Terrence A. Shimp et al. (eds), *1986 AMA Educators Proceedings*, American Marketing Association, Chicago, 1986, pp. 321–6; L. L. Manzer & S. J. Miller, 'An Examination of the Value–Attitude Structure in the Study of Donor Behavior', paper presented at annual meeting of American Institute for Decision Sciences, November 1978; L. Bozinoff & R. Cohen, 'The Effects of Personal Values and Usage Situations on Product Attribute Importance', in B. J. Walker et al. (eds), *An Assessment of Marketing Thought and Practice*, American Marketing Association, Chicago, 1982, pp. 25–9; R. E. Pitts & A. G. Woodside (eds), *Personal Values and Consumer Psychology*, Lexington Books, Lexington, MA, 1984; Walter A. Henry, 'Cultural Values Do Correlate with Consumer Behavior', *Journal of Marketing Research* 13, May 1976, pp. 121–7; Donald E. Vinson, Jerome E. Scott & Lawrence M. Lamont, 'The Role of Personal Values in Marketing and Consumer Behavior', *Journal of Marketing* 41, April 1977, pp. 44–50; and Kent L. Granzin & Kenneth D. Bahn, 'Do Values Have General Applicability to Retail Market Segmentation?', in Robert H. Ross, Frederick B. Kraft & Charles H. Davis (eds), *1981 Southwestern Marketing Proceedings*, The Southwestern Marketing Association, Wichita, KS, 1981, pp. 146–9; B. W. Becker & P. E. Conner, 'The Influence of Personal Values on Attitude and Store Choice Behavior', in B. I. Walker et al. (eds), *An Assessment of Marketing Thought and Practice*, American Marketing Association, Chicago, 1982, pp. 21–4; John S. Wagle & William O. Hancock, 'Matching Values Presented in Mass Media Vehicles to Promotional Messages: A Shortcut to the Marketing Concept', in Paul Thistlewaite, Dorrie Billingsly & John Berens (eds), *Proceedings*, Midwest Marketing Association, Macomb, IL, 1985, pp. 35–40.
27. Niles Howard, 'A New Way to View Customers', *Dun's Review*, August 1981, pp. 42–6.
28. Lynn R. Kahle, 'Social Values in the Eighties: A Special Issue', *Psychology & Marketing* 2, Winter 1985, p. 234.
29. Thomas P. Novak & Bruce MacEvoy, 'On Comparing Alternative Segmentation Schemes: The List of Values (LOV) and Values and Lifestyles (VALS)', *Journal of Consumer Research* 17, June 1990, pp. 105–9.
30. *The Roy Morgan Values Segments*, The Roy Morgan Research Centre Pty Ltd, Sydney, 1994.
31. Rob Lawson, Amy Rummel, Guenther Mueller-Heumann & Bruce Fiegler, 'A New Zealand Lifestyle Survey', *New Zealand Journal of Business*, 1990, pp. 22–35.
32. Hugh Mackay, *Reinventing Australia*, Angus & Robertson, Sydney, 1993, pp. 233–8.
33. Hyam Gold & Alan Webster, *New Zealand Values Today*, Alpha Publications, Palmerston North, 1990.
34. Don Poritt, 'Rejecting Perfection', *Australian Professional Marketing*, March 1994, pp. 23–4.
35. 'Prepare for the Future: Explore These Six Trends', *Marketing News*, 4 January 1985, p. 26.
36. Don Porritt, 'The Dynamics of Marketing Survival, *Australian Professional Marketing*, April 1994, pp. 34–5; and Gold & Webster, *New Zealand Values Today*, p. 15.
37. 'Company Motoring 1993', *Marketing*, June 1993, pp. 3–10.
38. Christopher Power, 'Value Marketing', *Business Week*, 11 November 1991, p. 133.

39. Bernard Berelson & Gary Steiner, *Human Behavior: An Inventory of Scientific Findings*, Harcourt, New York, 1964, p. 494.
40. Elizabeth C. Hirschman, 'Primitive Aspects of Consumption in Modern American Society', *Journal of Consumer Research* 12, September 1985, p. 145.
41. Hugh Mackay, *'The Mackay Report on Multiculture*, Mackay Research, Sydney, 1985.
42. Madeline Coorey, 'Lottery Move a Coup', *Australian*, 16 June 1994, p. 17.
43. Catherine Fox, 'SBS Gains Advertising Toe-hold', *Financial Review*, 7 September 1993, p. 43; and Tony Crease, 'Australia's Untapped Audience', *Marketing*, December 1993, pp. 53–4.
44. Fred Brenchley, 'Three Operators Target the Ethnic Pay-TV Market', *Financial Review*, 19 October, 1993, p. 42.
45. This section is largely based on information from a number of feature articles published in the *Australian*, 16 June 1994, pp. 16–18; and on 'Big Money in Ethnic Marketing', *Marketing*, June 1994, pp. 10–14.
46. David Bednall, Marketing Government Information to a Multicultural Audience, Working paper, David Syme Faculty of Business, Monash University, Melbourne, 1993.
47. Fiske, Hodge & Turner, op cit, Ref 13, pp. 52–4.
48. Roland Robertson, 'Mapping the Global Condition: Globalisation as the Central Concept', in Mike Featherstone (ed.), *Global Culture: Nationalism, Globalisation and Modernity*, Sage Publications, London, 1990, pp. 15-30.
49. Rosabeth Moss Kanter, 'Transcending Business Boundaries: 12 000 World Managers View Change', *Harvard Business Review* 69, May–June 1991, pp. 151–64.
50. Lawrence Stessin, 'Incidents of Culture Shock Among American Businessmen Overseas', *Pittsburgh Business Review*, November–December 1971, p. 1.
51. James A. Lee, 'Cultural Analysis in Overseas Operations', *Harvard Business Review* 44, March–April 1966, p. 44.
52. David K. Tse, Kam-hon Lee, Ilan Vertinksy & Donald A. Wehrung, 'Does Culture Matter? A Cross-cultural Study of Executives' Choice, Decisiveness, and Risk Adjustment in International Marketing', *Journal of Marketing* 52, October 1988, pp. 91–2.
53. Susanne C. Grunert, 'Consumer Values in West Germany: Underlying Dimensions and Cross-cultural Comparison with North America', *Journal of Business Research* 20, 1990, pp. 97–107.
54. This section is adapted from Rose Knotts, 'Cross-cultural Management: Transformations and Adaptations', *Business Horizons* 32, January–February 1989, pp. 30–2.
55. Edward T. Hall & Mildred R. Hall, *Hidden Differences Doing Business with the Japanese*, Anchor Press/Doubleday, Garden City, NY, 1987, pp. 16–18.
56. Hall & Hall, ibid, pp. 16–18.
57. Gold & Webster, op cit, Ref 33, pp. 63–9.
58. John McCallum, 'Secularisation in Australia between 1966 and 1985', *Australian and New Zealand Journal of Sociology* 23 (3), 1987, pp. 407–22.
59. Theodore Levitt, 'The Globalization of Markets', *Harvard Business Review* 83, May–June 1983, pp. 92–102.
60. Christine Dugas & Marilyn A. Harris, 'Playtex Kicks Off a One-ad-fits-all Campaign', *Business Week*, 16 December 1985, pp. 48–9.
61. 'Attitude Research Assesses Global Market Potential', *Marketing News*, 1 August 1988, p. 10.
62. Shalom H. Schwartz, *Advances in Experimental Social Psychology*, pp. 1–61.
63. Harper W. Boyd, Ronald Frank, William Massy & Mostafa Zoheir, 'On the Use of Marketing Research in the Emerging Economies', *Journal of Marketing Research* 1, November 1964, p. 23.
64. Rebecca Fannin, 'Seeing Is Believing', *Marketing and Media Decisions*, February 1988, pp. 51–2.

65. Rebecca Piirto, 'Global Psychographics', *American Demographics*, December 1990, p. 8; and 'Ad Agency Finds 5 Global Segments', *Marketing News*, 8 January 1990, pp. 9, 17.
66. Norbert Homma & Jorg Ueltzhoffer, 'The Internationalisation of Everyday-life-research: Markets and Milieus', *Marketing and Research Today*, November 1990, pp. 197–207.
67. Janette Martin, 'Beyond 1992: Lifestyle Is Key', *Advertising Age*, 11 July 1988, p. 57.
68. 'Europe '92: Cultural Borders Will Remain', *Futurist*, September–October 1990, pp. 57–8.
69. 'The Symbol of Truth', *Across the Board*, May 1991, p. 63.
70. Vem Terpstra, *International Dimensions of Marketing*, 2nd edn, PWS-Kent Publishing Company, Boston, MA, 1988, p. 92.
71. Alice Rudolph, 'Standardization Not Standard for Global Marketers', *Marketing News*, 27 September 1986, p. 3.
72. Nicole Seligman, 'Be Sure Not to Wear a Green Hat if You Visit Hong Kong', *Wall Street Journal*, 10 May 1979, p. 41.
73. Shoji, 'Custom-Made', *Business Tokyo*, March 1991, p. 18.
74. Jimmy Hafesjee, *Using the Media to Reach Ethnic Markets*, SBS, Sydney, 1994.
75. This section is based on Eion Scott, 'Can Marketers Straddle the Tasman?', *Marketing*, April 1993, pp. 11–17.
76. Pakeha is a Maori word used to designate non-Maori people and it is particularly applied to New Zealanders of European descent.

CHAPTER 4

SOCIAL CLASS

LEARNING OBJECTIVES

AFTER STUDYING THIS CHAPTER YOU SHOULD UNDERSTAND:

➡ the process of social stratification in societies;

➡ characteristics of the social-class system;

➡ how social class standing is measured and categorised;

➡ how social-class membership affects consumer behaviour;

➡ the role of social class in market segmentation.

A poor clergyman's wife with a sick husband was tempted by the handsome bunches [of grapes] which she saw in a shop window. She laid them down with a sigh when she was told the price. The shopman pitied her. "Tisn't the likes of you,' he said, 'that can afford them grapes; we keep them for the working men's ladies."[1]

This example from a 19th-century social history of the colonisation of Australia and New Zealand refers to an incident in an Auckland shop in 1895. It illustrates one of the perennial debates about social class and its relationship to income. Much of the debate concerning social class in consumer-behaviour research has centred around the relative merits of social class and income as predictors of behaviour, and this argument will be covered in detail later in this chapter.

Social class is one form of stratification by which we may attempt to divide society into more or less homogeneous groups of people with their own distinguishing modes of behaviour or lifestyles. *Social stratification* is the general term whereby people in a society are ranked by other members of a society into higher and lower social positions. Stratification is defined as 'structured inequalities between different groups'.[2] Historically, sociologists define four types of stratification across world societies: slavery, castes, estates and classes. The only form of stratification that is relevant to Australia and New Zealand is social class. Discussion of social class is often confused by reference to different terms such as 'prestige' and 'socioeconomic status'. These are often used interchangeably, especially by marketing practitioners. Other authors may keep them quite separate as they reflect different orthodoxies in social research.

It is impossible to escape some of this debate in this chapter, but we are not going to be dogmatic in our discussion. Along with the majority, we accept reference to measures of socioeconomic status as indicators of social class.

Australia and New Zealand have always prided themselves on the egalitarian nature of their societies, perhaps a reaction to British society with its characterisation of nobility, social class and privilege. Because of this, a discussion of social class does not always sit easy within our culture, and the dimensions of class are more difficult to pin down than in other less open and less socially mobile societies. *The Mackay Report on Social Class* makes it clear that Australians do relate to notions of class and, indeed, want to recognise a social hierarchy as it gives a sense of structure and order to society that offers individuals a degree of security.[3] This runs contrary to the 'Tall Poppy Syndrome', where Australians and New Zealanders have developed a reputation for 'cutting down the tall poppies'; that is, denigrating those who achieve some degree of excellence. Mackay argues that this behaviour pattern is a myth and that Australians (and we believe New Zealanders) are only irritated by those who *act* tall. Neither society is uncomfortable with the notion of success, but egalitarian ideals make both societies uncomfortable with the notion that success means superiority. Hence, they react negatively to displays of arrogance or smugness.

This distinction emphasises two important features about social class systems. First, they are supported by general normative beliefs regarding issues such as status and how it is conveyed. For example, individuals cannot merely determine their own class by their behaviour, including their consumption choices, if they do not have the other attributes such as the necessary educational and occupational characteristics. Secondly, social-class categories are descriptive and not normative items. There is no case in research using social class, or in its use by marketers to understand consumer behaviour, that implies that one class is better than another or superior in any way. In this chapter we are simply describing the class structure as researched in Australia and New Zealand. Some may resent such a discussion or be uncomfortable about it, feeling that it is unjust. However, social classes do exist and the concept can be useful to the marketer for understanding consumer behaviour and plotting a marketing strategy. In order to use it wisely, however, one must first understand its meaning.

We shall first discuss the nature of social class in Australia and New Zealand, including some of the problems associated with measurement. This will be followed by an examination of how consumer behaviour varies across different social classes. In this latter part of the discussion we have had to draw on some academic material from other countries. But we have constrained ourselves to findings that we believe can be generalised to Australia and New Zealand, and, in particular, to those findings that concur with the limited research available in the two countries.

THE NATURE OF SOCIAL CLASS

The term 'social class' has been defined as 'a large-scale group of people who share common economic resources which strongly influences the type of lifestyle they are able to lead'.[4] Ownership of wealth, together with occupation, are the chief bases for class differences. In contrast to other forms of social stratification, there are four key features in defining social classes:

1. Social classes are not established on any legal or religious provisions; they are relatively fluid and have no formal restrictions.

2. In part, an individual's class is achieved and not simply given as in a caste system; educational attainment and occupational choice allow an individual to achieve a particular position within the system.

3. Classes depend on economic differences between groups; that is, inequalities in the possession and control of material goods. By definition, this makes them directly relevant to the study of consumer behaviour.

4. Though social classes are strongly linked to interpersonal relationships, classes are *defined* through large-scale impersonal connections, not through individual personal ones as are other forms of stratification. For example, levels of pay and working conditions affect all people in specific occupational categories.

The study of social class in sociology is an extremely complex area with many different approaches and forms of measurement.[5] In order to clarify the concept further we are going to extend the review to emphasise six basic characteristics of social class. In doing this we are focusing on the aspects most pertinent to marketing and consumer behaviour, and it is acknowledged that we are presenting only some of the options available.

Social classes are multidimensional

Although based on economic resources, the concept of social class is a multidimensional one. *The Mackay Report on Social Class* indicates that Australians, like Americans, believe income is the most important dimension in ascribing social class, but that this is tempered by possessions, education and other features of social behaviour, such as care and maintenance of property.[6] Overall, the three most discussed components in research on social class in Australia and New Zealand are occupational class, income and education.[7]

In the United States the area of residence is also commonly considered as an element in social-class measurement. As we discussed in Chapter 2, the classification of residential neighbourhoods in Australia and New Zealand has tended to follow a separate evolution from social class for market segmentation. However, since 1990, indices developed by the Australian Bureau of Statistics have linked the two together, though neighbourhood residence is still not one of the measurement components.[8] These are discussed in more detail later in the chapter.

A further key feature that is emphasised in some approaches to social class, particularly those developed from a Marxian perspective, is the ownership of property and production within the economy, as this is strongly related to economic bases of power. Figure 4.1 gives a class schema developed by Wright known as the Exploitation of Assets model. It incorporates the ownership dimension and gives 12 different class locations. This class structure has been used fairly extensively by sociologists for analysing social-class-related issues in Australia, but it is not usually employed for commercial or policy research.[9] A useful feature of the scheme is that it makes explicit two of the characteristics on which occupational prestige is awarded—the skill assets and the organisational assets that are a feature of the occupation. These characteristics are fundamental to other evaluations of occupations for socioeconomic stratification, including the Australian Standard Classification of Occupations (ASCO).

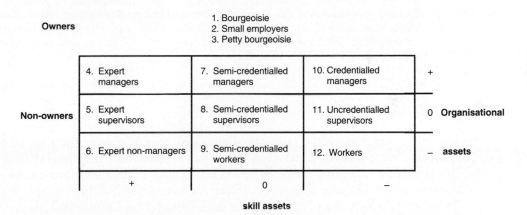

FIG. 4.1 Wright's Exploitation of Assets class schema   Source: J. H. Baxter et al., 'The Australian Class Structure: Some Preliminary Results from the Australian Class Project', *Australian and New Zealand Journal of Sociology* 25(1), 1989, pp. 100–17.

Most researchers see occupation as the key dimension of all those discussed. Occupation depends upon educational credentials and occupational incomes largely determine the level of living for most people, most of the time. Occupation is also known to be strongly correlated with the relationship aspects of social stratification—who mixes with whom—and is therefore important in determining the nature of peer groups for any individual.[10] For all these reasons, occupation (or measures of occupational status) is often used as a proxy for social class, but it must always be remembered that the true nature of the concept is a broader multidimensional one. Though education, income and occupation are positively correlated, the raw correlations are best described as modest-to-average (Table 4.1), and best explanations of consumer behaviour are likely to come from using all three variables.

TABLE 4.1 Correlation coefficients between income, occupation and education in Australia[a]

	Occupation	Education
Income	.51	.33
Occupation		.41

(a) All significant at p is less than 0.01.

Source: Jake M. Najman, 'The Measurement of Socioeconomic Inequality and Social Class in Australia: A Review of Past Practices and Recent Developments', *Community Health Studies* 12(1), 1988, pp. 31–41. (See also G. N. Marks, John S. Weston & Mark C. Weston, 'Class and Income in Australia', *Australian and New Zealand Journal of Sociology* 25(3), 1989, pp. 410–27. The authors demonstrate that these correlations could be improved if factors such as gender and working hours were controlled for.)

Social classes exhibit status

Thanks to the writings of the eminent sociologist Max Weber at the turn of the 19th century, we distinguish between the terms 'social class' and 'social status'. Social class is an objective measure based on an individual's economic ranking within society, while social status is a subjective assessment of their social standing. In practice, many people often interchange the terms 'status' and 'class' but it should be emphasised that though they are related, they are not equivalent concepts.[11] Social status is typically ascribed on the basis of wealth, lifestyle, education, hereditary factors, occupational prestige and individual achievements. Status, therefore, is a function not only of the social class to which an individual belongs, but also of personal and family characteristics.[12] For example, the fact that an individual is a scientist means that he or she has a high rank in the overall social system. However, a scientist employed by a prestigious research institute will have higher status or rank than a scientist employed by a small firm, even though both may be members of the same social class. Moreover, an individual's personal contributions to society will help determine his or her status. A scientist who discovers a breakthrough in laser technology, for example, will have higher status than another who has made no such significant contribution.

Each society subjectively establishes its own set of values. These values are reflected in the ideal types of people in that society. That is, those who more nearly conform to the ideal are accorded more respect and prestige, while those who conform less nearly are ranked lower by the society. In one country, members of the armed services may be accorded the greatest prestige; in another, politicians, educators or business people may be selected. The particular criteria used, as well as their relative weights, are determined by the values stressed by that society.

Social classes are hierarchical

Social classes have a vertical order to them, ranging from high social and economic standing to low standing. They exist as a position on the social scale. Individuals may be placed within a class on this hierarchy, based on appropriate socioeconomic-status criteria.

Social classes restrict behaviour

Interaction between the classes is limited, because most of us are more comfortable and find reinforcement with those 'like us' in terms of values and behaviour patterns. Consequently, members of the same social class tend to associate with each other and not to any large extent with members from another social class. The factor of limited interaction impedes interpersonal communication between different classes about advertising, products and other marketing elements.

Social classes are homogeneous

As a consequence of similar social standing within the hierarchy, social classes may be viewed as homogeneous divisions of society in which people within a class have similar attitudes, activities, interests and other behaviour patterns. For the marketer this means that groups of people are exposed to similar media, purchase similar products and services, and shop in similar stores. This homogeneity allows the marketer effectively to segment the market by social class and to develop appealing marketing mixes.

Social classes are dynamic

Social stratification systems in which people have some opportunity for upward or downward movement are known as *open systems*. People in *closed systems* have inherited or ascribed status; that is, they are born into one social level and are unable to leave it. For example, parts of rural India illustrate a caste, or closed, system, which has existed for thousands of years. Social inequality is rigidly enforced, creating a permanent social position assigned at birth and preventing any social mobility by the individual. The difference between a system based on earned or achieved status versus one based on inherited status is significant with regard to social mobility. Australia and New Zealand illustrate social-class, or open, systems which offer moderate opportunity for mobility. Although such a change can occur, it is usually not large and generally takes place over an extended time. Indeed, as hereditary aspects still play some part in determining status, a person from humble beginnings who makes it through the educational system and up the occupational and income ladder is not likely to throw off all the attributes of the original class background. Indeed, some people might fight determinedly to retain some aspects of their past life and contacts. The Welsh stage and film actor Richard Burton, who came from a mining family, is one such example. The clear transition in social class is likely to show up in the next generation within the family.

For much of the period since World War II we have lived with the myth of embourgeoisement. This was a popular notion that, with adequate social welfare systems and the breaking down of many old barriers to class, such as ownership of property and declining attention to hereditary status, everyone in society was becoming 'middle class'. Research in education began to dispel this myth in the 1970s when it was found that, even within systems of state education where there was apparent equal opportunity, the achieving pupils tended to be from higher social-class backgrounds. Access to particular educational resources depends on family resources and, particularly, parents' education. Therefore, though there is mobility in our systems in Australia and New Zealand, class systems tend to be perpetuated from generation to generation, and the concept is regarded as equally applicable in the 1990s as it was in earlier decades of the 20th century.

In fact, if we look at the income component of social class, there has been a marked widening in the distribution in recent years. Census data show that from 1976 to 1991 (using constant 1991 values) the proportion of Australian households with an income of more than $72 000 rose from 15 per cent to 30 per cent. At the same time, the proportion of households with an income of less than $22 000 rose from 20 per cent to 30 per cent. A similar widening of income distribution has also taken place in New Zealand over this period. Interpreting this information in a 1994 radio interview, the social researcher Hugh Mackay suggested that it was no longer appropriate to think in old terms of working, middle and upper classes. What we have now is a growing 'underclass' in society, which is characterised by a reliance on state benefits and various unofficial sources of income. What were the old-fashioned blue-collar working classes are now in the shrinking middle-income group together with the tradespeople and semiskilled white-collar people. At the top of the hierarchy there has been a large growth in professional, scientific and managerial positions that has expanded the range and size of the old upper-middle classes. Incidentally, many of these people also belong to dual-income households, accentuating the income differences across social classes. Such a polarity is likely to reduce social mobility and continue to make social class an important factor in explaining consumer behaviour. This situation is in contrast to some other countries, such as Finland, where an analysis of changes from 1955 to 1985 showed less variation in class structures across the country. There was also less relevance for social class in explaining levels of expenditure on some items such as alcohol and housing, though for other product classes it remained important.[13]

SOCIAL-CLASS MEASUREMENT AND CATEGORISATION

Broadly speaking there are three fundamentally different approaches to measuring social class. First, and most importantly, there are a series of objective measures, which depend largely upon the dimensions that are included in the study of class. Most of this section is devoted to reviewing the important Australian and New Zealand objective classifications.

Two other approaches are known as the *subjective method* and the *reputational method*. In the subjective method individuals are asked to rank themselves in the social-class hierarchy, while in the reputational method members of a community are asked to rank each other in the system. The subjective method is based on the argument that it is where individuals perceive themselves to be, or aspire to be, within the class system that is important in determining how they behave. This is an appealing notion, which is further developed in the discussion of self-concept in Chapter 8. However, research shows that, when reporting their view of their social class, most people are reluctant to categorise themselves as either the lower or the upper groups, and the middle class ends up with an unrealistically large share.[14] The reputational method relies on personal knowledge of the individuals and is only appropriate in restricted situations where a marketer might be investigating behaviour within a small community. The reputational method has been most widely employed by sociologists and, as the structure of social class depends on general normative beliefs, it is used to validate other measures of class such as those based on occupations.[15]

Objective methods of measurement

Objective methods fall into three broad types:

1. composite measures, which typically include education, income and occupation as discussed earlier;

2. measures based on a single proxy variable, typically occupation, and which allocate individuals to a series of strata, producing an ordinal (ranked) scale of groups from upper through middle to lower classes;

3. measures that seek to derive a continuous scale, or index, to denote a person's position in the hierarchy. Most usually this is based on occupational prestige. An extension to this is SEIFA. These are a series of indices for areas rather than individuals developed by the Australian Bureau of Statistics.

COMPOSITE MEASURES

Historically, the composite measures of social class most used in Australia and New Zealand are based on the three criteria of education, income and occupational status.[16] Usually generating this composite measure involves creating a distribution for each element and giving a person a score on each distribution for occupation, education and income. The scores are then totalled to provide a single index of social class. This score can be used directly as a measure of class but, in view of the problems outlined below, it is usually taken to allocate people to a class group. The data on social class and media behaviour given later in the chapter in Table 4.12(a) is based on this approach, using an index created by Morgan Research.

There are two main sets of problems with such composite measures. First, an interval-scaled distribution has to be generated from at best ordinal measures of occupations and education. This process requires extremely careful validation and repeated checking over time to ensure that the composite measures remain reliable. Secondly, the simple totalling of the distributions assumes that each element carries equal weight from individual to individual. We may have two marketing managers in equivalent positions with similar companies. One has earned the position in part through formal qualifications and progressed through a graduate trainee scheme with the company. The other has no degree and has reached the position by moving up the ranks from a lowly office job. It is a matter for debate whether education and occupation should get equal weighting in determining the social class of both people. For both these reasons, it is much better to use the composite score to allocate an individual to a broad group than it is to employ it directly as a measure of class.

MEASURES BASED ON SINGLE PROXY VARIABLE

In practice, only a few marketers and academic researchers go to the trouble of compiling composite measures of social class. Instead marketers typically make use of grading systems based on occupation as a proxy variable. Practical justification for this is taken from the fact that much evidence (though admittedly not all) suggests that composite measures do not produce better explanations of behaviour when used in statistical analysis.[17]

The most important occupational-based set of measures in Australia is the ASCO (Australian Standard Classification of Occupations) method.[18] This was developed by the Australian Bureau of Statistics in the 1980s as a comprehensive skills-based classification for the analysis of labour-force statistics, education planning and human resource management. It is based on the level of skill and the degree of specialisation, and therefore has both the dimensions covered in the employee part of the Wright model of class given earlier. There are four levels in the ASCO classification as shown in Table 4.2. At a base level ASCO defines 1079 individual occupations. These are aggregated into 282 unit groups at the second level. Units span industries but involve common tasks. At the third level the unit groups are collapsed into 52 minor groups, which are categorised by skill specialisation. Finally, these are aggregated to 8 major groups.

TABLE 4.2 An example of levels in the ASCO structure

Level	Code	Title
Major group	4	Tradesperson
Minor group	44	Building tradesperson
Unit group	4401	Carpenters and joiners
Occupation	4401-11	Carpenter

Source: Ian Castles, *A Guide to Major ABS Classifications*, Australian Bureau of Statistics, Canberra, 1991, pp. 19–21.

In total eight major groups are identified:

1. Managers and administrators
2. Professionals
3. Para-professionals
4. Tradespersons
5. Clerks
6. Salespersons and personal service workers
7. Plant and machine operators/drivers
8. Labourers and related workers

The ASCO classification was never intended as a measure of socioeconomic status but the major groups have obvious parallels with other SES classifications from overseas, and the classification has been adopted in that way. For example, in the United Kingdom professionals are placed ahead of managers and clerks ahead of tradespeople, but otherwise the schemes are the same. Because ASCO was not devised as a measure of class, a close investigation reveals a number of anomalies where individual occupations are graded in such a way that they cannot be seen to fit into our common understanding of social class, whatever our individual egalitarian standards. For example, prostitutes are included in the personal service category, which also includes funeral directors, and airline pilots are included with other transport workers in the para-professionals. A refinement of the ASCO scheme that aims to overcome these difficulties is given in Table 4.3. Here four levels of social class are given based on occupation and the anomalous occupations in the ASCO classification can be picked out as those away from the diagonal from upper left to lower right.[19]

Statistics New Zealand mainly use the International Standard Classification of Occupations (ISCO). This has nine groupings and is primarily designed to give information for different sectors of the economy. It does not reflect a hierarchy of social class in any way at all. The most important work on socioeconomic measurement in New Zealand are the Elley-Irving indices.[20] These were first developed in the 1960s and over the years have been revised to take account of

TABLE 4.3 An ASCO-based occupational status hierarchy for Australia

Grade		1. Managers and administrators (11.7%)	2. Professionals (11.8%)	3. Para-professionals (6.5%)	4. Tradespersons (15.3%)
	1.0	1.8 Magistrates (11p)	1.9 Doctors (23p)		
A	2.0	2.8 Legislators (11p)	2.0 Solicitors (26p) 2.2 Dentists (23p) 2.7 Building professionals (22) 2.8 Therapists (23p) 2.8 Scientists (21)	2.6 Pilots (33p)	
	3.0	3.0 General Managers (12) 3.2 Specialist managers (13)	3.1 Business Professionals (27)		
B		3.7 Managing supervisors (Sales) (15) 3.7 Managing supervisors (16)	3.5 Artists (28) 3.5 Social professionals (26) 3.5 School teachers (24) 3.5 Other teachers (25) 3.5 Miscellaneous professionals (29)	3.5 Medical science technicians (31) 3.5 Engineering/Building technicians (32) 3.5 Miscellaneous para-professionals (39) 3.6 Nurses (34) 3.6 Air/Transport technicians (33p)	
C	4.0	4.3 Farmers (14)		4.0 Police (35)	4.0 Electrical/Electronics (43) 4.4 Food preparers (47) 4.6 Building trades (44) 4.7 Printing workers (45) 4.7 Miscellaneous trades (49) 4.8 Metal fitters (41) 4.8 Other trades (42) 4.9 Mechanics and Panel beaters (46)
D	5.0				5.2 Gardeners (48)
	6.0				

Source: J. M. Najman & M. Bampton, 'An ASCO-based Occupational Status Hierarchy for Australia:

5. Clerks	6. Salespersons	7. Plant and machine operators/drivers	8. Labourers and related workers
(17.1%)	(12.4%)	(8.2%)	(14.4%)

3.4 Finance dealers (61)

4.3 Data/Machine operators (52)	4.2 Personal service (66)		
4.4 Numerical clerks (53)	4.3 Insurance/Real estate agents (61)		
4.6 Stenographers (51)	4.5 Miscellaneous sales (65)		
4.6 Miscellaneous clerks (59)	4.6 Sales representatives (62)		
4.8 Receptionists (56)			
4.8 Recording/ Dispatching (55)			
4.9 Filing clerks (54)			

		5.0 Engine/Boiler operators (73)	
		5.0 Mobile plant operators (72)	
	5.1 Sales assistants (63)		5.1 Agricultural labourers (82)
			5.1 Miscellaneous labourers (89)
			5.3 Construction labourers (84)
	5.4 Tellers (64)		
		5.6 Drivers (71)	
		5.6 Machine operators (74)	
			5.7 Trades assistants/Factory hands (81)
		6.0 Cleaners (83)	

new occupational groupings and other social changes, such as the changing position of women in society.[21]

The Elley-Irving indices are a further variation on the kind of measures that we have discussed so far. The scheme is devised as an objective index of occupational status and, using data from the New Zealand census, based on the levels of education and income of people participating in the occupations. Education and income are given equal weighting in the scheme. Thus, there is no actual measure of status as in the composite measure discussed earlier, but this is inferred from the two other variables—income and education.* Because some occupations are gender based, Elley and Irving produced two different classifications for males and females. These indices can attribute these different status to males and females for the same job, usually on account of women often receiving less remuneration than men. Only the male index was revised in the last Elley-Irving paper and we are awaiting promised revisions of both for the 1991 census. Table 4.4 gives a breakdown of the levels of male occupations in New Zealand. Farmers are the most problematical group in the whole index, because they show a tremendous variation in education and income. They are included in category 4 in the table but, because of their heterogeneity, Elley and Irving do suggest they could be relocated to a separate group comprising 6.3 per cent of male occupations.

TABLE 4.4 Socioeconomic classification in New Zealand (male labour force)

Socioeconomic level	Proportion of male population %	Example of occupations
1. Higher professional/administrative	7.5	Accountant, chiropractor, judge, ship's officer, university lecturer
2. Lower professional/technical	11.0	Armed forces officer, food technologist, managing director
3. Clerical/highly skilled	23.0	Business-services salesman, customs agent, production supervisor
4. Skilled	33.0	Carpenter, florist, coalminer, pest inspector, signwriter
5. Semiskilled	17.0	Bricklayer, lorry driver, housekeeper, shearer
6. Unskilled	8.5	Canner, food packer, groundsman, stockman, waiter

Source: W. B. Elley & J. C. Irving, 'The Elley-Irving Socio-economic Index 1981 Census Revision', *New Zealand Journal of Educational Studies* 20(2), 1985, pp. 115–28.

*In fairness to its creators, we must make it clear that Elley and Irving are explicit in saying their index was not devised as a measure of lifestyle, social class, material well-being or consumption. Most accurately it is an occupational index but, accepting the arguments of other sociologists and the high correlation between occupation and other status variables, we are able to use it as an effective proxy.

SINGLE INDEX MEASURES

The third type of objective measure is an index score of socioeconomic status, as opposed to the ranked series of groups described in ASCO and Elley-Irving. Such indices have significant advantages in the analysis of consumer behaviour because they are interval scales, and can be easily employed in many more statistical procedures. The most important scale for individuals in Australia and New Zealand is the ANU3 scale developed by Jones using the ASCO classification of individual occupations.[22] A status score is constructed for each occupation at the unit level by regression analysis of age, gender, sector of employment, weekly working hours, income, qualifications and age of leaving school. The raw scores on the regression analysis are rescaled to produce an index with the lowest scoring occupation receiving a 0 score and the highest a score of 100. Table 4.5 gives a sample of status scores for different occupations.

The most significant indices produced by the Australian Bureau of Statistics are SEIFA.[23] These are a series of five socioeconomic indices that have been developed to profile different areas in Australia. These areas can vary in size from an entire state, such as Queensland, down to the basic neighbourhood building blocks used for the census, and offer similar advantages to marketers as do the neighbourhood segmentation schemes discussed in Chapter 2. The five measures are:

1. urban index of relative socioeconomic advantage

2. rural index of relative socioeconomic advantage

3. index of relative socioeconomic disadvantage

4. index of economic resources

5. index of education and occupation

The indices of relative socioeconomic advantage and the index of socioeconomic disadvantage summarise variables relating to the economic resources of households, education and occupation. Several measures of each variable are included and these are combined by principal components analysis to produce a limited number of uncorrelated variables, which are used to derive an index for the area under analysis. To ease interpretation, all the indices have been standardised to have a mean of 1000 across Australia and a standard deviation of 100. Thus, an area with a high-advantage index will reflect an area with high incomes, a large proportion of tertiary-educated people and skilled occupations. A disadvantaged area focuses on low income, low educational attainment and high unemployment. It is normal for a high-advantage area to be also high disadvantage, and, in particular, some inner-city areas are strongly polarised and show high scores on both indices.

The index of economic resources excludes education and occupation variables but takes account of a wider range of income and expenditure items, including housing and car ownership variables. Unfortunately, the index misses savings and equities because the data was not collected in the 1991 census. The

TABLE 4.5 Socioeconomic status scores for Australian occupations, based on the Australian Standard Classification of Occupations

ASCO code	Occupation	Status Score
2303	Medical consultant	100.0
1101	Parliamentarian, ambassador	97.0
1103	Coroner, judge	96.1
2305	Dental specialist	88.7
2501	University lecturer	82.1
1317	School principal	82.0
2103	Geologist	79.2
1311	Computer systems manager	75.4
2209	Architect	73.6
2405	Secondary school teacher	69.2
1303	Marketing manager	66.1
2707	Systems designer	60.5
2807	Journalist	54.7
3305	Ship's master, ferry captain	54.6
2911	Librarian	53.0
6101	Stockbroker	49.8
3299	Mining technician	48.0
3909	Ambulance driver	41.7
4211	Aircraft maintenance staff	37.9
4307	Refrigeration technician	36.4
6603	Enrolled nurse	30.7
4505	Printer	26.2
5303	Insurance clerk	24.3
4407	Plasterer	23.4
5401	Filing clerk	19.6
7107	Train driver	13.3
7423	Tanner	11.4
6505	Waiter—formal	9.5
7203	Storeman	3.4
8407	Builder's labourer	1.9
8901	Usher, doorman	0.0

Source: Adapted from: F. L. Jones, 'Occupational Prestige in Australia: A New Scale', *Australian and New Zealand Journal of Sociology* 25(2), 1989, pp. 187–99.

inclusion of those items would have made it a good representation of wealth and therefore a better approximation of social class than solely income-based measures.

The index of occupation and education does not include any income variables. A high score indicates an area with a large number of higher skilled workers, rather than labourers, and a high proportion of people with tertiary qualifications, or undertaking tertiary level study. Because there is no income component in this index, it is a composite index least related to the concept of social class.

Table 4.6 provides an example of the summary SEIFA indices for the different Australian states. These tables are calculated at a postcode level and similar analysis could have been generated at other levels, such as collection districts or local government boundaries. Obviously, the Australian Capital Territory stands out as the area with highest advantage levels. Second to the Australian Capital Territory in the urban advantage index stands Western Australia. In the rural index, however, Victoria and Tasmania feature second and third, while Western Australia comes second-last. Obviously, close examination of SEIFA data can reveal many such trends, which would allow the marketer a better understanding of class variations in and between local areas.

TABLE 4.6 SEIFA summary area data for postcode level indices

State	Average	Quantile				
		10%	25%	50%	75%	90%
Index of relative socioeconomic disadvantage						
New South Wales	1001	919	962	1002	1040	1094
Victoria	1027	956	992	1032	1067	1099
Queensland	989	917	960	992	1022	1051
South Australia	994	905	952	994	1036	1094
Western Australia	992	907	964	1000	1031	1063
Tasmania	987	904	951	983	1031	1083
Northern Territory	931	829	862	967	990	1010
Australia Capital Territory	1071	983	1024	1088	1109	1136
Australia	**1003**	**923**	**966**	**1005**	**1045**	**1086**
Urban index of relative socioeconomic advantage						
New South Wales	998	923	949	975	1031	1119
Victoria	1003	930	958	987	1037	1113
Queensland	974	904	938	967	994	1058
South Australia	978	884	928	967	1016	1087
Western Australia	995	899	942	976	1046	1112

Continues

TABLE 4.6 SEIFA summary area data for postcode level indices *continued*

State		Quantile				
	Average	10%	25%	50%	75%	90%
Tasmania	957	886	929	948	1000	1047
Northern Territory	899	815	850	901	953	992
Australia Capital Territory	1073	904	1051	1065	1144	1171
Australia	**991**	**914**	**945**	**975**	**1027**	**1103**
Rural index of relative socioeconomic advantage						
New South Wales	1013	911	946	1004	1073	1132
Victoria	1033	928	963	1022	1095	1164
Queensland	997	890	919	978	1070	1131
South Australia	1008	902	938	984	1075	1155
Western Australia	978	884	913	949	1040	1123
Tasmania	1035	941	971	1027	1089	1162
Northern Territory	962	808	870	961	1009	1181
Australia Capital Territory	1107	909	961	1061	1247	1480
Australia	**1011**	**903**	**940**	**997**	**1076**	**1139**
Index of economic resources						
New South Wales	995	895	925	978	1047	1134
Victoria	991	910	936	973	1050	1093
Queensland	961	885	913	954	1000	1052
South Australia	952	867	893	935	1007	1080
Western Australia	966	897	919	950	1019	1072
Tasmania	942	860	901	935	980	1036
Northern Territory	933	792	867	949	1007	1039
Australia Capital Territory	1089	981	1024	1116	1141	1164
Australia	**977**	**889**	**919**	**962**	**1031**	**1092**
Index of education and occupation						
New South Wales	992	895	928	968	1049	1125
Victoria	998	918	949	984	1038	1106
Queensland	942	863	891	930	982	1039
South Australia	967	884	909	944	1014	1088
Western Australia	954	880	909	940	979	1057
Tasmania	950	853	896	934	992	1081
Northern Territory	994	894	951	989	1047	1082
Australia Capital Territory	1136	1056	1121	1134	1176	1197
Australia	**977**	**886**	**921**	**960**	**1024**	**1098**

Source: Ian Castles, *Socio-economic Indexes for Areas*, Cat. no. 2912.0, Australian Bureau of Statistics, Canberra, 1994, p. 7.

Such indices as SEIFA can be used for target-market selection, but they are complex to administer on surveys of customers, or potential customers. Also, as they are derived from census data, they are not even linked to the basic consumption data provided by the Australian Bureau of Statistics in the *Household Expenditure Survey*. These factors restrict their application, as it is difficult for the marketer to evaluate the success of the market-segmentation strategy.

Problems in social-class measurement

In spite of the many approaches used to measure and categorise social classes, there are a number of problems associated with the measurement of the concept. In fact, the variety of different approaches may be regarded as a good indicator of the difficulties. As one writer cautions, 'Social class is a conceptual tool and, lacking precise definition, is ultimately not susceptible to perfect measurement nor to absolute standards of validity in case placements'.[24] An analysis of the major research done on social-class measurement by marketers has found important shortcomings.[25] Following are a few of the problem areas:

1. When the ranking of social class is based simply upon an average of the person's position on several status dimensions, this ignores the inconsistencies that arise from an individual ranking high on one dimension (such as income) but low on another (such as education). Typically, the different components are given equal weighting and are treated as compensatory. Education may be a more important variable than income for ascribing class to a minister of the church, while income may be more important for the stockbroker.

2. A related issue is taking account of the diversity that exists within classes. That is, individuals, although in the same social class, may show considerable discrepancy in their ratings on the variables used to define the class. A good example of the problem is the place of farmers in the Elley-Irving scale. This inconsistency in strata variables, known as *status incongruency*, or *low status crystallisation*, presents difficulties not only in ranking individuals but also in understanding their behaviour.

3. A person's social class is generally assumed to be stable, and thus the effects of mobility are ignored. Even recalling that mobility is gradual, this may be especially important for companies such as banks, who have very long term relationships with customers and who wish to track that relationship over time.

4. It must be remembered that social classes are not discrete categories. Though individuals usually identify with the social class in which they are categorised, there are reference-group effects from other classes.

5. The social class of an entire family may be measured by examination of characteristics of only the wage-earner, thus ignoring characteristics of other family members.[26] Historically, social class for a household was determined on the basis of the occupation of the man as head of the

household. It is normal in the 1990s to measure both occupations for a couple, and to allocate on the basis of the higher grade. There can still be a difficulty in that one is choosing a single measure to represent a group of people in a household. Research has shown that households where the husband and wife are not in the same social class are less likely to share many duties around the home.[27] As this applies to childcare, and indoor and outdoor housework, it may well apply to purchasing decisions and shopping behaviour also, though research is required to substantiate this. Ideally, marketers should look at the social class of both partners when relating it to consumer behaviour.

6. The choice of simpler measures to denote class, in particular occupation, is also fraught with difficulties, and more so since our societies have developed a level of 'structural' unemployment. This not only makes the classification of individuals into strata more difficult but, if it persists from generation to generation as it has in the United Kingdom, fundamentally alters the nature of the class system and requires a different process of measurement to be adopted.

Resolution of these and other problems would make the concept of social class a more useful one for marketers.[28]

PSYCHOLOGICAL DIFFERENCES IN SOCIAL CLASSES

Much of our understanding of the relationship between social class and consumer behaviour stems from the work of Pierre Martineau in the 1950s.[29] Martineau proposed that class differences were reflected in psychological variations in decision making and consumption; hence, social class had more to offer in explaining behaviour than simple associations with income.

TABLE 4.7 Psychological differences between middle and lower class consumers

Middle class	Lower class
1. Pointed to the future	1. Pointed to the present and past
2. Viewpoint embraces a long span of time	2. Lives and thinks in a short span of time
3. More urban identification	3. More rural identification
4. Stresses rationality	4. Essentially non-rational
5. Has a well-structured sense of the universe	5. Vague and unclear structuring of the world
6. Horizons vastly extended or not limited	6. Horizons sharply defined and limited
7. Greater sense of choice making	7. Limited sense of choice making
8. Self-confident, willing to take risks	8. Very much concerned with security
9. Immaterial and abstract in thinking	9. Concrete and perceptive in thinking
10. Concerned with national happenings	10. World revolves around family and body

Source: Pierre Martineau, 'Social Classes and Spending Behavior', *Journal of Marketing* 23, October 1958, pp. 126–7.

American research in the 1980s re-examining these differences found that they generally still held true.[30] The most marked change was the switch in rural/urban focus, with many more people in the middle class having a rural orientation. (In many ways this was the odd item out in Martineau's original list, as other differences have far more to do with 'styles of thinking'.) Reasoning, choice making and the interpretation of events were all shown to be different between the classes, and still supported ideas about more rational, structured thinking styles in the middle classes as opposed to more emotional and limited approaches in the lower classes. One interpretation is that these differences may be the consequence of different educational styles and levels of achievement. Such an interpretation offers further evidence to support the links drawn earlier between education, income and occupation.

As well as these psychological differences, social class has also been shown to be related to attitudinal differences towards aspects of society such as education, law and order, women's liberation and politics. One important attitudinal difference for consumer behaviour is in spending. Without being extravagant, the lower classes are seen as readier to spend money and to emphasise cheapness in their buying. The middle classes, though occasionally they will spend a lot, watch their money more carefully and place less emphasis on cheapness.[31] Table 4.8 shows attitudinal differences between social classes in New Zealand. The categories—

TABLE 4.8 Attitudinal differences among social classes in New Zealand consumers

Upper classes:
- feel less alienated in society than middle and lower classes
- are more likely to regard themselves as leaders
- are less conservative
- are more ambitious
- feel less attracted to simplicity and more drawn to sophistication
- attach a higher importance to education
- attach less importance to children's obedience

Middle classes:
- are less concerned with appearance and fashion than upper and lower classes

Lower classes:
- are less career minded than middle and upper classes
- are more likely to be 'do-it-yourselfers'
- are more interested in local community events than national or international events
- exhibit more traditional attitudes towards roles within the family

Source: Extracted from R. W. Lawson, G. Mueller-Heumann, A. Rummel & B. Fiegler, *New Zealand into the 1990s: A Study of Consumer Lifestyles*, Department of Marketing, University of Otago, Dunedin, 1989.

upper, middle and lower—are each based on two of the Elley-Irving classes. The comparisons summarise important ways in which one of the groups differs from the other two. It is important to realise that there is not necessarily a simple linear relationship between social class and attitudes and behaviours. In most of these patterns there is no difference between the middle classes (i.e. numbers 3 and 4 in the Elley-Irving scale, the clerical and skilled groups) and either of the other two. In general terms, it is obvious that these findings show trends that are consistent with Martineau's propositions—the upper classes are shown as more outgoing and confident, while the lower classes are more focused on the shorter term (e.g. less career minded) and the local community. The differences concerning the family-role orientation are also consistent with other international findings. The lower classes had significantly different views, which emphasised that father should be the 'boss'; that the woman's 'place' was at home; and that children were the most important feature of family life.

Symbols of status

From the discussion of McCracken's work on culture in the last chapter, it is evident that people buy products for what the products mean as well as what they can do.[32] That is, products and services are seen to have personal and social meanings in addition to their purely functional purpose. This is an important notion in the context of social class, as the range of goods an individual possesses becomes an important method of displaying wealth and claiming the appropriate status in social hierarchy. Possessions, therefore, take the place of income as an indicator of status, as we are not likely to know how much others are paid. Consequently, there may be members of a society at each social-class level who seek to achieve a certain higher status by virtue of their possessions. It should be noted, however, that others at the same level may be content to save more and spend much less extravagantly. This idea was expressed long ago by Thorstein Veblen, who suggested that there is a tendency by some members of each social class to engage in *conspicuous consumption* while others spend more conservatively.[33] By 'conspicuous consumption', Veblen means consumers purchasing things that they do not really need so that others can see what they have done. The things consumers buy become 'symbols', telling others who they are and to which social class they belong. In Veblen's original portrayal, goods were seen as 'trickling down' from the upper classes through the different strata in society. Once they became commonplace among the status leaders, a new mode of expression would be adopted and the original products would be adopted by people in lower social classes.

In reality, the situation is far more complex than this and some products can only confer status within particular groups, such as among the young or among particular social classes or subcultures. Rather than 'trickle down', the term 'trickle across' is considered more appropriate, because diffusion often takes place across the strata in society. Each class level has its conspicuous consumers and its more conservative buyers. Illustrating the consumption differences between Upper Americans and Middle Americans, but of the same income level,

Coleman observes that the latter have a much greater frequency of ownership of motor boats, campers, utility trucks for sport or work, tractor lawn mowers, snow-blowers, remote-control televisions, backyard swimming pools, lakeside homes, late-model sports cars for their teenage college children, and large, expensive cars for themselves. In contrast, Upper Americans at the same income level spend a greater percentage of time and money on private club memberships, unique educational experiences for their kids, high-culture objects and events, and civic affairs. Their houses may be no more expensive but have the 'proper' address. Both groups are displaying their status using different sets of symbols.[34]

As we saw in our discussion of culture, a recent shift in values in Australia and New Zealand is the development of postmaterialism. One of the accepted consequences of this is that conspicuous consumption is viewed by the really wealthy as déclassé. They appear to be shunning prestige items, frivolity, and a lavish display of wealth—this ostentation is for the nouveau riche—because it's not socially acceptable. Such 'stealth wealth' means some people don't want to show off; they are more apt to buy quality items that are quieter and that don't scream money, glamour and glitz.[35]

Marketers have always catered to consumers who were looking for something to give them an edge, whether real or imagined, over their peers. The key to status symbols is their scarcity and social desirability. As such, they are marks of distinction, setting their owners apart from others. This need for prestige—to be admired, praised, envied and acknowledged by others—is vital in humans. Marketers should recognise that the use of prestige appeal rests on the following assumptions:

➡ The need for prestige or self-esteem is universal.

➡ Prestige is related to and satisfied by product or service purchases.

➡ The manifestation and satisfaction of this need vary across cultures.

➡ A company's multinational success depends on communicating and embodying product prestige in a way that is culturally appropriate for target segments.

The effectiveness of a product or service prestige appeal is conditioned on the basis of five factors:

1. It is relatively expensive—you are one of the select few who can afford it.

2. It is of high quality—you made a wise purchase decision and have shown your good judgment and impeccable taste.

3. It is in limited supply—not everyone can obtain it.

4. Not everyone can qualify for it—only a select few meet the standards for ownership.

5. It is purchased by a respected and admired group of people—you will be associated with these people and worthy of respect and admiration.[36]

TABLE 4.9 Symbols of success and accomplishment in Australia

Symbol	Proportion regarding it as success symbol
	%
Travelling for pleasure frequently	52
Having a successful investment strategy	41
Having a million dollars	36
Being really knowledgable about current affairs	34
Owning an expensive car	32
Giving large contributions to charity	27
Staying at a deluxe hotel	22
Wearing clothes made by a famous designer	19
Shopping at prestige stores	17
Owning expensive jewellery	16
Having the home professionally decorated	15
Having live-in help	14
Having a prestige or 'gold' card	10
Having a car phone	9
Drinking expensive wine	6

Source: Adapted from Paul Leinberger, 'Clued up on the Intelligent Consumer', *Australian Professional Marketing,* February 1993, p. 39.

BLURRING OF SYMBOLISM

At one time class differences in status and its symbols were an accepted fact of life in clothing, housing and furnishings, food, drink, speech and even religious affiliation. Today, however, views of status symbols are changing. Rapid advances in technology and communications have spread the desire for and availability of these material pleasures through all social classes. And as Australians and New Zealanders have become more affluent even those with moderate incomes are able to own their own homes, colour televisions, boats and all sorts of home appliances, and to take overseas vacations. Consequently, if 'perfectly ordinary' people can display expensive cars and fancy appliances, these things obviously have lost much of their effectiveness as status symbols.

One author notes that the luxury-goods market is being supported by middle-class people with up-market tastes. Although luxury-goods marketers attempt to create the impression that only millionaires buy their products, it is the 'pseudo-affluents'—those in the $40 000–$80 000 income range—who are purchasing these up-market indulgences. The genuinely affluent actually have many of the ordinary person's consumption habits. They view many of the luxury goods as toys for people who have not had very much financial success, and they are repulsed by their behaviour.[37]

Such a situation usually results in new symbols being adopted by higher social classes. Research in Australia in 1992 revealed an interesting list of consumption symbols that people associate with success and accomplishment, and this list is partly represented in Table 4.9.

The list emphasises the diversity of consumption symbols across Australian society and the potential difficulty in linking particular status symbols to social classes.

SOCIAL CLASS AND CONSUMER BEHAVIOUR

This section examines the most significant findings concerning the behaviour of various classes with regard to the products they buy, the places they shop, the promotions they respond to, the media they use, and their price-related behaviour.[38]

Products and services consumed

Product choice and usage differ among the social classes. A Finnish study showed that the product areas where social class explained most differences in the amount of money spent by consumers were tobacco (37 per cent of variance), clothing (42 per cent), cultural items (60 per cent) and tourism (22 per cent).[39] These appear to be typical findings for these product classes. For example, smoking is known internationally as a very class related consumption habit. Australian figures for 1989–90 show that it is highest among the unemployed (44 per cent), declining steadily as status rises, so only 17 per cent of professionals smoke.[40] There are items that are bought mainly by the upper classes, such as original paintings or etchings and exotic vacations, and others that are purchased mainly by lower classes, such as tools to complete their own car repairs. Over half the people who work regularly on their own cars come from the lower two socio-economic classes. However, the variations in buyer behaviour by social class are often much more subtle than this.

Table 4.10 gives a summary of ownership in 1989 for selected products in New Zealand. As we would expect, most of the figures show how the upper classes have higher levels of ownership, which is consistent with generally higher levels of income, and a less cautious approach to shopping, which means faster adoption of new products. One of the largest differences in the table relates to video cameras, which at that time were a relatively new-to-market product, adopted by only 5 per cent of the population. Obviously, at a *product-class* level, social class differences tend to disappear as the product becomes established and diffuses through the population. Other interesting variations in the table are the knitter/overlocker statistics, which accord with the do-it-yourself attitude expressed

The Wedgwood ad is a direct appeal to upper-class Australian and New Zealand lifestyles COURTESY OF WATERFORD WEDGWOOD AUSTRALIA LIMITED

by the lower classes; the superannuation funds, and the figures for caravans and yachts. Access to superannuation funds is evidently linked to occupations, but it is also consistent with the perspectives on time horizons discussed earlier. There are at least two contrasting explanations for why the lower classes may be prepared to invest more money on yachts and caravans than the middle classes. It may be that both are regarded as status symbols within the lower classes. Or a more traditional economic argument may be that the *opportunity* cost is fairly low in contrast to other forms of vacations. That is, the cost of alternative forms of holidays is greater than that of acquiring the boat or the caravan.

TABLE 4.10 Differences in product ownership by social class[a]

Product	Upper	Middle	Lower
Superannuation membership	123.7	107.0	52.8
Medical insurance	124.9	96.8	73.7
CD player	111.4	98.4	89.7
VCR	109.0	100.0	90.3
Second television	108.0	105.8	86.3
Video camera	152.3	109.1	38.6
Knitting machine and overlocker	90.9	101.0	109.6
Microwave oven	114.4	101.1	83.8
Dishwasher	133.0	89.5	73.3
Yacht or boat	118.6	78.4	97.9
Caravan	110.2	88.6	97.7

(a) Figures are indices based on a score of 100 for the total population.

Source: Extracted from R. W. Lawson, G. Mueller-Heumann, A. Rummel & B. Fiegler, New Zealand into the 1990s: A Study of Consumer Lifestyles, Department of Marketing, University of Otago, Dunedin, 1989.

In many other cases it is more appropriate to look at the proportion of a product or service consumed by different social classes rather than the number of people in each class who will be consumers of the product, because the frequency of use varies by social class. This approach is very important to marketers because it indicates to them where most value is likely to rest within the market, and sometimes it can be used effectively to help with volume segmentation strategies, which were outlined in Chapter 2. For example, in New Zealand the proportion of people who never play golf does not vary significantly between upper, middle and lower social classes (all between 76 and 82 per cent). However, among those who do play, the upper classes are twice as likely to play more than once a fortnight as the lower classes. The same basic trends exist with other recreational behaviours, such as attending gymnasiums, going fishing and camping, and playing sports such as bowls, squash, tennis and badminton. With betting on horse racing the example is reversed. Again, three-quarters of the population never bet, irrespective of social class. However, the more frequent gamblers, who bet more than once a week, are twice as likely to be from the lower classes.

Other products and services display different variations on frequency of use. For example, only 4 per cent of upper classes never visit a restaurant, but this figure rises to 12 per cent for middle classes and 20 per cent for lower classes. The proportion of heavy users, who visit restaurants more than once a fortnight, shows the reverse trend—35 per cent of upper classes, 27.5 per cent of middle classes and 20 per cent of lower classes. In between the heavy users and the non-users there is exactly the same proportion (60 per cent) of light users in each social class grouping. Similar trends occur for other entertainments such as attending the cinema and going to parties. Attempts to orientate marketing programs to heavy users may need to take into account social-class variations, but attempts to stimulate consumption among light users may need to ignore class effects and have message appeals that are more broadly based.

Book purchasing and library usage show a different pattern again. Here the proportion of heavy users does not vary by social class. Survey results show that 30 per cent of adult New Zealanders buy at least one book a fortnight, irrespective of their social class. There may, of course, be differences in the types and value of books purchased. However, only 13 per cent of upper classes had not bought within the preceding 12 months, rising to 18 per cent of middle classes and 28 per cent of lower classes. In this case, targeting regular buyers should embrace all social classes, but class considerations may be very relevant in deciding upon a strategy to increase consumption among light purchasers, or to move non-users to light buyers.

However, many products are purchased by a wide variety of consumers and so it becomes difficult to distinguish class differences in purchasing patterns. For example, all people purchase food, clothing and shelter items. Social-class differences come into view when we examine not just generic categories but types of products and particular brands purchased. Some illustrations of this relating to the media and credit cards are given in tables in the following sections, which look at shopping behaviour and promotional response patterns.

Shopping behaviour

Shopping behaviour also varies by social class. The following excerpt gives an Australian description:

> The design of shops and their use of space, as well as their location within the shopping complex, provide evidence that class differences do exist and are of commercial importance. The key opposition here is that between democracy or 'cheapness', on the one hand, and exclusiveness or 'money is no object', on the other. Centrepoint (Roselands) provides a clear example of this opposition at work. While the 'democratic' shops tend not to stress their own identity, and the 'middle-class' shops identify themselves as different but still available to all, the 'upper-class' shops—such as those on the Gallery level in Centrepoint—are exclusive. The windows of the upper-class shops have fewer goods in them, signalling the opposite of mass availability; their lighting is more subdued, with highlights on the individual commodity; and the shop behind the window is much less easily seen. The contrast in lighting styles between middle- and upper-class shop windows is a contrast in class taste and social presence.[41]

These two stores provide very different environments for consumers who wish to match their social status to their store choice   COURTESY OF MYER GRACE BROS DEPARTMENT STORES AND LOWES MENSWEAR

Thus, where we are not dealing with low-priced goods with mass avail-ability, such as those at newsagents, card shops or chemists, shoppers gener-ally have some idea of the social–status ranking of the store and will tend not to patronise those where they feel they do not 'fit', in a social-class sense.[42] The result is that the same products and brands may be purchased in different out-lets by members of different social classes.[43] American research has found a very close relation between store choice and social-class membership, indicating that it is wrong to assume that all consumers want to shop at glamorous, high-status stores. Instead, people realistically match their values and expectations with a shop's status and don't shop in retailers where they feel out of place.

Determining the 'social difference' between people and stores involves measuring the difference between a person's social class and the social class of a store's typical or stereotypical customers. In some research the social-distance measure has been related to the probability of frequenting stores. For example, the greater the social distance, the less likely a person is to shop at a given store. However, upper-class customers are less prone to shop at stores with lower-class stereotypes than lower-class customers are to shop at stores with upper-class stereotypes.[44] Therefore, an important function of retail promotion, including the advertising and store atmosphere, is to allow the shopper to make a social-class identification of stores.

In approaching the actual task of purchasing, the different social classes display a number of specific attitudinal differences that support the general psychological propositions discussed earlier. In particular, lower classes view themselves as:

➡ more cautious shoppers;

➡ less likely to try new and different products, particularly foods and restaurants;

➡ having higher levels of store loyalty;

➡ less confident in managing money;

➡ finding charge and credit cards more difficult to manage;

➡ less willing to adopt EFTPOS as a means of payment.[45]

One of the most important differences in shopping behaviour according to social class is in methods of payment and, in particular, in the use of plastic cards. Table 4.11 gives an indication of how card holdings vary by social class. Not only does the number of people in each class holding cards vary, but also Amex and Diners Club cards are clearly more associated with the upper classes, and the reader will recall that holding a gold card was one of the recognised status symbols listed early in the chapter. Furthermore, it is recognised that consumers from different social classes use bank credit cards for different purposes. Upper classes predominantly use them for convenience—that is, for money handling in place of cash—while lower classes use them as instalment credit. Such understandings are very important for the marketing strategies of both retailers and banks. It affects the nature of the credit service and its pricing in terms of fees or interest charges, as well as the kind of promotional appeals that it may be helpful to incorporate for each social group in a bank's or retailer's advertising of its credit plans.[46]

TABLE 4.11   Differences in credit card holdings by social class[a]

Credit card	Upper	Middle	Lower
Retail store cards	115.2	102.9	81.6
Visa, Mastercard or Bankcard	126.9	96.8	73.7
American Express or Diners Club	183.3	59.5	40.4

(a) Figures are indices based on a score of 100 for the total population.
Source: Extracted from R. W. Lawson, G. Mueller-Heumann, A. Rummel & B. Fiegler, *New Zealand into the 1990s: A Study of Consumer Lifestyles,* Department of Marketing, University of Otago, Dunedin, 1989.

Promotional response patterns

Important class differences exist with regard to promotional response. Social classes in Australia and New Zealand have differing media choice and usage patterns. Tables 4.12(a) and 4.12(b) give examples of differing magazine readership patterns by social classes and show how some magazines are generalist in appeal but others are strongly weighted to particular classes. Despite the different measures presented in the tables, some evidence of commonality between Australia and New Zealand can be gleaned from the similarity in profiles for magazines such as *Time, Reader's Digest* and the *Australian Woman's Weekly. Time* is strongest in the upper socioeconomic groups, *Reader's Digest* in the middle classes, while the *Australian Woman's Weekly* is spread across all classes, but slightly less well established in the upper groups.

TABLE 4.12(a)   Profiles of magazine readership in Australia by social class/quintiles[a]

General readers	AB	C	D	E	FG
Proportion of population	20.3%	19.1%	20.3%	20.4%	19.8%
	%	%	%	%	%
TV Week	13.3	19.5	23.5	22.7	20.9
Reader's Digest	19.8	20.5	20.7	19.9	19.1
Who Weekly	24.0	26.6	23.2	16.4	9.8
Simply Living	27.8	23.7	20.1	20.0	8.4
HQ	42.1	27.0	15.4	11.0	4.5
House & Garden	26.6	20.7	22.1	16.6	14.1
Belle	43.5	23.9	15.3	8.3	9.0
Time	44.9	24.1	13.9	10.7	6.5
Business Review Weekly	60.6	20.2	9.3	8.1	1.9
The Australian[b]	57.0	21.1	10.8	7.8	3.3

Continues

TABLE 4.12(a) Profiles of magazine readership in Australia by social class/quintiles[a] continued

Female Readers	AB	C	D	E	FG
Proportion of population	17.2%	19.1%	20.6%	21.8%	21.3%
	%	%	%	%	%
Australian Woman's Weekly	15.8	19.3	22.4	21.8	20.8
New Idea	12.4	18.9	21.8	22.6	24.3
Who Weekly	21.8	27.2	24.2	16.9	9.9
New Woman	27.6	24.4	20.2	17.3	10.5
Dolly	8.9	16.4	24.8	26.8	23.1
Girlfriend	9.1	14.6	24.2	27.3	24.6
Star	7.4	12.0	18.5	29.0	33.2
Mode	32.8	26.4	17.9	15.6	7.4
Vogue Australia	26.3	27.3	21.2	14.6	10.6
Male Readers	AB	C	D	E	FG
Proportion of population	23.6%	19.2%	19.9%	19.0%	18.4%
	%	%	%	%	%
People	8.9	16.4	27.3	26.7	20.6
Playboy	18.6	20.0	20.5	21.7	19.1
Street Machine	6.5	15.1	24.5	27.8	26.1
Rugby League Week	15.7	19.4	23.1	19.6	22.3
Bush Driver	22.3	18.9	22.7	21.5	14.7
Inside Sport	29.3	26.4	20.5	16.2	7.6

(a) Socioeconomic status groupings are based on a composite measure derived from education, income and occupation, which is divided into quintiles to produce five broad strata.
(b) Monday to Friday
Reprinted with permission from *Morgan Readership Survey: April 1994–March 1995*, The Roy Morgan Research Centre, Sydney.

The social classes also have different perceptions and responses to advertising and other promotional messages, responses that are significant in the development of proper marketing strategies. The basis of advertising differences directed at the various classes should be founded on the differing communication skills and interests of these groups. For example, advertising using surreal images and obscure puzzle meanings may be almost meaningless to lower-class people, who are unfamiliar with the subtle humour and baffled by the bizarre art. This certainly does not imply that they lack intelligence or wit, but merely that their communication skills or experiences have been oriented in a different way. Thus, their symbol systems are different, and they have a quite different approach to humour.[47]

TABLE 4.12(b) Profiles of magazine readership in New Zealand by social class[a]

Magazine	Upper	Middle	Lower
Listener	120.7	98.9	79.1
New Zealand Woman's Weekly	79.5	102.7	119.7
Time	128.0	94.5	76.8
TV Guide	68.0	106.6	128.7
Woman's Day	84.0	105.7	111.4
Reader's Digest	79.1	115.4	110.4
Metro	152.9	86.5	53.8
More	125.6	119.7	57.2
North and South	148.6	88.8	56.1
Australian Woman's Weekly	92.8	110.0	100.0

(a) Figures are indices based on a score of 100 for the total population.
Source: Extracted from R. W. Lawson, G. Mueller-Heumann, A. Rummel & B. Fiegler, *New Zealand into the 1990s: A Study of Consumer Lifestyles,* Department of Marketing, University of Otago, Dunedin, 1989.

In addition, certain voice and speech patterns may be more influential than others for specific consumer segments. Thus, speakers with 'upper-class' voices and speech patterns can appear more credible to higher classes than 'low-status' sounding speakers. In Australia and New Zealand this may mean importing people, particularly from the United Kingdom, for voice-overs in commercials. In Great Britain there are stronger speech differences associated with social class, and the use of actors such as Sir John Gielgud can clearly communicate an upper-class association for certain wines compared with a working-class Cockney accent used, for example, to promote paints and wallpapers.

Price-related behaviour

Research on price variables is extremely limited and most of what exists relates to specific studies of poor and disadvantaged groups, for example, the homeless. Research on consumers' knowledge of prices has not been successful in explaining variations between individuals, but some studies have shown that lower-class consumers may be more poorly informed about price and product alternatives.[48] In some respects this finding is contrary to the general assumption that lower classes are also more likely to buy products that are on 'special' or priced lower.[49] Many studies have found no correlation between social class and price awareness, and the conflicting signals from the results indicate a need for more research to develop a better understanding of price-related behaviour.[50]

Regarding price perceptions among the middle and working classes, an American shopping simulation showed that working-class home-makers have a greater reliance on the general belief that there is a price/quality association; that is, the higher the price of a product, the higher the quality. They perceive that they have an inability to discriminate between products, and are therefore forced to fall back on a general belief in order to handle the problem of which product to buy. Although the better educated homemakers in both classes held stronger beliefs that price and quality are related, they preferred lower priced product alternatives. They apparently felt capable of judging the product alternatives on their own merits rather than having to rely on general beliefs in price/quality to make a decision.[51] These findings emphasise the impact of education on class differences in behaviour and reflect differences in confidence between the classes.

THE ROLE OF SOCIAL CLASS IN SEGMENTING MARKETS

It is evident that the concept of social class should help us to understand better the behaviour of the various market segments. However, the marketing practitioner wants to know if segmentation on the basis of social class is an advantageous approach compared with other options. As described, there are many different measures that can be used for social class, and it is worthwhile substantiating that social class has more to offer in segmenting markets than other, more readily obtained and conceptually easier information, such as income.

Several American studies have addressed this issue and found contrasting results. It should be remembered that it is standard to use a composite measure of social class in the United States and not substitute a grade based solely on occupation as a proxy variable. In one major study researchers correlated more than 200 lifestyle items with both social class and income.[52] They found that, although most of the correlations were fairly low, the correlations obtained for social class were generally higher than those obtained for income. Additionally, items relating to culture and social interaction showed much higher correlations, suggesting that social class is a much better predictor in these areas. Cultural activities (such as concerts, ballet and bridge games) are available to people of almost any income level. The fact that some people choose to engage in them and others do not is one of the things that makes social class a meaningful concept. Social-interaction items (such as confidence, gregariousness and attractiveness) may result from upper-class people feeling a sense of belonging and recognition from having a secure place higher up in the social structure. However, consistent with the Australasian attitudinal differences described earlier, upper-social-class people also seem to have less interest in the home in general, and in children in particular, than do upper-income/lower-class individuals.

Other research has not shown this general tendency for social class to outperform income. One study showed that for a number of low-priced consumer packaged goods, both income and social class were found to correlate with buying behaviour. However, product usage generally proved to be more closely related to income than to social class.[53] A follow-up study, which included certain durable-goods items plus a few services, confirmed the earlier study by showing income to be superior to social class in segmenting the market for nearly all items.[54] This emphasises that many products appear to be classless in their appeal. For example, in the hotter parts of Australia, income, not social class, largely determines whether a family buys air-conditioning. If the family can afford to purchase air-conditioning, it does so.

One point that should be made very clear is that most of these studies comparing income and social class have based their findings on *use* or *non-use* of a product or service, rather than on *how often* that product or service was used. As we saw previously with the New Zealand data, social class showed more association with frequency of usage for some items rather than simple usage/non-usage. An American study looking at leisure and entertainment consumption confirms this conclusion. This research showed that income and stage in the life cycle were more highly related to *use* of all the entertainment activities than were age and social class. However, all four variables—especially social class—showed strong associations with the *frequency of use* of entertainment activities.[55] More research is needed on a broad variety of products before a generalisation of this finding is made.

Based on one thorough research study, the following tentative generalisations are possible regarding when social class or income, or a combination, is superior as a segmentation variable:[56]

1. Social class is superior to income for areas of consumer behaviour that do not involve high-dollar expenditures, but do reflect underlying lifestyle, value or home-maker role differences. Relevant products in this situation might include instant, frozen and canned convenience foods and beverages; snack foods; and wines. Social class is also superior for both method and place of purchase of highly visible, symbolic and expensive items such as living-room furniture.

2. Income is generally superior for products that require substantial expenditures, and which may no longer serve as symbols of status within a class or as status symbols to the upper-lower class (such as major kitchen and laundry appliances).

3. The combination of social class and income is generally superior for product classes that are highly visible, serve as symbols of social class or status within class, and require either moderate or substantial expenditure (such as clothing and make-up, automobiles and television sets).

Before attempting to use social class to segment markets, the marketer should remember three guidelines:

1. Social class may not always be a relevant consideration; that is, segmentation by other criteria, such as age and gender, is frequently more appropriate.

2. Benefits from social-class segmentation for undifferentiated products may be less than the costs incurred to achieve such segmentation.

3. Social-class segmentation is frequently most effective when used in conjunction with such additional variables as life-cycle stage and ethnic group.[57]

However, even for cases in which social class may have only limited application, it does provide the marketer with helpful insights—some of which may be specifically used in developing marketing strategies, and others of which at least offer an improved general understanding of consumer behaviour.[58]

SUMMARY

This chapter discussed the major implications of social class for consumer behaviour. We defined the concept of stratification and explained the nature of social class, including the bases on which it may be measured.

We learned that working with social class, while offering potential, is fraught with difficulties and limitations in its current stage of evolution. Nevertheless, we described much of what is presently known about reactions to products, promotions, shopping and prices among the different social classes.

A final subject of this discussion was the role of social class in market segmentation, and some comparisons of its performance with income as an alternative variable. The studies reviewed in this section showed mixed results for the employment of social class. There are at least two explanations for this.[59] First, it would clearly be wrong to expect every facet of consumers' lifestyles to be associated with social class. Also, there have been dramatic changes that have taken place in our societies' economic, social and cultural climates. For example, the universal exposure of all social classes to mass media and advertising may have diminished the differences in consumer behaviour between the classes.

MANAGERIAL REFLECTIONS

For our product or service situation:

1. What is the predominant social class of buyers?

2. Is there an important symbolism affecting its purchase?

3. What are the demographic and socioeconomic characteristics within social-class segments chosen as target markets?

4. How may the lifestyle of our social-class market be described?

5. Is social class a useful way to segment buyers?

6. What patterns are exhibited by target social-class segments with regard to product choice, shopping behaviour, and promotion and price responsiveness?

7. To what extent are social-class differences disappearing among our market segments?

DISCUSSION TOPICS

1. What is meant by the term 'social stratification'?

2. Discuss the use of social class as a market-segmentation approach.

3. Select one of the social-class categories and prepare a report on its lifestyle.

4. Find at least two manufacturers' ads for the same generic product (such as clothing) that you think are aimed at different social classes. Explain the differences in the ads.

5. Find three newspaper advertisements by local retailers that you think reach the different social classes. Explain the differences in the ads.

6. Classify the major department stores in your area according to your estimation of the social class of their customers. How do the marketing features of these stores differ?

7. Choose two sections of your town or city: one where residents are professional and business people and one where residents are mostly working class. How do the housing values differ? Does the appearance, architecture or decoration of homes differ? Are there stores in each area that differ in terms of merchandise and promotional policies?

8. Bring to class copies of magazines that were described in the chapter as appealing to certain social classes. Discuss their differences and similarities.

9. Are social-class differences diminishing? Prepare a report supporting your position.

REFERENCES

1. J. A. Froude, *Oceana: or England and Her Colonies*, London, 1886.
2. Anthony Giddens, *Sociology*, Polity Press, London, 1990, p. 206.
3. Hugh Mackay, *The Mackay Report on Class and Status*, Mackay Research, Sydney, 1986.
4. Giddens, op cit, Ref 2, pp. 207–10.
5. J. H. Baxter, P. R. Boreham, S. R. Clegg, J. M. Emmison, D. M. Gibson, G. N. Marks, J. S. Western & M. C. Western, 'The Australian Class Structure: Some Preliminary Results from the Australian Class Project', *Australian and New Zealand Journal of Sociology* 25(1), 1989, pp. 100–19.
6. Mackay, *The Mackay Report on Class and Status*; and Richard P. Coleman & Lee Rainwater, *Social Standing in America: New Dimensions of Class*, Basic Books, Inc., New York, 1978, p. 29.
7. Jake M. Najman, 'The Measurement of Socioeconomic Inequality and Social Class in Australia: A Review of Past Practices and Recent Developments', *Community Health Studies* 12(1), 1988, pp. 31–41.
8. Ian Castles, *Socio-economic Indexes for Areas*, Cat. no. 2912.0, Australian Bureau of Statistics, Canberra, 1994.
9. Baxter et al., op cit, Ref 5, pp. 100–19.
10. F. L. Jones, 'Stratification Approaches to Class Measurement', *Australian and New Zealand Journal of Sociology* 24, July 1988, pp. 279–84.
11. R. A. Omodei, 'Beyond the Neo-Weberian Concept of Status', *Australian and New Zealand Journal of Sociology* 18(2), 1982, pp. 196–213; and James E. Fisher, 'Social Class and Consumer Behavior: The Relevance of Class and Status', in Melanie Wallendorf & Paul Anderson (eds), *Advances in Consumer Research*, vol. 14, Association for Consumer Research, Provo, UT, 1987, pp. 492–96.
12. Fisher, op cit, Ref 11, pp. 492–6.
13. Timo Toivonen, 'The Melting Away of Class Differences? The Consumption Differences between Employee Groups in Finland 1955–1985', *Social Indicators Research* 26, 1992, pp. 277–302.
14. Robert C. Yeager, 'Caught in the Middle—I', *Across the Board*, November 1980, p. 24.
15. Francis Buttle, *The Elley-Irving Socio-economic Indices: Practical Problems in Their Use*, Research Report no. 6, Market Research Centre, Massey University, 1980, pp. 2–7.
16. A. F. Osborn & T. C. Morris, 'The Rationale for a Composite Index of Social Class and Its Evaluation', *British Journal of Sociology* 30 (1), 1979, pp. 39–60.
17. Najman, *Community Health Studies*, pp. 31–41; and G. R. Foxall, *Consumer Behaviour: A Practical Guide*, Croom Helm, London, 1982.
18. Ian Castles, *A Guide to Major ABS Classifications*, Australian Bureau of Statistics, Canberra, 1991, pp. 19–21.
19. J. M. Najman & M. Bampton, 'An ASCO-based Occupational Status Hierarchy for Australia: A Research Note', *Australian and New Zealand Journal of Sociology* 27 (2), 1991, pp. 218–31.
20. Buttle, *The Elley-Irving Socio-economic Indices: Practical Problems in Their Use*; and R. Johnston, *A Revision of Socio-economic Indices for New Zealand*, New Zealand Council for Educational Research, Wellington, 1983.
21. W. B. Elley & J. C. Irving, 'The Elley-Irving Socio-economic Index 1981 Census Revision', *New Zealand Journal of Educational Studies* 20 (2), 1985, pp. 115–28.
22. F. L. Jones, 'Occupational Prestige in Australia: A New Scale', *Australian and New Zealand Journal of Sociology* 25 (2), August 1989, pp. 187–99.
23. Castles, op cit, Ref 8.
24. Richard P. Coleman, 'The Continuing Significance of Social Class to Marketing', *Journal of Consumer Research* 10, December 1983, p. 276.

25. Luis V. Dominguez & Albert L. Page, 'Use and Misuse of Social Stratification in Consumer Behavior Research', *Journal of Business Research* 9, 1981, pp. 151–73.
26. Marie R. Haug, 'Social Class Measurement and Women's Occupational Roles', *Social Forces* 52, 1973, pp. 86–93.
27. J. H. Baxter, 'Gender and Class Analysis: The Position of Women in the Class Structure', *Australian and New Zealand Journal of Sociology* 24 (1), 1988, pp. 106–23.
28. See Terence A. Shimp & J. Thomas Yokum, 'Extensions of the Basic Social Class Model Employed in Consumer Research', in Kent B. Monroe (ed.), *Advances in Consumer Research*, vol. 8, Association for Consumer Research, Ann Arbor, MI, 1981, pp. 702–7; and Dominguez & Page, *Journal of Business Research*, pp. 151–73, for suggestions to overcome some of these problems.
29. Pierre Martineau, 'Social Classes and Spending Behavior', *Journal of Marketing* 23, October 1958, pp. 126–7.
30. Donald W. Hendon, Emelda L. Williams & Douglas E. Huffman, 'Social Class System Revisited', *Journal of Business Research* 17 (3), 1988, pp. 259–70.
31. Hendon et al., ibid, pp. 259–70.
32. Grant McCracken, 'Culture and Consumption: A Theoretical Account of the Structure and Movement of the Cultural Meaning of Consumer Goods', *Journal of Consumer Research* 13, June 1986, pp. 71–84.
33. Thorstein Veblen, *The Theory of the Leisure Class*, Macmillan, New York, 1899.
34. Coleman, op cit, Ref 24, p. 274.
35. Michelle Osborn, 'Conspicuous Consumption Is Déclassé', *USA Today*, 29 November 1991, pp. 1A–2A.
36. Richard T. Garfein, 'Cross-cultural Perspectives on the Dynamics of Prestige', *Journal of Services Marketing* 3, Summer 1989, pp. 18–19.
37. Cyndee Miller, 'Author Says Middle Class Buys Most Luxury Goods', *Marketing News*, 18 February 1991, p. 6.
38. Many conclusions in this section are drawn from data collected for the following lifestyle survey: R. W. Lawson, G. Mueller-Heumann, A. Rummel & B. Fiegler, *New Zealand into the 1990s: A Study of Consumer Lifestyles*, Department of Marketing, University of Otago, 1989.
39. Toivonen, op cit, Ref 13, p. 293.
40. Ian Castles, *Australian Social Trends*, Cat no. 4102.0, Australian Bureau of Statistics, Canberra, 1994, p. 62.
41. Adapted from John Fiske, Bob Hodge & Graeme Turner, *The Myths of Oz: Reading Australian Popular Culture*, Allen & Unwin, Sydney, 1987, pp. 107–9.
42. Martineau, op cit, Ref 29, pp. 126–7.
43. Sidney J. Levy, 'Social Class and Consumer Behavior', in Joseph W. Newman (ed.), *On Knowing the Consumer*, Wiley, New York, 1966, p. 153.
44. Douglas L. MacLachlan & John P. Dickson, 'Do People Avoid Some Stores Because of "Social Distance"?', *Channel of Communication*, Winter 1990, pp. 5–6.
45. Lawson et al., op cit, Ref 38.
46. H. Lee Mathews & John W. Slocum Jr, 'Social Class and Commercial Bank Credit Card Usage', *Journal of Marketing* 33, January 1969, pp. 71–8.
47. Martineau, op cit, Ref 29, p. 127.
48. Andrew Gabor & S. W. J. Granger, 'Price Sensitivity of the Consumer', *Journal of Advertising Research* 4, December 1964, pp. 40–4.
49. Frederick E. Webster Jr, 'The Deal-prone Consumer', *Journal of Marketing Research* 1, August 1964, pp. 32–5.
50. Rob Lawson, Juergen Gnoth & Kerry Paulin, 'Tourists' Awareness of Prices for Attractions and Activities', *Journal of Travel Research* 34 (1), 1995, pp. 3–10.
51. Joseph N. Fry & Frederick H. Siller, 'A Comparison of Housewife Decision Making in Two Social Classes', *Journal of Marketing Research* 7, August 1970, pp. 333–7.

52. James H. Myers & Jonathan Gutman, 'Life-style: The Essence of Social Class', in William D. Wells (ed.), *Life Style and Psychographics*, American Marketing Association, Chicago, 1974, p. 252.
53. James H. Myers, Roger R. Stanton & Arne F. Haug, 'Correlates of Buying Behavior: Social Class vs Income', *Journal of Marketing* 35, October 1971, pp. 8–15.
54. James H. Myers & John F. Mount, 'More on Social Class vs Income as Correlates of Buying Behavior', *Journal of Marketing* 37, April 1973, pp. 71–3.
55. Robert D. Hisrich & Michael P. Peters, 'Selecting the Superior Segmentation Correlate', *Journal of Marketing* 38, July 1974, pp. 60–3.
56. Charles M. Shaninger, 'Social Class versus Income Revisited: An Empirical Investigation', *Journal of Marketing Research* 18, May 1981, pp. 206–7.
57. Thomas S. Robertson, *Consumer Behavior*, Scott, Foresman, Glenview, IL, 1970, p. 129.
58. A. Marvin Roscoe, Arthur LeClaire & Leon Schiffman, 'Theory and Management Applications of Demographics in Buyer Behaviour', in Arch G. Woodside, Jagdish N. Sheth & Peter D. Bennett (eds), *Consumer and Industrial Buying Behaviour*, North Holland, New York, 1977, p. 75.
59. Ronald E. Frank, William F. Massy & Yoram Wind, *Market Segmentation*, Prentice-Hall, Englewood Cliffs, NJ, 1972, p. 49.

CHAPTER 5

SOCIAL GROUPS

LEARNING OBJECTIVES

AFTER STUDYING THIS CHAPTER YOU SHOULD UNDERSTAND:

➡ what is meant by the term 'social group', and how different group types may have relevance for consumer behaviour;

➡ the nature of status, roles, norms and socialisation properties exhibited by groups;

➡ how groups exert power over members' behaviour;

➡ how reference-group influence varies under differing conditions;

➡ the nature of reference-group influence on consumer behaviour.

As we continue to narrow our discussion of environmental variables this chapter examines ways in which groups affect consumer decision making. This is an important ingredient in the marketer's understanding of consumer behaviour. Our first task will be to define several group concepts essential to our discussion. Next we will examine the major characteristics of groups and group types. Finally, we shall discuss reference groups and their special relevance for the marketer in understanding consumer behaviour.

WHAT IS A GROUP?

Not every collection of individuals is a group, in the sense in which the term is used by sociologists. In fact, we can distinguish three different collections of people: aggregations, categories and groups. An *aggregation* is any number of people who are in close proximity to one another at a given time. A *category* is any number of people who have some particular attributes in common. A *group* consists of people who have a sense of relatedness as a result of interaction with each other.[1]

To illustrate these concepts, consider four people sitting on a bench at a university. They are an 'aggregation' as they are in close proximity. They may be a 'category' if they share some attribute such as all being undergraduates in commerce. They may also be a 'group' if they have a shared sense of relatedness through interaction; that is, if they are all friends or classmates in a consumer-behaviour course, for example.

Although our emphasis in this chapter is on groups, this does not mean that the marketer is not interested in aggregations and categories. These collections are frequently the focus for developing marketing strategies. For example, market segmentation typically does not involve social groups but instead uses categories such as people of similar ages or who have similar incomes.

CLASSIFICATION OF GROUPS

Groups may be classified according to a number of dimensions, including function, degree of personal involvement and degree of organisation.

Content or function

Most people view the content of groups in terms of their function. For example, we categorise them along such lines as students, factory workers, church members and so on. In fact, these are subtypes of the major kinds of groups that we encounter in a complex society, which could generally be categorised along such lines as family, ethnic, age, sex, political, religious, residential, occupational and educational.

Degree of personal involvement

By using this criterion, we can identify two different types of groups: primary and secondary. The hallmark of a *primary group* is that interpersonal relationships take place usually on a face-to-face basis, with great frequency and on an intimate level.[2] These groups have shared norms and interlocking roles. Families, work groups and even recreational groups (if individuals have some depth of personal involvement) are examples of such groups.

Secondary groups are those in which the relationship among members is relatively impersonal and formalised. This amounts to a residual category that includes all groups that are not primary, such as political parties, unions, occasional sports groups, and the Australian and New Zealand Marketing Institutes. Although such groups are secondary, the interpersonal relationships that occur may nevertheless be face-to-face. The distinction lies in the lack of intimacy of personal involvement.

This picture shows an informal primary group. The properties of this group will strongly influence the behaviour of the individual members, including what they choose to eat and drink, and how they dress   COURTESY OF NEW ZEALAND TOURISM BOARD

Degree of organisation

Groups range from those that are relatively unorganised to highly structured forms. We usually simplify this continuum into two types: formal and informal. *Formal groups* have a definite structure (e.g. they may have a president, vice-president, secretary and treasurer). They are likely to be secondary groups designed to accomplish specific goals, whether economic, social, political or altruistic. Rotary, the Rugby Football Union and the Labor Party are examples. *Informal groups* are typically primary groups, characterised by a relatively loose structure, a lack of clearly defined goals or objectives, unstructured interaction and unwritten rules. Because of the extent of their influence on individuals' values and activities, informal groups are probably of greater importance to us in seeking to understand consumer behaviour.

It should be evident from this discussion that the term 'group' is multifaceted and that groups have important influences on individuals, including on their activities as consumers. Primary informal groups have the greatest degree of impact on consumers and are therefore most important to marketers. From such groups consumers develop their product-consumption, shopping and media patterns. Consequently, these groups are generally most influential on consumers' buying behaviour. As a result, advertisers normally present their products within a primary-group setting, such as among friends, family or work groups.

Secondary informal groups probably are the next most influential to consumers and, therefore, are sometimes used in advertising efforts. For example, a new type of golf club, tennis racquet or snow ski may be featured in the appropriate friendly, competitive, but professional-looking surroundings, in which the product and user may be shown excelling and being rewarded with admiration. Primary and secondary formal groups are much less widely used by marketers because they have far less direct, intimate influence on consumer behaviour. In specialised situations, however, certain marketers may find them useful. For example, travel and insurance agents fairly commonly develop specific offerings for members of an organisation, such as state employees or university graduates. Sometimes the groups used are social ones, such as the bridge and bowling clubs used by National Insurance in New Zealand, because they tend to give the marketer access to more affluent older markets.

GROUP PROPERTIES

In order to understand the nature of groups better, we need to examine several other important concepts, including status, norms, role, socialisation and power, and their significance for consumer behaviour.

Status

Status refers to the achieved or ascribed position of an individual in a group or in society, and it consists of the rights and duties associated with that position. In Chapter 4, we referred to status in a hierarchical sense that related to prestige; however, this is only one of several different ways in which status may be classified. Status may also refer to some grouping on the basis of age or sex, family, occupation, and friendship or common interest.[3]

Norms

Norms were first introduced in our discussion of culture in Chapter 3. They are the rules and standards of conduct by which group members are expected to abide. For informal groups, norms are generally unwritten but are, nevertheless, usually quite well understood. For example, as a salesperson for a large business-machines company, you might be expected to live in a certain area of town, drive a certain type of car (perhaps a mid-sized Ford) and dress conservatively (such as in a navy-blue suit). Behaviour deviation outside these latitudes might result in slower advancement in the organisation. Thus, as employees or consumers, we often know what we can and cannot wear, drive, say and eat in order to be well accepted within the relevant group.

Role

This term is used to designate *all* of the behaviour patterns associated with a particular status. Role is the dynamic aspect of status and includes the attitudes, values and behaviour ascribed by the society to persons occupying this status. Roles not only refer to what we do, but are also strongly based on how others in society expect us to behave. Because the concept of role is such an all-embracing phenomenon, it is an extremely powerful tool with which to analyse behaviour. The social structure partially prescribes what sort of role behaviour is acceptable and thus what is expected. For instance, an upper-class husband who is a successful physician may feel that in his position he is expected to drive an expensive car, live in an exclusive neighbourhood, dress in fashionable clothes, attend the correct cultural activities and give generously to charities. Conversely, a lower-class husband who is an assembly-line worker may feel comfortable in a role in which he drives a utility truck, lives in rented housing, wears less fashionable clothes, and watches football in the pub while drinking jugs of beer with his friends.

Essentially, role theory recognises that one individual plays many different roles. This concept was expressed in a poetic way by Shakespeare in the following well-known passage:

> All the world's a stage,
> And all the men and women merely players:
> They have their exits and their entrances;
> And one man in his time plays many parts,
> His acts being seven ages.[4]

Not only does an individual, or consumer, enact many roles, but these roles may change over time, even during the course of a day. For example, a woman may have the role of wife, mother, employee, family financial officer, lover and Sunday school teacher, among others. Her behaviour in each of these roles will differ as she keeps 'switching hats', depending on her role at each moment.

Carrying the concept of playing a role further, Goffman suggests that the individual must not only learn lines (the group's special language), but also needs a costume (the group's accepted dress), props (the group's equipment or accoutrements), a set (where the group interacts), and a team or cast of players (the group members).[5]

Roles in groups (just as those in a play) are learned, but not every individual learns a given role in the same way.[6] Society allows some variation in role performance, but if too much latitude is taken, sanctions of some sort will be imposed. Thus, other people expect us to behave in a certain way and will reward conformity and punish nonconformity to those expectations.

Roles have a strong, pervasive influence on our activities as consumers. For example, other people have expectations regarding the products we buy to meet the needs of our roles. Just a few of the many consumption decisions directly affected include the places we shop, the clothes we wear, the cars we drive, the houses in which we live and the recreational activities in which we engage. Marketers, therefore, help individuals play their roles by providing the right costumes and props to be used in gaining acceptance by a particular group. It is the symbolic aspects of products that provide so much of the satisfaction that accrues from a product.

Because of the many roles we try to fulfil, whether at different times or simultaneously, we may develop *role conflict*, which means that two or more of our roles are incompatible with each other. The strain may often be evidenced in the behaviour of consumers. For example, many working women feel guilty about the compromises they see themselves making, particularly in the role of parent. The demands on a working mother's time may be more easily met by fixing the family quick and easy meals, particularly by using frozen TV dinners. However, in her role as a loving wife, mother and the family's gourmet cook, such product usage may be abhorrent to her and some resolution of this conflict will be necessary. A creative advertiser may suggest appeasement by showing her purchasing the company's prepared cooking sauces. Although easily prepared, when served with a meat or pasta base on the best dinner plates and garnished attractively, they resemble a gourmet meal.

Socialisation

Socialisation refers to the process by which a new member learns the system of values, norms and expected behaviour patterns of the group being entered. When new students arrive on a university campus, they soon learn from fellow students what is expected in the way of dress, eating patterns, class attendance and extracurricular activities. Residents new to a neighbourhood learn what patterns are expected in the group concerning home maintenance, lawns and landscaping, interior decoration and entertaining. Thus, individuals are continually engaging in the process of socialisation (although it is more intense at an early age) as they encounter new groups that have an impact on their lives. Consumer socialisation, therefore, is the process by which individuals acquire skills, knowledge and attitudes related to their effective functioning as consumers in the marketplace.[7] This is particularly relevant to young people and is an important dimension of family life. Consumer socialisation is also becoming increasingly formalised into school curricula as children complete studies on topics such as advertising and nutrition.

Power

Groups have power to influence their members' behaviour. Various sources of social power may operate in different social group situations, including reward power, coercive power, legitimate power, expert power and referent power.[8] Marketers also seek to use these forms of power to influence consumers, and power is an important component in understanding attitude-change strategies discussed later in the book.

REWARD POWER

This is based on the perception individuals have of others' ability to reward them. The strength of reward power increases with the size of the rewards an individual perceives another can administer. Rewards might include either tangible items such as money or gifts, or intangible things such as recognition or praise.

Social groups often have a great deal of reward power that they may dispense to their members. This 'carrot' approach can often result in the desired behaviour being exhibited by members. For example, Amway, which use direct-selling methods for their line of household products, make effective use of reward power in motivating their sales force. They hold large sales rallies where young salespeople, usually middle-class couples, watch a 20-minute colour film that features family scenes of successful Amway couples enjoying the fruits of their labours— swimming pools and cars.[9]

Marketers also use reward power directly and indirectly in order to influence consumers. Of course, they are able to reward consumers directly by providing high-quality products and services. In other situations marketers promise (implicitly, at least) the rewards of group acceptance, such as love, through use of a product. For example, advertising for Tegel chicken in New Zealand shows how group acceptance takes place through purchase and consumption of their product.[10]

COERCIVE POWER

This is the power to influence behaviour through the use of punishment or the withholding of rewards. Punishment, for our purpose, does not refer to the physical kind, but to more subtle psychological sanctions. For example, students may readily conform to the dress code of a particular group on campus and purchase the accepted clothing of this group in order not to be ridiculed by it. Commerce, drama, law and medical students are sometimes distinguished in this way by other students.

Marketers are also able to use coercive power effectively in certain situations. Inducing fear is one approach that may be taken by advertisers to some items such as life insurance, mouthwash, weight-reducing products and deodorants. Coercion occurs through showing the unfortunate consequences that could befall a consumer who fails to own or use such products. For example, the embarrassment of having 'onion breath' is brought to our attention by chewing-gum marketers.

Tupperware and other companies that sell products in social-group situations also make effective use of group coercive power. Group pressure may be strong because some people present at these sales parties tend to feel that if others are buying something they do not want to be embarrassed by not also making a purchase. They may feel that such an action would let the host and her friends down.[11]

LEGITIMATE POWER

This power stems from members' perception that the group has a legitimate right to influence them. We speak of such behaviours with expressions such as 'should' and 'ought to'. Many of these feelings have been internalised from parents, teachers and religious institutions. Thus, there is some sort of code or standard that the individual accepts and by virtue of which the group can assert its power. One small group in which legitimate power can be seen to operate is the family. Each member has a set of roles to carry out, which is legitimised by the other members.

Marketers are able to utilise this type of power in many situations by appealing to consumers' values. Appeals from charitable organisations such as Save the Children and Red Cross exert legitimate power, as do those for patriotic and nationalistic causes such as 'Buy Australian' or 'See New Zealand First'.

EXPERT POWER

This influence results from the expertise of the individual or group and is closely related to the discussion of opinion leadership and market mavens, or experts, in Chapter 7. Consumers regularly accept influence from those they perceive to have superior experiences, knowledge or skill. For instance, we may accept the recommendation of another person for a purchase we are about to make if we view that person as more knowledgeable than ourselves. Salespeople make effective use of this approach with their own product expertise.

Many advertisements use socially distant reference groups and rely on an expert's opinion about the product. For instance, Alison Holst is used for food and cooking appliances, Nigel Mansell promotes motor oils and Chris Amon advertises Toyota cars. Manufacturers may even 'create' experts when no one else seems suitable. For many years Colgate successfully used Mrs Marsh, a fictitious school teacher, to extol the virtues of good dental care (see photo). Another common practice is to create a 'generic' expert by using the appropriate uniform to create the impression of a doctor or scientist as an endorser for a product.

Information power, often related to expert power, stems from the 'logic', 'reasoning' or importance of the communication provided by the influencing agent.[12] Ads using information power may explain why the product is good, often citing available evidence such as price, quality of ingredients, performance and specifications.

REFERENT POWER

This influence flows from the feeling of identification an individual has with the group. As a consequence of this feeling of oneness, or desire for such an identity, the individual will wish to become a member or gain a closer association with the group. Identification with the group can be established or maintained if the individual behaves, believes or perceives as the group does. The stronger this identification with the group, the greater its referent power. In this chapter and in Chapter 7 we will look more closely at the use of referent power.

Advertisers often use referent power in promotions by encouraging consumers to be like or do the same thing as the individual advertising the brand. For instance, with many status-oriented products consumers are encouraged (either subtly or not so subtly) to obtain a similar status to that of the recommender by purchasing the item advertised. Colognes, clothing, cars and stereo equipment often use this approach. The use of celebrities is especially popular in these advertisements whereby consumers may aspire to have hair or skin like Rachel Hunter, for example. In other approaches, marketers may use slice-of-life commercials or testimonials from 'ordinary' consumers to show that other people experience the same problems and have found satisfaction with the recommended brand. The individual targeted by the advertisement may readily identify with that situation and be highly receptive to the brand.

Mrs Marsh was a powerful presenter for Colgate Fluoriguard for 13 years
COURTESY OF COLGATE-PALMOLIVE

REFERENCE GROUPS

Having discussed some important group concepts necessary for our interests, let us further examine the topic of reference-group influence.

Types of reference groups

Reference groups are used (that is, referred to) by individuals to determine their judgments, beliefs and behaviour. These groups may be of a number of types, as explained by the following classification system.[13]

MEMBERSHIP VERSUS NON-MEMBERSHIP

Membership groups are those to which the individual belongs. Membership in some groups is automatic by virtue of the consumer's age, sex, education and marital status. Before acting, consumers might consider whether purchase or use of a product would be consistent with their roles as members of one of these groups.

Non-membership groups are those to which the individual does not presently belong. Many of these groups are likely to be *anticipatory* or *aspirational* in nature; that is, they are groups to which the individual aspires to belong. Such aspirational groups can have a profound influence on non-members because of their strong desire to join the group. This pattern of behaviour is evident among upwardly mobile consumers who aspire to join higher status clubs and social groups.

POSITIVE VERSUS NEGATIVE

Reference groups can also be classified as to whether they attract or repel the individual. For instance, a *positive* reference group for the upwardly mobile consumer may be the 'country club crowd' in that city. There are *negative* groups, however, with which a person attempts to avoid being identified. For example, an individual who is trying to succeed as a new management trainee may attempt through speech, dress and mannerisms to back away from a lower-class background in order to have a greater chance of success in the job.

Reasons for accepting reference-group influence

Generally, consumers accept reference-group influence because of the perceived benefits in doing so. It has been suggested that the nature of social interactions between individuals will be determined by the individual's perception of the *profit* of the interaction. An interaction situation may result in *rewards* (such as friendship, information, satisfaction) but will also exact *costs* (lost time, money expended, alternative people and activities sacrificed). Individuals will attempt to maximise the difference between these rewards and costs; that is, the net profit from the social exchange. Thus, individuals will choose their groups and interact with members based upon their perception of the net profit of that exchange, rather than rewards or costs alone.[14]

At a more specific level, consumers may be seen to accept reference-group influence because of its role in providing informational, utilitarian and value-expressive benefits.[15] Table 5.1 presents a series of statements that typify these three types of reference-group influence situations.

INFORMATIONAL BENEFITS

One reason reference-group influence is accepted (or internalised) is that consumers perceive it as enhancing their knowledge of their environment and/or their ability to cope with some aspect of it (such as buying a product). Consumers

TABLE 5.1 Typical reference-group influences on brand decisions

Informational influence

1. Individuals seek information about various brands of the product from an association of professional or independent group of experts.
2. Individuals seek information from those who work with the product as a profession.
3. Individuals seek brand-related knowledge and experience (such as how brand A's performance compares with brand B's) from friends, neighbours, relatives or work associates who have reliable information about the brand.
4. Individuals are influenced to select a brand by observing a seal of approval of an independent testing agency (such as *Choice* or *Consumer*).
5. Individuals' observations of what experts do influence their choice of a brand (such as observing the type of car that police drive or the brand of television that repairers buy).

Utilitarian influence

1. To satisfy the expectations of fellow work associates, the individuals are influenced by their preferences in making a decision to purchase a particular brand.
2. Individuals' decisions to purchase a particular brand are influenced by the preferences of people with whom they have social interaction.
3. Individuals' decisions to purchase a particular brand are influenced by the preferences of family members.
4. The desire to satisfy the expectations that others have of them has an impact on individuals' brand choices.

Value-expressive influence

1. Individuals feel that the purchase or use of a particular brand will enhance the image that others have of them.
2. Individuals feel that those who purchase or use a particular brand possess the characteristics that they would like to have.
3. Individuals sometimes feel that it would be nice to be like the type of person shown using a particular brand in advertisements.
4. Individuals feel that the people who purchase a particular brand are admired or respected by others.
5. Individuals feel that the purchase of a particular brand helps to show others what they are, or would like to be (an athlete, successful business person, good mother and so on).

Source: Adapted from C. Whan Park & V. Parker Lessig, 'Students and Housewives: Differences in Susceptibility to Reference Group Influence', *Journal of Consumer Research* 4, September 1977, p. 105.

most readily accept the information sources that are thought to be most credible. A consumer using an informational reference group may:

1. actively search for information from opinion leaders or a group with the appropriate expertise; or

2. come to a conclusion through observing the behaviour of other people.

Therefore, actual physical interaction with the group is not necessary in this type of information search.

In this situation, then, the marketer may be able to appeal to consumers through the use of advertising testimonials from experts or even 'persons on the street', or by encouraging consumers to find out more about the brand from friends, neighbours or work associates. This personal source of information is often more influential in purchasing than commercial sources such as advertising and salespeople, as studies of food, small appliances and other products indicate. One of the key linkages in this process is the credibility of the influencer. A consumer contemplating a major appliance purchase will rely on friends, salespeople, or even product-rating magazines, if the information obtained is perceived as credible. Thus, consumers accept such expertise because of its informational benefits.

UTILITARIAN BENEFITS

This reason refers to pressure on the individual to conform to the preferences or expectations of another individual or group. In a product-purchasing situation, consumers will comply if:

1. they believe that their behaviour is visible or known to others;

2. they perceive that the others control significant sanctions (rewards or punishments);

3. they are motivated to realise the reward or avoid the punishment.

Visibility is very important in order for this normative influence to operate. As will be shown later in this chapter, in situations in which the product is visible or the effects from its use or non-use are visible, reference groups are able to exert strong normative influence. Products such as clothing and furniture are highly visible to others and therefore are quite susceptible to normative group influence. Even for items that are not themselves visible to others when in use (such as antiperspirant deodorants), normative influence is still likely to be strong, because the effects of non-use will be rather evident (e.g. body odour and a stained dress or shirt underarm area). Consequently, fear of group reaction will influence the product's use.

Thus, individuals accept influence from the group because they hope to attain certain specific rewards or avoid certain punishments controlled by the group. In effect, individuals learn to say or do expected things in certain situations, not because they necessarily enjoy doing so, but because it is instrumental in producing a satisfying social effect.

VALUE-EXPRESSIVE BENEFITS

To enhance or support their self-concepts, individuals may be motivated to associate with positive reference groups and/or dissociate from negative referents. Value-expressive reference-group influence is characterised by two different processes. First, individuals may utilise reference groups to express themselves or bolster their egos. Secondly, individuals may simply like the group and therefore accept its influence. Thus, an individual adopts behaviour derived from the group as a way of establishing or maintaining the desired relationship to the group and the self-image provided by this relationship. The individual may say what the group members say, do what they do, and believe what they believe in order to foster the relationship and the satisfying self-image it provides.

THE NATURE OF REFERENCE-GROUP INFLUENCE

Reference-group influence has the potential to be quite strong. This section describes several studies showing its importance in general as well as in a consumer-behaviour context.

One experiment showing that a group may induce strong pressure on an individual to conform involved groups of seven to nine college students brought together and instructed to judge the lengths of lines drawn on cards. All group members but one—the naive subject—were instructed to give an incorrect response. The naive subject answered after most of the group had answered, and thus found his or her judgment to be in opposition to that of the rest of the group. The result of the experiments with 123 naive subjects tested on 12 critical judgments was that 37 per cent of the total number of judgments conformed to the incorrect answers of the remainder of the group acting in unison.[16]

Other experiments have been conducted with similar goals but a different technique. Rather than allowing group members to have face-to-face oral communication with the group as in the situation above, individuals in these experiments were somewhat removed from each other, communicated only indirectly and were to some degree anonymous. The kind of yielding that occurred and its psychological significance were determined to be the same under both experimental approaches. However, the former situation imposed more powerful group pressure on the individual, resulting in a greater average amount of conformity.[17]

Another experiment provided an indication of the strength of the group norms in forcing conformity. Subjects were brought into a dark room and asked to judge the distance and direction of movement of a small point of light. Although the light was actually stationary, it appeared to move because of the autokinetic effect; that is, an illusion of movement due to small tremors in the eye. Group members arrived at a consensus that tended to be maintained when individual members were asked to give their judgments after the group had dispersed.[18]

Another researcher studied the influence of group pressure on consumer decision making and the effects of choice restriction by group pressure in the consumer decision-making process. Student subjects were instructed to evaluate and choose the best suit among three identical men's suits. Three group members (all confederates of the researcher) were instructed to select suit 'B', which then put pressure on the naive subject, who was questioned last, to agree with the group or to differ in his judgment and thus resist the group influence. It was found that individuals tended to conform to the group norm. The implication is that consumers accept information provided by their peer groups on the quality or style of a product that is difficult to evaluate objectively.

In addition, the study sought to determine the extent to which individuals might be controlled in a buying situation. The study's confederate subjects were instructed to give responses indicating that they were 'good guys' merely going along with the group consensus. The implication was that the naive subjects should also go along with the group. They were thus in a position of having to respond to an obvious effort at group pressure. In this situation the naive subjects tended to resist the pressure to conform and were more prepared to remain independent in their choices. We see the occurrence of this resistance in the marketplace when individuals conform to the group norms by keeping new products or adopting new styles, but maintain their independence by purchasing different colours or brands. This situation is known as *reactance*—whereby individuals are motivated to resist further reduction in their sets of free behaviours and to avoid compliance with the inducing agents, in this case their reference groups. It is possible, therefore, that too obvious an attempt to force compliance with a group may have the opposite effect on consumers, who may strike out in an independent direction to avoid going along with the group.[19]

In order for psychological reactance to occur two elements must be present.[20] First, a consumer must expect a measure of freedom to act in a given situation. Secondly, some threat must arise that infringes upon that important freedom. Sources of such threats may include social influence attempts by other people and impersonal barriers to action (such as product unavailability), or they may even be self-imposed, simply because the individual, by entering into the process of a decision, arrives at a point beyond which there will be an unwanted reduction in freedom.[21] When an individual's freedom to engage in a specific behaviour is threatened, the threatened behaviour becomes more attractive. Studies of retail advertisements in which limits are placed on consumers have shown increased attraction from the consumers. For example, in sales of limited duration, ads for one-day-only sales resulted in greater purchase likelihood than ads for sales of longer duration.[22] Another retail ad study showed that limits on soft-drink purchase quantity (e.g. a limit of two per customer, or four per customer) were capable of increasing attraction to the advertised product.[23] Reactance theory may help explain such situations as the following:

When the Coca-Cola company launched new Coke and abandoned their standard product recipe, many consumers in the United States were outraged because it threatened their freedom to obtain the familiar and constant product they had grown accustomed to.

Consumers refuse to buy when they consider that a salesperson is putting them under undue psycho-logical or time pressure. Reactance can occur in 'hard-sell' situations and also when products are sold in social-group situations, as discussed above. Dominant, an Australian home-network retailer, employ trial packs as their main sales technique and deliberately avoid pressure sales and therefore possible consumer reactance.

How do reference groups act as mediators of reactance processes? Studies have found, for example, that an individual's immediate group can suppress manifestations of reactance. When there is expected to be no future interaction between the individual and the group, the individual will tend to act contrary to the pressure (creating a boomerang effect). However, when future interaction is anticipated, subjects tend to conform to the group pressure; that is, the salient group apparently holds the reactance response in check.[24]

Reference groups may also influence shopping/purchasing patterns. A study of in-store shopping behaviour indicated that multiple shopping parties made many more changes in shopping plans than did single shoppers. Compared with single shoppers, less than half as many parties of three or more persons purchased as many items as planned.[25]

Another experiment was conducted to determine whether small, informal groups influence the formation of brand loyalty. In this study, consumers from pre-existing reference groups selected a loaf of bread from four identical loaves marked with different letters representing fictitious brands. Based on the individuals' choices, it was concluded that informal groups definitely influenced their members to conform with respect to brands of bread preferred. Moreover, the extent and degree of brand loyalty within a group was closely related to the behaviour of the informal leader.[26] A replication of this experiment, however, produced contrary findings. Evidence that group influence was not established was used to support the argument that products low in visibility, complexity and perceived risk, and high in testability are not likely to be susceptible to personal influence.[27]

The research approaches described above generally suggest that the responses of others establish a norm to which subjects comply. A recent study, however, suggests that such normative effects may have been too readily inferred from observations of unanimous or consensus behaviour among group members. In effect, people may use the product evaluation of others as a source of information about products; that is, they infer from such evaluations that the product is, indeed, a better product. Such a situation probably occurs regularly in shopping activities and in social groups.[28] Thus, in a situation where the basis for group agreement is normative, it may be that members go along with the group because, as a result of observing the group's reaction, they perceive the product differently.

A final research area has been the influence of group discussion versus lecture or one-way communication in changing consumer attitudes and behaviour. In one experiment, an attempt was made to change home-makers' meat consumption habits; half of the groups involved heard a lecture on the subject, while the other groups engaged in discussions. Although each group received the same information, results indicated that more individuals in the discussion groups used the recommended meats than did individuals in the lecture groups. Group interaction was found to be a strong influence in promoting changed attitudes and behaviour in various types of groups, even among groups whose members were initially strangers.[29]

The groups involved in most of these experiments were made up of subjects who either did not know each other initially or were only slightly acquainted. Imagine how much stronger and more significant the potential influence, then, from a group with which the individual strongly identifies or uses as a referent, such as family, close friends, or colleagues.

Decisions by social entities, other than a household, to purchase goods and services consumed by the entire group are a pervasive but much overlooked consumer research area. Such topics as how friends decide where to go to see a movie, to eat, to shop or on vacation, how co-workers decide on a radio station for background music, and how athletes choose their team's uniforms or equipment are all significant subjects for future study.[30]

THE VARIABILITY OF REFERENCE-GROUP INFLUENCE

Reference groups can be very potent influences on behaviour in general, and they may also be very influential on consumer behaviour. For example, before making a decision about purchasing a product, a consumer often considers what a particular group would do in the same situation, or what the group would think of the consumer for purchasing the product. This commonsense notion, however, has been difficult to apply meaningfully in specific marketing situations. The basic problem is one of determining which kinds of groups are likely to be referred to by which kinds of individuals in which kinds of situations in making which decisions, and of measuring the extent of this influence. Nevertheless, a start has been made in understanding this process. This section discusses some of what we now know about the variability of reference-group influence on consumers.

Variability among products

When the influence of reference groups on the purchase of a number of consumer goods was first studied, it was found that the 'conspicuousness' of a product is a strong determinant of its susceptibility to reference-group influence.[31] Conspicuousness may be of two forms. First, the item must be exclusive in some way. If virtually everyone owns it, it is not conspicuous in the first sense, even though it may be highly visible. Operationally, this has been defined as the distinction between luxuries (having a degree of exclusivity) and necessities (possessed by virtually everyone). In this sense, necessity does not equate to a basic item required for survival such as water, but to a product such as a refrigerator that is universally owned and an expected basic possession within our culture. Secondly, conspicuousness relies on the item being seen or identified by others. Thus, *where* an item is consumed has great relevance. A distinction may be made between publicly consumed products (which are seen by others) and privately consumed items (not seen by others). Reference groups may influence either the purchase of a product or the choice of a particular brand, or both.

Other consumer researchers have investigated the role of reference-group influence on product and brand choice for several product categories. One of these studies is summarised in Figure 5.1. It combines the concepts of public–private consumption and luxury–necessity items and, when applied to product and brand decisions, offers a set of eight reference–group influence relationships.[32]

1. *Publicly consumed luxury.* A product consumed in public view and not commonly owned or used (such as a yacht). In this case, whether or not the product is owned and also what brand is purchased are likely to be influenced by others. Relationships with reference-group influence:

    (a) Because it is a luxury, influence for the *product* should be *strong*.

    (b) Because it will be seen by others, influence for the *brand* of the product should be *strong*.

2. *Privately consumed luxury.* A product consumed out of public view and not commonly owned or used (such as a spa bath). In many cases, the brand is not conspicuous or socially important and is a matter of individual choice, but ownership of the product does convey a message about the owner. Relationships with reference-group influence:

    (a) Because it is a luxury, influence for the *product* should be *strong*.

    (b) Because it will not be seen by others, influence for the *brand* of the product should be *weak*.

3. *Publicly consumed necessity.* A product consumed in public view that virtually everyone owns (such as a wristwatch). This group is made up of products that essentially all people or most people use, although they differ as to what type of brand they use. Relationships with reference-group influence:

    (a) Because it is a necessity, influence for the *product* should be *weak*.

    (b) Because it will be seen by others, influence for the *brand* of the product should be *strong*.

4. *Privately consumed necessity.* A product consumed out of public view that virtually everyone owns (such as a mattress). Purchasing behaviour is largely governed by product attributes rather than the influences of others. In this group, neither products nor brands tend to be socially conspicuous, and the products are owned by nearly all consumers. Relationships to reference-group influence:

    (a) Because it is a necessity, influence for the *product* should be *weak*.

    (b) Because it will not be seen by others, influence for the *brand* of the product should be *weak*.

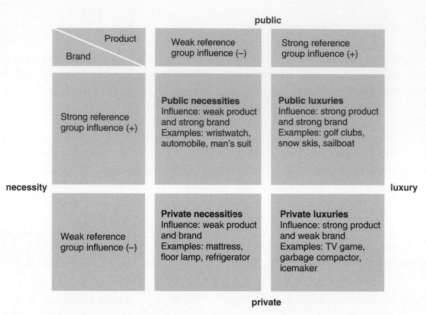

FIG. 5.1   Combining public–private and luxury–necessity dimensions with product and brand purchase decision   Source: William O. Bearden & Michael J. Etzel, 'Reference Group Influence on Product and Brand Purchase Decisions', *Journal of Consumer Research* 9, September 1982, p. 185.

More refinement is needed for understanding such reference influence, however. Research indicates, for example, that consumers perceive their own personal preferences strongly to outweigh reference groups' in arriving at their product and brand decisions. Table 5.2 presents evidence of the extent of reference-group influence for several product categories. It is clear that the perceived influence of reference groups is substantially underestimated by consumers. They view themselves as largely independent of the implicit social pressures exerted on their product and brand selection by reference groups. For major durables or 'family products', the greatest group influence comes from the family. Other reference groups are more influential in the case of products linked to social visibility or social status.

The marketer should also be aware that some shifting of product perceptions may occur over time. For example, a product may shift from a category in which reference-group influence is weak to another in which it is strong, especially through the use of heavy promotional efforts designed to create a favourable image and make a product or brand socially conspicuous. Products that are not publicly conspicuous, such as soap and men's underwear, could be brought out into the open in order to create more visibility, develop an image for them and stress the importance of the brand.[33] An important point to realise is that products may also slip in their degree of reference-group influence as they near saturation levels of ownership. Thus, attention to changing perceptions over a product's life cycle is important. This point is covered in more detail in Chapter 7, which deals with personal influence and the diffusion of innovations.

TABLE 5.2 Reference-group influence

Product	Referent on product usage				Referent on brand choice			
	Family	Friends	Work associates	Personal preference	Family	Friends	Work associates	Personal preference
	%	%	%	%	%	%	%	%
Air-conditioner	38.7	29.7	17.9	51.4	40.0	32.9	20.5	52.7
Beer	11.0	26.9	8.3	74.7	7.6	29.0	6.2	79.5
Canned peaches	36.2	3.4	0.7	72.6	35.6	4.1	1.4	73.8
Cars	43.2	28.3	17.2	82.2	44.5	31.0	18.6	82.9
Cigarettes	5.5	9.0	7.6	75.3	3.4	11.0	6.2	80.8
Clothing	27.4	34.5	17.2	80.8	27.2	35.2	11.0	86.3
Drugs	31.7	17.9	6.8	67.1	33.8	19.3	6.9	72.5
Furniture	50.7	13.1	6.2	81.5	45.9	22.1	9.0	78.3
Instant coffee	35.6	15.2	5.5	67.6	34.9	15.9	4.8	70.3
Laundry soap	37.7	9.0	2.8	86.2	40.4	9.7	2.1	68.3
Magazines	24.7	19.3	11.7	85.6	30.1	26.2	13.8	87.7
Radio	30.3	26.2	6.9	80.1	23.4	7.6	1.4	76.6
Refrigerators	45.2	24.8	16.6	52.7	41.4	30.1	13.0	61.0
Soap	29.5	13.1	4.8	80.1	34.9	7.6	1.4	76.6
Toilet soap	32.2	4.8	0	72.4	32.2	2.8	0	74.5
TV (colour)	44.5	26.2	12.4	69.9	46.2	35.6	15.1	71.2

Overall perceived group influence

Influence agent	Perceived group influence	Most important choice criterion
	%	%
Product usage:		
Family	33.2	24.7
Friends	18.8	6.2
Work associates	8.9	0.7
Personal preference		68.4
TOTAL		100.0
Brand choice:		
Family	32.6	22.6
Friends	21.4	14.4
Work associates	8.7	0
Personal preference		63.0
TOTAL		100.0

Source: William G. Lundstrum, William G. Zikmund & Donald Sciglimpaglia, 'Reference Group Influence on Product and Brand Choice: Update of a Classic Study', in Robert S. Franz, Robert M. Hopkins & Alfred G. Toma (eds), *Proceedings: Southern Marketing Association 1979 Conference*, Southern Marketing Association, Lafayette, LA, 1979, p. 264.

How may the kind of information presented in Figure 5.1 and Table 5.2 be used when making marketing decisions? The following advertising strategies may be adopted depending on the degree of reference-group influence found for the product or brand:

1. Where neither product nor brand appears to be associated strongly with reference-group influence, advertising should emphasise the product's attributes, intrinsic qualities, price and advantage over competing products.

2. Where reference-group influence is operative, the advertiser should stress the kinds of people who buy the product, reinforcing and broadening where possible the existing stereotypes of users. The strategy of the advertiser should involve learning what the stereotypes are and what specific reference groups enter into the picture so that appeals can be 'tailored' to each main group reached by the different media employed.[34]

Variability among groups

Reference-group influence has been shown to vary according to characteristics of the group or its type. For example, comparison of reference-group influence scores for students and home-makers across 20 products showed that there are significant differences between the groups in terms of the influence of reference groups on brand selection, and that students are generally more susceptible to reference-group influence.[35] Why? Possibly differences in needs or motivations among the groups result in different responses to reference-group influence. First, the lower age of students perhaps means that they are less familiar with products and have less product information, and face greater purchase risk than home-makers would. Secondly, social surroundings and daily activity differences exist between the groups. Students have more frequent social contacts, more interaction within groups that impose more rules and norms, and more visible behaviour subject to group pressure than do home-makers. Thirdly, hedonism may be stronger among students than among home-makers, and so they have more ego-involvement in their purchasing. The nature of involvement is fully explained in Chapter 9. Thus, we see that different groups exhibit different reference influences. Let's briefly examine a few of these group factors that seem to influence conformity.

Conformity may be related to *group cohesiveness*. One study of brand-choice behaviour found group cohesiveness and brand similarities to be positively related.[36] However, not all researchers have found group cohesiveness to be associated with group influence. Conformity also appears to be related to group size. One set of experiments showed that increasing the number of influencing members up to three increased the pressure toward conformity on the experimental subject, but beyond three, the influence was found to be no greater.[37]

Proximity to group members can influence conformity. For example, a study of elderly consumer social-interaction patterns found that more than 80 per cent of the exchange of information and advice about a new product occurred between persons living on the same floor of their residence.[38] This and other studies have indicated that influencers and influences live close to each other.

The *individual's relationship* to the group is another factor that influences conformity. An individual's social integration (such as the level of acceptance by other group members) and role in the group are factors that generally are positively related to the degree of group influence on the individual.[39] However, social comparison processes are at work even in socially distant reference groups.[40]

Similarity to the group's characteristics, outlooks and values is also important. Consumers are more likely to seek product information (and to trust this information) from friends with similar attributes. They are also more likely to choose the same products as do these friends. This suggests that a new product can be diffused fastest when the market possesses similar value orientations about similar types of products, because the likelihood of interpersonal communication and influence is greatest.[41]

Although similarity is likely to be important, one research study indicates that the single most important element of referent selection for 15 products commonly purchased by undergraduate males is *stage presence*, involving the referent's personal appearance or bearing.[42] The persuasive charisma resulting from this attribute may be very relevant in certain marketing situations. For instance, the marketer may often want to choose a model or potential referent having this attribute when promoting through advertising or personal selling.

Variability among individuals

The strength of reference-group influence varies not only among products and group types, but also among different consumers. In other words, some individuals are more susceptible to reference-group influence than others.[43] What individual characteristics seem to be associated with a consumer's susceptibility to reference-group influence? It appears that both demographic and psychological factors are relevant.

First, *personality* factors are important. Conformity has been found to vary by personality type and is positively related to the following personality traits: low intelligence, extroversion, ethnocentrism, weak ego, poor leadership, authoritarianism, need for affiliation, being a firstborn or only child, and feelings of personal inferiority or inadequacy.[44]

The type of *social character* of consumers may also affect reference-group influence. An important consumer typology related to this is Riesman's inner-directed and other-directed individual.[45] This theory describes inner-directed individuals as those who turn to their own inner standards and values to guide their behaviour. Early in childhood they are taught by parents, the church and other cultural institutions to accept and internalise these standards, and to use them as a frame of reference for future behaviour. These internalised values are relatively durable and change little over the individual's lifetime. Other-directed individuals depend on others around them for direction and guidance. They have been taught to look to other people for correct standards of behaviour and to be sensitive to the values and attitudes of their respected reference groups and associates. An analogy that distinguishes these two social-character groups is to think of inner-directeds as being equipped with a gyrocompass, while other-directeds are guided by radar.

A second set of factors relating to reference-group susceptibility is the consumer's *demographic* attributes. For example, differences in reference-group influence have been found between males and females, married couples and singles, younger and older people, and between different nationalities.[46] However, little consumer research allows for the summary of any consistent trends according to demographics.

Marketers should, therefore, carefully assess the extent to which reference group influence exists for their product, what type of influence appears to be more pervasive and how customer segments may differ in their responsiveness to such influences. The situational nature of such influence also needs to be understood. From such knowledge more effective marketing strategies may be developed incorporating referent power.

WHICH REFERENCE GROUP DOMINATES?

We see, then, that reference groups are highly relevant and potent influences in consumer decision making. But how do we identify the specific individual, group or groups who are most relevant to the consumer's behaviour? Unfortunately, at this stage we are unable to answer this question definitively; we simply are not sure which reference groups will be most important in a given buying decision. Thus, when a young woman goes to the shops to buy a new outfit, the ultimate choice may reflect her family, her church group, her boyfriend and his friends, or any other group. It is very difficult for the retailer to know which reference group generally dominates. Much depends on the individual's situation.

SUMMARY

This chapter has described social-group influences that impinge on the consumer. We first defined the term 'group' and distinguished small groups from other collections of individuals. We next described various types of groups classified along a number of dimensions. This was followed by a discussion of group properties including status, norms, role, socialisation and social power, which is the way in which consumers are influenced by their groups.

Reference groups were examined in detail because these are of great significance for the marketer. We defined important types of reference groups and reasons for consumers accepting reference-group influence, and described research on the nature of reference-group influence on individuals. We elaborated on the marketing implications of reference groups by discussing factors related to their level of influence and by citing their relevance in consumer decision making. Finally, we addressed the difficulty the marketer may have in identifying the consumer's relevant reference groups.

MANAGERIAL REFLECTIONS

For our product or service situation:

1. What classification of groups (primary/secondary, informal/formal) is most important in its purchase and consumption and how may these be incorporated in promotional messages?

2. How may it be related to various roles that consumers enact?

3. What types of social-group power are operative and how may we use that power to influence purchasers?

4. Is reference influence an important factor?

DISCUSSION TOPICS

1. What is meant by the term 'social group'? What are some types of social groups? Distinguish between the following types of groups:
   (a) primary versus secondary
   (b) formal versus informal
   (c) social group versus aggregation

2. Discuss the basic properties of a group. How do these properties relate to consumer behaviour?

3. What is a reference group? Name two reference groups that are important to you. In what way do they influence your consumer behaviour?

4. What groups do you belong to that you feel are not influential on you and your behaviour as a consumer?

5. Suggest a product not listed in Figure 5.1 over which reference groups would exert a strong or weak influence with regard to the purchase of the product and its brand or type. Explain.

6. Decide which of the consumers' reference groups would appear to be most important for the following purchase decisions:
   (a) a formal evening gown
   (b) selection of a physician
   (c) a new home
   (d) a basketball and warm-up suit

7. What factors appear to influence reference-group influence?

8. Identify advertisements that illustrate the marketer's use of each type of group power influence.

REFERENCES

1. David Dressler & Donald Cams, *Sociology: The Study of Human Interaction*, Knopf, New York, 1973, p. 259.
2. Charles H. Cooley, *Social Organization*, Scribners, New York, 1909, p. 23.
3. Ralph Linton, *The Cultural Background of Personality*, Appleton Century Crofts, New York, 1945.
4. William Shakespeare, *As You Like It*, act 2, scene 7, lines 140–3.
5. Erving Goffman, *The Presentation of Self in Everyday Life*, University of Edinburgh Social Sciences Research Centre, London, 1958.
6. David Krech, Richard S. Crutchfield & Egerton L. Ballachey, *Individual in Society*, McGraw-Hill, New York, 1962, p. 313.
7. George Moschis, *Consumer Socialisation: A Life-cycle Perspective*, Lexington Books, Lexington, MA, 1987; and Scott Ward, 'Consumer Socialization', *Journal of Consumer Research* 1, September 1974, pp. 1–14.
8. John R. P. French & Bertram Raven, 'The Bases of Social Power', in D. Cartwright (ed.), *Studies in Social Power*, Institute of Social Research, Ann Arbor, MI, 1959, pp. 150–67.
9. 'Soft Soap and Hard Sell', *Forbes*, 15 September 1975, pp. 72, 78.
10. Scott B. MacKenzie & Judy L. Zaichkowsky, 'An Analysis of Alcohol Advertising Using French and Raven's Theory of Social Influence', in Kent B. Monroe (ed.), *Advances in Consumer Research*, vol. 8, Association for Consumer Research, Ann Arbor, MI, 1981, pp. 708–12.
11. Ellen Graham, 'Tupperware Parties Create a New Breed of Super-saleswoman', *Wall Street Journal*, 21 May 1971, pp. 1, 18; and Flavia Krone & Denise Smart, 'An Exploratory Study Profiling the Party-plan Shopper', in Robert H. Ross, Frederick B. Kraft & Charles H. Davis (eds), *1981 Proceedings, Southwestern Marketing Association*, Wichita State University, 1981, pp. 200–3.
12. John L. Swasy, 'Measuring the Bases of Social Power', in William L. Wilkie (ed.), *Advances in Consumer Research*, vol. 6, Association for Consumer Research, Ann Arbor, MI, 1979, p. 341.
13. Francis S. Boume, 'Group Influence in Marketing and Public Relations', in Rensis Likert & Samuel Hayes Jr (eds), *Some Applications of Behavioral Research*, UNESCO, Paris, 1957, pp. 208–9; and Tamotsu Shibutani, 'Reference Groups as Perspectives', *American Journal of Sociology* 60, May 1955, pp. 562–9.
14. George Homans, *Social Behaviour: Its Elementary Forms*, Harcourt, Brace & World, New York, 1961; and Michael J. Ryan & E. H. Bonfield, 'The Fishbein Extended Model and Consumer Behaviour', *Journal of Consumer Research* 2, September 1975, pp. 118–36.
15. C. Whan Park & V. Parker Lessig, 'Students and Housewives: Differences in Susceptibility to Reference Group Influence', *Journal of Consumer Research* 4, September 1977, pp. 102–10; Herbert C. Kelman, 'Processes of Opinion Change', *Public Opinion Quarterly* 25, 1961, pp. 57–78; and M. Deutsch & H. B. Gerard, 'A Study of Normative and Informational Social Influences Upon Individual Judgment', *Journal of Abnormal and Social Psychology* 51; 1955, pp. 624–36.
16. Soloman E. Asch, 'Studies of Independence and Submission to Group Pressure: A Minority of One Against a Unanimous Majority', *Psychological Monographs* 70, 1956.
17. Krech, Crutchfield & Ballachey, op cit, Ref 6, p. 511.
18. Muzafer Sherif, *The Psychology of Social Norms*, Harper, New York, 1936, pp. 89–107.
19. M. Venkatesan, 'Experimental Study of Consumer Behaviour, Conformity and Independence', *Journal of Marketing Research* 3, November 1966, pp. 384–7.
20. For a review of reactance theory see Jack W. Brehm, 'Psychological Reactance: Theory and Applications', in Thomas K. Srull (ed.), *Advances in Consumer Research*, vol. 16, Association for Consumer Research, Provo, UT, 1989, pp. 72–75; Greg Lessne

& M. Venkatesan, 'Reactance Theory in Consumer Research: The Past, Present and Future', in Thomas K. Srull (cd.), *Advances in Consumer Research*, vol. 16, Association for Consumer Research, Provo, UT, 1989, pp. 76–8; and Mona A. Clee & Robert A. Wicklund, 'Consumer Behaviour and Psychological Reactance', *Journal of Consumer Research* 6, March 1980, pp. 389–405.

21. Clee & Wicklund, ibid, pp. 396–7.
22. Greg J. Lessne, 'The Impact of Advertised Sale Duration on Consumer Perceptions', in J. M. Hawes (ed.), *Developments in Marketing Science*, vol. 10, Academy of Marketing Science, Atlanta, 1987, pp. 115–17.
23. Greg J. Lessne & Elaine Notarantonio, 'The Effects of Limits in Retail Advertisements: A Reactance Theory Perspective', *Psychology and Marketing* 5, Spring 1988, pp. 33–44.
24. Clee & Wicklund, op cit, Ref 20, pp. 389–405.
25. Donald H. Granbois, 'Improving the Study of Customer In-store Behavior', *Journal of Marketing* 32, October 1968, p. 30.
26. James E. Stafford, 'Effects of Group Influence on Consumer Behaviour', *Journal of Marketing Research* 3, February, 1966, pp. 68–75.
27. Jeffery D. Ford & Elwood A. Ellis, 'A Re-examination of Group Influence on Member Brand Preferences', *Journal of Marketing Research* 17, February 1980, pp. 125–32.
28. Robert E. Burnkrant & Alain Cousineau, 'Informational and Normative Social Influence in Buyer Behaviour', *Journal of Consumer Research* 2, December 1975, pp. 206–15
29. Kurt Lewin, 'Group Decision and Social Change', in Harold Proshansky & Bernard Seidenberg (eds), *Basic Studies in Social Psychology*, Holt, New York, 1965, pp. 423–36.
30. James C. Ward & Peter H. Reingen, 'Sociocognitive Analysis of Group Decision Making Among Consumers', *Journal of Consumer Research* 17, December 1990, pp. 245–62.
31. Boume, op cit, Ref 13, pp. 208–9.
32. William O. Bearden & Michael J. Etzel, 'Reference Group Influence on Product and Brand Purchase Decisions', *Journal of consumer Research* 9, September 1982, pp. 184–5.
33. Sak Onkvisit & John Shaw, 'Self-concept and Image Congruence: Some Research and Managerial Implications', *Journal of Consumer Marketing* 4 (1), 1987, p. 21.
34. Boume, op cit, Ref 13, pp. 221–2.
35. Park & Lessig, op cit, Ref 15, pp. 103–4.
36. Robert E. Witt, 'Informal Social Group Influence on Consumer Behaviour', *Journal of Marketing Research* 6, November 1969, pp. 473–6.
37. John H. Murphy & William H. Cunningham, 'Correlates of the Extent of Informal Friendship-group Influence on Consumer Behavior', in Subhash C. Jain (ed.), *Research Frontiers in Marketing: Dialogues and Directions*, American Marketing Association, Chicago, 1978, pp. 130–3; and Ford & Ellis, op cit, Ref 27, pp. 125–32.
38. Leon G. Schiffman, 'Social Interaction Patterns of the Elderly Consumer', in Boris W. Becker & Helmut Becker (eds), *Combined Proceedings of the American Marketing Association*, American Marketing Association, Chicago, 1972, p. 451.
39. Jacqueline Johnson Brown & Peter H. Reingen, 'Social Ties and Word-of-mouth Referral Behavior', *Journal of Consumer Research* 14, December 1987, pp. 350–62; and Thomas S. Robertson, *Consumer Behavior*, Scott, Foresman, Glenview, IL, 1979, p. 74.
40. Benton A. Cocanougher & Grady D. Bruce, 'Socially Distant Reference Groups and Consumer Aspirations', *Journal of Marketing Research* 8, August 1971, pp. 379–81.
41. George Moschis, 'Social Comparison and Informal Group Influence', *Journal of Marketing Research* 13, August 1976, pp. 237–44.

42. W. Thomas Anderson Jr, Linda L. Golden & Joel Saegert, 'Reactional Analysis of Referent Selection in Product Decisions', in Subhash C. Jain (ed.), *Research Frontiers in Marketing: Dialogues and Directives*, American Marketing Association, Chicago, 1978, pp. 134–8.

43. William O. Bearden, Richard G. Netemeyer & Jesse E. Teel, 'Measurement of Consumer Susceptibility to Interpersonal Influence', *Journal of Consumer Research* 15, March 1989, pp. 473–81; and William O. Bearden, Richard G. Netemeyer & Jesse E. Teel, 'Further Validation of the Consumer Susceptibility to Interpersonal Influence Scale', in Marvin E. Goldberg, Gerald Gom & Richard W. Pollay (eds), *Advances in Consumer Research*, vol. 17, Association for Consumer Research, Provo, UT, 1990, pp. 770–6.

44. Lyman O. Ostlund, 'Role Theory and Group Dynamics', in Scott Ward & Thomas S. Robertson (eds), *Consumer Behavior: Theoretical Sources*, Prentice-Hall, Englewood Cliffs, NJ, 1973, p. 245.

45. Harold H. Kassarjian, 'Riesman Revisited', *Journal of Marketing* 29, April 1965, pp. 54–6; and Richard W. Mizerski & Robert B. Settle, 'The Influence of Social Character on Preference for Social Versus Objective Information in Advertising', *Journal of Marketing Research* 16, November 1979, pp. 552–8.

46. Donald W. Hendon, 'A New and Empirical Look at the Influence of Reference Groups on Generic Product Category and Brand Choice: Evidence from Two Nations', in *Proceedings of the Academy of International Business: Asia-Pacific Dimensions of International Business*, College of Business Administration, University of Hawaii, Honolulu, 1979, p. 757; and Robert T. Green, Joel G. Saegert & Robert J. Hoover, 'Conformity in Consumer Behavior: A Cross-national Replication', in Neil Beckwith et al. (eds), *1979 Educator's Conference Proceedings*, American Marketing Association, Chicago, 1979, pp. 192–4.

CHAPTER  6

FAMILY

SIGNIFICANCE OF THE FAMILY IN CONSUMER BEHAVIOUR

In Chapter 5 we examined the topic of social groups in order to understand their relevance to individuals and how marketers could use this knowledge. Now we turn to the family, not just as a type of small group, but as one that is often predominant in its influence over consumer behaviour.[1]

The family is both a *primary* group (characterised by intimate, face-to-face interaction) and a *reference* group (with members referring to certain family values, norms and standards in their behaviour). These two factors, however, are not the sole reasons accounting for the strength of the family's influence. Rather, it is, first, the fact that the bonds within the family are likely to be much more powerful than those within other small groups. Secondly, contrary to most other groups to which the consumer belongs, the family functions directly as a consumption unit in society. Thus, the family operates as an economic unit, earning and spending money. In doing this, family members must establish individual and collective consumption priorities, decide on products and brands that fulfil their needs, and also decide where these items are to be bought and how they are to be used in furthering family members' goals. Also, consumers' attitudes toward spending and saving and even the brands and products purchased have been moulded, often quite indelibly, by the families in which they grew up. Thus, marketers need to understand the nature of the family's influence on its members and the way in which purchase decisions are made by members so that they may effectively program their marketing mix. Table 6.1 illustrates several ways in which families differ from other groups.

TABLE 6.1 Differences between families and other groups

Family	versus	Other groups
Formation by marriage or birth		Formation by job or task
More permanent relationship		More contractual relationship
More interpersonal-relations oriented		More goal oriented
More intrinsic value seeking		More rational-oriented ties
Group-oriented (co-operative)		Self-oriented (competitive)

Source: Jong-Hee Park, Potriya S. Tansuhaj & Richard H. Kolbe, 'The Role of Love, Affection, and Intimacy in Family Decision Research', in Rebecca Holmon & Michael R. Solomon (eds), *Advances in Consumer Research*, vol.18, Association for Consumer Research, Provo, UT, 1991, p. 653.

The thrust of this chapter will be, first, to review several terms important in understanding this subject. Secondly, we shall describe the basic functions of the family. Next, we shall examine the family life-cycle concept and assess its meaning for the marketer. Family organisation and decision-making roles will then be discussed, incorporating marketing implications and examples. Finally, some aspects of the changing nature of the family in Australia and New Zealand will be discussed, along with implications for marketers who face this changing scene.

Families may be of different types. One basic distinction is between *nuclear* families and *extended* families. A nuclear family is recognised as the immediate group comprising husband, wife and children, while the extended family includes other generations and sibling relationships. The nuclear unit has become accepted as dominant form of family grouping in Western countries, but its importance varies across cultures. The extended aspects are usually considered much more important in most ethnic communities in Australia and New Zealand than in the white Anglo-Celtic group.

During their life, most people belong to two family groups: a family of *orientation* and a family of *procreation*. The family of orientation is the one into which they are born and is primarily responsible for their socialisation into the society, including their behaviour as consumers. The family of procreation is the one formed by marriage. Now that over one-third of all marriages formed in Australia and New Zealand end in divorce, it is obvious that a person may experience several combinations of orientation and procreation families, but the effects of such changes on consumer behaviour have not been studied. Most of the research that is reported in this chapter is based on nuclear families studied from a procreation perspective, that is, with a focus on husband/wife relationships. Unfortunately, the role of the extended family in consumer behaviour is virtually unknown.

FAMILIES AND HOUSEHOLDS

It is important to understand the difference between various terms that are frequently encountered when discussing the concept of family. First, we should distinguish between the terms 'family' and 'household', as market statistics may be gathered on either of these bases. A *household* includes the related family members and all the unrelated persons who occupy a housing unit (whether house, apartment, group of rooms or other). Thus, households may be of two main types: families and non-families. Most Australians and New Zealanders live in households. The ones who don't live in group quarters such as military barracks, prisons, nursing homes and college residences. The term 'family', however, is more limited, and refers to a group of two or more persons related by blood, marriage or adoption, and residing together as a household. Families comprise approximately seven out of 10 households. Table 6.2 shows how similar the basic household composition is in both countries and how the composition changed over the 1980s. Couples in a de facto relationship are classified with married couples.

TABLE 6.2   Household composition in Australia and New Zealand, 1981–1991

	Proportion of households			
	Australia		New Zealand	
Household composition	1981	1991	1981	1991
	%	%	%	%
Husband and wife only	22.1	23.5	21.3	23.7
Husband and wife with children	40.9	32.6	38.3	33.0
Lone parent with children	5.2	9.4	6.3	9.2
One family with others	7.2	6.9	7.8	5.6
Multiple families	n/a	1.5	1.4	1.7
Non family groups	4.6	4.5	6.1	5.8
One person households	18.0	21.6	18.2	20.0

Source: Extracted from Australian Bureau of Statistics and Statistics New Zealand. *Note: Because of different classifications between 1981 and 1991 in Australia it is not possible to separate out households with multiple families in 1981. Also, as the Australian figures are drawn from more than one source table, they do not total exactly 100%.*

The most important trends in these figures are the increasing number of one-parent families and the growth of single-person households. Growth in the latter has taken place across all age groups but is especially affected by the increasing number of elderly people in our societies. The added longevity of females over males means that there are increasing numbers of widows in single-person households. The 1991 Australian census identified a total of 4.7 million households with families. These are distributed across different family types as shown in Figure 6.1.

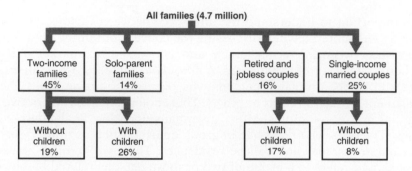

FIG. 6.1   Family types in Australia   Source: Australian Bureau of Statistics, *Census of Population and Housing 1991*, Cat no. 2821.0, Canberra, p.35

It should be noted that marketers are interested in the concept not only of families but also of households, as both may form the basis or framework of much consumer decision-making and buying behaviour. The marketer will use the concept that seems most relevant for segmenting markets and analysing decision processes. For instance, manufacturers of refrigerators, dishwashers, ranges and other kitchen appliances would probably find households to be the most relevant dimension in estimating market size, as purchase and replacement of these appliances would depend more on household formation than family formation. On the other hand, sellers of children's clothing and toys would probably be more interested in data on families.

FAMILY LIFE CYCLE

The concept of family or household life cycle has proven very valuable for the marketer, especially for segmentation activities. This section will describe the concept and discuss its application to consumer behaviour and marketing strategy.

Traditional life-cycle stages

The term 'life cycle' refers to the progressive stages through which individuals and families proceed over time. It was first developed by Joseph Rowntree in

1903 to describe the pattern of relative deprivation and prosperity experienced by a typical labourer in working London.[2] Figure 6.2 illustrates how Rowntree saw a person moving through economic cycles throughout his life and how these were related to critical events such as marriage, the birth and departure of children, and retirement.

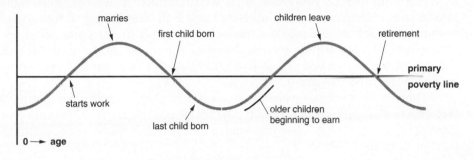

FIG. 6.2   The life cycle of a London labourer   Source: J. Rowntree, *The Life Cycle of a London Labourer*, Macmillan, London, 1903.

Though, in most instances, we are no longer discussing absolute levels of poverty, the fundamental basis of these economic cycles remains as one of the central features at the heart of the concept of the family life cycle. Trends in the number of women who continue working through child-rearing phases, and other developments such as pension and superannuation schemes, have eased the deprivation phases for many families, but they are not totally removed as committed expenditure on raising children and features such as health care in old age mean that these stages are still less affluent than other periods.

The most popular classification of stages for the family life cycle employed in marketing is that developed in the United States by Wells and Gubar.[3] They identified nine stages as follows:

1. Bachelor Stage: young, single people

2. Newly Married Couples: young, no children

3. Full Nest I: young married couples with youngest child under six

4. Full Nest II: young married couples with youngest child six or over

5. Full Nest III: older married couples with dependent children

6. Empty Nest I: older married couples with no children living with them and household head in labour force

7. Empty Nest II: older married couples with no children living with them and household head retired

8. Solitary Survivor I: older single people in labour force

9. Solitary Survivor II: older retired single people

In Australia and New Zealand it is necessary to make some minor adjustments to this classification to suit the local conditions. First, because of our much smaller populations, there are likely to be insufficient people in stage 8—older single people in the labour force—to make this group large enough to be of real practical interest to the marketer. The pattern of expenditures for this group closely parallels Empty Nest I, and the singles status is only really important for a limited number of products, such as vacations. A second local adjustment relates to the demarcation of Full Nest I and Full Nest II stages. Age six relates to commencing school and marks a transition in family life to a new set of needs and also extended possibilities for employment for many mothers. In New Zealand this transition is marked at age five and in Australia it varies between ages five and six according to state.

With the life-cycle concept the marketer is able to appreciate better how the family's needs, outlooks, product purchases and financial resources vary over time. The major family life-cycle stages and general effects on consumption are further described below.[4]

BACHELOR STAGE

At this stage of the life cycle earnings are relatively low because the individual is often just beginning a career. In spite of a low income, discretionary income is quite high, as there are few financial burdens that must be assumed. This group is generally recreation-oriented and high on fashion-opinion leadership. As a result, purchase patterns consist of vacations, cars, clothing, and various other products and services needed for the mating game. In addition, the establishment of residences away from the family usually necessitates the purchase of some basic furniture and kitchen equipment.

NEWLY MARRIED COUPLES

Even though they may have mortgage commitments, young couples are generally better off financially at this stage than when they were single. Both spouses are likely to be working and no longer in apprenticeships or tertiary education. They are also healthier financially than they will be in the next stage, which brings added demands on their resources. Couples at this stage have the highest purchase rate and the highest average purchase of durable goods, especially furniture and appliances. They also spend heavily on cars, clothing and vacations.

FULL NEST I

When their first child is born many women traditionally stop working, which causes a reduction in family income. As there is no uniform provision for paid maternity leave in either Australia or New Zealand, this is still a more critical phase for many families than in most OECD countries where statutory provisions make it easier for a woman to continue in employment if she desires. At the Full Nest I stage new demands are added to the family's purchasing requirements. For example, the increased family size may necessitate more space, so the family moves into a new home and purchases items necessary to fill the new environment. Furniture for the baby's room and other furnishing are bought, as well as such appliances as a washing machine, clothes drier and television set. In addition, many child-related expenses are now added, including baby food, baby medicines, doctor's visits and toys of all sorts. The parents are quite interested in new products and are susceptible to items they see advertised; however, they also grow more dissatisfied with their financial position and the amount of money available for savings.

FULL NEST II

In this stage the family's financial position has improved with the husband's advancement and perhaps, too, the wife's return to work. Families in this stage are still new-product-oriented, but tend to be less influenced by advertising because they have more buying experience. Products heavily purchased during this time include many foods (especially in larger packages and multiple-unit deals), cleaning materials, bicycles, and musical instruments and lessons.

FULL NEST III

During this stage the family's income continues to advance, more wives return to work and even the children may be employed. Although they are more resistant to advertising, these families have a high average expenditure for durable goods, primarily because of their need to replace older items. They purchase new, more tasteful furniture, luxury appliances, boats and cars. They also do more travelling and spend more on dental bills and magazines.

EMPTY NEST I

At this stage the family is most satisfied with its financial position and savings accumulation. Home ownership is at a peak, and major expenditures are necessary for home improvement. Although couples are less interested in new products, they do show an interest in travel, recreation and self-education. This spending pattern emphasises gifts and contributions, vacations and luxuries.

EMPTY NEST II

During this stage income is drastically cut. These couples stay at home more and spend more on medical appliances, medical care, and products that aid health, sleep and digestion.

SOLITARY SURVIVORS

If these individuals are still active in the labour force, their income is likely to continue to be good. Sometimes they may sell the home and spend more money on vacations, recreation and health-oriented items. Those who are retired will suffer a drastic cut in income, but will continue to have the same medical and product needs as other retired groups. During this stage individuals also have a special need for attention, affection and security.

A Modernised family life cycle

During recent years, many changes in the family have occurred, particularly smaller family sizes, the postponement of marriage and rising divorce rates. Thus, applying traditional family life-cycle schemes has resulted in the coverage of smaller and smaller proportions of the population. Applying the Wells and Gubar scheme to the 1981 New Zealand census data covered only 66.1 per cent of households and 62.3 per cent of the population.[5] As a result there have been many attempts to update the concept and make it more applicable to modern trends. The most comprehensive of these is diagrammed in Figure 6.3, and includes such stages as divorced single parents and middle-aged married without children. Such a flow chart helps to visualise the possible variety of different family life-cycle stages.

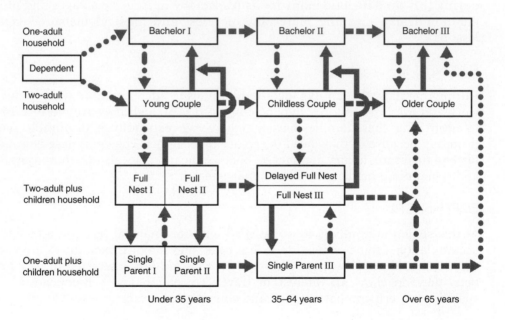

FIG. 6.3   The redefined family life cycle   Source: Mary C. Gilly & Ben M. Enis, 'Recycling the Family Life Cycle: A Proposal for Redefinition', in Andrew Mitchell (ed.), *Advances in Consumer Research,* vol. 9, Association for Consumer Research, Ann Arbor, MI, 1982, p. 274.

This modernised version has been slightly adapted to the local situation from the original groups described by Gilly and Enis.[6] The original groups were primarily based on the age of the female head of the household. In this adaptation more attention has been placed on the ages of the children, as we would argue that these are equally, if not more, important in determining the needs of the family, as well as the physical and financial constraints on the family's behaviour. The percentages on the right of each group indicate the proportion of households in New Zealand that fall into each category. Unfortunately, the exact form of statistics to reproduce the figures for Australia is not available from published data but we anticipate a very similar profile would result in view of the overall similarities in household composition between the two countries.

TABLE 6.3   A modernised family life cycle for New Zealand

Stage	Proportion of Population
	%
1. Bachelor I: head is 18–34, single (never married,divorced, separated, widowed), no dependent children	3.26
2. Young Couple: female head is 18–34, couple (married or unmarried), no children	5.28
3. Full Nest I: couple (married or unmarried), youngest child under 5	14.16
4. Full Nest II: couple (married or unmarried), school-age children, youngest child 5 or over	17.02
5. Single Parent I: single (never married, divorced, separated, widowed), youngest child under 5	2.36
6. Single Parent II: single (never married, divorced, separated, widowed), school-age children, youngest child 5 or over	3.60
7. Bachelor II: head is 35–64, single (never married,divorced, separated, widowed), no dependent children	7.39
8. Childless Couple: female head is 35–64, couple (married or unmarried), no dependent children	10.87
9. Full Nest III: couple (married or unmarried), youngest child 16 or over—probably still dependent or semi so	10.67
10. Single Parent III: head is 35–64, youngest child 16 or over	1.86
11. Bachelor III: head is 65 or older, single (never married, divorced,separated, widowed), no dependent children	9.55
12. Older Couple (Empty Nest): female head is 65 or older, couple (married or unmarried), no dependent children	7.73
Total households classified	93.75

Source: Adapted from Mary C. Gilly & Ben M. Enis, 'Recycling the Family Life Cycle: A Proposal for Redefinition', in Andrew Mitchell (ed.), *Advances in Consumer Research*, vol. 9, Association for Consumer Research, Ann Arbor, MI, 1982, p. 275; and data specially provided from Statistics New Zealand, *The 1991 Census of Population and Dwellings*, SNZ, Christchurch, 1993.

The advantage of this scheme can be seen immediately in the proportion of households classified. Only non-family groups, multiple-family households and households comprising families with other people present are not included in the scheme. In reality, many of the non-family groups and the families with others may involve a de facto husband and wife arrangement. For example, one-third of the 'families with others' category in New Zealand comprises a single parent with dependent children and other adults in the household. From published data it is impossible to tell what is the exact form of the group. For example, the other adult may be completely unrelated (e.g. a lodger), another generation of the same family, or a cohabiter and fulfilling the role of step-parent. Extending this argument, it is likely that from a practical point of view of considering market segment sizes, the figures in Table 6.3 probably slightly understate the Young Couple stage and Full-Nest stages.

Choice of an appropriate family life-cycle model is very much dependent upon the use that is to be made of it by the marketer or consumer researcher. In sociology, where most theoretical developments on the family life cycle have taken place, it is predominantly used as a *processual model*; that is, a model that allows for the study of individual families over time. For such studies, it is necessary to have a scheme, like the modernised version detailed above, which will allow the tracking of any family form. These longitudinal studies are very difficult to achieve, and are rare in either academic or marketing research. More usually, marketers employ the family life cycle for market segmentation, which is a form of cross-section analysis and does not involve tracking particular families over time. For this type of analysis, choice of a family life-cycle model is guided by other considerations. In particular, it is necessary to have a model that adequately classifies most of the population into groups large enough to be used for market segments, and sufficiently different in their consumer behaviour to make it worthwhile distinguishing them. For these reasons, family life-cycle classifications that distinguish smaller groups, like the three single-parent stages in the modernised version, are not relevant to most marketers in Australia and New Zealand. The needs of the single-parent groups very much follow those of the equivalent full-nest stages, and the most important distinguishing feature is the additional income constraints under which they are usually placed. This, in itself, makes them a less attractive proposition to marketers from the private sector. Also, since remarriage is very common, single-parent status may only be a temporary phenomenon before reversion to a full-nest position with a step-parent.[7] For segmentation purposes, the marketer will generally lose little from combining single-parent groups with their equivalent full-nest couples groups.

Relationship between family life cycle and consumer behaviour

Although 12 distinct stages were suggested above, there is no unanimity among research studies as to the most appropriate categorisation of life cycle. For example, the dividing line for terms such as 'young' and 'older' might be 40 years of age in one study and 45 in another, which makes it difficult to compare results among various research studies. In spite of these definitional difficulties there is, nevertheless, widespread agreement on the relationship between life cycle and consumer behaviour.

Research done using the family life-cycle model has revealed many consumption differences across household life-cycle stages, indicating that the model is a useful segmentation tool. For example, the financial services industry clearly recognises that as households act out different stages in the family life cycle various financial needs arise.[8] Research has shown that the family life cycle is a

Commonwealth Bank appeals to the youth market   COURTESY OF COMMONWEALTH BANK

key determinant of banking interest and behaviour.[9] Commonealth Bank, Westpac and Trustbank New Zealand have all used the family life cycle at different times for market segmentation. The advertisement above shows one approach used by Commonwealth Bank to target the young single market.

The family life-cycle model is a good predictor of individual attitudes and leisure activities. Analysis of inbound tourists to New Zealand, of whom the majority were Australian visitors, showed clearly different levels of expenditure and patterns of behaviour across different life-cycle segments. Length of stay, choice of accommodation, transport and activities followed are all strongly related to the stage of family life cycle. For example, visitors to New Zealand in Full Nest I and Full Nest II stages of the life cycle were almost entirely from Australia and making the trip in order to see friends and relatives. Consequently, they spent much less on all the usual tourist items, such as accommodation, than did other overseas visitors who were simply holidaying with no ulterior motives. Full Nest I and Full Nest II are stages of the family life cycle where funds for expenditure on discretionary items are usually at their lowest, and this choice of holiday is a relatively cheap option. In contrast, visitors in Empty Nest I, the most affluent stage, spent far more on top-grade hotels, rental cars, sightseeing activities and souvenirs.[10]

The family life-cycle model is also strongly related to food and beverage consumption, major and minor appliance ownership, dollar value of major household acquisitions (first and second homes, cars, boats), and dollar value of home entertainment devices (stereos, televisions, VCRs) and furniture.[11]

A dimension related to the family life-cycle concept is the household's acquisition pattern of durable goods. Research on this subject has sought to classify households based on their durable goods ownership and/or purchase plans. Thus, newly formed households start out with a set of durable goods acquired through gifts, purchases, lease/rentals, previous ownership, or as part of the first home dwelling. But because newly formed households are seldom able to purchase the complete set of durables needed to furnish a household, families must decide on an order of purchase and a decision plan for how the purchases will be made over time. Researchers have demonstrated the existence of some underlying priority pattern, or order in which household durables are bought. For example, 'comfort' products (such as washing machine, drier, dishwasher, freezer and microwave oven) were found to be acquired in a pattern.[12] A more extensive study that tracked the decision and purchase behaviour of the same households for 10 durable items over a 13-year period also found an order of acquisition for household durables.[13] Such findings can have relevance to marketers interested in forecasting consumer demand and targeting market segments.

Further evidence is provided by cross-national research studies, in which the sizes and compositions of household expenditures were found to be systematically related to the stage of the family life cycle.[14] Such findings are relevant to marketing managers when developing forecasts, for example. Demand for different product and service categories may be estimated from knowledge of the relationship between demand and stage in the life cycle and the predicted number of households in the various stages. A number of other studies have related shopping behaviour to life-cycle stage.[15]

A further important point is that time devoted to shopping varies with the stage of family life cycle. Ages of children seem particularly important in determining the amount of time available for shopping, and the pattern of time spent shopping by women in different stages of the life cycle is fairly complex. Table 6.4 shows how time spent decreases at the birth of the first child, then rises to a peak in the last part of Full Nest I when the children may well be taken on shopping trips. When all children are at school, time spent shopping declines once more and, after rising a little in Full Nest III, it declines again in the Empty Nest stage. Both the drop at the beginning of Full Nest II and in Empty Nest may be due to alternative pressures such as a return to the labour force on a part- or full-time basis.

TABLE 6.4 The effect of children on average weekly time spent shopping (hours)

	Time spent shopping	
Life-cycle stage	Married men	Married women
Under 45 years/no children	4.3	6.2
Youngest child 0–1 year	3.3	5.6
Youngest child 2–4 years	3.3	7.2
Youngest child 5–9 years	3.0	5.7
Youngest child 10–14 years	3.3	6.7
Youngest child 15 years and over	4.3	6.7
Over 45 years/no children	4.6	5.6

Source: Ian Castle, *Australian Social Trends 1994*, Cat No. 4102.0, Australian Bureau of Statistics, Canberra, 1994, p 123.

Life cycle versus age in segmenting markets

The reader may wonder whether the life-cycle concept offers a richer explanation of consumer behaviour than does a single variable, such as age. You will recall that we raised a similar question earlier when considering the merits of social class versus income in segmenting markets. Overall, the evidence heavily favours the use of life cycle as a way of segmenting markets.[16] One in-depth study on this subject found that for most items investigated, product consumption was more sensitive to life cycle than it was to age.[17] Obviously, there are always exceptions, and for some categories of products and services—for example, products tied to age-related physical difficulties, such as medical appliances and other medical-care items—the reverse is true.

Apart from difficulties in classifying a small percentage of the population, as illustrated above, the major disadvantage for marketers is that life-cycle data on customers are slightly more difficult to collect. Segmenting by life cycle requires information not only on the age of an individual, but also on marital status (or living arrangements), ages of children and occupational status (i.e. dependent, in the work force or retired). This is still relatively simple information to obtain compared with data required for other segmentation techniques, such as values and psychographics, but obviously more complex than age. Additionally, where this information is applied by organisations (such as banks) in a long-term relationship with particular customers, more effort is required to update records and keep an accurate track of customers.

For most products, however, life-cycle analysis allows the marketer to achieve a richer understanding of the market. A summary overview of life-cycle stages for family members and their consumer behaviour is presented in Table 6.5.

Beyond the life cycle: intergenerational influences

An important issue related to the concept of family life cycle concerns the degree to which family influence affects children's consumer behaviour later as adults. The family is the primary socialisation agent for each new generation. The transmission of attitudes, values and behaviours from parents to children is termed *intergenerational transfer*. This socialisation process results in the transmission of not only general social values and norms, but also skills and knowledge relevant to becoming successful consumers in a complicated marketplace. Through our families we first learn skills such as budgeting, attitudes and preferences toward products and brands, store choice and shopping patterns, the meaning of marketing communications and price–value judgments. The effect of such processes has only been hinted at because of the small number of studies on the influence of parents' consumption decisions on subsequent choices made by their adult children. But it appears that these effects may be strong.[18]

An example of how this intergenerational transfer works is provided by a North American study, which looked at the choice of camping as a form of family holiday. By far the most important explanatory variable was whether either spouse had been accustomed to camping holidays in their childhood. The study found very few instances where there was no childhood experience of camping.[19]

TABLE 6.5 Consumer elements by consumer life-cycle stage

Consumer element	Childhood	Adolescence	Early singlehood	Mature single	Newly married couples (young, no children)
Consumer characteristics	All needs provided by parents Little or no understanding of marketplace Marketplace limited to that of parents Limited cognitive ability Limited and unorganised product knowledge	Basic needs provided by parents Luxuries increasingly provided through part-time work Tastes and preferences evolving Susceptible to peer pressure to conform Limited product knowledge Limited understanding of marketplace Marketplace not solely limited to that of parents	Values and priorities unclear, therefore experimentation in lifestyle and associated consumption Highly mobile Few financial burdens Few assets Recreation-oriented Fashion opinion leaders Marketplace not limited by parents or legal restrictions due to age Wide product knowledge but little depth	Expectations of financial support by near relatives possible Discretionary income typically high Full marketplace accessible Wide product knowledge in depth likely Independent decision making	Resolution of lifestyle and values concerning consumption Lack of financial planning Financial condition better now than for near future High purchase of durables Wide product knowledge
Typical products and services	Toys Clothes Sweet treats Games Comic books	Records and CDs Bicycles Some personal-care products Toys Clothes Sporting goods	First care Basic home furnishings Home electronic equipment Vacations Sport equipment Education Personal-care products First use of credit Groceries	Tasteful home furnishings Appliances Travel Hobby-related purchases Better restaurants Savings for retirement House/condominium	Home equipment Durable furniture Cars Vacations Insurance

Continues

TABLE 6.5 Consumer elements by consumer life-cycle stage   *continued*

	Full Nest				Empty Nest			
	I	II	III	IV	I	II		
	Youngest child under 6	Youngest child 6 or older	Older married couples with dependent children	Single parenthood	Older married couples; no children at home, head in labour force	Older married couples; no children at home, head retired	Older solitary survivor, in labour force	Solitary survivor, retired
	Home purchase of primary concern Low liquid assets Conversion to one income likely Most susceptible to advertising and new products Dissatisfied with financial condition Change in lifestyle due to children Expansion of family influences on purchasing	Change in family risk patterns and concern for security Needs still expanding faster than income Consumption time scheduling difficult Some wives working Less susceptible to advertising Larger unit purchases	Ageing parents Recycling of products to younger siblings while protecting individual needs Heavy replacement of durables More wives working Hard to influence with advertising Wide product knowledge in depth likely Some children get jobs	Administration of consumption difficult Product knowledge of spouse lost Dissatisfaction with dual-parent role	Pre-retirement planning Home ownership at peak Typically in best financial position Not interested in new products Financial assistance to children	Drastic drop in income Want to keep home Product knowledge becoming obsolete	Income still good but likely to sell home Independent decisions now required due to absence of spouse	Drastic drop in income Independent decisions now required due to absence of spouse
	First house Day care Community services more important—schools, hospitals Baby food Toys Fast food Energy use high Bikes Baby furniture	Assortment increases due to expressed preferences Rapid usage of clothing Coats Magazines Non-necessary appliances Boats Recreational vehicles College expenses	Food expense at peak Dental services New furniture Larger house or remodelling Larger size packages Music lessons and instruments Fast food	Home security devices Buyable recreation for children Housekeeping services Day care Education for re-entry to job market	Travel Recreation Contributions Self-education Vacations Home improvements Savings for retirement Home security devices Hobby-related purchases	Medical care and products that aid sleep, health, digestion Leisure time equipment not formerly owned due to time constraints Household services for ageing Vacation home Restaurants	Household services Restaurants Similar to mature singlehood except for gifts to grown children Hobby-related purchases	Mass transportation Some product needs as other retired

Source: Ronald W. Stampfl, 'The Consumer Life Cycle', *Journal of Consumer Affairs* 12, Winter 1978, pp. 14–15.

It is important to realise that intergenerational transfer is not simply one-way. That is, not only do parents influence children but children also have the opportunity to influence their parents' consumer decisions.[20] Adult children may also have an important influence on the consumer decisions of their ageing parents. Figure 6.4 illustrates the process of intergenerational transfer of consumer-behaviour patterns between parents and children. A relevant question for the marketer is the extent to which this family influence carries over into our consumer behaviour as adults. It should be noted, too, that such influences may continue to be exerted between parents and children as each group ages. Considerable financial, emotional and practical support is known to exist within the extended dimensions of families but, because of the difficulties associated with researching such topics, there are no generalisable findings about its effects on consumer behaviour.[21]

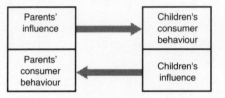

FIG. 6.4   Parent–child intergenerational influence on consumer-behaviour decisions

Changing family structures

Major shifts in demographics have already been reviewed in Chapter 2. Now we wish to emphasise some of the major changes that affect family structures and some of their consequences for consumer behaviour and marketing. The following are key points in recognising trends in family structures.[22]

1. Approximately two-fifths of all marriages end in divorce.

2. The number of one-parent families increased by 42 per cent between 1982 and 1992, and now 12 per cent of all lone parents with children are males.

3. Most divorced people remarry at some point.

4. The proportion of first marriages among all marriages has fallen from 90 per cent in the 1970s to 60 per cent in the 1990s.

5. Women are marrying much later. By the end of the decade in Australia 22 per cent of women are expected to be unmarried at age 35—the highest figure in history.

6. An estimated 25 per cent of people born in the 1960s will never marry.

7. The median age of married mothers having their first baby rose from 25 years to 28 years from 1982 to 1992.

8. The number of de facto couples has risen from 5 per cent in 1982 to 8 per cent in 1992. Of couples married in 1992, 56 per cent lived together in a de facto relationship prior to marriage.

Together with the changing age structure of the population, these trends have significant impacts on the size and nature of segments defined by the family life cycle. Following the modified Gilly and Enis scheme, these changes particularly emphasise the increasing importance of the three bachelor stages. Failure to marry, divorce and increased longevity of females all contribute to the increasing number of single-person households. For marketers, this presents special opportunities for products such as small apartments, small cars, single-serve meals and singles holidays. In Australia, like the United States, the growth in single-person households is also a trend that is recognised as having increased the importance of radio as a medium for recreation and companionship.[23] Unlike television, radio is essentially a conversation medium, and it provides an intimacy and involvement not offered by the other media. This is obviously an important consideration for marketers wishing to target advertising to bachelor groups.

Other implications from these changes for the family life cycle are the extension of the Young Couple phase, as age at first birth goes back, and the consequent shortening of the pre-retirement Childless Couple phase; that is, the Empty Nest I phase in older schemes such as Wells and Gubar. For some, the Childless Couple phase may be further shortened by trends to remarriage and second families.

FAMILY PURCHASING DECISIONS

This section probes more deeply into the nature of the decision-making process within the family, and its implications for consumer behaviour and marketing. Family purchasing decisions will be examined from four perspectives: role structure, power structure, stage in the decision-making process and family-specific characteristics. It is very important that the marketer understands who influences whom, and how, in the family buying process so that the proper marketing strategy may be developed.

Role structure

In our earlier discussion of the concept of roles, we described how society is structured by roles that are occupied (or played) by its members. So, too, does the family have its own structure, with each member playing a particular role. Thus, gender-role preferences reflect culturally determined attitudes toward the role of wife/husband and mother/father in the household. Perceptions of these gender roles affect the decision-making process and household decision behaviour.[24] Although several theories have been used to describe the structure of marital roles in decision making, from the standpoint of those interested in consumer behaviour, the following role categorisations appear to be perhaps the most helpful.

INSTRUMENTAL AND EXPRESSIVE ROLES

Generally, in traditional families among societies throughout the world, the husband is more likely to provide material support and primary leadership authority within the family, and the wife is more likely to provide affection and moral support. This distinction relates to what are known as instrumental and expressive needs of all small groups (including the family); that is, the need for leadership and fulfilment of the task on the one hand, and the need for morale and cohesion on the other.[25]

This differentiation of roles is known to result from small-group interaction. Leaders are produced who specialise in either *instrumental* functions (known as functional, or task, leaders) or *expressive* functions (social leaders). The former concern themselves with the basic purpose or goal of the group, while the latter attempt to reduce tension and give emotional support to members in order to maintain intragroup cohesion.[26] Within the family the instrumental role has typically been played by the father and the expressive role by the mother. That is, men tend to be task-oriented leaders, while women lead in social–emotional behaviour. The result of this is that in purchasing decisions husbands tend to concern themselves with functional product attributes and to exert more influence in deciding whether to buy and in closing the sale. Wives concern themselves more with aesthetic product attributes and with suggesting the purchase.[27]

Although the general role pattern cited above has been historically true, these roles are undergoing some degree of change today, particularly as more women enter the labour force. More will be said on changing roles in a later section of this chapter. For now it should merely be noted that wives may be just as likely to perform certain instrumental roles as their husbands do.[28]

PURCHASE PROCESS ROLES

There are several ways of viewing family-member roles as they relate to the purchase-decision and consumption process. In this context, there are six roles that may be performed by various family members.

First, one or another family member may be the *initiator*, or the individual who recognises the problem or need for the item. In this role the suggestion may be made by the wife, for example, that the household needs a food processor in order to prepare meals more easily. A second role is that of *influencer*, in which a person will inform or persuade others in a purchase situation. The influencer may also be thought of as an *opinion leader* in that this person exerts personal influence on other family members with regard to a particular purchase situation.

A third and related role is that of *information gatherer*, in which one or more individuals will secure information related to the possible purchase. This information may pertain to products or places of shopping. Often the individual most knowledgeable in the product category will gather information. For example, a husband may well gather information about a possible lawn-tractor purchase, while a wife may gather information about new financial services offered by a local bank.

The role of *decision maker* involves having authority to make the buying decision. The individual who makes this decision might be the same as the influencer or information gatherer, although not necessarily so. For instance, the wife may make the decision to purchase a microwave oven as well as the decision on which brand to buy, after having gathered information about various models available. Often the decision is a joint or shared one in which more than one family member participates. In other situations children were found to suggest which cereal brands their mothers should purchase when shopping. The mothers, however, were in the decision-maker position, and frequently disagreed with their children as to what cereal should be purchased.[29]

The *purchaser* role involves the act of purchase by one of the family members. In other words, the individual who buys the item in the store or, perhaps, places a telephone order for merchandise is acting in the role of purchasing agent for the family. The decider and purchaser need not necessarily be the same individual. For example, a teenage son or daughter may merely execute his or her parents' supermarket shopping list. In this situation (in which brands, sizes, and the like are specified), the youth is only a purchaser, not a decision maker. At other times, however, the purchaser may occupy a very strategic role in the brand decision. One study, for instance, found that nearly one-third of beer drinkers delegated the brand decision to the purchaser, and that the purchaser was aware of the consumer's preferences nine out of 10 times.[30]

A further role that is sometimes identified in family buying situations is the *gatekeeper*. This term was originally coined in organisational buying studies to refer to the person who controls access to information by other group members, and particularly access of sales representatives to different parts of an organisation. In family situations this role is less well studied and less well understood. Clearly parents will act as gatekeepers for children by controlling access to media. For example, they may control the quantity of time spent viewing television as well as the time of day at which television is watched.

Users are those who consume the product or service. A user may be the same person who performs each of the other roles, or it may be another person. The latter situation is often possible, for instance, in the case of a child for whom products such as clothing, toys and so forth are purchased.

For the marketer, it is important to distinguish each family member's role in order to develop an optimum marketing strategy. Assumptions made about such roles should be checked through consumer research so that the correct mix is aimed at the right individual. Knowledge of who generally performs which purchase and consumption process role within the family unit will aid in product planning and development, providing promotion messages and determining distribution decisions. More will be said about this topic in a later section.

ROLE LOAD

Another dimension of husband and wife roles in the family has to do with the role load of each spouse. Role load is the continuum of demands on a spouse's time, energy and other resources. One or both spouses may be overloaded in their household roles. Based on the four possibilities for role load shown in Figure 6.5, a variety of implications would occur for household consumer behaviour such as information acquisition, purchase decision making and the characteristics of the range of products and brands purchased.[31]

Husband role load

	overloaded			underloaded		
	Information acquisition	Purchase decision making	Assortment characteristics	Information acquisition	Purchase decision making	Assortment characteristics
overloaded	Truncated and individual information acquisition	Minimal joint decision making, especially for variants	Most incidence of convenience item, time-saving durables; diffused preferences for variants	Delegation to/assumption by husband	Joint decisions for budget allocation; variant decisions made by husband	Skewed towards wife; preferences of husband for variants
underloaded	Delegation to/assumption by wife	Joint decisions for budget allocation; variant decisions made by wife	Skewed towards husband; preferences of wife for variants	Extended joint search and information acquisition	Extended joint decision making	Least incidence of convenience items, time-saving durables; joint preferences represented

Wife role load (vertical axis label)

FIG. 6.5 Characteristics of household decisions under different husband and wife role loads

Power structure

This factor has to do with which family member is dominant or considered to be the family's head. A family may be *patriarchal,* in which case the father is considered to be the dominant member. In a *matriarchal* family the woman plays the dominant role and makes most of the decisions, while in the *egalitarian* family the husband and wife share somewhat equally in decision making. Although Australian and New Zealand families are still generally patriarchal and our societies are male-dominated, egalitarianism is a continuously emerging pattern.

PURCHASE INFLUENCE PATTERNS

Research on power relationships in the family has taken several directions. One approach to understanding the marital power structure in consumer decision making categorises the possibilities for dominance in the following way:

1. *autonomic,* in which an equal number of decisions is made by each spouse;

2. *husband dominant;*

3. *wife dominant;*

4. *joint,* or *syncratic,* in which most decisions are made by both husband and wife.[32]

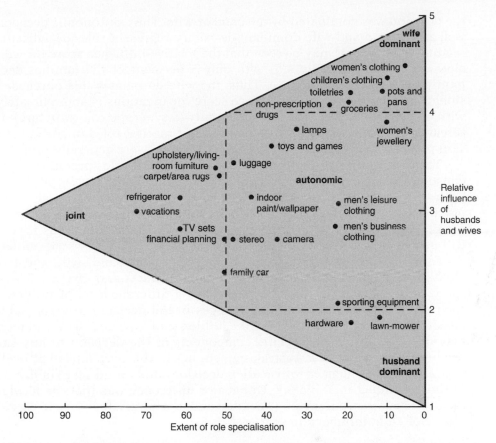

FIG. 6.6 Marital roles in 25 product/service decisions   Source: S. Amanda Putnam
& William R. Davidson, *Family Purchasing Behaviour: II Family Roles by Product
Category*, Management Horizons, A Division of Price Waterhouse, Dublin, OH,
1987, p. 7. Reprinted with permission.

A study using this concept measured the relative influence of Belgian husbands
and wives in purchase decisions for 25 representative products.[33] Similar
research on decision making by American husbands and wives was recently
conducted for businesses selling a wide variety of products. Figure 6.6 positions these decisions according to the four marital decision-making categories
of autonomic, husband dominant, wife dominant and joint. Each decision is
positioned in this figure according to two axes. The vertical axis is a scale of
the relative influence between husband and wife. Decisions can range along a
continuum from 1 (if respondents report husband specialisation) to 5 (if
respondents report wife specialisation). The horizontal axis is a scale of the
extent of role specialisation as measured by the percentage of families reporting that a decision is made jointly. Syncratic decisions, therefore, are those in
which more than half the respondents reported that the decision was joint;
while in the autonomic case, less than half the respondents indicated the decision was joint but there was no consensus among respondents as to whether

the decision was dominated by husband or wife. Thus, autonomic decisions, as well as husband-and-wife dominant decisions, represent role specialisation. In reading the figure, it may be seen that the relative-influence score for women's clothing is approximately 4.5, with only 5 per cent of the families deciding jointly on this item's purchase. Thus, the wife dominates this purchase decision. Similarly, the relative-influence score for vacations is approximately 3.1, with 65 per cent of families deciding jointly (a syncratic role structure). Other research of American couples' perceptions of marital roles in consumer decision processes also found that the Belgian results were generally supported.[34]

These and other studies have found that marital role specialisation in the consumer decision-making process varies significantly across product categories.[35] Results of these studies lead to the conclusion that joint decision making is most likely to occur for purchases that represent significant economic outlays, whereas routine expenditures for items viewed as necessities will probably be delegated to one of the spouses.

Table 6.6 presents data from an analysis of husband, wife and teenage child relative purchase influence for several products and services. The study shows that each family member may have a different level of influence for each product type and at different stages in the decision process. Table 6.7 adds to this idea by showing how the influence of husband, wife and teenager may differ according to specific components of the decision to buy various products. One of the few Australasian studies in this area looked at husband, wife and child influences for vacation decisions and found very similar results to those outlined in Table 6.7. One major difference was that the local study included activities pursued on vacation and, not surprisingly, there was a high degree of child influence in that area.[36]

TABLE 6.6   Family-member influence by stages of the decision process[a]

Product	Stages		
	I Initiation	II Search and evaluation	III Final decision
Television			
Husband	4.14	4.34	4.53
Wife	3.60	3.12	3.63
Child	2.19	1.79	1.88
Car			
Husband	4.70	4.88	4.91
Wife	3.52	2.98	3.53
Child	1.88	1.90	1.84
Vacation			
Husband	4.16	4.07	4.29
Wife	4.04	3.99	4.12
Child	2.72	2.45	2.64

Continues

TABLE 6.6   Family-member influence by stages of the decision process *continued*

	Stages		
Product	I Initiation	II Search and evaluation	III Final decision
Household appliance			
Husband	3.48	3.49	3.73
Wife	4.58	4.34	4.60
Child	1.76	1.71	1.73
Household furniture			
Husband	3.63	3.53	3.84
Wife	4.58	4.43	4.58
Child	1.96	1.79	1.87
Breakfast cereal			
Husband	2.64	2.51	2.60
Wife	3.64	3.66	3.88
Child	3.91	3.42	3.62

(*a*) Each score represents the average of the husband's, wife's and child's perceptions of family-member influence, as measured on a scale where 1 = no input at all and 6 = all of the input.

Source: George E. Belch, Michael A. Belch & Gayle Ceresino, 'Parental and Teenage Child Influences in Family Decision Making', *Journal of Business Research* 13, April 1985, p. 167.

TABLE 6.7   Family-member influence for specific decision areas[a]

Product	Husband	Wife	Child
Car			
When to purchase	4.62	3.41	1.58
How much money to spend	4.66	3.43	1.41
Make	4.52	3.31	1.88
Model	4.42	3.40	1.91
Colour	3.80	3.73	2.01
Where to purchase	4.62	2.86	1.39
Television			
When to purchase	4.27	3.67	1.81
How much money to spend	4.43	3.59	1.43
Brand	4.30	3.41	1.72
Model	4.18	3.47	1.76
Colour versus black/white	4.30	3.83	2.57
Where to purchase	4.20	3.31	1.49

Continues

TABLE 6.7 Family-member influence for specific decision areas[a] *continued*

Product	Husband	Wife	Child
Vacation			
Where to go	4.04	4.04	2.80
How much money to spend	4.28	3.83	1.76
How much time to spend	4.35	3.89	2.16
Where to stay	4.08	3.94	2.30
When to go	4.31	3.72	2.24
Household appliances			
What appliance to purchase	3.39	4.50	1.89
How much money to spend	3.79	4.15	1.85
Where to purchase	3.46	4.17	1.52
Style	3.06	4.58	1.73
Colour	2.89	4.66	1.77
Brand	3.30	4.47	1.66
Household furniture			
What furniture to purchase	3.51	4.46	2.10
How much money to spend	3.98	4.11	1.48
Where to purchase	3.50	4.25	1.54
Style	3.24	4.63	1.97
Colour	3.14	4.67	2.05
Fabric	3.09	4.66	1.85
Breakfast cereal			
What kind to buy	2.60	3.81	3.95
What brand to buy	2.42	3.90	3.68
What size	2.16	4.20	2.84
Where to purchase	2.07	4.43	2.29
When to purchase	2.14	4.37	2.75

(a) Each score represents the average of the husband's, wife's and child's perceptions of family member influence, as measured on a scale where 1 = no input at all and 6 = all of the input.

Source: George E. Belch, Michael A. Belch & Gayle Ceresino, 'Parental and Teenage Child Influences in Family Decision Making', *Journal of Business Research* 13, April 1985, p. 168.

It is important to remind ourselves that most of the studies summarised here are from the United States and, while there are very many similarities between the principles and patterns of consumer behaviour in the United States and Australia and New Zealand, there will be areas where the cultures diverge. One of these is recognised as practices of child rearing.[37] However, one Australian study examining children's influence still produced overall results consistent with previous work despite adopting a different approach. The research examined the number of times children made attempts to influence their parents *in stores* and noted their success rates for different products. The results have been collated into Table 6.8.

The number of influence attempts obviously reflects the children's interest in the product class. However, whether or not a child makes an influence attempt in

TABLE 6.8   Children's influence across different products

Product type	Influence attempt made	Influence attempt successful
	%	%
Clothing	85	57
Toys	90	10
Children's books	59	33
Chips, ice-cream, tomato sauce	57	30
Soft drinks	50	23
Toothpaste	20	10

Source: Mark A. Patton & Vicki H. Brinkworth, 'Children's Influence in Parents' Purchase Decision: A Western Australian Case Study', *Proceedings of the International Marketing Educators Conference, 14–16 April 1993, Bali*, Edith Cowan University, Perth, 1993.

store is situationally determined. Distractions such as the presence of toys or other children will diminish children's attempts to influence parents.

Consistent with other findings in the area, the success rate in this Australian study is dependent upon a number of features:[38]

1. *Intentions to buy*. Perhaps the most important factor, certainly in the first three situations in Table 6.8, is whether the parent has an intention to buy an item in the first place. That is, children may influence the item chosen but they carry less power in determining whether or not a purchase is made. For example, most parents intended to purchase clothing and, where the item was for the child's use, there was a very high success rate in influencing the parent to purchase a particular garment. With toys, children made far more attempts but had a very low success rate, because parents had no intention of making a purchase prior to the influence attempt.

2. *End user*. If the child is going to be the actual user of the product, the influence attempt is more likely to succeed.

3. *Age of child*. As children grow older the number of influence attempts they make decreases but their success rate improves. This is an obvious pattern of learned behaviour as the child learns what attempts are not likely to bring results and therefore are a waste of time. They also develop more sophisticated arguments and strategies to influence their parents. The researchers noted some children as young as seven and 10 years using some quite sophisticated arguments on price and value.

4. *Time pressures*. Where parents are in a hurry they are less likely to respond to cajoling by children.

ALTERNATIVE FAMILY DECISION-MAKING ROLE STRUCTURES

An extension of the role structure cited above is one based on the view that family decision making can fit one of four basic 'structures': parallel, hierarchical, ring and star (as shown in Fig. 6.7). A variety of hybrid configurations could be formed by combining these basic structures.

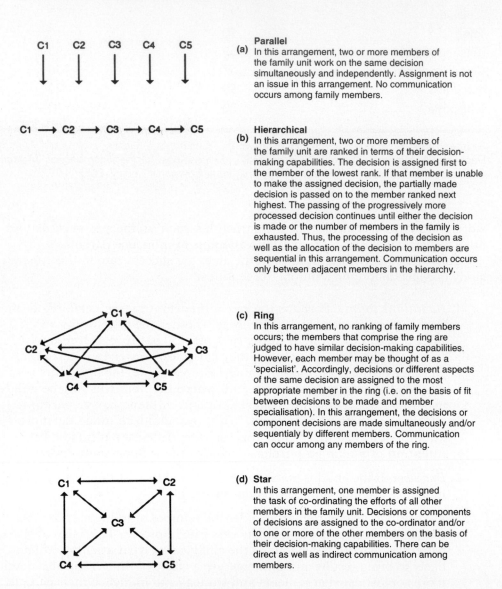

(a) Parallel
In this arrangement, two or more members of the family unit work on the same decision simultaneously and independently. Assignment is not an issue in this arrangement. No communication occurs among family members.

(b) Hierarchical
In this arrangement, two or more members of the family unit are ranked in terms of their decision-making capabilities. The decision is assigned first to the member of the lowest rank. If that member is unable to make the assigned decision, the partially made decision is passed on to the member ranked next highest. The passing of the progressively more processed decision continues until either the decision is made or the number of members in the family is exhausted. Thus, the processing of the decision as well as the allocation of the decision to members are sequential in this arrangement. Communication occurs only between adjacent members in the hierarchy.

(c) Ring
In this arrangement, no ranking of family members occurs; the members that comprise the ring are judged to have similar decision-making capabilities. However, each member may be thought of as a 'specialist'. Accordingly, decisions or different aspects of the same decision are assigned to the most appropriate member in the ring (i.e. on the basis of fit between decisions to be made and member specialisation). In this arrangement, the decisions or component decisions are made simultaneously and/or sequentially by different members. Communication can occur among any members of the ring.

(d) Star
In this arrangement, one member is assigned the task of co-ordinating the efforts of all other members in the family unit. Decisions or components of decisions are assigned to the co-ordinator and/or to one or more of the other members on the basis of their decision-making capabilities. There can be direct as well as indirect communication among members.

FIG. 6.7 Alternative structures within a multi-individual consumer unit   Source: Irene Raj Foster & Richard W. Olshavsky, 'An Explanatory Study of Family Decision Making Using a New Taxonomy of Family Role Structure', in Thomas K. Srull (ed.), *Advances in Consumer Research*, vol. 16, Association for Consumer Research, Provo, UT, 1989, pp. 666–7.

STRATEGIES TO RESOLVE CONFLICT

Family purchase decisions are often characterised by conflict over differences between the parties on several factors concerning the decision. For example, family members often have different views on who should make the purchase decision, how that decision should be made (such as how much information should be gathered) and who should implement the decision. Thus, the family purchasing-decision process is not always characterised by stability and easy agreement. Instead, conflict is quite likely, with families engaging in bargaining, compromising and coercing in order to arrive at a joint decision. Although the term 'conflict' is used here, it simply means that there is divergence or disagreement, whether explicit or implicit, between spouses on the rationale or outcome of a decision; that is, over purchase goals, decision alternatives or the decision process itself. Of course, there could be a range of conflict from much to little or none.[39]

Several strategies for resolving such conflicts may be adopted. The following six influence strategies have been suggested:[40]

1. *Expert*. A spouse might attempt to influence the other spouse by using superior information about decision alternatives.

2. *Legitimate*. A spouse might attempt to influence the other spouse based on his or her position in the household.

3. *Bargaining*. A spouse might attempt to gain influence over the other spouse now and allow reciprocal influence at some future date.

4. *Reward/Referent*. A spouse might attempt to gain influence over the other spouse by offering a reward.

5. *Emotional*. A spouse might attempt to influence the other spouse by using an emotional reaction.

6. *Impression management*. A spouse might attempt to influence the other spouse by using persuasion.

Research on the nature of joint purchase disagreements (particularly for large expenditures such as new cars, furniture, vacations and major entertainment appliances) has found that four approaches seemed to predominate as spouses dealt with each other:[41]

1. *Use of punishments, threats, authority, and negative emotion*. Strategies included refusing to do chores, threatening punishments, behaving angrily and stating that the spouse had no right to disagree.

2. *Use of positive emotion and subtle manipulation*. Strategies included putting the spouse in a receptive mood, appealing to the spouse's love and affection, and promising to do something nice in exchange for compliance.

3. *Use of withdrawal and egocentricity*. Strategies included denying affection, 'clamming up' and looking hurt.

This is a good illustration of a company targetting a particular family life stage   COURTESY OF AMP

4. *Use of persuasion and reason*. Strategies included the use of logic or persistence to change the other spouse's viewpoint.

Different decision-making strategies are likely for different situations. That is, depending on the family members, the product, the stage in the decision process and so forth, the strategies selected will vary. Much is dependent upon the individual situation and the characteristics of the people involved. A model of family decision making in Australia identifies five different sets of resources that affect the power of the family members over each other and the resolution approaches used:[42]

1. *Normative resources*. The cultural definitions of who has authority in a particular situation.

2. *Affective resources*. The level of commitment and the degree of dependence of the other person.

3. *Personal resources*. Personality, physical appearance and role competence of the people.

4. *Cognitive resources*. May reflect an extensive knowledge base pertinent to a buying decision, or may refer to the reasoning skills and abilities that influence the perception of power that a person holds.

5. *Economic resources*. Refers to the earning ability of individuals and is sometimes termed *resource contribution theory*. The principle states quite simply that the distribution of power over what is bought is derived from the amount of income contributed to the family.

CHANGING ROLES AND FAMILY PURCHASE DECISIONS

Changing role patterns of husbands and wives are having numerous effects.[43] Previous marriage patterns meant that there were generally no decisions to be made regarding the wife's chief life interest and sphere, nor the husband's. She concentrated on domestic activities and he concentrated on occupational efforts. Today, however, sex-role shifts toward egalitarianism mean that such a pattern is less inevitable, and many new and critical decisions must be made.[44] Increasing numbers of younger and better educated men and women are bargaining with each other about their chief life interests. And this is occurring not only among those soon-to-be or newly married, but also among couples married for some time. In such modern marriages there are virtually no non-negotiable issues; for example, where to live (near his work or hers), how many children to have and when, who will perform child-care and domestic chores, and how to spend *their* incomes.

In addition to the number of issues to be decided, there is also the matter of how this is negotiated. Women who have more traditional roles in marriage tend to negotiate with their husbands and try to persuade them to compromise on the basis of *collective* interest—what is best for the family group, for their marital relationship, for the children. A woman who has adopted modern roles tends to negotiate more in terms of her own *individualistic* interests—what is best for her. Such a strategy seems to result in achieving more equitable compromises in terms of reaching her goals.

Stage in the family purchase-decision process

The marketer is interested not only in the physical act of purchasing a product or brand, but also in the stages leading up to that decision. The research study on family participation and influence in purchasing behaviour presented in Table 6.6 found that roles and influence vary throughout the buyer decision-making process. Such knowledge can be of great help in formulating product, promotion, channel and pricing strategies. For some products wives are involved more heavily in the initiation, information-seeking and purchasing stages than are husbands. At other times, however, there is a greater tendency for husbands to participate in the decision process, particularly when the product is high-priced and technically or mechanically complex.

Studies have examined a wide variety of products and services with similar findings. Their data support the contention that the extent of husband–wife involvement varies considerably from product to product throughout the decision-making process.[45]

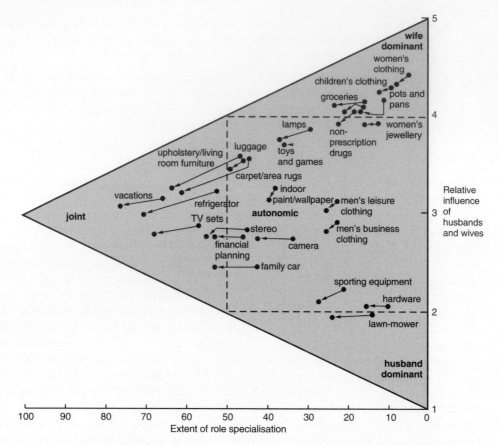

FIG. 6.8 Marital role changes in the decision process for 25 products/services
Source: S. Amanda Putnam & William R. Davidson, *Family Purchasing Behaviour: II Family Roles by Product Category*, Management Horizons, A Division of Price Waterhouse, Dublin, OH, 1987, p. 16. Reprinted with permission.

Figure 6.8 graphically illustrates the changes in marital roles occurring among a sample of American husbands and wives as decision making proceeds from search for information to final decision.

Family-specific characteristics

There are a number of additional variables that have been found to influence the nature of purchasing decisions made within the family. These include aspects related to culture, social class, family life cycle and sex-role orientation. Figure 6.9 shows how these may be put together to form a model describing family buyer behaviour.[46]

CULTURE

The roles of husbands and wives may differ dramatically from culture to culture, which may result in numerous differences in consumer decision making. One approach argues that the basic family systems encountered by the marketer around the world fall into three general patterns based on the degree of equality between the sexes. These can be illustrated as follows:

1. In Islamic cultures, the wife is generally in a subordinate and secluded role, with few rights and little control over the affairs of the family.

2. In the Latin American culture, the wife is freer but is still definitely a junior member of the partnership, with the husband having the final authority in all but minor matters.

3. In Australasian, European and North American cultures, the basic pattern is now equality as roles have shifted and male dominance has lessened. This latter region, for instance, evidences substantial similarity with regard to husband–wife involvement for a number of household activities.[47]

SOCIAL CLASS

Several studies on the relationship of socioeconomic class and joint participation in purchase decision making have indicated that a curvilinear relationship exists. That is, autonomy in decision making is most likely in upper and lower social classes, while joint decision making is most common among the middle class.

REFERENCE GROUPS AND SOCIAL INTERACTION

Although no research has been conducted on the role of reference groups in family purchase decisions, it is thought that such relationships are influential. Some authors indicate that the more social ties or connections spouses have with relatives or friends, the fewer joint or shared decisions they make. This is because some decisions may be made in consultation with friends or relatives rather than only with one's spouse.[48]

STAGE IN LIFE CYCLE

The nature of family decision making changes over the life cycle. For example, wives with preschool-aged children have considerably less independent responsibility for economic decisions than do other wives. In addition, families in early stages of the life cycle show a very high frequency of joint decisions.[49] However, evidence indicates that joint decision making declines over the life cycle. This tendency has been explained in terms of an increased efficiency or competence that people develop over a period of time in making purchasing decisions that are acceptable to their spouses. Such competence eliminates the need for extensive interaction.[50]

There is a suggestion, but it requires further research to substantiate the pattern, that joint decision making between spouses may become more important again after retirement. Several factors may contribute to this. Without working pressures, more time is available. A reduced income may mean that the financial risk associated with purchases may rise, bringing both partners into a decision. Finally, the power structure in the family is often altered after retirement, because the economic resources contributed to the family change as a salary is replaced by a pension.[51] A trend towards more joint involvement later in life might also be seen to fit with the data reported earlier in the chapter on time spent shopping, which showed an equalisation between men and women in the over-45s without children.

MOBILITY

Mobility, both social as well as geographic, tends to increase the extent of intrafamily communication and the degree of joint decision making. One researcher attributes this to the fact that movement away from stable primary groups such as family and close friends 'throws spouses upon each other'.[52]

FAMILY STRUCTURE

Based on a study of purchase-decision processes by families as opposed to couples without children, husbands tended to dominate decision making more in families, while joint decision making was more prevalent among couples.[53] Also, there are differences between married and cohabiting couples in terms of purchase involvement and participation. There is more autonomy and less female influence among unmarried than among married couples. However, these patterns vary from product to product and from decision stage to decision stage.[54]

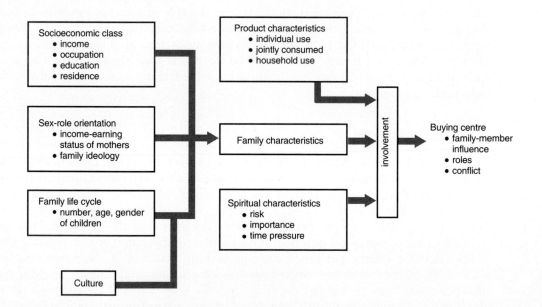

FIG. 6.9 A model of family buyer behaviour   Source: Christina Kwai-Choi Lee, 'A Model of Family Buyer Behaviour', *New Zealand Journal of Business* 14, 1992, p. 56.

Marketing implications of family purchasing decisions

It should be clear by now that the marketer's strategy is influenced at almost every turn by the nature of family role and decision-making patterns. Whether the marketer is concerned with product, promotion, channel or pricing decisions, family household purchase patterns must be well understood. Consider the following implications for promotion strategy.

Family roles and decision-making patterns impact strongly on the development of advertising and personal selling messages. For instance, the evaluative criteria by which a family will decide which brand of major appliance to purchase must be understood in developing the sales message. However, these criteria may vary among husbands and wives. For those decisions in which one spouse (such as the wife) dominates, messages may be developed with that segment in mind. However, where joint decision making prevails, the marketer may need to develop separate messages attuned to each party's buying criteria.

Similarly, differences in use of media among family members may necessitate using various message channels in order to reach influential or dominant family members. Reaching the purchaser may require one communication medium, while reaching the user may require another. For example, wives often are the purchasers of their husband's clothing. Consequently, a men's clothing manufacturer may use one campaign to reach men through male-dominated media and another campaign to reach women through female-oriented media, to encourage their purchase of the brand. Appealing to both segments with specific media and with appeals that are appropriate for each would be ideal, but this approach assumes a rather large budget.

A similar strategy is often called for when advertising products for which children are significantly involved in the purchase decision. For example, because children directly influence the choice of which fast-food establishment to patronise, Hungry Jacks, McDonald's and other chains find it necessary to appeal to children as well as to their parents. As a result, ads often feature people of all ages, with particular emphasis on families. Toy companies, likewise, often aim their ads at children as well as at parents. In fact, they do more than simply advertise; they systematically develop television programs that feature the product. In the case of the Teenage Mutant Ninja Turtles or Power Rangers, the whole product mix could be seen to include not just the toys but the television programs, films, collecting cards and other merchandising items.

THE CHANGING FAMILY

This section will examine ways in which changes are occurring among families in our cultures, and how these changes may be expected to affect the marketer.[55] Major changes in family structures were reviewed earlier in considering the family life cycle. The other most important area of change relates to the impact of changing sex roles on family processes and activities.

There is no doubt about which of the redefinitions of the past twenty years has had the most impact on the Australian way of life: it is the redefinition of gender roles which has taken place in the minds of roughly half the population—the female half.[56]

This quotation from Hugh Mackay makes two important points. First, it emphasises the speed of change. Though some of the trends that will be discussed could be discerned before the 1970s, it is only since that time that women have shaken off the status of 'second-class' citizens and been able to compete on virtually equal terms with men. This is not simply a comment on education and employment but perhaps more importantly reflects the treatment distributed by legal and financial services. Only since the 1970s have these two sets of institutions moved towards giving parity to males and females as *consumers*, and this has had a profound effect on their roles in society. Secondly, it is understood that males have been slow to recognise many of these changes and to comprehend the impacts on their roles in the family and society. News reports in 1994 showed how teenage boys are failing to cope with school systems where their female counterparts are not conforming to conventional stereotypes and are outperforming them in traditional male areas such as science and sports.

The changing role of women is thought to be best reflected in the proportion of married women in the workforce. This has risen from 32 per cent in 1970 to 53 per cent in 1990. Perhaps more importantly, 60 per cent of married women with dependent children are in the work force. This indicates how the revolution has started with the younger women in society and, hence, how we can expect these trends to continue. Rising participation in employment is only one aspect of changing female roles. It is easy to reflect that employment affects resource contribution to the family and therefore shifts the economic power within a family, affecting consumer decision making. But it is argued that the changes have been more fundamental than women simply entering into paid employment outside the home. Role definitions have changed with respect to romance and sex, parenting, household management, leisure, politics—in fact, every facet of life. This is reflected in the fact that it is not necessary in the 1990s for a woman to enter paid employment outside the home in order to acquire status. The choice to stay at home and manage the house and the family is now a respected one, and one that has even been given legitimacy by attempts in both Australia and New Zealand to produce national accounts taking this production into account.

This last point illustrates an important aspect of consumer behaviour that is often ignored when discussing the changing roles of women. That is that many women have simply changed the sector in the economy where they contribute to production. Instead of producing goods and services for the rest of the family to consume, they are now active in producing for other markets within the economy. Within the family, part of the woman's role has changed from a producer to a consumer. There is plenty of evidence to show that, in families where both spouses work full time, males have not generally taken on an equal share of household duties. Consequently, the woman remains the most important producer of household services, such as cooking and cleaning and typically marketers have responded with products that have made it possible for the woman to perform all these tasks in less time with less effort. Consumer durables such as microwaves, automatic washing machines and dishwashers all play their part in saving time and production effort for the woman. Similarly, improved cleaning agents and preprepared meals and sauces are all responses to the need to cut production time in the home. All this is to say that what has really changed is the way in which many women fulfil their traditional roles of mother, cook and cleaner, and that male participation in the household management has developed more slowly. Estimates show that the number of men involved in grocery shopping in Australia doubled between 1982 and 1992.[57] In part this growth was determined by the growth in male lone-parent households rather than an equalising or redistribution of roles in many married households. It is recognised that the degree of participation in household duties by husbands is generally unrelated to the amount of paid work being done by their wives. Extrapolating from what we know about family communication systems and participation in decision making, it is likely that education, social class and cultural norms are far more important than the pressure on family time caused by both spouses working outside the home.

One interpretation of the changing role of women is that it is associated with a redefinition of independence. Historically, marriage was seen as granting independence as the woman assumed responsibility for her own household instead of working within her mother's. Independence now emphasises the individual and not the family group. In this context it is part of a more general trend in society in the last 20 years where individualism, and competition between individuals, has been promoted above co-operation and collective welfare. The danger of this interpretation is that an equalising of status between males and females is not seen as a feature of a co-operative society. Clearly this need not be the case. However, it is important to recognise increased individualism in consumer behaviour. Many families operate as a loosely affiliated group of individuals rather than an integrated and heavily interdependent set; that is, in the sociological terms explained in the previous chapter, they are far less *cohesive*. A good illustration of how this trend has affected family life is the approach to mealtimes. For many families these are no longer occasions where all members assemble together. Instead family members often eat independently with a tendency to graze. The growing popularity of preprepared meals, microwaves, snack foods and takeaways all reflect this trend. Historically, mealtimes have been regarded as important occasions for family communication and unity. Nowadays, Mackay quotes examples of wives and mothers whose objective it is to assemble the family together for a meal on a weekly basis.[58]

Individualism also increasingly pervades the leisure and entertainment activities of families. In particular, the VCR is recognised as having liberated the family from the constraints of sitting together at particular times jointly to watch television. Programs are recorded and watched when convenient to any individual member of the family. Part of the same trend is the tendency for households to acquire multiple television sets—often so that children can watch their own programs in the convenience and privacy of their own rooms. A further item of new technology that increases individualism is the home computer. Although many computer games may be set up for multiple players, home computers are still single-user items at any particular moment, and they may take the attention of people for several hours at a session. All these technologies may reduce personal interaction within families.

Research on changing values, which was reviewed in Chapter 3, suggested that our societies are still committed to the family as a central institution. It is likely that the search for a return to traditional values in part reflects the instability in modern family life. The ambiguity in role structures, with the uncertainty that this occasions, and the unsteadiness of family group membership mean that the search for an idealised family lifestyle becomes ever more important. The more difficult it is to attain, the more important will be its expression in our values literature.

SUMMARY

This chapter described the influence of the family on consumer behaviour. First, the terms 'family' and 'household' were defined. Next, we described several types of families and the purpose of the family. The concept of family life cycle was examined in some detail. This progression of stages through which individuals and families proceed over time is found to be a primary determinant of the family's purchasing behaviour. In addition, it was suggested that life cycle offers a richer explanation of consumer behaviour than single variables such as age.

The nature of family purchasing decisions was discussed next from four vantage points: role structure and the influence of each family member based on his or her role in the family; power relationships within the family and their ability to explain the dominance of particular family members in various purchase decisions; the purchase decision and the varying roles and influences of particular family members at each stage of the process; and additional variables that are family-specific and have an influence on purchase decisions.

The final section of this chapter discussed the evolving family system, especially the changing roles of women and men, and suggested some of the effects on marketing activities likely to result.

MANAGERIAL REFLECTIONS

For our product or service situation:

1. Are families or households the target of greatest interest to us in marketing efforts?

2. Which family life-cycle stage is likely to be the most important in its consumption?

3. How does the family role structure play a part in its purchase and consumption?

4. What general patterns of purchase influence are exhibited among family members, and how do these influences change as the decision process continues?

5. How are changing female or male family roles influencing the marketing approaches necessary to reach and sell our prospects effectively?

DISCUSSION TOPICS

1. Distinguish between families and households. In what ways is each important to the marketer in analysing consumer behaviour?

2. Describe the traditional and more modern family life-cycle stages. What influence does life cycle have on consumer behaviour?

3. Explain how marketers of the following items would use the life-cycle concept in their strategies:
    (a) life insurance
    (b) pianos
    (c) retail banking
    (d) camping equipment

4. Describe the meanings of the following family roles:
    (a) instrumental and expressive
    (b) internal and external
    (c) purchase-process.
    What is their significance in terms of consumer behaviour and marketing strategy?

5. Referring to Figure 6.8 showing family decision-making power structures, explain how a marketer could use this information in developing marketing strategies (especially advertising and personal selling activities) for the following products:
    (a) living-room furniture
    (b) lawn mower
    (c) kitchenware
    (d) cars

6. Write a report on one of the following subjects, indicating specifically what some of the effects on consumer behaviour and marketing might be:
    (a) changing family values
    (b) changing role of women
    (c) divorce and alternative 'family' arrangements

7. Discuss the role of children in family decision making.

8. Identify three local restaurants (or other suitable retailers and services) and assess how each attracts a clientele in different stages of the family life cycle.

9. Interview local salespeople responsible for selling a range of items such as kitchenware, cameras, automobiles and living-room furniture. Ask about husband/wife influence in decision making and compare your results on the observations of salespeople with the research results summarised in this chapter.

REFERENCES

1. Elizabeth S. Moore-Shay & William L. Wilkie, 'Recent Developments in Research on Family Decisions', in Michael Houston (ed.), *Advances in Consumer Research*, vol. 15, Association for Consumer Research, Provo, UT, 1988, pp. 454–60.
2. Joseph Rowntree, *The Life Cycle of a London Labourer*, Macmillan, London, 1903.
3. William D. Wells & George Gubar, 'Life Cycle Concept in Marketing Research', *Journal of Marketing Research* 3, November 1966, pp. 355–63.
4. This summary of life-cycle stages has been adapted from the following sources: Wells & Gubar, *Journal of Marketing Research*, pp. 355–63; S. G. Barton, 'The Life Cycle and Buying Patterns', in Lincoln H. Clark (ed.), *Consumer Behavior*, vol. 2, New York University Press, New York, 1955, pp. 53–7; John B. Lansing & James N. Morgan, 'Consumer Finances over the Life Cycle', in Clark (ed.), pp. 36–51; and John B. Lansing & Leslie Kish, 'Family Life Cycle as an Independent Variable', *American Sociological Review* 22, October 1957, pp. 512–19.
5. Robert Lawson, 'A Modernised New Zealand Family Life Cycle', *New Zealand Journal of Business* 11, October 1989, pp. 52–64.
6. Mary C. Gilly & Ben M. Enis, 'Recycling the Family Life Cycle: A Proposal for Redefinition', in Andrew Mitchell (ed.), *Advances in Consumer Research*, vol. 9, Association for Consumer Research, Ann Arbor, MI, 1982, p. 275.
7. Peter McDonald, 'Household and Family Trends in Australia', in *Australian Bureau of Statistics 1994 Yearbook Australia*, ABS, Canberra, 1994, pp. 149–64.
8. Lurene Joseph & David Yorke, 'Know Your Game Plan: Market Segmentation in the Personal Financial Services Sector', *Quarterly Review of Marketing*, Autumn 1989, pp. 9-11.
9. L. V. Dominguez & A. Page, 'Formulating a Strategic Portfolio of Profitable Retail Segments for Commercial Banks', *Journal of Economics and Business* 36, 1984, pp. 189–206.
10. Rob Lawson, 'Tourism and the Family Life Cycle', *Journal of Travel Research* 29(4), 1991, pp. 12–18; and Rob Lawson, 'The Family Life Cycle', in S. Witt & L. Moutinho (eds), *The Handbook of Tourism Marketing and Management*, 1st edn, Prentice-Hall, 1989, pp. 147–50.
11. William D. Danko & Charles M. Schaninger, 'An Empirical Evaluation of the Gilly-Enis Updated Household Life Cycle Model', *Journal of Business Research* 21, 1990, pp. 39–57; and William D. Danko & Charles M. Schaninger, 'Attitudinal and Leisure Activity Differences Across Modernized Household Life Cycle Categories', in M. E. Goldberg, G. Gom & R. W. Pollay (eds), *Advances in Consumer Research*, vol. 17, Association for Consumer Research, Provo, UT, 1990, pp. 886–94.
12. R. F. Lusch, E. F. Stafford & J. J. Kasulis, 'Durable Accumulation: An Examination of Priority Patterns', in H. Keith Hunt (ed.), *Advances in Consumer Research*, vol. 5, Association for Consumer Research, Provo, UT, 1978, pp. 119–25.
13. Michael C. Mayo & William J. Qualls, 'Household Durable Goods Acquisition

Behavior: A Longitudinal Study', in Melanie Wallendorf & Paul Anderson (eds), *Advances in Consumer Research*, vol. 14, Association for Consumer Research, Provo, UT, 1987, pp. 463–7.

14. Robin A. Douthitt & Joanne M. Fedyk, 'Family Composition, Parental Time, and Market Goods: Life Cycle Trade-offs', *Journal of Consumer Affairs* 24, Summer 1990, pp. 110–33; and Johan Amdt, 'Family Life Cycle as a Determinant of Size and Composition of Household Expenditures', in William L. Wilkie (ed.), *Advances in Consumer Research*, vol. 6, Association for Consumer Research, Ann Arbor, MI, 1979, pp. 128–32.

15. Stuart U. Rich & Subhash C. Jain, 'Social Class and Life Cycle as Predictors of Shopping Behaviour', *Journal of Marketing Research* 5, February 1968, pp. 41–9; and Ben M. Enis & Keith K. Cox, 'Demographic Analysis of Store Patronage Patterns: Uses and Pitfalls', in Robert L. King (ed.), *Marketing and the New Science of Planning*, American Marketing Association, Chicago, 1968, pp. 366–70.

16. George P. Moschis, 'Socialization Perspectives and Consumer Behaviour', in Ben M. Enis and Kenneth J. Roering (eds), *Review of Marketing 1981*, American Marketing Association, Chicago, 1981, p. 49.

17. National Industrial Conference Board, *Expenditure Patterns of the American Family*, Life, New York, 1965.

18. Susan E. Heckler, Terry L. Childers & Ramesh Arunachalam, 'Intergenerational Influences in Adult Buying Behaviors: An Examination of Moderating Factors', in Thomas K. Srull (ed.), *Advances in Consumer Research*, vol. 16, Association for Consumer Research, Provo, UT, 1989, pp. 276–84; and L. Woodsen, T. L. Childers & P. R. Winn, 'Intergenerational Influences in the Purchase of Auto Insurance', in W. Locander (ed.), *Business Conference Proceedings*, American Marketing Association, Chicago, IL, 1976, pp. 43–9.

19. C. W. Cotton, *Family Socialisation and the Learning of Outdoor Recreation Use Patterns*, thesis, University of Utah, 1976.

20. Elizabeth S. Moore-Shay & Richard J. Lutz, 'Intergenerational Influences in the Formation of Consumer Attitudes and Beliefs About the Marketplace: Mothers and Daughters', in Michael Houston (ed.), *Advances in Consumer Research*, vol. 15, Association for Consumer Research, Provo, UT, 1988, pp. 461–7; and Karin M. Ekstrom, Patriya S. Tansuhaj & Ellen R. Foxman, 'Children's Influence in Family Decisions and Consumer Socialization: A Reciprocal View', in Melanie Wallendorf & Paul Anderson (eds), *Advances in Consumer Research*, vol. 14, Association for Consumer Research, Provo, UT, 1987, pp. 283–7.

21. Patricia Sorce, Lynette Loomis & Philip R. Tyler, 'Intergenerational Influence on Consumer Decision Making', in Thomas K. Srull (ed.), *Advances in Consumer Research*, vol. 16, Association for Consumer Research, Provo, UT, 1989, pp. 271–5; and Peter McDonald, 'Household and Family Trends in Australia', in *Australian Bureau of Statistics 1994 Yearbook Australia*, ABS, Canberra, 1994, pp. 149–64.

22. This section is largely developed from Hugh Mackay, 'Reinventing Australia', Angus & Robertson, Sydney, 1993, pp. 55–84; and McDonald, *1994 Yearbook Australia*, pp. 149–64.

23. Mackay, ibid, p. 79.

24. William J. Qualls, 'Household Decision Behavior: The Impact of Husbands and Wives' Sex Role Orientation', *Journal of Consumer Research* 14, September 1987, pp. 264–79.

25. Bernard Berelson & Gary Steiner, *Human Behavior: An Inventory of Scientific Findings*, Harcourt, New York, 1964, p. 314.

26. R. F. Bales, 'In Conference', *Harvard Business Review* 32, March–April 1954, pp. 44–50.

27. William F. Kenkel, 'Husband–Wife Interaction in Decision-making and Decision Choices', *Journal of Social Psychology* 54, 1961, p. 260.

28. Robert Ferber & Lucy Chao Lee, 'Husband–Wife Influence in Family Purchasing Behavior', *Journal of Consumer Research* 1, June 1974, pp. 43–50.
29. Lewis A. Berey & Richard Pollay, 'The Influencing Role of the Child in Family Decision Making', *Journal of Marketing Research* 5, February 1968, p. 72.
30. John S. Coulson, 'Buying Decisions within the Family and the Consumer Brand Relationship', in Joseph W. Newman (ed.), *On Knowing the Consumer*, Wiley, New York, 1967, p. 60.
31. Ellen Foxman & Alvin C. Burns, 'Role Load in the Household', in Melanie Wallendorf & Paul Anderson (eds), *Advances in Consumer Research*, vol. 14, Association for Consumer Research, Provo, UT, 1987, pp. 458–62.
32. P. G. Herbst, 'Conceptual Framework for Studying the Family', in O. A. Oeser & S. B. Hammond (eds), *Social Structure and Personality in a City*, Routledge, London, 1954.
33. Harry L. Davis & Benny P. Rigaux, 'Perceptions of Marital Roles in Decision Processes', *Journal of Consumer Research* 1, June 1974, pp. 51–62. (Note that the term 'syncratic' has become established in consumer behaviour to refer to joint decision making. The origin of this term is obscure to say the least and probably results from a corruption or misspelling of 'syncretic'.)
34. E. H. Bonfield, 'Perception of Marital Roles in Decision Processes: Replication and Extension', in H. Keith Hunt (ed.), *Advances in Consumer Research*, vol. 5, Association for Consumer Research, Ann Arbor, MI, 1978, pp. 300–7.
35. See for example, Arch G. Woodside, 'Dominance and Conflict in Family Purchasing Decisions', in M. Venkatesan (ed.), *Proceedings of the Third Annual Conference*, Association for Consumer Research, Chicago, IL, 1972, pp. 650–9; and Elizabeth H. Wolgast, 'Do Husbands or Wives Make the Purchasing Decisions?', *Journal of Marketing* 22, October 1958, pp. 151–8.
36. Sarah Todd & Rob Lawson, 'Family Decision Making for Vacations', in N. Piercy et al (eds), *Marketing into the New Millennium*, Marketing Educators Group, Cardiff, 1991, pp. 1212–28.
37. Mark A. Patton & Vicki H. Brinkworth, 'Children's Influence in Parents' Purchase Decision: A Western Australian Case Study', *Proceedings of the International Marketing Educators Conference 14–16 April 1993*, Edith Cowan University, Perth, 1993.
38. William R. Swinyard & Cheng Peng Sim, 'Perception of Children's Influence on Family Decision Processes', *Journal of Consumer Marketing* 4, Winter 1987, pp. 25–38.
39. Harry L. Davis, 'Decision Making within the Household', *Journal of Consumer Research* 2, March 1976, pp. 254–6; Michael A. Belch, George E. Belch & Donald Sciglimpaglia, 'Conflict in Family Decision Making: An Exploratory Investigation', in Jerry C. Olson (ed.), *Advances in Consumer Research*, vol. 7, Association for Consumer Research, Ann Arbor, MI, 1980, pp. 475–9; and Jagdish N. Sheth, 'A Theory of Family Buying Decisions', in Jagdish N. Sheth (ed.), *Models of Buyer Behavior*, Harper & Row, New York, 1974, p. 33.
40. William J. Qualls, 'Toward Understanding the Dynamics of Household Decision Conflict Behavior', in Michael Houston (ed.), *Advances in Consumer Research*, vol. 15, Association for Consumer Research, Provo, UT, 1988, pp. 442–8; and Rosann L. Spiro, 'Persuasion in Family Decision Making', *Journal of Consumer Research* 9, March 1983, pp. 393–402.
41. Margaret C. Nelson, 'The Resolution of Conflict in Joint Purchase Decisions by Husbands and Wives: A Review and Empirical Test', in Michael Houston (ed.), *Advances in Consumer Research*, vol. 15, Association for Consumer Research, Provo, UT, 1988, pp. 436–41.
42. Meredith Lawley, Janelle McPhail, Oliver Yau & Wayne Kwan, 'A Model of Family Decision Making: The Case of Australian Couples', *Proceedings of the Marketing Educators Conference 4–6 February 1992*, vol. 3, Edith Cowan University, Perth, pp. 685–99.

43. John Scanzoni, 'Changing Sex Roles and Emerging Directions in Family Decision Making', *Journal of Consumer Research* 4, December 1977, pp. 185–8.
44. Chankon Kim & Hanjoon Lee, 'Sex Role Attitudes of Spouses and Task Sharing Behaviour', in Thomas K. Srull (ed.), *Advances in Consumer Research*, vol. 16, Association for Consumer Research, Provo, UT, 1989, pp. 671–9.
45. See, for example, Arch G. Woodside & John F. Willenborg, 'Husband and Wife Interactions and Marketing Decisions', *Southern Journal of Business* 7, May 1972, p. 55; and L. Jaffe Associates Inc., 'A Pilot Study of the Roles of Husbands and Wives in Purchasing Decisions', Study conducted for *Life* magazine, 1965.
46. Christina Kwai-Choi Lee, 'A Model of Family Buyer Behaviour', *New Zealand Journal of Business* 14, 1992, pp. 50–60.
47. Susan P. Douglas, 'A Cross-National Exploration of Husband–Wife Involvement in Selected Household Activities', in William L. Wilkie (ed.), *Advances in Consumer Research*, vol. 6, Association for Consumer Research, Ann Arbor, MI, 1979, pp. 364–71.
48. James F. Engel, David T. Kollat & Roger D. Blackwell, *Consumer Behavior*, 2nd edn, Holt, New York, 1973, pp. 199–200; and Mira Komarovsky, 'Class Differences in Family Decision-making on Expenditures', in Nelson Foote (ed.), *Household Decision-making*, New York University Press, New York, 1961, p. 258.
49. Wolgast, op cit, Ref 35, p. 154.
50. Donald H. Granbois, 'The Role of Communication in the Family Decision-making Process', in Stephen A. Greyser (ed.), *Toward Scientific Marketing*, American Marketing Association, Chicago, IL, 1963, pp. 44–57.
51. Rob Lawson, The Family Life Cycle: An Examination of Demographic Relationships and Patterns of Tourist Behaviour in England and New Zealand, PhD thesis, University of Sheffield, 1987.
52. Komarovsky, op cit, Ref 48, p. 258.
53. Pierre Filiatrault & J. R. Brent Ritchie, 'Joint Purchasing Decisions: A Comparison of Influence Structure in Family and Couple Decision-making Units', *Journal of Consumer Research* 7, September 1980, pp. 131–40.
54. William C. Gaidis, Corbett F. Gaulden, Nabil Y. Razzouk & John L. Schlacter, 'Decision Making in the Household: A Comparison Between Married and Cohabiting Couples', *Akron Business and Economic Review*, Fall 1986, pp. 72–84.
55. This section is largely developed from Mackay, op cit, Ref 22, pp. 24–54; and Michael Gilding, *The Making and Breaking of the Australian Family*, Allen & Unwin, Sydney, 1991, pp. 110–33.
56. Mackay, op cit, Ref 22, p. 24.
57. Georgina Windsor & Jennifer Foreshaw, 'Supermarket Invasion by Mrs Men: an Ad Bonanza', *Australian*, 3 August 1994, p. 3.
58. Mackay, op cit, Ref 22, p. 80.

CHAPTER 7

PERSONAL INFLUENCE AND DIFFUSION

LEARNING OBJECTIVES

AFTER STUDYING THIS CHAPTER YOU SHOULD UNDERSTAND:

➡ the nature and significance to marketers of personal and word-of-mouth communications;

➡ how the communication and influence process operates between marketers and consumers;

➡ the characteristics of opinion leaders, and the reasons they influence others and their leadership is accepted;

➡ the nature of an innovation;

➡ how individuals move through stages in a process of product adoption;

➡ the characteristics of groups or categories of adopters making up the diffusion process by which an innovation spreads through a market;

➡ what factors influence the rate of diffusion for an innovation;

➡ what marketing strategies are appropriate in utilising the personal influence process.

This chapter further investigates the way in which individuals influence each other's behaviour as consumers. We shall first describe the nature of influence and then discuss its significance as evidenced by word-of-mouth communication among individuals. Next, models of the flow of communication will be examined to better understand how personal influence occurs. Then we shall discuss the nature and significance of opinion leadership in marketing, and the characteristics of leaders as well as followers. The concept of personal influence is strongly embodied in the process of adoption and diffusion of innovations; this topic will also be examined to understand better its significance to the marketer. Finally, we shall see how the marketer can use the concept of influence to advantage by incorporating opinion leadership as a cornerstone of promotional programs.

THE NATURE AND SIGNIFICANCE OF PERSONAL INFLUENCE

Personal influence is best described as the effect or change in a person's attitudes or behaviour as a result of communication with others. It can occur in a number of ways. The following distinctions can be made to indicate the multidimensional nature of this communication phenomenon:

1. Communication leading to influence may be *source-initiated* (by the influencer) or *recipient-initiated* (by the influencee).

2. Communication may result in *one-way* or *two-way* influence. That is, the individual may influence while being influenced.

3. Communication resulting in influence may be *verbal* or *visual*.[1]

Personal influence is frequently used synonymously with the term 'word-of-mouth' advertising or communication, even though the above classification indicates that they are not the same. Word-of-mouth is oral communication, so it is actually a subset of personal influence; however, we shall use the terms synonymously in this chapter.

Promotional activities conducted by the marketer are not the only or necessarily the most important influences on purchasing behaviour. There is evidence that favourable word-of-mouth communication can have more influence than the huge sums spent on advertising. Consequently, many companies advertise little and depend, instead, on word-of-mouth promotion. In the construction industry in Australia, for example, research shows that advertising and other promotion strategies have little or no impact on which company consumers will decide to have build their homes. Word-of-mouth is the determining factor for this product category.[2] Whether for durable goods or non-durables, products or services, word-of-mouth advertising has a big impact.[3] For example, it is so critical to the film industry that an executive of Paramount Pictures has remarked, 'Word of mouth is the most important marketing element that exists'.[4]

The marketer frequently tries to create a 'synthetic', or simulated, word-of-mouth program by using celebrities in advertising campaigns. These spokespeople enter our homes via the media and speak to us as if it were a one-to-one conversation. This simulated personal influence may be very effective.

It is clear that personal influence—whether actual or synthetic—can be quite convincing. The marketer is vitally interested in this process because a product's success appears dependent on it. It is very important, therefore, that mostly favourable, not unfavourable, communications take place. As one study of the spread of usage in a new food product in a married students housing complex showed, exposure to favourable word-of-mouth communication increased the probability of purchase, while exposure to unfavourable comments decreased the probability.[5] Therefore, it is vitally important that marketers effectively manage the personal influence and word-of-mouth communications process.[6] It is not something that can be left to chance.

Why is word-of-mouth communication so strong? There seem to be three main reasons for its dominant position in relation to impersonal media:

1. Consumers view word-of-mouth as reliable and trustworthy information that can help people to make better buying decisions.

2. In contrast with the mass media, personal contacts can provide social support and give a stamp of approval to a purchase.

3. The information provided is often backed up by social-group pressure to force compliance with recommendations.[7]

In order to understand better the way in which personal influence and word-of-mouth advertising occur, two models of the communication process will be presented in the following section.

COMMUNICATION AND INFLUENCE FLOW

Personal influence is necessarily dependent upon the process of communication. For years marketers assumed that communication was a one-way process, flowing from the marketer to consumers. Later the process of communication and influence was found not to be an exclusively direct flow, as had been originally supposed. Instead, influence can move from the mass media directly to influentials, or *opinion leaders*, who then through interpersonal networks pass on to their associates what they have seen or heard. However, there are several problems with this view. First, it suggests that an absolute leader exists for each informal group, when actually all group members have some amount of opinion leadership. Secondly, information is assumed to flow only from the mass media to opinion leaders who disseminate it to followers—in fact, followers are also in touch with mass media, but perhaps not to the same degree as leaders. Finally, it is not always *influence* that is transmitted interpersonally, but in some cases simply information, which may be relatively free of influence.[8] Because of these limitations, many communications researchers now suggest a multistep interaction model as a more accurate representation of personal influence.

Audiences are not simply passive receivers of communication. Instead, they have been found in several studies to be active seekers and important links in the flow of market information. Many audience members act as transmitters and receivers of information. One study found a similarity between opinion leaders and opinion seekers. In fact, almost two-thirds of opinion seekers also viewed themselves as opinion leaders in a product category, underscoring the view that opinion leadership is more of an exchange of opinion and information than a one-way flow of influence.[9] It has, furthermore, been suggested that the flow of communication may take place through three or more stages. Figure 7.1 presents a model of this process.

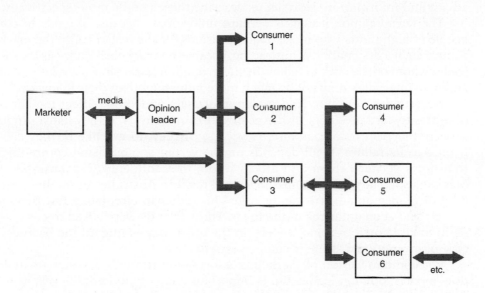

FIG. 7.1 A multistep model of communication

Consider the following examples of the different directions that a verbal flow of communication and personal influence may take between a source and a receiver:

1. *Source-initiated, one-way influence (this is most typical of the two-step flow model).* 'Ros told me how good her Dunlop radials are, so I decided to buy a set.'

2. *Receiver-initiated, one-way influence.* 'I asked Ros what kind of tyre she recommends.'

3. *Source-initiated, two-way influence.* 'I showed Mick our new Magic Chef stove. He really wants to buy one when his old stove gives out. His interest made me feel better about our range's higher price.'

4. *Receiver-initiated, two-way influence.* 'I asked Mick what he knew about electric ranges. We had an interesting discussion of the features of different brands.'

Of course, we could add additional levels to the flow and a visual mode of communication as well. The point is that obviously the communication process and flow of influence are very involved. In the next section we will more closely examine the nature of personal influence as effected through opinion leadership.

OPINION LEADERSHIP IN MARKETING

Opinion leaders were defined in Chapter 5 as those people who are able, in a given situation, to exert personal influence. They are the ones to whom others look for advice and information. Now, let us describe these people more specifically.

The term 'opinion leader' is perhaps unfortunate because it tends to connote people of high status who make major decisions for the rest of us. In the marketing context such a designation is misleading, because it erroneously suggests an absolute leader whom others seek to follow. In effect, opinion leadership is a relative concept, and opinion leaders may not be much more influential than their followers.[10]

Nevertheless, opinion leaders can informally and subtly affect the behaviour of others toward products, either positively or negatively. If they like a product or service, they can help to assure its success; if they do not like it, they can contribute to its failure. It all depends on the verbal and/or visual communication that flows between them and others whom they influence. For example, Hugh Mackay's son started a business in a rural town in Australia. Instead of spending a lot of money on advertising, he asked his father to circulate a few fliers to his friends and acquaintances in the town. Those friends were asked to circulate the fliers to all known 'opinion leaders' in the town. Depending on the business, this type of promotional strategy can be very effective.

For communication of marketing information through two-step or multistep flow models, opinion leadership is important and is found at all levels in society. Consumers tend to be influenced by those who are members of the same groups, people very much like themselves. Thus, every status level and every group will have opinion leaders, with the flow of influence being generally horizontal within them. However, the fact that opinion leaders are formed in all strata of society does not necessarily mean that they are equally effective or important to the marketer at each social level. In fact, personal influence appears to be more operative and to have greater importance and effectiveness at higher income and status levels.[11] These, then, are the levels that the marketer is often more concerned about reaching. Such opinion leaders may have an important impact on markets, as follows:

One out of every 10 adults is the trendsetter of the marketplace, according to one research organisation. These people are among the first to try new products and services. And because they are trendsetters, their approval of new items can ignite acceptance by the mass market. They were among the first to accept small cars, VCRs, jogging, CD players, bottled water and 'affinity' credit cards. They are better educated and earn more money than the average person, are typically married and in their 30s or 40s. They are categorised as influential if they have engaged in at least three public activities within the last year—such as running for political office, attending a public meeting or making a speech. They are attracted more than the average citizen to civic, local and national affairs, and are 'addicted' to television newscasts and newspapers. They seek product quality at a reasonable price, enjoy shopping in specialty stores and by mail, but do not like telemarketing sales calls.[12]

In Australia the use of census data can provide marketers with segmentation analyses of influential people. Companies such as Hermes Precisa Australia (see the following photo) provide geodemographic segmented data for companies to identify where their customers are living and what lifestyles they are leading. Opinion leaders can be identified in this way.

Inner City	% of Australian Households
1. High Living Materialists	1.88
2. Young Influentials	1.83
3. Student and Professional Cocktail	1.33
4. Bohemian Mix	3.11
5. Inner City Struggle	0.62
Higher Density Suburban	
6. Renters and Renovators	3.06
7. Post-War Migrants	4.97
8. Young Migrant Singles	2.05
9. Multicultural Blue Collar	4.59
Middle Suburban	
10. Affluentials in Prestige Areas	2.63
11. Wealthy and Wise	3.78
12. Middle Income, Older Families	4.22
Outer Suburban	
13. Established Investors	4.12
14. Qualified Achievers	6.06
15. Mature and Comfortable	5.71
16. Retired Singles and Couples	2.10
Urban Fringes	
17. Suburban Pioneers	2.19
18. New Homes, New Families	5.85
19. Older Communities	4.36
20. Blue Collar Fringe	3.64
21. Welfare Dependents	1.33
Country Towns	
22. Public Utility Towns	1.35
23. Provincial Families	6.26
24. Country Battlers	2.40
25. Self-Sufficient Lifestyles	2.78
26. Coastal and Country Retreats	2.54
27. Agricultural Service Towns	5.31
Agriculture and Outback	
28. Mining Communities	0.83
29. Outback Australia	0.33
30. Lifestyle Choice and Market Gardens	3.93
31. Homesteads and Farms	2.90
32. Grain and Livestock	1.94

MOSAIC   HPA HERMES PRECISA AUSTRALIA

Mosaic Tables   COURTESY OF HERMES PRECISA AUSTRALIA

Who are opinion leaders?

Because personal influence of opinion leaders is quite significant, marketers are obviously interested in trying to reach such influentials. To do so, however, requires that they first be identified and segmented. Perhaps they may then be reached with promotional messages and, in turn, will participate in additional communication and influence with their fellow group members.

CHARACTERISTICS

Numerous studies have been conducted attempting to identify opinion-leader characteristics. The research is not conclusive, but we have some understanding of the opinion leader's profile:

1. Opinion leaders have approximately the same social-class position as non-leaders, although they may have higher social status within the class.[13] This does not mean that personal influence does not flow across different class lines, but it is likely to be infrequent and of a visual rather than verbal nature.

2. Opinion leaders have greater exposure to mass media that are relevant to their area of interest.[14] For example, opinion leaders for women's fashions could be expected to have higher exposure to such magazines as *Vogue*. Similarly, automobile opinion leaders might be expected to read *Wheels* or *Modern Motor*. Exposure to relevant mass media provides them with information useful in enhancing their leadership potential.

3. Opinion leaders have greater interest in and knowledge of the area of influence than do non-leaders. This finding is closely related to their greater media exposure. Of course, knowledge is not a prerequisite for opinion-leader influence. Undoubtedly, much influence takes place by those who are ignorant of the topic of conversation.

4. Opinion leaders are more gregarious than non-leaders. This finding is logical, given that they must interact with those whom they influence. Thus, opinion leaders are generally more sociable or companionable.

5. Opinion leaders are more innovative than non-leaders. This does not mean, however, that they are *innovators* (the first people to purchase a new item). In fact, innovators and opinion leaders have been found in several studies to have differing characteristics and lifestyles. In the fashion market, for instance, the innovator is seen as an adventurer who is the earliest visual communicator of the newest styles aimed at the mass of fashion consumers.[15] The opinion leader, however, may be characterised more as an 'editor' of fashions, who defines and endorses appropriate standards.

6. Opinion leaders are more familiar with and loyal to group standards and values than are non-leaders. This refers to the fact that opinion leaders are vested with leadership authority by group members, and in order to maintain this position the individual has to reflect underlying norms and values for that area of consumption leadership. The clothing influential, for instance, cannot be too far ahead of or behind fashion, but must reflect the current norms in clothing.

7. Opinion leaders also appear to exhibit the personality trait of public individuation, which is a state in which they feel differentiated to some degree from other people and choose to act differently from them. People who are individuated could be expected to show high confidence, self-esteem, and ability to withstand criticism and rejection, and the need to be unique. Opinion leaders differentiate themselves by having greater knowledge of and interest in a particular product or issue than do opinion seekers. Moreover, opinion leaders demonstrate a willingness to stand out or be different in a group situation by disseminating information through word-of-mouth communication.[16]

'GENERAL' OPINION LEADERS

The question of whether generalised opinion leaders exist for a wide variety of products as opposed to specialised opinion leaders for each product has been the subject of much debate. Although research is often conflicting, it appears that there is *moderate* opinion leadership overlap across product categories; that is, general opinion leaders do appear to exist to some extent. One of the keys to this question seems to be the interest patterns of opinion leaders, with highest overlap existing among product categories involving similar interests.[17]

The existence of generalised opinion leaders or, more precisely, opinion leadership overlap, does not mean, however, that such individuals are opinion leaders for *all* product categories. One study of seven product-interest areas, for example, found that only about 3 per cent of the respondents were opinion leaders for at least five of the items.[18]

SITUATIONAL OPINION LEADERS

In the absence of a standardised, clear-cut opinion-leader profile applying across all products, and where influencers and influencees seem to be so much alike, how is the opinion leader distinguished from those who follow? It has been suggested that influence is related to the following factors:

1. *The personification of certain values (who one is)*. Thus, individuals who closely represent or personify group values are likely to be opinion leaders. For example, if some particular clothing style is valued by the group, the individual most closely representing this is likely to be influential.

2. *Competence (what one knows)*. An individual who is very knowledgeable about some topic valued by the group will probably be influential.

3. *Strategic social location (whom one knows inside and outside the group)*. For example, an individual who is available and active in the interpersonal communication process in the Rotary Club will have a better chance for a leadership position.[19]

Thus, influence takes place because opinion leaders personify group norms, exhibit competence and are accessible, with active communication between themselves and others. Because such leadership is situational and does not have a consistent pattern of characteristics across products, marketers might investigate the three characteristics cited above with regard to those who consume particular goods or services. In this way, they may uncover specific patterns, which could then guide marketing strategies.

Why opinion leaders attempt to influence others

Consumers, generally, do not speak about products or services unless they expect to derive some kind of satisfaction from the activity. We can categorise four reasons that opinion leaders engage in word-of-mouth communication about products or services.

PRODUCT-INVOLVEMENT

Use of a product or service may create a tension that may need to be reduced by way of talk, recommendation and enthusiasm to provide relief. For example, consumers often are fascinated by new items and feel they must tell someone what a good product they've found.

SELF-INVOLVEMENT

In this case, the emphasis is more on ways the influencer can gratify certain emotional needs. Product talk can achieve such goals as the following:

1. *Gaining attention.* People can have something to say in a conversation by talking about products rather than people or ideas.

2. *Showing connoisseurship.* Talk about certain products can show one is 'in the know' and has good judgment.

3. *Feeling like a pioneer.* The speaker likes to identify with the newness and uniqueness of products and their pioneering manufacturers.

4. *Having inside information.* The speaker is able to show how much more he or she knows about the product and its manufacturer than the listener (and thus how clever the speaker is).

5. *Suggesting status.* Talking about products with social status may elevate the speaker to the level of its users.

6. *Spreading the gospel.* The speaker may be able to convert the listener to using the product.

7. *Seeking confirmation.* The more followers accept the speaker's advice about the product, the more assured the speaker feels about his or her own decision.

8. *Asserting superiority.* Recommending products to listeners can help the speaker gain leadership and test the extent to which others will follow.

OTHER-INVOLVEMENT

In this case, product talk fills the need to give something to the listener, to share one's happiness or to express care, love or friendship.

MESSAGE-INVOLVEMENT

Talking may also be stimulated by great interest in the messages used to present the product. For example, advertising that is highly original and entertaining may be the topic of conversation, especially since most of us feel we are experts on effective advertising and can thus speak as critics.[20]

The involvement level of consumers, therefore, is a critically important dimension of their behaviour as opinion leaders and as innovators. The concept of enduring involvement—a continuing product interest and concern that goes beyond situational influences—is important to understanding opinion-leader behaviour. Research indicates that enduring involvement motivates opinion leadership, which, in turn, results in information sharing and innovative behaviour.[21]

Why followers accept personal influence

Marketers would certainly want to know the situational attributes under which opinion leadership will most likely occur so that they can actively cultivate the process. There are numerous product, individual and group characteristics that can be expected to influence the acceptance of opinion leadership by followers. Only a few of these will be cited here.[22]

Product characteristics are important in judging the significance of personal influence. For example, when products are highly visible or conspicuous (such as clothing as opposed to laundry detergents), they are more susceptible to personal influence. Products that can be tried or tested and compared against objective criteria are less susceptible to personal influence than those that cannot be tried. Product complexity may also give rise to personal influence, as would a product that consumers perceive to have a high amount of risk associated with its purchase.

Using these four factors to evaluate products helps the marketer to determine when opinion leadership is apt to be strong. For example, most food products would be expected to be associated with little opinion leadership, while small appliances would be thought to be subject to much more personal influence. However, one research study indicates that opinion seeking is not limited to particular types of goods but ranges across non-durables and durables, with the highest incidence occurring in the food category. Perhaps consumers use social communications more as a means of acquiring product information than as a means for reducing risk or evaluating complex products.[23] For example, research in Australia revealed that risk reduction was not a major factor in adoption of CD players.[24]

Individual consumer characteristics and group influences are also important in determining the extent to which opinion leadership will be operative. For example, individuals who are other-directed look to other people for behavioural guidance, in contrast to those who are inner-directed and rely on their own value systems for direction. Also, individuals who face new life experiences (such as newlyweds or retirees) may be very receptive to information and consequently quite susceptible to personal influence. In addition, aspirants to membership in particular groups are receptive to personal influence and may emulate the behaviour of group members. A final factor to be mentioned that affects acceptance of opinion leadership is the individual's personality. For example, some individuals are more persuasible than others.

The market maven

A view that broadens the concept of opinion leaders is that of the market maven. The term 'maven' is Yiddish and connotes a neighbourhood expert who has information ranging over several topics. 'Market mavens', therefore, are defined as individuals having information about many kinds of products, places to shop and other facets of markets, who initiate discussions with consumers and respond to their requests for market information.[25] This definition is similar to that of the opinion leader in that influence is derived from knowledge and expertise. However, it differs in that the market maven's expertise is of a more general market, rather than one of a product-specific nature. Market mavens do not have to be early purchasers of products or necessarily even users of products about which they have information. Other than the finding that market mavens are more likely to be women, there is no clear demographic or psychographic profile identified yet for these influencers.[26] However, they appear to be aware of new products earlier; provide information to other consumers across product categories; engage in general market-information seeking; show greater participation in market activities, couponing and reading advertisements; and have higher than average general media usage. They enjoy shopping and use browsing and shopping as an important way of learning about new products.[27] Mavens are much more likely to read both direct-mail advertising and local direct-mail classified newspapers than are non-mavens. Similarly, home-making magazines are more likely to be read by mavens, but news magazines are not effective with this group. Thus, direct mail and women's magazines are effective media vehicles to target for advertising efforts aimed at market mavens.[28]

While opinion leaders and early purchasers of products may be important prospects when diffusing information about new products, their usefulness may be limited in communicating other information such as changes in prices, availability of products, new stores and the like. Here, mavens may be useful targets for marketers because they appear to have knowledge about a wide array of goods and services, and about the process of acquiring them, and they are also active in providing other people with information and advice. Retailers and producers of low-involvement items (such as convenience goods), particularly, may find these influences very important in the spread of information. It appears that certain retail settings (such as grocery stores) are more commonly talked about than others (such as discount and department stores). However, mavens generally engage in significantly more frequent information provision about retailers than do other consumers.

ADOPTION AND DIFFUSION OF INNOVATIONS

The innovation adoption and diffusion processes will be discussed in this section to illustrate the way in which communication and interpersonal influence work with new products.

What is an innovation?

Product innovation is an essential element of the dynamic Australian economy and a critical activity for the marketer. As new and better products are developed they are launched in the marketplace, and their fate is determined by votes of consumers through their purchase or rejection of the products. New-product introductions are becoming more expensive, and the chances of product success are less than in previous years.[29] Thus, it is important to understand the nature of an innovation and how individuals and groups of consumers adopt them.

How innovative do you think these consumers are?
COURTESY OF NORMAN NICHOLLS

The term 'innovation' can be defined in several ways. One view based on consumer perceptions defines it as 'any idea, practice, or material artefact perceived to be new by the relevant adopting unit'.[30] Another view establishes a continuum or range of newness based on the product's effect on established consumption patterns. Under this concept three categories of innovation are classified as described below:

1. *Continuous innovations.* Have the least disrupting influence on established consumption patterns. Product alteration is involved, rather

than the establishment of a totally new product. Examples of these products are fluoride toothpaste, new-model car changeovers and menthol cigarettes.

2. *Dynamically continuous innovations*. Have more disrupting effects than do continuous innovations, although they do not generally alter established patterns. These may involve the creation of new products or the alteration of existing items. Examples of such products would include electric toothbrushes, electric cars, wall-sized television screens, and videophones.

3. *Discontinuous innovations*. Involve the establishment of new products with new behaviour patterns. Examples of these products would include televisions, computers and automobiles.[31]

The adoption process

Before we examine how products spread among population groups, we need to look at the process as it relates to individuals. The acceptance and continued use of a product or brand by an individual is referred to as 'adoption', although there are differing views about when this happens.[32] Figure 7.2 presents a simplified diagram of the adoption process. This model consists of the following stages:

1. *Awareness*. At this stage the potential adopter finds out about the existence of a product but has very little information and no well-formed attitudes about it.

2. *Comprehension*. This stage represents the consumers having knowledge and understanding of what the product is and can do.

3. *Attitude*. Here, the consumer develops favourable or unfavourable behavioural predispositions toward the product. Termination of the adoption process is likely at this stage if attitudes are not favourable.

4. *Legitimation*. Here, the consumer becomes convinced that the product should be adopted. This stage is predicated upon favourable attitudes toward the innovation, and the consumer may use information already gathered as well as additional information in order to reach a decision.

5. *Trial*. If possible, the consumer tests or tries the product to determine its utility. Trial may take place cognitively, whereby the individual vicariously uses the product in a hypothetical situation, or the consumer may actually use the product in a limited or total way, depending on the innovation's nature.

6. *Adoption*. At this stage the consumer determines whether or not to use the product in a full-scale way. Continued purchase and/or use of the item fulfils the adoption process.[33]

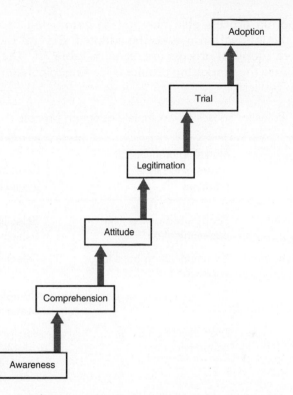

FIG. 7.2 The adoption decision process   Source: Adapted from Thomas S. Robertson, *Innovative Behavior and Communication*, Holt, New York, 1971. Reprinted by permission of the publisher.

Thus, adoption is seen to be a sequence of events through which individual consumers pass over a period of time. Some consumers pass through these stages early in a product's life while others may do so much later. In addition, the adoption process describes consumers who are actively involved in thinking about and considering a product.

The significance of the adoption process to the marketer is twofold. First, not all consumers pass through the adoption process with the same speed—some move swiftly, while others proceed more slowly. Secondly, the marketer's communication forms vary in their effectiveness over the different stages in the adoption process. These points can be important in assisting the marketer to develop an effective promotional program. It has been found, for example, that for early stages of the adoption process the mass media appear to be most effective in creating awareness; thus, the marketer would design awareness and interest-generating messages to be transmitted by such impersonal sources. At later stages in the adoption process, however, personal sources of information appear to become more important, so the marketer would desire to have effective personal selling and word-of-mouth communications at these points. This indicates, then, that as consumers move through the adoption process the amount of mass-media advertising might be decreased while the amount of personal selling is increased.

The adoption process also may not be completed by the individual, which means that the innovation will not be adopted. Several factors that may lead to an incomplete adoption process are listed in Table 7.1. The marketer should take care to minimise the marketing problems leading to consumer failure to complete the adoption process.

TABLE 7.1   Potential causes of incomplete adoption process

Acceptance process stage	Marketing-organisation causes of incomplete processes	Consumer causes of incomplete processes
Awareness	Poorly used or too little communication	Selective exposure Selective perception
Comprehension	Communication hard to understand	Selective retention
Attitude	Communication not persuasive	Complacency Suspended judgment
Legitimation	Poor source effect of communications	Peer-group pressure against adoption Laws regulating use of innovation
Trial	Behavioural response not specified in communications Poor distribution system	Alternative equally good Innovation not available
Adoption	Failure to develop new products and improve old products	Replaced by another innovation

Source: Adapted from Gerald Zaltman & Ronald Stiff, 'Theories of Diffusion', in Scott Ward & Thomas S. Robertson (eds), *Consumer Behavior: Theoretical Sources*, Prentice-Hall Inc., Englewood Cliffs, NJ, 1973, p. 451.

The diffusion process

In this section we shall discuss the nature of the process by which innovations spread. The marketer is vitally interested in this because it determines the success or failure of any new product brought to market. The marketer usually desires to secure the largest amount of adoption within the shortest period of time. Whether choosing such an accelerated strategy (as is the case for most continuous innovations) or taking an approach that moves more slowly (as might be taken with discontinuous innovations), marketers need to understand the diffusion process so that they can properly manage the spread of the new product or service.[34]

Although there are many limitations and weaknesses in much of the diffusion research that has been conducted by scholars, the research has helped us to understand the communication process for innovations and the social structure within which this occurs.[35]

We should first distinguish the concept of diffusion from that of adoption. As we saw earlier, the adoption process is an *individual* phenomenon, relating to the sequence of stages through which an individual passes from first hearing about a product to finally adopting it. The diffusion process, however, refers to a *group* phenomenon, indicating how an innovation spreads among consumers. The diffusion process, of course, necessarily involves the adoption process of many individuals over time.

Perhaps the best marketing-oriented definition of the diffusion process is 'the adoption of new products and services over time by consumers within social systems as encouraged by marketing activities'.[36] This definition recognises the various components of the process that are important in the spread of an innovation.

How does diffusion occur? Analysis of fashion life cycles and fashion diffusion provides some insights into the process. Several theories of fashion diffusion have been suggested.[37] First, the theory of upper-class fashion leadership postulates that fashions are initially adopted by the upper class and are then imitated by each succeeding lower class until they have 'trickled down' to the lowest class. The fashion industry has long emphasised elite-oriented fashion, and low-profile fashion designers and producers frequently copy the designs of their more famous counterparts. A second theory proposes that mass production combined with mass communications make new styles and information about new styles available simultaneously to all socioeconomic classes. Fashion diffusion, therefore, has the potential to start at essentially the same time within each class. This mass-market view is sometimes referred to as the horizontal-flow, or 'trickle-across', theory. A third and newer theory of fashion diffusion recognises that many new fashions have been initiated by subcultural groups such as youths, blue-collar workers and ethnic minorities. These innovations may range from new ideas (such as miniskirts), to customary artefacts of a culture or subculture, to styles resurrected from the past, or even to homemade inventions (such as the tie-dyed products pioneered by youth, which appeared in the 1960s). Whether a fashion is new or customary, the unique subculture style becomes admired and diffuses into the mass population where it is selectively assimilated into the dominant culture.

The fourth and most general theory of fashion diffusion suggests that nearly all creative or innovative individuals can become leaders of fashion trends if their innovative choices are reasonably in line with the social climate and lifestyles of the times. In this view, fashion leadership is not confined to the upper class but can emerge by a process in which collective tastes are formed by many people. Styles that most closely represent existing trends in consumers' tastes will slowly gain acceptance as the preferred fashion. Prestigious innovators who select this fashion will help to define better the public's tastes toward what should be the appropriate fashion and to legitimise the public's choices. There is evidence to support each of these theories of fashion diffusion.

Is this high or low fashion?
COURTESY OF AUSTRALIAN
TOURIST COMMISSION

The fashion-conscious or fashion-change agent of the population can be important to the spread of a new fashion. This group is a large and broadly fashion-oriented market segment. Many people in the population are interested in or oriented toward fashion monitoring, if not necessarily toward changing their wardrobes. For example, data consistently show that half the female population and 25 per cent of the male population have an active fashion consciousness. This group enjoys monitoring fashion magazines, fashion trends and new style offerings, and is broadly innovative and communicative. For a new style to obtain mass endorsement, fashion-change agents are important. This group, working across geographical regions and within personal social networks, is significant in the acceptance or rejection of a fashion object.[38]

As we see from the above description of the fashion-diffusion process, consumers who are enduringly involved with products are the ones who exercise an important position in the diffusion process. Such consumers tend to seek information on an ongoing basis, have considerable product knowledge and expertise, exert influence on other consumers' behaviour and buy new products.[39]

Diffusion also has a geographical dimension to it. For example, in the United States many social trends begin on the West Coast and work their way east. If current trends continue, the larger public will be expected to spend more time on shopping, playing sports, eating out and travelling than on housework and caring for children.[40]

Now, let's look more closely at the general process of diffusion and what it means for the marketer. We must remember that marketing actions should be designed to change the diffusion process to the firm's advantage.[41] Table 7.2 suggests how the proactive nature of marketing and competitive actions relate to various diffusion concepts.

TABLE 7.2 Marketing impact on diffusion

Diffusion concept	Marketing impact
The innovation	Marketing actions in product design and positioning are critical in the consumer perception of the innovation and its characteristics
The diffusion process	Marketing actions can influence the pattern and speed of diffusion for the total market and by segment, based on pricing, promotional expenditures and distribution intensity; competitive marketing actions have a similar effect
The adoption process	Marketing actions can modify the speed of adoption and the form of the adoption process; for example, via sampling programs that take consumers from awareness to trial
The communication process	Marketing change agents bear distinguishing characteristics from those in forming opinions; they are inherently self-serving and biased; advertising, personal selling and sales promotion are the dominant communication sources and can lead to purchase without 'objective, scientific authority'
Opinion leadership and personal influence	Marketing actions can both preclude the importance of personal influence and influence the occurrence of personal influence depending on objectives
Adopter categories	Marketing actions can be instrumental in determining who the innovator will be based on market segmentation decisions

Source: Thomas S. Robertson, 'Marketing's Potential Contribution to Consumer Behavior Research: The Case of Diffusion Theory', in Thomas C. Kinnnear (ed.), *Advances in Consumer Research*, vol.11, Association for Consumer Research, Provo, UT, 1984, p. 486.

CATEGORIES OF ADOPTERS

Because we know that people will not adopt an innovation all at the same time, we might classify consumers on the basis of time of adoption. In doing so, we will also discover that those who adopt new products at approximately the same time have similar characteristics. Armed with such knowledge, the marketer may thus be able to segment a market by adopter type, and aim strategies, in turn, at each group over time. Five adopter categories have been identified: innovator, early adopter, early majority, late majority and laggard. The characteristics of each group are summarised below.[42] The percentages that follow represent the proportion of all who adopt an innovation, which may only be a small proportion of the total market.

INNOVATORS (2.5 PER CENT OF A MARKET) The first to adopt new products, innovators are quite venturesome and eager to try new ideas. They have more risk capital (both material and social) and can afford to take calculated risks. Innovators are well educated, come from well-established families and are cosmopolitan, having friends outside the community. Their sources of information also transcend the local community, incorporating other innovators and impersonal and scientific sources. They may belong to state, regional or national organisations, and are respected by local community members for their success.

Robertson has distilled 21 studies of new-product diffusion and developed a profile of the innovative consumer. Because the studies span various product categories, sampling populations, research methodologies and definitions of innovation, the picture they provide of the consumer innovator must be viewed with caution. Nevertheless, Table 7.3 summarises these characteristics.

TABLE 7.3 A profile of the consumer innovator (as compared with the non-innovator)

Demographic factors	*Attitudinal and perceptual factors*
Higher income levels	More venturesome and perceives less
Often younger	risk in buying new products
Better educated	Perceives self as innovator
Higher occupational status	Has favourable attitudes toward new products
Social-interaction factors	*Consumption patterns*
Greater participation in friendship and organisational groups	Higher usage rate for innovative product category
Opinion leader	Marked willingness to buy new products
Socially mobile	
Favourably disposed to innovation	*Communication behaviour*
	Reads more print media

Source: Thomas S. Robertson, *Innovative Behavior and Communications*, Holt, New York, 1971, pp. 100–10.

EARLY ADOPTERS (13.5 PER CENT OF A MARKET)   The second group to adopt an innovation, this group is more socially integrated locally than are innovators, and it has the greatest degree of opinion leadership in most social systems. Early adopters are likely to hold positions of leadership within the community, and are respected as good sources of information and advice about the innovation. For this reason, they are very important in speeding the diffusion process. They watch the innovators and adopt when the innovation appears successful. They are just ahead of the average individual in innovativeness, so they are able to serve as role models for others in the market.

Early adopters have less risk capital than do innovators. They are younger than later adopters, higher in social status and above average in education. Early adopters subscribe to more magazines than later adopters (yet not as many as innovators). They also have been found to have the greatest contact with salespeople.

How important are innovators and early adopters in the success of new products? Quite significant, as General Electric have found in studies of their appliances. One study of a new cordless electric clothes brush, for example, obtained data from warranty cards for the new product and through personal interviews with early buyers. The company found that these early buyers directly influenced other consumers by talking about the product and by having it in their homes.[43]

Moreover, when the early adopters begin buying something new, retailers see the product moving and are likely to advertise it more heavily and feature it prominently in stores. This can enhance the retailer's image as an innovative store by handling 'hot' new products.

EARLY MAJORITY (34 PER CENT OF A MARKET)   The next to adopt an innovation, this group is the most deliberate of all adopter categories. The early majority may consider an innovation for some time before adopting; thus, their adoption period is longer than that of the two previous groups. They adopt an innovation just before the average member of a social system, which puts them in a crucial position to legitimise the new idea for others.

Those in the early majority are slightly above average in age and education, and in social and economic status. Although they belong to formal organisations, they are likely to be active members rather than leaders. They rely more heavily on informal sources of information than do earlier adopters. The early majority subscribe to fewer magazines and journals than do previous adopters, but they have considerable contact with salespeople. They are frequently the neighbours and friends of early adopters.

LATE MAJORITY (34 PER CENT OF A MARKET)   These people adopt an innovation just after the average consumer in the marketplace. This group can be described as 'sceptical' about new ideas and may yield only because of economic necessity or increasing social pressures. Those in the late majority are above average in age and below average in education, social status and income. They belong to few formal organisations and exhibit little opinion leadership, with communication patterns oriented primarily toward other late-majority members in their neighbourhood. There is little use of the mass media (e.g. fewer magazines are taken) but heavy reliance on informal sources of information and influence.

LAGGARDS (16 PER CENT OF A MARKET)   The last to adopt an innovation, this group is tradition-bound, making decisions based on what has been done in the past. Laggards are suspicious of innovations and perhaps of those who offer them. The adoption process for this group is quite lengthy; by the time a new product is finally adopted by this group, it has likely been superseded by another innovation.

Laggards have the least education, the lowest social status and income, and are the oldest of any adopter category. For example, in one Australian study, the average age of laggards in CD player adoption rates was found to be over 55.[44] They are the most local in orientation, which tends to be their immediate neighbourhood, and they communicate mostly with other laggards, who are their main sources of information. Laggards possess almost no opinion leadership, have little participation in formal organisations and subscribe to few magazines.

Although these categories and descriptions may vary for different products, they do provide the marketer with a helpful framework for managing an innovation's diffusion. One of the most important facets of the work in this regard will be the development of a sound promotional strategy. Clearly, adopter characteristics differ greatly among categories, and this requires that the marketer tailor promotions to appeal to each group over time. Table 7.4 illustrates the kinds of promotional approaches that appear to be most effective for each adopter category.

TABLE 7.4   How promotion varies by stage in the diffusion process

Adopter category	Successful promotional approaches
Innovator and early adopters	Stress excitement of ownership Explain how product is new and revolutionary Use sophisticated or technical messages and cosmopolitan appeals Use publicity for new-product announcements Use highly credible spokespersons Employ narrowly targeted special-interest and prestige publications Appeal to 'enthusiasts'—those highly involved in product category Use pioneering advertising in specialised mass media Use personal selling for high-learning products Distribute trial size of product to homes Use 'event marketing' to introduce new products to media and trade
Early majority	Use mass advertising to build brand preference Stress benefits and compare brands in ads Use demonstration-oriented advertising and house-party personal selling Rely on peer pressure to overcome deliberateness

Continues

TABLE 7.4 How promotion varies by stage in the diffusion process *continued*

Adopter category	Successful promotional approaches
	Use price-oriented ads to gain market share Employ sales-promotion tools such as coupons and trial sizes sold in stores Run dealer promotions to get them back to stock and display product Feature opinion leaders in ads and use testimonials
Late majority	Overcome scepticism by using guarantees and seals of approval Demonstrate product in store Use on-package coupons Stress extended warranty protection and service/repair centres Employ straightforward appeals Use mass advertising to support dealers of the brand
Laggards	Spend little on promotion because interest in product is disappearing.

Source: Thomas S. Robertson, *Innovative Behavior and Communications*, Holt, New York, 1971, pp. 100–10.

FACTORS INFLUENCING THE RATE OF DIFFUSION

The rate of an innovation's diffusion could range from several weeks to several decades, depending upon consumers' acceptance of the item, which, in turn, is determined by how the innovation is perceived by consumers. There appears to have been, over time, a general increase in the rate of adoption of innovations.[45] Thus, a rapidly shortening product life cycle appears to be occurring. This trend has importance to marketers, public policy makers and consumer researchers, because it may represent a significant change in consumption patterns. For example, more and more rapid adoption rates may preclude involved decision processes, so other purchase approaches may be increasing, such as conformity, imitation and recommendation. Even the adopter category distinctions may lose their usefulness as these cycles are shortened.

The marketer is generally interested in understanding how an innovation may be spread more rapidly among a relevant market. There are six product characteristics that seem to influence the rate and extent of adoption of an innovation: relative advantage, compatibility, complexity, trialability, observability and cost.[46] Descriptions of these characteristics follow:

1. *Relative advantage.* The degree to which an innovation is perceived as superior to preceding products or those with which it will compete. This might be reflected in longer life, easier maintenance or other measures. Products that have a strong relative advantage will be adopted more rapidly.

2. *Compatibility*. The degree to which an innovation is consistent with existing consumer values and past experiences of adopters. Acceptance will be retarded for new products that are not compatible with consumers' norms.

3. *Complexity*. How difficult the innovation is to understand and use. Diffusion will tend to be slowed for more complex items.

4. *Trialability (or divisibility)*. The extent to which an innovation may be tried on a limited basis. Where an item cannot be sampled on a small, less expensive scale, diffusion is retarded.

5. *Observability (or communicability)*. The conspicuousness of the innovation. New products that are highly visible in social situations are those that will be communicated most readily to other adopters.

6. *Cost*. The magnitude of the financial resources required to obtain and operate this innovation. Innovations high in cost would be expected to diffuse more slowly. However, one study indicates that cost does not appear to be significantly correlated with rate of adoption.[47]

The marketing implications of these characteristics are readily apparent. First of all, an innovation should exhibit some clear-cut advantages. In addition, products might be designed so that they could be evaluated on a limited basis (e.g. small trial sizes of a new toothpaste). With some products, however, such as cars and air-conditioners, trial is more difficult. Nevertheless, car test drives (or, in some cases, even extended car loans) and free home trials for appliances have been offered. Products should also be designed with minimum complexity and maximum compatibility (these also may make up part of the product's relative advantage). These features should then be stressed in promotional messages to potential adopters. If complexity and incompatibility are inherent in the innovation, promotion should seek to overcome these limitations (e.g. by stressing warranties or product-servicing facilities).

While product attributes must be carefully considered in developing an effective launch strategy for an innovation, the marketer must also consider target markets. For example, although innovative buyers may be perceived to be homogeneous, one researcher has identified segments of innovators having differing cognitive styles of decision making and problem solving.[48] Thus, each group might require a separate marketing mix at the launch stage of the product life cycle. With one group the marketer could emphasise continuity, harmony, and compatibility with existing products and lifestyles. With another group the marketer might need to suggest newness, discontinuity and novelty. Target segments and strategies would vary based on the range of newness of an innovation (from continuous to discontinuous).

Clearly not all consumers welcome an innovation. They may resist the disruption to their equilibrium that such change can bring, and act to maintain the status quo. A model of innovation resistance is presented in Figure 7.3, which proposes that characteristics of consumers, the innovation and propagation mechanisms have a direct effect on the process. Such a model can benefit marketing managers in at least three ways:

1. Marketers will be better able to design and develop successful new products.

2. Firms may be able to create consumer resistance to competitive products.

3. Consumer organisations could better prevent diffusion of potentially harmful or hazardous innovations.[49]

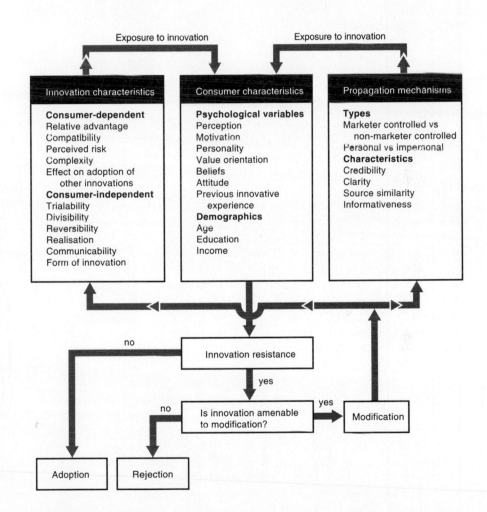

FIG. 7.3 A model of innovation resistance within a situational, cultural and social context   Source: S. Ram, 'A Model of Innovation Resistance', in Melanie Wallendorf & Paul F. Anderson (eds), *Advances in Consumer Research*, vol. 14, Association for Consumer Research, Provo, UT, 1987, p. 209.

Table 7.5 suggests a variety of strategies by which marketers may attempt to overcome consumer resistance to innovations.

TABLE 7.5 A classification of marketing strategies to overcome consumer resistance to innovation

Source of resistance (barrier)	Marketing strategy				
	Product strategy	Communication strategy	Pricing strategy	Market strategy	Coping strategy
Functional barriers					
Usage barrier	Develop a systems perspective (e.g. packaging); Integrate innovation with preceding activity (packaging)			Mandate usage (market development)	
Value barrier	Improve product performance (modification and development); Improve product positioning		Reduce price by lowering costs		
Risk barrier	Use a well-known brand name	Elicit endorsements and testimonials		Facilitate trial (increase market exposure)	
Psychological barriers					
Tradition barrier		Educate customers; Use change agents			Understand and respect traditions
Image barrier	Borrow a good image (brand name)	Make fun of negative image; Create a unique image			

Source: S. Ram & Jagdish N. Sheth, 'Consumer Resistance to Innovations: The Marketing Problem and Its Solutions', *Journal of Consumer Marketing* 6 (2), Spring 1989, p. 10.

'GENERAL' INNOVATORS

It was concluded earlier that there is a moderate amount of opinion-leadership overlap across product categories, with the greatest extent involving related product areas. A similar conclusion can be made with regard to innovators.[50] There is no 'superinnovator' who plays this part across a host of products. However, within a product category and perhaps between related product categories, some innovative overlap can be expected to occur, as seen in the following example:

When it comes to consumer electronics, 'taffies' should be watched carefully because they have been found to be a critical part of the success of new electronic products. No, taffies are not some unusual components made of silicon; they are the gadget freaks who enjoy snapping up the latest gee-whiz electronic products—even if it means skipping lunch for the next two months to pay for them. These people, sometimes considered oddballs, are almost infallible bellwethers of a new electronic product's chances for great success. According to the new head of one consulting firm who has studied them, 'If you fail with this group, you're doomed . . . If you succeed, your chances are very good, though not guaranteed, because other consumers view these people as the innovators—the experts they turn to for advice'. These Technologically Advanced Families—TAFs, or taffies, for short—are almost seven times more likely to have a personal computer than the general public is, and are also more likely to own a video cassette recorder.

Taffies are integrating consumer electronics into their lifestyles by planning their schedules on personal computers, waking up to digital alarms, cooking in microwave ovens, listening to portable stereos while headed to work or school and to their high-fidelity components during the evening, or using VCRs to watch time-shifted programs on their large-screen televisions. In contrast to the electronics buffs who used to lead the consumer electronic field, this group buys practical products that have mass-market potential. They investigate and make the decision as to whether a product offers enough performance for the price. Their actions determine the direction of the mass market, as their homes become the showcases for the products. They are not all affluent yuppies, as most taffies have mid-range incomes. As marketers learn about the lifestyles and attitudes of taffies, future electronic products may be enhanced in ways that will generate strong taffie appeal.[51] This information can be combined with data from the Australian Bureau of Statistics (ABS) to determine where innovators are most likely to live. For example, one Australian company, Hermes Precisa Australia, analyses ABS data to give geo-demographic profiles that can be used by companies to find localities of innovators, and other adoption categories of consumers.[52]

MARKETING IMPLICATIONS OF PERSONAL INFLUENCE

In this section we shall suggest various marketing strategies that effectively use the process of personal influence. Two cautions are in order, however. First, it should be remembered that opinion leadership is not equally active for all products—some products are very prone to personal influence, while others are not. Opinion leaders are more likely in product categories in which pleasure or satisfaction is derived from product usage or in which association with the product provides a form of self-expression. Consequently, using opinion leaders may be effective to diffuse information about such products as cars and personal computers but may be ineffective for products such as refrigerators and dehumidifiers. Secondly, it may be difficult and expensive to control the process of personal influence.

The marketer will want to address several questions when targeting prospects for a new product: the target market's innovative and early adoption propensities; its heavy volume potential; its susceptibility to influence; and the cost of reaching this group. This will require a systematic procedure utilising information from concept testing, product testing, test marketing and so forth.[53] If it is found that personal influence is potentially strong for the product, the marketer may desire to guide the process. There are several strategies that might be adopted: identifying and using opinion leaders directly; creating opinion leaders; simulating opinion leaders; stimulating opinion leadership; and stifling opinion leadership.

Identifying and using opinion leaders directly

There are two major difficulties in pursuing this strategy. First of all, locating opinion leaders who are influential over a particular product is most complicated. It is clear from the characteristics of opinion leaders, which were discussed earlier in this chapter, that these people are not easy to isolate. Moreover, for the consumer-goods marketer the task is likely to be hard because of the large number of consumers. In order to identify the leaders, the marketer would need to conduct difficult and expensive research on the product. Secondly, there is evidence that some opinion leaders may not be reached by certain advertising media any more effectively than the average consumer in a market would be.[54] Thus, direct appeal to personal influence may not always be the most effective approach.

If the direct approach is decided upon, however, the first step is to identify opinion leaders. There are several ways in which this may be done. One set of techniques involves measuring the degree of opinion leadership among consumers. Table 7.6 presents a questionnaire that has been effectively used to ascertain the degree of consumers' opinion leadership through survey research. In this instance, individuals would evaluate themselves on the leadership characteristic. Another approach to measuring opinion leadership involves the sociometric technique, which consists of asking group members to whom they go for advice and information about an idea. Finally, key informants in a group may be asked to designate the opinion leaders.

One of the best ways to identify those who may be influential for a company's product is to examine purchase records. For instance, many products today use a warranty card return system whereby the marketer can identify specific individuals who are early adopters of the product and identify the characteristics of these buyers. Of course, one disadvantage of relying exclusively on this approach is that not all buyers return these cards. Nevertheless, identifying and communicating with present owners may lead to effective incorporation of personal influence in marketing strategy.

TABLE 7.6   Opinion Leadership Scale

Items

Please rate yourself on the following scales relating to your interactions with friends and neighbours regarding cable television.

1. In general, do you talk to your friends and neighbours about cable television?

very often				never
5	4	3	2	1

2. When you talk to your friends and neighbours about cable television, do you:

give a great deal of information?				give very little information?
5	4	3	2	1

3. During the past six months, how many people have you told about cable television?

told a number of people				told no one
5	4	3	2	1

4. Compared with your circle of friends, how likely are you to be asked about cable television?

very likely to be asked				not at all likely to be asked
5	4	3	2	1

5. In a discussion of cable television, would you be most likely to:

listen to your friends' ideas?				convince your friends of your ideas?
5	4	3	2	1

6. In discussions of cable television, which of the following happens most often?

you tell your friends about cable				your friends tell you about cable
5	4	3	2	1

7. Overall in all of your discussions with friends and neighbours, are you:

often used as a source of advice?				not used as a source of advice?
5	4	3	2	1

Source: Terry L. Childers, 'Assessment of the Psychometric Properties of an Opinion Leadership Scale', *Journal of Marketing Research* 23, May 1986, p. 186, published by the American Marketing Association.

Study of past purchases may indicate which consumers are most likely to adopt new products. For example, by knowing that the most likely adopter of new telephone-system services, such as the videophone, would occur among those who had previously bought such equipment as push-button phones, extension phones and colour phones, the telephone company might assess available records to determine the households in the service area that would have the greatest likelihood of adopting the new equipment.

It is also significant to realise that early product triers also tend to be heavy users.[55] Thus, the marketer of a new product might engage in a two-step consumer identification program. First, heavy users of products within the same category as the to-be-introduced item should be characterised in terms of relevant background and behavioural variables so that a marketing program that appeals to these people can be developed. Secondly, once the product is introduced, description of the earliest triers should be obtained quickly so that the marketer may develop inducements for consumers with similar backgrounds.

Names and addresses of potential opinion leaders might be gathered not only from purchase records, but also from sponsorship of consumer contests, use of reader-service cards in magazines and similar activities. To illustrate, a major soup company received over 94 000 entries in a recent 'Creative Cooking Contest', in which original recipes were submitted. Once names of potential opinion leaders have been secured, the marketer is in a position to utilise their influence effectively. The opinion leaders may be reached through direct-mail advertising, if the cost is not prohibitive. They can also be provided with inside information about new products so that they are in a strategic position to pass along this information to others.

One approach that may work well is to obtain mailing lists containing names of people who have a high level of interest in a particular product category. In other words, identify the 'enthusiast' for this product.[56] These people are quite likely to be heavy readers of magazines relating to the product. For example, one study in Australia surveyed the car buff and found the following distribution of readership among car magazines:[57]

38 *Street Machine*
30 *Wheels*
20 *Motorsport News*
12 *Auto Action*
10 *Commodores*
10 *Motor*
 8 *Car Australia*
 5 Any at the newsagent
 4 All 4WD magazines
 4 *Street and Strip*
 4 *Fast Fours*
 4 *Open Wheel*
 4 *Motorcar Australia*
 4 *Modern Motor*
 1 *Ford book*
 1 *CHP*
 1 *Auto Car*
 1 *Hot Fours*
 1 *Australian Street Rodding*

1 *National Drag Racer*
1 General
1 *Motorbikes*
1 *Overlander*
1 Race programs
1 *American Auto*
1 *Motoring*
1 *Performance Street Car*

Opinion leaders could also be provided with free samples (if it were an inexpensive product),[58] discounts off the price of new products, or loan of the item (in the case of expensive durables).[59] For certain product categories, providing sampling for an even broader audience than simply opinion leaders is achieved through advertising. Fragrance strips providing a whiff of perfume or cologne have displaced sampling in stores for some companies, while cosmetics inserts carrying several shades of eye shadow, face powder and lipstick have been used by Cover Girl, L'Oreal and Revlon.

Another approach that has been successfully used is to have opinion leaders model or sell the product. For example, many clothing stores have established 'fashion advisory boards' on which high-school or university opinion leaders are placed. These fashion leaders may act as retail salespeople for the store, model the store's newest fashions for customers and appear in store advertising.

Creating opinion leaders

When opinion leaders cannot be easily identified or used, it may be possible to 'create' them. Such an approach is frequently attempted by aluminium-siding and swimming-pool manufacturers. Companies will typically select home owners (especially those with central locations in their neighbourhoods) and induce them to buy the product at a very low price if they will then demonstrate the product to others. The home owner opinion leader is, in effect, being created by the company.

Another successful use of this technique was reported in the introduction of a new pop record. The task was to transform an unknown song recorded by an unknown singer into a hit. The initial step was to seek out social leaders among the relevant buying public—high school students. Names of class presidents, class secretaries and sports captains selected from geographically diverse high schools were obtained. Although these students were social leaders, prior to the project they would not have been classified as opinion leaders for records because of their low ownership of this item. Next, the students were contacted by mail and invited to join a select panel to assist a manufacturer in evaluating new records. They were to receive free records and were encouraged to discuss their choices with friends. This inexpensive experiment provided very successful results. Several records reached the Top 10 charts in the trial cities while failing to make the Top 10 selections in any other cities. Thus, without promoters contacting any radio stations or record stores, records were pulled through the channels of distribution and made into hits.[60]

A number of companies have attempted to create opinion leadership by getting the product into the hands of people who have a great deal of public contact or exposure. Ford Motor Company have successfully utilised this approach. For example, when the Mustang was introduced, university newspaper editors, disc jockeys and flight attendants were loaned Mustangs, largely on the presumption that they were influential with regard to cars.[61]

Simulating opinion leadership

In this approach, personal influence is simulated by various means, especially advertising. Advertisers frequently simulate opinion leadership by approximating the position of the disinterested and non-commercial speaker who would engage in word-of-mouth communication. By taking such a position, the need for personal influence may be replaced to a certain extent by advertising.

There are several ways in which the marketer can simulate opinion leadership. One approach is that taken in promotions for many detergents, foods and laxatives, in which a person (the simulated opinion leader) tells another person about the virtues of the sponsored item. Commercials simulating opinion leadership also frequently use visual communication, whereby one shopper watches to see what another shopper (the opinion leader) purchases, then is seen to buy the same item based on this visual recommendation. Commercials of the sort in which a friend recommends the product to another often use non-professionals to enhance the believability and use a script written in authentic consumer language based on focus-group research.

Often the advertiser simulates personal influence by using a *testimonial* approach, in which the user of the product conveys a favourable experience or opinion about the item. One testimonial approach uses typical people in a seemingly unsolicited recommendation for the product. Commercials featuring ordinary-citizen recommendations, hidden-camera interviews and similar techniques may serve to influence viewers through a simulation of opinion leadership. Other testimonials often feature a famous actor or athlete as the endorser. Such celebrities are endowed with cultural meaning based on their status, class, gender, age, personality and lifestyle; and they transfer this meaning from themselves to the product, and from the product to the consumer.[62]

What effectiveness do celebrity endorsers have?[63] Not the automatic influence many marketers probably expect of them.[64] Celebrities will be most effective when there is a close match of personalities with products and advertising copy.[65] A review of hundreds of celebrity commercials over a 12-year period indicates that only 41 per cent obtained above-average scores in either brand awareness or attitude shift tests, and only 19 per cent were above average in both categories.[66] It appears that women, athletes and veteran actors scored best, while younger actors, comedian and non-entertainment personalities scored poorly. The effectiveness varies depending on the situation. For instance, a laboratory experiment of print advertising indicated that for the products of costume jewellery, vacuum cleaners and biscuits the best endorsers were celebrities, experts and typical consumers, respectively. Furthermore, these particular product-endorser combinations resulted in better overall attitude toward the product, greater intent to purchase the advertised product and more credibility for the endorser. However, regardless of the type of product, the celebrity endorser was most effective in sustaining brand-name recall and recall of the advertisement in the viewer.[67] Thus, if the advertiser most desires brand-name and advertisement recall, then a celebrity endorser is appropriate. If, on the other hand, the advertiser desires believability of the endorsement, overall attitude toward the advertised product and initial intent to purchase the advertised product, celebrities may only be best when the product purchase involves psychological or social risk. When the product involves financial, performance and/or physical risk, the advertiser might utilise an expert endorser. For products with little inherent risk, a typical-consumer endorser should be chosen.

Marketers who use celebrities in their advertising must be careful to follow certain regulations. In the United States, guidelines require, for instance, that celebrity or expert endorsers must actually use the product if the advertisements represent that they do and that the copy must represent the endorser's honest view of the product, with product claims substantiated.[68] Because of the potential problems of using celebrities (cost, death, scandal and the like), companies often create characters to star in their ads, with some achieving highly effective results.[69] The St George Dragon, Rice Bubbles' Snap, Crackle and Pop, and Capt'n Snooze provide instant identification for the company's products and set them apart from the competition.

The success of the testimonial approach depends on several things, therefore. First, the customer must believe that the speaker is talking to the interviewer spontaneously and disinterestedly (i.e. the speaker is not simply being paid to speak about a product). Secondly, the speaker needs a believable relationship to the product. Thirdly, the language that is used must sound authentic. In any event, it has been claimed that the use of a testimonial can increase advertising recall by 18 per cent, while a celebrity's testimonial will boost it 75 per cent.[70]

A final approach to simulating opinion leadership is to use a company's chief executive as the spokesperson for the product or service. It is claimed that commercials featuring company spokespersons generate three times the response of those using actors.[71] Examples of this practice abound in the media. More major companies are featuring bosses as spokespeople because the public tends to believe them. They can also be good motivators of the sales force, distributors and employees around the country.[72] Although credibility can be a major plus, the drawback is that the public may also perceive the company to be in bad financial or other shape. The ads may be seen as spreading unfavourable personal influence, because many corporations put their chief executives on the air when they are fighting an image problem. As the famous advertiser David Ogilvy advised, 'Only in the gravest cases should you show the clients' faces'.[73]

Table 7.7 illustrates which approaches are most believable categorised by educational level. College graduates are least likely to believe celebrity endorsements, hidden-camera interviews, or claims that products are new and improved.

TABLE 7.7 Educational influence on advertising believability

Ads that feature	Percentage of adults who find certain types of advertising believable, by educational attainment				
	All levels	Less than high school	High school graduates	Some college	College graduates
	%	%	%	%	%
Money-back guarantees	60	55	59	65	62
Products approved by health or medical groups	57	54	56	58	59
Claims based on survey results	46	45	48	48	41
Comparisons with competitors	38	38	39	37	36
Employees who make the product	37	41	39	34	31
Official products of sports teams or events	35	38	34	38	30
The president of the company	34	29	36	32	35
Hidden-camera interviews	29	34	32	29	19
New and improved products	26	33	25	26	22
Celebrity endorsements	25	27	27	25	18

Source: *Roper Reports*, The Roper Organization, 1990.

Stimulating opinion leadership

This strategy is designed to get people to talk about the product and thereby exert personal influence. One way this may be encouraged is by using a *teaser* promotional campaign. Such a technique provides only enough information about the new item to pique the customer's curiosity.

A second advertising strategy is to develop such highly entertaining or emotional campaigns that consumers engage in discussions about the product and its advertising. The Australian Gas Company ran a television advertising campaign using animals, such as koalas, lions and polar bears, anthropomorphising their daily activities and declaring 'Gas makes you feel more human'. Pepsi ran a very innovative advertising campaign integrating clips of deceased stars with current stars singing the Pepsi slogan. Most importantly, people looked forward to each new commercial. Some advertisers are even successful in having their slogans become adopted as part of the everyday language. The increase in zany television commercials by regional businesses trying to peddle their products with goofy, whimsical and sometimes downright obnoxious approaches is an attempt to get people to talk about and shop at these stores for their furniture, electronics, waterbeds, appliances and cars.[74]

A third advertising strategy attempts to instigate personal influence through having users disseminate product information and potential users request product information. Obviously, the marketer would desire only favourable word-of-mouth communications to be imparted about the product. This suggests that a monitoring system is needed to find out what present and potential customers are saying about the product and to help in the formulation of advertising strategies designed to react to word-of-mouth communication.

A final strategy is for the marketer to secure high visibility of the item. One approach is to use in-store demonstrations and displays at favourable locations. For example, one kit car company displays fully assembled cars in selected airports. Another approach is to have the product placed in a film or television show.[75] The use of brand-name products in movies comes about in several ways: producers may simply use a product without contacting the manufacturer; companies may solicit studios and pay for on-screen plugs; studios may solicit manufacturers for use of the product for a fee or for free; or brokers may try to get products of the companies they represent used on screen. The result of such usage and the implied endorsement that it represents can have a startling impact on the success of the product.[76] For example:

Wellcraft Marine built a $130 000 powerboat for action scenes in the television series 'Miami Vice', resulting in a sudden 21 per cent jump in sales for the company's entire line of watercraft.	Tom Cruise wore Ray-Ban Classic Aviator sunglasses in the movie *Top Gun*, causing a dramatic increase in sales and a substantial back order.

Contests and sweepstakes are another way to build visibility and interest. Similarly, when brand names are linked with athletes or athletic events in media coverage, corporate sponsors may score points in the marketplace. That is why so many companies are now involved in sports marketing. They act as official sponsors of a variety of athletic events, hoping to boost brand awareness among armchair and arena audiences and to reinforce the product image created from advertising. Such events also offer the chance for consumer product sampling.[77]

Stifling opinion leadership

There may be times when the marketer desires to stifle personal influence rather than encourage it. Negative personal influence may be the result of rumour, a poor product or misunderstanding among consumers. Whether negative information arises from external sources (e.g. '60 Minutes') or through an individual's own product experience, it can hurt the product's standing. Such information could influence people to avoid the brand, product, company, industry, idea or individual that is the focus of the information. Research indicates that even mild implied negativity can have serious consequences; and it can be even more powerful than positive information. Market share loss is an almost certain result of negative product publicity, but the good news from a study of such cases is that long-term effects can be made less severe when the company acts quickly and competently.[78]

When consumers spread negative word-of-mouth communication over dissatisfaction with a product or over a question or complaint that is ignored or unsatisfactorily resolved by the marketer, the effect may be quite damaging.[79] For example:

Although less than 3 per cent of a sample of communications received by Coca-Cola from consumers in a recent year consisted of complaints, customers who complained and weren't satisfied with the response typically told nine or 10 friends or associates about their experiences, and in 12 per cent of the cases they told more than 20 people. In addition, 30 per cent said they stopped buying Coca-Cola products, while another 45 per cent said they would buy less in the future.[80]

Another study indicated that 34 per cent of those dissatisfied with a personal-care product told others about their dissatisfaction.[81]

Firms have a range of response strategies available for negative publicity situations, including:

1. outright denial of all allegations;

2. no comment;

3. redirecting audience attention by emphasising tangential issues:

4. voluntary admission of guilt and wrongdoing;

5. implied admission of guilt and mandated compliance with governmental regulatory agencies' requests;

6. admission of guilt and voluntary corrective actions to make restitution.[82]

Although it is impossible to generalise, some research indicates that a proactive consumer-oriented approach implemented in a timely manner to redress negative publicity pays dividends.[83]

One condition under which unfavourable personal influence should be retarded exists when a damaging rumour surfaces about the company or its product. Rumours abound in our society; they are part of people's fascination with the grotesque. For example, the following unfounded business rumours have circulated among the public:

➡ McDonald's add worms to hamburger meat.

➡ False teeth dissolve if left overnight in a glass of Coca-Cola.

➡ KFC serve cooked cats and rats instead of chicken.

➡ Wearing some brands of men's underwear makes men sterile.

➡ Asian restaurants in Australia serve dog meat in their dishes.

➡ Procter & Gamble, whose century-old trademark is a man in the moon, are owned by the Reverend Sun Myung Moon's Unification Church. Others have claimed that the trademark is satanical.

➡ Life Savers' Bubble Yum bubble gum causes cancer and/or has spider eggs in it.[84]

In unfortunate cases such as these, the marketer must take immediate action to stop negative word-of-mouth communication and must build up a positive image.[85] It may well take a sustained effort to overcome the damage done by rumours. For example, Procter & Gamble, after years of fighting unwarranted attacks over their logo from misinformed consumers, dropped the logo from their packages and also modified it to remove any possible perception of unintended messages.

A final factor requiring slowing of personal influence results from consumer misunderstandings, and could lead to poor word-of-mouth communication if not corrected. For example, consumers may be operating the product incorrectly, leading to malfunctions. Perhaps the item needs to be redesigned or instruction manuals need rewriting to make them clearer. When the product is radically new, such problems are very likely to exist. In these cases demonstrations may be called for in stores, and more explicit commercials may be necessary, showing the product in use. Once again, the necessity of a system to monitor personal influence and word-of-mouth communication—both good and bad—is underscored.

SUMMARY

In this chapter we examined the concept of personal influence and its role in gaining acceptance of innovations. First, we described the way in which personal influence operates and found it to be a significant factor in new product adoption. We next discussed a multistep model of communication and influence flow.

The process of opinion leadership in marketing was discussed by describing the characteristics of those who are marketing opinion leaders and citing the nature of the process. We determined that moderate marketing-opinion leadership overlap exists, that opinion leadership is situational, and that influencers as well as those who are influenced have strong motivations to engage in word-of-mouth communication.

The adoption and diffusion processes were described and their significance for the marketer cited. The adoption process was seen to be an individual phenomenon—describing the stages through which an individual passes over a period of time in adopting a product. The innovation diffusion process, on the other hand, is a group phenomenon—it describes the categories of adopters who accept an innovation over a period of time. Both processes were related directly to the marketer through promotion-strategy implications.

Finally, several marketing strategies were suggested to utilise the process of personal influence. The marketer may desire to identify and use opinion leaders directly, create opinion leaders, simulate opinion leaders, stimulate opinion leadership, and/or stifle opinion leadership.

MANAGERIAL REFLECTIONS

For our product or service situation:

1. What communication and influence flows are exhibited between us and our customers?

2. Who are the opinion leaders relevant in this product category?

3. To what extent do our customers seek to influence others about the item?

4. What type of innovation is it considered to be, based on behavioural changes required of consumers?

5. Are there marketing or consumer barriers that may lead to an incomplete adoption process?

6. Which adopter category are we seeking in the diffusion process and how may the group be effectively marketed to?

7. Are there characteristics of the product that need modifying in order to encourage its rate and extent of adoption?

8. How may opinion leaders be identified and used directly?

9. Can additional opinion leaders be created?

10. Should attempts be made to simulate personal influence?

11. What techniques can be adopted to stimulate the process of personal influence?

12. Are we prepared to stifle negative opinion leadership?

DISCUSSION TOPICS

1. Describe the nature of personal influence. Why is it important to the marketer?

2. Describe the multistep model of communication discussed in the text. Why does it appear to be the most complete model of communication and influence?

3. Who are marketing opinion leaders? How do they differ from those they influence?

4. Think of a product or service about which you communicated by word-of-mouth recently. Were you the influencer or the person influenced? Which reasons for opinion leadership discussed in the text apply to this communication situation?

5. Locate several examples of new products (you might look in *Advertising Age*, *Business Week*, or *Australian Professional Marketer*). How would you classify each of these innovations in terms of its 'newness'?

6. Pick one of the products discovered from question 5 and describe how you would market the item.

7. How might promotion differ as consumers move through the adoption process?

8. Describe the adopter categories.

9. Categorise your friends according to their position among the adopter categories. Who tend to be innovators, opinion leaders, laggards?

10. Suggest a plan for using the process of personal influence in the following marketing situations:
    (a) a campus clothing store
    (b) a new food product
    (c) a new, sophisticated stereophonic receiver
    (d) a new sports car
    (e) a new novel

REFERENCES

1. Thomas S. Robertson, *Innovative Behavior and Communication*, Holt, New York, 1971, p. 170; and Deborah Sue Yeager, 'Markdown Mecca', *Wall Street Journal*, 6 July 1976, p. 1.

2. Paula M. Tidwell, *Understanding the New Home Buyer*, Tareena Constructions, Bathurst, NSW, 1993.

3. Paul M. Herr, Frank R. Kardes & John Kim, 'Effects of Word-of-Mouth and Product-Attribute Information on Persuasion: An Accessibility-Diagnosticity Perspective', *Journal of Consumer Research* 17, March 1991, pp. 454–62.

4. Barry L. Bayus, 'Word of Mouth: The Indirect Effects of Marketing Efforts', *Journal of Advertising Research* 25, June/July 1985, pp. 31–9.

5. Johan Arndt, 'Role of Product-related Conversations in the Diffusion of a New Product', *Journal of Marketing Research* 4, August 1967, pp. 291–5.
6. K. Michael Haywood, 'Managing Word of Mouth Communications', *Journal of Services Marketing* 3, Spring 1989, pp. 55–67.
7. Johan Arndt, *Word of Mouth Advertising: Review of the Literature*, Advertising Research Foundation, New York, 1967, p. 25.
8. Robertson, op cit, Ref 1, pp. 126–7.
9. Lawrence F. Feick, Linda L. Price & Robin A. Higie, 'People Who Use People: The Other Side of Opinion Leadership', in Richard J. Lutz (ed.), *Advances in Consumer Research*, vol. 13, Association for Consumer Research, Provo, UT, 1984, pp. 301–5.
10. Robertson, op cit, Ref 1, p. 175.
11. Myers & Reynolds, *Consumer Behavior*, p. 306.
12. Diane Crispell, 'The Influentials', *American Demographics*, March 1989, pp. 12–13; and 'Are you a Trendsetter?', *American Demographics*, October 1986, pp. 74–5.
13. Everett M. Rogers, *Diffusion of Innovations*, Free Press, New York, 1962, p. 241.
14. John O. Summers, 'The Identity of Women's Clothing Fashion Opinion Leaders', *Journal of Marketing Research* 7, May 1970, pp. 178–85; and Fred D. Reynolds & William R. Darden, 'Mutually Adaptive Effects of Interpersonal Communication', *Journal of Marketing Research* 8, November 1971, pp. 449–54.
15. Charles W. King, 'Fashion Adoption: A Rebuttal to the Trickle Down Theory', in Stephen A. Greyser (ed.), *Toward Scientific Marketing*, American Marketing Association, Chicago, 1964, pp. 108–25.
16. Kenny K. Chan & Shekhar Misra, 'Characteristics of the Opinion Leader. A New Dimension', *Journal of Advertising* 19, November 1990, pp. 53–60.
17. Charles W. King & John O. Summers, 'Overlap of Opinion Leadership across Consumer Product Categories', *Journal of Marketing Research* 7, February 1970, pp. 43–50.
18. David B. Montgomery & Alvin J. Silk, 'Patterns of Overlap in Opinion Leadership and Interest for Selected Categories of Purchasing Activity', in Philip R. McDonald (ed.), *Marketing Involvement in Society and the Economy*, American Marketing Association, Chicago, 1969, pp. 377–86.
19. Elihu Katz, 'The Two-step Flow of Communication: An Up-to-date Report on an Hypothesis', *Public Opinion Quarterly* 21, Spring 1957, p. 73.
20. Ernest Dichter, 'How Word-of-mouth Advertising Works', *Harvard Business Review* 44, November/December 1966, pp. 148–52.
21. Meera P. Venkatraman, 'Opinion Leadership, Enduring Involvement and Characteristics of Opinion Leaders: A Moderating or Mediating Relationship?', in M. E. Goldberg, G. Gom & R. W. Pollay (eds), *Advances in Consumer Reserach*, vol. 17, Association for Consumer Research, Provo, UT, 1990, pp. 60–7.
22. Robertson, op cit, Ref 1, pp. 191–209.
23. Feick, Price & Higie, op cit, Ref 9, p. 304.
24. G. Middleton & P. M. Tidwell, Transforming Elderly Laggards into Early Adopters: Is It Just a Matter of Risk Reduction?, Paper presented to Australian Marketing Conference, Adelaide, SA, 1994.
25. Lawrence F. Feick & Linda L. Price, 'The Market Maven: A Diffuser of Marketplace Information', *Journal of Marketing* 51, January 1987, p. 85.
26. Mark E. Slama & Terrell G. Williams, 'Generalization of the Market Maven's Information Provision Tendency across Product Categories', in M. E. Goldberg, G. Gom & R. W. Pollay (eds), *Advances in Consumer Research*, vol. 17, Association for Consumer Research, Provo, UT, 1990, pp. 48–52.
27. Feick & Price, op cit, Ref 25, pp. 93–4.
28. Robin A. Higie, Lawrence F. Fieck & Linda L. Price. 'Types and Amounts of Word-of-mouth Communications about Retailers', *Journal of Retailing* 63, Fall 1987, pp. 260–78.

29. 'Firm: Consumers Cool to New Products', *Marketing News*, 3 January 1986, pp. 1, 45.
30. Gerald Zaltman & Ronald Stiff, 'Theories of Diffusion', in Scott Ward & Thomas S. Robertson (eds), *Consumer Behavior Theoretical Sources*, Prentice-Hall, Englewood Cliffs, NJ, 1972, p. 426.
31. Thomas S. Robertson, 'The Process of Innovation and the Diffusion of Innovation', *Journal of Marketing* 31, January 1967.
32. John H. Antil, 'New Product or Service Adoption: When Does It Happen?', *Journal of Consumer Marketing* 5, Spring 1988, pp. 15–16.
33. Robertson, op cit, Ref 1, pp. 76–7.
34. Peter C. Wilton & Edgar A. Pessemier, 'Forecasting the Ultimate Acceptance of an Innovation: The Effects of Information', *Journal of Consumer Research* 8, September 1981, pp. 162–71; and Raymond J. Lawrence, 'The First Purchase: Models of Innovation', *Marketing Intelligence and Planning* 3 (1), 1985, pp. 37–72.
35. Everett M. Rogers, 'New Product Adoption and Diffusion', *Journal of Consumer Research* 2, March 1976, pp. 290–301; Vijay Mahajan & Eitam Muller, 'Innovation Diffusion and New Product Growth Models in Marketing', *Journal of Marketing* 43, Fall 1979, pp. 55–68; V. Solomon, E. Little & T. Parker, 'A Demonstration of a Theoretical Model for the Diffusion of Information through Word-of-mouth Communication', in P. Thistlethwaite, D. Billingsly & J. Berens (eds), *Proceedings*, Midwest Marketing Association, Macomb, IL, 1985, pp. 111–18; and Herbert Gatignon & Thomas Robertson, 'A Propositional Inventory for New Diffusion Research', *Journal of Consumer Research* 11, March 1985, pp. 849–67.
36. Robertson, op cit, Ref 1, p. 32.
37. George B. Sproles, 'Analyzing Fashion Life Cycles—Principles and Perspectives', *Journal of Marketing* 45, Fall 1981, pp. 116–24.
38. Charles W. King & Lawrence J. Ring, 'The Dynamics of Style and Taste Adoption and Diffusion: Contributions from Fashion Theory', in Jerry C. Olson (ed.), *Advances in Consumer Research*, vol. 7, Association for Consumer Research, Ann Arbor, MI, 1980, pp. 13–16.
39. Meera P. Venkatraman, 'Investigating Differences in the Roles of Enduring and Instrumentally Involved Consumers in the Diffusion Process', in Michael Houston (ed.), *Advances in Consumer Research*, vol. 15, Association for Consumer Research, Provo, UT, 1988, pp. 299–303.
40. John P. Robinson, 'It Came from California', *American Demographics*, July 1990, pp. 52–3.
41. Tina M. Lowrey, 'The Use of Diffusion Theory in Marketing: A Qualitative Approach to Innovative Consumer Behaviour', in Rebecca H. Holman & Michael R. Solomon (eds), *Advances in Consumer Research*, vol. 18, Association for Consumer Research, Provo, UT, 1991, pp. 644–50.
42. See Rogers, op cit, Ref 13, pp. 168–71; *The Adoption of New Products: Process and Influence*, Foundation for Research on Human Behavior, Ann Arbor, MI, 1959, pp. 1–8; and Gerald Zaltman, *Marketing: Contributions from the Behavioral Sciences*, Harcourt, New York, 1965, pp. 45–51.
43. 'Early Adopters in Aid in New Product Success, GE Finds', *Marketing Insights*, 24 April 1967, p. 14.
44. Middleton & Tidwell, op cit, Ref 24.
45. Richard W. Olshavsky, 'Time and the Rate of Adoption of Innovations', *Journal of Consumer Research* 6, March 1980, pp. 425–8.
46. Everett M. Rogers & F. Floyd Shoemaker, *Communication of Innovations*, Free Press, New York, 1971, pp. 137–57; and Gerald Zaltman & Melanie Wallendorf, *Consumer Behavior: Basic Findings and Management Implications*, Wiley, New York, 1979, p. 470.
47. Olshavsky, op cit, Ref 45, pp. 425–8.
48. Gordon Foxall, 'Marketing, Innovation and Customers', *Quarterly Review of Marketing*, Autumn 1989, pp. 14–18.

49. S. Ram, 'A Model of Innovation Resistance', in Melanie Wallendorf & Paul F. Anderson (eds), *Advances in Consumer Research*, vol. 14, Association for Consumer Research, Provo, UT, 1987, p. 212.

50. Thomas S. Robertson & James H. Myers, 'Personality Correlates of Opinion Leadership and Innovative Buying Behaviour', *Journal of Marketing Research* 6, May 1969, pp. 164–8; Robertson, op cit, Ref 1, pp. 110–12; and James W. Taylor, 'A Striking Characteristic of Innovators', *Journal of Marketing Research* 14, February 1977, pp. 104–7.

51. Len Strazewski, 'Families Tune in for Efficiency, Entertainment', *Advertising Age*, 9 January 1986, pp. 9–10; and Otis Port, 'The Gadget Freaks Who Can Make or Break a Product', *Business Week*, 19 August 1985, p. 81.

52. Promotional material supplied by Hermes Precisa Australia, Melbourne, (03) 9693 5500.

53. Philip Kotler & Gerald Zaltman, 'Targeting Prospects for a New Product', *Journal of Advertising Research* 16, February 1976, pp. 7–18.

54. Douglas J. Tigert & Stephen J. Arnold, *Profiling Self-designated Opinion Leaders and Self-designated Innovators through Life Style Research*, University of Toronto School of Business, Toronto, June 1971, pp. 28–9.

55. Fred W. Morgan Jr, 'Are Early Triers Heavy Users?', *Journal of Business* 52, 1979, pp. 429–34.

56. Stuart Elliot, 'How to Reach the Automobile Buff', *Advertising Age*, 22 June 1981, pp. S-16–S-18.

57. Provided by P. M. Tidwell, from a consulting project conducted by Market Research Services of Bathurst, 1994.

58. Alix Freedman, 'Free Product Samples . . . as Sales Tool', *Wall Street Journal*, 28 August 1986, p. 19.

59. Myers & Reynolds, op cit, Ref 11, p. 309.

60. Joseph R. Mancuso, 'Why Not Create Opinion Leaders for New Product Introductions?', *Journal of Marketing* 33, July 1969, pp. 20–5.

61. Grant McCracken, 'Who Is the Celebrity Endorser? Cultural Foundations of the Endorsement Process', *Journal of Consumer Research* 16, December 1989, pp. 310–21; and Linda M. Scott, 'The Troupe: Celebrities as Dramatis Personae in Advertisements', in Rebecca H. Holman & Michael R. Solomon (eds), *Advances in Consumer Research*, vol. 18, Association for Consumer Research, Provo, UT, 1991, pp. 355–63.

62. John C. Mowen, Stephen W. Brown & Meg Schulman, 'Theoretical and Empirical Extensions of Endorser Effectiveness', in Neil Beckwith et al. (eds), *1979 Educators' Conference Proceedings*, American Marketing Association, Chicago, IL, 1979, pp. 258–62; Jack Kaikati, 'The Current Boom in Celebrity Advertising', in John H. Summey & Ronald D. Taylor (eds), *Evolving Marketing Thought for 1980*, Southern Marketing Association, Carbondale, IL, 1980, pp. 68–70; and Arthur J. Bragg, 'Celebrities in Selling', *Sales and Marketing Management*, 4 February 1980, pp. 30–6.

63. Robert A. Swerdlow, 'Star Studded Advertising: Is it worth the Effort?', *Journal of the Academy of Marketing Science* 12, Summer 1984, pp. 89–102; and Charles Atkin & Martin Block, 'Effectiveness of Celebrity Endorsers', *Journal of Advertising Research* 23, February/March 1983, pp. 57–61.

64. Shekhar Misra & Sharon E. Beatty, 'Celebrity Spokesperson and Brand Congruence', *Journal of Business Research* 21, 1990, pp. 159–73.

65. James P. Forkan, 'Product Matchup Key to Effective Star Presenters', *Advertising Age*, 6 October 1980, p. 42.

66. Hershey H. Friedman & Linda Friedman, 'Endorser Effectiveness by Product Type', *Journal of Advertising Research* 19, October, 1979, pp. 63–71.

67. 'Bridges Case May Chill Use of Celebrities in Ads', *Marketing News*, 19 March 1990, p. 6; and Dorothy Cohen, 'FTC Issues Guidelines on Endorsements, Testimonials', *Marketing News*, 21 March 1980, p. 3.

68. Bourne Morris, 'Will a Personality Sell a Product Better? Pros and Cons', *Advertising Age*, 5 February 1975, pp. 43–4; and Bill Abrams, 'When Ads Feature Celebrities, Advertisers Cross Their Fingers', *Wall Street Journal*, 4 December 1980, p. 25.
69. Lawrence Ingrassia, 'As Mr. Whipple Shows, Ad Stars Can Bring Long-term Sales Gain', *Wall Street Journal*, 12 February 1981, p. 27.
70. 'Ads Should Focus on Products, Not Themselves', *Marketing News*, 12 August 1977.
71. Leslie Schultz, 'Not Quite Ready for Prime Time President', *Inc.*, April 1985, pp. 156–60.
72. Judith Dobrzynski & J. E. Davis, 'Business Celebrities', *Business Week*, 23 June 1986, pp. 100–7.
73. Ann M. Morrison, 'The Boss as Pitchman', *Fortune*, 25 August 1980, pp. 66–73.
74. Gordon M. Henry, 'And Now a Gag from Our Sponsor', *Time*, 19 May, 1986, pp. 71, 74.
75. Kevin Higgins, 'There's Gold in Silver Screen Plugs', *Marketing News*, 11 October 1985, p. 6.
76. Vernon Scott, 'Pulling the Plug on Movie Brand Names', *Hong Kong Standard*, 12 July 1988, p. 17.
77. Cheryl Waixel, 'Score One for the Sponsor', *World*, May–June 1986, pp. 38–42.
78. Marc G. Weinberger & Jean B. Romeo, 'The Impact of Negative Product News', *Business Horizons*, January–February 1989, pp. 44–50.
79. Marsha L. Richins 'Negative Word-of-mouth by Dissatisfied Consumers: A Pilot Study', *Journal of Marketing* 47, Winter 1983, pp. 68–78.
80. 'Marketing', *Wall Street Journal*, 22 October 1981, p. 29.
81. Betty Diener & Stephen Greyser, 'Consumer Views of Redress Needs', *Journal of Marketing* 42, October 1978, pp. 21–7.
82. Daniel L. Sherrell & R. Eric Reidenbach, 'A Consumer Response Framework for Negative Publicity: Suggestions for Response Strategies', *Akron Business and Economic Review*, Summer 1986 pp. 37–44.
83. Mitch Griffin, Barry J. Babin & Jill S. Attaway 'An Emperical Investigation of the Impact of Negative Public Publicity on Consumer Attitudes and Intentions', in Rebecca H. Holman & Michael R. Solomon (eds), *Advances in Consumer Research*, vol. 18, Association for Consumer Research, Provo, UT, 1991, pp. 334–41.
84. Jim Montgomery, 'Rumor-plagued Firms Use Various Strategies to Keep Damage Low', *Wall Street Journal*, 6 February 1979, pp. 1, 22; Michael Waldholz, 'Of Gingerbread Men with Pigtails, Rumor Problems at Entenmann's', *Wall Street Journal*, 1 October 1980, p. 31; and John E. Cooney, 'Bubble Gum Maker Wants to Know How the Rumors Started', *Wall Street Journal*, 24 March 1977, p. 1.
85. Sherrell & Reidenbach, op cit, Ref 82, pp. 37–44.

CASE STUDIES

CASE 1   SBS RADIO

SBS Radio is the sound of multiculturalism in Australia. It provides Australians from non-English-speaking backgrounds with a life-line—helping them not only to adjust to Australian life but also to maintain their cultural identity. SBS Radio started life in June 1975 when Radio 2EA and Radio 3EA started broadcasting for four hours a day in Sydney and Melbourne. One of the practical consider-ations that led to the setting up of the service was the need to inform ethnic communities about the government's new health-insurance scheme. SBS Radio's purpose is to provide news, practical assistance, entertainment and communications for Australians from non-English-speaking backgrounds. SBS Radio remained centred around Sydney and Melbourne until the 1990s. Approximately 40 per cent of Australia's non-English-speaking population live around Sydney and a further 30 per cent around Melbourne.

In December 1992, after representations from the SBS Board and community leaders, the government approved the establishment of a national SBS network. On Australia Day 1994 transmission was extended from Melbourne, Newcastle, Sydney and Wollongong to include Adelaide, Brisbane, Darwin and Perth. The service broadcasts from 6.00 am to midnight and includes pro-grams in over 60 different languages. Tuong Quang Luu, head of SBS Radio, argues that the service is unique in the world, and the national editor, Diane Willman, considers that SBS has played a highly significant role in the successful development of a multicultural society in Australia in the past 20 years. Willman says, 'I certainly can't think of another country, with the possible exception of Canada, that has made a policy of multicultur-alism work as effectively as Australia has done. I think SBS has played a very important role in making Australia a more tolerant society, and

one more aware and appreciative of cultural diversity'. As an example, Emanulle Tausinga, head of the Tongan language group in Sydney says, 'Tongans don't get much news about Tonga and see little of their own culture in Australia . . . The fact that the Tongan com-munity knows they are part of the picture at SBS is a very important point. It tells them that they are part of the Australian culture'.

Programming for the service is a mixture of national and local items. News, current affairs, segments on settlement and cultural affairs are viewed as national issues and are shared around the whole network, but other items very much reflect the interests of local communities. The allocations were made after two rounds of consultations between the SBS Board and a range of interest groups, includ-ing the Ethnic Communities Council, commu-nity organisations, Commonwealth and state service-providing agencies, politicians, and other media. After the first round of consulta-tions, SBS came up with a set of recommen-dations for time allocation and a draft program schedule. After considering the schedule the SBS Board undertook a second round of consultations, and the five criteria for the allocation of time were eventually raised by the communities themselves. These are:

1. the number of people who speak a partic-ular language in any community;

2. the proportion of people who are 55 years and over, which recognises the fact that older people tend to revert to their mother tongue and become more isolated;

3. the proportion of new arrivals in a com-munity, because new arrivals face particu-lar challenges in the process of integration and settlement;

4. the proportion of people in a community who lack a proficiency in English;

5. the proportion of unemployed people in a community, because there is a strong feeling that SBS has an obligation to help overcome the social and economic disadvantage of many people in the non-English-speaking background communities.

Even the 60 different languages do not fully represent the multicultural diversity of Australia. Many languages are common to different backgrounds, which have to be included in the content of the transmissions. For example, there are several examples where one language covers Australians originating from several different parts of the globe. The Portuguese-speaking community in Australia comes from places as diverse as Portugal, Brazil, East Timor, Macao, Angola, Malaysia and the Cape Verde Islands. The Spanish-speaking community comes from Chile, Argentina, Uruguay, El Salvador as well as Spain, and the Arabian-language group services people from 21 different Arab countries. Conversely, most Aboriginal programming takes place in English, which is the only common language available to the Aboriginal community who spoke something like 300 different languages before white settlement.

QUESTIONS

1. How would you summarise the planning and development of the national SBS Radio network?

2. Are there any suggestions you would make for improving the consultation process?

3. Summarise what you believe to be SBS Radio's main contribution to marketing in Australia.

This case study was prepared by Rob Lawson from material kindly supplied by SBS Ltd.

CASE 2 THE ROBOT TURTLE

A firm based in the United Kingdom, Systems Enterprises, is interested in finding an Australasian distributor for a new high-technology toy, the Robot Turtle. They have approached Julia Allen for this task. Julia graduated with a history degree, then worked in retail management for 11 years before returning to university to complete an MBA degree. She is now looking for business opportunities as she comes to the end of her course.

The Robot Turtle is designed to travel from point to point in a particular geometric pattern dependent upon a simple program developed by the child. It is being marketed as an educational toy that teaches children to program and understand robotics. The packaging states that the turtle is designed for children from 4 to 12 years and would carry a price of around $450 (AUS), $500 (NZ).

Julia has tested the product on her brother's children and feels the toy would be well received, but she does not feel she knows enough about the market to be confident in taking the opportunity. Systems Enterprises would give Julia exclusive distributor rights in both countries and expect her to invest in an inventory of 100 turtles. The turtles cost Julia $150 each.

Questions

1. What does Julia need to know about family buying behaviour before she decides on this opportunity?

2. Suggest how Julia might research the information she requires.

This case study was adapted by Rob Lawson from material supplied by Park Beede.

PART 3

INDIVIDUAL DETERMINANTS OF CONSUMER BEHAVIOUR

CHAPTER **8**

PERSONALITY AND SELF-CONCEPT

LEARNING OBJECTIVES

AFTER STUDYING THIS CHAPTER YOU SHOULD UNDERSTAND:

➡ the essence of several major theories of personality and their potential usefulness in understanding consumers;

➡ findings and limitations of early personality studies in the consumer-behaviour field and the implications for future research;

➡ the nature of self-concept theory, including how the self-concept develops and can influence the behaviour of consumers;

➡ the major applications of self-concept theory to consumer behaviour and marketing.

Marketers assume a link between an individual's personality and his or her behaviour as a consumer. Few laypeople would have any trouble with this assumption; it seems intuitively obvious that aggressive people like to buy such items as Rottweiler dogs with spiked collars, shy people tend to purchase conservative, traditional-style clothing, and flamboyant people with big egos are often the owners of flashy red cars. Such anecdotal evidence is not, however, particularly useful to a marketer looking for some consistent relationship between the totality of a person's make-up, or what he or she 'is', and the person's pattern of product choice and related behaviour.

In this chapter we examine personality and self-concept. While we draw heavily on work done by psychologists, the perspective is quite different. We approach these topics not as psychologists searching for a better understanding of human nature, but as marketers seeking variables that may help us to explain or predict some facets of people's behaviour as consumers.

The chapter begins with a fuller characterisation of the term 'personality'. Next, several of the theories that have been offered to explain the concept are reviewed briefly, and applied to consumer behaviour. A substantial section of the chapter is then devoted to the topic of consumers' self-concepts. Self-concept is probably more accurately considered as one of several approaches to personality, rather than as a unique concept in itself.[1] It warrants separate coverage, however, as the aspect of personality that appears to have the most relevance to marketers.

PERSONALITY

The 'intuitively obvious' relationship mentioned in the previous section rapidly becomes less intuitive and less obvious when we start trying to identify just what is meant by the term 'personality'. Despite the fact that the study of personality and its relationship to human behaviour can be traced back to the earliest writings of the Europeans, Greeks, Chinese and Egyptians, no agreement exists among behavioural scientists regarding the exact meaning of the term. Rather, a number of definitions have developed around different constructs of personality. These constructs span a broad range, from the Freudian perspective, with its emphasis on the subconscious and hidden motives, to trait theories, which seek to describe personality by the consistent characteristics and behaviour clearly exhibited by an individual, with many variants in between. Even the existence of personality as something unique within an individual is not universally accepted:

In our opinion, there is no personality as such. What exists is a living, active and purposeful organism, functioning and developing as a total integrated being.[2]

For our purposes, we do not need to agree on a formal definition. We will briefly review several major theories of personality, and consider their implications for consumer behaviour.

Some major personality theories

It certainly is not possible in the scope of this text to review all major concepts of personality. It should also be appreciated that to fully characterise even a few of the major theories would require a great deal of space. Therefore, the following paragraphs are offered as brief 'thumbnail' sketches of only some of the important aspects of several major personality theories.

Before we begin, the provision of some structure may assist your understanding of the material. The theories presented over the next few pages cover quite a range of perspectives, and comparisons between them are not always easily drawn. One useful way of categorising these theories is to recognise that while some are essentially *developmental* in their focus, others take a *current* perspective.[3] Developmental theories (psychoanalytic personalty theory, social theories) seek to explain personality by examining how it develops over the life of an individual; theories with a current perspective (trait and factor theories) focus on the individual's current psychological and physical characteristics to explain personality. While the two approaches are quite different, they can be considered to be complementary, with both needed to explain personality fully.

PSYCHOANALYTIC PERSONALITY THEORY

Freud, the father of psychoanalytic theory, proposed that every individual's personality is the product of a struggle among three internal forces: the id, the ego and the superego. According to Freud, the *id* is the source of strong inborn drives and urges such as aggression and sex. The id operates on what is called the *pleasure principle*; that is, it acts to avoid tension and seeks immediate pleasure. However, it tends to operate at a very subjective and unconscious level and is not fully capable of dealing with objective reality. Also, many of its impulses are not acceptable to the values of organised society. For example, when an individual is hot and thirsty, her id would urge her to grab something cold to drink. There would be no concern about how the drink was acquired or whether it belonged to someone else.

The *ego* comes into being because of the limitations of the id in dealing with the real world. Through learning and experience, the ego develops the individual's capabilities of realistic thinking and ability to deal appropriately with the environment. The ego recognises that acting solely in response to the urgings of the id rarely achieves the desired objectives. It operates on what is called the *reality principle*, which is capable of postponing the release of tension until that time when it will be effectively directed at coping with the external environment. To illustrate, although the thirsty individual's id would encourage her just to take a friend's drink, the ego might reason that asking the friend to share may take longer but may also result in a greater portion. Because it serves in this way as the organised focal point for effective action in the environment, the ego is said to be the executive of the personality.

The *superego* is the third component of personality. It constitutes the moral part of the individual's psychic structure, and develops through the individual internalising the values of society. It represents the ideal by defining what is right and good, and it influences the individual to strive for perfection. Therefore, it acts to control basic strivings of the id that could disrupt the social system and influences the ego to strive for socially approved goals rather than purely realistic ones. Continuing our thirst example, the superego may exert some pressure on the individual to purchase her own drink, or perhaps to offer part of her chocolate bar in exchange for a share of her friend's drink. Paying one's own way and sharing with a friend are both socially acceptable ways of dealing with the situation, which will also effectively fulfil the original need. Thus, the original basic need expressed by the id is transformed by the ego and the superego into an effective, socially acceptable behaviour.

According to Freud, the individual's total personality develops and is defined by the relationships between the id, ego and superego. The ego serves to administer the interaction between the moral standards of the superego and the often socially unacceptable desires and attempted expressions of the id. This moderating role usually results in realistic compromises between very basic strivings and accepted behaviour. (Those of you who watched the popular television series

'Herman's Head' will recognise this three-cornered tug-of-war as the basis of the program's humour; the id, ego and superego are represented by three totally incompatible people 'living' inside Herman's head, and constantly argue over how Herman should behave in particular situations. This non-academic treatment actually serves as quite a useful introduction to Freud's theory.) Many of these compromises are said to be accomplished at the unconscious level. In fact, Freudian psychology agues that a vast portion of our behaviour is unconsciously motivated or affected by subconscious factors that only occasionally reach our conscious level of awareness. Therefore, to fully understand the causes of behaviour and the interactions of personality, we must appreciate what factors are influencing the consumer at the unconscious and subconscious levels.

Although the ego is capable of resolving many of the conflicts that arise between the three personality components, on some occasions no resolution is achieved, and the individual is placed under considerable tension. It is usually at this time that *defence mechanisms* are enacted to deal with the tension. Defence mechanisms can be thought of as unconsciously determined techniques for avoiding or escaping from high levels of tension brought about by unresolved conflict between components of the personality.

Many defence mechanisms have been characterised, but only a few will be described here to give an impression of their general nature. One very basic form is called *repression*, or selective forgetting. Basically this mechanism allows the individual to minimise, or block out of the conscious mind, some aspects of the conflicting situation so that the conflict is no longer apparent. For example a consumer who enjoys football as an entertainment spectacle is in conflict about going to the games because he also feels that the sport is unnecessarily violent. If the ego cannot reach some sort of compromise, it is possible that the consumer may diminish the violent aspects of football in his mind. In this way he removes the conflict and can continue to watch the games. Freud theorised that these repressed feelings or impulses remain in our unconscious, and require substantial psychic energy to keep them from resurfacing in our consciousness.

Projection is the term used to describe the defence mechanism in which unacceptable feelings generated by the individual's id (or occasionally the superego) are ascribed by the individual to another person or group. Thus, an individual who openly criticises others for always rushing out to buy the latest fashion item may well be projecting her own similar urges on to others. In this way, she escapes the tension generated from realising that the feelings, which she feels are undesirable, are really her own.

In *identification*, in order to deal with a current conflict the individual unconsciously imitates the behaviour of another person whom the individual believes has successfully handled the same conflict. An example might be a young adult, faced with shopping for himself, going to the same Coles store and purchasing essentially the same products and brands that his mother did years previously.

Finally, the last defence mechanism to be mentioned here is *reaction formation*, in which unacceptable feelings or impulses are consciously expressed as opposites. There are two steps involved: first, the unacceptable feeling is repressed (i.e. made unconscious); then the opposite feeling is consciously expressed, in effect reinforcing the repression of the initial feeling. For example, a person harbouring hostile feelings towards her parents may repress these feelings, recognising that they are socially unacceptable. However, not satisfied with simply driving the unacceptable impulses from her conscious mind, the individual may go further, and shower her parents with gifts and other expressions of love.

Freud's theory of personality has been extremely influential, not only in psychology, but in many other fields (including marketing). The theory itself is so wide ranging that it is quite impossible to attempt any assessment of its 'correctness'. While certain aspects (e.g. the functioning of defence mechanisms) have been reasonably supported by empirical research, and therefore are generally accepted, many other aspects have not been supported. The theory has been generally criticised as vague, and relevant only to particular forms of behaviour.[4] However, Freud's ideas have dominated personality research for a good part of the last century, and will undoubtedly remain influential for some time to come.

APPLICATIONS OF PSYCHOANALYTIC THEORY Extending Freudian theory to marketing, it may be that product needs and wants are influenced by the kinds of unconscious drives and hidden motives described above. In the 1940s and 1950s Ernest Dichter, a Freudian psychologist, developed what came to be known as *motivational research*. Motivational research involves in-depth interviews with individuals in an effort to identify the often unconscious motives behind their behaviour as consumers. (Motivational research of this type should not be confused with the wider range of research into consumer motivation discussed in Chapter 9.) Some of Dichter's reported findings may look somewhat dubious to us today; however, his recommendations have certainly provided the basis for a number of advertising campaigns, and his basic approach is still in use. His more interesting findings include the following:

➡ The butcher is an extremely masculine figure, symbolising the primordial hunter, distributing the choice cuts from his prey. Eating steak is an attempt to gain some of the bull's strength. To barbecue the steak on an open fire fulfils our dreams of virility.

➡ Power tools symbolise manliness. Ownership of power tools provides a sense of omnipotence (absolute power and authority).

➡ A number of products (first car, first fountain pen) symbolise a coming of age, and thus take on a value far beyond their practical worth.

➡ An adult's response to charitable appeals can be compared with a child's response to toilet training. During the training, the child is the focus of much attention, praise (for the occasional successes) and encouragement from the parents. Once trained, the child has lost the means to attract this extra attention. Similarly, as potential donors to a charity, we receive flattering letters asking for donations, enhancing our self-image. If we donate, we fear the cessation of this attention and recognition and so, like the reticent child, we delay.[5]

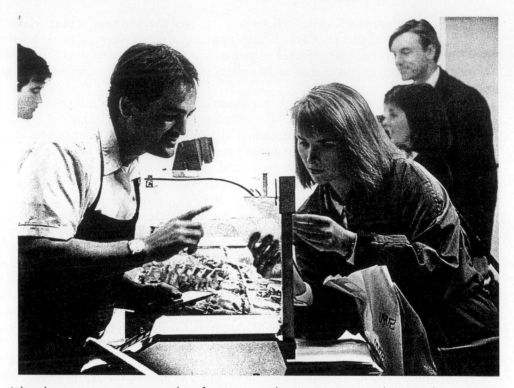

A butcher is seen as a masculine figure according to motivational research   COURTESY
OF AUSTRALIAN MEAT AND LIVESTOCK CORPORATION

Motivational research seeks to uncover the specific hidden motives relating to particular products. Psychoanalytic theory can also be applied at a more general level. One such application is the appeal to fantasy, which plays an important role in the operation of the pleasure principle of the id. Fantasy has been used in promotions for various products including perfume (Chanel No. 5), sports footwear (Nike) and jeans (Levi's).

Marketers have made many uses of symbols that appeal to the id in packaging and promotional messages. For example, some have argued that the shape of containers for various personal-care products (such as certain bottles for men's cologne) are clearly phallic. It is probably reasonable to suggest that designing promotional material that appeals to the id is easy; blatantly sexual or aggressive images could be expected to stimulate our basic instincts. A far more difficult task is to design an advertisement that appeals to the id without creating undue conflict with the superego. This task might be achieved by presenting the appeal to the id in a socially acceptable context (e.g. sexually suggestive images, with the participants clearly married), or simply by presenting the images in an artistic, or soft, manner rather than too blatantly.

Freudian applications to marketing are not restricted to sex and violence. Wish fulfilment, fantasy and escape from life's pressures are Freudian themes upon which appeals can be based.

Finally, an understanding of the operation of defence mechanisms can assist the marketer in developing marketing and promotional strategies. Identification is perhaps the most straightforward application. An ad showing an individual obviously suffering with the same kinds of conflicts as those afflicting the target market, then solving the problem using a particular product, would in effect be providing consumers with someone to identify with. A recent drink-driving advertisement in Queensland utilised this approach. The two young men in the car are obviously suffering a familiar internal conflict—it's Friday night, and they want to go out and have a good time (the id's influence), but they know that drink-driving is unacceptable behaviour (the superego). Possible solutions (one staying off the grog, both staying off the grog) are considered, with the final resolution being to limit themselves to a reasonable quantity of light beer (the ego's realistic

Marketers appeal to consumers' superego rationalisations
COURTESY OF CORBANS WINES LIMITED

compromise). The hope is that young people will recognise the conflict depicted as one they face themselves, and will identify with the characters in the ad and adopt the same reasonable solution.

Marketers may also try to use repression to their advantage. Marketers of personal luxury items might recognise that while the id may be encouraging an individual to purchase the item for the pleasure it will provide, the superego is probably pointing out the damage that an overly ostentatious lifestyle or excessive expenditure on unnecessary items might cause. Promotional messages pointing out how individuals have earned the luxury, or should buy the product as a statement of their position in life, may encourage repression of the superego's, rather than the id's, message.

SOCIAL THEORIES

Some of those who rejected Freud's id-based theory of personality reasoned that the individual develops a personality through numerous attempts to deal with others in a social setting. These social theorists, sometimes collectively called the neo-Freudian school, viewed individuals as striving to overcome feelings of inferiority and searching for ways to obtain love, security and a sense of community. Their argument minimised the role of id-based instincts that Freud emphasised. Instead, they stressed that childhood experiences in relating to others produce feelings of inferiority, insecurity and lack of love. These feelings motivate individuals to perfect themselves and also to develop methods to cope with anxieties produced by such feelings of inferiority.

The first major consumer-behaviour study using a neo-Freudian approach was based on the theoretical scheme of Karen Horney.[6] Horney identified 10 major needs acquired as a consequence of individuals attempting to find solutions to their problems in developing a personality and dealing with others in a social environment. These 10 needs were then classified into three major orientations, which describe general strategies for relating to others:

1. *Compliant orientation*. Those who move toward people and stress the need for love, approval, modesty and affection. These individuals tend to exhibit large amounts of empathy and humility, and are unselfish.

2. *Aggressive orientation*. Those who move against people and stress the need for power, strength and the ability to manipulate others.

3. *Detached orientation*. Those who move away from people. These individuals stress the need for independence, freedom and self-reliance in their dealings with others. An important consideration is that no strong emotional ties develop between them and others.

A CAD (Compliant, Aggressive, Detached) instrument was developed to measure people's interpersonal orientations within a consumer context. Results of the study indicated that different products and brands were used by individuals having different personality types. For example, it was found that 'compliant' types prefer known brand names and use more mouthwash and toilet soaps;

'aggressive' types prefer to use razors instead of electric shavers, use more cologne and aftershave lotions, and purchase Old Spice and Van Heusen shirts; and 'detached' types appear to have the least awareness of brands. Other research has found that the detached personality type appears to be less involved in purchasing than are compliant or aggressive types.[7]

Although such findings are interesting, social personality theories have not found great application in the consumer-behaviour area. Additional research is necessary to refine scales and to generate a wider base of findings from which to develop marketing strategies.[8]

TRAIT AND FACTOR THEORIES

The most popular personality concepts used in attempts to explain the behaviour of consumers have been trait and factor theories. A *trait* can be thought of as a readiness or tendency to respond (either in thought or action) in a similar fashion to a variety of different situations or stimuli.[9] An example of a trait might be punctuality—in a variety of different situations, a person possessing this trait would normally be expected to arrive on time, complete work on schedule and so on. Traits, then, are relatively stable personality characteristics that influence tendencies to behave. Trait theorists suggest that personality can be understood by studying the patterns of traits within an individual.

Trait theory has been questioned on at least two grounds. First, it has been suggested that the research evidence supporting the link between personality characteristics and behaviour across situations is weak, the implication being that traits, as defined above, do not exist. The second, more theoretical, issue concerns the nature of traits: Are they merely convenient *descriptors* of an individual's tendency to behave in certain ways, or are they actually useful in *explaining* these behaviours.[10] These issues should be carefully considered by marketers considering an application of trait theory; however, one recent review has reaffirmed the centrality of trait-based approaches in personality research. Specific research findings related to consumer behaviour will be considered later in this section.

Factor theories are a statistical extension of trait theories. Various researchers have generated quite lengthy lists of possible traits. Factor analysis is a technique that allows a researcher to examine a large set of variables and, by determining which ones appear to behave in a similar fashion over a large number of cases, identify some common underlying factors. In other words, factor analysis allows a researcher to identify groupings of apparently interrelated personality traits, which are linked to some common underlying factor. This underlying factor, then, might be considered to be a higher level, or source, trait. Researchers may then be able to consider a personality model based on a limited set of five or six source traits (factors).

Factor analysis provides valuable insights into the structure of personality, but it must be noted that the results are to some extent open to interpretation. The particular form of factor analysis used and the decision on the number of factors require some researcher judgment. Perhaps most critically, the factor is identified simply by the quantitative relationships between variables; it is up to the researcher to come up with a verbal description of the factor. This task is accomplished by interpreting the factor loadings (the correlations between the original measures and the factor score that is based on these measures). For example, consider a factor score that had strong loadings (correlations) with the personality measures of despondency, moodiness and pessimism. The researcher might use this information to label the factor as 'depression', or perhaps 'melancholy'. It is important to note that even though the naming of factors is guided by reference to the factor loadings, the actual naming of the factor is quite subjective.

APPLICATIONS OF TRAIT AND FACTOR THEORIES   In terms of their use in studying consumers, the advantage of trait and factor theories is that they are based on a number of readily available and standardised personality inventories and evaluative techniques. Using these techniques, a large number of researchers have tried to find a relationship between personality and the behaviour of consumers. These attempts have met with various degrees of success. Several representative studies are reviewed below to give the reader some appreciation of the nature of research in this area.

One researcher, using the Edwards Personal Preference Schedule (EPPS), collected data from almost 9000 consumer panel participants.[11] His results indicate a positive relationship between cigarette smoking and the traits of sex dominance, aggression and achievement needs among males. He also found personality differences between smokers of filter and non-filter cigarettes and among readers' preferences for certain magazines. However, a later analysis of this data suggested that personality traits accounted for only a small number of the differences among these groups.[12]

Another study, using the Gordon Personal Profile, found associations between certain personality traits and use of alcoholic beverages, automobiles, chewing gum, mouthwash and other products.[13] Unfortunately, in this as in many other studies, the associations were not very strong.

In what has now become a classic study, the EPPS was employed to determine if personality differences could be found between Ford and Chevrolet owners. Findings were that measurable personality differences were little value in predicting whether a consumer would own a Ford or a Chevrolet.[14] Many studies have re-examined this research, and the basic conclusion appears to be that personality traits are not very helpful in predicting consumers' brand choice for cars. However, some evidence indicates that they may be useful in predicting preferences for the type of car (e.g. sedan versus convertible).[15]

Other researchers have focused on a particular personality trait, the need for cognition.[16] The need for cognition (NC) refers to the extent to which an individual engages in or enjoys cognitive activity in the form of thinking. An individual high in NC would be likely to seek information from stimuli that require thinking. Conversely, a person low in NC would tend to shy away from such information and instead focus on background or more peripheral aspects of the stimulus in question.

Two recent experiments demonstrate the potential advertising implications of consumers' need for cognition. In one, attitudes of individuals high in NC were influenced more by the quality of arguments contained in an ad than were attitudes of others who were low in NC. In another experiment that exposed individuals to an ad, attitudes of those low in NC were influenced more by the endorser's attractiveness than were the attitudes of those high in NC. These results seem to suggest that individuals high in NC attended to stimuli that require thinking, whereas individuals low in NC were influenced more by peripheral cues.[17] These findings reveal an interesting aspect of personality that should be explored further.

Other studies have attempted to relate personality differences to innovativeness and to other consumer characteristics. As in previous cases, these studies have met with varying degrees of success.[18]

A critical review of personality theories

After reviewing more than 300 personality studies that have been conducted in consumer research, Harold Kassarjian and Mary Jane Sheffet concluded that results can best be described by a single word, 'equivocal'.[19] Although a few studies indicate a strong relationship between personality and aspects of consumer behaviour, some studies indicate no relationship, and the vast majority of studies suggest that if a relationship does exist, it is so weak that it is of little practical value to the marketer. Yet, experts still contend that personality is a critical variable in influencing consumers' purchasing processes. They argue that the lacklustre performance of previous studies is due to inappropriate research methods and an inadequate understanding of the role of personality in influencing consumers. Some of these criticisms are reviewed below to provide guidelines for evaluating future personality studies:

1. Personality tests have frequently been inappropriately employed in consumer studies. Often, a standard test designed by psychologists to detect general personality traits, or to use in clinical studies for understanding abnormal behaviour, is used to predict consumers' product or brand purchases. Because the test was not designed for such predictions, it is not surprising to find a low success rate in this type of use. Future efforts should employ tests that are designed for the specific needs of a consumer investigation.[20]

2. Personality tests have not always been carefully administered when used in consumer studies. Also, in a number of consumer investigations, standardised inventories have been arbitrarily shortened or modified.[21] Because such changes can seriously alter the validity and usefulness of a test, future modifications should be validated prior to their actual use.[22]

3. Many studies have searched for a relationship between personality and specific aspects of consumer behaviour (such as brand choice, brand loyalty over time, amount of product use). In many cases, the analysis was performed without much prior thought regarding why or how one should expect personality to relate to such behaviour.[23] In fact, as mentioned earlier, personality usually interacts with a variety of other

variables to influence general tendencies to behave. Specific actions will be strongly affected by the particular consumer situation as well as this general influence.[24] Therefore, it is more likely that personality would show stronger relationships with broad strategies and procedures that people adopt to deal with various consumer situations. More recent studies investigating such relationships between personality and general patterns of information acquisition and brand choice have tended to support these expectations.[25]

4. A sizeable number of consumer studies have focused on specific personality traits (like tolerance for ambiguity, rigidity, self-actualisation, need for affiliation) and their relationship to certain types of behaviour. This has led some to lose sight of the importance of the whole personality for understanding consumer behaviour. It must be remembered that each trait is only a partial component of the entire personality. Therefore, because traits can interact to result in a personality that is different from the sum of its parts, individuals are best understood through appreciation of the entire personality structure. Future investigations should be more strongly influenced by this perspective.[26]

One review of the status of personality investigations concludes that because of the above limitations, it is surprising that many previous studies were able to find *any* relationship between personality and consumer behaviour.[27] Future research must be more carefully designed and must employ more relevant tests of consumers' personalities.

SELF-CONCEPT

As noted earlier in this chapter, self-concept theory can be considered to be one approach to the study of personality, rather than a unique concept in itself. Most theories of personality focus on an objective assessment of what we are, but self-concept involves a more subjective view, or self-assessment. Another important point of differentiation is the inclusion in self-concept of our creations and possessions, extending the concept of 'what we are' beyond the internal element of personality. Both of these unique aspects are relevant to consumer behaviour, and make the concept worthy of particular attention.

William James has been credited with laying the foundations for self-concept theory in 1890. He described it as the sum total of what a man can call:

. . . not only his body and his psychic powers, but his clothes and his house, his wife and children, his ancestors and friends, his reputation and works, his lands and horses, and yacht and bank-account.[28]

More recently, Newcombe defined self-concept as:

. . . the individual as perceived by that individual in a socially determined frame of reference.[29]

Therefore, we can view the self-concept as a *person's perception of himself or herself*, which includes physical being, other characteristics such as strength, honesty and good humour in relation to others, and even extending it to include certain possessions and creations.[30] That the self can extend to possessions is illustrated by the following comments from a 40-year-old man:

> *Two years ago . . . I bought a wine-red Porsche 928 . . . Now when I pass by teenage girls on suburban streets, they stare and smile. When I pull up next to a snooty beauty in a black Rolls convertible, she winks. When I am out of the car in my own skin, the same women look at me, look through me, and virtually scream, 'Who is this geek with the grey hair and the glasses?'.*[31]

Although the self-concept is highly complex, it is well organised and works in a consistent way. To the outside observer, a person may appear to be behaving irrationally and inconsistently, but the individual taking such action is behaving according to a personal frame of reference. When this individual's point of view is known, it usually becomes clear that the behaviour is not inconsistent. For example, we may think a consumer is irrational to patronise a store that charges higher prices than its competition does for identical products. However, this loyalty may be shown because of the good service provided by the store or because the salespeople make each of their customers feel important, supporting some status component of the consumer's self-concept. Therefore, when viewed through the consumer's eyes, the slightly higher cost of the store loyalty may well be worth the money.

An example of status for consumer's self-concept

Alternative views of the self

Up to this point, self-concept has been discussed as if total agreement existed regarding its exact nature. The notion of self-concept as applied by consumer researchers derives from the broader concept of 'the self'. The self may be conceptualised as having two broad components: the *public* and the *private* self.[32] The public self encompasses how we are perceived by others. The private self has several components. One is the *self-concept* (sometimes called the 'actual' self), or how we see ourselves. Another important self is the *ideal self*, which is the person or self we would like to be. Various other elements of the internal self have been suggested: the *social self*—our perception of ourselves as we think other people see us;

the *ideal social self*—our perception of how we would like others to perceive us; and the *expressive self*—the ideal self or the social self, depending on situational and social factors.[33] Figure 8.1 graphically portrays these components of the self.

While this wide variety of perspectives on self-concept has led to a degree of confusion in the field, some researchers have recently argued that the various definitions should be viewed as complements to each other rather than as competing viewpoints.

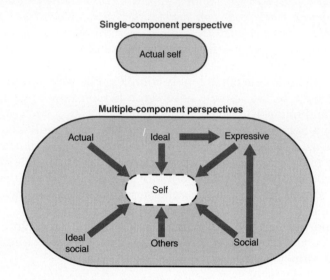

FIG. 8.1   Various viewpoints of self-concept

How the self-concept develops

Various theories have been proposed to explain how people develop their self-concepts. Social interaction provides the basis for most of these theories. Four particular views of self-concept development are presented below. Understanding how the self-concept develops helps us to identify possible marketing applications of the concept.

SELF-APPRAISAL

Some theorists believe that we fashion our self-concepts by looking at our own basic behaviour patterns, and appraising these patterns based on the standards of our society. For example, we might observe that we are less comfortable at parties than most other people, perhaps leading us to think of ourselves as shy, or even antisocial. We may then notice that we tend to spend a lot of time in individual as opposed to group activities, reinforcing the assessment already made. With repeated confirmation of this 'shyness' label, a portion of our self-concept emerges, playing a dominant role in how we view ourselves.

REFLECTED APPRAISAL

A second theory of self-concept development is termed 'reflected appraisal', or the 'looking-glass self'. This theory holds that we create or develop our self-concepts by interpreting how we see other people reacting to us. We search their reactions (both verbal and physical) for some indication of how they see us, and weave their assessments into how we see ourselves. Of course, both the reactions of others and our own interpretations are entirely subjective. Suggesting that we use others as a mirror in which to see our selves is therefore potentially misleading—the mirror is distorted by our own perceptions.

SOCIAL COMPARISON

The reflected appraisal theory gives a rather depressing picture of self-concept development, because it emphasises that people are passive and merely reflect the appraisals of others. The social comparison theory, however, states that our self-concepts depend on how we assess ourselves in relation to others. Thorstein Veblen, the major proponent of this theory, was curious as to why people so strongly desired to acquire more goods and services than were necessary to meet their physical needs. The *absolute* amount of products, property and services accumulated was not as important, he felt, as the amount *relative* to others.

> *The end sought by accumulation is to rank high in comparison with the rest of the community . . . So long as the comparison is distinctly unfavourable to himself [sic], the normal, average individual will live in chronic dissatisfaction.*[34]

This view of how people perceive themselves is dependent upon their perceptions of their status as compared to the social class, reference groups and other groups important to them. Remembering that our definition of self includes possessions, we should be able to extend social comparison theory and suggest that purchasing the 'right' products and brands could be seen by an individual as a means to improve the perceived social comparison—in a sense, then, 'we are what we buy'.

BIASED SCANNING

The last theory we shall discuss is concerned with motivation and biased scanning. In essence, this theory views self-concept development in terms of identity aspirations (what we would like to become—a desirable possible self) and biased scanning of the environment for information to confirm how well we are doing in achieving these aspirations. For example, a person who aspires (is motivated) to be a good lawyer will seek out information that confirms that he or she indeed is becoming, or has become, a good lawyer. Information that contradicts this aspiration will be blocked or devalued. With biased scanning our self-concepts tend to reflect the way we would like to be rather than an honest assessment.

As we can see, these theories of self-concept development take somewhat different views of how people see themselves. In reality, probably all of the theories are working to some extent. Our self-concepts are very likely shaped to varying degrees according to how we perceive ourselves relative to others, our levels of aspirations and biased selection of information about ourselves, the labelling of ourselves according to how we perceive society categorises us, and the reflected appraisals of significant others.[35]

Consistency of the self

Although theories vary on the development of a self-concept, psychologists agree that a person's conception of self displays a high degree of consistency, particularly in the short run. This relatively fixed structure of self is due to two conditions. First, as with many systems, self has an inertial tendency; that is, it tends to resist change. Secondly, after the self has become established, change becomes less likely because of selective perception of environmental information. That is, the self tends to interpret concepts in terms of the self.[36] Thus, ideas formed from a new experience are easily absorbed into the existing organisation of self when the experience is perceived as consistent with the existing structure. In contrast, ideas perceived as inconsistent with the present structure are either rejected or altered to fit the self, as they pose a threat to the individual.

Self-concept and consumer behaviour

Self-concept theory has attracted a lot of attention from marketers. The inclusion of material possessions in the definition of self, the various types of self and the range of possible explanations for the development of an individual's self-concept provide some direct and interesting links to consumer behaviour. Particularly fascinating is the possibility that not only might self-concept influence purchases, but purchases might also be affecting the self-concept. No doubt potential applications to consumer behaviour have occurred to you already while reading the foregoing discussion of self-concept.

The following two sections examine some interesting recent work done by consumer researchers and discuss some ways in which self-concept has been applied to marketing.

SELF-IMAGE/PRODUCT IMAGE CONGRUENCE

An area of considerable practical interest is the degree to which we as consumers might actually prefer certain products or brands because we perceive their images to be consistent with our views of ourselves. Thus, a business executive whose self-concept is young-at-heart and flamboyant may purchase a Rav 4 (a small four-wheel-drive vehicle described in the sales literature as 'an off-road sports car') rather than the expected Falcon sedan. Of course, the immediate question for the marketer is which of the various views of 'self' is relevant: the view of self as we believe ourselves to be (self-concept), as we would like to be (ideal or possible self), as we would like others to think of us (social self) or some other aspect of self-concept? One recent argument along this line is that the consumer's goals, as well as the situation confronted at any particular time, will determine which aspect of the self will influence behaviour.[37]

For example, the *ideal self* may be the predominant influence when we purchase swimwear (something sleek and sexy, consistent with the beautiful bodies we wish we had), while the *social self* may take over during the purchase of the clothes we wear to school or work (Hot Tuna, Country Road or whatever brand projects the image favoured by the social group we wish to present ourselves as part of), with the *actual self*, or *self-concept* likely to exert a stronger influence when we consider the purchase of a personal computer (a model that reflects an image consistent with our perceived needs and capabilities). This extension of self-concept theory into the consumer domain is known as *symbolic interactionism*—products that we wish to interact with in our personal environments are desired for their symbolic value in enhancing some aspect of our self-concept.

Figure 8.2 shows this process whereby the consumer's preferred brands are identified through a matching between self-image (self-image is used here to mean the overall combination of possible selves) and perception of various brand images. Congruity theory proposes that the greater the brand/self-image congruence, the more a brand will be preferred.

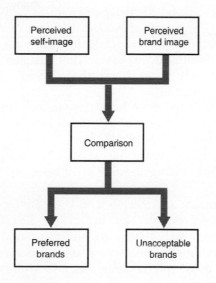

FIG. 8.2 A model of the brand-choice process as a function of self-concept and brand image

Although the findings have been somewhat inconsistent, there is a reasonable body of research evidence to support the proposition that self-image influences the products we buy, and how frequently we buy them. While it would seem naive to suggest that self-concept plays a role in even the most mundane everyday purchases, research results cover a wide range of products, including cars, beer, cigarettes, soap and toothpaste.[38]

MARKETING APPLICATIONS OF SELF-CONCEPT

Our understanding of self-concept and how it might apply to marketing is incomplete. Different interpretations of just what is meant by the 'self' can create uncertainty regarding its use in understanding consumers. Further, the self-image concept stresses consumers' self-awareness at the conscious level and tends to minimise the importance of subconscious or unconscious levels of influence. Such deeper mainsprings of behaviour can have an important influence on consumers' behaviour.

Despite these limitations, self-image and particularly the links between self and product image are powerful concepts that have many implications and applications in the field of consumer behaviour. Possible applications are in the areas of market segmentation, advertising, packaging, personal selling, product development and retailing.

Some people have suggested that companies can segment markets into more homogenous sets of self-image profiles. These self-descriptions could then serve as 'blueprints' useful to marketers in designing total marketing programs. It is argued that decisions based on markets segmented by consumer self-images view the consumer from the consumer's own point of view and thus embrace the marketing concept.[39]

Self-image/product-image congruence is quite heavily used in a variety of aspects of promotion. The choice of models, the setting, the copy and all the other basic elements all combine to communicate clearly an image for the products. When salespeople in clothing stores advise 'that suit just isn't you', they are applying the same concept, suggesting to you that there is an inconsistency between your image and that of the suit.

Even packaging reflects some attention to self-image/product-image congruence. Is a consumer whose image of himself is strongly masculine and outdoor-oriented likely to select a bath soap in a shiny pink wrapper with the brand name depicted in a soft flowing script? Or is a soap packaged in a bold green or blue wrap with strong angular print going to be more consistent with his self-image?

Analysis of consumers' self-images and their images of brands can also aid marketers in developing products. New brands can be created based on consumer self-image profiles for which there are no 'matching' brand images existing. Product categories having particular promise in this area include those that generate high ego involvement and have high social visibility among the upper social classes. Examples include home furnishings, clothing and cars, as opposed to such products as fingernail clippers and light bulbs.

One final comment regarding the self-image concept is important. Studies have suggested that self-image can be an important predictor of consumers' brand preferences. However, brand preferences are not necessarily translated directly into purchases. Constraining factors such as price and other individual or environmental influences can modify these brand preferences before they are acted upon.

PUBLIC SELF-CONSCIOUSNESS

A closely related concept to image congruence is self-consciousness. Unlike the everyday meaning we attach to self-consciousness, in this sense self-consciousness simply refers to 'a consciousness of self', with private self-consciousness being a tendency to focus on 'inner thoughts, feelings, desires, goals and intentions' and public self-consciousness a tendency to focus on 'the part of the self that others can observe and evaluate'; that is, a concern about what others think of us.[40]

People who are high in public self-consciousness tend to be particularly concerned with personal appearance, pay attention to fashion and are likely to 'go along with the group' in social situations, offering ample promotional opportunities to the marketer who is able to identify a segment of people high in public self-consciousness. Recent research has indicated that such people may be more likely to choose national brand names over bargain brands, presumably because of concern over what others may think of them if seen purchasing a bargain brand.[41] This finding could logically be extended to choice of store.

CULTURAL ANCHORING

The concept that people identify with certain products can be further extended to cultural anchoring, which occurs when 'a product becomes so inextricably a part of the consumer's life . . . that the "person/product interface" [becomes] an important parameter of the individual's self-concept'.[42] A familiar example might be the mobile telephone: the more the individual uses the product, the more essential a part of the person's life the product becomes. The user is virtually unable to consider going back to the 'pre-adoption' state, and product usage becomes part of the individual's self-concept. The originators of this concept suggest that the 'ego involvement' that results from anchoring can make the individual more susceptible to the next generation of innovative products, an idea that is of particular interest to marketers.

If anchoring truly occurs (it is a difficult concept to measure and therefore it is difficult to verify its existence), it is clearly important to marketers of technically oriented products. It has been suggested that to make a product highly 'anchorable':

➡ a technical product should be designed to be user-friendly as well as unique;

➡ trial should be encouraged through product loan, short-term leasing, demonstrations and so on;

➡ anchored users and technically credible endorsers should be shown in advertising;

➡ happy users reaping the benefits of use should also be shown in advertising (this approach induces anchoring through vicarious learning—learning by observing the experiences of others).[43]

BODY IMAGE

The image we hold of our physical self is also part of our overall self-image. Research consistently shows dissatisfaction with physical appearance among both sexes, with physique being a much greater concern than facial features to most individuals. Evidence suggests that dissatisfaction with body image is largely a female problem, with a recent review of body dissatisfaction literature indicating that 50–75 per cent of females who are of normal weight consider themselves to be too heavy, compared with only 25 per cent of males.[44]

The local evidence is consistent. A 1993 study of 1485 Australian university students found that body dissatisfaction and the drive to be thinner were stronger even among the most *under*weight female students than among the most *over*weight male students. Comparing the response of this group with the responses of a group of clinical anorexics, the pattern of responses of the normal-weight students most closely resembled the anorexic sample's responses.[45]

The marketing implications of these and similar findings in other countries are many. First, marketers can attempt to capitalise on the gap that many women apparently perceive between their 'ideal physical self' and their 'actual physical self'. The standard response to this situation is the use of thin models in advertising to pass on the implicit message that product use is linked to the achievement of a more slender body. For some products, however, it may be more appropriate to depict a larger woman, obviously comfortable with her size, with the implicit message that here is a product for women who are happy with themselves, like you. While there may be sound theoretical support for the use of larger women as models and spokespeople, there is no doubting the popularity of thin models in advertising. Attractiveness is an important characteristic in a model or spokesperson, and thinness is perceived to be an element of attractiveness. As was written in a popular Australian women's magazine recently:

> *Thin feels healthier, looks better, has a better sex-life, more boyfriends, a bigger house, a higher income—more choice in life, in fact—than fat, and statistics prove it. None of this is fair; it's just true.*[46]

The second implication of these studies that marketers must come to grips with is the social damage and personal suffering that these unrealistic body images may be causing. Although only a very small number of women develop true clinical bulimia or anorexia nervosa (1 per cent is the Australian estimate),[47] many more develop some symptoms of these disorders. In a small study conducted among 15–27-year-old Australian females some years ago, 17 per cent of the sample reported having experienced weekly binge eating and 5 per cent had abused laxatives.[48] In the United States it is estimated that 11 million women suffer from eating disorders.[49] Beyond this physical suffering, we must also consider the essentially unnecessary mental anguish of the millions of women dissatisfied with what are clinically 'normal' bodies.

While this issue may seem more a social than a marketing issue, we must consider the sources of these unrealistic body images. The high profile and pervasiveness of advertising have made it a popular target for some of the blame; however, anorexia nervosa has been around for a lot longer than advertisements showing ultra-thin models, suggesting other factors are involved. There is no doubting, though, that depiction of almost unnaturally thin ideal images in advertising reinforces an unrealistic body image and constitutes one element of a good environment for the development of eating disorders.

Is it, then, appropriate for marketers to be playing on women's body dissatisfaction in their advertising? Can advertisers be expected to use models who rate well nutritionally, but are perceived as overweight by most of the target audience? These are ethical issues that demand a thoughtful and well-reasoned response from marketers.

Putting the social issue aside, there are further implications here for marketers. Concern with body image has resulted in a surge of popularity for products such as slimming centres, health clubs, exercise equipment and nutritional supplements. Australian industry leaders Weight Watchers and Jenny Craig reported 20–25 per cent annual growth in their slimming-centre and diet-food business over the latter half of the 1980s.[50] Recent Australian research, however, suggests that body image may be becoming less important to many individuals, as the increasing pace of life and demands placed on our time push physical appearance further down our list of priorities.[51] There has also been a suggestion that the ideal body image is changing back to a fuller figure.[52] Certainly the idealised body image does seem to change over time, making today's ideal endorsers possible liabilities tomorrow.

SUMMARY

This chapter introduced the first of several individual determinants of consumer behaviour that are treated in Part 3 of the text. Two broad concepts were reviewed that attempt to take complete views of consumers. The concept of personality suggests that individuals possess quite stable and enduring properties, which influence them to respond in certain characteristic ways. Several major concepts of personality, including psychoanalytic, social and stimulus-response theories, were reviewed. The greatest amount of research regarding the relevance of personality to consumer behaviour has involved trait and factor theories. After reviewing a number of studies in this area, it appeared that even though research evidence has not offered a great deal of confirming support, experts still believe that personality plays a significant role in influencing consumers.

Attention next turned to the topic of consumers' self-concepts. A discussion of the development and different forms of self-concepts and their consistency over a period of time led to consideration of several areas of application to consumer behaviour. The evidence relating self-images to product and brand images certainly seems worthy of further study, and offers many possibilities to marketers willing to take the time to study their target market thoroughly. The related concept of public self-consciousness also appears useful in explaining some aspects of consumer behaviour. Cultural anchoring is a relatively new concept that may prove particularly relevant to marketers of technically sophisticated products. The chapter concluded with a consideration of the marketing opportunities and ethical issues surrounding body image.

MANAGERIAL REFLECTIONS

For our product or service situation:

1. What methods and problems exist for measuring the personality types of our consumers or consumer segments?

2. How might personality be expected to relate to consumers' behaviour toward our offerings and marketing efforts?

3. How might the field of psychographic research benefit our marketing activities?

4. In what areas does it appear reasonable to expect consumers' self-concept to be related to their behaviour toward our offerings?

5. Does the real self or ideal self appear to be more useful in understanding our customers' behaviour?

6. How might we practically determine the extent of congruence between consumers' self-image and their image of our offerings?

DISCUSSION TOPICS

1. Distinguish between the id, ego and superego in the Freudian personality scheme. Suggest the basic influence each might exert on a purchase decision.

2. Of what relevance is the personality concept to understanding consumer behaviour?

3. Describe the major characteristics of trait theories of personality, indicating their major advantages and disadvantages. Review their usefulness in explaining consumer behaviour.

4. Find at least three examples of promotions that appear to be using Freudian concepts. Be specific in describing which concepts are involved and how you think they are being used.

5. Cite at least two product examples in which it would appear that an understanding of consumers' psychographic profiles would be useful in describing their reaction to the products involved.

6. What are the significant limitations of the self-concept in explaining consumer behaviour?

7. Of what usefulness is it for a marketing manager to know that the self tends to be consistent?

8. Why is it important for the marketer to understand the distinction between consumers' self-image and ideal self-image?

REFERENCES

1. E. J. Phares, *Introduction to Personality*, 3rd edn, Harper Collins, New York, 1991, pp. 155–218; and L. A. Hjelle & D. J. Ziegler, *Personality Theories*, McGraw-Hill, New York, 1979, pp. 4, 287–330.
2. D. Magnusson & B. Torestad, 'A Holistic View of Personality: A Model Revisited', *Annual Review of Psychology* 44, 1993, p. 428.
3. Ibid, p. 428.
4. S. Feshbach & B. Weiner, *Personality*, 2nd edn, D. C. Heath & Company, Lexington, MA, 1986, p. 94.
5. E. Dichter, *Handbook of Consumer Motivations*, McGraw-Hill, New York, 1964; and R. Bartos, 'Ernest Dichter: Motive Interpreter', *Journal of Advertising Research* 26, 1986, pp. 13–20.
6. Joel B. Cohen, 'An Interpersonal Orientation to the Study of Consumer Behavior', *Journal of Marketing Research* 4, August 1967, pp. 270–8. Also see Joel B. Cohen, 'Toward an Interpersonal Theory of Consumer Behavior', *California Management Review* 10, Spring 1968, pp. 73–80.
7. Mark Slama, Terrell Williams & Armen Tashchian, 'Compliant, Aggressive and Detached Types Differ in Generalized Purchasing Involvement', in Michael J. Houston (ed.), *Advances in Consumer Research*, vol. 15, Association for Consumer Research, Provo, UT, 1988, pp. 158–62.
8. See, for example, Jon Noerager, 'An Assessment of CAD-A Personality Instrument Developed Specifically for Marketing Research', *Journal of Marketing Research* 16, February 1979, pp. 53–9.
9. E. J. Phares, *Introduction to Personality*, 3rd edn, HarperCollins, New York, 1991, p. 221.
10. Magnusson & Torestad, op cit, Ref 2, p. 433.
11. Arthur Koponen, 'Personality Characteristics of Purchasers', *Journal of Advertising Research* 1, 1960, pp. 6–12.
12. Robert Brody & Scott Cunningham, 'Personality Variables and the Consumer Decision Process', *Journal of Marketing Research* 5, February 1968, pp. 50–7.
13. William T. Tucker & John Painter, 'Personality and Product Use', *Journal of Applied Psychology* 45, October 1961, pp. 325–9.
14. Franklin B. Evans, 'Psychological and Objective Factors in the Prediction of Brand Choice', *Journal of Business* 32, October 1959, pp. 340–69.
15. See Alan S. Marcus, 'Obtaining Group Measures from Personality Test Scores: Auto Brand Choice Predicted from the Edwards Personal Preference Schedule', *Psychological Reports* 17, October 1965, pp. 523–31; Gary A. Steiner, 'Notes on Franklin B. Evans' "Psychological and Objective Factors in the Prediction of Brand

Choice"', *Journal of Business* 34, January 1961, pp. 57–60; Charles Winick, 'The Relationship among Personality Needs, Objective Factors, and Brand Choice: A Re-examination', *Journal of Business* 34, January 1961, pp. 61–6; and Ralph Westfall, 'Psychological Factors in Predicting Product Choice', *Journal of Marketing* 26, April 1962, pp. 34–40.

16. John T. Cacioppo & Richard E. Petty, 'The Need for Cognition', *Journal of Personality and Social Psychology* 42, 1982, pp. 116–31.

17. Curt Haugtvedt, et al., 'Personality and Ad Effectiveness: Exploring the Utility of Need for Cognition', in Michael J. Houston (ed.), *Advances in Consumer Research*, vol. 15, Association for Consumer Research, Provo, UT, 1988, pp. 209–12.

18. See Charles M. Schaninger & Donald Sciglimpaglia, 'The Influence of Cognitive Personality Traits and Demographics on Consumer Acquisition', *Journal of Consumer Research* 8, September 1981, pp. 208–16; Raymond L. Horton, 'Some Relationships between Personality and Consumer Decision Making', *Journal of Marketing Research* 16, 1979, pp. 233–46; Thomas S. Robertson, *Innovation and the Consumer*, Holt, New York, 1971; and Louis E. Boone, 'The Search for the Consumer Innovator', *Journal of Business* 43, April 1979, pp. 135–40, for representative findings.

19. Harold H. Kassarjian & Mary Jane Sheffet, 'Personality and Consumer Behavior: An Update', in Harold H. Kassarjian & Thomas S. Robertson (eds), *Perspectives in Consumer Behavior*, Prentice-Hall, Englewood Cliffs, NJ, 1991, pp. 281–303.

20. See William D. Wells, 'General Personality Tests and Consumer Behavior', in Joseph W. Newman (ed.), *On Knowing the Consumer*, Wiley, New York, 1966, pp. 187–9; and Kathryn E. A. Villani & Yoram Wind, 'On the Usage of "Modified" Personality Trait Measures in Consumer Research', *Journal of Consumer Research* 2, December 1975, pp. 223–8.

21. Ibid.

22. See George Brooker, 'Representativeness of Shortened Personality Measures', *Journal of Consumer Research* 5, September 1978, pp. 143–4; and Villani & Wind, op cit, Ref 20, pp. 223–8.

23. Kassarjian & Sheffet, op cit, Ref 19, pp. 281–303.

24. See Robert A. Peterson, 'Moderating the Personality Product Usage Relationship', in Ronald C. Curhan (ed.), *1974 Conference Proceedings*, American Marketing Association, Chicago, 1975, pp. 109–12.

25. See Shaninger & Sciglimpaglia, op cit, Ref 18, pp. 208–16; and Horton, op cit, Ref 18, pp. 233–46.

26. See Stewart Bither & Ira Dolich, 'Personality as a Determinant Factor in Store Choice', in M. Venkatesan (ed.), *Proceedings of the Third Annual Conference*, Association for Consumer Research, College Park, MD, 1972, pp. 9–19; Robert A. Peterson & Louis K. Sharpe, 'Personality Structure and Cigarette Smoking', in Barnett A. Greenberg (ed.), *Proceedings: Southern Marketing Association 1974 Conference*, Southern Marketing Association, 1975, pp. 295–7; and Larry Percy, 'A Look at Personality Profiles and the Personality–Attitude–Behavior Link in Predicting Consumer Behavior', in Beverlee B. Anderson (ed.), *Advances in Consumer Research*, vol. 3, Association for Consumer Research, Ann Arbor, MI, 1976, pp. 119–224.

27. Harold H. Kassarjian & Mary Jane Sheffet, 'Personality and Consumer Behaviour: One More time', in Edward M. Mazze (ed.), *1975 Combined Proceedings*, American Marketing Association, Chicago, IL, 1975, pp. 197–201.

28. William James, *The Principles of Psychology*, vol. 1, Henry Holt & Company, New York, 1890, p. 291.

29. Theodore M. Newcombe, *Social Psychology*, Holt, New York, 1950, p. 328.

30. See Donald Snygg & Arthur W. Combs, *Individual Behavior*, Harper, New York, 1949, p. 57; William James, *Psychology*, Henry Holt & Company, New York, 1890, p. 176;

and Russell Belk, 'Possessions and the Extended Self', *Journal of Consumer Research* 15, September 1988, pp. 139–68.

31. Benjamin H. Stein, 'The Machine Makes This Man', *Wall Street Journal*, 13 June 1985, p. 30.

32. R. Baumeister & D. Tice, 'Four Selves, Two Motives and a Substitute Process Self-regulation Model', in R. Baumeister (ed.), *Public Self and Private Self*, Springer-Verlag, New York, 1986, pp. 63–74.

33. See, for example, M. Joseph Sirgy, 'Self-concept in Relation to Product Preference and Purchase Intention', in V. V. Bellur (ed.), *Developments in Marketing Science*, vol. 3, Academy of Marketing Science, Marquette, MI, 1980; G. David Hughes & Jose L. Guerrero, 'Automobile Self-congruity Models Reexamined', *Journal of Marketing Research* 8, February 1971, pp. 125–7; and J. Michel Munsen & W. Austin Spivey, 'Assessing Self-concept', in Jerry C. Olson (ed.), *Advances in Consumer Research*, vol. 7, Association for Consumer Research, Ann Arbor, MI, 1980, pp. 598–603.

34. Thorstein Veblen, *The Theory of the Leisure Class*, Mentor Books, New York, 1958, p. 42, a reprint from Thorstein Veblen, *The Theory of the Leisure Class*, Macmillan, New York, 1899.

35. For additional views on principles influencing the development of the self, see Rosenberg, *Conceiving the Self*, pp. 62–77.

36. Snygg & Combs, op cit, Ref 30, p. 57.

37. Carolyn Turner Schenk & Rebecca H. Holman, 'A Sociological approach to Brand Choice: The Concept of Situational Self Image', in Jerry C. Olson (ed.), *Advances in Consumer Research*, vol. 7, Association for Consumer Research, Ann Arbor, MI, 1980, pp. 610–14.

38. P. M. Tidwell, et al, *Current Psychology*, December 1991.

39. Wayne DeLozier & Rollie Tillman, 'Self Image Concepts—Can They Be Used to Design Marketing Programs?', *Southern Journal of Business* 7, November 1972, p. 11.

Note: References 40–52 were not completed by Paul Rainbird before his untimely death.

CHAPTER 9

MOTIVATION AND INVOLVEMENT

LEARNING OBJECTIVES

AFTER STUDYING THIS CHAPTER YOU SHOULD UNDERSTAND:

➡ the nature of motives and their role in influencing consumers;

➡ some of the basic categories of motives;

➡ how motives energise consumers and give direction to their activities;

➡ how motives interact with each other to affect consumers' behaviour;

➡ the use of motivation research methods for discovering consumers' motives and the problems associated with their use;

➡ the nature of consumer involvement and its influence on consumers.

Anyone interested in consumers soon becomes concerned with what 'turns them on'—the forces that activate and direct their behaviour. This is more than a subject of idle curiosity for marketing managers, as many of their decisions are based on knowledge or assumptions about the general forces activating consumers.

It would be surprising if any one variable could fully explain what initiates and guides consumers' actions. Nevertheless, the concept of motivation plays an essential role in any such understanding. This chapter begins by defining motives, indicating their importance and influence, and discussing some methods of classifying them. Attention then turns to what arouses motives, how they are expressed in consumer behaviour and what factors influence how they are structured together. Next, several particular aspects of motivational influences are discussed, and we then turn to a brief review of the somewhat controversial subject of motivation research. The topic of involvement is addressed next. After characterising the concept, we review its dimensions and indicate how it is related to motivation. Finally, some of the marketing implications of involvement are discussed.

THE NATURE AND ROLE OF MOTIVES

The nature of motives

A number of writers have drawn distinctions between motives and related concepts such as needs, wants and drives.[1] For our present purposes, these distinctions are not very helpful and will be avoided. We will view a *motive* as an inner state that mobilises bodily energy and directs it in selective fashion toward goals usually located in the external environment. This definition implies that motives involve two major components:

1. a mechanism to arouse bodily energy;

2. a force that provides direction to that bodily energy.

The arousal component activates general tension or restlessness but does not provide direction for release of this energy. It might be compared to the generally random thrashing about that newborn babies often show. The directive aspect of motives focuses such aroused energy toward some goal in the individual's environment. That is, when our hunger is aroused, we are usually directed toward particular foods.

Various concepts have been offered to explain how motives exert their directional influences on consumers. Earlier views held that instincts beyond the individual's control provided the direction for behaviour. Later it was stressed that basic needs (hunger, thirst and the like) impelled people toward action. This view also held that behaviour instrumental in satisfying a need would become associated with it and have a higher likelihood of occurring in future situations involving the same need arousal.

These somewhat simplistic views of motivation have been found lacking, because they imply that people are impelled by various forces and have very little conscious control over the direction of their own actions. For this reason, a *cognitive* orientation has gained in popularity.[2] It emphasises the role of mental processes such as planning, evaluation and goal selection in directing behaviour. This suggests that consumers have a very active role in selecting their goals, evaluating the relative usefulness of products in terms of these goals, and consciously orchestrating their behaviour in terms of these products.

The role of motives

As has already been noted, the role of motives is to arouse and direct behaviour. The arousal component activates bodily energy so that it can be used for mental and physical activity. In their *directive* role, motives have several important functions for guiding behaviour.[3] These are discussed below.

DEFINING BASIC STRIVINGS

Motives influence consumers to develop and identify their basic strivings. Included among basic strivings are very general goals such as safety, affiliation or achievement, or other desired states that consumers seek to achieve. Motives serve to guide behaviour in a general way across a wide variety of decisions and activities.

IDENTIFYING GOAL OBJECTS

Although there are exceptions, people often view products or services as a means by which they can satisfy their motives.[4] In fact, consumers often go one step further and think of products as their goals, without realising that they merely represent ways of satisfying motives.

This motivational push that influences consumers to identify products as goal objects is of great interest to marketers, particularly because it appears that it can be influenced. Certainly, the features designed into a product can affect the degree to which consumers may accept it as a goal or means for achieving some goal. Much effort is also spent on developing promotions that persuade consumers to consider products as objects useful for achieving some motive.

INFLUENCING CHOICE CRITERIA

Motives also guide consumers in developing criteria for evaluating products. Thus, for a car buyer strongly influenced by the convenience motive, features such as electronic speed control and automatic driver-seat adjustments would become more important choice criteria than would styling or the number of kilometres on the clock.

It appears that marketers are also capable of influencing consumers' choice criteria. This could occur because consumers are not consciously aware of their own motives. For example, a salesperson for air-conditioners may remark that one model is more efficient than others, thereby making the consumer realise that operating economy is important to the choice. At other times people are aware of their motives but unsure of the specific criteria to use in their product evaluations. The marketer can inform consumers of the importance of particular criteria and how well the product meets these criteria.

DIRECTING OTHER INFLUENCES

At a more fundamental level, motives affect the individual determinants of perception, learning, personality, attitudes and how people process information. This also results in directional influences on behaviour. For example, motives influence information processing, which in turn regulates how we interpret and respond to our environment. These influences are discussed in greater detail in the remaining chapters of this section.

CLASSIFYING MOTIVES

Since the early 1900s many thousands of motive concepts have been suggested to account for the great diversity of human behaviour.[5] The need to group so many suggestions into a more manageable set of general categories soon became apparent. A variety of classification schemes ranging from the simplified to the complex have been proposed.

Simplified schemes

A number of classification methods are simplified so that they group motives on the basis of one unique characteristic of interest. Several of particular relevance to understanding consumers are highlighted as follows.

PHYSIOLOGICAL VERSUS PSYCHOGENIC

One scheme categorises motives according to their underlying sources. *Physiological* motives are oriented toward directly satisfying biological needs, such as hunger, thirst and pain-avoidance. Conversely, *psychogenic* motives focus on the satisfaction of psychological desires. Examples include the seeking of achievement, affiliation or status. It is interesting to note that consumers often can satisfy physiological needs at the same time as they are satisfying psychogenic motives. For example, sharing a favourite drink with friends after a touch-football game satisfies affiliation needs as well as one's thirst.

Although general agreement exists about the number and nature of physiological motives, there is less consensus about their psychogenic counterparts. However, a common characteristic of such psychological motives is that they are learned. This learning can occur throughout life, but the childhood socialisation process probably accounts for a majority of these acquired motives. The nature of this learning will be explored in Chapter 11.

Learned, or secondary, motives exert a very important influence on people. In fact, many argue that in economically developed societies, psychogenic motives dominate over physiological ones in affecting consumers' goals and acquisition of products to attain or express these goals. This is a significant consideration for marketers involved in the design of products and advertising appeals.

CONSCIOUS VERSUS UNCONSCIOUS

Motives also differ in the degree to which they reach consumers' awareness. Conscious motives are those of which consumers are quite aware, whereas a motive is said to be unconscious when the consumer is not aware of being influenced by it.

It has been suggested that people are not conscious of some motives because they don't want to confront the true reason for their purchase. To illustrate, purchases of expensive clothes are frequently justified in terms of the clothes' 'fit' or durability rather than the status they are expected to display. Sometimes consumers simply may not be aware of the true motives behind many of their purchases; for example, we really don't understand why we prefer certain colours over others.

POSITIVE VERSUS NEGATIVE

Motives can exert either positive or negative influences on consumers. Positive influences attract consumers toward desired goals, while negative ones direct them away from undesirable consequences. Positive attractions exert the predominant influence, but a few very important cases of negative forces do exist. One example of a negative force is fear, which can play an important role in some purchases such as toothpaste, for decay prevention, and insurance, to protect loved ones.

A comprehensive scheme

Although the above distinctions provide a useful perspective, they are limited because only one characteristic serves as the basis of classification. A more comprehensive method using four two-pole motive tendencies has been suggested by McGuire.[6] As shown in Table 9.1, the relevant distinctions are cognitive/affective (mental deliberation versus emotional reactions), preservation/growth (maintenance of equilibrium versus self-development), active/passive (self-initiated action versus reactive tendencies) and internal/external (achievement of new internal states versus new relationships with the environment). These four means of classification are not intended to be mutually exclusive. In fact, when used together they provide an interesting basis for appreciating 16 major motivational influences on consumer behaviour. Each is briefly characterised in Table 9.1.

TABLE 9.1   A comprehensive classification of major motive influences

| | | Active | | Passive | |
		Internal	External	Internal	External
Cognitive	Preservation	1. Consistency	2. Attribution	3. Categorisation	4. Objectification
	Growth	5. Autonomy	6. Exploration	7. Matching	8. Utilitarian
Affective	Preservation	9. Tension reduction	10. Expressive	11. Ego-defensive	12. Reinforcement
	Growth	13. Assertion	14. Affiliation	15. Identification	16. Modelling

Source: Adapted from William J. McGuire, 'Some Internal Psychological Factors Influencing Consumer Choice', *Journal of Consumer Research* 2, March 1976, pp. 302–19.

The description and classification of motives provide useful perspectives for understanding consumers. However, it must be remembered that motives have only a general influence on behaviour. Their exact effect is modified by environmental conditions and the consumer's existing states, such as attitudes and knowledge. Consequently, although we may know that a given motive *can* activate and guide behaviour in a particular direction, this does not necessarily enable us to predict that it *will* do so. One study has shown that many of the motivational taxonomies do not predict ultimate product purchases.[7] Also, any given behaviour, such as the purchase of a particular product, can be influenced by many motives. This means that by merely observing consumers' actions we are often not in a good position to specify the motives that are influencing them. These comments demonstrate the need for marketers to understand more about the structuring and operational characteristics of motives, such as how they are aroused, what influences their strength and why they persist over time. It is to these and similar issues that we now turn.

TABLE 9.2 Sixteen major motivational influences identified by McGuire

1. *Consistency.* Motivation to maintain a coherent and organised view of the world. *Example:* Learning that the cereal we considered nutritious really is not very high in food value, and consequently feeling 'uncomfortable' and attempting to find an explanation for this inconsistency.

2. *Attribution.* Motivation to understand or infer causes for various occurrences. This is focused in three major directions: inferences as to the causes of various events; attempts to understand our own attitudes, values and so on from the behaviour we see ourselves engaging in; and inferences about the reasons other people act the way they do. *Example:* The meaning we derive from information in our environment, such as promotional messages, being strongly influenced by attribution inferences.

3. *Categorisation.* Motivation to categorise complex information in order to organise and deal with it more easily. *Example:* Dividing clothing into formal, casual and 'hang-around' categories.

4. *Objectification.* Motivation to use 'objective', external information instead of internal reflection to draw conclusions about our values, attitudes and the like. This is similar to attribution but more passive in nature. *Example:* Using the amount of ski equipment purchased as a measure of the degree we enjoy the sport.

5. *Autonomy.* Motivation to seek individuality and personal growth through self-actualisation and development of a distinct identity. *Example:* Reading various self-help books in order to improve ourselves.

6. *Exploration.* Motivation to seek stimulation through new events or circumstances. *Example:* Impulse buying or switching from favourite to other brands to generate some excitement in our lives.

7. *Matching.* Motivation to develop mental images of ideal situations and regularly compare (match) perceptions of actual situations to these ideals. A strong matching motive implies that internal standards, not characteristics of other brands, are more important criteria for judging products. *Example:* Comparing a new car model to our ideal car rather than to other brands.

Continues

TABLE 9.2 Sixteen major motivational influences identified by McGuire *continued*

8. *Utilitarian*. Motivation to use the external environment as a valuable resource for information and skills to help solve life's problems. *Example:* Doing a lot of 'window shopping' to see how available products can help around the home.

9. *Tension reduction*. Motivation to reduce or avoid any tension that is generated when needs are not being satisfied. *Example:* Avoiding new brands because they generate uncertainty (and tension) regarding how well they will perform.

10. *Self-expression*. Motivation to project our identities to others. *Example:* Purchasing an Alpha Romeo Spider to reflect our enjoyment of the sporty life in the fast lane.

11. *Ego-defensive*. Motivation to protect ourselves from social embarrassment and other threats to feelings of self-worth. *Example:* Purchasing underarm deodorant, dandruff shampoo, strong denture adhesive or carpet freshener to avoid the potential of social disgrace.

12. *Reinforcement*. Motivation to act in ways that have previously resulted in rewarding situations. *Example:* Consistently arguing with the car mechanic because such behaviour was necessary in the past to get the car fixed properly.

13. *Assertion*. Motivation to strive for competition, power and success. *Example:* Using some products, such as the latest software, to get ahead of the pack.

14. *Affiliation*. Motivation to seek acceptance, affection and warm personal contact with others. *Example*: Becoming a member of a service organisation such as Lions or Rotary.

15. *Identification*. Motivation to develop new identities and roles to enhance our self-concepts. Acting these roles out in social settings allows expression of values and development of feelings of importance. *Example:* Patronising certain 'gathering spots' frequented by young professionals in an attempt to belong or identify with that group.

16. *Modelling*. Motivation to imitate other individuals with whom we identify or empathise. *Example:* Buying G.I. Joe, Rambo, Gladiators or similar toys.

Source: Based on William J. McGuire, 'Some Internal Psychological Factors Influencing Consumer Choice', *Journal of Consumer Research* 2, March 1976, pp. 302–19.

MOTIVE AROUSAL

The arousal concept concerns what actually energises consumers' behaviour. Remember from our earlier discussion that although arousal activates bodily energy, it provides little, if any, direction to behaviour.

Triggering arousal

A variety of mechanisms can trigger the arousal of motives and energise consumers. The following may work alone or in combination to activate behaviour.[8]

PHYSIOLOGICAL CONDITIONS

One source of arousal acts to satisfy our biological needs for food, water and other life-sustaining necessities. Not attending to such a bodily need generates an uncomfortable state of tension. When this tension is sufficiently strong, arousal occurs to provide the energy necessary to satisfy the need. The consumer's previous experience and present situation will strongly influence the directions any heightened activity will take.

COGNITIVE ACTIVITY

Humans engage in considerable cognitive activity (thinking and reasoning) even when the objects of their thoughts are not physically present. This thinking, considered by some to be daydreaming or fantasy, can also act as a motive trigger. One way this occurs is when consumers deliberate about unsatisfied wants. For example, thinking about a lack of physical activity can arouse energy to remedy the situation.

SITUATIONAL CONDITIONS

The particular situation confronting consumers may also trigger arousal. This can occur when the situation draws attention to an existing physiological condition, as when noticing an advertisement for Slice soda suddenly makes you aware of being thirsty. Here, the need for liquids may have been present, but not yet strong enough to trigger arousal. Seeing the advertisement draws attention to the condition and leads to activity.

Situational conditions can also work alone to generate motive arousal. This appears to occur when circumstances draw consumers' attention to the disparity between their present state and something viewed as a better condition. For example, a consumer may see an advertisement stressing how compact disc players enhance the pleasure of listening to music. Such a message might, by itself, be responsible for triggering the aroused state.

STIMULUS PROPERTIES

Certain properties of external stimuli themselves also seem to have the power to generate arousal.[9] These *collative properties* include the characteristics of novelty, surprisingness, ambiguity and uncertainty. Stimuli possessing a sufficient amount of these properties have the potential of drawing attention to themselves by arousing an individual's curiosity or desire for exploration. As such, they represent a special type of situational condition.

Stimuli with arousal potential are important for marketers because they can be used to attract and focus consumers' attention. This represents an opportunity to present information, facilitate consumers' processing of that information, and increase involvement and interest in the product. Therefore, a great deal of effort is devoted to incorporating stimuli with arousal potential into promotions and packaging. An important aspect of this effort is to choose stimuli that will draw attention to the marketer's message or product as well as to themselves.[10]

Optimal stimulation and arousal

Historically, consumers have been viewed mainly as tension avoiders. Similar to the operation described for physiological triggers, events creating tension were seen as generating arousal, which initiated tension-reduction activity. From this, we might be tempted to conclude that, as external variables can also generate tension, consumers might *consistently* seek to minimise such environmental stimulation. However, at best, this conclusion describes only certain activity patterns. Casual observation and research evidence both suggest that in many situations consumers do not act to minimise external sources of stimulation. In fact, consumers often wish to increase stimulation. Sudden purchases of different brands 'just for a change', window-shopping activity, the trial of many new products, and the great interest many consumers show in various intriguing products such as *Dungeons & Dragons* have been cited as evidence of this desire.

We do not presently know a great deal about the exact causes underlying such behaviour. However, several theories suggest the existence of a motivation to seek variety or novelty, or to explore stimuli that are seemingly inconsistent with our expectations.[11] This was noted in McGuire's motive classification scheme reviewed earlier. One element common to most of these explanations is that consumers' *optimum* stimulation level is at a moderate (not minimum) magnitude. Therefore, depending on conditions, consumers may seek increases or reductions in their external stimulation.

The theory proposed by Streufert and Driver serves to explain such behaviour.[12] In this scheme, the stimulation consumers derive from their environment is determined by the amount of incongruity or disparity existing between their stored knowledge about the environment and the information that they receive from it. For example, a large disparity between what a consumer 'knows' about a brand and the experiences the consumer actually has while using it would generate considerable stimulation. However, if the consumer's beliefs and knowledge are confirmed through use of the brand, little stimulation is likely to occur.

Based on past experiences, each consumer is seen as adapting to and expecting a certain average level of incongruity, or stimulation, from the environment.[13] This level, called the *General Incongruity Adaptation Level* (GIAL), becomes the optimum amount of stimulation derived from the environment. Therefore, more or less than the optimum amount will be uncomfortable and is likely to motivate behaviour designed to return to the optimum. The type of behaviour that will be engaged in is influenced by the magnitude and direction of the difference between present levels of environmental stimulation and the GIAL.

These relationships are shown in Figure 9.1. The degree of incongruity, or stimulation, generated by differences between stored knowledge about the environment and actual experiences is represented on the X-axis. The amount of affect (degree of liking) of the stimulation is represented on the Y-axis. This ranges from negative levels through zero, which is represented by the horizontal line, to positive levels. The parabolic-shaped curve shows the relationship between levels of stimulation and the degree of liking or affect that the consumer will exhibit. Note that the optimum level of stimulation (GIAL), shown on the X-axis, corresponds to the greatest degree of consumer satisfaction. Also, note that this value is somewhat *above* the zero point on the X-axis, showing that the optimum amount of environmental stimulation is at a moderate level.

Figure 9.1 also shows that very low and very high levels of stimulation produce negative affects, while moderate deviations from the GIAL produce positive affects. In fact, there are four ranges or zones of stimulation values that a given stimulus might generate for a consumer. If the stimulus falls into Zone 1, the resulting stimulation will be very low, generating the negative affect of considerable boredom. A rather active search for completely new, more stimulating experiences is to be expected in this situation. This behaviour is quite descriptive of consumers who have become extremely familiar with and actually bored by a brand that they have purchased repeatedly for a considerable period of time.

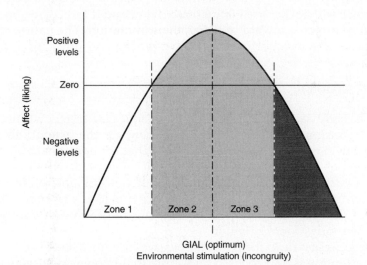

FIG. 9.1 A diagram based on Streufert and Driver's theory of the relationship between optimum stimulation and affect

In Zone 2 stimulation is still below optimum, but not enough to generate negative affects. Consequently, new stimulus experiences will not be sought. Instead, the consumer will be passively receptive to new stimulus situations, and will probably devote some effort to exploring existing stimuli in greater depth. Both of these activities are taken to yield moderate increases in stimulation. Consumers facing Zone 2 levels of stimulation include those who are only slightly bored by their existing brands. As such, they may be susceptible to negative information about these brands coming from other consumers or, as in the attack of Pepsi on Coke, producers of competitive brands.

Zone 3 levels of stimulation are slightly above optimum but still within levels that the consumer perceives favourably. Therefore, the motivation to seek new sources of stimulation is not high. Passive reception of other stimuli and examination in greater depth of existing stimuli are likely to occur. In both cases, the goal is to reduce stimulation levels. Consumers who have purchased a new product or brand and then learn that it is a little too different, novel or complex are likely to experience Zone 3 levels of stimulation.

In the fourth zone, present levels of stimulation are so high above optimum that they are quite uncomfortable to the consumer, and they yield negative affects. Additional stimulation certainly will not be sought. In fact, consumers will be motivated to escape from the uncomfortable state and actively seek other more familiar stimuli that will bring them closer to optimum. People in this situation are frequently seen as avoiding unfamiliar or novel brands and preferring known, standard brands. They are also susceptible to advertisements that make brands appear less novel.

To summarise, the theory suggests that the types of information a consumer will seek and be receptive to are a function of the present level of stimulation being received from the environment. If stimulation levels are below optimum, the consumer will be disposed to increase them, and if levels are above optimum, action will be directed toward reducing the stimulation. The nature of the actions will depend on the particular stimulation zone the consumer is facing.

Effects of arousal

We have already seen that several mechanisms can trigger arousal to release energy for consumers' actions. Factors influencing the extent and direction of aroused behaviour will be discussed shortly. What is important to note here is that the intensity of arousal acts to regulate the amount of effort consumers will devote to a particular motivating situation. Higher amounts of arousal result in greater attention to stimuli that may have been previously ignored. This increases the chances that the consumer will become aware of information useful in dealing with the motivational situation.

The process just described is quite passive in nature, because the consumer's increased attention is only focused on stimuli that happen to be available. Arousal can also expand the consumer's available information by energising an active search process, which can involve asking questions of salespeople, reading *Choice* or *Consumer*, or making a point of having a conversation with a friend about a particular product.

Arousal also influences the cognitive activity (thinking and evaluating) devoted to decision making about alternative goods and services. This influence involves regulating the effort allocated to interpreting potentially informative stimuli, such as the energy-efficiency rating of a refrigerator. It also involves allocating effort to reviewing stored knowledge about brands by using decision rules to evaluate and choose among purchase alternatives.

Utilitarian and hedonic expressions of motives

The discussion thus far may give the impression that consumers are rather deliberate, calculating entities who are motivated to assess rationally the functional worth of products according to their usefulness in meeting certain utilitarian goals. However, for some time it has been recognised that this is not the only way consumers are motivated to evaluate products—as early as 1924 Copeland suggested that consumers also have a set of emotional desires that influence product choices.[14] Yet, much of the existing research in consumer behaviour has tended to focus on how consumers react to the functional, utilitarian properties of products and services.

Recently some have argued for an increased emphasis on the 'feeling', or experiential, aspects of consumer behaviour.[15] This viewpoint, termed the 'hedonic perspective', notes that consumers often seek products or services at least partially for the anticipated sensory stimulation, appreciation of beauty, fun or other experiential aspects of consumption. The product consumption generates an emotional 'high', which is pleasurable in itself.

An implication of this viewpoint is that consumers are likely to evaluate products/services differently depending on the degree to which they are expected to yield functional or hedonic benefits. Goods such as detergents and word processors would probably be viewed as utilitarian in nature by many, and therefore would tend to generate significant cognitive (thinking-oriented) evaluation of functional characteristics. However, goods and services such as high-fashion clothes, athletic clubs and opera would tend to encourage focus on product symbolism, and physical and psychological stimulation—hedonic-related experiences. Notice that these expected benefits are less tangible, and more symbolic and personal in nature, than functional ones.

Of course, many products or services are likely to be perceived by consumers as incorporating both types of attributes. Also, it is likely that the market contains segments of consumers who are prone to focus on functional benefits and other segments more prone to seek hedonic benefits. These differences present challenges regarding the product/service benefits to communicate to consumers through advertising. A focus on utilitarian benefits of a product to an audience interested in hedonic benefits is likely to be unsuccessful, as is a focus on experiential benefits to those interested in functional aspects of the good. Therefore, the marketer needs to make appropriate choices about what type of advertising appeals to use.

In addition, the method of communication is also an important decision variable. For functional properties, a predominantly verbal, cognitive appeal is likely to be successful; while for hedonic properties, pictorial imagery, symbolism and even fantasy themes have better potential for tapping the emotional properties of expected benefits.[16] Therefore, the types of benefits consumers expect from certain products/services can significantly influence the focus of the marketing program.

MOTIVE STRUCTURING

Motives do not act on consumers in an arbitrary manner, but fit together in a unified pattern. This suggests the existence of a priority scheme, or structuring mechanism, for motives.

Motive hierarchy

The concept of a hierarchy underlies many schemes offered to explain the structuring of motive influences. The most influential motive is seen as enjoying the most dominant position in the hierarchy, the second most influential holds the second most dominant position, and so on through the entire list. To be useful, however, the hierarchy concept must also help to explain what factors influence the relative ordering of motives.

MASLOW'S HIERARCHY

Perhaps the most widely known hierarchy was proposed by A. H. Maslow. His scheme classified motives into five groupings and suggested the degree to which each would influence behaviour.[17] Although this theory certainly is relevant to the topic of motive classification discussed earlier, its treatment has been reserved until now because of its importance to the structuring concept.

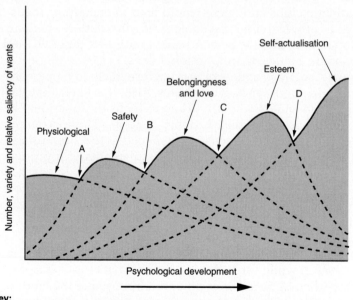

Key:
Physiological: motives that seek basic body requirements including water, food and oxygen
Safety: motives for security, protection and stability in one's life
Belongingness and love: motives oriented towards affection and affiliation with other
Esteem: motives orientated towards achievement, prestige, status and self-confidence
Self-actualisation: motives relating to self-fulfilment and maximising one's potential

FIG. 9.2   A diagram of Maslow's motive hierarchy, depicting the predominance of motives and the number and variety of wants recognised for each motive   Source: David Krech, Richard S. Crutchfield & Egerton L. Ballachey, *Individual in Society*, McGraw-Hill, New York, 1962, p. 77.

Maslow proposed that motives could be classified into five basic categories: physiological, safety, belongingness and love, esteem and self-actualisation. As depicted in Figure 9.2, he also suggested that these groupings are arranged in ascending order, with physiological motives occupying the first position on the hierarchy and self-actualisation occupying the last step. The degree to which each motive category is essential to existence and survival was seen to define its *prepotency*, or initial importance. The first ordering of motives is then determined by their relative prepotency. The most prepotent motives (physiological) would have the greatest influence on behaviour until they are adequately satisfied. At that point the next most prepotent motive—safety—would begin to dominate behaviour. We would expect this to influence various purchase behaviours, such as the use of unleaded petrol, burglar alarms, studded snow tires and other similar features or products. Car manufacturers have used safety in their advertising campaigns, as seen in the following photos. If the consumer is capable of adequately satisfying each succeeding motive category, self-actualisation will finally tend to dominate behaviour. The pattern of succeeding motive influence is also depicted in Figure 9.2. Points A through D define the places where higher level motives will begin to assume dominance over more prepotent, but adequately satisfied, motives.

It is also important to note that even after being passed on the hierarchy, a motive can assume temporary dominance over behaviour. This will occur as a result of *deprivation*—the extent to which the motive is not being adequately satisfied. The degree to which deprivation can affect the structuring of motives and assume temporary dominance over consumers' actions is easily appreciated if you recall the last time you were extremely hungry.

Maslow also argued that as individuals progress from being dominated by physiological motives toward self-actualisation, they grow psychologically, developing more wants and seeking a greater variety of ways to satisfy particular motives. Thus, in our economy, consumers dominated by the 'higher' motives of esteem or self-actualisation will be expected to show interest in a greater variety of products and services than consumers dominated by 'lower' motives. Of course, this focus on goods and services does not necessarily hold for individuals or people from other cultures with less materialistic tendencies.

We carry safety further.

Volkswagen don't just aim to meet commercial vehicle safety requirements. The new front-engined, front-wheel drive VW Transporter actually exceeds many passenger car safety levels. And with its German engineering and reliability, independent rear suspension, walk-through cab and class leading 5.4m³ versatile load space, it takes the entire category a step ahead. Panel Van and Window Van from $24,990*. For details see your nearest Volkswagen dealer or telephone 008 819 057.

New Transporter

COURTESY OF VOLKSWAGEN

Commodore Acclaim delivers twins.

Affordable, family safety has been taken into another dimension with driver,

and now passenger airbag, standard on the new Holden Commodore Acclaim.

 No other large Australian family car

offers the same level of protection, while only Commodore Acclaim includes the

unique combination of Anti-lock Braking and Independent Rear Suspension. That's

why Commodore Acclaim continues to be recognised

HOLDEN
Commodore Acclaim
There's nothing quite like a Holden.

by experts as the safest Australian family car, ever.

COURTESY OF GENERAL MOTORS-HOLDEN'S AUTOMOTIVE LTD

Although Maslow's scheme is useful for a general understanding of motives, it has limited use in attempting to predict specific behaviour.[18] Of particular concern is that consumers are continually influenced by motives that they have apparently passed on the hierarchy. For example, even in our economy, safety (second on the hierarchy) still appears to motivate many consumer decisions. Some suggest that the theory accounts for this, because even though the focus is on dominant motives, the hierarchy still allows for the influence of other motives not in a dominant position. This is said to explain fluctuating behaviour under conditions of a stable hierarchy. However, the mechanism regulating this process has not been well defined.

HIERARCHY DYNAMICS

Difficulties in explaining changing behaviour patterns using a relatively stable motive hierarchy have led some theorists to suggest a goal hierarchy to help bridge the gap between motives and behaviour.[19] Motives can then be viewed as exerting a relatively stable influence on goals, while opportunities, constraints and changing conditions in the consumer's environment may be seen as exerting a dynamic influence. The interaction of these two forces can then lead to changes in goal importance and flexible behaviour patterns.

Aspiration levels also help to explain how dynamic consumer goals can occur under the influence of relatively stable motives. A level of aspiration may be thought of as a goal that can be influenced by a number of factors to change either up or down over time. Therefore, as consumers approach achievement of a goal, they can still be influenced by the same motive structure to strive for even higher levels of achievement. The goal moves ever upward, causing us to run faster and faster to reach it but, like Alice and the Queen in *Through the Looking Glass*, we never make it. For example, hunger can easily be satisfied by very basic foodstuffs such as beans and milk, but most consumers set their sights 'higher' for foods such as burgers and chips. Influences on consumers' levels of aspirations include:

1. *Achievement*. Success yields rising aspiration levels, while failure tends to result in a decline in such goals.

2. *Reality orientation*. Usually aspirations are set to reflect the individual's assessment of what levels of achievement are within reach.

3. *Group influences*. Consumers' aspirations are influenced by individuals in membership and reference groups.[20]

A further influence on motive and goal structuring is learning. As indicated earlier under the discussion of classifying motives, consumers can acquire (learn) new motives from dealing with their environment. Much of this occurs during the childhood socialisation process. The acquisition of these *secondary* motives results in restructuring the hierarchy. This occurs because secondary motives are often quite strong and therefore can significantly influence behaviours. Consider, for example, how the learned needs for social approval so strongly influence purchase decisions, from personal-care products to cars.

Motive combinations

It is convenient to discuss motives separately, as if they influence consumers independently and one at a time. In fact, they often interact, leading to a combined influence or to situations in which they conflict and exert opposing influences on behaviour.[21]

MOTIVE LINKING

Because motives can differ in how specific they are, it is possible for a linking to occur at various levels of generality. For example, safety may be made up of more specific motives, including ones relating to security and protection. Therefore, achievement of a specific motive can be a means of approaching a more general motive that is viewed as the goal.[22] This is referred to as the means–end linking of motives. A linking that might exist to influence purchase of a bike lock is depicted in Figure 9.3. Here, we see that safety has been linked to the more specific motives of protection and security. In turn, these have been linked to strength, dependability and durability properties of the product. All of these factors can exert a combined influence on the consumer.

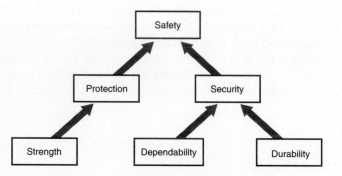

FIG. 9.3   A means–end linking for a bike-lock purchase   Source: John A. Howard & Jagdish N. Sheth, *The Theory of Buyer Behavior*, Wiley, New York, 1969, p. 107.

MOTIVE BUNDLING

It is very important to realise that a given product can satisfy various motives at the same approximate level of specific influence. This results in the bundling, or combining, of influences on consumers' decisions. To illustrate, for a car purchase, a desire for transportation can bundle with motives for achievement, social recognition, safety and economy.

MOTIVE CONFLICT

Motives can also conflict with each other to affect how consumers interact with the marketplace. A major contributor to the topic of motive conflict is Kurt Lewin.[23] He viewed motives as influencing the attracting or repelling forces of goals in the individual's environment. The degree to which a product or service satisfies a motive will therefore determine its attracting (positive) force, and how adverse it is to a motive will influence its repelling (negative) force.

In Lewin's view, conflict is most likely when motives are of approximately equal strength. Three principal cases are possible: approach–approach, avoidance–avoidance and approach–avoidance conflict. These terms refer to psychological tendencies for attraction or repulsion, not necessarily actual physical movement.

APPROACH–APPROACH CONFLICT   This is a situation in which conflict exists between two desirable alternatives, such as when a consumer must decide how to allocate purchasing dollars between a home-exercise centre and a microcomputer (see Fig. 9.4(a)). These situations can lead to a period of temporary indecision and vacillation between alternatives. Permanent indecision is rare, however, because approach–approach conflict is said to be unstable. Instability occurs because the pull toward a positive goal increases as one approaches it, and declines as one moves away. Therefore, a slight tendency to accept one alternative can lead to resolving the conflict quickly. Such resolution can occur through exposure to information useful in evaluating the alternatives. Promotional literature and salespeople's comments play a crucial role in this process.

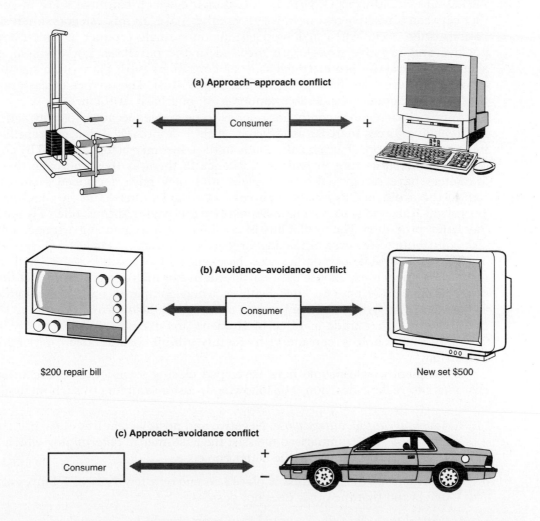

(a) Approach–approach conflict

+ ← Consumer → +

(b) Avoidance–avoidance conflict

− ← Consumer → −

$200 repair bill   New set $500

(c) Approach–avoidance conflict

Consumer ←→ + −

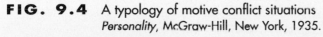

FIG. 9.4   A typology of motive conflict situations   Source: Kurt Lewin, *A Dynamic Theory of Personality*, McGraw-Hill, New York, 1935.

AVOIDANCE–AVOIDANCE CONFLICT   This situation occurs when consumers face choices between two alternatives, both of which are perceived as being negative in nature. For example, when the television set with which a family has been perfectly happy becomes seriously 'ill', the alternatives may be a hefty repair bill or the large expense of a replacement set (see Fig.9.4(b)). Such situations are characterised as being stable because consumers tend to vacillate between undesirable alternatives. Vacillation occurs because approaching a negative alternative leads to a stronger repulsion by it. Such situations often lead to considerable search for information (window shopping, reading ads and making inquiries) but often stop short of a purchase commitment.

APPROACH–AVOIDANCE CONFLICT   Situations in which consumers are in conflict between a positive and negative alternative make up this category. Such situations often occur when making decisions on a single product in which both positive and negative aspects are involved in the purchase. For example, to acquire an attractive product such as a car, consumers must part with a sizeable amount of scarce purchasing dollars (see Fig. 9.4(c)). These types of cash outflows can generate considerable amounts of purchase avoidance.

Approach–avoidance conflict also tends to be stable, because both attracting and repelling forces increase as the goal object is approached; but the repelling force increases more sharply. This results in the consumer being attracted by goal objects but experiencing increasing resistance to them as they approach them. Marketers have recognised this problem, and they have developed means to reduce the avoidance aspect of such conflicts. Banks offer loans in which you 'borrow in June and start paying in September' and major airlines offer 'Fly Now, Pay Later' programs. The availability of credit cards and financing arrangements also contribute to the ease of making large expenditures.

Approach–avoidance conflict also happens in more subtle ways, such as when consumers must choose between alternative brands of a given product that have both positive and negative features when compared with one another. Choosing a Ford over a Holden because of its styling also means sacrificing the traditionally higher trade-in value of Holdens, for example. When faced with such important choices, consumers frequently exhibit considerable conflict and indecision.

Consequently, salespeople have developed closing techniques to encourage customers to make a decision. The following is just a sampling of such methods:

1. *Advantage/disadvantage close.* Negative and positive features of each alternative are summarised to assist the customer in determining which alternative appears to be the better choice.

2. *Critical feature close.* Stress is placed on one or a few 'critical' features of one brand that the other does not possess.

3. *Critical time close.* If one brand is in short supply, or a special sale is about to end, emphasising the immediacy of the decision can convince a consumer to purchase.

HOLDEN STATESMAN VERSUS FORD FAIRLANE.
DON'T TAKE NO FOR AN ANSWER.

FEATURES	HOLDEN STATESMAN SERIES II	FORD FAIRLANE GHIA
3 Year or 100,000km Powertrain Warranty	YES	NO
5 litre V8 Engine	YES	NO
IRS & Optional ABS Combination	YES	NO
Variatronic Power Steering	YES	NO
Security Alarm System	YES	NO
Door Deadlocks	YES	NO
Long Range Fuel Tank	YES	NO
Height Adjustable Seat belts: Front and Rear	YES	NO
Twin Chrome Exhaust Tailpipe Ends	YES	NO
Passenger Seat Lumbar Support	YES	NO
Body Colour Door Handles	YES	NO
Side & Rear Skirts	YES	NO
Glovebox Drink Cooler	YES	NO
Driver's Side Lockable Glovebox	YES	NO
Headlamps Auto Off with Programmable Delay	YES	NO
Road Speed Sensitive Intermittent Wiper Dwell	YES	NO
Rear Lamp Failure Warning	YES	NO
Safety Triangle	YES	NO
Memory Height on Power Antenna	YES	NO
Illuminated Centre Console Storage Bin	YES	NO
Illuminated Passenger's Vanity Mirror	YES	NO
Auto Time Delay on Power Windows	YES	NO

The 1993 Holden Statesman Series II is the biggest Holden ever built, and has many distinct advantages over the Fairlane Ghia. One of which is the level of standard features you get for your money.

Independent Rear Suspension (IRS), for instance, endows the Statesman with supreme ride and handling which is further enhanced by Variatronic road speed sensitive power steering. It is exceptionally light when parking, yet firmly responsive at speed.

And your safety was top of mind with the development of Statesman's optional Anti-lock Braking System (ABS). It ensures that you remain in total control, even when braking hard in the wet.

The advanced Holden 5.0 litre MPFI V8 engine produces 165kW and 385Nm, yet it can still return 9.5l/100km on the highway and 16l/100km in the city. Or Holden's refined V6 engine will provide you with 127kW and 293Nm, yet return 8l/100km on the highway and 13l/100km in the city.

All this, including Holden's 2 Year or 50,000km New Vehicle Warranty, 3 Year or 100,000km Powertrain Warranty and 24 Hour HoldenWise Roadside Service and Roadside Ultra, which comes at no extra cost.

So when you get the very best value in a Holden Statesman Series II, why settle for second best?

Holden Statesman Series II

Australia's Own Luxury Car.

Examples of approach–avoidance conflict   COURTESY OF GENERAL MOTORS-HOLDEN'S AUTOMOTIVE LTD

Self-concept

Although a consumer's motive structure exhibits some flexibility over time, there remains a central theme or organisation to the structure. One factor influencing this organisation is the individual's self-concept, as discussed in Chapter 8. That is, consumers possess certain images of themselves, and these self-concepts exert organising influences on their motives. One important effect of these influences on motives is reflected in the types of goods purchased, as consumers appear to prefer some products and brands that are consistent with their self-concepts. Thus, we would expect to see individuals who view themselves as successful business people drive cars, own homes, join clubs and interact with social groups that reflect this self-image.

MOTIVATION RESEARCH

We have noted that many consumers are unaware of the motives influencing their purchase behaviour. Some motives may not reach the consumer's consciousness, and others may be repressed because to deal with them may be uncomfortable. This presents difficulty to the marketer, who needs to understand consumers in order to design the most effective mix of marketing offerings. Any direct attempts to determine such motives, say by interviewing consumers, may only yield 'surface' explanations or rationalisations that hide true strivings.

The concept of *motivation research* has been offered as a means of identifying consumers' true, underlying purchase motives. The term is typically not used to describe just any type of research on motivational issues. It refers to certain research techniques and, to some extent, ways of interpreting information about motivation generated by these techniques. Briefly stated, disguised and indirect techniques are used in an attempt to probe consumers' inner motives without arousing defence mechanisms that can generate misleading results.

In practice, motivation research has yielded provocative and sometimes strange conclusions. For example, earlier findings included:

➡ Many men don't like to fly because they fear that if the plane crashes they will be blamed by their families for not being killed in a decent fashion, such as in a car crash.

➡ When she is baking, a woman is unconsciously and symbolically re-enacting the process of giving birth.

➡ Men who use suspenders have an unresolved castration complex.[24]

The novelty of these interpretations is at least partially explained by the central role of fantasy, unconscious antisocial strivings and sex in Freudian psychology, which has apparently strongly influenced conclusions drawn from many motivation-research studies.

There have also been a number of other criticisms levelled at motivation researchers.[25] First, sample sizes are frequently small because of the costly nature of in-depth interviewing. This has created doubt in relation to conclusions made about the entire population of consumers. Secondly, motivation-research studies have generated inconsistent findings, and this leaves the marketer in a quandary as to what action should be taken. Thirdly, some findings are difficult for the marketer to capitalise on. For example, of what practical use is it to know (assuming it is true) that suspender-wearers have a 'castration complex'? Finally, and perhaps most importantly, motivation researchers have been criticised for improperly employing research techniques borrowed from psychologists. In psychology, these techniques are used in conjunction with knowledge of a patient's history and normal standards of behaviour to serve as references. The lack of such standards in marketing make it difficult to determine whether many motivation-research findings are truly representative of most consumers.

Despite its potential limitations, motivation research has been a valuable research tool in a number of situations. For example, in a now-classic study, Haire discovered evidence suggesting that initial resistance to Nescafé instant coffee may have been due to more than just its taste characteristics. Projective methods revealed that women believed users of the instant product were lazy and not particularly good wives. Thus, it was argued, they would not be quick to adopt it themselves.[26]

More recently, well-known advertising agencies have used forms of projection and other motivation-research techniques to understand consumers. For example, BBDO Worldwide use a method called *Photosort*, where consumers look at a photo deck showing various types of people and are asked to indicate which brands of a product they feel these people would use. The type of people the consumers associate with the brand gives insight into how consumers view the brands themselves. Advertising campaigns for Honda, GE Australia, Visa and others have been based on insights developed from this method.[27]

Australian studies have provided data for marketing decisions of major industrial giants such as Optus, General Motors and the Australian building industry. Lions Clubs have also used motivational research to improve their operations.[28] Therefore, it appears that properly conducted motivation-research-oriented studies, employed with other information, can provide valuable information about consumers.

INVOLVEMENT

Consumers exhibit different levels of involvement depending on the product they are buying. For example, consider a consumer faced with two different buying situations. The first involves a new pair of running shoes. Because the consumer runs an average of 25 kilometres per week, and thus is really 'into' the sport, her interest in running shoes is very high. She talks with another runner and considers a change in brands. She then carefully reads advertisements in several issues of running magazines. She makes the purchase decision based on a detailed evaluation of her own running style and the magazine's ratings of shoes. The entire decision-making process takes two weeks.

The same consumer realises that she has driven her car several thousand kilometres since purchasing it without changing the oil. The next time she finds herself in Big W she goes to the automotive section and looks at the different brands of oil and oil filters available. Although she has seen many television advertisements for car products, none of them has really captured her attention. Consequently, these brands are not on her mind during her first trip into the automotive section. She looks on the charts available in the store to determine which filter and oil she needs for her car, and purchases the least expensive brand available. The entire process occupies only a portion of one Saturday afternoon and involves very little effort.

These two buying situations differ considerably in terms of the energy devoted to purchase decisions. Unfortunately, many marketers assume that, typically, consumers are actively involved to the extent described in the first example. Although this may describe many situations, it appears lacking for a wide variety of other circumstances that resemble our second example—consumers having little personal concern about their consumption activities and adopting a rather detached, reactive stance to stimuli that reach their awareness. Therefore, a major concern in this relatively new area of inquiry is how the level of involvement affects the amount of effort consumers give to learning about products and deciding which brands to buy.

Unfortunately, many American-owned companies assume that levels of consumer involvement are the same for both Americans and Australians, although research has shown there are differences.[29]

TABLE 9.3 Comparing American and Australian involvement with certain products

High involvement	Australia	United States
Airlines	4.51†	4.27
Bicycles	4.76	4.17
Cameras	4.81	4.82
Cars	4.95	4.58
Cassette players	4.56	4.75
Stereos*	4.86	3.75
TVs	4.56	4.42
Telephones	3.42	3.08
Wash and dry*	4.39	4.70
Low involvement		
Beer*	2.50	1.71
Dishwashing detergent (soap)	1.87	1.75
Luncheon meat*	2.41	1.58
Mayonnaise*	2.26	1.42
Peanut butter	1.76	1.67
Pickles*	1.58	1.58
Shampoo*	2.67	1.83
Toilet paper	1.63	1.50
Tomato sauce (ketchup)*	1.88	1.25

* Interesting similarity or difference.
† Means scores on a scale from low = 1 to high = 5.

Source: P. M. Tidwell, Involvement as a Function of Brand Frequency: Comparing Americans and Australians, Paper presented to International Marketing Educators and Researchers' Conference, Griffith University, Qld, 2–5 July 1995.

Herbert Krugman proposed the concept of involvement to characterise differences in the intensity of interest with which consumers approach their dealings with the marketplace.[30] As might be expected for a relatively new concept, full agreement has not yet been reached regarding its exact nature.[31] However, most definitions acknowledge that involvement:

1. is related to the consumer's values and self-concept, which influence the degree of personal importance ascribed to a product or situation;

2. can vary across individuals and different situations;

3. is related to some form of arousal.

On the basis of a review of these and other characteristics, it has been suggested that involvement incorporates the critical properties of intensity, or degree of arousal, and directional influence.[32] Although involvement as characterised above may not be identical to motivation, the two concepts appear closely related in important aspects. That is, as our example showed, in some given situation individuals may perceive important links between a product or service and themselves, in terms of values the product or service can express or needs it can fulfil—they will feel connected to it in some way. This will lead to the individuals being interested in the product or service and activating energy toward it. That is, they will be motivated to act toward the product or service. The stronger the felt link (degree of involvement) the more intense the motivated state will be experienced.

Dimensions of involvement

The concept of involvement appears to have a number of important dimensions, which are outlined in Figure 9.5 and described in the following paragraphs.[33]

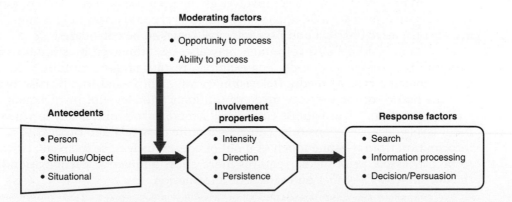

FIG. 9.5 A diagram of the major dimensions of involvement   Source: Based on J. Craig Andrews, Srinivas Durvasula & Syed H. Akhter, 'A Framework for Conceptualizing and Measuring the Involvement Construct in Advertising Research', *Journal of Advertising* 19, 1990, pp. 27–40; and Judith L. Zaichkowsky, 'Conceptualizing Involvement', *Journal of Advertising* 15 (34), 1986, pp. 4–14.

ANTECEDENTS

A variety of variables are thought to precede involvement and influence its nature and extent. These *antecedents* can be viewed as bases or sources that interact with each other to generate the degree of involvement the consumer will experience at any particular time. It is helpful to group the variables into person, stimulus/object and situational categories.

PERSON   Among the variables encompassed within the person category are personal needs, values, experiences and interests. For example, a person who strongly values body fitness is more likely to be interested in the fat and fibre content of breakfast foods as well as their vitamin levels.

STIMULUS/OBJECT   Products or stimuli that consumers perceive to be closely related to their values, interests, experiences and so on are likely to lead to higher levels of involvement. Therefore, we should not expect a given product to generate the same level of involvement for all consumers—the product will *interact* with the personal variables just described to generate a unique level of involvement for every person.

The degree to which the consumer perceives various product alternatives to be different can also affect the level of involvement.[34] The substitutability of brands, number of brands available and product performance features all influence this perceived differentiation and the resulting level of involvement.[35]

The amount of risk consumers perceive in their purchase decisions can also influence the degree of felt involvement. This *perceived risk* is derived from consumers' perceptions of the chances of making a purchase decision that they will in some way regret, combined with perceptions of the potential degree of resulting unfavourable consequences.[36] The unfavourable consequences can be in the form of financial loss, physical loss or psychological harm, among others. Thus, while purchase of a lawn-mower involves giving up a considerable sum of money, if its safety features are inadequate or its noise level could anger neighbours, there are also negative physical and psychological issues to be considered.

Consumers' levels of involvement may also be influenced by stimuli used to promote products and brands. For example, results of some studies have suggested that the type of media (television, print, radio) used to advertise brands and the nature of the message given can influence the level of involvement consumers generate.[37] Television is considered generally to require only low involvement levels because a consumer can view it quite passively and process very little information from it—tune much of it out of consciousness, so to speak. However, to be processed, print media requires more effort and active participation from the consumer as a reader and seeker of information.

SITUATIONS   The type of situation consumers face can also influence the level of involvement that they will experience. One such situational influence can be the use that will be made of the product.[38] Thus, purchase of rope for a clothes line may not involve a consumer much at all. On the other hand, if rope is needed for a child's swing set, the same consumer may become quite involved in the purchase process. Another situational influence could be the occasion for which a purchase is being made. While the purchase of a coffee mug might not normally be very involving, when the purchase is being made for a gift the level of involvement might increase substantially. A further situational influence may occur as a result of environmental change, such as news that a given over-the-counter drug is now suspected of posing certain health risks. In all of these situations consumers' values, interests, and so on combine with specific circumstances in their environment to generate a given level of involvement.

MODERATING FACTORS

Several variables or conditions may exist to limit or constrain the impact of antecedents on consumers' state of involvement.[39] For example, a consumer watching a stereo component advertisement, which would normally be of interest because stereos are highly relevant to the consumer's needs, is distracted from the ad by the doorbell ringing. In another case, a portion of a newspaper article about the possible allergic reactions one can have to a fibre supplement might be unavailable because it was used to clean the cat box. These circumstances limit the consumer's *opportunity to process* information and consequently will influence the level of involvement experienced.

In a similar vein, the consumer's *ability to process* information may influence the level of involvement that is experienced. If consumers have little knowledge of a particular product, they might not be able to understand some of the information available in advertisements and consequently not evaluate alternative brands as completely as they otherwise would.

INVOLVEMENT PROPERTIES

Involvement may be thought of as an internal state that the consumer experiences. As mentioned earlier, this internal state has arousal properties and, like motivation, it also has a directional influence on how consumers will behave. As an internal state, involvement may be viewed as having three main properties: intensity, direction, and a level of persistence.

INTENSITY   The property of intensity refers to the degree of involvement that the consumer experiences. Typically, involvement has been viewed in terms of two broad categories—high and low. Recently some researchers have incorporated additional levels to understand how consumers act with regard to product and brand information in their environment.[40] An important contribution of these schemes is their implications for understanding how consumers process information. However, for our purposes, it is sufficient only to draw distinctions between high and low involvement levels.

Traditionally, a highly involved consumer is defined as one who is very interested in differences between particular brands of a product and is willing to invest considerable energy in decision making about purchasing them. As in the example about buying running shoes, this interest often generates an active search for information as well as increased attention to relevant brand advertisements. In addition, highly involved consumers, rather than just passively accepting information, tend to evaluate critically the negative and positive implications of received information. Attitudes are formed about specific brands from the beliefs that consumers develop from such critical evaluations.

When consumers operate under low-involvement conditions, they are passive receivers of information who engage in virtually no active information search about alternative brands. Also, advertisements or other information actually reaching these consumers' attention will only be processed at a very superficial level, receiving little meaningful evaluation. Very low levels of brand awareness and comprehension will be the result. Further, consumers do not appear to develop distinct attitudes about brands from such information.

DIRECTION   The property of direction refers to the focus, or target, of involvement. Antecedent conditions will strongly influence this focus. Possible targets are actual products such as cars and perfume. The target might also be a purchase decision itself; as when involvement is temporarily high because the purchase decision poses considerable risk, even though the consumer is not particularly enamoured with the product category.

The involvement target may also be advertisements about the product.[41] Some media appear to involve consumers more than others. For example, as mentioned earlier, it has been argued that compared with print media, television typically does not generate very high involvement. However, many television advertisers attempt to develop advertisements that heighten this level. The attractiveness or expertise of a spokesperson may be of assistance in this regard. In other cases, the mood or theme set by the advertisement can generate higher levels. For example, Cathy Freeman, gold medallist in the 1994 Commonwealth Games, has increased consumers' levels of involvement in her television commercials as a result of her political statements at those games.

PERSISTENCE   A third involvement property deals with the length of time the consumer remains in a state of involvement. Sometimes consumers experience a long-term personal interest in one or more products. Anglers, naturalists, stereo buffs, gourmets and car enthusiasts are examples of some who appear to have this ongoing personal interest. Such continuing heightened commitment is termed *enduring involvement*, as it defines a base line of long-term interest in a product or other object.

Situational involvement refers to the temporary involvement that occurs as a result of the consumer's situation; the situation, rather than some long-term interest in the object itself, defines the object's relevance. Purchase situations such as buying a gift for a close friend, lacking knowledge about brands or anticipating the pleasure to be derived from the purchase can significantly influence a consumer's involvement in the brand-choice decision being confronted. Situational factors can temporarily lead to high levels of involvement for the consumer, even for products that generate low levels of enduring involvement.

RESPONSE FACTORS   The response dimension characterises how a consumer behaves under different involvement conditions. That is, it describes the mental and physical actions or reactions the consumer engages in. Therefore, the response dimension is a function of the type of involvement generated and the situations confronted.

Some response characteristics have already been mentioned in our earlier discussion. However, it is useful to provide a fuller view of their nature here. Generally, we can view the response dimension as including different patterns of information search and acquisition, the mental processing of information to evaluate products and make decisions about them, and postdecision behaviour.

In one study comparing high- and low-involvement products, Australians were shown to prefer significantly different decision strategies from those preferred by Americans.[42] See Table 9.4 for further details and Chapter 14 for further explanation of the decision strategies.

TABLE 9.4 Percentage of decision strategy preference for significantly different categories

Products	Lexicographic		Sequential elimination		Conjunctive		Simple additive		Weighted additive		Phased decision		Affect referral	
	US	OZ	US	OZ	US	OZ	US	OZ	US	OZ	US	OZ	US	OZ
Beer	23.3	28.4	14.8	7.9	6.3	7.5	4.4	3.0	3.3	6.0	3.7	1.5	12.2	22.4
Bicycles	20.0	20.9	12.6	14.9	8.1	14.9	10.4	6.0	7.4	14.9	4.4	4.5	6.0	10.4
Cameras	25.2	19.4	7.8	10.4	10.7	7.5	9.0	11.9	11.5	13.4	8.5	11.9	9.6	14.9
Cars	24.4	19.4	8.1	9.0	9.6	11.9	8.5	6.0	12.6	13.4	9.6	10.4	9.3	17.9
Tape players	25.9	25.4	13.0	10.4	11.1	11.9	11.1	7.5	8.5	11.9	5.9	10.4	6.7	14.9
Pickles	18.9	9.0	31.1	35.8	7.8	11.9	5.2	3.0	4.4	3.0	3.7	0	7.8	3.0
Luncheon meat	18.5	16.4	28.9	38.8	10.7	7.5	7.8	1.5	4.1	1.5	1.9	1.5	8.9	6.0
Stereos	21.1	13.4	9.3	9.0	7.4	13.4	10.4	11.9	9.6	13.4	5.9	11.9	12.6	13.4
TV sets	20.4	10.4	6.3	6.0	10.7	17.9	11.1	9.0	10.0	14.9	4.1	11.9	14.1	16.4
VCRs	20.7	9.0	10.0	14.9	7.4	13.4	11.1	7.5	8.1	10.4	5.9	13.4	10.7	13.4

Source: P. M. Tidwell & W. Marks, 'American versus Australian Consumer Decision Making: An Analysis of Decision Rules Used in Limited Problem-solving Behaviour', *Asia Pacific Advances in Consumer Research* 1, 1994, pp. 148–52.

As already mentioned, some research has indicated that high involvement generates rather intense efforts on the part of the consumer for attending to and actively searching out sources of product and brand information. In fact, one study found that consumers high in enduring involvement for a product engaged in a regular, ongoing search for information about it.[43] This is to be contrasted with the search activity that may increase shortly before purchasing a product due to high situational involvement.

Conversely, low involvement is said to result in a consumer engaging in little if any active search for information. Here, exposure to products occurs mainly through ads and other information that the consumer happens to confront as a result of engaging in other activities (such as watching television). Because of this lack of interest, little attention is devoted to these sources. Consequently, only modest amounts of information may be acquired about a specific brand, even after many exposures to ads for it. Also, awareness level for brands may be low.[44]

After acquiring information, consumers process it to determine its meaning. The steps undertaken in this information-processing stage have been viewed in terms of a *hierarchy of effects*, because they appear to describe the mental processes that lead to a purchase decision. A variety of hierarchies have been proposed under one common assumption—the consumer is highly involved. However, a different hierarchy of effects has been proposed for low-involvement conditions.[45] The essence of each hierarchy that is relevant to our present discussion is presented in Figure 9.6.

Cognition in the high-involvement hierarchy refers to the knowledge and beliefs about brands that consumers derive from evaluating information. Active search and attention to information foster learning about advertisements and other product information. In addition, consumers engage in considerable thinking about this information to determine its consistency with their existing brand knowledge and beliefs. Sometimes this is referred to as a *central route* to processing, because consumers deal with information they feel is central to the evaluation process.[46] Critical evaluation and rejection of information inconsistent with existing beliefs are likely to occur. Rejection can happen through the consumer's use of arguments to counter information or advertising claims ('the price is low, but I'll bet the service is bad') and through attempts to discredit the source of the information. Alternatively, consistent information is likely to generate strong supportive arguments (thoughts that support the position of the source). The result is a new or modified set of beliefs about alternative brands.

As the second stage in the high-involvement hierarchy suggests, evaluation of beliefs in a positive and negative sense leads the consumer to form attitudes about

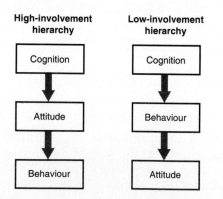

FIG. 9.6 The hierarchy of effects under high- and low-involvement conditions

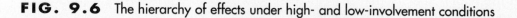

the brands and their relative desirability. Thus, the degree to which consumers are persuaded by the ad will be reflected in a change in their attitudes. Studies have suggested that persuasive effects are more persistent under high-involvement conditions.[47] Resulting behaviour is believed to be strongly influenced by the changed attitudes that the consumer holds. Thus, a consumer who has had a favourable change in attitude toward the product may be expected to seek more positive information about it and/or have a greater likelihood of purchasing it.

Cognition in the low-involvement hierarchy differs considerably from its counterpart under conditions of high involvement. Attention levels are low because the consumer has little desire to process information for the purpose of evaluating brands. Despite exposure to many advertisements, knowledge about brands is also very low. In fact, the consumer may not even be consciously aware of the brand name. Consequently, beliefs about brands are not well founded and are unlikely to be strong enough to support formation of clearly defined brand attitudes.

Another consequence may occur after a consumer is exposed to numerous advertisements about a particular brand. The name can become sufficiently familiar for the consumer to recognise it when shopping for the product. Because the consumer has no strong attitude about any of the specific brands, this familiarity may be a sufficient reason for purchasing the brand. That is, purchase decisions may be made based on associating the brand with non-central cues such as pleasing background music or an expert-looking spokesperson. This is sometimes referred to as a *peripheral route* to processing information. Therefore, as the second stage in the low-involvement hierarchy shows, purchase behaviour occurs before strong brand attitudes have developed. After purchasing and experiencing the product through direct use, the consumer is likely to develop some attitudes about it. However, these attitudes may never become very strong because of the low importance of the product to the consumer.

Marketing implications of involvement

Two essential conclusions emerge from the above review:

1. For numerous products or situations, many consumers are quite uninterested in learning about alternative brands and their characteristics.

2. Consumers may make many purchase decisions without first developing clear brand attitudes or even having much knowledge about alternative brands.

Given that involvement can vary across consumers and situations, these conclusions have a number of marketing-strategy implications.[48] A primary consideration is to determine whether any strategy should account for different levels of involvement. If only a small proportion of the market operates on a low-involvement condition for the brand in question, it may not be economical to consider changing strategies. However, if sizeable portions of the potential market might relate to the company's offerings at either level of involvement, then some manner of coping with these different levels would seem highly desirable. One strategy might be to differentiate marketing communications for each condition. For example, high-involvement messages would entail longer advertisements and considerable amounts of more complex information. In addition, because of its higher involvement demands, print media may be the more appropriate choice for advertising assertions.[49] For the low-involvement advertisements, short visually oriented messages with little information content could be frequently repeated to foster brand awareness. Many of these might be placed on television because of its lower demands for viewer concentration and the potential for frequent advertising insertions.

The picture may even be slightly more complicated. Earlier we suggested that antecedents of involvement will influence the nature of consumers' responses. Evidence suggests also that some antecedents exert a stronger influence than others. For example, one study found that the amount of risk perceived in a purchase will more strongly influence how extensive the decision process will be than other antecedents such as the product's perceived pleasure value.[50] Also, the consumer's tendency to allow exposure to advertising messages does not seem highly related to risk importance but is strongly influenced by the product's perceived pleasure value. Such results need to be verified by additional research. If they are confirmed, these findings imply that marketers will benefit from discovering the sources of consumer involvement before designing marketing strategies for their products or services.

A second involvement-related strategy would be an attempt to move low-involvement consumers to higher levels.[51] Of course, the specific situation will determine the feasibility of this alternative. If conditions appear favourable, various methods may be considered. These could include creating controversy (the Pepsi challenge, comparative advertisements and so on), linking the product to a high-involvement issue (linking air bags in cars to the protection of loved ones) or changing the product to add features that might increase involvement levels.

A third strategy option is also possible—segmenting consumers into high- and low-involvement groups and tailoring marketing programs for each.[52] Take the example of writing pens. Low-involvement consumers could be catered to with inexpensive models that are rather nondescript and disposable. Frequent television commercials could remind mass audiences of the brand name. Conversely, those concerned with conveying an image with their pen might be willing to spend more than $30 and even as much as $900. These instruments would be made of distinctive materials, and have high-class styling and a quality finish. Promotions detailing the many product features might be placed in exclusive magazines such as the *Architectural Digest*, *The Bulletin*, *Vogue* or *Belle* to attract high-income readers.

This section has introduced the involvement concept, suggested its general potential for influencing the behaviour of consumers and indicated its implications for marketing strategy. We will build on this introduction in subsequent chapters to show the relevance of involvement to the variables under discussion.

SUMMARY

Motives were defined as inner states that mobilise and direct bodily energy toward goal objects located in the environment. After several schemes for classifying motives were reviewed, the concept of arousal was treated. The major ways motives can be triggered were shown to be through physiological conditions, situational conditions and cognitive activity. Although the concept of tension is central to motive arousal, it was indicated that the primary goal of consumers is not always to reduce environmental stimulation. Rather, the optimum level of stimulation appears to be above zero and this suggests that, depending on prevailing conditions, consumers may seek to decrease or increase stimulation levels. Perhaps this is because of a curiosity motive.

The concepts of motive hierarchies and levels of aspiration were shown to be central to an understanding of motive structuring. However, a practical view of such structuring must consider that motives interact to combine their influence (linking or binding), or conflict with each other.

Next, the topic of motivation research was briefly reviewed. It appears that after an early flush of popularity, perhaps associated with overzealous application, the discipline has matured to a point in which its valid contributions can be usefully combined with other methods to understand consumers' motives.

Discussion then turned to the highly related concept of consumer involvement. After involvement was characterised, attention focused on its dimensions, including levels (high and low), types (enduring and situational), antecedents and response characteristics, including consumers' hierarchy of effects. Finally, some marketing implications of involvement were reviewed.

MANAGERIAL REFLECTIONS

For our product or service situation:

1. What motives might influence choice criteria?

2. What factors are likely to trigger arousal and how can they be influenced?

3. What motives might combine to influence purchases? Which might put the consumer into conflict and how might the consumer be able to resolve such conflict?

4. How might motivation-research methods help to give us insight into consumers?

5. To what degree are consumers influenced by enduring involvement?

6. Should segmentation be based on involvement levels?

DISCUSSION TOPICS

1. What is a motive? Indicate the various roles motives play in influencing behaviour.

2. Find three examples of advertisements that appeal to psychogenic motives. Be prepared to discuss the appropriateness of the association between the product and the motive.

3. Discuss the problems unconscious motives pose for implementing the marketing concept.

4. What general factors can trigger motive arousal? Cite at least two examples of each type.

5. It has been argued that at times consumers seem to increase levels of environmental stimulation as well as strive to reduce them. Review this argument, and suggest situations as well as marketing strategies that could relate to such occurrences.

6. Briefly review Maslow's motive hierarchy and the concept of prepotency. Cite at least three products that might appeal to an individual at each stage of the hierarchy. Can you suggest any product for which a marketer might be able to appeal to at least three of the states at the same time?

7. Of what interest is the concept of 'levels of aspiration' to the marketer? What relevance does this concept have to the problem of energy shortage and depletion of resources?

8. Review the concepts of motive linking and motive bundling. Show how they can apply to the purchase of a tracksuit.

9. Define each of the major types of motive conflicts and cite a personal experience that fits each of these situations. Be sure to indicate the specifics involved, including any relevant products, the duration of the conflict and how it was resolved.

10. Construct two high-involvement and two low-involvement consumer scenarios, and suggest marketing strategies to accommodate them.

REFERENCES

1. See Joe Kent Kerby, *Consumer Behavior Conceptual Foundations*, Dunn-Donnelly, New York, 1975; Johan Arndt, 'How Broad Should the Marketing Concept Be?', *Journal of Marketing* 42, January 1978, pp. 101–3; and Gerald Zaltman and Melanie Wallendorf, *Consumer Behavior: Basic Findings and Management Implications*, Wiley, New York, 1979.

2. See Abraham K. Korman, *The Psychology of Motivation*, Prentice-Hall, Englewood Cliffs, NJ, 1974.

3. Portions of this section follow the discussion in John Howard & Jagdish Sheth, *The Theory of Buyer Behavior*, Wiley, New York, 1969, pp. 105–18.

4. One exception is the case of anxiety in which consumers suffer from a lack of direction to their arousal.

5. See G. W. Allport & II. S. Odbert, 'Trait-Names: A Psychological Study', *Psychological Monographs* 47 (1), 1936.

6. See William J. McGuire, 'Some Internal Psychological Factors Influencing Consumer Choice, *Journal of Consumer Research* 2, March 1976, pp. 302–19; and William J. McGuire, 'Psychological Motives and Communication Gratification', in J. G. Blumer & E. Katz (eds), *The Uses of Mass Communications: Perspectives on Gratifications Research*, Sage Publications Inc., Beverly Hills, CA, pp. 167–96.

7. P. M. Tidwell & A. C. Graesser, Working paper based on Masters thesis, Memphis State University, 1989.

8. Some of this section follows David Krech, Richard S. Crutchfield & Egerton L. Ballachey, *Individual in Society*, McGraw-Hill, New York, 1962, pp. 84–7.

9. See, for example, D. E. Berlyne, *Conflict, Arousal and Curiosity*, McGraw-Hill, New York, 1960; Werner Kroeber-Riel, 'Activation Research: Psychobiological Approaches in Consumer Research, *Journal of Consumer Research* 5, March 1979, pp. 240–50; and P. S. Raju & M. Venkatesan, 'Exploratory Behavior in the Consumer Context: A State of the Art Review', in Jerry C. Olson (ed.), *Advances in Consumer Research*, vol. 7, Association for Consumer Research, Ann Arbor, MI, 1979, pp. 258–63.

10. For factors to consider in this decision see Werner Kroeber-Riel, *Journal of Consumer Research*, pp. 240–50; and Kathy A. Lutz & Richard J. Lutz, 'The Effects of Interactive Imagery on Learning: Application to Advertising', Paper No. 40, University of California, Los Angeles Center for Marketing Studies, March 1976.

11. See M. Venkatesan, 'Cognitive Consistency and Novelty Seeking', in Scott Ward & Thomas S. Robertson (eds), *Consumer Behavior Theoretical Sources*, Prentice-Hall: Englewood Cliffs, NJ, 1973, pp. 354–84; and P. S. Raju, 'Theories of Exploratory Behavior: Review and Consumer Research Implications', in Jagdish N. Sheth (ed.), *Research in Marketing*, vol. 4, JAI Press, Greenwich, CT, 1981, pp. 223–49.

12. S. Streufert & M. J. Driver, 'The General Incongruity Adaptation Level (GIAL)', Technical Report 32, Dorsey Press, Homewood, IL, 1971.

13. This discussion follows Raju, op cit, Ref 11, pp. 223–49; and Raju & Venkatesan, op cit, Ref 9, vol. 7, pp. 258–63.

14. Melvin T. Copeland, *Principles of Merchandising*, A. W. Shaw, New York, 1924, pp. 155–67.

15. See Elizabeth C. Hirschman & Morris B. Holbrook, 'Hedonic Consumption: Emerging Concepts, Methods, and Propositions', *Journal of Marketing* 46, Summer 1982, pp. 92–101; Morris B. Holbrook & Elizabeth C. Hirschman, 'The Experiential Aspects of Consumption: Consumer Fantasies, Feelings, and Fun', *Journal of Consumer Research* 9, September 1982, pp. 132–40; William J. Havlena & Morris B. Holbrook, 'The Varieties of Consumption Experience: Comparing Two Typologies of Emotion in Consumer Behavior', *Journal of Consumer Research* 13, December 1986, pp. 394–404; and T. C. Srinivasan, 'An Integrative Approach to Consumer Choice', in Melanie Wallendorf & Paul Anderson (eds), *Advances in Consumer Research*, vol. 14, Association for Consumer Research, Provo, UT, 1987, pp. 96–101.

16. See Holbrook & Hirschman, ibid, pp. 132–40.

17. A. H. Maslow, 'A Theory of Human Motivation', *Psychological Review* 50, 1943, pp. 370–96; and Holbrook & Hirschman, op cit, Ref 15, pp. 132–9.
18. See Frederick Herzberg, 'Retrospective Comment', in Howard A. Thompson (ed.), *The Great Writings in Marketing*, Commerce, Plymouth, MI, 1976, pp. 180–1; and van Raaij & Wandwossen, 'Motivation-Need Theories and Consumer Behavior', for critiques of Maslow's contributions.
19. As an example, see James R. Bettman, *An Information Processing Theory of Consumer Choice*, Addison-Wesley, Reading, MA, 1979.
20. George Katona, *The Powerful Consumer*, McGraw-Hill, New York, 1960, p. 130.
21. Some of this section follows Howard & Sheth, op cit, Ref 3, pp. 105–18.
22. See Bettman, op cit, Ref 19, pp. 19–22, for an illustration.
23. Kurt Lewin, *A Dynamic Theory of Personality*, McGraw-Hill, New York, 1935.
24. See Ernest Dichter, *Handbook of Consumer Motivations*, McGraw-Hill, New York, 1964, for these and other interesting motivation research findings.
25. See N. D. Rothwell, 'Motivational Research Reinstated', *Journal of Marketing* 19, October 1955, pp. 150–4.
26. Mason Haire, 'Projective Techniques in Marketing Research', *Journal of Marketing* 14, April 1950, pp. 649–56.
27. Rebecca Piirto, 'Measuring Minds in the 1990s', *American Demographics*, December 1990, pp. 31–5.
28. P. M. Tidwell, Understanding the New Home Buyer, Consulting report commissioned by Tareena Constructions. Contact Market Research Services of Bathurst for further information on (015) 259 964.
29. P. M. Tidwell, Involvement as a Function of Brand Frequency: Comparing Americans to Australians, Paper presented to International Marketing Educators and Researchers' Conference, Griffith University, Qld, 2–5 July 1995.
30. H. E. Krugman, 'The Impact of Television Advertising: Learning without Involvement', *Public Opinion Quarterly* 29, Fall 1965, pp. 349–56.
31. Anthony G. Greenwald, Clark Leavitt & Carl Obermiller, 'What Is Low Consumer Involvement?', in Gerald J. Gorn & Marvin E. Goldberg (eds), *Proceedings, Division 23 Program of the 88th Annual Convention*, American Psychological Association, Montreal, 1980, pp. 65–74.
32. Andrew A. Mitchell, 'Involvement: A Potentially Important Mediator of Consumer Behavior', in William L. Wilkie (ed.), *Advances in Consumer Research*, vol. 6, Association for Consumer Research, Ann Arbor, MI, 1979, pp. 191–6.
33. This discussion draws from J. Craig Andrews, Srinivas Durvasula & Syed H. Akhter, 'A Framework for Conceptualizing and Measuring the Involvement Construct in Advertising Research', *Journal of Advertising* 19, 1990, pp. 27–40.
34. Pradeep K. Korgaonkar & George P. Moschis, 'An Experimental Study: Cognitive Dissonance, Product Involvement, Expectations, Performance and Consumer Judgment of Product Performance', *Journal of Advertising* 11, 1982, pp. 32–44.
35. Judith L. Zaichkowsky, 'Conceptualizing Involvement', *Journal of Advertising* 15, 1986, pp. 4–14, 34.
36. See Donald F. Cox (ed.), *Risk Taking and Information Handling in Consumer Behavior*, Division of Research, Graduate School of Business, Harvard University, Boston, 1967, pp. 23–108; and Gilles Laurent & Jean-Noel Kapferer, 'Measuring Consumer Involvement Profiles', *Journal of Marketing Research* 22, February 1985, pp. 41–53.
37. See Ivan L. Preston, 'A Reinterpretation of the Meaning of Involvement in Krugman's Model of Advertising Communication', *Journalism Quarterly* 47, Summer 1970, pp. 287–95; and Peter Wright, 'Analyzing Media Effects on Advertising Response', *Public Opinion Quarterly* 38, Summer 1974, pp. 192–205.
38. See Russell W. Belk, 'Effects of Gift-giving Involvement on Gift Selection Strategies', in Andrew Mitchell (ed.), *Advances in Consumer Research*, vol. 9. Association for Consumer Research, Ann Arbor, MI, 1981, pp. 408–11; Keith Clarke & Russell W. Belk, 'The Effects of Product Involvement and Task Definition on Anticipated

Consumer Effort', in H. Keith Hunt (ed.), *Advances in Consumer Research*, vol. 5. Association for Consumer Research, Ann Arbor, MI, 1978; Marsha L. Richins & Peter H. Bloch, 'After the New Wears Off: The Temporal Context of Product Involvement', *Journal of Consumer Research* 13, September 1986, pp. 280–5; and Judith Lynne Zaichkowsky, 'Measuring the Involvement Construct', *Journal of Consumer Research* 12, December 1985, pp. 341–52.

39. Andrews, Durvasula & Akhter, op cit, Ref 33, pp. 27–40.
40. See Andrew Mitchell, 'The Dimensions of Advertising Involvement', in Kent B. Monroe (ed.), *Advances in Consumer Research*, vol. 8, Association for Consumer Research, Ann Arbor, MI, 1981, pp. 25–30; and Greenwald, Leavitt & Obermiller, op cit, Ref 31, pp. 65–74, for two different views of a three-level scheme.
41. Carolyn L. Castley, 'Meta Analysis of Involvement Research', in Michael J. Houston (ed.), *Advances in Consumer Research*, vol. 15, Association for Consumer Research, Ann Arbor, MI, 1988, pp. 554–62.
42. P. M. Tidwell & W. Marks, 'American versus Australian Consumer Decision Making: An Analysis of Decision Rules Used in Limited Problem-solving Behavior', *Asia Pacific Advances in Consumer Research* 1, 1994, pp. 148–52.
43. Peter H. Bloch, Daniel L. Sherrell & Nancy M. Ridgway, 'Consumer Search: An Extended Framework', *Journal of Consumer Research* 13, June 1986, pp. 119–26. It should be noted that some recent evidence suggests that search activity may be a function of whether a product serves functional or expressive roles. See Banwari Mittal, 'Must Consumer Involvement Always Imply More Information Search?' in Thomas K. Srull (ed.), *Advances in Consumer Research*, vol. 16, Association for Consumer Research, Ann Arbor, MI, 1989, pp. 167–72.
44. Jacques E. Brisoux & Emmanuel J. Cheron, 'Brand Categorization and Product Involvement', in Marvin Goldberg, Gerald Gorn & Richard Pollay (eds), *Advances in Consumer Research*, vol, 17, Association for Consumer Research, Ann Arbor, MI, 1990, pp. 101–9.
45. See Michael L. Ray, 'Marketing Communication and the Hierarchy-of-effects', in Peter Clark (ed.), *New Models for Mass Communication Research*, Sage Publications Inc., Beverly Hills, CA, 1973, pp. 147–76; and Krugman, op cit, Ref. 30, pp. 349–56.
46. Richard E. Petty & John Cacioppo, 'Central and Peripheral Routes to Persuasion: Application to Advertising', in Larry Percy & Arch Woodside (eds), *Advertising and Consumer Psychology*, Lexington Books, Lexington, MA, pp. 3–23.
47. See Richard E. Petty & John Cacioppo, *Communication and Persuasion: Central and Peripheral Routes to Attitude Change*, Springer-Verlag, New York, 1986.
48. See Michael L. Rothschild, 'Advertising Strategies for High and Low Involvement Situations', in John C. Maloney & Bernard Silverman (eds), *Attitude Research Plays for High Stakes*, American Marketing Association, Chicago, 1979, pp. 74–93; Tyzoon T. Tyebjee, 'Refinement of the Involvement Concept: An Advertising Planning Point of View', in John C. Maloney & Bernard Silverman (eds), *Attitude Research Plays for High Stakes*, American Marketing Association, Chicago, 1979, pp. 94–111; Richard Vaughan, 'How Advertising Works: A Planning Model', *Journal of Advertising Research* 20, October 1980, pp. 27–33; and Greenwald, Leavitt & Obermiller, op cit, Ref 31, pp. 65–74.
49. Herbert E. Krugman, 'The Measure of Advertising Involvement', *Public Opinion Quarterly* 30, 1966, pp. 583–96.
50. Laurent & Kapferer, op cit, Ref 36, pp. 41–53.
51. Rothschild, op cit, Ref 48, pp. 74–93.
52. See Tyebjee, op cit, Ref 48, pp. 107–8.

CHAPTER 10

INFORMATION PROCESSING

It is important for the marketer to understand how consumers acquire and handle the information available from stimuli in their environment. This chapter introduces the nature and role of information processing. It begins with a brief overview of the concept. Major aspects of information acquisition, selective attention to stimuli and the task of deriving meaning from these stimuli are then discussed in greater depth. The application of these concepts to a number of marketing-decision problems is reviewed. Additional information-processing topics are also treated later in the learning and attitude chapters, as well as in Parts 4 and 5 of the text.

OVERVIEW OF INFORMATION–PROCESSING ACTIVITIES

It is often helpful to view consumers as problem solvers who use information in an attempt to satisfy their consumption goals. From this perspective, *consumer information processing* may be thought of as the acquisition of stimulus inputs, the manipulation of these inputs to derive meaning from them and the use of this information to think about products or services. More specifically, five of the major ways in which consumers use information derived from their environment are:

1. to understand and evaluate products and services;

2. to attempt to justify previous product choices;

3. to resolve the conflict between buying or postponing purchases;

4. to satisfy a need for being informed about products and services in the marketplace;

5. To serve as a reminder to purchase products that must be regularly replenished (soaps, beverages and the like).[1]

It is important to realise that, as its definition implies, information processing is not the end result of activity, but the actual process that consumers engage in when dealing with their environment.

Information processing can be conceptualised within a framework. The framework shown in Figure 10.1 can be arranged into four groupings:

1. stimuli that serve as the raw material to be processed;

2. the stages of processing activities, which are linked by arrows and are mainly internal to the consumer;

3. situational and consumer characteristics that can influence the nature of these processing activities;

4. an executive system that guides the process by regulating the type and intensity of processing activities engaged in at any time.

Each of these is briefly characterised in the following text.

Stimuli may be thought of as units of energy such as light and sounds that can excite our sensory receptors. We have receptors for internally produced stimuli, such as hunger pangs, as well as receptors for the five senses of taste, touch, smell, vision and hearing. Typically, a given stimulus does not exist in isolation, but is part of a larger stimulus situation comprising many individual stimuli.

The *acquisition process* enables consumers to confront certain stimuli in their environment and begin to process them. *Exposure*, which is part of the acquisition process, occurs in a wide variety of ways, but two major categories

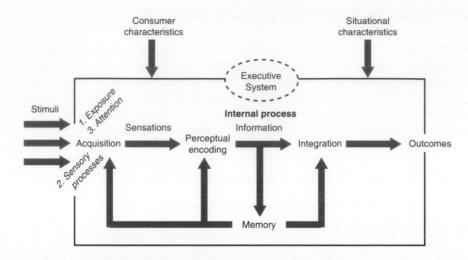

FIG. 10.1 An information-processing framework

exist: active search and passive reception. In active search, the consumer's executive system serves as a guide to seek out specific types of stimuli, such as the nutritional content per serving in a can of soup. As Figure 10.1 shows, this information may already exist in memory, or it can be part of the external environment. The way in which the search process is conducted will be influenced by the consumer's motives, and it is mainly within conscious control. Conversely, in passive reception, consumers confront stimuli in the process of living their daily lives. Exposure to advertisements and news reports on various products, and acquiring information as a by-product of normal shopping activities are both examples of the passive-reception mode of stimulus acquisition.

Through the exposure process of both active search and passive reception the consumer is capable of acquiring an almost infinite number of stimuli. Because the consumer has limited capacity to process this amount of data, two major mechanisms reduce the number of stimuli to manageable proportions. First, sensory receptors have limited sensitivity, which means that our *sensory processes* produce sensations for only a specific range of stimulus values. Secondly, we selectively devote *attention* to only a small proportion of the resulting sensations, and we literally ignore the rest. Therefore, with certain exceptions to be discussed later, stimuli that are capable of producing sensations and then attracting the consumer's attention are the main focus of further processing efforts.

Sensations may be thought of as electrical impulses with no innate meaning that are produced by our receptors. A *perceptual encoding process* involves several activities that allow the consumer to interpret these raw inputs. The process can be thought of as constructing mental symbols, such as words or images, to represent sensations in order to derive meaning from them. Of course, characteristics of the stimulus itself will strongly influence how it will be represented. Research has shown significant differences between high- and low-involvement products on perceptual identification tasks.[2] As Figure 10.1 shows, however, another major influence is the information already stored in memory. That is, the meaning we derive from stimuli is greatly affected by our previous experiences. It is for this reason that the perpetual encoding process is said to develop personal meaning, called *information*, from raw stimulus inputs. Thus, consumers act on their own interpretation of the world, as opposed to what actually may exist.

Figure 10.1 indicates that information generated by perpetual encoding can be stored in *memory* for future use, and it can also be directly transferred to the *integration* stage of processing. Here, the consumer combines and arranges various informational inputs to reach conclusions about the environment. For example, information on the package size, number of servings, price and brand name of several supermarket products could be arranged in various ways to be meaningful in the consumer's mind. Information available from memory as well as material obtained directly from the environment represent inputs to this integration process.

A major goal of information processing is to deal effectively with the environment. Therefore, *outcomes* of information-processing activities are likely to affect evaluation, attitudes and, eventually, observable behaviour. Information that has been integrated involves *attitudes* when the consumer's beliefs or feelings about a particular object (brand, product, purchasing action and so on) are developed or changed. These attitudes can be held by the consumer to influence later actions toward the object. For example, if the consumer's attitudes toward purchasing a pair of jeans are positively influenced by an advertisement, this is likely to increase the probability of a later purchase.

Consumers' attitudes are positively influenced by this advertisement
COURTESY OF JUST JEANS

A second outcome can occur more directly. Information can be processed for the purpose of product *evaluation* choice, and immediate purchase. Here, the consumer, rather than forming attitudes to influence later decisions, makes a brand choice as the information is processed. For example, while hearing about an accountant's qualifications a consumer will make a decision about using the accountant based on whether the qualifications are professional or academic.[3]

In some cases, the consumer may not think the evaluation or choice task has high importance. This usually results in a brief process of review. Here, various rules of thumb (select the lowest priced alternative and so on) may be employed to *minimise* choice effort. However, when the evaluation and choice situation is perceived to be quite important, considerable effort is likely to be devoted to the process.

Information processing is strongly influenced by *consumer characteristics*. For example, previous attitudes can affect how the consumer will evaluate a particular brand, and the evaluation process can, in turn, result in attitude change or development of new brand attitudes. Other consumer characteristics exerting a major influence on information processing are the consumer's motives and involvement, personality, attributes and learning. *Situational characteristics* can also play a role. For example, the consumer's environment is sometimes overloaded with potential information, and some selection of stimuli for processing must be made. At other times the environment may generate such little stimulation that the consumer begins looking for more.

Information-processing activities do not act independently of each other. Rather, each activity needs to be co-ordinated with others so that intelligible meaning can be derived from stimuli. The *executive system* is the mechanism that co-ordinates various information-processing activities. It also serves as a command centre that directs attention and organises processing energies toward those stimuli that are potentially more relevant to the consumer's goals.

The vast majority of information-processing activities are internal to the consumer and therefore unobservable. Two notable exceptions are portions of the stimulus-acquisition process (the number of stores shopped, salespeople consulted and so on) and certain overt responses (such as brands purchased). Figure 10.1 recognises these overt activities by showing that stimulus acquisition and outcomes are not completely encompassed within the internal framework (lines of the box). Although such overt actions can be directly observed, the majority of information-processing activities must be studied by determining their influence on other variables and measures.

The preceding paragraphs presented a brief overview of the major activities involved in information processing. Discussion now turns to a more detailed review of two of these components: acquisition and perceptual encoding. Subsequent chapters will treat other activities in greater depth.

INFORMATION ACQUISITION

The term 'information acquisition' describes the set of activities or means by which consumers are exposed to various environmental stimuli and begin to process them. As mentioned in the overview, exposure occurs in two major ways: when consumers are motivated actively to *seek* information and when they passively receive stimuli that are confronted in daily activities. We will discuss aspects of the active search process first.

Active search

Consumers often actively seek and selectively acquire information that has potential usefulness for achieving their consumption goals. The first stage in this process appears to be the *internal search*, because of the relative ease with which it can be accomplished compared with the external search. Internal search involves scanning memory for stored information that is relevant to the purchase situation under consideration. This available information has been previously acquired from passive reception experiences as well as through active external searches.[4] Consequently, it can include information derived from advertising claims, personal experiences, product test reports, previous solutions to similar purchase problems and interactions with other consumers.

The internal search will tend to be rather deliberate and comprehensive when the consumer views a situation as important, when the purchase decision is a difficult one, and when the amount of information in memory is considerable or complex. In other situations, such as during the regular replenishment of one's usual brand of bath soap, the memory scan may be so automatic that it never even reaches conscious awareness.

In what appears to be the majority of cases, information acquired from an internal memory scan is sufficient for the consumer's needs. Consequently, the consumer will make a decision without seeking any external information. For the remaining situations, the consumer is not satisfied with existing knowledge and becomes sufficiently motivated to engage in external search.

The amount of external search varies considerably across individuals and different purchase situations. Factors affecting this amount include:

1. market conditions, such as price and feature differences between brands;
2. situational factors, including conditions of store crowding and the urgency of need;
3. buying strategies that consumers may adopt, such as brand or store loyalty patterns;
4. individual factors, including the level of involvement and self-confidence.

Chapter 14 will explore these factors in greater depth.

Passive reception

In the passive-reception mode, consumers confront and acquire information in the process of living their daily lives. For example, when watching a television program, casually talking to a friend or searching for literature about house paints, a consumer could be exposed to information about aluminium house siding. This information might be stored away for a future time when the need to address the issue of house siding arises. As this situation demonstrates, passive reception occurs when consumers acquire information that they are not presently seeking. Instead of having a plan of search, individuals respond to environmental stimuli to which they are exposed.

Although virtually any type of stimulus may be passively acquired, substantial amounts of certain types of information are likely to be received in this manner.[5] Knowledge of the existence of various products, a significant amount of learning about product attributes and their advantages, and at least some knowledge about the quality of products can be gained through conversations with friends or other passive means.

The way in which passive reception occurs has important practical implications, because consumers' daily living patterns selectively influence their exposure to advertisements and other sources of consumption-related information. For this reason, marketers spend considerable time and effort on studies of consumers' selective media habits (magazines read, television programs watched) and activity patterns (shopping habits) that lead to exposure opportunities.

Recent changes in technology seem to have significantly altered the passive reception of television advertisements. Traditionally, when television shows broke for commercials, unless viewers got up to change the channel or left the room for some reason, they were confronted with advertising messages. Attention may not have been focused on the messages but exposure did occur. However, with the arrival of VCRs and remote-control units in millions of households the situation has changed. Many viewers use remote-control units to switch rapidly to other channels during commercial breaks and thereby avoid commercial messages. This behaviour has become known as *zapping*. A similar form of commercial avoidance also became popular with the technological breakthrough of 'windows' on televisions. Here the viewer can partition a section of the television screen to show an additional channel. Thus, while advertisements are on one channel the viewer can watch another show through the window.

The use of VCRs has also affected exposure to advertisements. When viewers prerecord programs for enjoyment at a later time the remote-control unit allows them to fast-forward through commercial breaks. On many VCR units the resulting picture is distorted and has no sound, and so this so-called *zipping* results in very little exposure to the advertising messages.

Because these behaviours serve to limit consumers' exposure to advertising content, they are of considerable interest to researchers and those responsible for developing marketing communications.[6] Consequently, additional information on the nature and effect of zapping, zipping and similar technology-aided behaviour should become available. However, one response by advertisers has already been developed—the *chameleon* advertisement. Here the ad is designed to mimic an actual show such as a news show or talk show. The intent is to keep viewers' attention by simulating the content of an actual show and thereby postponing or eliminating zapping behaviour.[7]

Sensation

The exposure mechanisms of active search and passive reception produce many more stimuli than the consumer is capable of processing. Two of the gatekeeping mechanisms that reduce this 'blooming confusion' to more manageable proportions involve consumers' physiological limitations: awareness thresholds and differential thresholds.

AWARENESS THRESHOLD

Any given stimulus may be either too small or too weak to notice, or so great that it also escapes awareness. Consumers' zones of stimulus awareness can be identified by defining two thresholds:

1. *Absolute threshold*. The minimum value of a stimulus capable of being consciously noticed.

2. *Terminal threshold*. The maximum value of a stimulus capable of being consciously noticed.

To illustrate, the average person's absolute and terminal thresholds for sound pitch are about 20 and 20 000 cycles per second, respectively. Those familiar with audio equipment will notice that this is the exact range stereo manufacturers concentrate on when designing their equipment.

The threshold concept implies that we can determine precise values that mark the boundaries of stimulus awareness. This is misleading, because these limits for any given stimulus differ among individuals and even for the same individual over a period of time. Therefore, thresholds must be viewed as being somewhat variable and are usually defined by the stimulus value that goes undetected 50 per cent of the time.

Consumers' absolute thresholds are often of more interest to marketers than are terminal thresholds, because of their greater relevance to product designs. For example:

⇒ Common household light bulbs pulsate at 50 cycles per second but appear to have a constant intensity.

⇒ Television sets produce an apparent full-screen image by rapidly scanning the entire screen with a narrow beam of light.

⇒ In another application, because adults differ significantly in their taste sensitivity to beer, experts have segmented the consuming public into three distinct groups: discriminating individuals mainly concerned with the taste of beer; discriminating individuals influenced by price and other variables; and non-discriminating consumers.[8] Marketing strategies directed at such segments could differ significantly.

DIFFERENTIAL THRESHOLD

Many sellers have made changes in their offerings only to find that they went unnoticed in the marketplace. This suggests that consumers also have limited sensitivity for noticing differences between different stimulus values. The differential threshold defines this sensitivity as the smallest detectable difference between two values of the same stimulus. For example, if Coca-Cola were interested in whether consumers could detect a difference in sweetness between two different sugar concentrations of a drink, they would need to examine consumers' differential threshold for sweetness.

To determine the differential threshold for a stimulus, the measurer commonly changes its intensity in very small amounts, as in a hearing test. The consumer's threshold is said to occur when he or she first notices that the stimulus has changed. The difference between this value and the starting value is often referred to as the *just noticeable difference (jnd)*.

WEBER'S LAW   As with absolute thresholds, consumers also differ in their ability to detect differences between stimulus values, and this sensitivity varies with conditions. However, numerous studies have revealed a general relationship known as Weber's Law, which states that the stimulus change needed to reach the differential threshold (produce a just noticeable difference) is a constant *proportion* of the starting stimulus value. Weber's Law can be expressed as:

$$\frac{\triangle S}{S} = K$$

where S =   the initial stimulus value

$\triangle S$ =   the smallest change in the stimulus capable of being detected:
the just noticeable difference (jnd)

K =   the constant of proportionality

Expressing the equation as $\triangle S = K \cdot S$ suggests that if we know the values of K and S, we could predict how large a change in the stimulus is necessary before consumers detect the change. To illustrate, assume that through testing we found that 1 gram ($\triangle S$ = 1) had to be added to a 10 gram container of liquid soap (S = 10) before consumers detected a change in its weight. This would yield a constant of proportionality of K = 1/10 = 0.1, allowing us to predict that:

1. consumers will not detect a change in the weight of the larger 50 gram economy bottle of the soap unless at least 5 grams are added to or removed from it;

2. consumers will be able to detect a 3 kilogram addition to a 20 kilogram portable television.

Two points should be noted with regard to Weber's Law: first, there are different constants of proportionality for different stimuli such as weight, colour and size; and, secondly, the law is not universal in its applicability, because individuals differ and because it does not predict well near absolute or terminal thresholds. However, refinements have been made to the basic law and it appears to hold fairly well over the majority of stimulus range.

APPLYING WEBER'S LAW   Marketers can apply Weber's Law to predicting how consumers will respond to differences between marketing variables or changes in these variables.[9] Sometimes the goal is to have consumers detect differences, and at other times it is to have differences escape their attention. For example, because the cost of candy ingredients fluctuates widely there is a constant search for more stably priced substitutes. According to one report, this led to the discovery by Peter Paul Inc. that tasters could not distinguish between one type of chocolate made with vegetable oil and another made with traditional cocoa butter.[10] However, a second firm found that most consumers could detect a difference between a chocolate substitute and the real thing.

A second way to hold prices constant in times of changing costs is to change the size or amount of the product slightly. For example, during a 23-year period a well-known chocolate manufacturer changed the price of their basic milk chocolate bar only three times, but varied its weight 14 times.[11] It should be noted that many of these changes escaping consumers' awareness were weight *increases* allowed by declining costs. Similar changes (increases as well as decreases) have occurred in numerous packages and products, including newspapers, bathroom tissues and soft drinks.

Another application of Weber's Law lies in the battleground of brand competition. Here producers of major brands, such as Tip Top's Hyfibe bread, seek to distinguish their products as quite different from those of private competitors. However, some competing firms seek to produce similar products using less costly ingredients or components that might escape consumers' notice, thereby obtaining a differential price advantage. Also, packages of some privately labelled grocery products bear a striking resemblance to those of major brands.[12] Presumably, this discourages shoppers from detecting any noticeable differences existing between the brands.

Pricing decisions may also make use of Weber's Law—many merchants have noted that price reductions of at least 15 per cent are usually needed to attract consumers to sales. This experience is supported by experimental evidence suggesting that consumers do possess an awareness threshold for price changes.[13]

Attention

A research study conducted some time ago suggested that the average American adult is aware of seeing less than 100 major media advertisements per day. However, the daily advertising exposure rate for a typical consumer has been estimated to range as high as 3000 or more. This suggests that although exposure and sensory processes both selectively filter stimuli for information processing, additional points of selectivity must also exist. One such filtering mechanism is *attention*, which can be viewed as the allocation of processing capacity to stimuli. That is, attention regulates the amount of additional processing that a stimulus will receive. Generally, the more processing capacity that is devoted to a stimulus, the greater will be the consumer's awareness and comprehension of it.

VOLUNTARY AND INVOLUNTARY ATTENTION

Consumers allocate their attention on both a voluntary and an involuntary basis. For voluntary attention, consumers deliberately focus on stimuli because of their relevance to the task at hand; for example, they might carefully review the manufacturer's specifications on a microwave oven that they are about to purchase. Consumers' motives, knowledge and expectations about what information will be found serve to guide this selective attention.[14]

Conversely, involuntary attention occurs when the consumer confronts novel or unexpected stimuli that seem interesting or distinctive in some way, even though they may be unrelated to the current goal or activity at hand. Funny, 'catchy' or otherwise unusual advertisements often fall into this category. Many other stimuli that consumers confront in their daily lives are also handled by the involuntary attention process.[15] In fact, most of the stimuli that consumers process reach awareness via involuntary attention.

Both types of attention play a useful role for consumers. Voluntary attention facilitates progress toward immediate goals by concentrating processing capacity on the most task related stimuli and filtering out others, while involuntary attention allows consumers to be generally knowledgeable about the environment by keeping them in touch with stimuli that are potentially relevant to a variety of their interests.

CHARACTERISTICS OF ATTENTION

We have already noted that the consumer's attention is selectively allocated to only certain stimuli. Before turning to factors influencing this process, three characteristics of attention having important implications for marketers should be mentioned.[16] First, consumers can only attend to a limited number of items at any one time. This limit appears to be from five to seven 'chunks' of information, in which a chunk is an organised grouping of data or informational inputs. An example would be how telephone numbers are arranged into three major chunks to facilitate their retention: STD, prefix, suffix. This five-to-seven-chunk capacity shows that consumers' attention spans can be quite limited.

Secondly, many stimuli require attention to be processed, while others that are very familiar to the consumer do not.[17] Because a consumer's span of attention is limited, those stimuli that require attention cannot all be processed at the same time. The consumer must allocate this limited resource to them in some type of sequence or order; while one is being processed, other cannot be attended to (e.g. when we are unable to read something and listen to a radio message at the same time). Conversely, stimuli not requiring attention can be received *simultaneously* from several channels and will be automatically transferred to the next stage of processing. To illustrate, when exposed to a television advertisement for Qantas, consumers might be able visually to process physical attributes of the plane (colour, shape, size of the interior) and think about how much people seem to enjoy the flight at the same time as they are listening to the tune accompanying the visual presentation.

A third characteristic of attention is that it can be allocated to stimuli on a rapid basis. One set of studies found that processing occurred at the rate of 26 items per second.[18] This speed tends to compensate for consumers' limited attention spans.

Marketers should give serious consideration to these attention characteristics because they can significantly influence the effectiveness of various efforts to communicate with consumers.

Another area of concern is the many factors, both within and outside the marketer's control, that influence how consumers allocate their attention among stimuli. These influences mainly affect involuntary attention, and they can be categorised into stimulus and individual factors.

SELECTIVE ATTENTION: STIMULUS FACTORS

Certain characteristics of stimuli themselves attract attention. Generally, these include emotion-arousing properties (colours, pleasant phrases), physically intense values (loud noises, bright colours), and novel or surprising characteristics.[19] More specifically, the following are mentioned because of their particular importance to promotional campaigns

COLOUR Historically, colour advertisements have been found to attract more attention than those presented in black and white. However, the higher cost of using colour may result in capturing less attention per advertising dollar spent.[20] Also, because the attraction power of colour may be a result of its novelty, common use of it in any medium such as television may reduce its attention-attracting power, unless more intense or unusual hues are employed—a practice increasingly used lately.[21]

NOVELTY AND CONTRAST Stimuli that stand out against their background attract attention. Novel stimuli achieve this through unique images, shapes, sounds and colours (the advertisement for Hitachi is an example). Novelty can also be achieved through messages that seem at odds with commonly held beliefs.

Contrast also attracts attention. Reversals (white printing on black background) in print media, and changes in volume levels (louder or softer) for television or radio advertisements are examples of contrast effects used to capture attention.

SIZE AND POSITION In print media, attention increases with the size of an advertisement, but appears to grow in proportion to the square root of the ad's area. Thus, to double its attention-attracting power, an advertisement would have to be quadrupled in size.

Position also is an important influence as the following findings illustrate. First, in terms of layout, ads with vertical splits (pictures on one side and copy on the other) and haphazard arrangements of pictures appear to discourage at least some readers.[22] Secondly, in terms of placement on a page, position does not seem to have an effect unless many ads share the page, in which case the upper

An example of novelty and contrast COURTESY OF HITACHI AUSTRALIA LTD

right-hand corner appears advantageous.[23] Thirdly, there appears to be an attention advantage for magazine ads placed in the first 10 pages or next to related editorial matter, but, due to high page traffic, position within a newspaper is not as critical.[24]

HUMOUR Spokespeople in television commercials are frequently shown in strange or embarrassing situations, cracking jokes, getting pies in the face, being bitten by dogs or doused with water or coloured liquids, and crashing into various objects. All of these situations, plus more subtle approaches, are attempts to employ humour in advertising. In fact, estimates are that between 15 and 42 per cent of television and radio advertising employs some form of humour, usually designed to attract attention.[25]

Although practitioners generally appear to believe that humour can attract attention, there has not been a great deal of research conducted in an advertising context to test this belief.[26] Based on the evidence that is available, a tentative conclusion appears to be that humorous messages in advertising can generally attract audience attention. However, it also appears that the effectiveness of humour depends on the characteristics of audience members, and varies according to their sex and racial background.[27]

A wide variety of other stimulus factors have been employed to attract consumers' attention. These include 'scratch and sniff' strips in printed promotions, inflatable sections of billboards and signs with moving parts. Because a detailed treatment of each is beyond the scope of this chapter, we now turn to individual factors influencing attention.

SELECTIVE ATTENTION: INDIVIDUAL FACTORS

In addition to stimulus characteristics, individual attributes of consumers themselves also influence whether a given stimulus will receive attention. Some of these individual factors are discussed below.

ATTENTION SPAN   We have already noted that consumers' attention spans, as measured by the number of items processed at any time, are quite limited. The time that stimuli can hold a consumer's attention also appears to be rather short—perhaps only a matter of seconds. Therefore, attention must be repeatedly captured, even for something as brief as a 15-second spot commercial on television. So advertisers use a variety of stimulus factors not only to capture, but also to hold, consumers' interest.[28]

ADAPTATION   Prolonged exposure to constant levels of stimulation results in consumers not noticing the stimuli. This gradual adjustment to stimuli is called *adaptation*. For example, an air-conditioned building at first appears quite cool to us, but a short time later we adapt to the temperature and become less aware of it. Similarly, consumers adapt to various marketing stimuli such as price levels and advertising messages. This helps to explain why marketers search for fresh advertising approaches and try to offer new and improved products.

PERCEPTUAL VIGILANCE AND DEFENCE   The concept of *perceptual vigilance* explains consumers' heightened sensitivity to stimuli that are capable of satisfying motives, or stimuli that are personally relevant and generate higher levels of involvement. This suggests that consumers will pay increased attention to marketing stimuli relevant to aroused states.[29] It also may explain why comparative advertising claims are said to attract the attention of more consumers.[30] Based on this concept, it has been suggested that less expensive, small- or medium-sized print advertisements may be more economically effective than large ones for reaching the attention of motivated consumers.[31]

Individuals are also capable of *perceptual defence*; that is, decreasing their awareness of threatening stimuli. For example, one study found that only 32 per cent of a sample of smokers consistently read articles relating smoking to lung disease, while 60 per cent of a group of non-smokers read the articles.[32] Apparently, smokers feel threatened by such information, and their perceptual defence mechanisms allow them to ignore it.

The topic of perceptual defence has relevance in advertising, particularly to the use of fear appeals to promote products such as burglar alarms and smoke detectors. Of course, the danger of fear appeals is that they may be so threatening to consumers that they lead to perceptual defences against the entire message. For example, an advertisement showing burned children to draw viewers' attention to the need for home alarms would probably fail because consumers want to avoid thinking of such a tragedy.

Our discussion of the acquisition process has focused on three major subcomponents: exposure—the means by which consumers come in contact with stimuli; sensation—the means by which only certain stimulus values produce messages for further processing; and attention—the means by which processing capacity is allocated to stimulus sensations. Focus turns now to how consumers derive meaning from these raw sensory inputs.

PERCEPTUAL ENCODING

Because sensations generated by stimuli are only a series of electrical impulses, they must be transformed into a type of language that is understandable to the consumer. This is accomplished by *perceptual encoding*, which is the process of assigning mental symbols to sensations in order to interpret them or give them meaning. These symbols can be words, numbers, pictorial images or other representations. The symbols are also used to remember stimuli and to do any subsequent thinking about them.

The manner in which stimuli are encoded will be influenced by a number of factors, including the individual's ability to process the sensations, the motivation to process them and the opportunity (adequate time and so on) to process them.[33] Thus, we see that perceptual encoding is a highly individualised process that is used to derive personal meaning from stimulus experiences. Any actions or subsequently thoughts will be based on interpretations derived from stimuli rather than on the stimuli themselves.

Stages in the encoding process

Two major activities involved in encoding appear to be feature analysis and a synthesis stage.[34] In *feature analysis*, the consumer identifies main stimulus features and assesses how they are organised. In the *synthesis stage*, organised stimulus elements are combined with other information available in the environment and in memory to develop an interpretation of the stimulus. How consumers react to a Nissan Serena, as in the following photo, illustrates these stages. First they would assess the basic size, shape, colour and other prominent features of the vehicle. Then they would organise these characteristics into a unified whole and appreciate them as a type of motorised vehicle rather than as separate components of glass, steel, rubber and so on. However, even in the unlikely event that all consumers develop the same unified whole during the feature-analysis stage, each would interpret it differently depending on his or her individual experiences. In fact, it can be said that there are three major influences on the synthesis stage: stimulus features, contextual influences and memory factors.[35]

The biggest difference between a
Serena and a Tarago is the value.

For a start the Serena will save you
over $5,000*.

And you still get all the luxury
features that you'd expect. Like
central locking, power mirrors and
windows. The TI even has twin
electric sunroofs and the comfort of
separate front and rear automatic
climate control.

Serena is more like a car than
a bus, even a family of seven will
love Serena's quiet interior that makes
every journey a pleasure.

The 2.0 litre DOHC EFI engine
provides loads of power, while
calmly delivering almost 10% better
fuel economy than Tarago†.

And Serena's tiny turning circle
will leave Tarago searching for a
parking spot.

Like all Nissan passenger cars
Serena comes with the reassurance of
the 3 year/100,000 km warranty and,
should you ever need it, the Nissan
24 Hour Roadside Assistance.

So talk to your Nissan Dealer about
the new Serena today. Just quietly, it
makes driving serener.

It's Serena than Tarago.

Just wait 'til you drive it.

* RRP Serena ST $34,435, Tarago GLi $39,635 as at 1.2.94, excludes on-road and dealer delivery costs. † Based on AS2877 figures for manual transmission Serena ST and Tarago GLi. 23MSB

An example of attitudes
COURTESY OF NISSAN

We have already mentioned that major aspects of the stimulus will influence the interpretation process. To this must be added the stimulus context. That is, the stimulus being focused on in any particular situation is surrounded by a wide variety of other stimuli, which form a context that can significantly influence our interpretation of the so-called focal stimulus.[36] For example, a regular newspaper advertisement for a new car carrying a price of $16 500 may be perceived differently if it is accompanied by the words 'Drastically Reduced' and 'Manufacturer's Suggested List Price—$20 000'. Marketers are well aware of the potential influence of contextual stimuli and frequently use them to promote and position their offerings. The use of highly active and dynamic people in McDonald's commercials and the western scenes in Marlboro cigarette ads are additional illustrations.

Consumers' experiences and knowledge will also strongly influence how they interpret a stimulus situation. An expanding body of evidence suggests that consumers interpret stimuli by attempting to categorise them along with other stimuli already contained in memory. Much of this is done automatically without conscious deliberation. A benefit of this categorisation process is that similar stimuli can be efficiently responded to in much the same way, instead of treating each as a novel situation requiring a different reaction. The categorisation process also influences the consumer to interpret a stimulus based on its resulting category membership as well as its actual features.[37] That is, the meaning the consumer ascribes to the stimulus will be partly due to its actual features (and context) and partly due to the meaning associated with its category. For example, a consumer is confronted with a new brand of food product that is positioned as a breakfast food. It is packaged like a breakfast bar, but the consumer notices that it contains the same ingredients as most candy bars. The issue confronting the consumer is whether to categorise the food as a snack food or breakfast-food item. We can see from this example that how consumers categorise a product influences the meaning that they will ascribe to it.

Research suggests that consumers perceive *degrees* of match between any stimulus and a given category to which it might be assigned. That is, the match does not have to be perfect in order to be assigned to a given category. However, the more a given stimulus is perceived to be typical of a given category, the greater the likelihood that it will be assigned to that category.[38] This so-called *typicality* appears to be influenced by the match of attributes between stimuli in the category and the stimulus being evaluated, whether the stimulus has certain valued attributes, and the frequency with which it is encountered.[39] For example, a research paper presented at a recent conference in Australia examined the typicality of product attributes for fast-food restaurants. Restaurateurs could use this information to position their product in terms of the most atypical product attributes, or a new product could enter the market using the most typical product attributes to gain market share.[40]

Consumers also appear to categorise products at different levels of generality.[41] For example, a camcorder could be grouped into a product class-level category (video recorder), a product type-level category (8 mm portable) and at the brand level (Sony Handycam Sport). Categorisation at the product class level allows little meaning to be ascribed to the video recorder (takes video images, uses video tape). However, categorisation at the product type level allows significantly more inferences about its nature (uses micro cassettes, is compact, takes good pictures, has zoom lens). Categorisation at the brand level increases the meaning that may be ascribed to the product, but not to a great degree (well made, water-resistant). Therefore, the greatest potential for inferring meaning from the stimulus appears to exist at the product type level. Consumers with greater experience and knowledge in a given product area are likely to have a greater number of well-defined categories at each of the levels mentioned above. Consequently, they will be able to categorise and ascribe meaning to related stimuli with greater ease and in less processing time than would other consumers with less expertise.

Depth of processing refers to the degree of effort the consumer expends in developing meaning from stimuli. If little effort is expended, a great deal of meaning will not be derived. However, at deeper levels of processing the stimulus is represented with symbols that are more meaningful to the consumer. For example, reading the ingredients listed on a type of snack-food package could lead the consumer to the relatively shallow interpretation 'it's mainly sugar' or to the deeper 'it's a fattening and unhealthy food'. Here, we can see that the deeper level of processing results in a more personally relevant representation and interpretation of the stimulus. We will return to this depth-of-processing concept in the next chapter when we consider its relevance to learning and memory.

Influences on encoding

A wide variety of factors influence the encoding process. Although some were briefly mentioned previously, it is useful to give more detailed treatment to several major influences. The first group of influencing factors is more relevant to feature-analysis activities, while the second group has its primary influence on the synthesis stage.

FACTORS INFLUENCING FEATURE ANALYSIS

Much of feature analysis involves mentally arranging sensations into a coherent pattern, which is often called a *gestalt* (pronounced 'goh-shtält'). In fact, this process has been the prime interest of gestalt psychologists, and much of this section is based on their work. Although visual examples are primarily used here, many of the principles can also be applied to other stimuli.

FIGURE–GROUND   This is one of the most basic and automatic organisational processes perceivers impose on their work. Two properties of this innate perceptual tendency are:

1. the figure appears to stand out as being in front of the more distant background;

2. the figure is perceived to have form and to be more substantial than the ground.

An example of the way in which the figure–ground process operates is shown in Figure 10.2. Most individuals organise this stimulus situation as a white goblet (figure) on a black ground rather than as two faces (figure) with a white ground separating them.

Print advertisements frequently employ figure–ground techniques to assist readers in organising symbols and other material that the marketer deems most important.

PROXIMITY   In this organisation process, items close to each other in time or space tend to be perceived as being related, while separated items are viewed as being different. The uses of proximity in promotions are many. Mentholated cigarettes are shown in beautiful, green, springlike settings or against a deep blue sky to suggest freshness. Soft drinks and fast foods are usually shown being enjoyed in active, fun-oriented settings, and sporty cars are frequently pictured at

FIG. 10.2   An example demonstrating figure–ground perception

racetracks or in other competitive situations. Also, in comparative advertising, the promoted brand is usually shown in the good company of other respected brands and separated from presumably inferior alternatives.

SIMILARITY   Assuming that no other influence is present, items that are perceived as being similar to one another will tend to be grouped together. This, in turn, can influence the pattern one perceives in a conglomeration of items.

The principle of similarity has been used in various ways to influence consumers' perceptions. For example, some car manufacturers have attempted to develop certain style similarities between their products and the BMW in the hope that consumers will conclude that the cars are also similar in other important respects. This must have led to concern at BMW, because they responded with advertising messages stressing that their car is a standard that other carmakers have tried to copy but have done so unsuccessfully, as similar looks do not necessarily mean similar cars.

CLOSURE   Frequently consumers organise incomplete stimuli by perceiving them as complete figures. In other words a figure such as an opened circle would tend to be filled in by the individual to result in perception of a whole. Research suggests that under certain conditions this tendency toward closure can be an effective advertising device, because it motivates consumers mentally to complete the message.[42] This can focus attention and facilitate learning and retention. The Commonwealth Bank used closure in the 'Which bank?' campaign, leaving the consumer to answer the question, or fill in the blank.

It should be mentioned that not all incomplete advertising messages appear to be remembered better than completed ones. Further investigation of closure is needed to determine both the nature and effectiveness of its role in advertising.

FACTORS INFLUENCING SYNTHESIS STAGE

Many additional factors influence how consumers develop meanings from stimuli that have undergone feature analysis. The major effect of these influences is to predispose the individual toward interpreting stimuli in a certain way. Five major categories of influences are learning, personality, motivation, attitude and adaptation levels.

LEARNING Learning influences consumers to categorise stimuli by developing their abilities to identify stimulus attributes used in discrimination and levelling. In *discrimination*, consumers learn those attributes useful in distinguishing between items in order to categorise them differently. For example, we learn to distinguish fresh from stale bread, and traditional from contemporary furniture. Of course, there is no guarantee that all consumers will learn valid methods of discrimination. It depends on their prior experiences, as in the case where consumers rejected a new, quiet food processor because they incorrectly perceived it as having less power than older, noisier models.[43] This was perhaps a result of their experience with powerful and noisy appliances in the past.

As we have already seen, learning can also influence the categorisation process whereby similar but not identical stimuli are classified by the consumer into the same perceptual group and therefore generate the same response. For example, when instant coffee was first introduced, many families made clear distinctions between it and percolated or drip coffee. However, over time, *levelling* has taken place to the extent that when coffee is now offered, no distinction is usually made as to its type.

PERSONALITY AND MOTIVATION Consumers' personality characteristics also influence the meaning they derive from stimuli. To illustrate, one study found that individuals who find it difficult to tolerate uncertain situations tend to be influenced by seals of approval, such as those of the Australian Heart Association or Nursing Mothers' Association, to a greater degree than do other consumers.[44] The meaning individuals derive from stimuli is also influenced by their motivational state. This has been demonstrated in one study in which hungry subjects 'saw' more food-related items in ambiguously shaped stimuli than did subjects who were not hungry. Such findings help explain why certain products may be highly valued by some groups of consumers and deemed rather useless by others.

ATTITUDES For our present purpose, consumers' attitudes may be thought of as predispositions to understand and respond to objects and events in consistent ways. That is, attitudes act as frames of reference that affect consumers' tendencies to interpret stimuli from the environment. These frames of reference are influenced by the consumers' values and beliefs that have been developed from previous processing experiences.

The greater the consistency of a given stimulus with currently held attitudes, the more likely the consumer will interpret it in a way consistent with these attitudes. Thus, if a consumer has a negative attitude toward Toyota and sees one stalled on the roadside, the situation is likely to be interpreted as evidence of an inferior product rather than as an isolated problem with a quality car. However, a neighbour's high praise for a Toyota during an eight-year period will make it very difficult for the consumer to maintain a consistent negative attitude toward Toyota.

Because attitudes predispose consumers to interpret stimuli in consistent ways, they often lead to efficient processing. That is, many stimuli can be quickly interpreted without a great deal of processing effort being allocated to them. It must also be realised that the resulting meaning consumers derive from these stimuli is very strongly influenced by their predispositions as well as by characteristics of the stimuli themselves. Chapter 12 will discuss these issues in greater depth.

ADAPTATION LEVEL   Our discussion of selective attention noted that consumers tend to adapt to rather constant stimulus levels. This process leads to the formation of *adaptation levels*, which are standards of reference used to judge new stimulus situations. To demonstrate, assume that two individuals must judge the heaviness of this textbook. Prior to the test, however, one is required to sort envelopes and the other is assigned to moving office furniture. It seems reasonable that, due to their different standards of reference, the mail sorter will judge the text to be heavier than would the furniture mover. In fact, results of many experiments have verified this expectation.[45] They have also demonstrated that adaptation levels can be influenced to move by exposing the individual to different stimulus values. This means that the standard of reference for judging stimuli is a *sliding scale* that can change over time.

The concept of an adaptation level serving as a sliding frame of reference suggests that consumers adapt to levels of service, products and other marketing variables, and those become standards by which new situations are judged. Consider how some of the advertisements employing sexual themes are accepted today, and compare this with how they would have been judged just 15 years ago.

A basic conclusion of the above discussion is that perceptions are *subjective*. Consumers derive meaning from stimuli only by interpreting them in relation to the present situation, their experiences, and their physical and psychological states. This presents both problems and opportunities to the marketing manager. Problems are encountered because it cannot be assumed that consumers will perceive products and other marketing variables in the same way that the marketer does. Opportunities arise from determining how consumers perceive these variables and from using this insight to design more competitive offerings.

Information load

Earlier in the chapter, it was shown that the environment produces many more stimuli than consumers are capable of dealing with. Awareness thresholds, and other mechanisms were mentioned as means consumers have for reducing the number of stimuli to more manageable proportions. Of course, at any time there is no guarantee the consumer will be able to handle all stimuli that succeed in passing through these filtering mechanisms. Some researchers contend, based upon studies they have conducted, that another threshold exists—an upper limit on the amount of information that consumers can effectively deal with in their decision-making processes.[46]

Consumers' *information load* has traditionally been defined in terms of the number of brands and/or the number of attributes per brand that are available for processing. The position of these researchers, then, is that consumers' exposure to an amount of information that exceed their threshold point will generate conditions of information *overload*. Further, when they are experiencing information overload, consumers will make poorer decisions (ones that can benefit them less) than they would make under conditions of less information. This may occur despite the possibility that consumers will feel more confident with decisions based on large amounts of information. Thus, consumers facing information overload may fall back on simple 'rules of thumb' to manage the situation. That is, they may adopt decision rules such as choosing the most familiar brand name, choosing the way their friends did, or choosing the brand that seems the easiest to justify to themselves or to others. The implication here is that an overload condition not only involves attention and other information-acquisition mechanisms, but also may influence perceptual encoding, integration, evaluation and decision rules.

The research methods used and data generated on the topic have been the subject of considerable reanalysis, study and debate.[47] Because of this, we are not in a position to conclude positively whether and under what conditions information overload can occur.[48] We will return to this topic in Part 5 when consumerism issues are considered.

MARKETING IMPLICATIONS

In the previous sections we have discussed the information-processing activities involved in acquiring and interpreting stimulus experiences. Subsequent chapters treat memory factors, the information-integration stage, and evaluation and choice activities in as much depth. At this point, however, it is useful to review briefly some marketing applications of the material already examined.

Product factors

The relevance of information processing to consumers' product evaluations has already been mentioned in this chapter. We would expect that product evaluations are, at least in part, based on consumers' attempts to evaluate *directly* physical product attributes, often called *intrinsic cues*, such as size, shape and grade of ingredients. However, evidence suggests that, for many goods, buyers can have difficulty in distinguishing between different offerings on the basis of such direct product attributes. For example, one study found that subjects could discriminate between Pepsi-Cola and Coca-Cola in 'blind' taste tests (taste tests where brand identification is hidden from the subjects), but they had difficulty distinguishing each of them from another cola.[49] Such evidence led to a serious promotional war when Pepsi attempted to gain market share from Coke by using an advertising focus stressing taste difference between the brands. The strategy was to show large number of cola drinkers, many with Coke as their favourite brand, preferring Pepsi over Coke in blind taste tests called the 'Pepsi Challenge'. Early advertising responses from Coca-Cola just encouraged consumers to stick to 'the real thing'. However, because the Pepsi Challenge had considerable success, Coke responded more strongly, and hostilities broke out between the two soft-drink giants. Coke aggressively criticised and ridiculed Pepsi's testing methods, and the advertising debate that ensued became quite intense—so much so that some believe the promotional war, which has not completely subsided, had damaging effects on brand images in the soft-drink industry.[50] Despite such dangers, the apparent success of Pepsi, as measured by sales increases, has led other companies to attempt similar strategies. For example, Australian car manufacturers, fast-food chains and health-insurance companies use comparative advertising in print and television media.

A very important issue raised by the above discussion is whether consumers' differential thresholds are typically sensitive enough to discriminate between brands. If differences between some brands go undetected in taste tests in which consumers attempt to 'tune in' their discriminatory powers, perhaps even larger differences escape notice in everyday consumption activity.

For other non-food products, consumers may be capable of using intrinsic cues to discriminate between brands, but may not be able to determine whether these differences are important in predicting which brand will provide greater satisfaction. For example, how many would be capable of identifying the 'best' grade of carpeting without expert help? Given these problems, it is not surprising to find that product perceptions are often influenced by other factors. That is, in order to form impressions of products, consumers process additional stimuli that are not physical characteristics of the product itself. These features, often called *extrinsic cues*, could be packaging characteristics, advertising messages, statements of friends and many other pieces of information from a wide variety of sources.[51] To illustrate, studies have shown that the addition of a faint, not consciously noticed perfume to women's hosiery can lead consumers to prefer them strongly over identical but unscented alternatives.[52] Also, bread wrapped in cellophane was judged by consumers to be fresher than identical bread wrapped in waxed paper.[53]

Some evidence suggests that consumers' product perceptions are most likely to be influenced by extrinsic cues when the product is complex in nature.[54] Generally, however, little is known about how consumers select such cues to form interpretations, or what the conditions are that influence this process. What is known suggests four propositions that are worthy of consideration:

1. Certain extrinsic cues are more likely than others to be selected for use in judging products. The selection will be influenced by consumers' experiences as well as the types of cues available.

2. The way in which extrinsic cues are encoded can strongly influence consumers' product evaluations. For example, the cellophane wrapping on a food item could be encoded as 'packaging', but it also could be encoded as 'freshly kept food', 'protected food' or something similar. Each method of encoding is likely to have a different influence on product perception.

3. The consumer may not be able to encode certain extrinsic cues in a meaningful way. These cues would then have little if any subsequent effect on how the product is interpreted. The listing of certain packaged-food ingredients such as sodium ascorbate, calcium propionate and propyl gallate might fit this description.

4. Available extrinsic cues may lead the consumer to develop additional *inferential beliefs*, or interpretations, of the product. An inferential belief is one formed without a direct basis in the existing stimulus situation. For example, an advertisement that only mentions the whitening ability of a laundry detergent might also lead some consumers to interpret the brand as having clothes-softening properties. This could occur because ads for other brands claim to have both properties, and consumers have associated the two in their minds. However, as the present advertisement makes no softening claim, such interpretations are based on inference and do not have a basis in the stimulus situation.[55] Another study revealed that consumers infer brand character from the type of people who tend to use the product, and that their own personality characteristics are highly correlated with those characteristics to which they are brand loyal.[56]

We now turn to a special example of cue utilisation in the discussion of how consumers process the information content of price. The question of interest here is: what meaning do consumers derive from the price variable?

Price considerations

Traditional microeconomic theory has apparently influenced many marketers to assume that consumers use price only as an indicator of product cost. Consumers' use of price in this way will generate the classic down-sloping demand curve, as portrayed in Figure 10.3(a), where lower prices result in greater quantities of the product being demanded. However, considerable evidence suggests that the meaning consumers derive from the price variable is much more complex in nature.[57]

PSYCHOLOGICAL PRICING

Much discussion of how consumers encode price information has focused on the concept of 'psychological pricing'. This suggests that there is greater consumer demand at certain prices and that this demand decreases at prices above *and below* these points. Such a situation is described by the ratchet-type demand curve in Figure 10.3(b). Prices P_1, P_2 and P_3, respectively, are seen to generate a greater quantity demand than other prices in their immediate range.

One aspect of psychological pricing is the frequently observed retail practice of odd-pricing. Here, it is said that prices ending in an odd number (such as 5, 7 or 9) or just under the round number (such as 96 or 98 as opposed to 100) generate significantly higher demand than related round-numbered prices. However, this argument is usually based on retailers' experiences and has not yet been confirmed by rigorous testing.

PRICE AND PRODUCT QUALITY

Another important price-perception topic is what has become known as the price–quality proposition, which holds that consumers tend to use price as an indicator of the quality or the satisfaction potential of a product. The use of a price as an extrinsic product cue in this way is not unreasonable when consumers lack confidence or ability to judge product attributes directly. For example, previous purchase experiences may lead to an awareness that higher quality products tend to cost more. Adages such as 'You get what you pay for' also act to reinforce this association. Given the uncertainty arising from attempts to evaluate today's technically complex products directly, consumers may rely on these previous experiences to conclude that higher priced products are of higher quality. This, in turn, suggests that consumers may suspect the quality of some products that bear very low prices.

Based on the above argument, we can see how price may hold a dual informational role for consumers—as an indicator of product cost and as an indicator of product quality. Therefore, consumers' demand for a product will depend on the relative degree to which they use price as a measure of cost and quality. This can be shown by the unusual-shaped demand curve in Figure 10.3(c). The upper portion of the curve has a rather traditional shape, reflecting consumers' use of price primarily as a measure of cost; lower prices generate greater quantity demanded. However, when the use of price as an indicator of product quality begins to dominate consumers' purchase decisions, lower prices can lead to a drop in quantity demanded. This situation is reflected in the backward-bending portion of the demand curve in Figure 10.3(c).

Given such an important implication, a number of researchers have sought to determine the extent to which consumers might use price as an indicator of product quality. To do this, they developed experimental situations in which only the price of a product was allowed to change across various testing situations. These studies found that respondents tended to prefer the higher priced alternative, especially when brands were expected to differ considerably in terms of quality. Further studies determined that the price–quality relationship varied across products, and it was highest when consumers faced risky situations and when their confidence in directly judging the quality of products was low.[58]

More recent investigations have researched a variety of products and perhaps more realistic shopping situations. These findings are more complex in nature, as they suggest that price is not always the most important influence on quality perception, especially when brand names are known and experience with the product is great.[59] Further, the importance of price in influencing perceptions may depend on the amount of perceived quality variability between brands in the

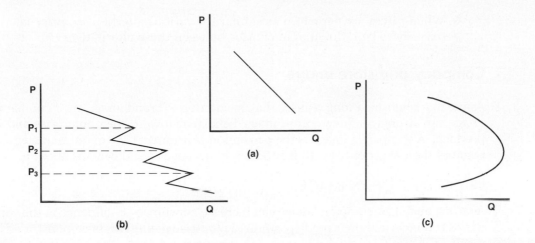

FIG. 10.3   Potential shapes of the demand curve under conditions of different consumer perceptions of the price variable

marketplace and on specific product-quality aspects being evaluated.[60] Therefore, overall product perceptions are probably the result of a combination of information derived from price, other extrinsic cues and judgments of intrinsic product characteristics.[61]

Several other conclusions have been derived from studies of how consumers react to the price variable. A review of this research offers the following summary.[62]

1. Consumers appear to use price as an indicator of product quality as well as an indicator of purchase cost.

2. Consumers also tend to develop reference prices as standards for judging prices that they confront in the marketplace.

3. Reference prices are not constant, but are modified by market experiences. Therefore, the consumer's exposure to prices somewhat higher than the reference price is likely to result in an upward adjustment of the reference price. The opposite is likely for exposure to prices somewhat below the reference price.

4. Buyers appear to develop a range of acceptable prices around the standard, or reference, price. Prices outside the range (above *or below*) are likely to be judged as inappropriate for the product in question and may result in a decreased willingness to purchase.

5. Certain factors (such as brand name, store image) can mitigate the strength of the perceived price–quality relationship and actually overshadow it for some products in some situations.[63]

6. When prices are perceived as similar for various alternatives, price is unlikely to be influential in choices between these alternatives.

Company and store image

Astute marketers have long realised that, in addition to brand image, their company's image can strongly influence consumers' behaviour toward their enterprise and its products. A company's image is the perception consumers have of its character as a result of their experiences with it and their knowledge of and benefits about it.

IMPORTANCE OF AN IMAGE

A strong and clear company image can increase consumers' confidence in the company's products and their predisposition to purchase them. This is demonstrated by results of a study in which a sample of women were 14 per cent more likely to try a new product offered by Heinz than a new product offered by a large but unspecified food company.[64] Such evidence has encouraged many firms to change their names or company logos in an effort to refine their images. In addition, as companies diversify, merge or acquire new operations, it often seems appropriate to rename the organisation to reflect its new dimensions or make a break with its old identity. Thus, United Aircraft became United Technologies and Mobil Oil Corporation became Mobil Corporation. Such changes can be quite expensive—it has been reported that in the early 1970s Humble Oil spent more than $100 million to change their name to Exxon.[65] The popular media used by marketers in Australia to communicate their brand image to the customers are shown in Table 10.1.

TABLE 10.1   Media used to convey brand image

Media	Percentage of total advertising budget
	%
1. Printed material	48.5
2. Television	34.0
3. Radio	9.2
4. Outdoor	6.8
5. Cinema	1.4

Source: Commercial Economic Advisory Service of Australia.

Because the way in which consumers perceive a company can influence their reactions to its offerings, managers are very concerned with their firms' images, even when a name change is not being considered. For example, the negative way in which business people can be portrayed in various entertainment shows is thought by many executives to create a general image problem for business.

Consumers' patronage of a particular retail store can also be significantly influenced by their perception of its image or 'personality'.[66] Store image may be defined as 'the way in which the store is defined in the shopper's mind, partly by its functional qualities and partly by an aura of psychological attributes'.[67] This implies that perception of a store image is derived not only from functional attributes of price, convenience and selection of merchandise, but also from the influence of variables such as architecture, interior design, colours and advertising. Therefore, consumers can develop images of stores regardless of whether retailers consciously attempt to project a specific image. Recent research suggests that the types of store attributes that consumers use when constructing images vary according to the image component being developed. For example, brand name seems the most important cue for forming impressions about the quality of merchandise, while the number of salespersons per department appears to most strongly influence images about the quality of service.[68]

MEASURING STORE IMAGES

Although a variety of methods exist to measure store images, one frequently used is the semantic differential profile. Here, a list of important tangible and intangible store-image attributes are first identified. Then a sample of consumers is asked to respond to 7-point scales that have antonym words or phrases at the ends of the scales. A consumer is asked to mark the position that most clearly corresponds to his or her perception of the store-image component being measured. This can also be done for competing stores in the same study. Mean or median responses can then be calculated to yield an *image profile* for each store in question. Figure 10.4 serves as an illustration by portraying image profiles found for two competing shopping centres in rural Australia.

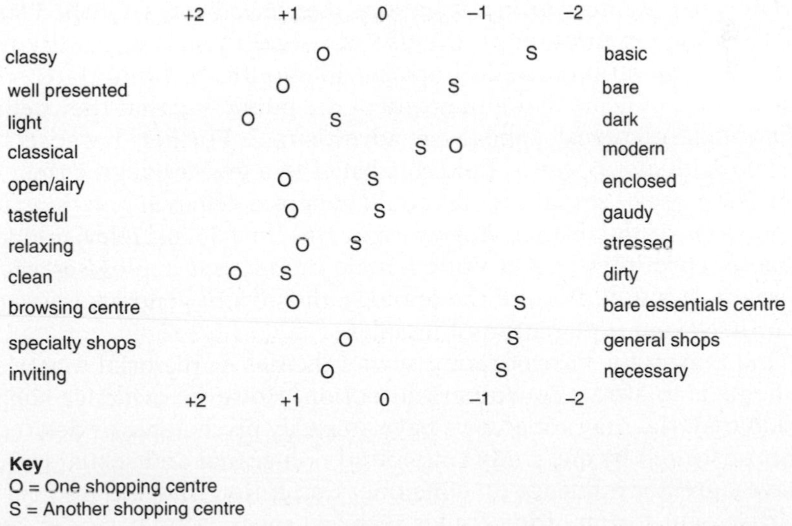

	+2	+1	0	−1	−2	
classy			O		S	basic
well presented		O		S		bare
light	O	S				dark
classical				S O		modern
open/airy		O	S			enclosed
tasteful		O	S			gaudy
relaxing		O	S			stressed
clean	O	S				dirty
browsing centre		O			S	bare essentials centre
specialty shops		O		S		general shops
inviting		O		S		necessary
	+2	+1	0	−1	−2	

Key
O = One shopping centre
S = Another shopping centre

FIG. 10.4 Semantic differential results for two shopping centres' images

It should be concluded from the above discussion that measurement of store image reveals only positive/negative image information using a semantic differential (word difference or opposite). For example, one store may be perceived as progressive and another as conservative, neither of which is necessarily a good or bad trait. Research has also revealed some other interesting findings, particularly the fact that stores do have distinctive images or personalities. Also, different stores appear to attract specific socioeconomic segments, and consumers in different social classes, stages of family life cycle or other market segments are likely to perceive a different store differently.[69] All of these findings suggest that stores may be more successful in appealing to specific target segments as opposed to the mass market.

Advertising issues

Applications of information processing to advertising have been cited throughout the chapter. Two other areas that draw considerable attention are use of sex in advertising and the controversy over subliminal advertising.

SEX IN ADVERTISING

The use of sexually attractive models and sexually suggestive themes in advertising has a long history. It is therefore surprising that little is generally known about specific consumer reactions to these methods of promoting products. Because the recent promotional trend has been toward a dramatic increase in the use of more explicit sexual themes and pictures, the need for research in this area is even greater.[70] Of course, it should be kept in mind that the findings of such research may pertain only to the culture in which the investigation was conducted.

The small number of investigations that have been published suggest that, in at least some circumstances, the use of sexual themes or nudity in promotions may have a small favourable impact and significant limitations.[71] For example, some studies indicate that a majority of the public say that they believe too much use is made of sexual appeals in advertising.[72] Further, because feminists and older individuals appear to hold this belief to a greater degree than do others, an advertiser's use of sexual themes could generate negative reactions from substantial portions of the market. For example, the Just Jeans' television advertisement for men's corduroys uses a nude female model, but apologises up front for the 'cheap sexist stunt'. Despite the apology, the ad *still* generates negative reactions due to its sexual exploitation of females.

One reason for incorporating sexual themes or pictorial material into advertisements is to attract consumers' attention. However, evidence suggests that use of such material may not always have an easily predictable or desired effect.[73] This is demonstrated by one study that found non-sexual and sexual romantic themes to have a greater influence on consumers' attention than did nudity.[74] Also, a print advertisement for an office copier received much greater reader response when the bikini-clad model standing beside it was removed. One explanation is that the model that was employed to attract attention drew attention *away* from the advertising message.[75]

Of course, attracting attention is only one purpose of advertising. Consumers must also remember the brand name and advertising message in a favourable manner. It is interesting to note that studies have found that although consumers' recognition or recall of an advertisement may increase through the use of sexual illustrations, no strong positive influence could be detected for the brand being advertised.[76] Other research indicates that even the higher recognition of advertisements may be confined mainly to the visual material and not to the verbal content.[77]

A further concern is how the use of sexual content influences consumers' perceptions of the advertisement and advertised brand. Here again, evidence does not consistently favour the use of sexual content in ads. One study found that ads employing female nudity were perceived by consumers as being less appealing than those without nude models. Also, the products advertised using nude models were perceived as being of lower quality.[78] However, results of this and other studies suggest that several other factors can influence how consumers will react to products advertised using sexual content. First, and quite predictably, consumers' predispositions toward sexual themes appear to be an important determinant of their reaction to ads containing such material. Secondly, reactions to nudity seem to be negative when the viewer is a member of the same sex as the nude model.[79] Thirdly, the use of sexual themes may be perceived as acceptable for certain products, such as ones designed to increase allurement (perfume, aftershave, body oil and the like).[80] Finally, the people present in the viewing situation may also influence how consumers react to a given sexual theme.[81]

Thus, the decision to use sexual themes in advertising is not a simple, straightforward one. The product to be advertised, the situations involved and the predispositions (attitudes toward sexual themes and sexual exploitation) of various market segments are all important considerations when making such a decision. There needs to be a sound evaluation of advertising content and market characteristics before employing sexual themes to promote any specific product.

SUBLIMINAL ADVERTISING

The technique called subliminal advertising has sparked considerable controversy in promotional and scientific fields. You may recall from earlier discussions that the absolute threshold identifies the minimum value of a stimulus capable of being consciously noticed. Because this is also referred to as a *limen*, the term 'subliminal perception' means perception of stimuli that are below the level needed to reach conscious awareness.

Potentially, this could be achieved in at least three major ways:

1. by presenting visual stimuli for a very brief duration;

2. by presenting auditory messages through accelerated speech at low volume levels;

3. by embedding or hiding images or words in pictorial material.[82]

The purported benefit of using such techniques in advertising is that a subliminal message will not be strong enough to arouse consumers' selective attention and defence mechanisms, but it will have enough strength to influence them at an unconscious level.

The first widely known test of subliminal advertising was conducted by Vicary during the 1950s.[83] During picture-theatre tests more than 45 000 unsuspecting viewers were presented with filmed messages every five seconds, with each message said to be 1/3000 of a second in duration. The two messages employed were 'Eat popcorn' and 'Drink Coca-Cola'. By comparing sales receipts during the test period with those from a previous period, it was reported that popcorn sales increased 58 per cent and Coca-Cola sales rose 18 per cent.

These results quickly generated concern regarding unethical uses of subliminal methods. However, closer examination of Vicary's research raised questions as to its validity. As one review stated, 'There were no reports of even the most rudimentary scientific precautions, such as adequate controls, provisions for replication, etc.'.[84] The lack of information on these provisions does not generate much confidence in the results.

Other efforts to influence audiences subliminally have not been able to document the strong positive effects reported by Vicary.[85] Nevertheless, a number of applications of subliminal or nearly subliminal messages in print and audio media have been developed. These include attempts to deter shoplifting and influence purchases, self-help audio tapes (quit smoking, build self-confidence) and efforts at reducing radio audience stress and increasing the motivation of employees.[86] The use of subliminal messages is claimed to be fairly prevalent in television advertisements.[87] Also, popular books on the subject have charged that effective subliminal images are embedded in many print advertisements, and that messages are also subliminally incorporated into movies and pop music.[88] In fact in a sensational legal case, parents sued the heavy-metal group Judas Priest, claiming that their teenage children committed suicide because a subliminal message allegedly implanted in the album *Stained Class* made them want to kill themselves.[89]

Unfortunately, because careful steps have not been taken to measure the influence of these messages on the intended audience, their effects have not been well documented. This seems to have led some to take a lighter approach to the issue. Toyota has touted its Paseo model with television ads where the 'main' message refers to practical aspects of the car, while words such as 'sexy', 'wild' and 'exciting' flash on the screen in fast, but easily perceived durations.[90]

More carefully controlled experiments suggest that although subliminal messages may be capable of arousing basic drives such as thirst and hunger, evidence of their influence on attitudes or specific motives directing consumers toward particular brands has not been shown to be strong.[91] However, a review of studies from the field of psychology suggests that subliminal messages might be capable of influencing consumers' specific but unconsciously held desires.[92]

In conclusion, some evidence suggests that under certain conditions subliminal perception may occur. However, considerable technical problems result when attempting to capitalise on this perceptual process by developing subliminal advertising messages in a commercial setting. First, the speed of the message must be determined. This may be especially difficult when one considers that the absolute thresholds of various consumers may differ by a considerable amount. Secondly, the message itself must be brief and simple, as anything longer than a few words would probably be too complex to comprehend. Furthermore, we have seen how consumers' motives, personality and other individual determinants influence selective perception of stimuli above the absolute threshold. There is no guarantee that these factors would not operate on subliminal stimuli. Thus, the subliminal message 'Drink Coke' could be distorted into 'Stink Coke', or some other meaning not desired by the marketer.

Furthermore, because subliminal messages may arouse only basic drives, they may initiate behaviour that is not always specifically beneficial to the advertiser. Thus, a subliminal message for Pepsi may increase a consumer's thirst enough for a trip to the refrigerator for a glass of cordial or another liquid refreshment that is on hand. Also, if such messages can appeal to consumers' unconscious motives, the problems of identifying and dealing with such motives appear to be quite large. Therefore, it seems safe to conclude that, at present, subliminal advertising does not hold the threat of turning consumers into automatons who are at the mercy of marketers. In fact, minimal evidence regarding its effectiveness, technical difficulties associated with its use and unknown consequences of employing it give little reason for advertisers wholeheartedly to embrace subliminal advertising.[93]

SUMMARY

This chapter examined the topic of information processing and its role in influencing consumer behaviour. First, an overview of major concepts identified the important processes of information acquisition, perceptual encoding, memory, integration, evaluation and choice. The importance of the executive system in directing these activities, as well as the influences provided by consumers and situational characteristics, was also reviewed.

Several of these topics were then treated in greater depth. Discussion first focused on information acquisition. Here, active search for and passive reception of stimuli were shown to be the two major activities for acquiring information. Active search involves scanning both internal (memory) and external sources. Internal search provides sufficient information to the consumer in most situations, but external search will be used where presently held information is inadequate.

The nature of external search was then examined. A primary conclusion is that consumers do not appear to engage in a great deal of external-search activity. Passive reception of information was briefly treated. Attention then turned to the topic of how consumers acquire sensations from stimuli. Here, the nature and marketing implications of consumers' awareness and differential thresholds were discussed. The selective nature of consumers' attention to stimuli was then treated. Various stimulus properties, as well as characteristics of consumers themselves, were shown to have a great influence on attention. Perceptual encoding was the next major topic. Encoding involves assessing how the main features of a stimulus are organised (feature analysis) and then combining this information with other available information to interpret (encode) the stimulus. A wide variety of stimulus and individual factors can influence this perceptual encoding process. The influence of the categorisation process on how consumers will respond to products was seen to be very important.

The chapter then switched to a consideration of the marketing implications of information-processing material that had been presented. Product and price factors, company images, sex in advertising and subliminal advertising were highlighted.

MANAGERIAL REFLECTIONS

For our product or service situation:

1. How often do consumers engage in active search for, as opposed to passive reception of, information?

2. To what degree are differential and absolute thresholds an important consideration?

3. How can we be creative in capturing consumers' attention with our advertisements?

4. In what ways can we influence how consumers categorise and interpret our products and advertisements?

5. To what extent is information overload a potential problem for consumers?

6. To what extent are intrinsic product cues important in consumers' perceptions of the product?

7. To what degree is there a price–quality perception among consumers?

8. What is our company's image? Are we satisfied with this image? What factors might be changed in an attempt to alter this image?

DISCUSSION TOPICS

1. What is information processing? Distinguish between the various activities that constitute the information-processing function.

2. It is often said that the information-acquisition activity is selective in nature. In what ways is this so? What implications does this have for understanding consumer behaviour?

3. Review that portion of the chapter dealing with consumers' attention processes and then select several advertisements from various media (print, television and so on). Describe these advertisements and evaluate them in terms of their potential for attracting consumers' attention. If possible, include examples of the advertisements.

4. The resemblance of certain private-brand packaging to the packaging of nationally known brands has been so close at times that the products have been described as look-alikes. Visit a supermarket and bring back two packaged products to demonstrate this. Also, while you are there, make an effort to determine the prevalence of this phenomenon. In what ways might it influence the behaviour of consumers?

5. Assume that consumers have heightened awareness of the following prices for various models in a product line: $11.70, $15.21 and $19.77. Using Weber's Law, predict the next highest price in the line that would generate heightened awareness.

6. Bring to class print advertisements that use each of the following techniques for influencing perceptual encoding:
    (a) similarity
    (b) figure–ground
    (c) closure
    Be prepared to assess how effectively these techniques have been employed.

7. Write up a procedure that you would employ for conducting a taste test to determine:
    (a) if your fellow students can discriminate between three brands of cola;
    (b) if they have a preference for any particular cola based on taste alone.
    Indicate the variables that might influence the results and how you would design an experiment to minimise their influence.

8. Choose any two restaurants or pubs that are frequented by students at your college. Measure their image profiles by designing a number of semantic differential items and administering them to a random sample of your fellow students. What conclusions can you draw from your data?

REFERENCES

1. Jagdish N. Sheth, 'How Consumers Use Information', Faculty working paper No. 530, College of Commerce and Business Administration, University of Illinois at Urbana-Champaign, 1978, pp. 14–18.
2. W. Marks, P. M. Tidwell & C. L. Spence, 'Brand Frequency and Product Involvement: The Application of a PC-based Perceptual Learning Routine to Psychology and Marketing', *Psychology and Marketing* 8 (4), 1991, pp. 299–310.
3. M. E. Scott, D. J. Weekes & P. M. Tidwell, 'The Effect of Qualifications and Membership of Professional Accounting Bodies on the Individual's Choice of Accountants', *Journal of Professional Services Marketing* 14, 1996.
4. See Howard Beales et al., 'Consumer Search and Public Policy', *Journal of Consumer Research* 8, June 1981 p. 22, for a more comprehensive discussion of this issue and its implications for public policy.
5. See Beales et al., ibid, p. 13.
6. See Avery Abernethy & Herbert Rotfield, 'Zipping through TV Ads Is Old Tradition— but Viewers Are Getting Better at It', *Marketing News*, 7 January 1991, pp. 6, 14; Thomas J. Olney, Morris B. Holbrook & Rajeev Batra, 'Consumer Responses to Advertising: The Effects of Ad Content, Emotions, and Attitude toward the Ad on Viewing Time', *Journal of Consumer Research* 17, March 1991, pp. 440–53; and Stuart Elliott, '"Chameleon" Ads Mimic TV', *USA Today*, 12 June 1989, p. 5b.
7. Ibid.
8. 'Does Taste Make Waste?', *Forbes*, 1 June 1974, p. 24.
9. Some of the following discussion follows Richard Lee Miller, 'Dr Weber and the Consumer', *Journal of Marketing* 26, January 1962 pp. 57–61; and Steuart Henderson Britt, 'How Weber's Law Can Be Applied to Marketing', *Business Horizons* 18, February 1975, pp. 21–9.
10. L. Paul Gilden, 'Sampling Candy Bar Economics', *New Englander* 22, January 1976, p. 32.
11. 'Hidden Costs', *Wall Street Journal*, 15 February 1977, p. 1.
12. See 'Checkout Counter Look-alikes', *Money*, May 1976, pp. 71–2.
13. Joseph Uhl, Consumer Perception of Retain Food Price Changes, Paper presented to First Annual Meeting of the Association for Consumer Research, 1970.
14. Raymond Bauer & Stephen Greyser, *Advertising in America: The Consumer's View*, Harvard University Press, Cambridge, MA, 1968, p. 178.
15. See Esther Thorson, 'Consumer Processing of Advertising', in James H. Leigh & Claude R. Martin Jr, (eds), *Current Issues—Research in Advertising*, vol. 12, University of Michigan, Ann Arbor, 1990, pp. 197–230.
16. Much of this section follows the discussion in Andrew A. Mitchell, 'An Information Processing View of Consumer Behavior', in Subhash C. Jain (ed.), *Research Frontiers in Marketing: Dialogues and Directions*, American Marketing Association, Chicago, 1978, pp. 189–90.
17. Walter Schneider & Richard M. Sheffrin, 'Controlled and Automatic Human Information Processing: I. Detection, Search and Attention', *Psychological Review* 84, 1977, pp. 1–66.
18. S. Sternberg, 'High Speed Scanning in Human Memory', *Science* 153, 1966, pp. 652–4.
19. See Geraldine Fennell, 'Attention Engagement', in James H. Leigh & Claude R. Martin Jr, (eds), *Current Issues and Research in Advertising*, University of Michigan Press, Ann Arbor, 1979, pp. 17–33, for a much fuller discussion of these factors.
20. J. W. Rosenberg, 'How Does Color, Size, Affect Ad Readership?', *Industrial Marketing* 41, May 1956, pp. 54–7.
21. Rafael Valiente, 'Mechanical Correlates of Ad Recognition', *Journal of Advertising Research* 13, June 1973, pp. 13–18.

22. Stephen Baker, *Visual Persuasion*, McGraw-Hill, New York, 1961.
23. 'Position in Newspaper Advertising: 1', *Media/Scope*, February 1963, p. 57. This finding is contrary to much previous research; see Melvin S. Hattwick, *How to Use Psychology for Better Advertising*, Prentice-Hall, Englewood Cliffs, NJ, 1950, pp. 145–50.
24. See Hattwick, ibid, p. 155; and 'Position in Newspaper Advertising: 1', ibid, p. 57.
25. See Pat Kelly & Paul J. Soloman, 'Humor in Television Advertising', *Journal of Advertising* 4, Summer 1975, pp. 33–5; Peter Lubalin, 'Humor in Radio', *ANNY*, 4 November 1977, p. 22; and Dorothy Markiewicz, 'Effects of Humor on Persuasion', *Sociometry* 37, 1974, pp. 407–22.
26. See Markiewicz, ibid, pp. 407–27 and Brian Sternthal & Samuel Craig, 'Humor in Advertising', *Journal of Marketing* 37, October 1973, pp. 12–18.
27. See Sternthal & Craig, *Journal of Marketing*, pp. 12–18; and Thomas J. Madden & Marc G. Weinberger, 'The Effects of Humor on Attention in Magazine Advertising', Working Paper 81–19, School of Business Administration, University of Massachusetts, Amherst, 1981.
28. Allan Greenberg & Charles Suttoni, 'Television Commercial Wear-out', *Journal of Advertising Research* 13, October 1973, pp. 47–54.
29. See, for example, Richard L. Celsi & Jerry C. Olson, 'The Role of Involvement in Attention and Comprehension Processes', *Journal of Consumer Research* 15, September 1988, pp. 210–24; and Deborah J. MacInnis & Bernard J. Jaworski, 'Information Processing from Advertisements: Toward an Integrative Framework', *Journal of Marketing* 53, October 1989, pp. 1–23.
30. Cornelia Pechmann & David W. Stewart, 'The Effects of Comparative Advertising on Attention, Memory, and Purchase Intentions', *Journal of Consumer Research* 17, September 1990, pp. 180–91.
31. See Alvin J. Silk & Frank P. Geiger, 'Advertisement Size and the Relationship Between Product Usage and Advertising Exposure', *Journal of Marketing Research* 9, February 1972, pp. 22–6, which credits this hypothesis to Leo Bogart.
32. Charles F. Cannell & James C. MacDonald, 'The Impact of Health News on Attitudes and Behavior', *Journalism Quarterly* 33, July/September 1956, pp. 315–23.
33. Joseph Cherian & Marilyn Jones, 'Some Processes in Brand Categorizing: Why One Person's Noise Is Another Person's Music', in Rebecca H. Holman & Michael R. Solomon (eds), *Advances in Consumer Research*, vol. 18. Association for Consumer Research, Ann Arbor, MI, 1991, pp. 77–83.
34. See Bettman, pp. 79–82; and Peter H. Lindsay & Donald A. Norman, *Human Information Processing*, Academic Press, New York, 1972, pp. 115–47.
35. Bettman, p. 79.
36. See Harry Helson, *Adaptation-level Theory*, Harper & Row, New York, 1964; Kent B. Monroe, 'Objective and Subjective Contextual Influences on Price Perception', in Arch Woodside at al. (eds), *Consumer and Industrial Buying Behavior*, North-Holland, New York, 1977, pp. 287–96; Kent B. Monroe, Albert J. Della Bitta & Susan L. Downey, 'Contextual Influences on Subjective Price Perceptions', *Journal of Business Research* 5, December 1977, pp. 277–91; Russell W. Belk, 'Situational Variables and Consumer Behavior', *Journal of Consumer Research* 2, December 1975, pp. 157–64; and Donald R. Lichtenstein & William O. Bearden, 'Contextual Influences on Perceptions of Merchant-supplied Reference Prices', *Journal of Consumer Research* 16, June 1989, pp. 55–66.
37. Eloise Coupey & Kent Nakamoto, 'Learning Context and the Development of Product Category Perceptions', in Michael J. Houston (ed.), *Advances in Consumer Research*, vol. 15, Association for Consumer Research, Provo, UT, 1988, pp. 77–82; and Mita Sujan, 'Consumer Knowledge: Effects on Evaluation Strategies Mediating Consumer Judgments', *Journal of Consumer Research* 12, June 1985, pp. 31–46.

38. See, for example, Eleanor Rosch & Carolyn Mervis, 'Family Resemblances: Studies in the Internal Structure of Categories', *Cognitive Psychology* 7, October 1975, pp. 573–605.

39. Barbara Loken & James Ward, 'Alternative Approaches to Understanding the Determinants of Typicality', *Journal of Consumer Research* 17, September 1990, pp. 111–26.

40. P. M. Tidwell, W. Marks, A. E. Graesser & C. L. Abercrombie, 'Family Resemblance as a Function of Familiarity: An Analysis of Fast-food Restaurants in America', in B. Sharp (ed.), *Southern Marketing Theory and Applications*, University of South Australia, Adelaide, SA, 1994, pp. 128–48.

41. See Joseph W. Alha & J. Wesley Hutchinson, 'Dimensions of Consumer Expertise', *Journal of Consumer Research* 13, March 1987, pp. 411–54; Mita Sujan & Christine Dekleva, 'Product Categorization and Inference Making: Some Implications for Comparative Advertising', *Journal of Consumer Research* 14, December 1987, pp. 372–8; and Joan Meyers-Levy & Alice M. Tybout, 'Schema Congruity as a Basis for Product Evaluation', *Journal of Consumer Research* 16, June 1989, pp. 39–54.

42. Norman Heller, 'An Application of Psychological Learning Theory to Advertising', *Journal of Marketing* 20, January 1956, pp. 248–54; and Dev Pathak, Gene Burton & Ron Zigli, 'The Memory Impact of Incomplete Advertising Slogans', in Henry Nash & Donald Robin (eds), *Processing of the Southern Marketing Association Conference*, 1977, pp. 269–72.

43. Robert Froman, 'You Get What You Want', in J. H. Westing (ed.), *Readings in Marketing*, Prentice-Hall, Englewood Cliffs, NJ, 1953, p. 231.

44. Thomas L. Parkinson, 'The Use of Seals of Approval in Consumer Decision-making as a Function of Cognitive Needs and Style', in Mary Jane Schlinger (ed.), *Advances in Consumer Research*, vol. 2, Association for Consumer Research, Chicago, IL, 1975, pp. 133–40.

45. Harry Helson, *Adaptation-level Theory: An Experimental and Systematic Approach to Behavior*, Harper & Row, New York, 1964.

46. See Jacob Jacoby, Donald E. Speller & Carol A. Kohn, 'Brand Choice Behavior as a Function of Information Load', *Journal of Marketing Research* 11, February 1974, pp. 63–9; Jacob Jacoby, Donald E. Speller & Carol A. Kohn, 'Brand Choice Behavior as a Function of Information Load: Replication and Extension', *Journal of Consumer Research* 1, June 1974, pp. 33–42; and Jacob Jacoby, Donald E. Speller & Carol A. K. Berning, 'Constructive Criticism and Programmatic Research, Reply to Russo', *Journal of Consumer Research* 2, September 1975, pp. 154–6. See also Debra L. Scammon, 'Information Load and Consumers', *Journal of Consumer Research* 4, December 1977, pp. 148–55, for additional relevant evidence.

47. See Edward J. Russo, 'More Information Is Better: A Re-evaluation of Jacoby, Speller and Kohn', *Journal of Consumer Research* 1, December 1974, pp. 68–72; John O. Summers, 'Less Information Is Better?', *Journal of Marketing Research* 11, November 1974, pp. 467–8; William L. Wilkie, 'Analysis of Effects of Information Load', *Journal of Marketing Research* 11, November 1974, pp. 462–6; and Naresh K. Malhotra, Arun K. Jain & Stephen W. Lagakos, 'The Information Overload Controversy: An Alternative Viewpoint', *Journal of Marketing* 46, Spring 1982, pp. 27–37.

48. See Naresh K. Malhotra, 'Information Load and Consumer Decision Making, *Journal of Consumer Research* 8, March 1982, pp. 419–30; Roger J. Best & Michael Ursic, 'The Impact of Information Load and Variability on Choice Accuracy', in Melanie Wallendorf & Paul Anderson (eds), *Advances in Consumer Research*, vol. 14, Association for Consumer Research, Provo, UT, 1987, pp. 106–8; Kevin Lane Keller & Richard Staelin, 'Effects of Quality and Quantity on Decision Effectiveness', *Journal of Consumer Research* 14, September 1987, pp. 200–13; Robert J. Meyer & Eric J. Johnson, 'Information Overload and the Nonrobustness of Linear Models: A Comment on Keller and Staelin', *Journal of Consumer Research* 15, March 1989, pp. 498–503; and Kevin Lane Keller & Richard Staelin, 'Assessing Biases in

Measuring Decision Effectiveness and Information Overload', *Journal of Consumer Research* 15, March 1989, pp. 504–8.

49. F. J. Thumin, 'Identification of Cola Beverages', *Journal of Applied Psychology* 46, October 1962, pp. 358–60.

50. See 'Coke-Pepsi Slugfest', *Time*, 26 July, pp. 64–5; 'The Cola War', *Newsweek*, 30 August 1976, p. 67; 'One Sip Not a Taste Test, Coke Tells New Yorkers', *Advertising Age*, 16 August 1976, p. 6; and Peter W. Bernstein, 'Coke Strikes Back', *Fortune*, 1 June 1981, pp. 30–6.

51. See Donald F. Cox, 'The Sorting Rule Model of the Consumer Product Evaluation Process', in Donald F. Cox (ed.), *Risk Taking and Information Handling in Consumer Behavior*, Harvard Business School, Cambridge, MA, 1967, pp. 324–69; Jerry C. Olson & Jacob Jacoby, 'Cue Utilization in the Quality Perception Process', in M. Venkatesan (ed.), *Proceedings, 3rd Annual Conference of the Association for Consumer Research*, Association for Consumer Research, College Park, MD, 1972, pp. 167 79; Jerry C. Olson, 'Inferential Belief Formation in the Cue Utilization Process', in H. Keith Hunt (ed.), *Advances in Consumer Research*, vol. 5, Association for Consumer Research, Ann Arbor, MI, 1978, pp. 706–13; Robert E. Burnkrant, 'Cue Utilization in Product Perception', in H. Keith Hunt (ed.), *Advances in Consumer Research*, vol. 5, Association for Consumer Research, Ann Arbor, MI, 1978, pp. 724–9; and John Wheatley & John S. Y. Chiu, 'The Influence of Intrinsic and Extrinsic Cues on Product Quality Evaluations of Experts and Non Experts', in Neil Beckwith et al. (eds), *1979 Educators' Conference Proceedings*, American Marketing Association, 1979, pp. 205–9. See also Allison & Uhl, 'Influence of Beer Brand Identification on Taste Perception', for an excellent example of how marketing efforts can influence brand perceptions.

52. D.A. Laird, 'How the Consumer Estimates Quality by Subconscious Sensory Impressions', *Journal of Applied Psychology* 16, June 1932, pp. 241–6; and *Women's Wear Daily*, 28 January 1961, p. 15.

53. Robert L. Brown, 'Wrapper Influence on the Perception of Freshness in Bread,' *Journal of Applied Psychology* 42, August 1958, pp. 257–60.

54. Burnkrant, op cit, Ref 51, pp. 724–9.

55. See Olson, op cit, Ref 51, pp. 706–13 for a discussion of this topic.

56. P. M. Tidwell, D. D. Morgan & C. T. Kenny, 'Brand Character as a Function of Brand Loyalty', *Current Psychology* 2 (4), 1992, pp. 347–53.

57. For excellent reviews of this evidence, see Kent B. Monroe, 'Buyers' Subjective Perceptions of Price', *Journal of Marketing Research* 10, February 1973, pp. 70–80; Jerry C. Olson, 'Price as an Informational Cue: Effects on Product Evaluations', in Arch G. Woodside, Jagdish N. Sheth & Peter D. Bennett (eds), *Consumer and Industrial Buyer Behavior*, North-Holland, New York, 1977, pp. 267–86; Kent B. Monroe & Susan M. Petroshius, 'Buyers' Perceptions of Price: An Update of the Evidence', in Harold H. Kassarjian & Thomas S. Robertson (eds), *Perspectives in Consumer Behavior*, 3rd edn, Scott, Foresman, 1981, pp. 43–55; and Valarie A. Zeithaml, 'Consumer Perceptions of Price, Quality and Value: A Means-End Model and Synthesis of Evidence', *Journal of Marketing* 52, July 1988, pp. 2–22, upon which much of this section is based.

58. See Benson Shapiro, Price as a Communicator of Quality: An Experiment, PhD thesis, Harvard University, 1970; and Zarrel Lambert, 'Price and Choice Behavior', *Journal of Marketing Research* 9, February 1972, pp. 35–40.

59. See, for example, Robert A. Peterson, 'Consumer Perceptions as a Function of Product, Color, Price, and Nutrition Labeling', in William D. Perreault Jr (ed.), *Advances in Consumer Research*, vol. 4, Association for Consumer Research, Atlanta, GA, 1977, pp. 61–3.

60. Michael Etgar & Naresh K. Malhotra, 'Determinants of Price Dependency: Personal and Perceptual Factors', *Journal of Consumer Research* 8, September 1981,

pp. 217–22; and Akshay R. Rao & Kent B. Monroe, 'The Moderating Effect of Prior Knowledge on Cue Utilization in Produce Evaluations', *Journal of Consumer Research* 15, September 1988, pp. 253–64.

61. Jacoby, Olson & Haddock, 'Price and Product Composition Characteristics'.
62. Monroe and Petroshius, op cit, Ref 57, pp. 43–55.
63. See, for example, Carl Obermiller, 'When Do Consumers Infer Quality from Price?', in Michael J. Houston (ed.), *Advances in Consumer Research*, vol. 15, Association for Consumer Research, Provo, UT, 1988, pp. 304–10.
64. National Probability Sample in Great Britain, Market and Opinion Research International Cooperative Image Study, Spring 1970, reported by Robert Worcester, 'Corporate Image Research', in Robert Worcester (ed.), *Consumer Market Research Handbook*, McGraw-Hill, London, 1972, p. 508.
65. 'Humble Exxon in; Esso out', *National Petroleum News*, June 1972.
66. See, for example, Ponpun Nickel & Albert I. Wertheimer, 'Factors Affecting Consumers' Images and Choices of Drugstores', *Journal of Retailing* 55, Summer 1979, pp. 71–8; B. Rosenbloom, *Retail Marketing*, Random House, New York, 1981; and James M. Kenderdine & Jack J. Kasulis, 'The Relationship between Changes in Perceptions of Store Attributes and Changes in Consumer Patronage Behavior', in Robert F. Lusch & William R. Darden (eds), *Retail Patronage Theory: 1981 Workshop Proceedings*, Center for Economic and Management Research, University of Oklahoma, Norman, OK, 1981, pp. 100–5.
67. Pierre Martineau, 'The Personality of the Retail Store', *Harvard Business Review* 36, January/February 1958, pp. 47–55.
68. David Mazursky & Jacob Jacoby, 'Exploring the Development of Store Images', *Journal of Retailing* 62, Summer 1986, pp. 145–65.
69. See William Lazer & Robert G. Wyckham, 'Perceptual Segmentation of Department Store Marketing', *Journal of Retailing* 45, Summer 1969, pp. 3–14; and William D. Haueisen, 'Market Positioning: A New Segmentation Approach', in Robert F. Lusch & William R. Darden (eds), *Retail Patronage Theory: 1981 Workshop Proceedings*, Center for Economic and Management Research, University of Oklahoma, Norman, OK, 1981, pp. 86–92.
70. See, for example, Gail Bronson, 'King Leer: Sexual Pitches in Ads Become More Explicit and More Pervasive', *Wall Street Journal*, 18 December 1980, pp. 1, 14; and Christopher Rowley, 'Sex in Advertising', *Scan* 29, April 1981, pp. 12–15.
71. See, for example, Michael S. LaTour, Robert E. Pitts & David C. Snook-Luther, 'Female Nudity, Arousal, and Ad Response: An Experimental Investigation', *Journal of Advertising* 19 (4), 1990, pp. 51–62.
72. See, for example, Gordon L. Wise, Alan L. King & J. Paul Merenski, 'Reactions to Sexy Ads Vary with Age', *Journal of Advertising Research* 14, August 1974, pp. 11–16; and Deborah K. Johnson & Kay Satow, 'Consumers' Reactions to Sex in TV Commercials', in Keith H. Hunt (ed.), *Advances in Consumer Research*, vol. 5, Association for Consumer Research, Ann Arbor, MI, 1978, pp. 411–14.
73. See Michael S. LaTour, 'Female Nudity in Print Advertising: An Analysis of Gender Differences in Arousal and Ad Response', *Psychology & Marketing* 7, Spring 1990, pp. 65–81.
74. Bruce John Morrison & Richard C. Sherman, 'Who Responds to Sex in Advertising?', *Journal of Advertising Research* 12, April 1972, pp. 15–19.
75. See Baker, *Visual Persuasion*; and Gordon Patzer, *The Physical Attractiveness Phenomena*, Plenum Press, 1985.
76. See Robert Chestnut, Charles LaChance & Amy Lubitz, 'The Decorative Female Model: Sexual Stimuli and the Recognition of Advertisements', *Journal of Advertising* 6, Fall 1977, pp. 11–14; Major Stedman, 'How Sexy Illustrations Affect Brand Recall', *Journal of Advertising Research* 9, March 1969, pp. 15–19; Raymond L. Horton, 'The Effects of Nudity, Suggestiveness, and Attractiveness on Product

Class and Brand Name Recall', in Vinay Kothari (ed.), *Developments in Marketing Science*, vol. 5, Academy of Marketing Science, Nacogdoches, TX, 1982, pp. 456–9; and Jessica Severn, George E. Belch & Michael A. Belch, 'The Effects of Sexual and Non-sexual Advertising Appeals and Information Level on Cognitive Processing and Communication Effectiveness', *Journal of Advertising* 19 (1), 1990, pp. 14–22.

77. Leonard N. Reid & Lawrence C. Soley, 'Another Look at the "Decorative" Female Model: The Recognition of Visual and Verbal Ad Components', in James H. Leigh & Claude R. Martin Jr (eds), *Current Issues and Research in Advertising—1981*, Graduate School of Business Administration, Division of Research, University of Michigan, Ann Arbor, 1981, pp. 123–33.

78. Robert A. Peterson & Roger A. Kerin, 'The Female Role in Advertisements: Some Experimental Evidence', *Journal of Marketing* 41, October 1977, pp. 59–63.

79. See Donald Sciglimpaglia, Michael A. Belch & Richard F. Cain Jr, 'Demographic and Cognitive Factors Influencing Viewers' Evaluations of Sexy Advertisements', in William Wilkie (ed.), *Advances in Consumer Research*, vol. 6, Association for Consumer Research, Ann Arbor, MI, 1979, pp. 62–5; and Michael A. Belch et al., 'Psychophysiological and Cognitive Responses to Sex in Advertising', in Andrew Mitchell (ed.), *Advances in Consumer Research*, Ann Arbor, MI, 1982, pp. 424–7.

80. Sciglimpaglia, Belch & Cain, ibid, pp. 62–5; and Deborah K. Johnson & Kay Satow, 'Consumers' Reactions to Sex in TV Commercials', in Keith H. Hunt (ed.), *Advances in Consumer Research*, vol. 5, Association for Consumer Research, Ann Arbor, MI, 1978, pp. 411–14.

81. Sciglimpaglia, Belch & Cain, op cit, Ref 79, pp. 62–5; and Johnson & Satow, ibid, pp. 411–14.

82. Timothy E. Moore, 'Subliminal Advertising: What You See Is What You Get', *Journal of Marketing* 46, Spring 1982, pp. 38–47.

83. See H. Brean, 'What Hidden Sell Is All About', *Life*, 31 March 1958, pp. 104–14.

84. James V. McConnell, Richard L. Cutter & Elton B. McNeil, 'Subliminal Stimulation: An Overview', *American Psychologist* 13, May 1958, p. 230.

85. See M. Mannes, 'Ain't Nobody Here but Us Commercials', *Reporter*, 17 October 1957, pp. 35–7; and 'Subliminal Ad Okay If It Sells: FCC Peers into Subliminal Picture on TV', *Advertising Age* 28, 1957.

86. See, for example, 'Secret Voices', *Time*, 10 September 1979, p. 71; Neil Maxwell, 'Words Whispered to Subconscious Supposedly Deter Thefts, Fainting', *Wall Street Journal*, 25 November 1989, p. 25; Fred Danzig, 'Relaxed Radio Soothes—But Subliminally', *Advertising Age*, 15 September 1980, p. 34; Bernie Whalen, 'Threshold Messaging Touted as Antitheft Measure', *Marketing News*, 15 March 1985, pp. 5–6; and 'Subliminal Ad Tactics: Experts Still Laughing', *Marketing News*, 15 March 1985, pp. 6–7.

87. 'Subliminal Messages Sneak into Mexican Ads', *Providence Sunday Journal*, 10 July 1988, p. A-5.

88. See Wilson Bryan Key, *Subliminal Seduction*, Prentice-Hall, Englewood Cliffs, NJ, 1973; Wilson Bryan Key, *Media Sexploitation*, Prentice-Hall, Engelwood Cliffs, NJ, 1976; and Wilson Bryan Key, *The Clomplate Orgy*, Prentice-Hall, Englewood Cliffs, NJ, 1980.

89. Judy Keen, 'Nevada Judge Will Decide Landmark Suit', *USA Today*, 16 July 1990, pp. 1–2.

90. Cleveland Horton, 'Toyota Double Talk', *Advertising Age*, 10 June 1991, p. 53.

91. See Del Hawkins, 'The Effects of Subliminal Stimulation on Drive Level and Brand Preference', *Journal of Marketing Research* 7, August 1970, pp. 322–6; John G. Caccavale, Thomas C. Wanty III & July A. Edell, 'Subliminal Implants in Advertisements: An Experiment', in Andrew Mitchell (ed.), *Advances in Consumer Research*, vol. 9, Association for Consumer Research, Ann Arbor, MI, 1982,

pp. 418–23; William E. Kilbourne, Scott Painton & Danny Ridley, 'The Effect of Sexual Embedding on Response to Magazine Advertisements', *Journal of Advertising* 14, 1985, pp. 48–56; Larry T. Patterson & Mary Ann Stutts, 'Subaudible Radio Messages: Did I Hear What I Think I Heard?', in David Klein & Allen Smith (eds), *Proceedings, Southern Marketing Association Conference*, Southern Marketing Association, 1985, pp. 20–2; Myron Gableet et al., 'An Evaluation of Subliminally Embedded Sexual Stimuli in Graphics', *Journal of Advertising* 16 (1), 1987, pp. 26–9; and Anthony G. Greenwald et al., 'Double Blind Tests of Subliminal Self-help Audiotapes', *Psychological Science* 2, March 1991, pp. 119–22; Timothy E. Moore, 'The Case Against Subliminal Manipulation', *Psychology & Marketing* 5, Winter 1988, pp. 297–316; Anthony R. Pratkanis & Anthony G. Greenwald, 'Recent Perspectives on Unconscious Processing: Still No Marketing Applications', *Psychology & Marketing* 5, Winter 1988, pp. 337–53; and Nicolaos E. Synodinos, 'Review and Appraisal of Subliminal Perception within the Context of Signal Detection Theory', *Psychology & Marketing* 5, Winter 1988, pp. 317–36.
92. Joel Saegert, 'Another Look at Subliminal Perception', *Journal of Advertising Research* 19, February 1979, pp. 55–7.
93. See Moore, op cit, Ref 82, pp. 38–47.

CHAPTER 11

LEARNING AND MEMORY

LEARNING OBJECTIVES

AFTER STUDYING THIS CHAPTER YOU SHOULD UNDERSTAND:

➡ the principal elements of learning;

➡ various ways learning can occur and the implications of this for understanding consumer behaviour;

➡ the role of behaviour modification in consumer behaviour;

➡ factors influencing consumers' rate and degree of learning and loss of learned material;

➡ the major characteristics and operating mechanisms of memory systems and their impact on consumers' behaviour.

Consumers' learning is an important component of their behaviour. Learning certainly occurs intentionally, as when a problem is recognised and information is acquired about products that might solve the problem. However, as our example illustrates, consumer learning also can occur unintentionally and this type of learning can strongly influence the behaviour of consumers.

One benefit of the learning mechanism is that consumers are able to adapt to a changing environment. Consequently, knowledge of learning principles can be useful in understanding how consumers' wants and motives are acquired, and how their tastes are developed. Also, appreciation of learning and memory processes can aid our understanding of how frequently to repeat advertising messages; how visual symbols, songs and other techniques can facilitate consumers' learning and memory regarding products and promotions; and how consumers develop habitual purchase patterns for some goods.

389

This chapter begins by defining learning and describing what it is that we learn. Secondly, major elements of the learning process are reviewed. Next, several ways by which consumers can learn are described and characterised, followed by a number of additional learning topics particularly useful for understanding the behaviour of consumers. Finally, consumers' memory and the process of forgetting are addressed.

CHARACTERISING LEARNING

Before going further, it is useful to adopt a definition of learning. Several introductory comments concerning the nature of learned material will also provide a beneficial foundation.

Learning defined

Very simply, learning can be viewed as a relatively permanent change in behaviour occurring as a result of experience. The implications of this definition are fairly subtle and therefore require some explanation.

First, as before, the term 'behaviour' is used to refer to non-observable cognitive activity as well as to overt actions. Therefore, it is possible for learning to occur without there being any change in observable behaviour. Changes in consumers' attitudes resulting from exposure to new information about a brand demonstrate this point. Secondly, learning results in relatively permanent changes in behaviour. This excludes changes brought about by fatigue or other short-lived influences such as drugs. Thirdly, as our definition of learning stresses experience, we must exclude the effects of physical damage to the body or brain, and of natural human growth.

Types of learned behaviour

Nearly every type of behaviour we exhibit as humans has been learned. The following paragraphs provide some specific examples.

PHYSICAL BEHAVIOUR

Generally, we learn many physical behaviour patterns useful in responding to a variety of situations faced in everyday life. For example, all healthy humans learn to walk, talk and interact with others. As consumers, we also learn methods of responding to various purchase situations. These may take the form of learning to act dissatisfied when hearing the first price quote on a car, or learning to read closely the fine print in purchase contracts. Consumers may also learn certain physical activity through the process termed *modelling*, in which they mimic the behaviour of other individuals, such as celebrities. This suggests the important influence of learned physical behaviour.

SYMBOLIC LEARNING AND PROBLEM SOLVING

People learn symbolic meanings that enable highly efficient communication through the development of languages. Symbols also allow marketers to communicate with consumers through such vehicles as brand names (Kodak and Sony), slogans ('We try harder' for Avis) and signs (McDonald's golden arches). As mentioned previously, the marketer intends for these symbols to connote positive images of the company to consumers as well as keeping the firm's name familiar to them.

Consumers can also engage in problem-solving learning by employing the processes of thinking and insight. *Thinking* involves the mental manipulation of symbols representing the real world to form various combinations of meaning. This often leads to *insight*, which is a new understanding of relationships involved in the problem. As we have noted, many consumer efforts can be viewed as problem-solving behaviour. One use of thinking and problem solving is that they enable consumers to evaluate mentally a wide variety of products without having to purchase them. For example, a person might be interested in a car burglar alarm but then begins to reflect on how the car is typically used—at home it is parked in a locked garage and at work it is left in a car park supervised by the company's security force. This may lead the person to conclude that for most of the time a burglar alarm is not going to be very useful, and the money would be better spent elsewhere.

AFFECTIVE LEARNING

Humans learn to value certain elements of their environment and dislike others. This means that consumers learn many of their wants, goals and motives, as well as what products satisfy these needs. Learning also influences consumers' development of favourable or unfavourable attitudes toward a company and its products. These attitudes will affect the tendency to purchase various brands.

We discovered in earlier chapters that consumers' interactions within a social system can have a significant influence on their learning of tastes. This is quite obvious for products such as whisky and tobacco, where it is said that one has to 'acquire a taste' for the product. However, the same process is at work regarding the vast majority of foods, clothes and other goods. The process that influences such learning includes sanctions and social pressure by group or family members.

The discussion of what we learn could easily fill the remaining pages of this chapter. However, it is more appropriate to turn our attention to the principal elements of learning and other issues of importance to the understanding of these processes. Before doing so, it should be mentioned that although much consumer learning occurs through direct experiences with the use of products and services, it would be incorrect for marketers to assume that these direct experiences are outside their area of influence. In fact, a number of opportunities exist for marketers to affect consumer learning through such direct product experiences.[1] To understand these options, marketers need to consider carefully how learning and memory factors influence consumers. We now turn our attention to these topics.

Principal elements of learning

As will be demonstrated shortly, consumers learn in several basic ways. However, four elements seem to be fundamental to the vast majority of situations: motive, cue, response and reinforcement.[2] The exact nature and strength of these components influence what will be learned, how well it will be learned and the rate at which learning will occur.

MOTIVE

As noted in Chapter 9, motives arouse individuals, thereby increasing their readiness to respond. This arousal function is essential, as it activates the energy needed to engage in learning activity. In addition, any success at achieving the motivating goal, or avoiding some unpleasant situation, tends to reduce arousal. Because this is reinforcing, such activity will have a greater tendency to occur again in similar situations. Thus, marketers strive to have their brand or its name available when relevant consumer motives are aroused, because it is expected that consumers will learn a connection between the product and motive. For this reason, we see advertisements for Goldair heaters shortly before winter and Coppertone suntan lotion during the summer.

CUES

A cue may be viewed as a stimulus not strong enough to arouse consumers, but capable of providing *direction* to motivated activity. That is, it influences the manner in which consumers respond to a motive. The shopping environment is packed with cues, such as promotions and product colours, which consumers can use to choose between various response options in a learning situation. For example, when we are hungry we are guided by certain cues, such as restaurant signs and the aroma of food cooking, because we have learned that these stimuli are associated with food preparation and consumption.

RESPONSE

A response may be viewed as a mental or physical activity the consumer makes in reaction to a stimulus situation. Responses appropriate to a particular situation are learned over time through experience in facing that situation. As we have noted, the occurrence of a response is not always observable. Therefore, it must again be emphasised that our inability to observe responses does not necessarily mean that learning is not taking place.

Chapter 9 introduced the concept of a motive hierarchy, and a similar situation exists for responses. Before learning occurs our innate characteristics order responses to a stimulus from the most likely to least likely response. Thus, a hungry baby is more likely to cry or exhibit sucking behaviour than to exhibit other responses. Over time, learning will modify the response hierarchy so that other responses have a greater chance of occurring. In this way, consumers are able to adapt to changing environmental conditions.

REINFORCEMENT

Perhaps the most widely acceptable view of reinforcement is anything that follows a response and increases the tendency for the response to recur in a similar situation.[3] Because reinforced behaviour tends to be repeated, consumers can learn to develop successful means of responding to their needs or changing conditions.

One important type of reinforcement is achieved through reducing motive arousal. This occurs through removing a *negative reinforcer* (something that generates discomfort and is avoided) or receiving a *positive reinforcer* (something that generates pleasure and is sought). An example of the former is taking an aspirin to relieve a headache, while the latter is exemplified by playing a sport for the fun of it. In either case, reducing motive arousal is reinforcing to the consumer. For example, drinking 7-Up on a hot day or purchasing a ticket for a ski weekend can both reduce motive arousal for the consumer.

In other situations, punishment through mental or physical discomfort is applied as a negative reinforcer. Such circumstances can result in learning to avoid something or to discontinue some behaviour pattern. All of these situations demonstrate that reinforcement is a general term that involves more than just receiving or giving rewards. It should be noted here that a number of learning experiments have not involved the introduction of positive or negative reinforcers.[4] Often it appears that just the accomplishment of a learning task is by itself a reinforcing experience. Thus, consumers may learn about products merely by mentally evaluating their relevance to solving consumption problems. Window-shopping activity and informal discussions with friends or salespeople may be aspects of such learning behaviour.

Another point to consider is that our behaviour can be reinforced so subtly that we may not even be aware that the reinforcement has occurred.[5] Simple social gestures such as a nod, smile or frown are often powerful in their influence. This type of behaviour can be observed in certain television commercial featuring a lead character who speaks directly to viewers while one or more other characters are seen engaged in some activity in the background. Close observation of these background players will sometimes reveal that they nod approval or use other body language to support important points the lead character is making. This suggests that consumers can be encouraged to develop attitudes and patterns of behaviour toward brands without becoming aware that such changes are occurring.

CLASSIFYING LEARNING

Various theories have been developed to explain different aspects of learning.[6] These theories, however, can be grouped into several major categories for the focus of our present discussion. As Figure 11.1 depicts, the first major division is between the connectionist and cognitive schools of thought. While *cognitive* interpretations place emphasis on the discovery of patterns and insight, *connectionists* argue that what humans learn are connections or associations between stimuli and responses. The connectionist school may be further subdivided on the basis of the type of conditioning employed. Each of these subdivisions will be discussed in turn.

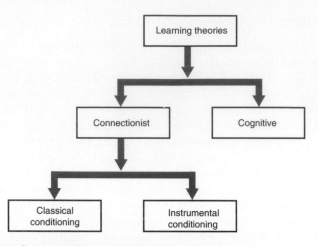

FIG. 11.1 A classification of learning theories

CONNECTIONIST THEORIES

Some learning theorists maintain that learning involves the development of connections between a stimulus and some response to it. That is, the association of a response and a stimulus is the connection that is learned.

Several members of this group minimise the importance of reinforcement to learning, while others stress its crucial role. We shall sidestep this debate by adopting the reinforcement viewpoint, because of its attractiveness in explaining consumers' learning behaviour.[7] Reinforcement is employed in conjunction with two fundamentally different methods of learning connections: classical and instrumental conditioning.

CLASSICAL CONDITIONING

Essentially, classical conditioning (sometimes called respondent conditioning) pairs one stimulus with another that already elicits a given response. Over repeated trials the new stimulus will also begin to elicit the same or a very similar response.

To appreciate the process involved, it is useful to review the experiment conducted by Pavlov, who pioneered study of classical conditioning.[8] Pavlov reasoned that because food already caused his dog to salivate, it might be possible to link a previously neutral stimulus to the food so that it too would make the dog salivate. This would demonstrate that the dog had learned to associate the neutral stimulus with the food. Pavlov used a bell as the neutral stimulus. His experiment is diagrammed in Figure 11.2.

The term 'unconditioned stimulus' is used for the food because conditioning is not required for it to cause the dog to salivate. This built-in stimulus–response connection is represented by the solid arrow. Because the salivating response also does not require learning, it is termed the 'unconditioned response'. The bell is referred to as the 'conditioned stimulus', because conditioning is required to learn a connection between it and the food. Pavlov accomplished this by ringing the bell every time he presented the dog with food. After a significant number of conditioning trials the dog learned a connection between the bell and the food. In fact, the association was strong enough for the bell alone to become capable of causing the dog to salivate. The dotted arrow connecting the bell and the food symbolises the learned connection between these stimuli, and the second dotted arrow indicates that the bell can now cause the dog to salivate.

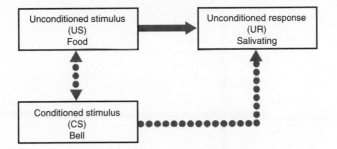

FIG. 11.2   A representation of classical conditioning

In this situation a natural reflex of salivating to food was employed as the unconditioned stimulus. It is important to note, however, that classical conditioning does not require use of reflexive stimuli, and the dog could now be conditioned to a new stimulus by using the bell as the unconditioned stimulus. Learning new associations between stimuli in this manner is termed *second-order conditioning*. Because evidence suggests that humans are capable of even further levels of conditioning, this concept is more generally referred to as higher order conditioning.[9]

Higher order conditioning can be useful for understanding how consumers acquire secondary motives that were described in Chapter 9.[10] Here, goals that once had no motivating abilities can become associated with reinforcing stimuli and take on motivating properties themselves. For example, the achievement motive may be acquired by a child because rewarding praise was given to him or her for accomplishing certain tasks. Later this achievement motive can influence the purchase of various products to assist in accomplishing tasks.

INSTRUMENTAL CONDITIONING

The method of instrumental conditioning (also called operant conditioning) also involves developing connections between stimuli and responses, but the process involved differs from classical conditioning in several important respects. Although classical conditioning relies on an already established stimulus–response connection, instrumental conditioning requires the learner to discover an appropriate 'correct' response—one that will be reinforced.

The principles of this type of learning can best be illustrated by employing the same 'box' that B. F. Skinner made famous with his pioneering work in the area.[11] Assume that we place a pigeon in a box. On one wall is a button that when pressed will deliver food to the pigeon. In this case, the button is the conditioned stimulus. When placed in the box, the pigeon can respond in a variety of ways, shown as R_1 through R_n in Figure 11.3. Eventually it will push button R_3, receive the food and eat it with great enjoyment. Here, the food, which represents a positive reinforcer, is the unconditioned stimulus.

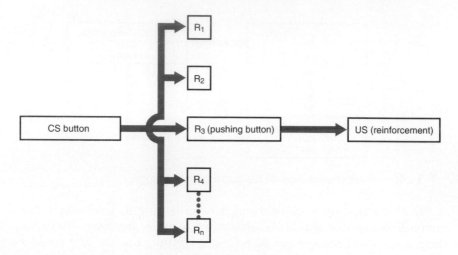

FIG. 11.3   A representation of instrumental conditioning

Most likely, the pigeon will not immediately associate pushing the button with receiving the food. Other responses will occur, but only a push of the button will lead to reinforcement. Therefore, over a number of reinforced trials the pigeon will learn a connection between the stimulus (button) and response (pushing). This can lead to very rapid repetition of the process—perhaps until the bird becomes ill from consuming too much food, which, as we know, also leads to learning.

DISTINCTIONS BETWEEN CONDITIONING METHODS

A number of distinctions can be made between classical (respondent) and instrumental (operant) conditioning. Three of the most important ones are summarised in Table 11.1. Note that while classical conditioning is dependent on an already established connection, instrumental conditioning requires the learner to discover the appropriate response. For this reason, instrumental conditioning involves the learner at a more conscious and purposeful level than does classical conditioning.[12]

A second distinction between these two methods concerns the *outcome* of the learning situation. In classical conditioning the outcome is not dependent on the learner's actions, but with instrumental conditioning a particular response can change the learner's situation or environment. The response then is *instrumental* in producing reinforcement or making something happen in the environment; hence the name for this type of conditioning.

TABLE 11.1   Important distinctions between classical and instrumental conditioning

Classical (respondent) conditioning

1. It involves an already established response to another stimulus.
2. The outcome is not dependent on the learner's actions.
3. It influences development and changes in opinions, tastes and goals.

Instrumental (operant) conditioning

1. No previous stimulus–response connection is necessary.
2. The learner must discover an appropriate response.
3. The outcome is dependent on the learner's actions.
4. It influences changes in goal-directed behaviour.

Source: Based on David Krech et al., *Psychology: A Basic Course*, Knopf, New York, 1976, pp. 50–61.

Because of the above differences, each conditioning method is suited to explaining different types of learning. Learning to adapt and control one's environment is better explained by instrumental conditioning, because it requires that the learner discover the response that leads to reinforcement. Alternatively, classical conditioning is often more useful in explaining how consumers learn brand names and acquire or change their opinions, tastes and goals. That is, the material to be learned in such cases is associated with stimuli that already elicit favourable or unfavourable experiences.

Cognitive interpretations

Instead of viewing learning as the development of connections between stimuli and responses, cognitive theorists stress the importance of perception, problem solving and insight. This viewpoint contends that much learning occurs not as a result of trial-and-error or practice but through discovering meaningful patterns that enable us to solve problems. These meaningful patterns are termed *gestalts*, and were discussed in Chapter 10. Cognitive theories of learning rely heavily on the process of insight to explain the development of gestalts.

Wolfgang Kohler's work with apes provides an interesting example to understand better this view of learning.[13] In one experiment, he placed a chimpanzee in a cage with a box, and hung bananas from the top of the cage beyond reach even if the chimp jumped. After failing to reach the food, the chimp suddenly solved the problem by placing the box under the bananas and jumping from it to reach the food. This suggested that the chimp's learning was not a result of trial-and-error, but a consequence of deliberation and sudden insight into a solution. This feeling of insight is familiar to all of us when we suddenly 'see' the solution to a problem situation.

Although the chimp in Kohler's experiment was rewarded by reaching the bananas, the reward is not so apparent in many cognitive learning situations. For example, no observable reward is present when the student solves a difficult problem in statistics. However, the concept of *closure* is viewed as having important reinforcing properties in the cognitive viewpoint. As long as an individual has not solved a problem, a state of incompleteness produces tension to motivate continued search for a solution. Problem solution results in closure, which reduces the motivating tension and is reinforcing.

Applying alternative learning concepts to consumer behaviour

We should not be dismayed by alternative explanations of how consumers learn. In fact, it is useful to have these alternatives, as the nature of what consumers learn probably influences the method they use to learn it.

As we have noted, cognitive interpretations stress problem-solving behaviour and the learners' active understanding of situations confronting them. It is not 'blind' or rote behaviour, as the learning of connections can be. This view is therefore most useful in understanding how consumers learn which stores, methods of shopping or products will best meet their needs. For example, it can take the form of learning about the uses and benefits of products new to the market, especially if they represent significant innovations. It can also explain how consumers learn about existing products for which they have developed a recent interest or need.[14] In either case, this type of learning is not a simple process of consumers discovering the objective 'truth' about products or services. It is influenced by how consumers perceive the problem at hand and their familiarity with the information they confront. This is especially so when consumers confront information in the environment that is vague or confusing.[15]

Connectionist theories of learning are appropriate to understanding a variety of other aspects of consumer behaviour. As has already been noted, classical conditioning is useful for explaining how consumers acquire tastes and motives. Advertisers also employ the concept by showing their brands in pleasant, exciting or otherwise emotionally positive surroundings. For example, beers and other cold drinks are often shown in refreshing swimming-pool or beach settings, and fast-food products are often shown being consumed in fun-filled social gatherings. Here, the concept of classical conditioning applies to the advertiser's plan for repeated association of a brand with the positive surroundings, which will lead to consumers developing a preference toward the brand.

Figure 11.4, which parallels Figure 11.2, suggests how this would occur using a happy situation as the unconditioned stimulus. The setting (such as a family gathering) is selected because it already elicits pleasant feelings from

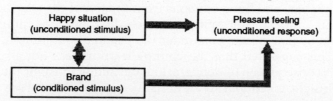

 **FIG. 11.4** *How classical conditioning can be used to develop pleasant feelings towards an advertised brand*

An advertising example of the use of classical conditioning
COURTESY OF ACI NEW ZEALAND GLASS MANUFACTURERS

consumers—the unconditioned response. Repeated association of the brand with this setting will enable the brand itself to generate similar pleasant feelings. This should increase consumers' preferences for it.

The ACI glass ad shows how bottle shapes have become associated with products—the shape is the conditioned stimulus to evoke product and sensations. Recent consumer research in universities and for advertisers such as Coca-Cola has suggested that this type of advertising strategy has considerable potential for influencing consumers' brand preferences.[16] However, additional investigation indicates that the associations fostered by such advertisements are not very strong after the consumer has had only a small number of advertising exposures.[17] Other research suggests that more investigation is needed to explore fully the usefulness of classical conditioning to advertising applications.[18]

Certain types of habitual behaviour are also explained through classical, or respondent, conditioning. For example, many consumers automatically purchase particular brands such as Sellotape for sticky tape because they have developed strong associations between the brand name and the generic product. In other examples, people talk about 'Xeroxing' when they mean taking a photocopy, or 'Hoovering' when they mean using a vacuum cleaner. This is often an advantage accruing to marketers who first develop a product that dominates the market. In still other cases, consumers habitually purchase particular brands merely because their parents did. Here, consumers often have made such a strong association between a particular brand and an activity or a need that they may give little consideration to the brand's suitability.

Instrumental, or operant, conditioning is useful for understanding consumer learning where conscious choices resulting in positive or negative reinforcement are made. The obvious case is consumers' purchase and evaluation of products. Favourable experiences will result in positive reinforcement of the particular choice. Of course, learning to avoid certain products because of negative reinforcement from bad experiences with them is also possible. This is strong justification for the marketer's stress on satisfying the customer.

Advertisements depicting satisfied buyers can also result in consumers learning a connection between a brand and favourable experiences. Other types of promotional efforts, including cash rebates, free product samples, trial periods or low introductory prices, also make use of instrumental conditioning. The goal is to structure a situation so that consumers are given rewards as a consequence of having performed an activity that is desired by the marketer.

Many other applications of both cognitive and connectionist learning could be cited. However, we now turn our attention to other useful concepts of consumer learning.

ADDITIONAL CONSUMER-LEARNING CONCEPTS

A number of other aspects of learning have importance for those interested in the behaviour of consumers. Although the following topics by no means exhaust the list of useful concepts, they are representative of the ways in which learning concepts can be used to understand consumers.

The behaviour-modification perspective

The emphasis in a behaviour-modification perspective (BMP) of learning is on a set of intervention techniques designed to influence the behaviour of individuals. That is, focus is placed on how environmental events (stimuli, reinforcements and the like) can be modified to bring about changes in the way people act.[19] In fact, a segment of BMP advocates, containing those who are referred to as 'behaviourists', completely discards the role of internal psychological processes (such as needs, attitudes) and the concept of learning when studying behavioural changes in people. Behaviourists argue that it is sufficient just to consider changes in behaviour and the environmental events that appear capable of influencing such behaviour, rather than also attempting to *explain* what internal forces within the individual relate these two events together. A less radical view, which is adopted here, proposes retaining explanations of internal processes and blending them with consideration of environmental influences.[20] Therefore, we will view the BMP as having a distinct focus but sharing certain principles, such as conditioning and reinforcement, with theories of learning that also incorporate internal psychological processes to explain behaviour.

Several areas of environmental influence can be considered as within the BMP domain: classical (respondent) conditioning, instrumental (operant) conditioning, modelling and ecological design. Both classical and instrumental conditioning have already been discussed. The examples given for classical conditioning were sufficient to demonstrate how environmental variables could be used to influence consumers' behaviour. Although examples were also provided for instrumental conditioning, it is useful to discuss five additional topics in this area (reinforcement schedules, shaping, discrimination, modelling and ecological design) to show how they can be used to influence behaviour change.

REINFORCEMENT SCHEDULES

It is not necessary to reinforce every 'correct' response in order for learning to occur. Different reinforcement schedules, however, lead to different patterns of learning. *Continuous-reinforcement* schedules, which reward every correct response, yield rapid changes in behaviour. Conversely, *partial-reinforcement* schedules yield a slower rate, but also result in learning that is more permanent in nature. This may at least partially explain why consumers' negative attitudes toward brands are usually very difficult to reverse. That is, negative attitudes can be acquired through partial reinforcement because a few unsatisfactory experiences with a brand can occur over a period of time. This can result in consumers being highly resistant to positive information about the brand, especially if the marketer is the source of such information.

In a different vein, partial-reinforcement schedules can also represent an economical alternative for marketers. Because many marketing forms of reinforcement (such as free gifts and special offers) can cost considerable sums of money, finding a way to cause changes in consumers' behaviour without having to reward every learning experience represents an attractive opportunity.

SHAPING

The term 'shaping' refers to influencing a large change in behaviour over time by reinforcing successively closer approximations to that behaviour. The thinking behind the idea of shaping is described by an ancient proverb: 'A journey of a thousand miles is started with but a single step.' That is, although it might be very difficult to achieve a rather large or complex change in consumers' behaviour in one step, a series of smaller changes leading to the same end point may be much less difficult.

An example of shaping would be to offer consumers special prizes to visit a retail store over several weeks and, while they are there, encouraging them to purchase items by using discounts, special sales or rebates. The behaviour of travelling to the store is rewarded, and purchasing at the store is also reinforced. In this way it is expected that consumers will adopt the behaviour of regularly shopping at the store after the special reinforcements are withdrawn. Many similar examples of shaping exist in the selling and consumer-behaviour area.

DISCRIMINATION

Learning to discriminate between various objects or events is important for consumers, because it helps them to adapt to their environment. Discrimination is learned over time when the same response to two similar but noticeably different stimuli leads to different consequences (reinforcement). Stimuli that the consumer can use to distinguish between various items in their environment are often termed *discriminative stimuli*.

Consumers make frequent use of discrimination learning. New or different brands as well as different models within the same producer's line must be distinguished, even though they might differ in only a few features. Products that provide rewarding service must also be distinguished from those that are relatively inferior. Of course, a great deal of marketing effort encourages such discrimination learning. Here, the goal is to reinforce consumers' attention to the uniqueness of a brand. In fact, brand names, logos and trademarks are quite useful discriminative stimuli, but unique colours, shapes and packages also have utility. In another quite different and interesting case, patrons of a small retail shop were personally telephoned and thanked for shopping at the store. Reaction to this *distinctive* reinforcement was very favourable—sales increased 27 per cent during the test period.[21] This attests to the impact of reinforcement on consumers' discrimination learning.

MODELLING

The term 'modelling' refers to learning that occurs as a result of the individual observing both the behaviour of others and the consequences of that behaviour. This can lead to the learning of new behaviour, a change or strengthening of existing behavioural tendencies or the facilitation of previously learned responses.

In the marketing discipline, demonstrations, advertisements and other promotional means can be used to develop the appropriate modelling scenarios. In fact, the technique is employed quite extensively for some of today's most successful products.[22] The usual procedure is to produce a television advertisement that depicts one or more individuals engaging in certain behaviour and receiving a reinforcement. The reinforcement can be in the form of social approval or avoidance of embarrassment, or in the form of direct product benefits or satisfactions. Examples include consumers avoiding problems because they took the right kind of health insurance as promoted by Medibank Private in Australia and Susan Devoy in New Zealand, and people chewing gum to eliminate social embarrassment caused by onion and garlic breath.

ECOLOGICAL DESIGN

The concept of ecological design involves a deliberate attempt to manipulate aspects of the environment to achieve changes in behaviour. Building and landscape architects have made extensive use of ecological principles for the purpose of directing traffic patterns, focusing office work flow and achieving crowd control. However, similar principles have also been used in the field of marketing. Consider the efforts made to design nightclubs as exciting environments, as well as the placement of displays and demonstrations in central areas of shopping malls to attract shoppers' attention and influence their purchase behaviour. Perhaps more obvious examples would include the physical layout of supermarkets to encourage high shopper exposure to a wide variety of merchandise, and the use of racks at checkout counters to display a variety of convenience or 'impulse' items to the waiting customer.

The potential of ecological design for affecting the behaviour of consumers is considerable. For example, in one study the tempo of background music was found to influence the pace with which consumers walked through the store—faster music resulted in a faster pace. Also, consumers treated to slower paced music were found to spend significantly more than those treated to music with a faster tempo.[23] We can expect other advances in this field, especially those directed at the use of design to influence consumers' moods, perceptions and attitudes.

The above comments have provided only a brief review of the BMP, which grew out of work by B. F. Skinner and other behaviourally oriented psychologists. A few examples were given of its application to the field of marketing. Table 11.2 presents an excellent summary of additional areas of application and methods for their achievement.

It should be mentioned that the BMP has not enjoyed a high level of awareness and appreciation among those interested in marketing or the behaviour of consumers. Despite this, many of the practical marketing tactics that have been developed without knowledge of the field appear to be quite consistent with it. As the perspective achieves wider exposure and effort is devoted to exploring its marketing applications, further insights should lead to the development of more effective tactics. Also, when combined with more internally oriented viewpoints, the perspective could prove quite beneficial in describing how the purchase–consumption process works.[24]

Stimulus generalisation

When a given response to a stimulus has been learned, it will tend to be elicited not only by the original stimulus involved in the learning situation but also by stimuli that are similar to it. This process, called *stimulus generalisation*, appears to occur automatically unless stopped by discrimination learning.[25] Stimulus generalisation simplifies the consumer's life, because it means that learning a unique response to every stimulus is not necessary. One response can be used for similar stimuli unless there is some important reason to learn to discriminate between them.

The *gradient of generalisation* relates the degree of similarity between two stimuli to the likelihood that both will generate the same response. It has been found that the greater the resemblance between a given stimulus and another that already causes a response, the greater the chance that it will generate the same response.[26] Conversely, the more dissimilar two stimuli are, the smaller the likelihood of stimulus generalisation occurring. As noted in Chapter 10, some producers of private brands make use of the gradient concept by packaging products to closely resemble national brands. Other firms 'ride the coat-tails' of success of pioneering companies by offering highly similar products. The sudden appearance of various caffeine-free soft drinks and sugarless gums are cases in point.

TABLE 11.2   Some illustrative applications of the behaviour-modification perspective in marketing

A. Some applications of respondent-conditioning principles		

1. Conditioning responses to new stimuli

Unconditioned or previously conditioned stimulus	Conditioned stimulus	Examples
Exciting event	A product or theme song	Gilette theme song followed by sports event
Patriotic events or music	A product or person	Patriotic music as background in political commercial

2. Use of familiar stimuli to elicit responses

Conditioned stimulus	Conditioned response(s)	Examples
Familiar music	Relaxation, excitement, 'good will'	Christmas music in retail store
Familiar social cues	Excitement, attention, anxiety	Sirens sounding or telephones ringing in commercials

B. Some applications of operant conditioning principles	

1. Rewards for desired behaviour (continuous schedules)

Desired behaviour	Reward given following behaviour
Product purchase	Trading stamps, cash bonus or rebate, prizes, coupons

2. Rewards for desired behaviour (partial schedules)

Desired behaviour	Reward given following behaviour
Product purchase	Prize for every second or third etc. purchase Prize to a fraction of people who purchase

3. Shaping

Approximation of desired response	Consequence following approximation	Final response desired
Opening a charge account	Prizes etc. for opening account	Expenditure of funds
Trip to point-of-purchase location	Loss leaders, entertainment or event at the shopping centre	Purchase of products
Product trial	Free product and/or some bonus for using	Purchase of product

continues

TABLE 11.2 Some illustrative applications of the behaviour-modification perspective in marketing *continued*

4. Discriminative stimuli

Desired behaviour	Reward signal	Examples
Entry into store	Store signs Store logos	50% off sale K-mart's big red 'K'
Brand purchase	Distinctive brandmarks	Levi tag

C. Some applications of modelling principles

Modelling employed	Desired response
Instructor, expert, salesperson using product (in ads or at point-of-purchase)	Use of product in technically competent way
Models in ads asking questions at point-of-purchase	Ask questions at point-of-purchase that highlight product advantages
Models in ads receiving positive reinforcement for product purchase or use	Increase product purchase and use
Models in ads receiving no reinforcement or receiving punishment for performing undesired behaviours	Extinction of or decrease in undesired behaviours

D. Some applications of ecological modification principles

Environmental design	Specific example	Intermediate behaviour	Final desired behaviour
Store layout	End of escalator, end-aisle, other displays	Bring a customer into visual contact with product	Product purchase
In-store mobility	In-store product directories, information booths	Bring consumer into visual contact with product	Product purchase
Noises, scents, lights	Flashing lights in store window	Bring consumer into visual or other sensory contact with store or product	Product purchase

Source: Adapted from Walter R. Nord & J. Paul Peter, 'A Behavior Modification Perspective on Marketing', *Journal of Marketing* 44, Spring 1980, pp. 42–3, published by the American Marketing Association.

The generalisation gradient also helps us to understand the marketing approach of introducing 'new' products that often bear a considerable resemblance to their predecessors. This encourages consumers to generalise learned attitudes and preferences from the old product to the new model. The family brand strategy and brand extensions employ similar methods. Here, the family brand name is prominently associated with the new product, as in the case of a General Motors car or a Panasonic radio. The intention is that consumers' favourable perceptions and attitudes about the family name will be generalised to the new product. Of course, the danger of such a strategy is that unfavourable experiences on the part of consumers with one product in the family line may lead to generalising poor impressions toward the entire group of products.

Rate and degree of learning

Learning of all but the simplest tasks appears to follow a rather common pattern, which has become known as a *learning curve*. A typical curve is displayed in Figure 11.5, where the amount learned is measured on the Y-axis and the number of practice trials is shown on the X-axis. The characteristic shape of this curve demonstrates that the rate of learning is quite rapid during initial stages. However, in later stages, as the amount learned accumulates, the rate of additional learning per trial decreases. This demonstrates the highly effective nature of practice in early stages of learning and its diminishing effect in later trials. It also demonstrates that even though the rate of learning is high initially, many practice trials are needed to ensure a large amount of total learning.

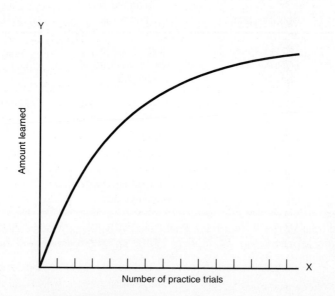

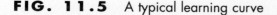
Number of practice trials

FIG. 11.5 A typical learning curve

It is important to note that repetition of an advertisement appears to lead to a learning curve similar to the one in Figure 11.5.[27] In these cases, the number of times the advertising message is repeated is measured along the X-axis and the extent of consumers' learning of the message is measured along the Y-axis. Of course, marketers must determine whether this general pattern fits their particular products and situations.[28] For example, it may not describe learning in some low-involvement situations in which fewer repetitions might be necessary for storing simple facts, such as brand names, away in memory.[29] Where the curve is appropriate, there are several implications regarding the use of advertising to encourage consumer learning. First, as the curve demonstrates, a marketer must be willing to repeat an advertising message a significant number of times. This is also why a brand name may be repeated several times in just one advertisement. Secondly, the curve demonstrates that after repeating messages many times, the marketer is paying for small increases in consumer learning. Further, evidence suggests that advertising messages are subject to *wearout* and manipulation by audience members. That is, as the number of message repetitions increases, boredom can result, inattention can increase, and audience members may switch from rehearsing the message to generating and attending to their own less positive thoughts about the message.[30] This type of evidence might tempt the marketer to stop advertising after a time. However, as will be demonstrated shortly, if a message is not repeated, consumers tend to forget most of it very rapidly. This indicates the need to repeat advertisements merely to *maintain* consumers' level of learning. One strategy that might reduce wearout and other negative consequences of repetition is to repeat the basic content of an advertising message while periodically changing the method of doing so. As well as maintaining consumer interest such variety has the advantage of encouraging consumers to engage in deeper processing of the basic message in order to facilitate learning and memory.[31] It may also encourage positive feelings toward the brand.[32] In addition, one study found that when consumers have little motivation to process the advertisement, small 'cosmetic' changes (colour, background and so on) in the basic ad led to greater attitude change. But when motivation to process the ad was high, variation in emphasis on different important product features, as a means of changing ad elements while maintaining the basic theme, had the greatest influence on consumers' attitudes.[33] Means of accomplishing such a strategy include using different spokespeople, employing various beginnings and endings to the ads, and adopting different themes, scenarios or backgrounds for the message. Close attention to advertisements on television will reveal that such techniques are employed.

Although the foregoing general patterns of consumer learning appear to exist, a number of variables influence the rate and strength of the process. One of these factors is briefly reviewed below.

PRACTICE SCHEDULES

If only the time actually spent on a learning task is considered, periods of practice separated by rest intervals achieve much more efficient learning in many situations than do learning periods with no rest. The term *distributed practice* refers to learning sessions with rest periods, while learning without rest periods is known as *massed practice*. Aside from its obvious relevance to students' study habits, practice schedules have implications regarding the proper scheduling of advertising messages over time. Given that distributed practice is an effective learning technique, the marketer is interested in the optimum time interval to plan between advertising repetitions in order to generate the greatest amount of consumer learning. This has sparked a considerable amount of research in the advertising field.[34]

Extinction

We can 'unlearn' material or behaviour that has been previously learned. This unlearning process is termed *extinction* and occurs when, over time, a learned response is made to a stimulus but reinforcement does not occur. The greater the number of non-reinforced trails, the less likely the response is to occur; but complete extinction is rare. Also, *spontaneous recovery*—the sudden reappearance of an extinguished response—reduces the chance of complete extinction. Resistance to extinction also strengthens when:

1. impelling motives are strong;

2. the number of previously reinforced trials is large;

3. the amount of reward during learning trials is large;

4. reward is delayed during the learning process;

5. a partial reinforcement schedule occurs during learning.

Resistance to extinction at least partially explains why consumers are slow to change many tastes, shopping patterns and consumption habits. For example, many find it difficult to reduce or eliminate sweets, coffee or smoking. Similarly, others who have developed strong brand or store loyalties over time resist making changes, even if their regular brands or stores are not currently providing the rewards they once did. This poses a great challenge to marketers attempting to draw patronage away from competition.

Forgetting

It is important to distinguish between extinction and the process of forgetting. Extinction will occur when a previously learned response continues to be made but is no longer reinforced. *Forgetting* can be defined as the loss of retained material because of non-use or interference from some other learning task. As can be inferred from this definition, *retention* is the amount of previously learned material that is remembered.[35]

The process of forgetting, and how it can be minimised, has been of more concern to marketers than has extinction. This is so not only because it is a more significant problem, but also because marketers can influence the proces by repeating advertising messages to encourage consumers' retention. To determine the extent of their success, they employ various measures of advertising retention. The two most commonly used methods are:

1. *Recall*. The consumer tells an interviewer the advertisement she remembers seeing recently. She may not be prompted at all (unaided recall), or may be given some guidance (aided recall) such as the product category involved.

2. *Recognition*. The consumer is presented with an advertisement or series of advertisements and is asked to indicate which ones he has seen recently.

Both methods of measuring retention are used frequently but, as shown in Figure 11.6, the level of retention as measured by recognition is typically greater than indicated by the recall method. Of course, the most appropriate technique will depend on promotional goals and the specific situation, such as the type of product involved. However, the marketing manager must be aware of which technique is being employed to evaluate properly the success of the promotional effort.

Note from Figure 11.6 that, regardless of the measure of retention used, the fastest rate of forgetting occurs soon after learning has occurred. As the time since the last learning trial increases, forgetting continues, but its rate slows considerably. This was dramatically demonstrated in one marketing experiment in which the percentage of people who could remember a specific advertisement dropped by 50 per cent only four weeks after the last repetition.[36]

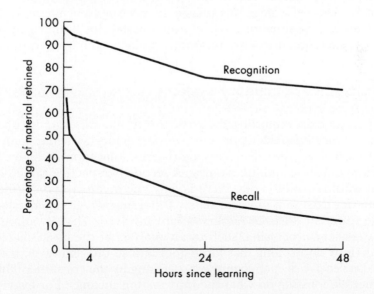

FIG. 11.6 A graph showing loss of retention as measured by recognition and recall methods   Source: C. W. Luh, 'The Conditions of Retention', *Psychological Monographs* 31, 1922, pp. 1–87.

The characteristic shape of retention curves explains the marketer's concern for repeating advertisements to combat the forgetting process. However, designing effective methods to minimise forgetting requires some understanding of human memory. We now turn our attention to this topic.

MEMORY

As everyone's experience has demonstrated, material that consumers have 'learned' is not always readily retrievable by them. Some information, such as popular brand names or the location of merchandise in a supermarket, is easily 'remembered'. Other information appears to end up lost, or at least it does not appear to be readily obtainable. This section of the chapter focuses on the structure and operation of consumers' memory. The discussion picks up where we left off in the information-processing chapter. Here we are concerned with the storage and retrieval of information after it has been acquired and has undergone initial processing.

Memory processes are of considerable importance to the understanding of consumers. This is so because, to a large extent, consumers act on the basis of their *cognitions* (their knowledge or beliefs about the world), which are stored in memory and influence how incoming stimuli are interpreted. Cognitions also form the basis for attitudes, behavioural intentions and brand choice, which are treated in the next two chapters. On a more concrete level, consider the goal of a marketer who strives to have consumers retain a brand name or information about it. The challenge is great because there are thousands of different brands advertised on a national or regional scale in Australasia. In more densely populated countries with larger markets the situation may be even tougher for brand managers. In a very real sense, each brand vies for a prominent place in consumers' memory.[37]

Characteristics of memory systems

Several views exist regarding the structure of memory and its operation.[38] One, termed the *multiple-store* approach, views memory as being composed of three distinct storage registers (sensory, short-term, long-term), which differ in capacity, storage duration and functioning. A second perspective, which has been quite popular until recently, is that there is only one memory and distinct storage registers do not exist in a physical sense. Different storage registers appear to exist because different *levels of processing* are involved. That is, stimuli can receive shallow sensory processing, such as an analysis of the basic characteristics of a new car (four doors, long, has large boot and so on). However, the same stimuli might also receive deeper cognitive processing by the consumer. This involves the consumer elaborating on what the information means.[39] For example, the shape of a car may lead the consumer to consider how many people it can seat comfortably, how much luggage it can hold, how fast it might go and how good its fuel economy might be. Different levels of processing exist because humans have limited processing capacity to allocate across a variety of incoming stimuli. Also, information receiving deep levels of processing will enjoy a more complex and longer lasting memory, while shallow processing is likely to result in only temporary storage.

A third conception of memory, called the *activation model,* also makes use of the single-memory-store concept.[40] In this currently popular view, consumers are seen as having one large memory store, but at any given time only a portion of that memory can be activated into what we might think of as 'working memory' that is available for use by the consumer. The result is that at any moment only a fraction of memory can be used by the consumer. Consequently, the remaining portions that are not activated will not be available to recall material held in memory or to help process incoming information.

Information the consumer confronts often serves to activate portions of memory that hold material related to the situation at hand. For example, when viewing a sporty-looking car, the consumer is likely to activate memory elements related to sports-car attributes such as style and performance. Information about other sports cars is also likely to be activated. As this information is related to additional material the consumer also holds in memory, the other information is also likely to be activated. This chain-reaction type of activation across related memory elements is termed *spreading activation*. Of course, what memory elements are 'related' is determined by the consumer's personal experiences. Also, activation is only temporary, which means that the portion of memory dealing with incoming information will not stay active unless effort is expended to maintain it.

It has been argued that although the three models of memory are distinct in terms of their emphasis, they are not necessarily incompatible.[41] For example, one could view short-term memory in the multiple-store model as that part of memory which is being *activated* and performing a certain function at a given *level* of processing. Other points of commonality can also be found. Therefore, although there are limitations in taking the multiple-store viewpoint, for purposes of exposition, we shall discuss memory in terms of this model.[42]

We must be careful to note, however, that each component should *not* be viewed as a physically separate entity, but as a distinct process, or functioning, of memory that has certain unique characteristics. The diagram in Figure 11.7 showing the three components—sensory, short-term and long-term memory—will facilitate our discussion.

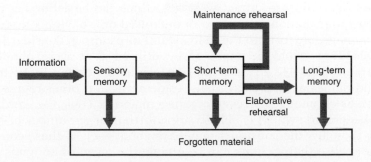

FIG. 11.7 A representation of memory systems

SENSORY MEMORY

As Figure 11.7 shows, information is first received by sensory memory. Input is in the form of sensations that have been produced by the sensory receptors. Memory registers exist for sensations being produced through the visual, auditory and other sense organs. The capacity of these registers is very large—they are capable of storing all that the sensory receptors transmit. They also appear to represent this information faithfully in forms that closely resemble the stimuli themselves. A good illustration of the nature of these representations is the after-image we 'see' in our 'mind's eye' immediately after observing an object and closing our eyes. This example also illustrates the duration of sensory memory. Information is stored for only a fraction of a second and will be lost through decay (fading away), unless sufficient attention is allocated to it so that it can be analysed and transferred to short-term memory for further processing. This initial information analysis is conducted in terms of physical characteristics (such as size, colour, shape), which is the process of feature analysis described in Chapter 10. Advertisers concentrate a great deal of effort on designing stimuli in their ads to be vivid and easily recognised in order to draw attention and to provide strong sensory impressions for consumers.

SHORT-TERM MEMORY

To a large extent, short-term memory can be viewed as the work space for information processing. That is, it is a portion of memory activated to temporarily store and process information in order to interpret it and comprehend its meaning. This is accomplished by combining incoming information with other information (past experiences, knowledge and the like) stored in long-term memory. The reader should refer back to the previous chapter on information processing to re-emphasise some of the points in this section.

Although the duration of this memory register is considerably longer than that of the sensory register, it still is very brief, lasting less than one minute. The capacity of short-term memory is also quite limited. Approximately seven items or groupings of items are all that can be sorted at any one time.[43]

Material residing in short-term memory does not bear a one-to-one correspondence with the real world. Instead, the process of *coding* is used to organise information into a more easily handled and remembered format. The primary method of this coding is termed *chunking*, which can be defined as the method of assembling information into a type of organised unit having a more understandable or manageable form to the individual. For example, consider how the number 1800432251 could be more easily utilised if it were chunked into the configuration 1800 432 251 as a toll-free telephone number in Australia.

Brand names as well as symbols, trademarks and other representations can also serve as chunking devices to organise material. Thus, the word 'McDonald's' or the Mastercard symbol is able to bring forth a large number of informational items or thoughts the consumer may have about each of these companies. Also, when we realise that a chunk can be among the seven or so items a person can simultaneously hold in short-term memory, we should appreciate that the capacity of seven items or chunks is not as limited as one might initially suspect.

It appears that to employ the chunking process an individual must be prepared to receive the incoming information. For example, a radio advertisement involving a telephone number should alert consumers that a number will be mentioned so that they will be prepared to chunk it into an exchange plus a four-digit number. Without such preparation, the material may be forgotten before chunking can be used. In addition, the telephone number should be announced in chunked form to facilitate memory.

As Figure 11.7 demonstrates, rehearsal is required to maintain information in short-term memory or to transfer it to long-term memory. If rehearsal does not occur, the information will be forgotten through the process of decay. However, it appears that the type of rehearsal involved differs depending on whether the goal is to retain material in short-term memory for additional processing or to transfer it to long-term memory. The process of *maintenance rehearsal* involves the continual repeating of information so that it can be held in short-term memory.[44] For example, after hearing a new brand name of interest, the consumer might keep on repeating it silently until able to write it down. The type of rehearsal used to transfer information to long-term memory is frequently called *elaborative rehearsal*, because it appears to involve relating the new information to prior experiences and knowledge in order to derive meaning from it. This is considered to entail 'deeper' levels of processing rather than mere repetition of the information.

LONG-TERM MEMORY

This memory system can be thought of as the relatively permanent storehouse for information that has undergone sufficient processing. Material can be maintained in long-term memory from as little as a few minutes to as long as many years. In addition, this system has the capacity to store an almost unlimited amount of information.

A predominant key to coding material for storage in long-term memory is *meaningfulness*, the personal understanding an individual can derive from the information. That is, through elaborative rehearsal individuals use their existing knowledge to interpret incoming information and code it in a way that is consistent with their existing cognitive structures (knowledge bases). The degree of success in accomplishing this will affect how well the new information can be retained and made available for future use.[45]

Some people claim that we never really forget anything that has been transferred to long-term memory.[46] Instead, they argue, what is forgotten is the key that tells us where the material is located in our memory. Of course, such a position is difficult to prove or disprove. We therefore will sidestep this issue by expanding the term 'forgetting' to refer to a general inability to access material that has been stored in long-term memory. Given this, we can now state that material, instead of just decaying over time, appears to be forgotten from long-term memory as a result of other learning interfering with retention of that material. The interference concept holds that material can be forgotten in two basic ways. In *retroactive inhibition*, new learning interferes with material already in long-term memory and the material in memory is forgotten. This could occur, for example, when studying concepts in this chapter results in forgetting material studied in the chapter on information processing. In *proactive inhibition*, material already in memory interferes with the remembering of new material. In either case, the greater the similarity between two sets of different material, the more they will interfere with each other, especially if several ads are competing for the consumer's attention.[47]

The above paragraphs presented an overview of the sensory memory, short-term memory and long-term memory systems. Their duration, capacity, type of coding and major forgetting mechanisms were noted. These characteristics are also summarised in Table 11.3. At this point, it is useful to explore long-term memory in somewhat greater depth. Our attention is focused on this system because of its central role in interpreting new stimulus situations and its functioning as a store-house for what consumers know about their world.

TABLE 11.3 Characteristics of memory systems

Memory system	Duration	Capacity	Type of coding	Major forgetting mechanism
Sensory memory	Fraction of a second	All that perceptual sensors can deliver	Quite direct representation of reality	Decay
Short-term memory	Less than one minute	Approximately seven items	Indirect— chunking	Decay
Long-term memory	Up to many years	Almost unlimited	Indirect— clustering via meaningfulness	Interference

Source: Adapted from David Krech et al., *Psychology: A Basic Course*, Knopf, New York, 1976, p. 83. Copyright © Alfred A. Knopf Inc.

CONTENT OF LONG-TERM MEMORY   Because long-term memory is a depository for the wide variety of material that a person can learn, it stands to reason that different ways should exist for storing or coding this information. Evidence suggests that this is so.[48] As indicated in the previous section, one heavily used method of coding involves semantic concepts and the associations between them. By *semantic concepts*, we mean a person's general abstracted knowledge about facts, objects and their attributes, and other aspects of the world. Therefore, the individual does not perform semantic coding by directly representing an object in memory. Instead, it is stored in a generalised form that has meaning for the individual. Because of this, each of us may store an object in a different way. For example, some people might conceptualise an Apple computer as a powerful method of performing business or household tasks, while others might conceptualise it primarily as a home-entertainment device. Still others might think of it as a learning tool for their children. In each case, the same object will be represented in memory differently, and each representation is likely to be associated with emotions and other already existing memory concepts that are similar to it.

Other material coded into memory includes chronological representations of events that have occurred in the past. That is, we often store information about happenings by coding them as a sequence of events that occur in a certain time order. The notion of *scripts* appears to be one example of such coding.[49] A script is a representation in memory of a series of actions occurring in some particular type of past situation. What seems to be important is that a well-defined script tends to influence the consumer's expectations about what actions will occur at a future time when a similar situation occurs. As a result, it tends to guide behaviour. Therefore, we can see that the name 'script' was chosen because the representation in memory resembles an outline of actions that actors follow in a play or movie. An example might be the script that guides behaviour when purchasing a new pair of slacks: find an appropriate size, choose a colour, make a comparison with other available brands with similar prices and quality, select a brand, try on two different sizes to select the best fit and so forth.

Scripts are believed to be useful to consumers because they can be activated automatically when the consumer confronts a familiar situation, and because they guide behaviour without requiring much thought or deliberation from the consumer.[50] This relatively automatic behaviour also has a number of implications for marketing strategy. For example, it suggests that for many products consumers may not be highly conscious of some of their purchasing patterns. Also, these patterns may be resistant to influence attempts because they are so well established in long-term memory, even though the nature of scripts may vary across consumers for the same situation.[51] An example of a consumer script for shopping is given in Chapter 15.

A third method of coding information into long-term memory appears to be *visual* in nature. That is, people appear to use mental images to represent certain information, especially when something tangible such as a physical object is involved.[52] To demonstrate this, we only have to try to remember what is hung on a given kitchen wall in our home. Most people will accomplish this by recalling a 'mental picture' of the wall and its contents. It has been shown that using such mental images to store information often leads to a very strong long-term memory for the material.[53]

The strong memory potential for visually coded information has important implications for those who design packaging, company logos and promotional messages.[54] However, evidence suggests that more is involved than just the old conclusion that 'a picture is worth a thousand words'. This is so because certain types of verbal stimuli that are not accompanied by any visual presentations also appear capable of influencing consumers to develop distinct mental images.[55] In addition, some methods of designing pictures, graphics and similar presentations appear to be more effective than others for facilitating consumers' visual memory. Research has shown that interactive images are more effective for influencing consumers to remember brand names than are normal visual presentations.[56] In this context, an *interactive image* is one that becomes part of the brand name or visually integrates the brand name with the product or service being provided. The following illustration gives an example of an interactive image from a Yellow Pages advertisement in New Zealand. In order to use interactive imagery to its full potential, marketers will have to design their visual presentations carefully.

SHOP AROUND BY PHONE-

LET THE YELLOW PAGES™ HELP YOU.

YELLOW PAGES™
LET YOUR FINGERS DO THE WALKING

An example of interactive imagery in advertising Yellow Pages shop around by phone
COURTESY OF YELLOW PAGES
NEW ZEALAND

There is also evidence that other formats are used for coding information into long-term memory, including auditory (coding by sounds), gustatory (coding by taste) and olfactory (coding by smells) methods of representation.[57] These various methods do not appear to be completely independent. Instead, they interact to influence the retention and retrieval of information.

It has been suggested that the various methods of long-term memory coding can be grouped into three general categories, which interact with each other: episodic memory, procedural memory and semantic memory.[58] In *episodic memory*, a record of events in an individual's personal life is stored according to the time order in which the events occurred. Facts are stored independently of each other and more in terms of how and when they occurred, rather than in terms of the meaning they have. Therefore, retrieval of such information requires that we 'play back the tape' from a starting point. For example, when asked how much liquid we had to drink today, most of us would probably try to remember by tracing our steps from when we got up in the morning. Statements reflecting episodic memory include: 'I bought that sweater the day the Wallabies played the All Blacks in Brisbane' and 'Myer always have a sale early in the New Year'.

Our *procedural memory* holds knowledge about skills and methods for dealing with facts, concepts and episodes. Therefore, it is a memory for knowing *how* to perform certain functions or tasks, and it plays an important role in problem-solving behaviour. Statements reflecting procedural memory include 'When buying a car, always offer the seller less than the stated price', 'A new coat of paint adheres better if the old coat is lightly sanded first' and 'Always check unit prices before buying packaged food products'.

Our *semantic memory* contains general knowledge we have about the world—facts and concepts, as well as objects and their attributes. It seems that this knowledge is not linked to the means or the time period in which it was obtained. For example, most of us have stored information about Uncle Toby's Weet-Bix, but we usually cannot remember when or how we acquired this information. Because of this, retrieval of material from semantic memory can be direct without the need to 'replay' a sequence of events as in episodic memory. Another important characteristic of semantic memory is that it is associational in nature. That is, new information is related to existing stored knowledge so that associations are formed between elements and they develop into a type of meaningful cognitive structure. Statements reflecting semantic memory include 'Stereo systems can be expensive', 'Compact disc players produce better sound than cassette systems' and 'Adidas soccer balls have a good reputation'. How such knowledge can be associated in a memory structure is addressed next.

STRUCTURE OF LONG-TERM MEMORY It is currently believed that long-term memory is organised into numerous groupings or packets of information. Various types of packets have been suggested by researchers.[59] However, one of the most frequently mentioned schemes is the associative-network model of long-term memory for facts and events. We have already described aspects of this model, but it is useful to look at it in a little more detail.

The network model depicts long-term memory as an interconnected system of 'nodes' representing the information (often referred to as concepts) being stored. It may be useful to visualise this system as resembling a fishing net. Knots of the net may be thought of as nodes of information located at various places in the brain, and the string between these knots can be viewed as connections or relationships between the concepts. As our earlier discussion of spreading activation indicated, activation of one part of the memory net is likely to activate any other information that is connected by strings of the net. This view was given greater support quite recently when scientists using X-rays were able to see various points on subjects' brains being activated when they were asked to recall certain information.

Figure 11.8 shows how a consumer's memory for Mainland butter might be represented using this model. The first thing to note is that a hierarchial structure is involved. That is, the general category of dairy products is shown at the top of the figure and butter is seen as one of these products, which share a number of common characteristics and uses. Next, we see that Mainland butter is one of several brands of butter of which the consumer is aware. Finally, the consumer's knowledge of various characteristics of Mainland butter are shown.

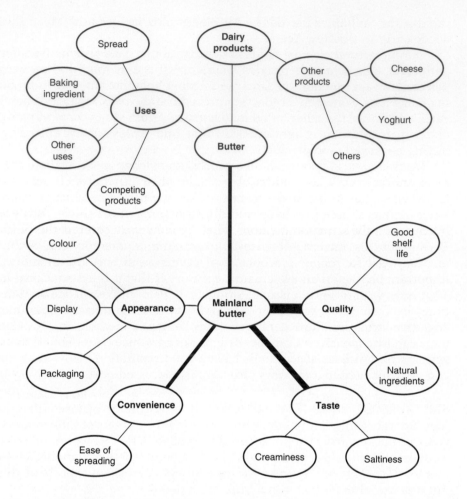

FIG. 11.8 An illustration of a memory network

We can also see from the figure that each concept in memory is integrated into an organised structure involving at least one other concept. This is shown by the connecting lines, which also represent the strength of the indicated relationship—the thicker the line, the stronger the association between concepts. Specifically, the lines show that the consumer has remembered Mainland butter as one brand in the product class, and also has associated quality, taste, appearance and convenience concepts with the product. The 'quality' concept is most strongly linked to Mainland, followed by the 'taste' concept, while appearance is the weakest of the linkages. Each of the concepts also has particular characteristics that have made enough of an impression on the consumer to be remembered. A good understanding of these structures is particularly important for marketers when they wish consumers to learn new information about existing products or when they may wish to develop brand extensions. For example, Mainland may wish to add other products to their range using the Mainland name. Brand extensions that share attributes relevant to existing concepts strongly linked to Mainland will be easiest to develop.

It should be clear that this view of long-term memory depicts a highly organised structure of knowledge and beliefs about the world. Progressive marketers have shown interest in this because it implies that an awareness of consumers' memory structures is useful in predicting how they will interpret and respond to new inputs, such as product information and promotions. However, as discussed in the following paragraphs, evidence has been accumulating recently that adds weight to the need to understand consumers' cognitive structures.

Surprisingly, it is possible for memory to contain more than what was received from the environment. That is, associations between concepts in memory are not part of the environment, but are actively formed by consumers when they attempt to interpret and remember incoming information. This is especially likely when the situation contains what the consumer perceives to be incomplete information.[60] One consequence of this is that consumers can develop beliefs about a specific product without ever receiving information directly relevant to those beliefs.[61] As an example, assume that a consumer interested in portable electric heaters examines several brands and finds that all have a built-in safety device that turns the unit off when it is tipped over. It is then quite possible that when seeing another brand this consumer might infer that it also has this safety feature, without ever directly evaluating the new brand. Because of the way in which they are formed, such beliefs are termed *inferential beliefs*.

Another, closely allied process also occurs while consumers confront new material and attempt to interpret it for storage in long-term memory. This involves what has become known as *cognitive response*—positive or negative thoughts generated by the consumer as a result of being exposed to information.[62] When information is in the form of advertising messages, the major forms of cognitive response are generated thoughts that support the message; refute or diminish the message; or degrade the *source* of the message so that its impact can be minimised. We will examine this in greater detail when dealing with consumers' attitudes. What is important to understand here is that these self-generated thoughts can be stored in long-term memory along with the information that generated them. This means that they also become part of long-term memory and can be retrieved to influence the interpretation of future information. For example, while watching a television commercial for a brand of personal computer, a consumer might think, 'Basically, they just look like fancy game machines to me'. If this concept is associated with personal computers in the long-term memory, it could be retrieved at some future date to have a strong influence on the interpretation of additional messages about personal computers. How this could occur is the subject of the next section.

Retrieval of information

Retrieval is the process of accessing information in long-term memory and activating it into consciousness. The retrieved data may then be combined with other material available in short-term memory, elaborated on and formed into a coherent package of meaningful information. Therefore, retrieval may be viewed as the means of transferring information from long-term memory into the activated work space of short-term memory so that it can be processed further.

Several factors are important influences on the process of retrieval. One is the extent of original learning—the more thoroughly material is learned, the easier it should be to retrieve. As we have seen, the thoroughness of learning is a function of the degree of elaborative processing used to fit material into a cognitive structure, as well as the amount of rehearsal involved. A second factor influencing retrieval appears to be the goals involved in the original learning situation. For example, evidence suggests that consumers have better recall for information when their original purpose is to commit it to memory rather than to use it to choose between various brands.[63] A third major influence on retrieval is the context of the situation. Context is important because it contains cues providing guidance as to which portion of long-term memory should be accessed. For example, assume that we hear the word 'ring' mentioned. It is quite possible that this word is stored in several parts of our cognitive structure to represent something a telephone does, a dirt line on a short collar, something worn on a finger or a layer of scum in the bathtub. The context in which the word is used will strongly influence what aspects of memory will be retrieved.

As previously mentioned, because concepts in long-term memory are associated or linked with other concepts, retrieval typically involves bringing a packet of interrelated information to consciousness. Usually an environmental event will trigger a search of long-term memory, and elements of the context will influence which node or nodes will be activated. Other concepts that are strongly linked to the activated nodes are themselves likely to be activated, but concepts that are weakly linked or not linked at all are unlikely to be activated. The result is that when a situation initiates a search of long-term memory, activated concepts, as well as material they are linked to, are likely to be retrieved and reach conscious attention. These interrelated informational items may be combined with other material in short-term memory, and may then be modified or expanded upon for use in a variety of ways.[64] In fact, some evidence suggests that consumers' decisions may be influenced merely by the number of positive and negative attributes remembered about the brand or the number of dimensions in which one brand outperforms another, rather than how important these attributes may actually be to the consumer.[65]

The example illustrated in Figure 11.9 can help to explain the interrelationships involved. Assume that while shopping in a department store a customer asks a salesperson about a particular Panasonic colour television set. The customer is told that the set is a 50 centimetre table model of all solid-state design. The salesperson also mentions that the set is mostly handcrafted and it has an excellent warranty. As shown in Figure 11.9, this information represents environmental input into the initial stage of short-term memory. The term 'initial' is being used here to indicate the status of memory stores at the start of some event.

As we know, information can only be maintained if it is rehearsed. The solid arrow from initial short-term memory to expanded short-term memory represents maintenance of a portion of the newly acquired information through rehearsal. Specifically, information about the size of the set and its warranty has been maintained, while the remaining items have been lost from memory.

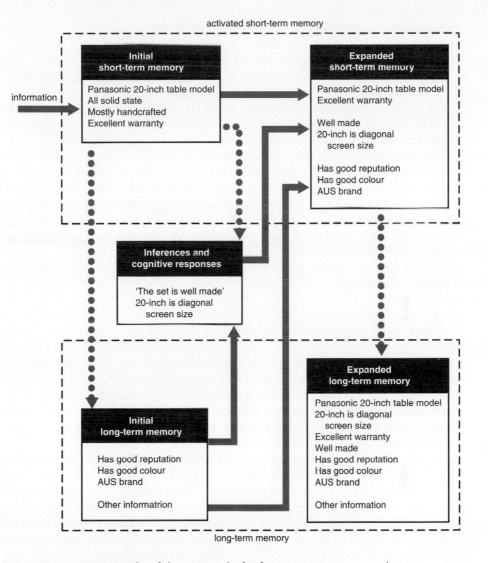

activated short-term memory

long-term memory

FIG. 11.9   An example of the retrieval of information into active, short-term memory and the interrelationship between memory elements

On the basis of previous experience, the consumer has retained certain beliefs and knowledge about Panasonic television sets.[66] The figure shows that this material is stored in initial long-term memory along with other information that is not relevant to the situation. The dotted arrow entering this part of the figure indicates that information from the salesperson has activated long-term memory. The solid arrow leading from this part to expanded short-term memory shows that activation has resulted in three items of information being transferred from long-term memory to the consumer's conscious attention.[67]

The salesperson's comments are also shown by a dotted arrow as activating the consumer's inferential and cognitive responses. Thus, even though the salesperson never really stated it, the consumer has inferred that the 50 centimetre measurement represents screen size as measured on the diagonal.[68] We also see that the salesperson's comments have stimulated the consumer to generate a supportive cognitive response—'the set is well made'. The solid arrow leading from initial long-term memory to these conclusions suggests that they are at least partially influenced by what resides in memory as well as by what transpires in the situation at hand. The inference and cognitive response are then transferred to expanded short-term memory to be combined with other material.

We can now see that short-term memory is 'where it all comes together'. To use a cooking analogy, a pinch of this is added to a measure of that and a dash of something else. Elaborative rehearsal develops a meaningful pattern from material received from the environment, from inferences and cognitive responses, and from the retrieval of information in long-term memory. As shown in Figure 11.9, the result is that long-term memory now holds an expanded and coherent packet of information about the Panasonic television set. This is available for immediate use, such as deciding on a purchase, and it is also available in long-term memory for future reference.

Advertising applications of memory concepts

Numerous memory concepts have significant implications for the field of advertising. The following conclusions represent only a sampling of the useful guidelines that are available. While some are drawn directly from our previous discussion, others represent extensions of that material.[69] Of course, these conclusions are generalisations that might not apply in specific cases.

1. *Advertising messages with unique aspects have a greater potential for being remembered*. This occurs because material with unusual aspects is least affected by the interference process of forgetting. This is one factor that motivates advertisers to seek novel approaches and themes for their messages (see the Arnott's Biscuits advertisement). Another potential benefit is that products characterised by ads as somewhat unique may lead to a more favourable evaluation by consumers.[70]

2. *The order in which material is presented seems to influence how well it will be retained, with the middle portion being most easily forgotten*. This apparently occurs because the beginning and ending of messages stand out the most and interfere with remembering material in between (retroactive and proactive inhibition). The implication is that the most important parts of advertising messages should be placed at the beginning or end, or both. Conversely, some direct-mail advertisers bury the price of their merchandise in the middle of a long letter so as to minimise its negative impact on a purchase decision.

3. *Messages that encourage immediate rehearsal of material stimulate its retention*. Maintenance rehearsal keeps material in short-term memory. Elaborative rehearsal will encourage the transfer of material to long-term

In a world gone mad, we're just quietly crackers.

Arnott's Stoneground Wheat Crackers are made with the finest natural ingredients and the very best whole wheat. Ground the same way since 1863.

Arnott's Biscuits use novelty to convey product benefits COURTESY OF ARNOTT'S BISCUITS

memory. This is why some radio and television advertisers encourage listeners to repeat a telephone number or address several times, and also attempt to develop some meaningful pattern to the numbers.

4. *More information can be processed and retained if it is chunked.* Because the capacity of short-term memory is approximately seven items, chunking can be viewed as a way to package a greater amount of information efficiently. This suggests that advertisers should attempt to find appropriate methods of chunking information for consumers so that they can deliver a greater amount of message content in the limited time or space at their disposal.

5. *The amount of information that can be transferred to long-term memory is a function of the time available for processing.* When recall of a message will be required, approximately five to 10 seconds is required to transfer one chunk of information to long-term memory through memorisation. The amount of information that an advertiser presents should therefore be tailored to the amount of time available for processing and the way the information can be packaged.[71]

6. *Memory is cue-dependent, and the presentation of relevant cues will stimulate recall.* Apparently, certain cues present during the learning context become associated with the material in memory. Their presentation at a later date facilitates recall of the learned material.[72] This process can be very effectively employed by designing packages and point-of-purchase displays to contain the same cues used in advertisements for the product. For example, just as skiing reminds some consumers of ice beer, the word 'blimp' reminds others of Goodyear.

7. *Material retained in long-term memory can be quite different from the information presented in a learning situation.* This is so because some information will be lost from short-term memory, the consumer may generate inferences and cognitive responses, and material will also be drawn from long-term memory. It is important for advertisers to understand these activities, and their potential in any specific situation for influencing the meaning that consumers derive from promotional messages.

8. *Material that is meaningful to the individual is learned more quickly and therefore has a greater chance of being retained than does non-meaningful material.* Apparently, meaningful material actively involves the individual's

I had
all
the
words
prepared
but
the
diamond
said it
brilliantly.

A Diamond Engagement Ring. A month's salary that lasts forever.
For a free leaflet write to the Diamond Information Centre, 234 Sussex Street, Sydney 2000.
A diamond is forever.   De Beers

This advertisement shows how previously learned associations may be used to promote a product   COURTESY OF DE BEERS

mental capacities, and this leads to its greater retention. Therefore, the strong recommendation that has been made for some time is to design advertisements that stimulate consumers' mental involvement, thereby making messages meaningful to them. However, the marketer should develop the specific meaning desired for the message, rather than relying on chance for consumers to determine what meaning they will derive from it themselves. Some methods of accomplishing are outlined in the following list. Of course, the specific situation will dictate the degree to which they are appropriate:

(a) *Visual material*. Information presented as visual content is frequently more memorable than information presented verbally. This suggests that, where possible, advertisers should find ways to 'say it with pictures' rather than conveying information with advertising copy.[73]

(b) *Interactive imagery*. Use of pictures, symbols and other visual devices that depict how two concepts or properties relate to each other can be a highly effective aid to consumers' memory. Such imagery can be used to link a specific brand to particular needs or to a general product group. A splendid example is using the image of the sun kissing an orange for the Sunkist brand of oranges.

(c) *Showing mistakes*. During demonstration of mechanical skills, performance or decision making, it is often useful to show how things should *not* be done, as well as how they should be done. Another technique, which also heightens involvement, is to simulate situations as if the viewer were actually experiencing them.

(d) *Incomplete messages*. Leaving some messages open-ended so that consumers must become involved to complete them has been found to increase retention.[74] Incomplete messages have also been found to positively influence brand attitudes, purchase intentions and brand choice for highly involved consumers, but not for consumers having low involvement.[75] This may be quite overtly done by simply not completing the entire message, or it may be more subtly accomplished by having the announcer ask a question or pose a decision problem for the viewer to answer.

(e) *Mnemonic techniques*. The art of mnemonics (ne-mon-ics) involves the development of a pattern for a series of seemingly unrelated facts so that they can be more easily remembered.[76] Therefore, any technique that allows consumers to 'see' some pattern for associating otherwise meaningless facts will usually be helpful. This is often the case with free phone numbers. A television advertiser who wants a viewer to respond immediately by, for example, phoning for a catalogue, will use a simple, easily recalled pattern of numbers. Numbers such as 1800 109 109 (one of American Express's local numbers) are easily recalled.

Again, it should be stressed that the above list of general guidelines regarding consumers' memory is not by any means exhaustive. In addition, the specific situation must be considered before employing any of them. However, the list is illustrative of the potential benefits of applying such concepts to the design of marketing communications.

SUMMARY

This chapter dealt with two of the fundamental methods by which consumers are able to adapt to their environment. The influence of learning and memory processes was seen to be pervasive, affecting behaviour from consumers' basic likes and dislikes to typical methods of shopping. After some introductory comments about the nature of learning, attention turned to principal learning elements—motives, cues, response and reinforcement. Next, some of the basic methods by which consumers learn were introduced. Distinctions between cognitive and connectionist schools of thought were highlighted, and the usefulness of each of the concepts to understanding consumer learning was addressed. Cognitive theories appear best suited for understanding problem-solving behaviour, while classical conditioning is useful for explaining rote, less conscious learning. Instrumental conditioning falls between these extremes.

Attention then turned to some additional learning topics, including behaviour modification, generalisation and discrimination, learning rate, extinction and forgetting. Behaviour modification was seen to have considerable potential for marketers interested in influencing the actions of consumers over time. The last major section dealt with consumers' memory systems. Although various ways of viewing memory exist, it is most useful for us to view memory as comprising three sets of component processes: sensory memory, short-term memory and long-term memory. The nature of these memory components and their interrelationships were discussed. Especially important was the discussion of how consumers may integrate information from a current situation with information stored in memory and with cognitive responses and inferences that they have constructed. All of these factors were seen as inputs consumers combine in their activated work spaces for the purpose of interpreting the stimulus situation they are currently facing. Finally, a number of useful guidelines for advertisers were drawn from the list of memory concepts that have potential applicability.

MANAGERIAL REFLECTIONS

For our product or service situation:

1. What is the potential for using classical conditioning in our advertising?

2. How might an attempt to structure product trials or introductions make effective use of instrumental conditioning?

3. What implications do stimulus generalisation and discrimination have for our marketing efforts?

4. What are the major potential uses of the behaviour-modification perspective?

5. What are the practical implications for the major memory system characteristics summarised in Table 11.3?

6. What are the common characteristics of consumers' semantic memory structure for our offerings?

7. What types of inferential beliefs are consumers likely to form from our marketing communications?

DISCUSSION TOPICS

1. What is learning? Briefly indicate its importance to understanding consumer behaviour.

2. What method of learning (classical conditioning, instrumental conditioning or cognitive) seems best able to explain:
   (a) smoking cigarettes
   (b) purchasing an air-conditioner primarily for reducing the humidity in a hot, humid room
   (c) writing Sellotape on a shopping list instead of sticky tape?

3. What are stimulus generalisation and discrimination learning, and how are they important to the marketer?

4. Draw a learning curve, and discuss its implications for repeating a given advertising message to consumers.

5. Add a typical retention curve to the end of the learning curve drawn for question 4. Discuss the implications of these curves for advertisers.

6. Design examples of how a marketer could employ the following behaviour-modification elements:
   (a) shaping
   (b) modelling
   (c) classical conditioning

7. Suggest some circumstances in which an advertiser might be more interested in using the recall method for measuring retention rather than the recognition method. Do the same for the recognition method as opposed to the recall method.

8. Compare and contrast the sensory memory, sort-term memory and long-term memory systems. Indicate the relevance of each to advertising strategies.

9. Cite some suggestions you would give to advertisers who were concerned with consumers remembering the following:
   (a) the instructions to start a rotary lawn-mower safely. One should make sure that the deflector chute or grass bag is attached, no objects or debris are next to the mower, the left foot is placed on the mower and the right foot is placed well back.
   (b) a brand name for earth-moving equipment. It should be one that contractors will remember and associate with their need for such equipment.
   (c) how to pronounce the airline name Alitalia so that they will not be reluctant to ask for it on their trips to Europe.

10. Choose a brand name for a particular product. Develop your semantic network (as in Fig. 11.8) for this brand. Be sure to include where the specific brand fits into a hierarchial structure of the product class and where it fits into the set of alternative brands.

    This may also be tried with other people to contrast different structures. Select three willing participants and choose a brand that is familiar to all three. Using the free-association technique (you mention key words, then the subject relates what comes to mind), attempt to discover the semantic network for this brand.

11. Select a product and develop three advertising or product introduction or trial scenarios that would make use of learning or memory principles discussed in the chapter. Be specific in discussing how the particular principles are being applied.

REFERENCES

1. See Stephen J. Hoch & John Deighton, 'Managing What Consumers Learn from Experience', *Journal of Marketing* 53, April 1989, pp. 1–20.
2. Much of this section is based on John Dollard & Neal Miller, *Personality and Psychotherapy*, McGraw-Hill, New York, 1950, pp. 25–47.
3. Winfred F. Hill, *Learning: A Survey of Psychological Interpretations*, Chandler, San Francisco, 1963, p. 225.
4. Hill, ibid, pp. 100–12.
5. Leonard Krasner, 'Studies of the Conditioning of Verbal Behaviour', *Psychological Bulletin* 55, 1958, pp. 148–70.
6. See Ernest R. Hilgard & Gordon H. Bower, *Theories of Learning*, 3rd edn, Appleton-Century-Crofts, New York, 1966, for a comprehensive review of these theories.
7. The two schools of thought are referred to as the 'reinforcement' and 'contiguity'

advocates. See Hill, op cit, Ref 3, pp. 31–89, for a review of their differences and many similarities.

8. Ivan Pavlov, *Conditioned Reflexes, An Investigation of the Psychological Activity of the Cerebral Cortex*, ed. & trans. G. V. Anrep, Oxford University Press, London, 1927.

9. Clark L. Hull, *Principles of Behavior*, Appleton-Century-Crofts, New York, 1943, p. 94.

10. See Francis K. McSweeney & Calvin Bierley, 'Recent Developments in Classical Conditioning', *Journal of Consumer Research* 11, September 1984, pp. 619–31.

11. B. F. Skinner, *The Behavior of Organisms: An Experimental Analysis*, Appleton-Century-Crofts, New York, 1938.

12. See Terence A. Shimp, 'Neo-Pavlovian Conditioning and Its Implications for Consumer Theory and Research', in Thomas S. Robertson & Harold H. Kassarjian (eds), *Handbook of Consumer Behavior*, Prentice-Hall, Englewood Cliffs, NJ, 1991, pp. 162–87, for a review of Pavlovian conditioning that argues that much greater cognitive activity is involved in this form of conditioning than was previously thought.

13. Wolfgang Kohler, *The Mentality of Apes*, Harcourt, Brace & World, New York, 1925.

14. See Alan R. Andreasen & Peter G. Durkson, 'Market Learning of New Residents', *Journal of Marketing Research* 5, May 1968, pp. 166–76.

15. See Hoch & Deighton, op cit, Ref 1, pp. 1–20.

16. See Gerald J. Gorn, 'The Effects of Music in Advertising on Choice Behavior: A Classical Conditioning Approach', *Journal of Marketing* 46, Winter 1982, pp. 94–101; Calvin Bierley, Francis K. McSweeney & Renee Vannieuwkerk, 'Classical Conditioning of Preferences for Stimuli', *Journal of Consumer Research* 12, December 1985, pp. 316–23; and 'Coca-Cola Turns to Pavlov . . . Car Buyers . . . 90-second Ads', *Wall Street Journal*, 19 January 1984, p. 31.

17. James Kellaris & Anthony Cox, 'The Effects of Background Music in Advertising: A Reassessment', *Journal of Consumer Research* 16, June 1989, pp. 113–18.

18. See Chris T. Allen & Thomas J. Madden, 'A Closer Look at Classical Conditioning', *Journal of Consumer Research* 12, December 1985, pp. 301–15.

19. See Michel Hersen, Richard M. Eisler & Peter M. Miller (eds), *Progress in Behavior Modification'*, vol. 25, Sage Publications, Newbury Park, CA, 1990, for some recent findings in areas other than marketing.

20. See Walter R. Nord & J. Paul Peter, 'A Behaviour Modification Perspective on Marketing', *Journal of Marketing* 44, Spring 1980, pp. 36–47; Michael L. Rothschild & William C. Gaidis, 'Behavioral Learning Theory: Its Relevance to Marketing and Promotions', *Journal of Marketing* 45, Spring 1981, pp. 70–8; and J. Paul Peter & Walter R. Nord, 'A Clarification and Extension of Operant Conditioning Principles in Marketing', *Journal of Marketing* 46, Summer 1982, pp. 102–7, upon which much of this discussion is based.

21. J. Ronald Carey et al., 'A Test of Positive Reinforcement of Customers', *Journal of Marketing* 40, October 1976, pp. 98–100.

22. See Rom J. Markin & Chem L. Narayana, 'Behavior Control: Are Consumers Beyond Freedom and Dignity?', in Beverlee B. Anderson (ed.), *Advances in Consumer Research*, vol. 3, Association for Consumer Research, Ann Arbor, MI, 1976, p. 225.

23. Ronald E. Milliman, 'Using Background Music to Affect the Behavior of Supermarket Shoppers', *Journal of Marketing* 46, Summer 1982, pp. 86–91.

24. Nord & Peter, op cit, Ref 20, pp. 36–47. Also for a challenging and provocative assessment of behaviourist contributions to consumer behaviour and marketing see Gordon R. Foxall, *Consumer Psychology in Behavioural Perspective*, Routledge, London, 1990.

25. Bernard Berelson & Gary A. Steiner, *Human Behavior: An Inventory of Scientific Findings*, Harcourt, Brace & World, New York, 1964, pp. 138–9.

26. C. I. Hovland, 'The Generalization of Conditioned Responses: I', *Journal of General Psychology* 17, 1937, pp. 125–48.

27. See Hubert A. Zielske, 'The Remembering and Forgetting of Advertising', *Journal of Marketing* 23, January 1959, pp. 239–43; and Julian L. Simon & Johan Arndt, 'The

Shape of the Advertising Response Function', *Journal of Advertising Research* 20, August 1980, pp. 11–28.

28. Michael L. Ray, Alan G. Sawyer & Edward C. Strong, 'Frequency Effects Revisited', *Journal of Advertising Research* 11, February, 1971, pp. 14–20.

29. See Herbert Krugman, 'What Makes Advertising Effective?', *Harvard Business Review* 53, March–April 1975, pp. 96–103; and Howard Kamin, 'Advertising Reach and Frequency', *Journal of Advertising Research* 18, February 1978, pp. 21–5.

30. See Bobby Calder & Brian Sternthal, 'Television Commercial Wearout: An Information Processing Perspective', *Journal of Marketing Research* 17, May 1980, pp. 173–86; and George E. Belch, 'The Effects of Television Commercial Repetition on Cognitive Response and Message Acceptance', *Journal of Consumer Research* 9, June 1982, pp. 56–65.

31. See Joel Saegert & Robert Young, 'Comparison of Effects of Repetition and Levels of Processing in Memory for Advertisements', in Andrew Mitchell (ed.), *Advances in Consumer Research*, vol. 9, Association for Consumer Research, Ann Arbor, MI, 1982, pp. 431–4.

32. See Alan G. Sawyer, 'Repetition and Affect: Recent Empirical and Theoretical Developments', in Arch Woodside, Jagdish Sheth & Peter Bennett (eds), *Consumer and Industrial Buyer Behavior*, North-Holland, New York, 1977, pp. 229–42; and Belch, op cit, Ref 30, pp. 56–65.

33. See David W. Schumann, Richard E. Petty & D. Scott Clemons, 'Predicting the Effectiveness of Different Strategies of Advertising Variation: A Test of the Repetition-Variation Hypotheses', *Journal of Consumer Research* 17, September 1990, pp. 192–202.

34. See Edward C. Strong, 'The Use of Field Experimental Observations in Estimating Advertising Recall', *Journal of Marketing Research* 11, November 1974, pp. 369–78, for one such investigation.

35. Howard H. Kendler, *Basic Psychology: Brief Version*, W. A. Benjamin, Menlo Park, CA, 1977, p. 448.

36. Zielske, op cit, Ref 27, pp. 239–43.

37. See Joseph W. Alba, J. Wesley Hutchinson & John G. Lynch Jr, 'Memory and Decision Making', in Thomas S. Robertson & Harold H. Kassarjian (eds), *Handbook of Consumer Behavior*, Prentice-Hall, Englewood Cliffs, NJ, 1991, pp. 1–49, for a review of the influence of memory factors on consumer decision making and choice behaviour.

38. See James Bettman, *An Information Processing Theory of Consumer Choice*, Addison-Wesley, Reading, MA, 1979, pp. 139–43.

39. John R. Anderson, *Cognitive Psychology and Its Implications*, W. H. Freeman & Company, New York, 1985, p. 170.

40. See John R. Anderson, *The Architecture of Cognition*, Harvard University Press, Cambridge, MA, 1983, Ch. 3; and Allan M. Collins & Elizabeth F. Loftus, 'A Spreading Activation Theory of Semantic Processing', *Psychological Review* 82, 1975, pp. 407–28.

41. Bettman, op cit, Ref 38, pp. 139–43.

42. See Dawne Martin & Pamela Kiecker, 'Parallel Processing Models of Consumer Information Processing: Their Impact on Consumer Research Methods', in Marvin Goldberg, Gerald Gorn & Richard Pollay (eds), *Advances in Consumer Research*, vol. 17, Association for Consumer Research, Provo, UT, 1990, pp. 443–8.

43. See George A. Miller, 'The Magical Number Seven, Plus or Minus Two: some Limits on Our Capacity for Processing Information', *Psychological Review* 63, 1956, pp. 81–97.

44. Peter H. Lindsay & Donald A. Norman, *Human Information Processing: An Introduction to Psychology*, 2nd edn, Academic Press, New York, 1977, p. 319.

45. See Joel Saegert, 'A Demonstration of Levels-of-processing Theory in Memory for Advertisements', in William L. Wilkie (ed.), *Advances in Consumer Research*, vol. 6, Association for Consumer Research, Ann Arbor, MI, pp. 82–4; Leonard N. Reid &

Lawrence C. Soley, 'Levels-of-Processing in Memory and the Recall and Recognition of Television Commercials', in James H. Leigh & Claude R. Martin Jr (eds), *Current Issues and Research in Advertising, 1980*, The University of Michigan, Ann Arbor, 1980, pp. 135–45; and Joel Saegert, 'Comparison of Effects of Repetition and Levels of Processing in Memory for Advertisements', in Andrew Mitchell (ed.), *Advances in Consumer Research*, vol. 9, Association for Consumer Research, Ann Arbor, MI, 1982, pp. 431–4.

46. See Allan G. Reynolds & Paul W. Flagg, *Cognitive Psychology*, Winthrop Publishers, Cambridge, MA, 1977, pp. 144–7.

47. Raymond R. Burke & Thomas K. Srull, 'Competitive Interference and Consumer Memory for Advertising', *Journal of Consumer Research* 15, June 1988, pp. 55–68.

48. Reynolds & Flagg, op cit, Ref 46, pp. 139–44, 163–70.

49. See R. P. Abelson, 'Psychological Status of the Script Concept', *American Psychologist* 36, 1981, pp. 715–29.

50. See Lorne Bazinoff, 'A Script Theoretic Approach of Information Processing: An Energy Conservation Application', in Andrew Mitchell (ed), *Advances in Consumer Research*, vol. 9, Association for Consumer Research, Ann Arbor, MI, 1982, pp. 481–6, for an elaboration and some examples.

51. Jeffrey J. Stoltman, Shelley R. Tapp & Richard S. Lapidus, 'An Examination of Shopping Scripts', in Thomas K. Srull (ed.), *Advances in Consumer Research*, vol. 16, Association for Consumer Research, Provo, UT, 1989, pp. 384–91.

52. Different methods of storing information do not necessarily require different storage registers. Rather, material processed in different ways (visual, verbal) may just be represented in different ways in long-term memory. See, for example, Zenon W. Pylyshyn, 'What the Mind's Eye Tells the Mind's Brain: A Critique of Mental Imagery', *Psychological Bulletin* 80, July 1973, pp. 1–24; and John R. Anderson & Gordon H. Bower, *Human Associative Memory*, Winston, Washington, DC, 1973.

53. See Allan Paivio, *Imagery and Verbal Processing*, Holt, New York, 1971.

54. For more information on the effects of visual information, see Terry Childers & Michael Houston, 'Conditions for a Picture-superiority Effect on Consumer Memory', *Journal of Consumer Research* 11, September 1984, pp. 643–54; Terry Childers, Susan Heckler & Michael Houston, 'Memory for the Visual and Verbal Components of Print Advertisements', *Psychology & Marketing* 3, Fall 1986, pp. 137–50; Meryl Gardner & Michael Houston, 'The Effect of Verbal and Visual Components of Retail Communications', *Journal of Retailing* 62, Spring 1986, pp. 64–78; and Ruth Smith, Michael Houston & Terry Childers, 'The Effects of Schematic Memory on Imaginal Information Processing: An Empirical Assessment', *Psychology & Marketing* 2, Spring 1985, pp. 13–29.

55. See, for example, Kathy A. Lutz & Richard J. Lutz, 'Imagery-eliciting Strategies: Review and Implications of Research', in H. Keith Hunt (ed.), *Advances in Consumer Research*, vol. 5, Association for Consumer Research, Ann Arbor, MI, 1978, pp. 611–20; Larry Percy, 'Psycholinguistic Guidelines for Advertising Copy', in Andrew Mitchell (ed.), *Advances in Consumer Research*, vol. 9, Association for Consumer Research, Ann Arbor, MI, 1982, pp. 107–11; Morris B. Holbrook & William L. Moore, 'Feature Interactions in Consumer Judgments of Verbal versus Pictorial Presentations', *Journal of Consumer Research* 8, June 1981, pp. 103–11; and H. Rao Unnava & Robert E. Burnkrant, 'An Imagery-processing View of the role of Pictures in Print Advertisements', *Journal of Marketing Research* 28, May 1991, pp. 226–31.

56. Kathy A. Lutz & Richard J. Lutz, 'Effects of Interactive Imagery on Learning: Applications to Advertising', *Journal of Applied Psychology* 62, 1977, pp. 493–8.

57. See Reynolds & Flagg, op cit, Ref 46, pp. 163–70.

58. Lyle E. Bourne Jr, Roger L. Dominowski & Elizabeth F. Loftus, *Cognitive Processes*, Prentice-Hall, Englewood Cliffs, NJ, 1979, pp. 10–11.

59. See Andrew A. Mitchell, 'Models of Memory: Implications for Measuring Knowledge Structures', in Andrew A. Mitchell (ed.), *Advances in Consumer Research*, vol. 9, Association for Consumer Research, Ann Arbor, MI, 1982, pp. 45–51; and Anderson, op cit, Ref 39, Ch. 3.

60. Gary T. Ford & Ruth Ann Smith, 'Inferential Beliefs in Consumer Evaluations: An Assessment of Alternative Processing Strategies', *Journal of Consumer Research* 14, December 1987, pp. 363–71.

61. See Jerry C. Olson, 'Inferential Belief Formation in the Cue Utilization Process', in H. Keith Hunt (ed.), *Advances in Consumer Research*, vol. 5, Association for Consumer Research, Ann Arbor, MI, 1978, pp. 706–13; and Philip A. Dover, 'Inferential Belief Formation: An Overlooked Concept in Consumer Behavior Research', in Andrew Mitchell (ed.), *Advances in Consumer Research*, vol. 9, Association for Consumer Research, Ann Arbor, MI, 1982, pp. 187–9.

62. Peter L. Wright, 'The Cognitive Processes Mediating Acceptance of Advertising', *Journal of Marketing Research* 10, February 1973, pp. 53–62.

63. See Gabriel Biehal & Dipanker Chakravarti, 'Information-presentation Format and Learning Goals as Determinants of Consumers' Memory Retrieval and Choice Processes', *Journal of Consumer Research* 8, March 1982, pp. 431–41.

64. When the consumer is exposed to several competing ads, interference effects may inhibit the consumer from accessing relevant information available in memory. See Burke & Srull, op cit, Ref 47, pp. 55–68; Kevin Lane Keller, 'Memory Factors in Advertising: The Effect of Advertising Retrieval Cues on Brand Evaluations', *Journal of Consumer Research* 14, December 1987, pp. 316–33; and Kevin Lane Keller, 'Memory and Evaluation Effects in Competitive Advertising Environments', *Journal of Consumer Research* 17, March 1991, pp. 463–76, for a discussion of this and related topics.

65. See Joseph W. Alba & Howard Marmorstein, 'The Effects of Frequency Knowledge on Consumer Decision Making', *Journal of Consumer Research* 14, June 1987, pp. 14–25.

66. Recent research suggests that the consumer's memory does not just influence judgments about brand attributes but also strongly influences whether the brands themselves may be recalled and available for inclusion in the consumer's set of viable alternatives. See Prakash Nedungadi, 'Recall and Consumer Consideration Sets: Influencing Choice without Altering Brand Evaluations', *Journal of Consumer Research* 17, December 1990, pp. 263–76.

67. If new information can be easily categorised by the consumer, he or she can more quickly retrieve it and use it to influence judgments about new product situations. Without such information, new product information is likely to be evaluated more closely on each dimension. See Mita Sujan, 'Consumer Knowledge: Effects on Evaluation Strategies Mediating Consumer Judgments', *Journal of Consumer Research* 12, June 1985, pp. 31–46.

68. Relationships that the consumer may perceive between brand features accessible in memory and information that is missing in the brand-perception situation currently being faced are more likely to influence the consumer's inferences than are prior overall evaluations of brands. See Alan Dick, Dipankar Chakravarti & Gabriel Biehal, 'Memory-based Inferences During Consumer Choice', *Journal of Consumer Research* 17, June 1990, pp. 82–93.

69. For additional guidelines, see Steuart Henderson Britt, 'How Advertising Can Use Psychology's Rules of Learning', *Printer's Ink* 252, September 1955, pp. 74 ff.; and Steuart Henderson Britt, 'Applying Learning Principles to Marketing', *MSU Business Topics* 23, Spring 1975, pp. 5–12.

70. Joan Meyers-Levy & Alice M. Tybout, 'Schema Congruity as a Basis for Product Evaluation', *Journal of Consumer Research* 16, June 1989, pp. 39–54.

71. James R. Bettman, 'Memory Factors in Consumer Choice: A Review', *Journal of Marketing* 43, Spring 1979, pp. 37–53.

72. See John G. Lynch Jr & Thomas K. Srull, 'Memory and Attentional Factors in Consumer Choice: Concepts and Research Methods', *Journal of Consumer Research* 9, June 1982, pp. 18–36; and Keller, op cit, Ref 64, pp. 316–33.

73. See John R. Rossiter, 'Visual Imagery: Applications to Advertising', in Andrew Mitchell (ed.), *Advances in Consumer Research*, vol. 9, Association for Consumer Research, Ann Arbor, MI, 1982, pp. 101–6.

74. See, for example, James T. Heimbach & Jacob Jacoby, 'The Zeigarnik Effect in Advertising', in M. Venkatesan (ed.), *Proceedings of the Third Annual Conference*, Association for Consumer Research, College Park, MD, 1972, pp. 746–57.
75. Alan G. Sawyer & Daniel J. Howard, 'Effects of Omitting Conclusions in Advertisements to Involved and Uninvolved Audiences', *Journal of Marketing Research* 28, November 1991, pp. 467–74.
76. See Naresh K. Malhotra, 'Mnemonics in Marketing: A Pedagogical Tool', *Journal of the Academy of Marketing Science* 19, Spring 1991, pp. 141–9, for a review of this memory aid.

CHAPTER 12

ATTITUDES

The topic of attitudes has been one of the most important subjects of study in the field of consumer behaviour. Widespread investigations of attitudes among marketing academics and practising marketers support this statement. Attitude research forms the basis for developing new products, repositioning existing products, creating advertising campaigns and predicting brand preferences, as well as general purchase behaviour. Understanding how attitudes are developed and how they influence consumers is a vital ingredient to the success of any marketing program.

Material presented in Chapters 9 and 10 provides a useful perspective for our discussion in this chapter. Recall from Chapter 9 that the role of attitudes differs depending on the level of consumer involvement in a purchase situation. It was argued that in low-involvement situations, attitudes toward a brand are formed *after* a purchase has been made, when the brand is being evaluated through actual use. However, in high-involvement situations, consumers are seen as forming attitudes about brands and then making a purchase decision based on these attitudes. This means that in high-involvement cases, attitudes are formed on the basis of product evaluations that are made *prior* to purchase. Therefore, they represent one outcome of the information-processing activities that are shown in Figure 10.1, in the chapter on information processing. The high-involvement perspective is most relevant to our discussion of attitudes in this chapter. That is, the sequence of steps an involved consumer takes can be thought of as:

1. processing information;

2. forming attitudes;

3. making choices in the marketplace, guided by these attitudes.

In this chapter, we explore how attitudes are formed and organised. The functions of attitudes in our daily lives and their relationship to purchase behaviour are then discussed. Additionally, we describe several well-known attitude models and theories that help us to measure and predict consumer behaviour.

Many marketers are attempting to change consumer attitudes through the use of persuasive messages. Thought must be given to various characteristics of the audience that will receive these communications, the type of spokespeople or various sources to use in these communications, and the content of messages that will be delivered. In addition, care must be taken to arrange the background of these messages and understand the nature of situations surrounding consumer decisions to purchase the advertised product or service.

As we have just suggested, the persuasive communication process appears capable of influencing attitude change among consumers. It should be kept in mind, however, that many of the methods for influencing attitude change that will be discussed in this chapter are also useful for encouraging the development of new attitudes—for example, toward new products. The reader should also note that the degree of success in changing consumers' attitudes depends on how strongly existing attitudes are held. Those that are strongly entrenched are difficult to change, while neutral and weakly held attitudes are much easier to influence.

The chapter discusses strategies for changing consumers' attitudes and reviews the general nature of the communication process used to accomplish these strategies. Several major components of such communications are discussed in terms of their influence on attitude change. First, various communication sources and their potential effects are addressed. Different properties of the message itself are then treated. Finally, characteristics of the intended audience that affect its receptivity to persuasive communications are examined.

DEFINITIONS OF ATTITUDE

Social psychologists, unfortunately, do not agree on the precise definition of an attitude. In fact, there are more than a hundred different definitions of the concept.[1] However, four definitions are more commonly accepted than others. One conception is that an attitude is how positive or negative, favourable or unfavourable, or pro or con a person feels toward an object.[2] This definition views attitude as a feeling or an evaluative reaction to objects. A second definition represents the thoughts of Allport, who views attitudes as 'learned predispositions to respond to an object or class of objects in a consistently favourable or unfavourable way'.[3] This definition is slightly more complicated than the first because it incorporates the notion of a readiness to respond toward an object. A third definition of attitude popularised by cognitively oriented social psychologists is: 'an enduring organisation of motivational, emotional, perceptual and cognitive process with respect to some aspect of the individual's world'.[4] This views attitudes as being made up of three components:

1. the *cognitive*, or knowledge, component;

2. the *affective*, or emotional, component;

3. the *conative*, or behavioural-tendency, component.

This conception of attitude has been used successfully in Australian marketing research to predict demand for new products.[5]

More recently, theorists have given more attention to a new definition of attitude, which has generated much research and has been useful in predicting behaviour. This definition explicitly treats attitudes as being multidimensional in nature, as opposed to the unidimensional emphasis taken by earlier definitions. Here, a person's overall attitude toward an object is seen to be a function of the strength of each of a number of beliefs the person holds about various aspects of the object, and the evaluation the person gives to each belief as it relates to the object.[6] A *belief* is the probability a person attaches to a given piece of knowledge being true.

This last definition has considerable appeal, because it has been shown that consumers perceive a product (object) as having many attributes, and they form beliefs about each of these attributes. For example, a consumer may believe strongly that Listerine mouthwash kills germs, helps prevent colds, gives people clean, refreshing breath, and prevents sore throats. If this consumer evaluates all five of these attributes as favourable qualities, according to the definition the consumer would have a strongly favourable overall attitude toward the brand. On the other hand, a second consumer might believe just as strongly as the first consumer that Listerine possesses all five of these traits, but may not evaluate all attributes as favourably as the first consumer does. Therefore, this consumer's overall attitude toward the brand would be less favourable. This idea will be discussed in more detail later in the chapter.

It has been important to provide all four attitude definitions because the majority of attitude studies have been based on them. In fact, results of this research serve as the basis of this chapter.

CHARACTERISTICS OF ATTITUDES

Attitudes have several important characteristics, or properties: namely, they have an object; they have direction, intensity and degree; they have structure; and they are learned.

Attitudes have an object

By definition, attitudes must have an object. That is, they must have a focal point—whether it be an abstract concept, such as 'ethical behaviour', or a tangible item, such as a motorcycle. The object can be a physical thing, such as a product, or it can be an action, such as buying a lawn-mower. In addition, the object can be either one item, such as a person, or a collection of items, such as a social group; it also can be either specific (Garibaldi Smallgoods) or general (imported meats).

Attitudes have direction, degree and intensity

An attitude expresses how a person feels toward an object. It expresses *direction*— the person feels either favourable or unfavourable toward, or for or against, the object; *degree*—how much the person either likes or dislikes the object; and *intensity*—the level of sureness or confidence of expression about the object, or how strongly a person feels about his or her conviction. Although degree and intensity might seem the same and are actually related, they are not synonymous. For example, a person may feel quite strongly that a Honda ride-on mower is very poorly made but at the same time the person may have very little conviction, or feeling of sureness, that this attitude is right. This indicates a negative attitude where the *degree* of negative feeling is quite strong but the *intensity* is weak. Thus, this attitude could be more easily changed in a favourable direction than could the attitude of a person who feels a strong conviction that Honda mowers are poorly made.

The direction, degree and intensity of a person's attitude toward a product have been said to provide marketers with an estimate of the person's readiness to act toward, or purchase, the product. However, a marketer must also understand how *important* the consumer's attitude is in relation to other attitudes, and the situational constraints, such as ability to pay, that might inhibit the consumer from making a purchase decision.

Attitudes have structure

As explained below, attitudes display organisation, which means that they possess interattitudinal centrality and internal consistency. They also tend to be stable, to be generalisable and to have varying degrees of salience.

The structure of human attitudes may be viewed as a complex Meccano set erected in a type of circular pattern. At the centre of this structure are the individual's important values and self-concept. Attitudes close to the hub of this system are said to have a high degree of *centrality*. Other attitudes located farther out in the structure possess less centrality.

Attitudes do not stand in isolation. They are associated (tied in) with each other to form a complex whole. This implies that a certain degree of *consistency* must exist between them. That is, because they are related, there must be some amount of 'fit' between them, or conflict will result. Also, because the more central attitudes are related to a larger number of other attitudes, they must exhibit a greater degree of consistency than more peripheral attitudes do.

Because attitudes cluster into a structure, they tend to show *stability* over time. The length of time may not be infinite, but it is far from being temporary. Also, because attitudes are learned, they tend to become stronger, or at least more resistant to change, the longer they are held.[7] Thus, newly formed attitudes are easier to change and less stable than are older ones of equal strength.

Attitudes tend to be *generalisable*. That is, a person's attitude toward a specific object tends to generalise toward a class of objects. Thus, a consumer who purchases a Porsche that develops mechanical difficulties may believe that all Porsches and Volkswagen products, and possibly all German-made products, are poorly constructed. Consumers tend to generalise in such a manner in order to simplify their decision making.

Among all of the attitudes in a person's attitudinal structure, some are more important, or *salient*, to the person than others. For example, an Australian consumer might feel that 'buying Australian' is more important than saving money, and so she might purchase an Australian car that costs more than a comparable foreign car. Also, the 'buy-Australian' attitude can be closely tied to attitudes of creating Australian jobs, keeping money at home and the like, which thereby support the 'buy-Australian' attitude and increase its salience. The Eureka! advertisement targets this attitude.

Attitudes are learned

Just as a golf swing, a tennis stroke and tastes are learned, so are attitudes. They develop from our personal experiences with reality, as well as from information from friends, salespeople and news media. They are also derived from both direct and indirect experiences in life. Thus, it is important to recognise that learning precedes attitude formation and change, and that principles of learning discussed in Chapter 11 can aid marketers in developing and changing consumer attitudes.

The buy Australian attitude is targeted with this advertisement   COURTESY OF EUREKA

FUNCTIONS OF ATTITUDES

Attitudes serve four major functions for the individual: the adjustment function, the ego-defensive function, the value-expressive function and the knowledge function.[8] Ultimately, these functions serve people's need to protect and enhance the images they hold of themselves. In more general terms, these functions are the motivational bases that shape and reinforce positive attitudes toward goal objects perceived as need satisfying, and/or negative attitudes toward other objects perceived as punishing or threatening. These situations are diagrammed in Figure 12.1. The functions themselves can help us to understand why people hold the attitudes they do toward psychological objects.

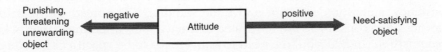

FIG. 12.1   Attitude development and function based on perceived need satisfaction or harm avoidance

Adjustment function

The adjustment function directs people toward pleasurable or rewarding objects and away from unpleasant, undesirable ones. It serves the utilitarian concept of maximising reward and minimising punishment. Thus, the attitudes of consumers depend to a large degree on their perceptions of what is need satisfying and what is punishing. Because consumers perceive products, services and stores as providing need-satisfying or unsatisfying experiences, we should expect their attitudes toward these entities to vary in relation to their experiences.

Ego-defensive function

Attitudes formed to protect the ego or self-image from threats help fulfil the ego-defensive function. Actually, many outward expressions of such attitudes reflect the opposite of what people perceive themselves to be. For example, a consumer who has made a poor purchase decision or a poor investment may staunchly defend the decision as being correct at the time or as being the result of poor advice from another person. Such ego-defensive attitudes help us to protect our self-image and often we are unaware of them.

Value-expressive function

Whereas ego-defensive attitudes are formed to protect a person's self-image, value-expressive attitudes enable the expression of the person's centrally held values. Therefore, consumers adopt certain attitudes in an effort to translate their values into something more tangible and easily expressed. Thus, a conservative person might develop an unfavourable attitude toward bright clothing and instead be attracted toward dark, pinstriped suits.

Marketers should develop an understanding of what values consumers wish to express about themselves, and they should design products and promotional campaigns to allow these self-expressions. Not all products lend themselves to this form of market segmentation, however. Those with the greatest potential for 'value-expressive' segmentation are ones with high social visibility. Parker pens, Country Road clothes and Ferrari cars are examples.

Knowledge function

Humans have a need for a structured and orderly world and therefore seek consistency, stability, definition and understanding.[9] The need for structure determines what consumers are motivated to learn about, or defines areas of knowledge acquisition. In addition, the need to know tends to be specific. Therefore, an individual who neither plays golf nor wishes to learn the sport is unlikely to seek knowledge or an understanding of the game. This will influence the amount of information search devoted to this topic. Thus, out of our need to know come attitudes about what we believe we need or do not need to understand.

In addition, attitudes enable consumers to simplify the complexity of the real world. As was pointed out in Chapter 10 on information processing, the real world is too complex for us to cope with and so we develop mechanisms to simplify situations. We saw that this involves sensory thresholds and selective attention, and it also involves attitudes. Attitudes allow us to categorise or group objects as a way of knowing about them. Thus, when a new object is experienced we attempt to categorise it into a group that we know something about. In this way the object can share the reactions we have for other objects in the same category. This is efficient because we do not have to spend much effort reacting to each new object as a completely unique situation. Consequently, we often find consumers reacting in similar ways to ads for 'going out of business' sales, 'limited time' offers, 'Australian-made' goods and so on. Of course, there is some risk of error in not looking at the unique aspects or new information about objects but, for better or worse, our attitudes have influenced how we feel and react to new examples of these situations.

SOURCES OF ATTITUDE DEVELOPMENT

The preceding section not only discussed the functions of attitudes but also provided us with an initial understanding of how and why attitudes develop. All attitudes ultimately develop from human needs and the values people place upon objects that satisfy those perceived needs. This section discusses sources that make us aware of needs, their importance to us, and how our attitudes develop toward objects that satisfy needs.

Personal experience

People come into contact with objects in their everyday environment. Some are familiar, while others are new. We evaluate the new and re-evaluate the old, and this evaluation process assists us in developing attitudes toward objects. For example, consider a gourmet cook who has searched two months for a new food processor only to have it break down three months after purchase. Through direct experience, this consumer will re-evaluate the earlier attitude toward the processor.

Our direct experiences with sales representatives, and products, services and stores help to create and shape our attitudes toward the products they sell, and those market objects. However, several factors influence how we will evaluate such direct contacts:

1. *Needs.* Because needs differ and also vary over time, people can develop different attitudes toward the same object at different points in their lives.

2. *Selective perception.* We have seen that people operate on their personal interpretations of reality. Therefore, the way people interpret information about products, stores and so on affects their attitudes toward them.

3. *Personality.* Personality is another factor influencing how people process their direct experiences with objects. How aggressive–passive, introverted–extroverted and so on people are will affect the attitudes they form.

Group associations

All people are influenced to one degree or another by other members in the groups to which they belong. Attitudes are one target for this influence. Our attitudes toward products, ethics, warfare and a multitude of other subjects are influenced strongly by groups that we value and with which we associate or wish to associate. Several groups, including family, work and peer groups, and cultural and subcultural groups, are important in affecting a person's attitude development.

Influential others

A consumer's attitude can be formed and changed through personal contact with influential persons such as respected friends, relatives and experts. Opinion leaders are examples of people who are respected by their followers and who may strongly influence the attitudes and purchase behaviour of followers.

To capitalise on this type of influence, advertisers often use actors who look or act like their intended audiences. People tend to like others who are similar to themselves, because they believe that they share the same problems, form the same judgments and use the same criteria for evaluating products.[10] Another application that advertisers use to influence audience attitudes is the so-called 'slice-of-life' commercial. These commercials show 'typical' people confronting 'typical' problems and finding solutions in the use of the advertised brand. Examples include ads for Pert shampoo (to solve dandruff problems), Colgate toothpaste (to fight cavities) and Beaurepaires (to fix punctures).

Figure 12.2 is a pictorial summary of what we have learned so far. The diagram is a simple representation of the concepts that have been discussed in the previous sections. It shows that several sources provide consumers with information and influence about products, services, retail stores and other objects. The individual selectively receives and distorts the information according to his or her individual needs, values and personality, and according to how well the information 'fits' with currently held beliefs and attitudes. This processed information initiates either development, change or confirmation in the consumer's beliefs about the product and the importance of each of the product's attributes to the consumer and his or her current needs. Out of this process is synthesised a general attitude toward a product. This represents a rather traditional view of attitudes. Admittedly, this model also is an oversimplification. However, it presents a concise picture of psychological and external elements often claimed to be involved in the process of forming attitudes toward products. Also, it should be pointed out that the process is dynamic; it continues to change over time.

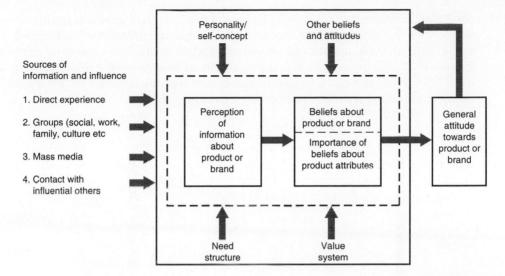

FIG. 12.2 A simple diagram of the interrelationships of an attitude toward a product or brand and other psychological processes

ATTITUDE THEORIES AND MODELS

This section describes several attitude theories and models.[11] Although at first glance some may appear to be somewhat complicated, their essence is usually quite simple and useful in understanding the role of attitudes in consumer behaviour.

Attitude theories primarily are concerned with how attitudes develop and change. Three of the more popular viewpoints are founded on the general principle that *the human mind strives to maintain harmony or consistency among currently perceived attitudes.* If the mind perceives an inconsistency within its attitude structure, mental tension develops to return the structure to a consistent state. The three classical theories based upon the consistency principle are congruity, balance and cognitive dissonance. Newer multiattribute attitude theories are discussed after a consideration of these traditional views.

Congruity theory

A basic understanding of the congruity model can be gained through consideration of the following examples. Assume that a consumer initially holds positive attitudes toward the rock group U2 (positive scale value of +2) and negative attitudes toward a particular brand of electric guitar (negative scale value of –2), as illustrated in Figure 12.3. Then the consumer sees an advertisement where the U2 group makes positive statements about this brand of electric guitar. Given this situation, the consumer will have inconsistent attitudes: 'U2, whom I like, said nice things about a brand of guitar that I don't like'. The consumer is now in a state of *incongruity*, which produces uncomfortable tension that must ultimately lead to resolution of the incongruous state. The congruity model predicts that a person in this situation would develop a less favourable attitude toward the U2 group and also a more favourable attitude toward the brand of electric guitar, as shown in part (b) of Figure 12.3. The model predicts a movement of two units of each attitude toward each other (the centre in this case), because the consumer perceives both objects as being of equal strength but in opposite directions of the zero neutral point.

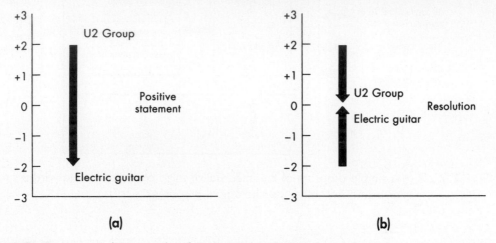

FIG. 12.3 A simple example of incongruity resolution

Most of the time the resulting equilibrium point is not determined so simply. Figure 12.4 presents another situation of a consumer's initial attitudes toward the U2 group and a brand of electric guitar. Note that the scale distance between the two concepts is 4 units as before, but resolution is not the midpoint between the two concepts (+1) as we might expect. Instead, the model predicts that resolution would occur at +2, reducing the consumer's perceived attitude of U2 by only 1 scale unit and increasing the attitude toward the electric guitar by 3 scale units.

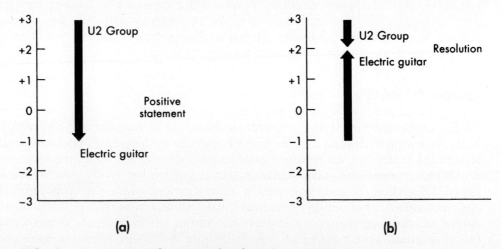

FIG. 12.4 A more complex example of resolving incongruity

Although the mathematics used to predict the resolution point will not be presented here, a smaller attitude shift on U2 than on the electric guitar is intuitively understandable.[12] Strong attitudes are more difficult to change than are weak or moderate ones. Thus, the stronger positive attitude toward U2 exerts greater pull on the weaker negative attitude toward the guitar. This idea suggests that when consumers develop a strong dislike toward a brand, the company marketing efforts required to improve these attitudes will be tremendous, and may not be worth the expense. The company may be better off in many cases either: to drop the brand and reintroduce it under another name, if promotional positioning has been the problem; or to introduce a new reformulated brand, if product quality, design or formulation has been the problem. Conversely, if the consumer holds an extremely positive attitude toward the brand, considerable unfavourable experiences and word-of-mouth influence would be required before the attitude deteriorated significantly.

It should be noted that although the model predicts resolution at a value of +2 in Figure 12.4, there are qualifications. First, if the information the consumer heard is perceived to be totally unbelievable, it can be rejected, and no attitude change will occur. In this instance, the information would be totally discounted. Secondly, if the consumer experiences only some disbelief instead of total disbelief, only a slight attitude change will occur.[13] This qualification for disbelief adds further strength to the marketing examples previously mentioned. Specifically, consumers who hold extremely negative attitudes toward a brand not only will be difficult to change, but will ignore or discount information to the contrary.

The congruity principle is used frequently in marketing.[14] Advertisers often use hired celebrities to endorse brands, services, organisations and causes. Athletes speak against drug use among young people; film actors endorse various kinds of beauty aids; and racing-car drivers promote brands of tyres, spark plugs and other car accessories. Of course, the intent is to have consumers who hold positive attitudes toward a source (the person making such favourable statements about an object) to develop a positive value association between the source and the object.

Balance theory

Several balance models have been developed, all of which are based upon the pioneering work of Fritz Heider.[15] According to balance theory, a person perceives his or her environment in terms of *triads*. That is, a person views himself or herself as being involved in a triangular relationship in which all three elements (persons, ideas and things) have either positive (liking, favourable) or negative (disliking, unfavourable) relationships with each other. This relationship is termed *sentiment*.

Unlike in the congruity model, there are no numerical values used to express the degree of unity between elements. Instead, the model is described as *unbalanced* if the multiplicative relationship among the three elements is negative, and *balanced* if the multiplicative relationship is positive. To illustrate, consider the consumer situation expressed as three statements: 'I like large, luxurious cars', 'I don't like energy-wasting products' and 'I believe large, luxurious cars waste energy'. This situation is described by the triad shown in Figure 12.5. Notice that the structure is not in balance, because there is a positive relationship on two sides of the triad and a negative relationship on the third side, and this results in a negative multiplicative product.

Because the relationship presented in the example is unbalanced, it will produce tension for the consumer. It may be possible to 'live with' the tension and do nothing to resolve it. However, if sufficient tension exists, it is likely that attitude change will occur regarding at least one element in the triad in order to restore balance to the system. These attempts at resolution can result in the consumer disliking large, luxurious cars; believing that large, luxurious cars are not really energy-wasting products; or liking energy-wasting products (e.g. they create jobs and provide psychological satisfaction). As we can see, rationalisation can help to change our perceptions of relationships and thus our attitudes.

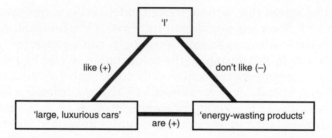

FIG. 12.5 A graphic representation of an unbalanced attitudinal structure

Cognitive dissonance

The theory of cognitive dissonance was developed in 1957 by Leon Festinger.[16] Festinger describes cognitive dissonance as a psychological state that results when a person perceives that two cognitions (thoughts), both of which the person believes to be true, do not 'fit' together; that is, they seem inconsistent. The resulting dissonance produces tension, which serves to motivate the individual to bring harmony to inconsistent elements and thereby reduce psychological tension.

Dissonance can arise in three basic ways. First, any *logical inconsistency* can create dissonance. For example, 'All candy is sweet; my candy is sour'. Secondly, dissonance can be created when people experience *inconsistency either between their attitudes and their behaviour or between two of their behaviours*. For example, Margaret actively praises Nike training shoes on many occasions and then purchases a pair of New Balance training shoes. This is an example of an inconsistency between two behaviours. On the other hand, if David strongly dislikes gambling but bets on the outcome of football games, a discrepancy would exist between his attitude and his behaviour. Thirdly, dissonance can occur when a strongly held *expectation is disconfirmed*. To illustrate, Michael expects to find significant savings at a sidewalk sale but finds only unstylish and damaged merchandise.

In all three cases dissonance is not automatic. It is necessary for a person to perceive the inconsistency; otherwise, no dissonance will occur. Some people are very capable of holding an attitude that contradicts their behaviour without perceiving the contradiction. Therefore, they suffer no dissonance.

Regardless of its source, cognitive dissonance arises *after* a decision has been made. The decision, in effect, commits the person to certain positions or attitudes, when prior to that time that person was capable of adjusting his or her attitudes or behaviour to avoid dissonance.

People experiencing cognitive dissonance have three major ways of reducing it:

1. rationalisation,

2. seeking additional information that is supportive of or consistent with their behaviour;

3. either eliminating or altering some of the dissonant elements, which can be accomplished either by forgetting or suppressing dissonant elements, or by changing their attitudes so that they are no longer dissonant with other attitude or behaviour.

Each of these strategies may be used alone or in combination.

To illustrate these methods, consider Diane, who has purchased a Nikon 35 mm, single-lens reflex camera outfit for $650 after seriously considering other brands, such as Pentax, Canon and Minolta, in the same general price range. Besides investing $650, she has also invested much thought and searching time and a considerable amount of ego in the purchase decision. Therefore, the amount at stake in this purchase is significant. After evaluating the pros and cons of each brand of camera, she has selected the Nikon. Subsequent to the purchase, Diane finds her camera hard to focus and the lenses difficult to change. Furthermore, the strap on the carrying case breaks. She now begins to doubt the wisdom of her purchase. A tension arises from her two beliefs that: 'Nikons are well-constructed precision cameras' and 'My Nikon is difficult to focus for clear pictures, it takes too much time and effort to change lenses, and the strap on the carrying case has broken'.

Diane can reduce the tension arising from these two cognitions by *rationalising* that any fine camera can have its faults and the retailer probably treated the carrying case roughly, causing the eventual strap break. Or she might *seek information* that reinforces her belief that Nikon cameras are among the very best in the world—such as rapid film advancement, nice styling and a solid shutter click, indicating durability—thereby amplifying the strong points of the camera. Finally, a third option is to *change her opinion* toward Nikon cameras. 'They are not good cameras. I should have purchased a Canon'.

This example illustrates a very common type of marketing-related phenomenon—*postpurchase dissonance*. Postpurchase dissonance occurs when a person makes a decision to buy one brand from among several alternative brands within a product category. The dissonance becomes particularly strong when the consumer makes a large commitment in the purchase. Such commitment refers not only to the amount of money, but also to the investment of time, effort and ego,

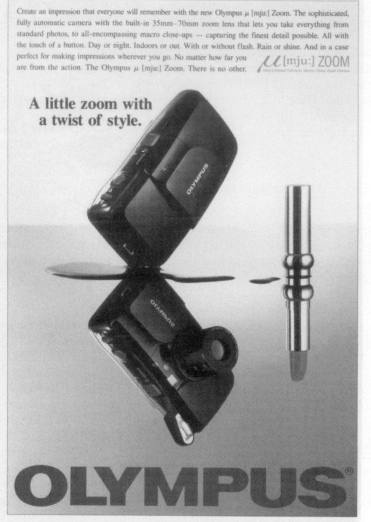

Create an impression that everyone will remember with the new Olympus μ [mju:] Zoom. The sophisticated, fully automatic camera with the built-in 35mm-70mm zoom lens that lets you take everything from standard photos, to all-encompassing macro close-ups — capturing the finest detail possible. All with the touch of a button. Day or night. Indoors or out. With or without flash. Rain or shine. And in a case perfect for making impressions wherever you go. No matter how far you are from the action. The Olympus μ [mju:] Zoom. There is no other.

μ [mju:] ZOOM

Ultra-Compact Full-Auto 35mm–70mm Zoom Camera

A little zoom with a twist of style.

OLYMPUS®

The information in this advertisement could be used to reduce post-purchase dissonance
COURTESY OF OLYMPUS

as was illustrated in the previous example. Therefore, a purchase decision involving choice among brands of chewing gum at a supermarket checkout counter is unlikely to produce much perceptible dissonance. Goods requiring consumers to commit much of themselves or their money, however, are likely to generate considerable postpurchase dissonance. In general, therefore, durable and luxury goods are more likely to produce dissonance than are convenience goods, because they usually require larger consumer investment in time, ego and money.

During purchase decisions, dissonance can result when the consumer recognises that alternative brands have both positive and negative characteristics. Therefore, after making a decision, the consumer realises that some relatively undesirable traits of the selected brand have been acquired while some relatively desirable traits of the alternative brands have been forgone. At this point the consumer may even rate the unchosen alternatives higher than the brand purchased.

In the consumer's mind, the positive attributes of unchosen brands and the negative characteristics of the chosen brand are emphasised. This period of post-purchase process is called the *regret* phase, and it usually is very brief. The next phase is termed the *dissonance reduction period*. In this stage the consumer is very likely to evaluate the chosen brand more positively than at the time of purchase, and may evaluate the unselected brands less positively.

Multiattribute models

In recent years the adequacy of earlier attitude theories and models has come under question. An important criticism has been the lack of attention paid to the complexity and interactions of attitude components. In fact, early work employed only one-component definitions of attitude by focusing exclusively on a person's overall feelings or evaluative reactions toward objects. Later theories expanded on this view by stressing that attitudes have three major components: the *cognitive* component, which accounts for the individual's perceptions and knowledge about an object; the *affective* component, which describes the individual's feelings or emotional reactions (like/dislike) toward the object; and the *conative* component, which encompasses a tendency to act in certain ways toward the object. Unfortunately, although the importance of the three-component view of attitudes was widely recognised, many marketers continued to employ measures that only focused on the affective component for determining an individual's overall evaluation of an object. As a consequence, it was difficult to determine the basis of a person's overall attitude and how it might be possible to influence this attitude to change.[17] Of course, as we might expect, the basis, or reasons, for holding an attitude and the factors that might influence it to change over time are two considerations of high importance for the design of marketing strategies. Therefore, attitude measures that continued to focus only on the affective component were of limited usefulness to marketers.

Rosenberg and Fishbein pioneered new models of attitudes that have overcome many of the shortcomings of previous theories.[18] Because marketers and consumer behaviourists have given more attention to the Fishbein model, it will be reviewed here as an example of multiattribute attitude models.[19]

FISHBEIN'S ATTITUDE MODEL

Fishbein's position is that people form attitudes toward objects on the basis of their *beliefs* (perceptions and knowledge) about these objects. Beliefs are in turn acquired by processing information obtained from direct experiences with objects and from communications about them received from other sources. Therefore, to understand consumers' attitudes adequately, we must determine the beliefs that form the basis of these attitudes. Notice how this view is consistent with the view of high-involvement consumer activities that has been presented in this text; information processing leads to cognitions or beliefs about products, which, in turn, lead to attitudes that are involved in the evaluation of products.

Because any object such as a product has numerous attributes (size, features, shape and the like), individuals will process information and form beliefs about many of these individual attributes. Positive or negative feelings are also formed on the basis of the beliefs held about these attributes. Therefore, Fishbein's model is constructed so that a person's overall attitude toward some object is derived from the person's beliefs and feelings about various attributes of the object. This is why we refer to it as a *multiattribute* attitude model.

Fishbein's attitude model can be expressed in equation form as:

$$A_o = \sum_{i=1}^{n} b_i e_i$$

where A_o = the person's overall attitude toward the object

b_i = the strength of the person's belief that the object is related to attribute i (such as the strength of the belief that Wrangler jeans are durable)

e_i = the person's evaluation or intensity of feelings (liking or disliking) toward attribute i

n = the number of relevant beliefs for that person

We can see that the model explicitly incorporates the cognitive (belief) and affective (evaluation) components of attitudes. It also accounts for the strength or intensity of these elements. The conative component, to be discussed in more depth shortly, is related to these two components.

The model states that to determine a person's overall attitude toward some object, it is first necessary to determine those beliefs that have the most influence on this attitude. These most relevant beliefs, called *salient* beliefs, frequently do not exceed nine in number.[20] The overall attitude toward an object can then be obtained by multiplying the belief score by the evaluation score for each attribute and then summing across all relevant beliefs to obtain the value A.

An example will reinforce our understanding of the model. Assume that we want to determine a consumer's overall attitude toward a certain brand of wristwatch, and that through questioning we have been able to identify five beliefs that appear to be salient for this consumer. The strength of each belief can be measured on a bipolar scale such as the following:

The wristwatch is high in price

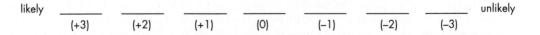

likely ___ ___ ___ ___ ___ ___ ___ unlikely
   (+3)   (+2)   (+1)   (0)   (–1)   (–2)   (–3)

The consumer's response to this scale would indicate the degree to which the consumer believes that the wristwatch possesses the attribute in question—in this case, a high price. If we were attempting to assess the attitudes of more than one consumer, we could question a sample of them and then select as salient beliefs those that are most frequently mentioned. The entire group of consumers would then be asked to respond to these salient beliefs, as indicated above.

After obtaining belief scores, the consumer would be asked to evaluate each product attribute for which a salient belief exists. This is frequently accomplished on the following type of scale:

A high price for wristwatches is:

extremely good	moderately	slightly	neither/nor	slightly	moderately	extremely bad
(+3)	(+2)	(+1)	(0)	(−1)	(−2)	(−3)

Be careful to note that these evaluation scores measure the consumer's feelings about each attribute itself (high price, accurate time and so on). They do *not* measure how much the consumer is pleased or displeased that the brand in question possesses the attribute.

Table 12.1 presents hypothetical results of these data-collection efforts. As the model requires, each of the consumer's belief scores is now multiplied by its respective evaluation score to obtain the last column of the table. Adding all of the products in this column reveals that the consumer's overall attitude toward the brand stands at +5. This represents a slightly positive attitude toward the brand when compared with a maximum attainable attitude score of +45. The consumer's attitude toward other wristwatch brands could also be calculated and compared with this brand. For the additional brands, it would only be necessary to obtain new belief scores because, as mentioned, the evaluation score measures feelings toward general product attributes and therefore does not vary across brands.

TABLE 12.1 Calculating a consumer's attitude toward a brand of wristwatch

Salient beliefs	Belief Strength (b_i)	Evaluation Score (e_i)	Product ($b_i e_i$)
Keeps accurate time	+3	+2	+6
Has waterproof case	+2	+2	+4
Has day/date calendar	+1	+3	+3
Is high in price	+3	−2	−6
Has digital display	+2	−1	−2

$$\text{Overall attitude score: } A_0 = \sum_{i=1}^{5} b_i e_i = +5$$

It is important to note how differences in belief scores and evaluation scores can influence the consumer's overall attitude toward the product. For example, note in Table 12.1 that the first two salient beliefs both have the same evaluation score of +2. However, because the consumer's beliefs that this brand of wristwatch keeps good time (+3) are stronger than the beliefs that it has a waterproof case (+2), the time–accuracy attribute contributes more to the overall attitude toward the brand. Conversely, notice that the first and fourth salient beliefs both have the same belief strength, but they differ considerably in terms of evaluation scores (+2 versus −2), yielding *offsetting* contributions to the consumer's overall attitude. This points out an important characteristic of this type of attitude model—in addition to being multiattribute in nature, it is also a *compensatory* model. This means that the product of belief and evaluation scores on one brand attribute can be offset, or *compensated* for, by the products derived from one or more other attributes. The implication is that a poor response to one feature of a brand does not necessarily cancel this brand out in the consumer's eyes.

These last comments demonstrate an important potential of multiattribute models. As has been stated:

> *The potential advantage of multiattribute models over the simpler 'overall affect' approach (unidimensional model) is in gaining understanding of attitudinal structure. Diagnosis of brand strengths and weaknesses on relevant product attributes can then be used to suggest specific changes in a brand and its marketing support.*[21]

That is, information regarding consumers' beliefs and evaluations generated by a multiattribute model provides important knowledge relevant to marketing strategy. The information can be used to suggest changes in brand attributes, modifications of promotional messages to better acquaint consumers with existing brand attributes and the identification of new market opportunities. More will be said about these strategies in the next chapter.

MODEL LIMITATIONS   Marketers were quick to capitalise on the potential of Fishbein's model and similar multiattribute models for predicting the behaviour of consumers. Consequently, many studies were undertaken to establish the strength of this attitude–behaviour linkage. Unfortunately, these studies did not always yield a highly positive relationship. Several reasons have been offered for these results:

1. Consumption situations can vary, and the situation will influence the strength of the attitude–behaviour relationship.[22] In fact, evidence suggests that consumers' attitudes toward a given brand can actually vary depending on the situation.[23]

2. Time usually elapses between when consumers form attitudes and when they are ready to act on these attitudes. During that time many variables, both expected and unexpected, can intervene also to influence behaviour. For example, an unexpected need for a new family car could quickly postpone or cancel plans to purchase a home VCR.

3. A distinction must be made between attitudes toward objects and attitudes toward behaving in a certain way toward these objects. For example, many consumers could have a favourable attitude toward Chevrolet Corvettes, but, because of their cost, few would realistically have a favourable attitude toward purchasing one. Consumers' attitudes toward some type of behaviour are influenced by their evaluation of the perceived consequences (positive and negative) of taking such action. Therefore, these attitudes are more relevant for predicting consumers' actions than are attitudes toward the objects themselves.

4. Consumers are often influenced by their *perceptions* of what others will think of their actions. Therefore, even though a consumer may have a favourable attitude toward making some purchase, he or she may refrain from doing so because of a perception that important others may not approve of the action. This influence is referred to as a *subjective norm*.

These considerations convinced attitude theorists that it was inappropriate to expect attitude-toward-object models successfully to predict behaviour. New modelling efforts were necessary to account for the additional complexity introduced by such factors. Fishbein responded with the behavioural intentions model.[24]

FISHBEIN'S BEHAVIOURAL INTENTIONS MODEL

The revised model offered by Fishbein, and contributed to by Ajzen, can be presented in diagram form as shown in Figure 12.6. Here, we see that behaviour is a function of a person's intention to behave in a certain manner and other intervening factors. This means that intention to behave cannot be expected to be a perfect predictor of behaviour.

Two factors are seen to influence the person's intention to act in a certain manner: the person's attitude toward acting in that manner; and subjective norms, which, as we said, are the individual's perceptions of how important others will react to such behaviour. The relative influence of each of these factors will determine the exact nature of the person's behavioural intentions. The figure also shows that attitudes toward behaviour are determined by beliefs and evaluations that the consumer holds about the consequences of behaviour. Subjective norms are determined by the consumer's beliefs about reactions of others regarding the intended behaviour, and the consumer's motivations to comply with their standards for behaviour.

Fishbein expressed these relationships in equation form as:

$$B \approx BI = w_1(A_B) + w_2(SN)$$

where B = the person's actual behaviour, which is approximately equal to BI

BI = the person's intention to behave in a specific manner

A_B = the person's attitude toward performing that behaviour

SN = the subjective norm regarding this behaviour

w_1, w_2 = weights representing the relative influence of A_B and SN, respectively, on the behavioural intention

As the model shows, to predict behaviour one must determine the individual's attitude toward the specific behaviour in question (A_B), and the individual's subjective norm (SN) regarding that behaviour. Each of these would then be weighted by w_1 and w_2 respectively (which add up to 1.0), to reflect its relative importance in influencing the behavioural intention. Such weights would be

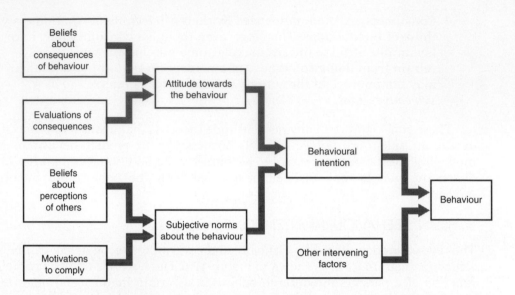

FIG. 12.6 The relationship of components in Fishbein's behavioural intentions attitude model

derived by regression analysis from a preliminary study. The weighted components would then be combined to yield a measure of behavioural intention to be used for prediction. We can see, therefore, that use of the model requires determination of its two components inferior—A_B and SN. Each of these is discussed, in turn, below.

The individual's attitude toward performing the specific behaviour (A_B) is expressed as:

$$A_B = \sum_{i=1}^{n} b_i e_i$$

where A_B = the individual's overall attitude toward performing the specific behaviour

b_i = the person's belief that performing that behaviour results in consequence i

e_i = the person's evaluation of consequence i

n = the number of relevant behavioural beliefs

It will be noticed that the *structure* of this component is identical to the model for attitude toward objects that was discussed earlier. As was stated before, relevant beliefs must be determined and then these beliefs and the accompanying evaluations must be measured on scales. The important change here is that beliefs and evaluations are about certain *actions* and the consequences of these actions, rather than about attributes of an object.

The subjective norm component of the behavioural intentions model can be expressed as follows:

$$SN = \sum_{i=1}^{k} b_i m_i$$

where SN = the individual's subjective norm regarding the specific behaviour

b_i = the individual's normative belief that reference group or person i thinks the individual should or should not perform the behaviour

m_i = the individual's motivation to comply with the thoughts of referent i

k = the number of relevant referents

An example will provide more meaning to these formulas. Assume that a consumer is considering the purchase of a chartered vacation package for a two-week period during the first half of July. To simplify the situation, also assume that she is only interested in choosing between two vacation packages—one to England and one to Japan. The consumer's behavioural intention toward these alternatives will be a function of her attitude toward purchasing each, and of the subjective norms she holds about each purchase. These components are examined in turn below.

As our formula for A_B shows, to determine the consumer's attitude toward purchasing either vacation package, we must first identify the salient beliefs she holds toward the consequences of a purchase. Often these can be obtained through a questioning process. However, if the attitudes of a large number of consumers had to be measured, questioning a sample of them would identify the most frequently held salient beliefs. In either case, once consumers' salient beliefs regarding the consequences of actions have been identified, we would need to measure their belief strengths and their evaluations of these consequences. The difference between the scales that would measure these variables and the ones used for Fishbein's earlier attitude model is that now focus is on the *consequences* of purchase *behaviour* rather than on the attributes of the object.

Table 12.2 presents results that we could have obtained from our consumer. The first column identifies six salient beliefs this consumer holds about the consequences of purchasing the two chartered vacation packages. Notice that the statements refer to a specific time interval for the actions. The second and third columns represent the degree to which the consumer believes these consequences describe the England trip and Japan trip, respectively. The fourth column represents the consumer's evaluation of the consequences described in column 1. Notice that these evaluations would be the same for the various trips, because they reflect feelings about consequences and not feelings about the extent to which such consequences would result from particular trips.

The last two columns present the product of belief and evaluation scores for each trip; the sum of these columns shows that the consumer holds a more favourable attitude toward taking the England trip (+14) than she does the Japan trip (+7).

TABLE 12.2 Calculating a consumer's attitude toward purchasing different vacation packages

Salient beliefs about consequences	Belief strengths (b_i)		Motivation to comply (m_i)	Product ($b_i e_i$)	
	England trip	Japan trip		England trip	Japan trip
Taking the England/Japan vacation package in July will:					
Increase my social contacts	+2	+2	+3	+6	+6
Provide a restful vacation	+2	+1	+1	+2	+1
Improve my mental attitude	+1	+3	+2	+2	+6
Be expensive	+2	+3	–2	–4	–6
Make me a more interesting person	+1	+3	+2	+2	+6
Involve difficult language skills	–2	+2	–3	+6	–6
Overall attitude toward purchase: $A_B = \sum_{i=1}^{6} b_i e_i =$				+14	+7

Now, in order to determine the consumer's subjective norm for purchasing either vacation package, we must first identify the groups and individuals who have the most influence on her regarding the behaviour in question. These are called the *salient referents*. Often this information can be obtained through a questioning process. Assume for our purposes that there are three individuals who are salient referents for this consumer: her brother, a special friend and her boss.

We next must identify the consumer's beliefs about thoughts or reactions of these people regarding her purchase of each of the vacation trips. Her motivation to comply with these thoughts must also be measured. This information could be obtained from the following types of measurement scales:

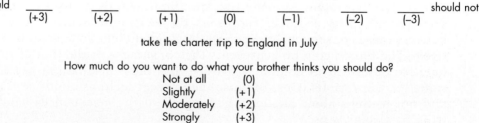

Table 12.3 summarises the results of our data collection regarding the subjective norm component in much the same way as previous tables have done. It is useful to notice how the consumer's motivation to comply weights the

perceptions of salient referent opinions. For example, she believes that both her special friend and her boss hold the same opinions about the Japan trip, but because she is more motivated to comply with her friend's opinion, it carries more weight in influencing her subjective norm. Overall, we see from a summation of the last columns that the subject norm considerably favours the Japan trip (+11) over the England trip (+1).

TABLE 12.3   Calculating a consumer's subjective norm toward purchasing different vacation packages

Salient referents	Normative belief strength (b_i)		Motivation to comply (m_i)	Product $(b_i m_i)$	
	England trip	Japan trip		England trip	Japan trip
Brother	+2	+1	+1	+2	+1
Special friend	−1	+2	+3	−3	+6
Boss	+1	+2	+2	+2	+4
Selective norm: $SN = \sum_{i=1}^{3} b_i m_i =$				+1	+11

The last ingredients needed to determine our consumer's behavioural intentions are weights that reflect the relative importance of her attitude toward behaviour and her subjective norm. Recall that these weights would have to come from regression analysis of a preliminary study. Assume that such an investigation generated weights of .4 and .6 for the attitude and subjective norm components, respectively. We now can substitute these weights and information from Tables 12.2 and 12.3 into the equation that was presented earlier and is repeated below:

$$BI = w_1(A_B) + w_2(SN)$$

For the England trip we find that $BI = .4(14) + .6(1) = 6.2$ and for the Japan trip $BI = .4(7) + .6(11) = 9.4$. We see that, in this case, even though the consumer's attitude strongly favours the England trip, her subjective norm strongly favours the Japan trip. Because the subjective norm carries more weight in her decision making on this issue (.6 versus .4), the prediction is that she intends to purchase the Japan trip. However, recall from our earlier discussion and Figure 12.5 that, because of other influencing factors, the consumer's behavioural intentions will only be an approximation of her actual behaviour.

MODEL EVALUATION   A number of issues and limitations of the Fishbein behavioural intentions model still need to be resolved.[25] Nevertheless, evidence accumulating from tests of the model has been quite encouraging.[26] Our ability to predict the behaviour of consumers has improved when compared with earlier attitude-toward-object models. However, what appear to be just as important are the implications this model has for marketers in terms of factors influencing consumers' intentions to behave. These attitudinal and subjective-norm components help our understanding of reasons for consumers' behaviour, and also suggest alternative marketing strategies for effecting changes in consumers' attitudes and intentions to behave. These practical implications will have much of our attention in the next section.

THE PERIPHERAL ROUTE TO DEVELOPING ATTITUDES

Fishbein's view of how consumers develop attitudes has been described as a theory of reasoned action. This is because the models are *belief-based*. That is, the models assume that consumers will, in a very conscious and deliberate fashion, first develop beliefs about individual attributes of an object and then carefully combine these beliefs to forge an overall attitude about the object. Notice that the focus here is on *conscious* attitude development by consumers, with stress on the processing of *verbal* information in the form of cognitions (thoughts or beliefs about objects, such as buying a particular brand).

However, other evidence has accumulated to suggest that consumers may develop attitudes through other processes that do not depend on conscious and deliberate thought.[27] A laboratory experiment to test attitude formation regarding facial tissues serves as an example.[28] Separate groups of subjects were shown different advertisements for four fictitious brands of tissues. Three ads contained no verbal information beyond the fictitious name of the facial tissue (identified only by a letter of the alphabet) but did contain a half-page colour photograph. One showed a soft, fluffy kitten with the facial-tissue box, one used a sunset over an ocean and another showed a presumed neutrally evaluated abstract painting. The fourth ad contained a verbal claim about the softness of the tissues, but no picture. Study results indicated that subjects formed significantly different impressions of the advertised tissues. Both the kitten and sunset ads created more positive brand attitudes than did the verbal message or the picture of the abstract painting. Also, subjects exposed to the ad showing the soft, fluffy kitten rated the facial tissues as significantly softer than did any of the other groups. Fishbein's attitude model did not successfully predict these attitude scores of the subjects. Given such results, one implication is that those who would employ Fishbein's belief-based model to assess consumers' brand attitudes might stand the risk of misrepresenting these attitudes to some degree.

Why do consumers act in this way? What mechanism might be involved? A quite popular theory is that there might be two routes to attitude development and change, and that each works under different circumstances.[29] These two routes are termed the central and peripheral routes to processing. In the *central route*, consumers form attitudes in a conscious and deliberate manner, as described by Fishbein's behavioural intentions model. This is sometimes referred to as a *systematic-processing strategy*. However, as in the facial-tissue experiment, the *peripheral route* enables consumers to form attitudes without engaging in conscious thought about how the advertising message describes the object or its attributes. Rather, in this process, sometimes called a *heuristic-processing strategy*, consumers form attitudes by associating the object in question with seemingly incidental cues that accompany it. In an advertisement these may be background music; colour; the spokesperson's looks, behaviour or perceived trustworthiness; or similar characteristics such as the soft kitten in the experiment. Looking at various magazine ads will reveal that some appear to rely on such a process because they contain so little concrete information about the brand and its characteristics.

One way this process might operate is through classical conditioning. We saw in the last chapter on learning that repeated pairing of a neutral stimulus with one that evokes positive reactions can lead to the neutral stimulus evoking similar reactions. Therefore, classical conditioning would imply that if advertisers repeatedly show their brand associated with stimuli such as fluffy kittens and pleasant music, the positive reactions generated by these stimuli will tend to become associated with the advertised brand. This might then increase consumers' positive evaluations of the brand more than their cognitive beliefs about the brand and its attributes could account for.

What determines which route consumers are likely to use to develop their attitudes? The *Elaboration Likelihood Model* (ELM) proposes that, for any situation, the consumer's level of involvement and ability to process information will be critical determinants.[30] If involvement levels are high (if personal relevance and so on is high) and the consumer is able consciously to understand the object and its attributes, the central route is likely to be employed. That is, elaboration is likely—deliberate thinking about the object and its attributes is likely. However, if involvement levels are low, economic implications are not that important or the consumer is having difficulty understanding the object or its attributes, conscious elaboration is unlikely and the consumer will probably be influenced by cues that are incidental to the object in question.[31]

The ELM with its associated central and peripheral routes to attitude development, has been the focus of considerable research interest in the past few years. A number of studies suggest that the theory has usefulness.[32] However, recent findings have raised concern over some of its components, and other studies now suggest that peripheral processing may also influence consumers' *beliefs* as well as change overall attitudes toward brands.[33] If confirmed with additional research, this would suggest that peripheral processing can work to supplement (as opposed to substitute for) central belief-based processing. In either case, what is clear is that given the large number of advertisements that stress the visual presentation and often convey little verbal information, those interested in consumers' attitudes should be eager to learn more about these fascinating new proposals on the effects of advertisements.

STRATEGIES FOR CHANGING ATTITUDES AND INTENTIONS

Some strategies for influencing changes in consumers' attitudes toward certain behaviours have already been identified. Other strategies exist, however, that accomplish changes in behavioural intentions without directly affecting attitudes. Because Fishbein's behavioural intentions model links these concepts so closely together, the various change strategies are discussed collectively below. Although many factors can influence the marketer's choice among these alternatives, one fundamental consideration should be the degree of involvement that consumers are experiencing with the product.

Low-involvement strategies

In Chapter 9 we noted that under low-involvement conditions consumers are not likely to make brand choices on the basis of attitudes established through developing clearly formulated beliefs about the product or service. In essence, their interest is too low to spend time thinking about products and evaluating them in a rational and deliberate fashion. Given this, it is generally unproductive for marketers to develop communications designed to develop or modify thought-intensive prepurchase beliefs about their brands among consumers. In the preceding chapter on attitude development, we also noted that it seems possible to change a consumer's attitudes by a variety of cues that are among the incidental stimuli in the advertisement itself or are part of the situation in which the advertisement is being perceived by the consumer.[34] This seems especially so in low-involvement situations. Consequently, one potential low-involvement strategy may be to change consumers' attitudes by using *peripheral cues* to encourage favourable reactions toward advertisements used to promote the brands. Such cues might include pictures, colour, attractive spokespeople or characters, the creative placement of ad components and music in broadcast ads.[35] Some of these mechanisms will be treated in the last portion of this chapter. What is important to appreciate here is that the ensuing favourable reactions these mechanisms can generate among consumers toward the advertisement itself would then be expected to become associated with the product being advertised.

The options that remain stress capitalising on a means to transform the situation into one characterised by high involvement. Success here would allow use of high-involvement attitude-change methods to influence brand choices. How can this increase in prepurchase involvement be accomplished? A list of options suggested by various researchers has been compiled:

1. *Link the product or service to an involving issue*. Because issues are often more involving than are products, this linkage could increase involvement regarding the product. Linking a breakfast cereal to problems of deficient performance among school children who have not had a wholesome breakfast would be one example.

2. *Link the product to a presently involving personal situation*. On some occasions a message can be targeted to audiences at the time they are engaged in an activity related to the product. At this time their interest could be sufficiently high to qualify as high involvement. An example might be radio advertisements for a suntan lotion during midday hours of summer weekends.

3. *Develop high-involvement advertisements.* Because consumers' involvement in a product is low, it does not necessarily mean that they cannot become involved in advertisements for the product. The use of humour, dramatic events or other methods can create an involving advertisement to which the product could then be linked. Examples might include the active scenes in many sportswear commercials and other television ads showing the humorous woes of people who failed to use the advertised brand.

4. *Change the importance of product benefits.* This option is quite difficult to pursue, because it attempts a frontal attack on consumers' perceptions of product benefits. To illustrate, if consumers could be convinced that the fibre content in dried cereal is very important to their health, they might become more involved in their choice of cereal. The brands that possess this attribute are then likely to be the recipient of favourable consumer attitudes.

5. *Reveal or introduce important product characteristics.* New attributes can be associated with a product, and consumers can also be made aware that some favourable attributes have been product characteristics for a long time. These attributes have the potential for increasing involvement levels. The absence of caffeine and sugar or the addition of calcium in a number of soft drinks certainly appears to capture the interest of many consumers because of its implications regarding the health and appearance of the body. Fortification of milk and other foods with vitamins represents another example.[36]

In all of these cases, the attempt has been to increase involvement levels among consumers to the point where they will form attitudes prior to purchase and use these attitudes to influence their purchase decisions. We now turn to strategies designed for conditions in which these prepurchase attitudes are likely to be formed.

High-involvement strategies

Potentially, a variety of strategies are available for changing consumer attitudes under high-involvement conditions. Before implementing such strategies, however, the marketer must be clear on whether the attempt is to change consumer attitudes about the brand, or whether it is to change attitudes about behaving toward the brand. Consumer attitudes about behaving toward a brand are more closely related to their intentions to purchase. Therefore, we will focus on attitudes toward behaviour in the following discussion.

Figure 12.7 is based on Fishbein's behavioural intentions model and closely parallels portions of Figure 12.6. It suggests a variety of potential strategies for influencing change in consumers' attitudes toward behaviour.[37]

Employing the same reasoning as Fishbein used to develop his model, we can argue that behavioural change is a function of changes in behavioural intentions

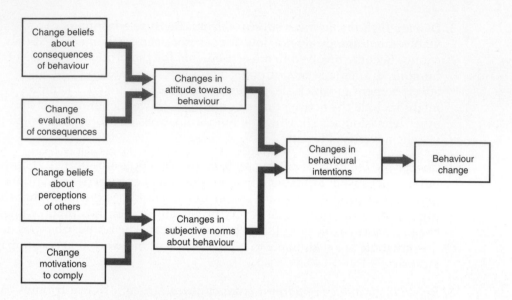

FIG. 12.7 Some strategy options for attitude change in high-involvement conditions
Source: Martin Fishbein & Icek Ajzen, *Belief, Attitude and Behavior; An Introduction to Theory and Research*, Addison-Wesley, Reading, MA, 1975, p. 407.

and other intervening factors. Changes in behavioural intentions are related to changes in attitudes toward the behaviour and changes in subjective norms about the behaviour. All of these, in turn, are functions of their components. These relationships suggest the following potential strategies:

1. *Change existing beliefs about the consequences of behaviour.* Consumers often hold incomplete or incorrect beliefs about the consequences of purchasing and using particular brands. Modification of those beliefs that will positively influence attitudes can increase intentions to purchase. One way to accomplish this is for advertisements to focus on brand benefits. Here, the message would be that purchase of the brand will yield certain beneficial results (consequences) for the consumer. As an example, consider the following message: 'Users of Top Flight golf balls get up to 14 more metres per drive than users of other brands'. Of course, a second option is for advertisements to suggest that few negative consequences will result from purchasing the brand. Stress on a low price is one such method.

2. *Change consumers' evaluation of the consequences of a particular action.* Consumers may believe that using a brand will lead to certain consequences, but these consequences are not evaluated very positively. Measures taken to increase evaluations of the consequences can have positive results. For example, an advertisement for Listerine mouthwash has stressed that its strong taste is associated with effectiveness in killing germs and giving fresh breath—'It tastes strong because it is strong'.

Potential results are more positive evaluations of the strong taste and enhancement of attitudes toward the brand.

3. *Introduce new belief/evaluation combinations.* In some cases, marketers can add or delete product attributes and generate positive consequences for the consumer. In other cases, the presence or absence of existing product attributes can be stressed in terms of their favourable consequences for the consumer.

4. *Change existing normative beliefs.* In some situations, consumers may hold favourable attitudes toward certain behaviours but be reluctant to take action because of unfavourable reactions on the subjective norm component. In other words, consumers believe that others who are important to them will not react favourably to the actions in question. This can be an important consideration with regard to the purchase of certain clothing items and other socially visible products. Although it may be difficult, the possibility exists that changes in such beliefs can be achieved. For example, promotions may simulate group settings in which people with whom consumers might identify express favourable reactions to purchasing the advertised brand. Given sufficient realism, such advertisements may weaken consumers' beliefs that people important to them will have negative reactions to purchase of the brand.

5. *Change motivations to comply with subjective norms.* A second strategy to modify the subjective norm component of behavioural intentions is to alter consumers' motivations to comply with the influences of people important to them. One way this can be accomplished is to diminish or increase the perceived importance or status of these influential others for at least the decision in question. For example, advertisements for a particular brand might stress the importance of being an individual and not always heeding the opinions of friends or important others.

6. *Introduce new normative components.* Subjective norms can also be influenced by the addition of new normative components that will be strong in their influence on the consumer. This can be done through introducing additional individuals the consumer deems important, or additional norms that the consumer might think important. Promotions showing how family, friends and so on react to certain purchase decisions and why these reactions might be important to the consumer are possibilities, as is introducing new standards of behaviour that others may expect.

The above review suggests that a variety of potential strategies exist for influencing attitude change among consumers in high-involvement situations. Selection of one or more strategies will be affected by the competitive environment, consumers' existing conditions, knowledge and beliefs, characteristics of the product and related factors. A few comments are useful on several of these issues.

Experience has shown marketers that it is much easier to change the intensity of attitudes than it is to change their direction. For example, if consumers have negative attitudes toward a brand, it would be a difficult task to transform these attitudes into positive ones. Efforts may be successful in reducing the intensity of negative attitudes, but the pay-off involved in such endeavours would be questionable. In such cases, the frequent recommendation is to 'Go with the flow', which could mean withdrawing the brand, or redesigning or reformulating it and introducing it to consumers under another name so that it will be given a fighting chance in the marketplace. For brands that receive generally favourable consumer acceptance, the strategy is typically to identify and concentrate on those components that yield the most positive change in attitudes for a given amount of investment in promotion.

Related to this discussion is the point that weakly held attitudes are easier to change than ones that are strongly held. Attitude strength has a variety of sources. One is the strength of the consumer's beliefs. The more confident a consumer is about his or her brand beliefs, the more difficult it is to change the beliefs. For example, two consumers may believe that Dunlop tyres will yield only moderate levels of tread wear. However, one's beliefs may be much stronger than the other's. It would be more difficult to convince the consumer with strong beliefs that Dunlop give excellent tread wear. Strong beliefs are formed through personal experience and from information about products that is clear and readily available for a period of time. Weaker beliefs tend to exist under opposite conditions.

A second influence on attitude strength is the degree of involvement a consumer has with the product in question. Greater involvement reflects more personal relevance of the product to the consumer. Consequently, an involved consumer is likely to hold stronger beliefs about the brands in question. Additional evidence suggests that the more involved consumer will be less willing to accept statements that diverge from beliefs held about a brand.[38] The degree of divergence that will be accepted is referred to as the consumer's *latitude of acceptance*. Conversely, statements that are accepted will fall into the consumer's *latitude of rejection*. The implication is that highly involved consumers are likely to hold strong beliefs about a brand and accept only those advertising claims that deviate very little from these beliefs. On the other hand, consumers who are not highly involved will have wider latitudes of acceptance, and their attitudes can be changed by the more discrepant advertising claims. As a consequence, more advertising dollars will probably have to be expended to change gradually the brand beliefs of highly involved consumers, while more rapid change with fewer resources may be possible for the less involved consumers.

A final point to mention here is that typically it appears to be easier to change consumers' beliefs than it is to change their evaluations of the consequences of certain actions. This is probably so because evaluations are based on consumers' need structures, which are more enduring and central to their values and self-concepts than are beliefs about purchasing a particular brand.

Discussion in the previous paragraphs has focused on strategies for making absolute changes in consumers' brand or purchase attitudes. Of course, in most situations consumers face competing brands and perceive them relative to each other. Therefore, a potential strategy not yet mentioned would be for the marketer to increase a brand's *relative* attitude standing by encouraging consumers to develop more negative attitudes toward competing brands. This would require communications that directly attack competing brands, or initiate or encourage damaging rumours about these brands. Generally speaking, there has been very little of this type of behaviour in the marketplace. In addition to the ethical issues that speak against it, such efforts are likely to result in damaging counterattacks from competitors. The ensuing battle would probably hurt all those involved. Therefore, we will not discuss such strategies further.

THE COMMUNICATION PROCESS

The primary means available to marketers for influencing attitude change is the design and implementation of persuasive communications. Properly designed communications benefit from an appreciation of the general nature of the communication process. A simplified model of this process is shown in Figure 12.8 and described in the following paragraphs.

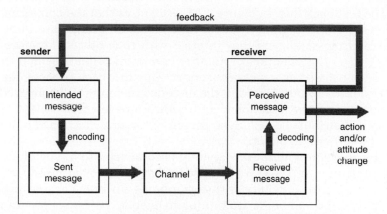

FIG. 12.8   A simplified model of the communication process

The sender initiates a communication message. This individual or group has as an objective the transmission of an intended message to one or more individuals acting as receivers. In marketing, the sender usually represents a company or its brand, and the intended message is usually conceived of as a mechanism to change consumers' attitudes toward the brand or toward purchasing it.

An intended message is the meaning a sender wishes to convey to receivers. In order to deliver this intended meaning, however, the message must be suitably formed for transmission in the channel selected for its delivery. That is, the intended message must be encoded into symbols making up the actual message, which represent thoughts of the sender. These symbols are usually words, but often they involve pictures and actions of the sender. Whatever the method, the important goal of the sender is to encode the message in a way that will maximise the likelihood that the receiver will interpret it in a way that matches the sender's intended meaning.

The sent (actual) message is transmitted over a channel of communication. In marketing, the potential channel alternatives are varied, ranging from radio to in-store displays and personal messages. Therefore, considerable deliberation must be taken to select the channel with characteristics most appropriate to the message involved.

The sent message is acquired by one or more receivers. However, received messages are rarely identical to sent messages. Characteristics of the channel of transmission are one set of factors accounting for this difference. For example, it is very difficult to reproduce accurately product colours and textures on television or in newspapers. Consequently, the received message can differ significantly from the sent message.

The received message is transformed into a perceived message through the receiver's information-processing activities. That is, the message is *decoded*—received symbols are transformed back into meaning or thoughts by the receiver. As we have seen, an individual's experiences, as well as the context in which the message is perceived, will influence any meaning derived from the message. Attitude change and/or actions will then be based on this perceived message.

The feedback loop in Figure 12.8 recognises that the communication process involves a two-way flow. That is, individuals or groups are both receivers and senders of messages, and they interact with each other. Therefore, feedback can be viewed as the initiation of another communication in which the receiver can now be construed as a message sender. This feedback process enables the original sender to monitor how well the intended meaning was conveyed and received. In many marketing situations, communications are transmitted via mass media to widely distributed consumers; therefore, accurate feedback information is very rare and difficult to obtain.

The concept of *noise* is frequently used to refer to a type of disruption in the communication process. We have seen that a variety of noise sources exist. The sender may have difficulty with formulating an intended message, and further problems can occur while attempting to encode a message for transmission. The channel of communication itself is capable of interfering with a message. The receiver may also introduce noise through the decoding process. Of course, the feedback loop may contribute additional noise. Therefore, each state of the communication process is susceptible to message distortion.

In order to appreciate the persuasive communication process, it is necessary to understand three general kinds of factors that operate to influence beliefs, attitudes and behaviour. They are source, message, and receiver factors.[39] These three sets of factors interact to produce intended and unintended communication effects. For simplicity, each set of factors is next examined one at a time. However, the reader should continually bear in mind that these factors are interactive.

SOURCE FACTORS

What characteristics do certain individuals, companies or groups possess that facilitate their effectiveness in changing the views and attitudes of others? This section discusses major characteristics of persuasive communication sources. The major types of marketing communication sources are reviewed first, and factors influencing their persuasiveness are discussed next.

Marketing communication sources

In a marketing context, several sources can be employed in an attempt to reach consumers with persuasive communications. These can be used alone or in combination to produce a combined source effect on consumers. Six prominent marketing source effects are briefly described in the following paragraphs.

Consumers perceive *companies* as sources of information, and some are seen as highly credible while others are viewed with suspicion. Most consumers feel that Procter & Gamble and Sterling, for example, are trustworthy companies.

Because of their face-to-face contacts with current and prospective customers, *sales representatives* themselves are viewed by consumers as information sources. Also, salespeople who are viewed as knowledgeable (expert) and trustworthy often are more persuasive than those not so highly regarded.[40] In addition, evidence suggests that consumers are more receptive to salespeople from highly credible companies than from unknown or low-credibility companies.[41]

Consumers use the *media* extensively for product information. Although media are actually channel links between companies and consumers (receivers), people view them as sources; thus, it is important to understand their effects on persuading consumers to purchase products.

Companies typically employ individuals as representatives in advertising. In fact, on-camera *spokespeople* appear in a significant portion of television advertising. Effective hired promoters such as Luke Egan, Greg Norman and Michael Jordan are ones who have established reputations for themselves, often in occupations unrelated to the advertised product. Surprisingly, among Australians Michael Jordan is better known than other Australian athletes, according to one report.[42]

Spokespeople are used to persuade consumers to buy products COURTESY OF UNCLE TOBYS CO. PTY LTD

At the local level, *retailers* often act as sources for marketing communications. A department store that has a good local reputation may more easily sell unknown brands than less reputable stores might. Also, specialty shops are successful in selling unknown brands because of their perceived expertise in the product line, such as cameras, rugs and stereo equipment.

Although we have described each of the above marketing sources separately, in reality there are *combined source effects* that interact to produce a persuasive impact on consumers. Therefore, producers must carefully select hired promoters, media and retailers to deliver persuasive brand messages.

Influences on source effectiveness

A variety of factors can influence the persuasiveness of those who transmit marketing communications. Among many factors influencing the ability of sources to change attitudes are their credibility, their similarity to audience members, and their attitudes toward themselves, the message and audience members. This section reviews these major influences.

CREDIBILITY AND ITS EFFECTS

Perhaps the most investigated source factor in persuasion is credibility or believability. A long-held conclusion from numerous early research studies has been that highly credible sources achieve greater attitude change among consumers than do those having less credibility. We should be careful to note here that credibility rests in the eyes of receivers. That is, receivers must *perceive* a source as credible, regardless of whether or not the source *is* honest, trustworthy, knowledgeable and so on. Thus, if a consumer *perceives* Michael Jordan as a credible source for basketball shoes, when Jordan promotes the advantages of Nike the consumer would be expected to be persuaded by the message to a greater degree than if someone else who the consumer perceives as a less credible source had spoken the same words.

This general finding about the effectiveness of highly credible sources for generating attitude change seems like common sense to many of us. However, more recent evidence suggests that the impact of source credibility is complex, depending on a number of specific conditions. Some of these are addressed in the following sections. In this discussion we are assuming that conditions of high involvement exist, so consumers are actively attending to the communications being sent.

INFLUENCE OF RECEIVER'S OPINION The initial opinion of audience members appears to be one important influence on the impact of source credibility. Specifically, when receivers already hold opinions that are opposite to those presented in a message, highly credible sources are likely to generate more attitude change than will sources of lower credibility. However, when audience opinions already favour positions presented in a message, highly credible sources have not been found to be more effective than sources of lower credibility in generating attitude change. In fact, some research even suggests that sources of lower credibility will be more effective in generating attitude change.[43]

To appreciate why these statements may have validity, we must understand that communications can generate cognitive responses among consumers. Recall from the section on memory in Chapter 11 that *cognitive response* refers to thoughts a consumer will retrieve from long-term memory upon exposure to a communication such as an advertising message. Those responses most relevant to our discussion here are *counterarguments*—thoughts stored in long-term memory that are used to contradict aspects of the message being received; and *support arguments*—thoughts stored in long-term memory that are used to support aspects of the received message. Counterarguments are generated by receivers when messages oppose their initial opinions, and support arguments are developed for messages consistent with initial positions. One interesting finding is that highly credible sources appear to have such significant believability that they tend to block cognitive responses.[44] This means that when receivers are initially opposed to information in a message, highly credible sources will tend to block counterarguments. The message is therefore likely to be accepted without much modification, yielding a considerable change in attitudes. However, the same message received from sources having lower credibility will be critically reviewed. This will generate counterarguments, tending to neutralise points made in the message. Therefore, the amount of attitude change will be less than what a highly credible source could achieve.

What happens when receivers' initial opinions or beliefs are consistent with the content of a message? The message transmitted from a highly credible source will again be accepted without much critical examination. However, because it is consistent with the receiver's existing position, a large amount of attitude change is unlikely. Conversely, as before, the same message received from a less credible source will be critically reviewed and will generate cognitive responses. Because the cognitive responses will now be in the form of support arguments, the resulting attitude change can be greater than that achieved by the highly credible source.

Important practical implications can be drawn from this analysis. First, marketers may usually want to avoid developing communications that oppose consumers' opinions because of their requirements for a highly credible source. As the task of achieving very high credibility in a marketing context is quite difficult, often expensive and sometimes impossible, an alternative to consider carefully is using communications consistent with consumers' positions. However, when fighting rumours, bad publicity and various other forms of unwarranted consumer beliefs, marketers may need to design communications that oppose consumers' positions. In these cases, it would be quite important to carefully identify and use sources that will have high credibility for the specific situation at hand.

MESSAGE DISCREPANCY CONDITIONS   A topic closely related to the above discussion is message discrepancy. Highly discrepant messages do not completely oppose receivers' initial opinions, but are quite deviant from the receivers' beliefs. Marketers encounter such situations when they wish to demonstrate extraordinary products such as Super Glue or to make claims about their offerings that differ considerably from current beliefs in the target market. Similar to the situation of negative initial opinions, very credible sources are most effective in achieving attitude change for highly discrepant messages. As before, the explanation appears to be that high credibility minimises cognitive responses, which are likely to be counterarguments in cases of high discrepancy.[45] For messages of little discrepancy, counterarguments are less likely, while support arguments will be more prevalent. Therefore, under such conditions less credible sources can be effective in achieving attitude change.

What are the strategy implications of these findings? If the marketer can achieve a high-credibility standing in the target market, discrepant promotional claims can be employed to yield considerable attitude change. However, as we have noted, very high levels of credibility are often difficult to achieve. In such cases, the suggestion has been to design only mildly discrepant messages.

LOW-CREDIBILITY EFFECTIVENESS   Are there situations in which highly credible sources can actually *inhibit* attitude change in an audience? Research suggests that there are. In fact, we have already mentioned one such situation—when audience members hold initial opinions that are in agreement with points to be made in the message. A second situation appears to be when the marketer wishes to change consumers' behaviour directly and have this lead to later attitude change.[46] This could occur when free brand samples or trials are offered to encourage development of favourable attitudes.

In other situations, high credibility may be most effective in changing attitudes, but using less credible sources is more feasible. Here, a potential strategy is to improve the amount of attitude change that can be achieved with low-credibility sources. One method to accomplish this is to develop a situation in which sources will argue against their own interests. By doing so, the communicators appear to establish credibility, because it becomes obvious to audiences that they have nothing to gain by arguing for someone else's position. For example, in one advertisement the spokesperson states that he is not getting 'one red cent' for endorsing the advertised product.

Low-credibility sources can also increase their persuasiveness if they are identified *after*, rather than *before*, presenting their messages. The reason is that audience members will attend to a message if they do not know it is from a low-credibility source. Otherwise, they will selectively ignore a presentation if they strongly suspect the credibility of the source.

Care must be taken in using these strategies. Their implementation can be difficult and can cause problems for other aspects of the message. Therefore, it probably would be wise to consider other options before embracing such strategies.

THE SLEEPER EFFECT   The above review suggests that under certain circumstances highly credible communicators can significantly influence attitude change. However, a valid question is whether we can expect this change in attitudes to be long lasting. Research evidence suggests that the initial effect can dissipate rather rapidly, which is not completely surprising given our understanding of the learning curve. However, a startling finding of early research was that an audience exposed initially to a low-credibility source develops opinions more closely in line with the source as time passes.[47] This result became known as the 'sleeper effect'.

Consideration of both findings would lead us to predict that as time passes opinion change achieved by high- and low-credibility sources would tend toward equality. Figure 12.9 graphically illustrates this conclusion, which drew the attention of astute marketers interested in long-run attitude change.

The explanation offered for these findings is that receivers tend to forget message sources more rapidly than they forget message content. Thus, as the 'enhancing' and 'depressing' effects of high- and low-credibility sources dissipate what will tend to remain is message content, which is the same in both cases.

Unfortunately, additional research has not shown consistent support for the sleeper effect.[48] This means that we cannot unquestioningly accept that small amounts of initial attitude change achieved by using a low-credibility source will increase over time. A further finding adds one more piece to the puzzle: if original sources are reinstated (allowed to reintroduce their position), the effect is to restore audience opinion levels nearly to the points they were right after initial message exposure.[49] In effect, reintroduction of a source tends to yield the same effect as when it was initially used. Figure 12.10 graphically summarises these points. Note how the dashed lines duplicate the situation shown in Figure 12.9. Therefore, the assumption being used here is that, other things being held constant, the sleeper effect is valid and a decline in attitude change will occur over time for the highly credible source. The new solid lines in this figure now indicate that reinstatement of each source tends to hold attitude change levels near their original conditions. If we were to assume that the sleeper effect was not valid, the dashed and solid lines for the low-credibility source would coincide and run horizontally.

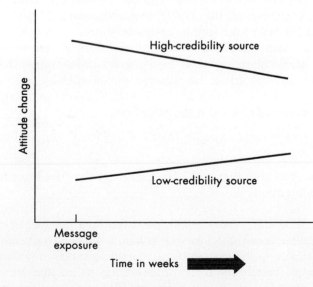

FIG. 12.9 An illustration of attitude-change convergence predicted by early research evidence on source credibility effects over time

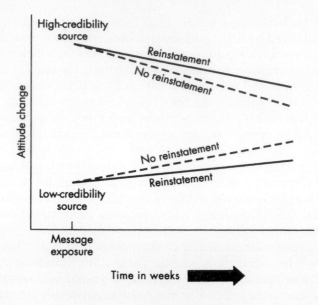

FIG. 12.10 An illustration of the effects of reinstatement of long-run attitude change; conditions of a 'sleeper effect' are assumed

The evidence presented above and summarised in Figure 12.10 tends to favour use of a high-credibility source when situations discussed in the previous sections warrant it. Recent evidence also suggests that for audiences experiencing high levels of message involvement highly credible expert sources should be introduced early in the communication to enjoy their greatest impact.[50] Also, typical marketing applications, such as advertising repetition, could easily involve source reinstatement, which would act to maintain favourable attitude-change levels initially achieved with the highly credible source. Therefore, whether or not a sleeper effect does exist would only influence the *degree* to which a highly credible source would generate more long-run attitude change than one of low credibility. Combined conditions favouring a low-credibility source would be:

1. the existence of a valid sleeper effect;

2. a relatively large expense involved in identifying and using a highly credible source;

3. as suggested in Figure 12.10, a strategy that does not involve source reinstatement.

BASES OF CREDIBILITY   Our conclusion is that in a number of circumstances, using a highly credible communicator can enhance the persuasiveness of marketing messages. Practically speaking, therefore, many marketers may wish to identify sources that have high credibility in communicating to an audience about a particular brand. But what factors influence the credibility of a source in the eyes of an audience? Five major bases are trustworthiness, expertise, status or prestige, likability and an assortment of physical traits. Each of these is discussed in this section.

A source will be perceived as more credible if the audience views him or her as honest or trustworthy, and this is related to the degree the source is perceived as having an *intention to manipulate*. If the audience believes that the communicator, no matter how generally honest, has something to gain personally by the message, then any persuasive attempts will lose effectiveness.

This idea suggests one reason advertising and personal selling are generally less effective than the advice of a trusted friend for changing consumer attitudes. Advertisers have attempted to overcome this problem to some extent by using 'candid interviews' with consumers who were not aware that they were giving testimony to a company's brand. Other similar approaches, such as disguised brand tests, have been used by advertisers to reduce their perceived 'intention to manipulate'. This technique has been used for Kelloggs Corn Flakes, Surf's Cold Power, Pepsi, beer, nappies and feminine pads.

Another basis of source credibility is *perceived expertise*. That is, when an audience views a communicator as having higher qualifications than others to speak on a topic, the communicator will be more persuasive than a person viewed as less qualified. This is why experts in a field related to a company's product often are used to promote its brands. An example would be Shane Warne and Laurie Daley for Nike shoes.

A communicator whom an audience perceives as high in *status or prestige* is often more credible than one perceived as low in these attributes. As we have learned, society 'confers' status and prestige upon individuals according to the roles they occupy. For example, a physician is generally regarded as having higher status and prestige than a nurse, and a scientist usually has more prestige than an engineer. Marketers often attempt to obtain as endorsers of their products individuals who have obtained high status. Examples include using Professor Julius Sumner-Miller to endorse Cadbury chocolates and Peter Brock as a spokesman for motor oil. It should be noted that although the concepts of prestige and expertise overlap, they are not synonymous.[51]

The *physical characteristics* and other features of communicators can also influence their credibility, although the effect of these attributes on actual behaviour is less well documented.[52] For example, age, gender, colour, dress and likability, as well as general attractiveness, can affect source credibility. Regarding physical attractiveness, the general wisdom has been that attractive spokespeople are generally preferred to less attractive ones, because their physical appearance enhances their credibility. However, recent evidence suggests that this enhancing power of attractiveness may only exert its positive influence when consumers perceive that the product is in some way related to physical attractiveness.[53] Regarding age, older people tend to be influential on younger people in many cultures. The tendency for youth to accept their elders' advice and influence might be largely because the younger generation perceives older people as having had more experience in life, viewing them as more 'expert'.

This discussion has focused on the influence of source credibility in achieving attitude change. Two other groups of source factors that can also be important are briefly reviewed in the following sections.

ATTITUDE OF THE COMMUNICATOR

Communicators are more persuasive when they have positive attitudes toward themselves, their messages and their receivers.[54] Within a marketing context, a sales representative who has a positive attitude toward himself or herself is one who has self-confidence. The self-confidence is perceived by the prospective buyer and can influence the decision to buy.

Sales representatives are trained to show positive attitudes toward their products and sales presentations (their messages). That is, they are trained to *believe* in the products they are selling and what they say about them.

SIMILARITY WITH AUDIENCE Another finding regarding communication sources is that people are persuaded more by a communicator they perceive to be similar to themselves.[55] That is, people seem to be influenced by others who are like themselves. Similarity can be perceived in a variety of ways, such as personality, race, interests, self-image and group affiliations. This has led some marketers to use so-called slice-of-life advertisements. For example, ads for Nescafé coffee, Sunlight dishwasher detergent and Colgate toothpaste attempt to show 'typical' people finding satisfaction with their products.

MESSAGE FACTORS

It is important to understand what components make up a persuasive message. This section discusses three sets of message factors: message structure, message appeal and message code.

Message structure

Message structure refers to how the elements of a message are organised. Four structures that have been extensively studied are message sidedness, order of presentation, conclusion drawing and repetition.

MESSAGE SIDEDNESS

A message can be either one-sided or two-sided. A *one-sided message* is one in which only the strengths of the communicator's position are described. For example, advertisements for BMW automobiles often only address their advantages and don't mention any of their possible weaknesses or the possible advantages of competing cars. A *two-sided message*, on the other hand, presents the strengths of the communicator's position as in the one-sided message, but it also admits either to weaknesses in the communicator's position or to some strengths in the opposite position. In a marketing context, the typical method of implementing the two-sided approach would be for the spokesperson to mention one or two weaknesses in the company's products or to admit to one or two strong features of competitors' products. Advertisements for Listerine, for example, claim effectiveness but admit to less than perfect taste.

Two questions arise regarding message sidedness. First, why would anyone want to admit to weaknesses in his or her own product or mention the strengths of competing products? Secondly, is the one- or two-sided message approach more effective? Insight into the first question is found in discussion of the second. Either approach might be more effective than the other depending upon the message and conditions under which the message is presented. Relevant issues that have been suggested are: the audience members' initial opinions on the issue; their exposure to subsequent counterarguments or counterinformation; the audience's educational level; and characteristics of the message itself.[56]

Regarding the first condition, a one-sided argument may be more effective when audience members are already in agreement with the communicator's position. The rationale for this is that a one-sided message will tend to confirm what the audience members already believe, and therefore foster *cognitive responses* by these consumers in the form of *support arguments* that will reinforce their initial position. A two-sided message can be more effective for an audience *not* in initial agreement with the communicator's stance, because the audience tends to view the communicator as more objective and honest (credible), since he or she is admitting to the merits of the audience's initial position. This approach will minimise the audience's use of counterarguments because the communicator is now perceived as trustworthy. Fewer counterarguments should then result in greater acceptance of the communicator's message.[57] This line of reasoning is derived from what has become known as *inoculation*, or *immunisation*, theory. In essence, this theory holds that, just as people are inoculated with vaccines composed of weakened disease cultures to increase their resistance to diseases, exposure of audience members to weakened forms of counterarguments will tend to immunise them from generating their own and perhaps stronger form of counterarguments.[58]

Arguments regarding the second issue mentioned above—audience exposure to subsequent counterarguments or counterinformation—closely parallel the line of reasoning just used regarding cognitive responses.[59]

A third issue mentioned above for determining whether to use a one-sided or two-sided message is the educational level of an audience. Some evidence suggests that two-sided messages are more persuasive for better educated audiences, whereas a one-sided message may be more effective in changing attitudes of less educated audiences. Because better educated people generally are more perceptive in 'seeing' both sides of an argument anyway, a communicator may gain more in admitting the strengths of opposing views or weaknesses in his or her own position. As we have just argued, by doing this the communicator is established as being more objective and credible in the eyes of the audience. This will tend to reduce counterarguments by the audience, which could be harsher than what the communicator is likely to address in a two-sided appeal. Less educated people are not as capable of seeing other sides of an issue and therefore are more likely to accept the arguments that they hear. To present both sides might confuse them or provide negative information about the product that they would not have developed for themselves. Therefore, a two-sided approach does not appear attractive for such an audience.

Finally, the fourth issue mentioned above is the effect of message characteristics themselves on the relative effectiveness of one- and two-sided messages.

One review of this topic identified several key characteristics that may influence choice between these two alternatives:

1. *How important the audience will perceive the negative information to be.* The more important the shortcomings are perceived to be, the more trustworthy the source will tend to be perceived. However, even given this, the more important the shortcomings are to consumers, the less effective the message is likely to be at enhancing favourable attitudes toward the communicator's product or position.

2. *The audience's perception of whether the communicator is revealing the negative information voluntarily.* If the perception is that the communicator is revealing information only because of legal reasons, the communicator is not likely to gain much benefit from doing so. This is likely to be the case for product warnings such as those appearing on cigarette packs and other products.

3. *How highly correlated the potentially negative attributes are to other potentially desirable attributes featured in the message.* If consumers relate the negative information to some other positive product elements, addressing the negatives with a two-sided appeal may also increase consumers' attention to the positive elements and lead to a more favourable impression. Of course, if negative attributes are not perceived by the consumer as being related to positive ones, then this potentially positive effect will not occur.[60]

Based on this review, it seems reasonable to conclude that often two-sided messages may not produce a favourable result for the communicator due to the variety of factors that influence their effect on consumers.[61] Therefore, it appears wise for marketers to use this technique with caution, and only after careful consideration of the conditions existing in the situation at hand.

MESSAGE ORDER

What is the best order in which to present persuasive arguments in an advertising message? Should the most important parts to the communicator be presented at the beginning, middle or end? If a two-sided message is used, should the marketer use a pro-con or con-pro order? For a series of advertisements in a medium such as television, does the first or last ad have an advantage in influencing attitude change? This section briefly addresses these questions and reviews some of the evidence relevant to them.

CLIMAX VERSUS ANTICLIMAX ORDER   A *climax order* refers to ordering message elements whereby the strongest arguments are presented at the end of a message. An *anticlimax order* refers to the presentation of the most important points at the beginning of a message. When the most important materials are presented in the middle of a message, it is referred to as a *pyramidal order*. Figure 12.11 graphically describes these three alternatives.

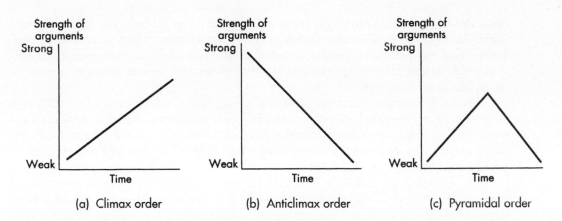

FIG. 12.11   Three orders of message presentation

On the basis of research findings, the following tentative guidelines can be offered regarding the ordering of messages:

1. An anticlimax order tends to be most effective for an audience having a low level of interest in the subject being presented.

2. A climax order tends to be most effective for an audience having a high level of interest in the subject being presented.

3. The pyramidal order is the least effective order of presentation.

The first two generalisations can be explained in terms of audience interest. Where interest is low, the stronger, more interesting points in a message have the greater potential for gaining audience attention, and therefore they should be placed first (anticlimax order). In this way, a communicator is better able to get the message across and thus effect change in the audience. However, with this approach the communicator also must be careful of avoiding an audience 'let down' when the weaker points in a message follow.

When audience interest in the subject is high, there is no need to present the stronger points first, because the message will be attended to out of interest. Therefore, the climax order should be used, because points made at the end of the message exceed expectations created by the points initially presented.[62]

The lesson marketers must learn from these statements is that for low-interest products an anticlimax order appears effective. In addition, in some cases each method can perhaps be strengthened by presenting the important points at *both* the beginning and end of the message—in the form of an introduction and summary of important points. However, very little if any justification exists for a pyramidal order.

RECENCY AND PRIMACY EFFECTS   Two additional questions were raised previously. When presenting a two-sided message, should the points favourable to the advertiser's brand be presented first or second? If many competing messages are involved, as they are in magazines and during commercial breaks on television, does the first or last communication tend to have the advantage? Both of these issues involve the subject of primacy and recency effects. When the material presented first produces the greater opinion or attitude change, a *primacy effect* has occurred. When material presented last produces the greater change, a *recency effect* has been observed.

Research into the question of which presentation of order is more effective when using a two-sided message has not been very conclusive. It appears that sometimes a primacy and sometimes a recency effect is observed. The reasons for these contradictory findings is not at all clear. Therefore, we will not even offer tentative guidelines on this subject.

The evidence on whether it would be better for a promotional message to appear first or last in a series of messages is also not clear. However, many advertisers who favour evidence suggesting a primacy effect are willing to pay a premium for early placement in a magazine or during a commercial break. Others act the same way regarding placement at the end of a series of advertisements. Each set of advocates can point to research evidence supporting their position. More investigation of the factors accounting for such contradictory findings is certainly needed.

CONCLUSION DRAWING

Is it better to draw a conclusion for consumers at the end of a message or let them draw their own conclusion from the information presented in the communication? Investigations of this question suggest that for some consumers, attitude change is most effectively achieved by drawing a conclusion for them in the marketing communication. If this is not done, they may either draw the 'wrong' conclusion or no conclusions at all, and therefore the intended attitude change will not occur.

However, research has also found that involvement levels are an important consideration when conclusions are implied but not explicitly drawn for consumers.[63] Under conditions of high involvement, omitted but implied message conclusions are likely to be inferred by intelligent consumers, and this is likely to lead to favourable attitude change. Those consumers having low-involvement are less likely to make such inferences. Therefore, conclusion drawing appears appropriate for consumers expected to be operating under low-involvement levels.

REPETITION

In Chapter 11 we saw that repetition of persuasive messages can be beneficial in encouraging rehearsal, transferring information to long-term memory and forestalling forgetting. Other benefits were also suggested. That is, some research evidence indicates that increased repetition of an advertising message can, by itself, encourage consumers to develop positive feelings toward the brand.[64] This suggests that consumers can be changed in a positive direction through frequent advertising exposures. Conditions that appear to produce such an effect are when the audience initially favours the message position and when a 'soft-sell' (as opposed to a 'hard-sell') is employed.

Even under the conditions just cited, marketers should not expect continuous positive change among consumers from increased repetitions of a communication. At some point, message *wearout* occurs. Here, the positive effects of repetition diminish as repetition occurs because of audience boredom, inattention and increased cognitive response activity that is less positive in content than the message.[65] The conclusion from these studies is that moderate levels of advertising repetition over time appear positively to influence attitudes as well as rehearsal and memory. The effects of wearout can probably be forestalled by employing a series of messages having a central theme with unique components to provide different information and some novelty.

Message appeals

The foregoing review summarised some major conclusions regarding the structuring of messages to achieve maximum attitude change. We now turn our attention to message appeals and how they can be used to enhance the persuasiveness of messages.

FEAR APPEALS

In some situations it seems reasonable for marketers to consider using fear in their attempts to persuade consumers. That is, fear of physical danger, social disapproval or other consequences seems potentially useful in influencing consumers' attitudes and/or behaviour toward the advertised brand. In fact, fear appeals have been employed to promote the use of a wide range of goods from toothpaste to life insurance. In addition, fear appeals have been used to promote social causes such as encouraging safe driving and the use of seat belts (especially among teenagers), preventing heart disease and the spread of AIDS, and reducing cigarette smoking. For example, to encourage safe driving, very graphic video scenes of actual accidents are shown, exposing viewers to the moans and screams of victims.

The earliest fear research appeared to suggest that as the intensity of a fear appeal increases its effectiveness in persuading audiences will decrease.[66] One explanation is that strong, fear-evoking message components (such as the gore and moans in the 'safe-driving' videos) cause consumers to set up perceptual *defence mechanisms* to screen out the fearful aspects of the message. However, in doing so they also reject the rest of the message—they 'throw the baby out with the bath water', so to speak. The result of these and other early findings was that most advertisers became reluctant to use fear appeals for promoting their products or services.

Several years later, other investigations began to uncover additional results.[67] The conclusions can be summarised by what has become known as the 'inverted-U' argument: low fear appeals are not effective because they generate little motivation for attitude change, and high fear appeals also tend to yield little attitude change because, as said above, they activate defence mechanisms. Therefore, moderate fear appeals, which provide sufficient motivation but do not activate perceptual defences, appeared most effective in generating attitude change. Figure 12.12 diagrams this proposed inverted-U relationship between the intensity of fear appeals and amount of attitude change likely to be achieved.

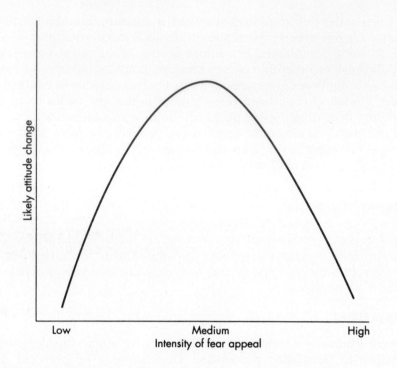

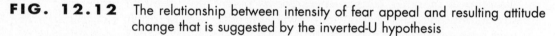

FIG. 12.12 The relationship between intensity of fear appeal and resulting attitude change that is suggested by the inverted-U hypothesis

However, more recently, others have been arguing that perhaps it is inappropriate to draw general conclusions about any given level of fear appeal, because numerous factors may influence how consumers will respond to the appeal.[68] For example, factors that may influence the persuasiveness of fear appeals include source credibility, audience characteristics, the context of the message presentation and the type of fear appeal used:

1. Highly credible sources may be more effective in employing fear to change attitudes, because their credibility tends to block counterarguments that consumers use to protect themselves from fear-evoking messages.

2. Characteristics of an audience can influence the degree to which they are persuaded by fear appeals. Receivers who are high in self-esteem, are effective in coping with tension and do not perceive themselves as particularly vulnerable to the feared consequences appear to be more persuaded by high-fear appeals than are receivers who do not have these characteristics. This suggests that marketers must investigate their target audience in order to determine whether a high fear appeal is warranted. For example, people who perceive themselves as having very risky occupations might not be receptive to high-fear appeals for occupational-related disability insurance.

3. Certain conditions in the environment (such as humour or use of a third party to bear the feared consequences) can distract audience attention away from a strong fear appeal and increase message persuasiveness.

4. Evidence also suggests that fear appeals are more effective when they focus audience attention on the specific danger or threat, and the practical steps that may be taken to avoid any undesirable consequences. Messages that dwell on the unpleasant circumstances without suggesting practical ways to avoid them will tend to be less persuasive.[69]

This last point has given rise to a new perspective on the use of fear appeals—the *protection motivation theory*.[70] According to this theory, four processes influence how individuals will respond to threatening information presented in a fear appeal. Individuals will:

Isn't your entire lifestyle riding on your income?

Whichever way you look at it, your income provides for just about everything that makes family life secure and comfortable.

An income not only pays for day to day expenses it also allows for longer term accomplishments like your children's education and savings for a brighter future.

At Australian Casualty & Life, our purpose is to protect the long term financial security of Australians. That's why we're a leader in income protection.

We have the enviable track record of processing over 85% of claims within 48 hours. And since 1971, we've processed over 40,000 income protection claims totalling more than $120 million.

Australian Casualty & Life is a member of an Australian owned financial group with assets owned and under management totalling in excess of $30 billion world-wide. So we'll be here when you need us.

Talk to Australian Casualty & Life about income protection now.

Our policy is service.

Australian Casualty
& Life

NSW: (02) 413 4344   Australian Casualty & Life Limited (ACN 000 333 844)   VIC: (03) 890 4999
QLD: (07) 831 9533   NTH QLD: (077) 21 5721   SA: (08) 31 6077   WA: (09) 325 7388   TAS: (002) 31 0033

One example of fear appeal COURTESY OF AUSTRALIAN CASUALTY & LIFE

1. determine how severe the threat is to them;

2. determine how likely the threat is to occur;

3. determine what action might be able to remove the threat—the coping response;

4. determine how able they are is to carry out the coping-response behaviour.[71]

The result of a consumer's evaluation of the threat is typically the *protection motivation*—a motivation to adopt certain behaviours to protect himself or herself. This is different from fear itself, because it is intended behaviour designed to cope with a threat, rather than an emotion that is felt by the individual (fear).

Protection motivation theory is an attractive concept for marketers because it suggests guidelines for designing communications to motivate consumers to respond to threatening situations. Based on the above four points, a fear appeal in an advertisement should:

1. provide information about the severity of any threat;

2. suggest the probability of its occurrence;

3. indicate effective coping responses;

4. show how easily the coping response can be used.

For example, an advertisement for a muffler franchise might address the danger of asphyxiation from a defective muffler, provide evidence on how many such cases occur per year, explain how a sound muffler minimises these risks, and show how easy it is to stop into a conveniently located shop and get an exhaust-system check/repair in a short time, even without an appointment. A number of recent promotional messages appear to be making use of this concept regarding the use of coping behaviour suggestions in fear appeals.

DISTRACTION

Some evidence suggests that pleasant forms of distraction can often work to increase the effectiveness of persuasive appeals in encouraging attitude change.[72] Sales representatives often practise this principle when they take clients out to dinner. Advertisers can also use such pleasant forms of distraction as music or background activity.

The explanation for the effectiveness of distraction on attitude change has been that it retards counterargumentation. That is, distraction tends to make receivers lose their trains of thought or forget to argue against the message. This, according to the explanation, would result in greater message acceptance.

Studies have shown conflicting evidence on the distraction concept.[73] Also, in some cases, distraction may actually reduce receivers' attention to the message. Therefore, evidence is still not clear regarding the effectiveness of this method of increasing attitude change and the conditions that influence it.

PARTICIPATION

As was discussed earlier in the text, active audience participation is a means of gaining attention to and enhancing the learning of a message. Similarly, participation can increase the effectiveness of a persuasive appeal.[74] Marketers have learned the value of giving product samples to prospective customers, encouraging trial use of their products and providing coupons for trial purchase. In addition, they often develop television advertisements that place the viewers in the position of vicariously 'trying' a product by using well-developed camera angles and other production techniques that make them feel a part of the commercial.

HUMOUR

Estimates are that between 15 and 42 per cent of radio and television advertising employs humorous appeals. Print media also contain many similar messages. Some brands, such as Toyota and Daewoo cars, Tooheys and Hahn beers, and Energizer batteries, have developed extensive campaigns based on humour. However, other companies hardly give it serious consideration, arguing that amusing circumstances are not universal in appeal and wear out quickly, often humour is not really appropriate for the product being advertised and it consumes too much advertising time or space.

Daily experience and research evidence seem to support the contention that humour is not universal in its appeal. For example, studies investigating reactions to three basic types of humour (hostile, sexual and nonsensical) find that females and males differ in their perception as to what is amusing.[75] Also, much humour is culturally determined and therefore responses to any 'humorous' message may be quite different across groups. However, a variety of benefits have been suggested for humorous appeals, including:

1. Humour attracts attention.

2. Humour can increase retention of the advertising message.

3. Credibility of the source can be enhanced with humour.

4. Attitude toward the advertisement can be enhanced with the use of humour.

5. Counterarguments may be minimised with the use of humour because it acts to distract the audience from making cognitive responses.[76]

Despite these proposed benefits, research evidence has not consistently and systematically shown humour to have a superior effect on consumers when compared with non-humorous appeals.[77] For example, humorous messages may attract greater attention, but they may also have a detrimental effect on message comprehension and recall. (In an advertising context, one can sometimes counter this potential problem by focusing the humour on product attributes expected to be instrumental in influencing attitudes.) In addition, a number of studies have not found humour to increase viewers' attention to message content.[78]

Certainly, universal agreement does not yet exist on the exact benefits of humorous appeals. However, it has been suggested that for humour to be successful, the advertised product should be 'appropriate' for the use of humorous appeals, the humour should contribute to the main point of the message and the humour should be tasteful.[79] In addition, recent evidence suggests that humour is more effective in changing consumers' attitudes and choices when the audience already holds positive evaluations of the advertised product.[80]

EMOTIONAL VERSUS RATIONAL APPEALS

Should marketers use emotional or rational appeals in promoting their products? As the reader might guess, neither approach has been shown to be generally superior to the other. This seems understandable, because the effectiveness of appeals is likely to be a function of the underlying motives consumers have for considering the product, as well as other factors such as involvement and the type of processing (central versus peripheral) being used by the consumer.

When emotional appeals appear to be appropriate, the following points have been offered as guidance for constructing the appeal:

1. Use emotionally charged language, especially words that have a high personal meaning to the target consumers.

2. If the brand or message is unfamiliar to the audience, associate it with well-known ideas.

3. Associate the brand or message with visual or nonverbal stimuli that arouse emotions.

4. The communication should be accompanied by nonverbal cues, such as hand motions, which support the verbal message.[81]

COMPARATIVE APPEALS

The term 'comparative advertising' refers to advertising messages that make some form of comparison between the promoted brand and some other brand or brands. In a strict sense, this would involve comparisons with one or more *specifically* named or recognised brands of the same generic product in terms of one or more *specific* products or attributes.[82]

Prior to the 1970s comparative advertisements were quite rare, especially on television. However, in more recent times they have become more prevalent. Some of the more widely known comparative campaigns include the Avis Corporation stating, 'We try harder', compared with Hertz, and showing service attributes as their claim to superior performance. And, of course, Pepsi met Coke head-on in the now-famous 'Pepsi Challenge' comparative campaign in the United States. In Australia, Holden versus Ford cars, and Drive versus Cold Power laundry detergents are known for comparative campaigns. In all of these cases, and in a number of others, quite favourable sales results accrued to the company initiating the comparative appeal.

However, although many advertising practitioners extol the benefits of comparative appeals, research evidence has suggested a number of potential problems. These include the following:

1. Comparative ads have not been shown to be significantly more effective in increasing brand awareness.

2. Comparative ads may result in information overload for at least some consumers.

3. Comparative ads may be perceived as offensive, and the sponsoring company may be perceived as less trustworthy.

4. Comparative themes may encourage consumers' involvement and, as a consequence, lead to more counterarguments against the message. This can generate a 'boomerang' effect and depress brand attitudes rather than generating more favourable ones. However, use of two-sided comparative ads (where some minor disadvantages for the brand are mentioned) appear to reduce such counterarguments.

5. The effect of comparative ads may be influenced by various sources, and audience and situational conditions. For example, those loyal to the advertised brand may tend to respond more favourably than others. Also, some evidence suggests that such ads may be more effective for the brand that is not the present market leader.[83]

These situations suggest that more still needs to be known about the effects of comparative ads on consumers' attitudes and other response variables.

Message codes

The way in which marketers assemble and use message codes, including the language used in advertisements, can have a dramatic effect on the impact of their messages.[84] Three broad classes of message codes are verbal, nonverbal and paralinguistic.

VERBAL CODES

The verbal code is a system of word symbols that are combined according to a set of rules, as in the English language. Although a variety of alternatives exist for devising verbal code structures, advertisers tend to use modifier words, such as adjectives and adverbs, to elicit favourable emotions within a consumer. For example, the same factual information is conveyed by using either of the following advertising messages, but one conveys the facts with words higher in emotion:

1. The new plastic product resembling leather will soon be available to shoe manufacturers.

2. The fabulous new plastic product that out-leathers leather will soon replace all other products used in the manufacture of superior quality shoes.[85]

The advertiser is likely to use the second statement, because it expresses the same idea but with more highly charged modifiers.

NONVERBAL CODES

Nonverbal codes are extremely important in persuasive communication, and they have not been given the attention they deserve in published research.[86] For example, a communicator's facial expressions, gestures, posture and dress can affect how a receiver responds to a message.

Sales representatives have found the study of nonverbal communications extremely helpful in better understanding prospective customers and in meeting sales resistance. Astute representatives can tell when a client is bored, receptive, doubtful, critical, interested and so forth by observing nonverbal cues such as crossed legs, body lean, hand gestures and mannerisms. Advertisers also are aware of the importance of nonverbal communications in television and print advertisements, particularly those that use models.

PARALINGUISTIC CODES

Paralinguistic codes are those that lie between the verbal and nonverbal codes. They primarily involve two components—voice qualities and vocalisations.[87]

Voice qualities refer to such speech characteristics as rhythm pattern, pitch of voice and precision of articulation. They can communicate urgency, boredom, sarcasm and other feelings. *Vocalisations*, on the other hand, are sounds such as yawns, sighs and various voice intensities that reflect certain emotions.

Advertisers are very careful to select models whose tonal qualities match the product message. For example, when facial soaps, body creams and shampoos that are soft and gentle are being promoted, the model's voice tends to be quite soothing. However, advertisements for pick-up trucks, tools and some heavy-duty cleansers typically employ low, powerful-sounding voices.

RECEIVER FACTORS

To be a persuasive communicator and an effective marketer, it is important to adopt a 'know your audience' position. In our discussion throughout this chapter, we have already focused on a number of receiver factors that affect the persuasiveness of communications. For example, we have noted that the effectiveness of fear and humour appeals depends on characteristics of audience members. This section briefly deals with three additional general receiver characteristics that deserve mention. These are the receiver's personality traits, mood and belief types.

Personality traits

Behavioural research has shed light on the relationship between personality traits and persuasibility. Among these traits are self-esteem and rich imagery.

SELF-ESTEEM

Self-esteem refers to a person's feelings of adequacy and self-worth. In general, research has suggested that people who have low self-esteem tend to be more persuasible than those with high self-esteem.[88] This generalisation appears to be particularly true in situations in which people are motivated by social approval. Researchers believe that people who feel inadequate are more persuasible because they lack confidence in their judgments and therefore tend to rely upon the opinions of others.

RICH IMAGERY

People who are high in rich imagery, or who live out much of their lives through dream worlds and fantasy, are more persuasible than those who are not high in rich imagery. With this information, companies such as Nissan have developed successful advertising themes, which stress a number of situations that audience members could fantasise about. The brand is then associated with these situations.

Mood

Another factor that can influence consumers is their mood state. Mood may be defined as a temporary and mild positive or negative feeling that is generalised and not tied to any particular circumstance.[89] Moods should be distinguished from emotions, which are usually more intense, tied to specific circumstances and often conscious (moods may not reach awareness). In one sense, the effect of a consumer's mood can be thought of in much the same way as can our reactions to the behaviour of our friends—when our friends are happy and 'up', that tends to rub off on us, but when they are 'down', that can have a negative impact on us. Similarly, consumers operating under a given (positive or negative) mood state tend to react to stimuli in a direction consistent with that mood state.[90] Thus, for example, we should expect to see consumers in a positive mood state evaluate products in a more favourable manner than they would when not in such a state. In addition, mood states appear capable of enhancing consumers' memory.[91]

Moods appear to be readily influenced by marketer actions. For example, the tempo, pitch and volume of music has been shown to influence behaviour such as the amount of time spent in supermarkets or intentions to purchase products.[92] In addition, advertising can influence consumers' moods, which, in turn, are capable of influencing consumers' reactions to products. For example, as we mentioned earlier when we discussed peripheral routes to attitude change, marketers sometimes design ads for the main purpose of evoking positive feelings among consumers, under the expectation that these positive feelings will then be associated with the product being advertised.

There is also another way in which moods can influence consumers and their reactions to advertisements.[93] Consumers may just happen to be in a particular mood that was not influenced by any advertisements, but that mood will now influence how an advertisement is able to influence their attitudes toward the brand being advertised. For example, consumers who are in a positive mood when seeing an advertisement for Sony televisions are likely to react more favourably to advertising information about the brand, and this should lead to more positive attitudes toward it. One explanation for this occurrence is that the positive mood reduces the likelihood of negative cognitive responses such as counterargumentation. It may also be that a positive mood tends to reduce the motivation to spend time *thinking* about messages (elaborative processing or rehearsal) and this leads to accepting the messages at 'face value'.[94] The issues relating to how consumers' moods influence their behaviour are still relatively unexplored, although recent evidence suggests that when the mood of a television advertisement (happy or sad) is consistent with the mood of program content (happy or sad), viewers react more favourably than when the two elements are not consistent.[95] Therefore, the effect of mood may be more complex than just the expectation that a happy audience mood is always preferable for the advertiser. Additional research is likely to lead to exciting insights for marketing applications.

Belief types

As indicated elsewhere in this chapter, a receiver's existing attitude and belief structure can be an opportunity for, or an obstruction to, persuasive marketing communications.[96] The direction of attitudes and the strength of beliefs are two factors that were mentioned as particularly important in influencing change. Three basic belief types influence the commitment that consumers will have regarding their knowledge. Of course, these in turn will influence the difficulty in changing attitudes. *Central beliefs* form the core of a person's cognitive structure. Because they are deeply connected to so many other beliefs, they are quite resistant to change. This was suggested in our discussion of memory structure in Chapter 11. *Derived beliefs* are an outgrowth of central beliefs. For example, 'Retailers should be free to charge whatever prices they feel are appropriate' is a belief derived from a central belief about freedom. As the name implies, *central-free beliefs* exist separate and apart from other beliefs in the consumer's cognitive structure. 'I believe that Al's market is the best in town' is an example.

In order of difficulty, central beliefs are the hardest to change, derived beliefs are the next most difficult and central-free beliefs are the easiest to change. Marketers should avoid attacking central beliefs and instead should see them as opportunities. That is, messages that are aligned with central beliefs are readily acceptable, because they reinforce already strongly held attitudes. Similarly, beliefs derived from more central ones may be used as a basis for an advertising theme. In this way the beliefs are not attacked, but instead are used as a means of enhancing the value of the advertised brand. The lesson to be learned is that a consumer's psychological barriers should be avoided and turned into opportunities.

SUMMARY

This chapter introduced the concept of attitudes, described their basic characteristics and reviewed their functions. Various sources of attitude development also served as a focus for discussion.

Several theories and models of attitudes were depicted. Specifically, the congruity, balance and cognitive dissonance views were treated. Although these viewpoints provide significant insight, recent attention has turned to multiattribute attitude models. The attraction of these models lies in their explicit recognition that attitudes have more than one dimension. This focuses attention on the factors that contribute to overall attitudes (product attributes, consequences of actions) and how they are evaluated by the consumer. The practical implications for marketing strategies that result from understanding these factors were addressed.

Belief-based models offered by Fishbein were discussed in some detail as representatives of these multiattribute attitude concepts. These models stress that consumers develop attitudes by forming beliefs about objects, such as products, and then consciously and deliberately use these beliefs to form an overall attitude toward the object. Fishbein's earlier model of attitude-toward-objects was seen as an important contribution to thinking in the area. Its limitations in predicting consumer behaviour were also discussed. This model has given way to a newer concept of behavioural intentions, in which consumers' intentions to behave in a specific way are seen as a function of their attitudes toward that behaviour and their subjective norms.

Finally, a section reviewed the concept of peripheral routes to developing attitudes. In contrast with belief-based theories, these viewpoints stress how attitudes may be formed without consumers consciously developing beliefs about objects and then deliberately forming attitudes based on these beliefs. Rather, in at least certain situations, it seems that consumers may, in a largely unconscious manner, also use peripheral cues (cues that are seemingly non-essential to the situation at hand) such as a spokesperson's voice or good looks to develop attitudes toward products. This has significant implications for our understanding of consumer behaviour.

This chapter then focused on the important marketing goal of attitude change. First, basic strategies of attitude change for low-involvement situations were introduced. Fishbein's model of behavioural intentions then served as a basis for suggesting strategies for changing attitudes under conditions of high involvement. Next, a simple model of the communication process was presented. Then the many factors capable of influencing attitudes via communications were categorised into source, message and receiver factors.

The category of source factors was discussed first. This category contains properties or characteristics of message senders. In marketing, these include salespersons, companies, hired promoters, media, and other marketing sources of product and brand information. A number of source characteristics, including credibility and similarity to the audience, were discussed. Especially with regard to the sleeper effect of source credibility, the influence of the particular situation was stressed.

The impact of message factors was the next topic of attention. Message structure and message appeals were topics of primary concern here. A discussion of one- versus two-sided messages concluded that, due to a variety of conditions, two-sided messages may not produce the favourable results anticipated. Message order, conclusion drawing and the effect of repetition were discussed next. The pyramidal order appears to be the least preferred; debate exists regarding recency versus primacy; conclusion drawing appears appropriate for consumers expected to be operating under low-involvement levels; and the benefits of repetition must be appreciated with consideration for the wearout problem.

Message appeals were the next topic of consideration. Conditions affecting the effectiveness of fear appeals were treated, and insights offered from protection motivation theory were reviewed in an effort to increase understanding of how fear appeals may be effectively used. Other message appeals were reviewed, and prominent among them were humour and comparative appeals. Humour was seen to have several benefits, but universal agreement does not yet exist on the exact nature of all benefits. Comparative appeals have been shown to pose a number of problems as well as potential benefits. More research is needed in these areas. Message codes were briefly reviewed before attention turned to receiver factors. Here, audience characteristics of personality (self-esteem and imagery) as well as mood and belief types were addressed. Strategies to handle situations arising from these characteristics were suggested.

MANAGERIAL REFLECTIONS

For our product or service situation:

1. What experiences are likely to be influential in forming attitudes toward our offering?

2. How might congruity theory and balance theory be useful in understanding consumers' attitudes?

3. What are likely sources of dissonance related to our offerings, and how might we influence the dissonance process?

4. Of what potential benefit is Fishbein's attitude model? What are its potential limitations?

5. How might we successfully employ Fishbein's behavioural intentions model?

6. What are some of the 'other intervening factors' that might result in a difference between consumers' intentions to behave and their actual behaviour?

7. What are the potential implications of consumers' attitudes toward our advertisements?

8. What low- or high-involvement strategies appear to have the greatest potential for changing consumers' attitudes toward purchasing our brands?

9. What insights does the communication-process model described in Figure 12.8 provide for our promotional efforts?

10. What are the major marketing communication sources for our organisation?

11. What are the implications of source credibility for our firm's communications?

12. Do two-sided messages have potential benefits for our marketing communications?

13. Do fear, humour, or emotional appeals appear to have any significant potential for our promotional messages?

14. Do comparative appeals appear beneficial for our advertisements?

15. Which types of message codes appear appropriate for our broadcast advertisements?

16. What are the unique characteristics of our consumers that may influence how they respond to our promotions?

DISCUSSION TOPICS

1. Several definitions of attitude exist. What appears to be the emphasis of the more recent definitions?

2. What are the major characteristics of attitudes? Assume an attitude regarding a specific product, and use this as an example to demonstrate each characteristic.

3. What are the functions of an attitude? Can you cite specific personal experiences that demonstrate each of these functions?

4. What are the sources of attitude development? Can you foresee how these sources might conflict with one another in their influence on developing attitudes? If so, cite an example to demonstrate your point.

5. Review the attitude theories of congruity, balance and cognitive dissonance. Highlight their major characteristics.

6. Some advertisements make highly exaggerated claims for a brand, claims that probably cannot be fulfilled. Using your knowledge of cognitive dissonance, assess the wisdom of this technique.

7. Distinguish between the Fishbein attitude model and earlier attitude theories. What implications does this comparison have for predicting consumer behaviour?

8. It has been argued that the consequences of action referred to in Fishbein's behavioural intentions model can be linked to the concepts of consumers' perceived benefits and benefit segmentation. Discuss this argument.

9. Think of a product, or action toward a product, about which you hold an attitude. Did you use a compensatory method in formulating this attitude? If so, explain how. If not, explain why you think this is the case.

10. Who are the major marketing communicators of a firm?

11. What major factors assist a source in being perceived as credible? Cite specific advertising examples of the use of each factor.

12. What is the sleeper effect, and, if it were shown to exist, what implications would there be for the communicator?

13. What recommendations would you make to a communicator regarding the following aspects of message structure:
    (a) message sidedness?
    (b) order of presentation?
    (c) message code?

14. What suggestions would you offer regarding drawing a conclusion in a marketing communication? Watch a number of television advertisements and try to determine the extent to which these suggestions are being followed.

15. What conclusions can you offer regarding the effective use of message appeals? Can you point out any specific advertisements that might not be following these conclusions?

16. Under what conditions might a highly credible source detract from the persuasiveness of a message?

17. If you were going to present a speech to Asia-Pacific business leaders on 'The Declining Quality of Australia's Goods and Services', what guidelines could you employ from this chapter?

18. Suggest the characteristics of some fear appeals that might be used for:
    (a) the Heart Foundation of Australia attempting to persuade people to check their blood pressure regularly;
    (b) Dunlop steel-belted radial tyres;
    (c) NRMA disability insurance;
    (d) a Tandy burglar-alarm system for the home.

19. When might a manager want to employ comparative appeals?

REFERENCES

1. Martin Fishbein, 'The Relationship between Beliefs, Attitudes, and Behavior', in Shel Feldman (ed.), *Cognitive Consistency*, Academic, New York, 1966, pp. 199–223.
2. The term 'object' is used here to include abstract concepts such as enjoyment, as well as physical things.
3. Gordon W. Allport, 'Attitudes', in C. A. Murchison (ed.), *A Handbook of Social Psychology*, Clark University Press, Worcester, MA, 1935, pp. 798–844.
4. D. Krech and R. Crutchfield, *Theory and Problems in Social Psychology*, McGraw-Hill, New York, 1948.
5. P. M. Tidwell, Consumer Demand for the Multi-purpose Entertainment Teaching Complex (METCOM) in Bathurst, Consulting Report for the Bathurst City Council, Charles Sturt University and Bathurst Arts Council, 1993. Contact Market Research Services of Bathurst, NSW, for more information.
6. Martin Fishbein, 'A Behavior Theory Approach to the Relations between Beliefs about an Object and the Attitude toward the Object', in Martin Fishbein (ed.), *Readings in Attitude Theory and Measurement*, Wiley, New York, 1967, p. 394.
7. T. M. Newcomb, R. H. Turner & P. E. Converse, *Social Psychology*, Holt, New York, 1965, p. 115.
8. Daniel Katz, 'The Functional Approach to the Study of Attitudes', *Public Opinion Quarterly* 24, 1960 pp. 163–204.
9. See, for example, Mark P. Zanna, 'Attitude-Behavior Consistency: Fulfilling the Need for Cognitive Structure', in Thomas K. Srull (ed.), *Advances in Consumer Research*, vol. 16, Association for Consumer Research, Provo, UT, 1989, pp. 318–20.
10. M. Wayne DeLozier, *The Marketing Communications Process*, McGraw-Hill, New York, 1976, p. 81.
11. This section is based largely upon the works of Charles E. Osgood, George J. Suci and Percy H. Tannenbaum, *The Measurement of Meaning*, University of Illinois Press, Urbana, 1957; Milton J. Rosenberg et al., *Attitude Organization and Change*, Yale University Press, New Haven, CT, 1960; Leon A. Festinger, *A Theory of Cognitive Dissonance*, Stanford University Press, Stanford, CA, 1957; Roger Brown, *Social Psychology*, Free Press, New York, 1965; and Martin Fishbein & Icek Ajzen, *Belief Attitude Intention and Behavior*, Addison Wesley, Reading, MA, 1975.
12. For a thorough treatment of the mathematics involved in predicting the resolution of such cases, see Osgood, Suci & Tannenbaum, ibid, pp. 199–207.
13. See Jonathan L. Freedman Jr, Merrill Carlsmith & David O. Sears, *Social Psychology*, Prentice-Hall, Englewood Cliffs, NJ, 1970, p. 263; and Charles E. Osgood & Percy H Tannenbaum, 'The Principle of Congruity in the Prediction of Attitude Change', *Psychological Review* 62, 1955, pp. 42–55.
14. Some of the ideas in this section are attributable to Brown, op cit, Ref 11, pp. 566–670.
15. Fritz Heider, 'Attitudes and Cognitive Organizations', *Journal of Psychology* 21, January 1946, pp. 107–12.

16. See Festinger, op cit, Ref 11.

17. See Fishbein & Ajzen, op cit, Ref 11, pp. 11–13; and Icek Ajzen & Martin Fishbein, *Understanding Attitudes and Predicting Social Behavior*, Prentice-Hall, Englewood Cliffs, NJ, 1980, pp. 18–20.

18. See Milton J. Rosenberg, 'Cognitive Structure and Attitudinal Affect', *Journal of Abnormal and Social Psychology* 53, November 1956, pp. 361–72; Martin Fishbein, 'An Investigation of the Relationship between Beliefs about an Object and the Attitudes toward That Object', *Human Relations* 16, 1963, pp. 233–40; and Martin Fishbein, 'Attitude and the Prediction of Behavior', in Martin Fishbein (ed.), *Readings in Attitude Theory and Measurement*, Wiley, New York, 1967, pp. 477–92.

19. Some examples are Arch G. Woodside & James D. Clokey, 'Multi-attribute/Multi-brand Models', *Journal of Advertising Research* 14, October 1974, pp. 33–40; Frank M. Bass & W. Wayne Talarzyk, 'An Attitude Model for the Study of Brand Preference', *Journal of Marketing Research* 9, February 1972, pp. 93–6; Michael B. Mazis, Olli T. Ahtola & R. Eugene Klippel, 'A Comparison of Four Multi-attribute Models in the Prediction of Consumer Attitudes', *Journal of Consumer Research* 2, June 1975, pp. 38–52; and James R. Bettman, Noel Capon & Richard J. Lutz, 'Multi-attribute Measurement Models and Multi-attribute Theory: A Test of Construct Validity', *Journal of Consumer Research* 1, March 1975, pp. 1–14.

20. Ajzen & Fishbein, op cit, Ref 17, p. 63.

21. William L. Wilkie & Edgar A. Pessemier, 'Issues in Marketing's Use of Multi-attribute Attitude Models', *Journal of Marketing Research* 10, November 1973, p. 428.

22. See William O. Bearden & Arch G. Woodside, 'Interactions of Consumption Situations and Brand Attitudes', *Journal of Applied Psychology* 61, 1976, pp. 764–9.

23. See Kenneth E. Miller & James L. Ginter, 'An Investigation of Situational Variation in Brand Choice Behavior and Attitude', *Journal of Marketing Research* 16, February 1979, pp. 111–23.

24. See Martin Fishbein, op cit, Ref 6, pp. 477–92; and Ajzen & Fishbein, op cit, Ref 17.

25. See, for example, Paul R. Warshaw, 'Predicting Purchase and Other Behaviors from Generally and Contextually Specific Intentions', *Journal of Marketing Research* 17, February 1980, pp. 26–33; Michael J. Ryan & E. H. Bonfield, 'Fishbein's Intentions Model: A Test of External Pragmatic Validity', *Journal of Marketing* 44, Spring 1980, pp. 82–95; and Russell Fazio, Martha Powell & Carol Williams, 'The Role of Attitude Accessibility in the Attitude-to-behavior Process', *Journal of Consumer Research* 16, December 1989, pp. 280–8.

26. See, for example, Richard L. Oliver & Philip K. Berger, 'A Path Analysis of Preventive Care Decision Models', *Journal of Consumer Research* 6, September 1979, pp. 113–22; Ryan & Bonfield, ibid, pp. 82–95; and Blair Sheppard, John Hartwick & Paul Warshaw, 'The Theory of Reasoned Action: A Meta-analysis of Past Research with Recommendations for Modifications and Future Research', *Journal of Consumer Research* 15, December 1988, pp. 325–43.

27. See, for example, Terence A. Shimp, 'Attitude toward the Ad as a Mediator of Consumer Brand Choice', *Journal of Advertising* 10, 1981, pp. 9–15; Andrew A. Mitchell & Jerry C. Olson, 'Are Product Attribute Beliefs the Only Mediator of Advertising Effects on Brand Attitude?', *Journal of Marketing Research* 18, August 1981, pp. 318–32; Gerald J. Gorn, 'The Effects of Music in Advertising on Choice Behavior: A Classical Conditioning Approach', *Journal of Marketing* 46, Winter 1982, pp. 94–101; Carl Obermiller, 'Varieties of Mere Exposure: The Effects of Processing Style and Repetition on Affective Response', *Journal of Consumer Research* 12, June 1985, pp. 17–46; and Chris Janiszewski, 'Preconscious Processing Effects: The Independence of Attitude Formation and Conscious Thought', *Journal of Consumer Research* 15, September 1988, pp. 199–209. See Thomas Madden, Chris Allen & Jacquelyn Twibel, 'Attitude toward the Ad: An Assessment of Diverse Measurement

Indices under Different Processing "Sets"', *Journal of Marketing Research* 25, August 1988, pp. 242–52, for some concerns about the methods involved in this research.

28. Mitchell & Olson, ibid, pp. 318–32.
29. Richard Petty & John Cacioppo, 'The Elaboration Likelihood Model of Persuasion', in *Advances in Experimental Social Psychology*', vol. 19, Academic Press Inc., New York, 1986, pp. 123–205.
30. Richard Petty, John Cacioppo & David Schumann, 'Central and Peripheral Routes to Advertising Effectiveness', *Journal of Consumer Research* 10, September 1983, pp. 135–46.
31. See ibid; and Shelly Chaiken, 'Heuristic versus Systematic Information Processing and the Use of Source versus Message Cues in Persuasion', *Journal of Personality and Social Psychology* 39, 1980, pp. 752–66.
32. See, for example, Paul Miniard, Peter Dickson & Kenneth Lord, 'Some Central and Peripheral Thoughts on the Routes to Persuasion', in Michael Houston (ed.), *Advances in Consumer Research*, vol. 15, Association for Consumer Research, Provo, UT, 1988, pp. 204–8; Judith Hennessey, Mary Bitner & Carl Obermiller, 'The Elaboration Likelihood Model: Limitations and Extensions in Marketing', in Elizabeth Hirschman & Morris Holbrook (eds), *Advances in Consumer Research*, vol. 12, Association for Consumer Research, Provo, UT, 1985, pp. 420–5; Catherine Cole et al., 'The Elaboration Likelihood Model (ELM): Replications, Extensions and Some Conflicting Findings', in Marvin Goldberg, Gerald Gorn & Richard Pollay (eds), *Advances in Consumer Research*, vol. 17, Association for Consumer Research, Provo, UT, 1990, pp. 231–6; and Paul Miniard, Sunil Bhatla & Randall Rose, 'On the Formation and Relationship of Ad and Brand Attitudes: An Experimental and Casual Analysis', *Journal of Marketing Research* 27, August 1990, pp. 290–303.
33. See, for example, Miniard, Dickson & Lord, ibid, pp. 204–8; Hennessy, Bitner & Obermiller, in *Advances in Consumer Research*, pp. 420–5; Catherine Cole et al., ibid, pp. 231–6; Miniard, Bhatla & Rose, ibid, pp. 290–303; Scott MacKenzie, Richard Lutz & George Belch, 'The Role of Attitude toward the Ad as a Mediator of Advertising Effectiveness: A Test of Competing Explanations', *Journal of Marketing Research* 23, May 1986, pp. 130–43; Russell Laczniak & Les Carlson, 'Examining the Influence of Attitude-toward-the-ad on Brand Attitudes', *Journal of Business Research* 3, 1989, pp. 303–11; Susan Middlestadt, 'The Effect of Background and Ambient Color on Product Attitudes and Beliefs', in Marvin Goldberg, Gerald Gorn & Richard Pollay (eds), *Advances in Consumer Research*, vol. 17, Association for Consumer Research, Provo, UT, 1990, pp. 244–9; and Pamela Homer, 'The Mediating Role of Attitude toward the Ad: Some Additional Evidence', *Journal of Marketing Research* 27, February 1990, pp. 78–86.
34. See C. Whan Park & S. Mark Young, 'Consumer Response to Television Commercials: The Impact of Involvement and Background Music on Brand Attitude Formation', *Journal of Marketing Research* 23, February 1986, pp. 11–24; Douglas M. Stayrnan & David A. Aaker, 'Are All the Effects of Ad-induced Feelings Mediated by A_{Ad}', *Journal of Consumer Research* 15, December 1988, pp. 368–73; and Homer, *Journal of Marketing Research*, pp. 78–86, for a discussion of whether peripheral cues affect attitudes directly through their effect on brand beliefs, indirectly by influencing attitudes toward the advertisement, or through some combination of these two routes (termed the dual mediation hypothesis).
35. See Chris Janiszewski, 'The Influence of Print Advertisement Organisation on Affect toward a Brand Name', *Journal of Consumer Research* 17, June 1990, pp. 53–65, for an interesting perspective on the effect of the subconscious on processing of placement attributes.
36. Henry Assael, *Consumer Behavior and Marketing Action*, Kent, Belmont, CA, 1981, p. 91.
37. Richard J. Lutz, 'Changing Brand Attitudes through Modification of Cognitive Structure', *Journal of Consumer Research* 1, March 1975, p. 49, has discussed some of these strategies.

38. See John L. Lastovicka & David M. Gardner, 'Components of Involvement', in John C. Maloney & Bernard Silverman (eds), *Attitude Research Plays for High Stakes*, American Marketing Association, Chicago, 1979, pp. 53–73; and C. W. Sherif, M. Sherif & R. E. Nebergall, *Attitude and Attitude Change: The Social Judgment Involvement Approach*, Yale University Press, New Haven, CT, 1965.

39. One might validly suggest that channel factors should be included in this list. However, for purposes of this chapter, these effects are included within the source, because consumers frequently view a medium as a source of information and influence.

40. Arch C. Woodside & J. William Davenport, 'The Effect of Salesman Similarity and Expertise on Consumer Purchasing Behavior', *Journal of Marketing Research* 11, May 1974, pp. 198–202.

41. Theodore Levitt, 'Communications and Industrial Selling', *Journal of Marketing* 31, April 1967, pp. 15–21.

42. News report broadcast by Stereo 2BS Radio, Bathurst, NSW, June 1995.

43. See, for example Brian Sternthal, Ruby Dholakia & Clark Leavitt, 'The Persuasive Effects of Source Credibility: Tests of Cognitive Response', *Journal of Consumer Research* 4, 1978, pp. 252–60; D. Bock & T. Saine, 'The Impact of Source Credibility, Attitude Valence, and Task Sensitization on Trait Error in Speech Evaluation', *Speech Monographs* 37, 1975, pp. 342–58; and Robert R. Harmon & Kenneth A. Coney, 'The Persuasive Effects of Source Credibility in Buy and Lease Situations', *Journal of Marketing Research* 14, May 1982, pp. 255–60.

44. See Sternthal, Dholakia & Leavitt, ibid, pp. 252–60.

45. See Brian Sternthal, Lynn Phillips & Ruby Dholakia, 'The Persuasive Effect of Source Credibility: A Situational Analysis', *Public Opinion Quarterly* 42, 1978, pp. 285–314; and Daniel R. Toy, 'Monitoring Communication Effects: A Cognitive Structure/Cognitive Response Approach', *Journal of Consumer Research* 9, June 1982, pp. 66–76.

46. See Ruby Dholakia & Brian Sternthal, 'Highly Credible Sources Persuasive Facilitators or Persuasive Liabilities?', *Journal of Consumer Research* 3, March 1977, pp. 223–32.

47. See Carl Hovland & Walter Weiss, 'The Influence of Source Credibility on Communication Effectiveness', *Public Opinion Quarterly* 15, 1951, pp. 635–50; Herbert Kelman & Carl Hovland, 'Reinstatement of the Communicator in Delayed Measurement of Opinion Change', *Journal of Abnormal and Social Psychology* 48, 1953, pp. 327–35; and Carl Hovland, Arthur A. Lunsdaine & Fred D. Sheffield, *Experiments on Mass Communications*, Princeton University Press, Princeton, NJ, 1949, pp. 188–9.

48. See, for example, N. Capon & J. Hulbert, 'The Sleeper Effect: An Awakening', *Public Opinion Quarterly* 37, 1973, pp. 333–58; and C. Gruder et al., 'Empirical Tests of the Absolute Sleeper Effect Predicted from the Discounting Cue Hypothesis', *Journal of Personality and Social Psychology* 36, 1978, pp. 1061–74.

49. Kelman & Hovland, op cit, Ref 47, pp. 327–35.

50. See Pamela M. Homer & Lynn R. Kahle, 'Source Expertise, Time of Source Identification, and Involvement in Persuasion: An Elaborative Processing Perspective', *Journal of Advertising* 19 (1), pp. 30–9.

51. For a more complete discussion, see E. P. Bettinghaus, *Persuasive Communication*, 2nd edn, Holt, New York, 1973, p. 10.

52. See E. Aronson & B. Golden, 'The Effect of Relevant and Irrelevant Aspects of Communicator Credibility on Opinion Change', *Journal of Personality* 30, 1962, pp. 135–46; Gordon Patzer, *The Physical Attractiveness Phenomenon*, Plenum, New York, 1985; Marjorie Caballero, James Lumpkin & Charles Madden, 'Using Physical Attractiveness as an Advertising Tool: An Empirical Test of the Attraction Phenomenon', *Journal of Advertising Research*, August–September 1989, pp. 16–22;

and Susan Petroshius & Kenneth Crocker, 'An Empirical Analysis of Spokesperson Characteristics on Advertisement and Product Evaluations', *Journal of the Academy of Marketing Science* 17 (3), 1989, pp. 217–25.

53. Michael A. Kamins, 'An Investigation into the "Match Up" Hypothesis in Celebrity Advertising: When Beauty May Be Only Skin Deep', *Journal of Advertising* 19 (1), 1990, pp. 4–13.
54. David K. Berlo, *The Process of Communications*, Holt, San Francisco, 1960, pp. 45–8.
55. M Karlins & H. I. Abelson, *Persuasion*, 2nd edn, Springer, New York, 1970, p. 128.
56. See C. Hovland, A. Lumsdaine & F. Sheffield, *Experiments in Mass Communication*, vol. 3, Princeton University Press, Princeton, NJ, 1948; also see Linda Golden & Mark Alphert, 'The Relative Effectiveness of One-sided and Two-sided Communication for Mass Transit Advertising', in H. Keith Hunt (ed.), *Advances in Consumer Research*, vol. 5, Association for Consumer Research, Ann Arbor, MI, 1978, pp. 12–18.
57. See Michael Kamins and Henry Assael, 'Two-sided versus One-sided Appeals: A Cognitive Perspective on Argumentation, Source Derogation, and the Effects of Disconforming Trial on Belief Change', *Journal of Marketing Research* 23, February 1987, pp. 29–39; and William Swinyard, 'The Interaction between Comparative Advertising and Copy Claim Variation', *Journal of Marketing Research* 5, May 1981, pp. 175–86.
58. See Stewart W. Bither, 'Resistance of Persuasion: Inoculation and Distraction', in Arch Woodside, Jagdish Sheth & Peter Bennett (eds), *Consumer and Industrial Buying Behavior*, North-Holland, New York, pp. 243–50; Michael Etgar & Stephen A. Goodwin, 'One-sided versus Two-sided Comparative Message Appeals for New Brand Introductions', *Journal of Consumer Research* 8, March 1982, pp. 460–5; and Kamins & Assael, ibid, pp. 29–39.
59. See Michael A. Kamins & Lawrence J. Marks, 'Advertising Puffery: The Impact of Using Two-sided Claims on Product Attitude and Purchase Intention', *Journal of Advertising* 16 (4), 1987, pp. 6–15.
60. Cornelia Pechmann, 'How Do Consumer Inferences Moderate the Effectiveness of Two-sided Messages?', in Marvin Goldberg, Gerald Gorn & Richard Pollay (eds), *Advances in Consumer Research*, vol. 17, Association for Consumer Research, Provo, UT, 1990, pp. 337–41.
61. See Manoj Hastak & Jong-Won Park, 'Mediators of Message Sidedness Effects on Cognitive Structure for Involved and Uninvolved Audiences', in Marvin Goldberg, Gerald Gorn & Richard Pollay (eds), *Advances in Consumer Research*, vol. 17, Association for Consumer Research, Provo, UT, 1990, pp. 329–36; and Pechmann, ibid, pp. 337–41.
62. C. I. Hovland, I. L. Janis & H. H. Kelley, *Communication and Persuasion*, Yale University Press, New Haven, CT, 1953, p. 119.
63. Frank Kardes, 'Spontaneous Inference Processes in Advertising: The Effects of Conclusion Omission and Involvement on Persuasion', *Journal of Consumer Research* 15, September 1988, pp. 225–33.
64. See Alan G. Sawyer, 'Repetition and Affect: Recent Empirical and Theoretical Developments', in Arch Woodside, Jagdish Sheth & Peter Bennett (eds), *Consumer and Industrial Buyer Behavior*, North-Holland, New York, 1977, pp. 229–42; and George E. Belch, 'The Effects of Television Commercial Repetition on Cognitive Response and Message Acceptance', *Journal of Consumer Research* 9, June 1982, pp. 56–65.
65. See Bobby Calder & Brian Sternthal, 'Television Advertising Wearout: An Information Processing View', *Journal of Marketing Research* 17, May 1980, pp. 173–86; and James M. Munch & John L. Swasy, 'Rhetorical Question, Summarization Frequency, and Argument Strength Effects on Recall', *Journal of Consumer Research* 15, June 1988, pp. 69–76.

66. I. Janis & S. Feshbach, 'Effects of Fear-arousing Communications', *Journal of Abnormal and Social Psychology* 48, 1953, pp. 78–92.

67. See L. Berkowitz & D. R. Cottingham, 'The Interest Value and Relevance of Fear-arousing Communication', *Journal of Abnormal and Social Psychology* 60, 1960, pp. 37–43; A. S. DeWolf & C. N. Governale, 'Fear and Attitude Change', *Journal of Abnormal and Social Psychology* 69, 1964, pp. 119–23; H. Leventhal, R. P. Singer & S. Jones, 'Effects of Fear and Specificity of Recommendation upon Attitudes and Behavior', *Journal of Personality and Social Psychology* 2, 1965, pp. 20–9; C. A. Insko, A. Arkoff & V. M. Insko, 'Effects of High and Low Fear-arousing Communications upon Opinions toward Smoking', *Journal of Experimental Social Psychology* 1, August 1965, pp. 254–66; and Michael L. Ray & William L. Wilkie, 'Fear: The Potential of an Appeal Neglected by Marketing', *Journal of Marketing* 34, January 1970, pp. 54–62.

68. See, for example, Herbert Rothfeld, 'Fear Appeals and Persuasion: Assumptions and Errors in Advertising Research', in Claude R. Martin Jr (ed.), *Current Issues Research in Advertising*, vol. 11, University of Michigan, Ann Arbor, 1989, pp. 21–40.

69. See Brain Sternthal & C. Samuel Craig, 'Fear Appeals: Revisited and Revised', *Journal of Consumer Research* 1, 1974, pp. 22–34; John J. Burnett & Robert E. Wilkes, 'Fear Appeals to Segments Only', *Journal of Advertising Research* 20, October 1980, pp. 21–4; and John J. Burnett & Richard L. Oliver, 'Fear Appeal Effects in the Field: A Segmentation Approach', *Journal of Marketing Research* 16, May 1979, pp. 181–90.

70. Ronald Rogers, 'Cognitive and Physiological Processes in Fear Appeals and Attitude Change: A Revised Theory of Protection Motivation', in John Cacioppo & Richard Petty (eds), *Social Psychophysiology*, Guilford Press, New York, 1983, pp. 153–76.

71. For recent work in this area, see John F. Tanner Jr, Ellen Day & Melvin Crask, 'Protection Motivation Theory: An Extension of Fear Appeals Theory in Communication', *Journal of Business Research* 19, 1989, pp. 267–76; and John F. Tanner Jr, James Hunt & David Eppright, 'The Protection Motivation Model: A Normative Model of Fear Appeals', *Journal of Marketing* 55, July 1991, pp. 36–45.

72. M. Karlins & H. I. Abelson, *Persuasion*, 2nd edn., Springer, New York, 1970, p. 15.

73. See Stewart W. Bither, 'Effects of Distraction and Commitment on the Persuasiveness of Television Advertising', *Journal of Marketing Research* 9, February 1972, pp. 1–5; and David Gardner, 'The Distraction Hypothesis in Marketing', *Journal of Advertising Research* 10, December 1970, pp. 25–31.

74. See Hovland, Janis & Kelley, op cit, Ref 62, pp. 228–37; also see W. Watts, 'Relative Persistence of Opinion Change Induced by Active Compared to Passive Participation', *Journal of Personality and Social Psychology* 5, 1967, pp. 4–15.

75. See Thomas W. Whipple & Alice E. Courtney, 'How Men and Women Judge Humor: Advertising Guidelines for Action and Research', in James H. Leigh & Claude R. Martin Jr (eds), *Current Issues and Research in Advertising*, University of Michigan, Ann Arbor, 1981.

76. See, for example, Brian Sternthal & C. Samuel Craig, 'Humor in Advertising', *Journal of Marketing* 37, October 1973, pp. 12–18; Thomas Madden & Marc Weinberger, 'Humor in Advertising: A Practitioner View', *Journal of Advertising Research* 24, 1984, pp. 23–9; and Calvin Duncan, 'Humor in Advertising: A Behavioral Perspective', *Journal of the Academy of Marketing Science* 7, Fall 1979, pp. 285–306.

77. See Duncan, ibid, pp. 285–306; Sternthal & Craig, ibid, pp. 12–18; and Amitava Chattopadhyay & Kunal Basu, 'Humor in Advertising: The Moderating Role of Prior Brand Evaluation', *Journal of Marketing Research* 27, November 1990, pp. 466–76.

78. See, for example, Jennings Bryant, Alan Silberberg & Scott Elliott, 'Effects of Humorous Illustrations in College Textbooks', *Human Communication Research* 8, Fall 1981; and Calvin Duncan & James Nelson, 'Effects of Humor in a Radio Advertising Experiment', *Journal of Advertising* 14, 1985, pp. 33–40.

79. See Cliff Scott, David Klein & Jennings Bryant, 'Consumer Response to Humor in

Advertising: A Series of Field Studies Using Behavioral Observation', *Journal of Consumer Research* 16, March 1990, pp. 498–501; and Kenneth Runyon, *Advertising*, Charles Merrill, Columbus, OH, 1979.

80. Chattopadhyay & Basu, op cit, Ref 77, pp. 466–76.

81. E. P. Bettinghaus, *Persuasive Communication*, 2nd edn, Holt, New York, 1973, pp. 160–1.

82. William L. Wilkie & Paul W. Farris, 'Comparison Advertising: Problems and Potential', *Journal of Marketing* 39, October 1975, pp. 7–15.

83. See Stephen B. Ash & Chow-Hou Wee, 'Comparative Advertising: A Review with Implications for Further Research', in Richard Bagozzi & Alice Tybout (eds), *Advances in Consumer Research*, vol. 10, Association for Consumer Research, Ann Arbor, MI, 1983, pp. 370–6; George E. Delch, 'An Examination of Comparative and Noncomparative Television Commercials: The Effects of Claim Variation and Repetition on Cognitive Response and Message Acceptance', *Journal of Marketing Research* 18, August 1981, pp. 333–49; William R. Swinyard, 'The Interaction between Comparative Advertising and Copy Claim Variation', *Journal of Marketing Research* 18, May 1981, pp. 175–86; Terence A. Shimp & David C. Dyer, 'The Effects of Comparative Advertising Mediated by Market Position of Sponsoring Brand', *Journal of Advertising* 3, Summer 1978, pp. 13–19; Gerald J. Gorn & Charles B. Weinberg, 'The Impact of Comparative Advertising on Perception and Attitude: Some Positive Findings', *Journal of Consumer Research* 11, September 1984, pp. 719–27; Norman Turgeon & David Barnaby, 'Comparative Advertising: Two Decades of Practice and Research', in James H. Leigh & Claude R. Martin Jr (eds), *Current Issues and Research in Advertising*, vol. 11, University of Michigan, Ann Arbor, 1989, pp. 41–65; and Michale Bixby & Douglas Lincoln, 'Legal Issues Surrounding the Use of Comparative Advertising: What the Nonprescriptive Drug Industry Has Taught Us', *Journal of Public Policy & Marketing* 8, 1989, pp. 143–60.

84. See Martha Rogers, 'Using Psycholinguistics as a Theoretical Basis for Evaluating and Copytesting Advertising Messages', in John D. Leckenby (ed.), *Proceedings of the 1988 Conferences of the American Academy of Advertising*, American Academy of Advertising, Austin, TX, 1988, pp. RC112–17; and Richard Jackson Harris, Ruth Sturm, Michael Klassen & John Bechtold, 'Language in Advertising: A Psycholinguistic Approach', in James H. Leigh & Claude R. Martin Jr (eds), *Current Issues and Research in Advertising 1986*, vol. 9. University of Michigan, Ann Arbor, 1986, pp. 1–26.

85. Bettinghaus, op cit, Ref 81, pp. 121–2, in reference to G. L. Trager, 'Paralanguage: A First Approximation', *Studies in Linguistics* 13, 1958, pp. 1–12. Also see Larry Percy, 'Psycholinguistic Guidelines for Advertising Copy', in Andrew Mitchell (ed.), *Advances in Consumer Research*, vol. 9, Association for Consumer Research, Ann Arbor, MI, 1982, pp. 107–11, for some practical guidelines for using verbal codes.

86. For a recent exception, see Patrick L. Schul & Charles W. Lamb Jr, 'Recoding Nonverbal and Vocal Communications: A Laboratory Study', *Journal of the Academy of Marketing Science* 10, Spring 1982, pp. 154–64.

87. Bettinghaus, op cit, Ref 81, pp. 121–2, in reference to G. L. Tragar, 'Paralanguage: A First Approximation', *Studies in Linguistics* 13, 1958, pp. 1–12.

88. See I. L. Janis, 'Personality Correlates of Susceptibility to Persuasion', *Journal of Personality* 22, 1954, pp. 504–18; F. J. Divesta & J. C. Merivan, 'The Effects of Need-oriented Communications on Attitude Change', *Journal of Abnormal and Social Psychology* 60, 1960, pp. 80–5; and I. L. Janis & C. I. Hovland (eds), *Personality and Persuasibility*, Yale University Press, New Haven, CT, 1959, pp. 55–68.

89. Meryl Gardner, 'Mood States and Consumer Behavior', *Journal of Consumer Research* 12, December 1985, pp. 281–300.

90. Rajeev Batra & Douglas Stayman, 'The Role of Mood in Advertising Effectiveness', *Journal of Consumer Research* 17, September 1990, pp. 203–14.
91. See Gardner, op cit, Ref 89, p. 283.
92. See Judy Alpert & Mark Alpert, 'Music Influences on Mood and Purchase Intentions', *Psychology & Marketing* 7, Summer 1990, pp. 109–33; and Gordon C. Bruner II, 'Music Mood and Marketing', *Journal of Marketing* 53, October 1990, pp. 94–104.
93. Ronald Paul Hill, 'The Effects of Advertisements on Consumers' Mood States: An Interactive Perspective', in Michael J. Houston (ed.), *Advances in Consumer Research*, vol. 15, Association for Consumer Research, Provo, UT, 1988, pp. 131–4.
94. Batra & Stayman, op cit, Ref 90, pp. 203–14; and David Kuykendall & John Keating, 'Mood and Persuasion: Evidence for the Differential Influence of Positive and Negative States', *Psychology & Marketing* 7, Spring 1990, pp. 1–9.
95. See Michael A. Kamins, Lawrence J. Marks & Deborah Skinner, 'Television Commercial Evaluation in the Context of Program Induced Mood: Congruency versus Consistency Effects', *Journal of Advertising* 20, June 1991, pp. 1–14.
96. This discussion is based in part upon Bettinghaus, op cit, Ref 81, pp. 59–61.

CASE STUDIES

CASE 1 ## THE NEW ZEALAND HONEY INDUSTRY

Honey is produced in all areas of New Zealand. The total domestic sales value in 1991 was $14 million, but the industry is suffering from stagnant demand and accelerating competition within the industry and from other competing products such as jams. The industry consists of a very large number of part-time apiarists, and around six hundred producers who produce enough honey to make it their major or sole source of income. A sizeable proportion of production is controlled by a handful of very large producers. Honey production is very dependent on 'airspace', or the size and vegetation cover of the area over which bees from a particular hive can gather honey. As a result, the South Island crop is very nearly as large as that of the North Island.

Table 1 *Honey production by district, 1990–91*

Production district	No. of beekeepers		Annual production	
	1990	1991	1990	1991
			tonnes	tonnes
Whangarei	1580	1307	660	668
Hamilton	659	649	1154	1067
Tauranga	656	619	1296	1470
Palmerston North	1391	1340	894	811
Blenheim	54	505	548	265
Lincoln	783	768	2774	1965
Alexandra	593	780	1503	1054

Beekeepers do not own their own airspace. Airspace is usually made available to beekeepers through agreements with local farmers. The beekeeper may pay the farmer for this privilege, or the farmer may give the airspace free to a good beekeeper in recognition of the important role that bees play in the pollination of major crops such as apples and kiwi fruit. All beekeepers with more than 50 hives are members of the National Beekeepers Association, a national body representing the interests of apiarists across the country. The association is primarily involved in co-ordination, research and lobbying, rather than in the marketing of honey. The association is based in Wellington, and is supported by a levy on hives. The levy is 48c per hive. Each hive produces between 20 and 30 kilograms of honey per year. Non-varietal honey commands a price of around $2 a kilogram ex-hive.

DOMESTIC CONSUMPTION PATTERNS

Honey consumption does not vary widely across the country on a per-capita basis. Thus, consumption is heavily skewed toward the North Island. Industrial customers account for a small percentage of the honey produced. New Zealand has an exceptionally high per-capita consumption of honey compared with other developed countries. Consumption has been steady in New Zealand for a considerable time.

EXPORT AND IMPORT

Exports are normally in the form of bulk commodity honey in 40-gallon (180-litre) drums for blending into consumer products abroad. The international market is dominated by honey sold in this form. The assessment of quality on the international commodity market is based largely on colour; the lighter the colour of the honey, the higher the price paid for it. This pricing policy is also reflected in the prices that producers receive for their product when selling to honey processors in New Zealand. The major import markets for international honey commodities are the United States, Europe, and particularly eastern Asian countries such as Malaysia and Korea.

Some countries such as Korea have barriers to the entry of commodity honey but, in general, international honey is a small and relatively free market dominated by low-cost producers such as China and Argentina. The competitive advantage of these major producers is based on the reduced labour rates paid during the production of this highly labour-intensive commodity. Australia is a significant honey producer, but at present Australian honey is barred from New Zealand along with most other commodity-type honeys.

Some attempts to export honey in value-added form have occurred. After an initial success, most of these products have been undermined by opportunist dumping exports from other organisations within New Zealand. Most processed exports have been directed at the European market, particularly Germany and Austria. Recently exports of processed product to South-east Asia, and in particular to Korea and Malaysia, have been increasing. This is largely as a response to barriers to the commodity product, but also in response to an increasing demand for luxury packaged food products in these markets. There is currently no organisation in New Zealand that either actively controls or promotes the export of honey on the scale of other large producer boards.

At present, production exceeds demand in New Zealand, leading to a surplus on the domestic market and subsequent pressure to export. Of approximately 8000 tonnes produced in 1991, 2000 were exported, largely in commodity form but with a significant value-added sector, largely directed at eastern Asian markets. There are other exports of importance, including wax and package bees, especially queen bees, which are mainly sent to the United States.

Imports of honey to New Zealand are controlled via health regulations, most of which are related to the control of American foul brood. The temper of government at present would indicate that protection of the domestic market will certainly not be increased, and may be reduced, especially with respect to Australian honey.

TYPES OF HONEY

Several honey types are produced. Most on sale in New Zealand are blended honeys, sold either as a whipped semi-solid product or as a clear viscous liquid, the difference in appearance being solely a factor of the processing of the honey rather than a difference in the honey as produced by the bees. These blended honeys are sold under a variety of brand names and trademarks. The colour of these honeys depends on the individual honeys blended into them. Recently there has been a trend toward honeys derived from specific plant species. Some, such as viper's bugloss or rata, are sold on appeal of the flower concerned, or on flavour and appearance. Others such as manuka are sold on their supposed therapeutic qualities and command a significant premium as a result. Honey sold in the comb is a very small, high-premium sector of the market.

PROCESSING

The processing required for honey to be sold on the consumer market is minimal. Honey harvested from hives is centrifuged to remove comb fragments, dead bees and other undesirable impurities. The relatively low cost of centrifuges allows even the smaller producers to process honey to this stage. The resultant clear viscous fluid may then be whipped to produce the opaque stiff honey familiar to most consumers. At this point it is ready to be shipped off to honey packagers or industrial customers, or is packaged for final consumption by the producers themselves.

SELLING CHANNELS

A couple of the larger North Island producers package and sell their own products. However, most of the full-time producers tend to sell into larger processors and packagers, which act as marketing agents and possess brand names that are locally or nationally recognised. Some of these packagers are owned by the producers and return their profits to them. Others are private entities and profit centres in their own right. The health requirements for the packaging of honey are extremely relaxed when compared with other animal products.

Therefore, honey can be packaged by any producer with a very small capital outlay beyond the centrifuges, which are required to modify comb honey into a form that the major packagers will accept as an input. Many of the smaller producers package and sell their product directly onto the local market. There are a few intermediaries between packagers and the final consumer, or retail store.

CUSTOMERS

Consumers

A small amount of honey is sold directly by producers to consumers. This is a small but highly significant market, as such direct sellers have few of the overheads associated with the producer retail chains. They can, as a result, undercut retailers almost at will while still maintaining an adequate margin. Not surprisingly, there are signs that producer interest and activity in this segment are increasing.

Retailers

Retailers can be divided into two main groups:

1. *Independents*. Independents consist of two further groups: outlets such as dairies and small supermarkets, which make their income primarily from the sale of foodstuffs, and retailers such as tourist shops and service stations, which sell honey along with other foodstuffs as an opportunistic sideline. The souvenir-style shops normally demand a very different product from the usual honey pottle (tub). Statistics would suggest that sales to the first of these groups are declining, while sales to the latter are increasing sharply.
2. *Supermarkets*. Supermarkets are the dominant channel through which honey reaches the consumer, controlling over 85 per cent of the retail market. The power and concentration of the supermarkets are increasing rapidly, as is the concentration of the buying function within these organisations. Despite this, supermarket buying is more decentralised in New Zealand than in almost any other country.

Owner-managers tend to make a great many purchase decisions on the spot without reference to head office. This practice is particularly prevalent in the honey sector, with a great many local producers supplying quite large retail outlets directly.

Industrial buyers

Industrial consumers can be divided into two main groups. It is presumed, though not known, that they account for about 25 per cent of the honey sold in New Zealand:

1. *Large-scale industrial users*. These tend to buy directly off large producers in crude commodity form.
2. *Small-scale industrial users and food service outlets*. The buying habits of these organisations are completely unknown.

THE NEW ZEALAND HONEY CONSUMER

Usage patterns

New Zealand has one of the highest per-capita honey-consumption rates in the world. Over 80 per cent of households possess honey and hold it on a regular basis. Honey is overwhelmingly used as a spread on bread or other baked products. Its usage as a cooking agent is light but has a widespread penetration, with over 50 per cent of households using it regularly as a cooking aid.

Purchase patterns

The purchase cycle for honey appears to be about once a month. Honey rarely finds its way onto the weekly shopping list, and a significant number of households buy only once every three months or even more infrequently.

Attitudes

Consumers normally treat honey as a spread. Brand awareness is low. Decisions as to brand are not made until the consumer reaches the supermarket. Preferences are not clear-cut. Most associate darker colour with increased flavour, and the main problem cited with respect to honey is difficulty in spreading the product on bread. Honey is occasionally used as a substitute for sugar, with health reasons normally being cited.

Purchase criteria

In the absence of any other criteria, consumers select their honey largely on the basis of price. The only honey that appears to be consistently asked for, and that commands a premium, is manuka honey, due to its widely publicised therapeutic properties.

Demographics

Honey is unusual in that there are no strong demographic trends in the volume purchased. Information relating usage patterns to demographics is not available.

EXISTING HONEY PRODUCTS

Consumer products

Consumer honey is sold in three forms: comb, creamed and normal:

1. *Comb honey*. This is sold in two forms: either as a section of the comb sliced out of the tray taken from the hive and placed in a shallow tin, or as a lump floating in a (clear) pottle of normal honey. Comb honey is a particularly large seller to tourists.

2. *Normal honey*. This is sold in the form in which it is collected from the centrifuge. It is a clear viscous fluid with the appearance and consistency of golden syrup. Many consumers do not favour this honey due to its tendency to dribble off the spoon when being transferred from pottle to bread. Normal honey has a tendency to crystallise in storage.

3. *Creamed honey*. This is normal honey whipped to include air bubbles. Creamed honey varies in consistency from not much stiffer than uncreamed honey to concrete, depending on the degree of whipping and the conditions under which it is stored after creaming. Major consumer grouses about this product are its inconsistency, and its tendency to rip the centre out of slices of bread.

Consumer-product packaging

Consumer-product packaging is dominated by two forms:

1. *Opaque pottle*. This is the old 'standard' packaging consisting of a push-resealable plastic pottle, both lid and pottle being opaque. The manufacture, brand and other information are normally printed directly onto the plastic in one or two colours. The plastic pottle comes in a variety of sizes from 250 grams to 2 kilograms.

2. *Clear pottle*. This is the more modern of the two packaging systems, and the one in which the more modern 'varietal' honey types are found. The package consists of a clear square, jar-style plastic pottle with a white screw-top and usually carries a paper label with multiple colours. Comb honey is occasionally presented in these pottles. This type of packaging is almost exclusively in quantities of 500 grams. Occasionally manuka and other premium honeys are packaged in 250 gram pottles.

There are a few other packages for tourist and specialist honeys, but they are usually developments of the two major types detailed above.

PRICES AND MARGINS

The honey producers are coming under increasing pressure, particularly from supermarkets, with respect to price.

QUESTIONS

1. Is it possible to identify market segments that the honey industry could use for strategy development?

2. How important is consumer involvement within the different segments?

3. Suggest strategies that the industry might develop to stimulate demand, and explain how these would work in terms of concepts from consumer behaviour.

Source: This case study was prepared by Rob Hamlin, Department of Marketing, University of Otago, New Zealand.

CANTERBURY REGIONAL BLOOD TRANSFUSION SERVICE

Andrea Fisher, manager of the Canterbury Regional Blood Transfusion Service (CRBTS), reflected on the figures she had just finished putting together for her annual report. Donations of blood for the year ended 31 June 1993 totalled 18 460, almost 8 per cent short of the target 20 000 donations (each donation comprises one unit or 450 millilitres of blood) for the year (see Fig. 1). By itself this shortfall was not insurmountable, but it was particularly worrying because it continued a trend in the availability of this vital supply for the

region's health service. Clearly, some new initiatives were essential to retain and increase donors to ensure adequate supplies of life-saving blood in the short and long terms.

New Zealand's free donor-based system for blood collection and distribution, internationally noted in the past for its success, operates through six main regional centres of which Christchurch is one. Collection and preliminary processing of blood at each centre are supervised by a director, who is also responsible for ensuring that sufficient blood is

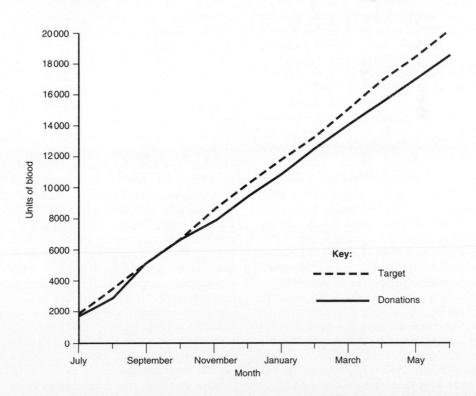

Fig. 1 Cumulative number of units of blood sought (target) and received (donations) by the Canterbury Regional Blood Transfusion Service in the year ending 31 June 1993

available to satisfy needs. Advertising and publicity are the principal means of recruiting donors, and the national advertising budget for 1991 amounted to about $15 000 (the advertising budget for Melbourne's blood service serving a similar-sized population was $200 000 for the same year). Budget cuts and changing public attitudes since 1991 have resulted in a marked decline in donors both regionally and nationally. Only 150 000 units of blood were collected across the whole country during the year to June 1990, just 86 per cent of the targeted 175 000. Such shortfalls can be made up from stocks of frozen New Zealand blood held at the Commonwealth Serum Laboratories in Melbourne. However, these stocks will disappear in the future if donations continue to fall short of targets.

A number of activities to increase donor numbers were tried with varying success, but more usual commercial marketing activities are not appropriate for several reasons. First, no payments or rewards can be offered as inducements to attract donors, because these are likely to attract persons in high-risk categories with respect to various blood problems and diseases (e.g. HIV sufferers, hepatitis B and C sufferers). Secondly, resources available are inadequate to support such inducements. Thirdly, no charges are made for blood provided because of the widely held principle that blood that is given freely by voluntary donors should be available free of charge to those who need it.

Thus, like equivalent services elsewhere around the world, the CRBTS relies heavily upon a pool of loyal donors, periodic publicity campaigns and visits to major employers for blood. These, however, are no longer sufficient to ensure an adequate supply of blood in the changed social and economic environment of the 1990s. The perceived risk of infection with the various blood-related diseases when giving blood, notably HIV, along with a more self-centred attitude in difficult economic times appear to have been responsible for some of the increase in loyal donor retirements to 4065 in 1992–93, or about 26 per cent of total donors on file (32 per cent more CRBTS donors retired in 1992–93 compared with 1990–91). In addition, harder economic times and high unemployment have been blamed for the greater reluctance of the public to make time to visit donation centres to give blood.

A careful system involving appointments for previous donors being mailed out a week in advance and confirmed by telephone the day before has not helped. Earlier opening (8.00 am) has helped and, on some days, all facilities are full immediately. However, processing requirements and budgetary constraints limit flexibility in this respect. The lengthy processing of donated blood must commence almost immediately, so collection normally finishes at 1.00 pm on most days to avoid the significant costs of paying staff overtime or penalty rates. Total donations decreased by 5.3 per cent over the last two years, and recruitment of new donors declined by 9.6 per cent over the same period. In the past, new donors were usually brought in by a loyal donor, but this also has dropped off, perhaps due to a combination of the above factors.

Promotional campaigns, notably publicity through television and radio, continue to be particularly successful. Typically, each press release or other publicity activity is followed by a marked increase in new donors. Equally typically, however, this increase is normally a brief surge in numbers that disappears within two or three days. More sustained or frequent publicity campaigns are not attempted because it is believed that the general public would quickly tire of such stories and their effectiveness would quickly diminish. Larger scale promotional efforts have been useful in the past when business sponsorship of these was possible. At present, however, the service lacks sufficient resources to fund such campaigns itself and the opportunities for obtaining corporate sponsorship have diminished drastically. Sponsors seem very unwilling to become associated with anything to do with blood because of its link to HIV and other diseases. They fear that their organisation will, in some tenuous and irrational way, become linked to these insidious diseases in consumers' minds. Further, businesses seem more reluctant to sponsor causes while economic conditions remain tight.

A specially designed and fully staffed Mobile Unit (now out-dated) has been a major source of donations. This large, buslike facility transports equipment to major employers and important shopping centres within the city, suburbs and outlying rural communities. Once the equipment is set up in a cafeteria, conference room, church or school hall, donors can give blood with minimal effort and disruption to their daily routines. Such visits are usually preceded by advance notice to the larger employers, as well as the placing of posters at strategic locations nearby. Once again, donations collected by the Mobile Unit have decreased substantially in recent years. Apparently, the general reluctance to give blood applies to the Mobile Unit also. In addition, it seems that employers are now much more reluctant to allow employees time off work to give blood at the unit, even though it may be located within or very close to their premises.

A special letter drop to all households in one suburb of the city was undertaken by the local Lions Club, a community service organisation, in association with New Zealand Post Marketing. Response to this initiative was very disappointing, with less than 10 donors coming to the Mobile Unit (located in a main shopping centre) on the specified morning as a result of the letter drop.

The CRBTS has very little good information on why people do or do not give blood. The manager had been given a copy of a survey of blood-donor behaviour undertaken by a market-research firm in 1986. This showed that only one-third of the total New Zealand adult population had given blood and that just 16 per cent were regarded as active donors (had given blood in the past two years). The typical donor at that time tended to be male (61 per cent), aged 25–39 years (41 per cent), live in metropolitan areas and small cities (65 per cent) and belong to middle socio-economic levels (52 per cent). The study provided no real guidelines for developing programs likely to increase donations, although there was a little information on lapsed and non-donors (see the following table).

Thus, Andrea Fisher believed that some new approaches to attracting and retaining donors were required urgently. However, she and her board had run out of practical ideas capable of being implemented within the present resources.

Table 1 Results of a survey of a multistage, stratified, random sample of 1000 adults (15 years and over) resident in New Zealand undertaken by personal interview in 1986

Reason for not giving blood	Lapsed donors (n = 226)	Non-donors (n = 626)
	%	%
Blood perceived unsuitable—ill, too old[a]	51	39
Apathy—haven't got around to it	20	22
Inconvenient—location	13	4
Low profile—never asked, don't know where	10	15
No particular reason	8	12
Adverse effect—get sick	7	2
Emotional reaction—dislike thought	5	17
Don't know	1	2
Scared of getting AIDS	0	1
Other	0	1

(a)People aged 16–65 years in good health and not belonging to 'at risk' social groups in terms of various diseases are accepted as first-time donors. Existing donors may give blood until age 70.

QUESTIONS

1. What motivations are consumers displaying in reference to donating blood?

2. What suggestions could you make to help the Canterbury Regional Blood Transfusion Service recruit more donors?

This case study was prepared by Graham Fenwick, Department of Management, University of Canterbury, New Zealand.

Sources: Canterbury Regional Blood Transfusion Service, *Donor Manager's Report, July 1992–June 1993*, CRBTS, Canterbury, 1993; New Zealand Blood Transfusion Service, *1993 New Zealand Blood Transfusion Services (BTS): Information Booklet*, Ministry of Health, Wellington, 1993; and D. Telford, 'Blood Cuts', *Listener & TV Times*, 1 April 1991, pp. 34–5.

CASE 3 — MAPPING TOURIST PERCEPTIONS OF HOLIDAY DESTINATIONS

This research used *multidimensional scaling* and *image association* techniques to provide a perceptual map of the position of Queenstown, a New Zealand tourist resort, relative to other New Zealand destinations, in the minds of New Zealand domestic tourists. The resulting maps and image analysis sought to uncover dimensions and attributes by which domestic New Zealand tourists positioned domestic holiday destinations, and to give a clear visual representation of differences in perceptions and attitudes about Queenstown among important domestic target markets.

QUEENSTOWN—THE DESTINATION

The resort of Queenstown lies on the foreshore of Lake Wakatipu, the second largest of the southern lakes located deep in the heart of New Zealand's South Island. The lake is surrounded by steep mountains clad in tussock, bracken fern and isolated strands of beech forest. This backdrop of scenic beauty contributed much to the alpine splendour that originally attracted visitors to the region. Today Queenstown is a vibrant alpine resort with a multitude of activities and attractions. The resort offers a diverse range of sightseeing opportunities, and it is well placed to cater for a variety of tourist segments. Queenstown is probably best known as New Zealand's premier ski resort, but it also has a well-developed tourism infrastructure, with activities ranging from bungi-jumping to

jetboating and whitewater rafting, and many different nightclubs and restaurants. Queenstown also lies close to some of the finest walking tracks in the country and the surrounding countryside offers a rich resource for a great variety of outdoor pursuits.

However, in recent years, there was a feeling among some tourism operators in Queenstown that domestic tourists were preferring other holiday destinations to that of Queenstown. People living in Otago and Southland, the two provinces closest to Queenstown, seemed to prefer Wanaka, Alexandra and other smaller Central Otago holiday spots. As well, North Island residents, especially those from Auckland, were favouring holidays to Australia over a holiday in New Zealand. They considered Australia to be better value for money than a trip to the South Island, which many considered expensive to reach.

It was decided a study of how Queenstown was positioned along important attributes relative to other domestic destinations might provide initial information that could be used to develop a domestic tourism marketing strategy for Queenstown.

THE RESEARCH

The research objectives were:

1. to establish the images associated with domestic holiday destinations by the New Zealand domestic market;

2. to represent the 'perceived position' of domestic destinations held by the domestic population based on a set of relevant attributes;

3. to examine the image and position of Queenstown in the eyes of relevant domestic publics; in particular, to examine any differences in attitudes held about Queenstown by geographic segments of the New Zealand population.

Population and sample

Two geographic samples were drawn from the New Zealand population:

1. *Auckland region—the potential market.* Auckland is the biggest urban market in New Zealand, and has the largest number of New Zealanders with high discretionary spending power. This sample was chosen because it was considered to represent a large potential market for Queenstown currently untapped (i.e. a small number of Aucklanders currently visit Queenstown).

2. *Coastal Otago/Southland Region—the existing market.* Queenstown draws most of its domestic market from this area (59.8 per cent) and it was seen as representing the existing domestic visitor market to Queenstown.

Table 1 *Ratings and rankings of destinations on selected attributes by Auckland respondents*

Attribute	Destinations									
	Akld	Chch	Cor	Rot	Que	Tau	Na/H	Dun	Nel	Wan
Value for money	(a)3.58 (b)(7)	3.30 (2)	3.15 (1)	3.85 (8)	4.32 (10)	3.36 (3)	3.47 (5)	3.47 (5)	3.45 (4)	3.99 (9)
Easy to reach	1.75 (1)	3.30 (4)	3.48 (5)	2.46 (2)	4.51 (9)	2.87 (3)	3.73 (6)	4.28 (8)	4.07 (7)	5.02 (10)
Nightlife and entertainment	2.33 (1)	3.77 (4)	5.81 (10)	3.70 (2)	3.71 (3)	4.39 (5)	4.66 (70)	4.42 (6)	4.91 (8)	5.29 (9)
Peaceful and quiet	5.06 (10)	3.05 (6)	1.66 (2)	3.64 (9)	2.78 (4)	3.35 (8)	3.04 (5)	3.08 (7)	2.49 (3)	1.20 (1)
Sports/rec facilities	2.41 (1)	2.86 (3)	3.53 (10)	3.15 (5)	2.61 (2)	3.06 (4)	3.43 (8)	3.47 (9)	3.25 (7)	3.18 (6)
Cultural experience	3.45 (2)	3.90 (3)	4.51 (7)	2.14 (1)	4.19 (5)	4.58 (8)	4.39 (6)	4.11 (4)	4.66 (9)	4.78 (10)
Beautiful scenery	2.93 (9)	2.22 (6)	1.67 (3)	2.10 (4)	1.33 (1)	2.73 (7)	3.03 (10)	2.73 (7)	2.17 (5)	1.58 (2)
Different	3.38 (6)	3.21 (5)	2.34 (3)	1.78 (1)	1.89 (2)	3.90 (9)	4.01 (10)	3.38 (6)	3.40 (8)	2.38 (4)
Climate	2.90 (5)	3.72 (9)	2.49 (2)	3.18 (6)	3.39 (7)	2.29 (1)	2.72 (4)	4.74 (10)	2.66 (3)	3.57 (8)
Shopping	2.14 (1)	3.48 (2)	5.22 (10)	3.51 (3)	3.82 (4)	3.86 (5)	4.18 (6)	4.30 (7)	4.30 (7)	4.78 (9)
Summer resort	2.89 (6)	3.96 (8)	1.79 (1)	2.88 (5)	4.16 (10)	1.87 (2)	2.59 (3)	4.08 (9)	2.04 (4)	3.51 (7)
Summer and winter resort	3.55 (5)	3.45 (4)	4.29 (9)	2.83 (2)	2.62 (1)	4.33 (10)	4.05 (7)	4.03 (8)	3.69 (6)	3.12 (3)

(a)   3.58 = Aggregate mean rating score of destinations on an attribute, 1 being good and 7 meaning poor, e.g. Auckland rates 3.58 out of 7 on Value for money.

(b)   (7) = Aggregate mean rank of destinations on particular attribute, e.g. Auckland ranks 7th out of the 10 destinations on Value for money.

Table 2 *Ratings and rankings of destinations on selected attributes by Otago/Southland respondents*

Attribute	Destinations									
	Akld	Chch	Cor	Rot	Que	Tau	Na/H	Dun	Nel	Wan
Value for money	3.78 (7)	2.82 (1)	3.58 (5)	4.07 (9)	5.01 (10)	3.75 (6)	3.52 (4)	2.82 (1)	3.31 (3)	3.83 (8)
Easy to reach	3.79 (5)	2.10 (2)	4.89 (10)	3.98 (6)	2.58 (3)	4.37 (9)	4.10 (8)	1.87 (1)	3.98 (6)	3.30 (4)
Nightlife and entertainment	2.21 (1)	2.87 (2)	5.02 (10)	3.98 (5)	3.11 (3)	4.26 (7)	4.25 (6)	3.83 (4)	4.43 (8)	5.00 (9)
Peaceful and quiet	5.94 (10)	4.01 (9)	2.54 (2)	3.98 (8)	3.50 (5)	3.54 (7)	3.53 (6)	3.28 (4)	2.86 (3)	2.40 (1)
Sports/rec facilities	2.89 (6)	2.60 (2)	3.18 (8)	3.48 (10)	2.64 (3)	3.17 (7)	3.25 (9)	2.61 (1)	2.83 (5)	2.82 (4)
Cultural experience	3.51 (2)	3.77 (3)	4.28 (8)	2.62 (1)	4.01 (5)	4.17 (7)	4.04 (6)	3.79 (4)	4.34 (9)	4.88 (10)
Beautiful scenery	3.90 (10)	3.16 (8)	2.28 (4)	2.44 (5)	1.25 (1)	2.75 (4)	3.31 (9)	2.89 (7)	2.20 (3)	1.67 (2)
Different	3.69 (7)	3.96 (9)	2.84 (4)	2.09 (2)	1.88 (1)	3.72 (8)	4.12 (10)	3.53 (6)	3.28 (5)	2.63 (3)
Climate	3.20 (9)	3.16 (8)	2.68 (5)	2.82 (7)	2.70 (6)	2.58 (3)	2.65 (4)	4.37 (10)	1.81 (1)	2.42 (2)
Shopping	1.90 (1)	2.23 (2)	4.50 (9)	3.74 (8)	3.40 (3)	3.89 (6)	3.86 (6)	3.40 (4)	3.65 (5)	4.50 (9)
Summer resort	3.24 (9)	3.23 (8)	2.50 (3)	2.73 (5)	2.84 (7)	2.58 (4)	2.83 (6)	3.57 (10)	1.80 (1)	2.40 (2)
Summer and winter resort	3.79 (6)	3.55 (4)	3.93 (10)	3.34 (3)	1.58 (1)	3.89 (8)	3.90 (9)	3.80 (7)	3.78 (5)	1.96 (2)

(a)   3.78 = Aggregate mean rating score of destinations on an attribute, 1 being good and 7 meaning poor, e.g. Auckland rates 3.78 out of 7 on Value for money.

(b)   (7) = Aggregate mean rank of destinations on particular attribute, e.g. Auckland ranks 7th out of the 10 destinations on Value for money.

Data collection and questionnaire design

A mail questionnaire was sent to a total of 1800 people—900 in the Auckland area and 900 in the Otago/Southland regions. The questionnaire was sent in a personally addressed envelope, with a covering letter attached to the questionnaire and a free-post return envelope for the return of the questionnaire. An incentive to reply was provided in that those who returned the questionnaire went into a draw for an $800 travel prize.

The *destination set* was derived from those destinations that had the highest percentage of

'person visits' made by the New Zealand domestic population and the relevance of the destination as a competitive threat to Queenstown. Ten destinations made up the destination set. The *attribute set* was taken from an initial set of attributes gathered from past research, both within New Zealand and overseas, which had looked at attributes important in destination choice. These attributes were broken down into those that were consistent across most studies and those that were universal across regional and international boundaries. The attributes were then pretested among tourism specialists, both

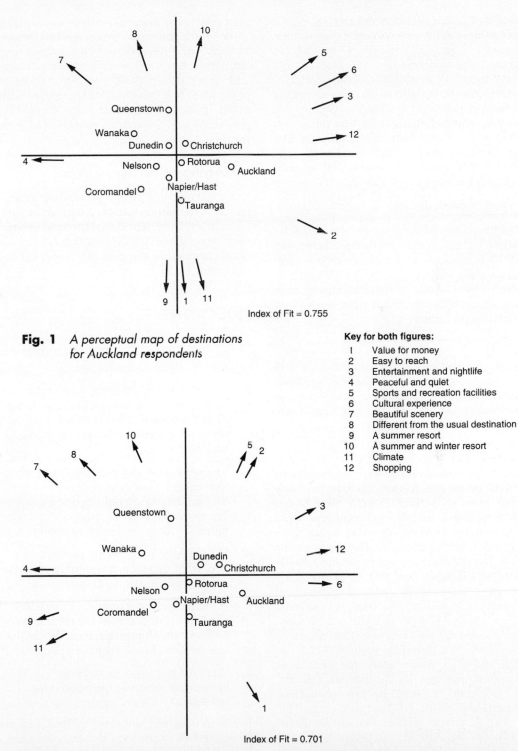

Fig. 1 *A perceptual map of destinations for Auckland respondents*

Index of Fit = 0.755

Key for both figures:

1 Value for money
2 Easy to reach
3 Entertainment and nightlife
4 Peaceful and quiet
5 Sports and recreation facilities
6 Cultural experience
7 Beautiful scenery
8 Different from the usual destination
9 A summer resort
10 A summer and winter resort
11 Climate
12 Shopping

Index of Fit = 0.701

Fig. 2 *A perceptual map of destinations for Otago/Southland respondents*

academics and practitioners, and among a small sample of the general public. From these pretests it was found necessary not only to include those attributes that were relevant to a New Zealander's overall destination decision-making criteria, but also to take account of the 'scenario-dependent' destination choice; for example, whether the holiday was taken primarily to go skiing, boating or shopping. The final set consisted of 22 attributes. For the purpose of this case, the number of relevant attributes has been limited to 12.

Method of analysis

Stimulus (destination) space generation of the positioning maps was performed using the MDPREF (multidimensional preference scaling) program written by J. D. Carroll and J. J. Chang, where aggregate mean ratings of each destination on the attributes given were taken to derive a perceptual map.

RESULTS

The final useable sample consisted of 809 respondents, or 45 per cent of the questionnaires sent out. The response rate from the Auckland region was 44 per cent, and from Otago/Southland 56 per cent.

Image analysis

The image associations with Queenstown showed quite clearly that Aucklanders saw Queenstown in a different light from Otago and Southland people. Respondents were asked to write down the first images that came to mind when thinking of the destinations listed. The predominant image of Queenstown among Aucklanders was that of 'skiing' (28.2 per cent), followed by 'attractive, beautiful scenery' (19.1 per cent), the 'lake' (8.8 per cent) and 'mountains' (7.8 per cent). In comparison, Otago/Southland residents saw Queenstown as being 'attractive, beautiful scenery' (17.3 per cent), and then, interestingly, the next most common image was 'for the tourists, touristy' (16.3 per cent), followed by 'expensive' (10.6 per cent) and 'skiing' (10.1 per cent).

The Auckland market was broken down into those who *have* visited Queenstown and those who *have never* visited Queenstown. This produced some dramatic differences in image association. The major images of Queenstown by those who *have* visited Queenstown were 'attractive, beautiful scenery' (23.6 per cent) and 'snow skiing' (18.0 per cent), while for those who *have never* visited Queenstown, the major images of the resort were 'skiing' (41.6 per cent) and 'beautiful scenery' (13.3 per cent).

Uncovering the perceptual maps

Using the aggregate mean scores (see Tables 1 and 2) of the ratings assigned each destination on each attribute, perceptual maps were developed using the MDPREF program. The results of this perceptual mapping exercise are shown in Figures 1 and 2.

QUESTIONS

1. What would the *image associations* suggest to you about how Queenstown is seen by different market groups?

2. Examine the positioning map of domestic New Zealand tourist destinations. What does the position that Queenstown occupies suggest? What are its strengths and weaknesses?

3. The position of the attributes suggests there may be underlying dimensions driving the position of the destinations. Try to assign labels to these dimensions based on the grouping of attributes.

4. Using all the information presented to you, what domestic positioning strategy would you suggest for Queenstown?

5. What further research do you consider needs to be undertaken for the marketers of Queenstown to understand better the market(s) in which they are operating?

6. What do you consider to be the underlying rationale for positioning strategies?

This case study was prepared by Dr J. Cossens, Department of Marketing, University of Otago, New Zealand.

CASE 4 ATTITUDE VERSUS REALITY: SILVERPEAKS BAY ORGANIC FOODS

The growth in demand for foods grown under organic principles has been a worldwide phenomenon in most developed countries. Concern for the environment and for personal health has been reflected in a desire for insecticide-, pesticide- and herbicide-free products. New Zealand has also witnessed a growing demand for food grown under such conditions, and a small number of retailers have attempted to meet this demand.

Jim had set up an organic food growers co-op in Dunedin, New Zealand, under the name Silverpeaks Bay Organic Foods (SBOF), and operated a retail outlet that sold organically grown products. The co-op not only provided the growers with the opportunity to sell their products through one retail outlet, but also allowed non-grower co-op members and the residents of Dunedin the opportunity to buy organically grown produce from a Dunedin retail outlet. Up until now, most organically grown produce had been sold 'at the farm gate'. The new co-op allowed customers the chance to buy a range of organic produce and products in one shop. Jim sold only 'certified' organic produce, which meant that only growers accredited with either the Demeter or the BioGro organic certification could sell products through the co-op retail outlet.

Jim had been operating for about 18 months from an old church close to Otago University, which at that time had around 12 000 students and 2000 staff. While the rents were cheap and the shop was close to the university, it was a long way from the main shopping area in Dunedin. Sales had been steadily climbing and the co-op now had 260 members, but Jim felt things could be going better. He also felt he didn't know a lot about his existing customers or whether he should be targeting other groups as well. So Jim decided to conduct some market research to provide a demographic and psychographic profile of his co-op members, whom he considered represented the majority of his existing customers; and information on how the general public felt about organic food and the principles behind it. From this information he felt he would be in a better position to develop promotions targeting particular groups. He had also wondered whether the location of his retail outlet was hampering store patronage and hoped the research would help him make a decision on the store's location.

Jim developed a questionnaire, which he sent out with his co-op newsletter to co-op members. It asked them questions about their attitudes to a wide range of environmental and health issues, and he also sought their opinions about SBOF. The second group in his study represented what he considered to be typical supermarket shoppers. He was particularly interested in the attitudes of mothers with young and teenage children. He sought the opinions of this important shopping group by holding a series of focus groups and using more informal discussions as well as a questionnaire similar to that given to the co-op members.

The results of the research were very interesting. The survey of existing co-op members revealed a distinct group of people who shopped at the 'church'. Overall, this group tended to be well educated, predominantly female and with higher household incomes. However, there was a polarisation within the group, with a hard core of what might be called 'alternative lifestyle' people. They had relatively low household incomes, lived a semi-rural lifestyle, and were very committed to environmental issues and organic farming. Many of this group were also local growers serving the co-op. The other group was made up of well-educated, often professional people, with few children and higher than average household incomes.

The demographic profile of co-op members clearly showed a high level of education among members, with this showing through in occupational groupings; in particular, there was a high representation of professional workers (especially those working at the university), teachers, nurses, students, and technical and skilled people.

Price sensitivity was not as high in the co-op member sample as it was among the panel groups. Other differences between the co-op members and the female shopper panels were in food-attribute importance; panel members were looking for more convenience foods, were more price conscious, more concerned about fat-free/reduced-fat products, not as concerned about environmentally safe, spray-free and organic products. They also wanted convenience in how they bought groceries; that is, they wanted to buy as much as they could when buying the weekly groceries in the supermarket.

These differences in attitude could be attributed to several factors. The panel groups were predominantly mothers with young and teenage families, and convenience in food preparation was important because of their busy lives; buying food for families was often budget-based and thus price conscious; concerns for the environment, spray-free and organic foods were often overridden by convenience, lack of choice and price. But also a lack of knowledge about organic food, and the dangers of sprays and residues contributed to such attitudes.

There was strong support among the panel groups for:

- a clear and easy-to-understand certification system;
- the need for more spray- and residue-free foods;
- the need for more environmentally sensitive foods;
- the need for more organic foods.

Many of the panel members were concerned about eating fresh fruit with pesticide residues and 77 per cent considered there was some danger in eating fruit and vegetables sprayed with pesticides. Lack of availability of organic produce in supermarkets, lack of awareness about SBOF and a lack of knowledge about organically grown foods were felt to be the three biggest factors preventing more people from buying organic foods. It was also felt there was little promotion of organics and organic-food outlets/producers.

Other areas that it was felt needed to be addressed to gain buyer support for organic food among the wider Dunedin population were availability and continuity of supply, competitive pricing with conventional foods, and variety and range in the organic product offering.

Availability and continuity of supply, more competitive pricing, and a greater range and variety of organic products were the most important factors preventing present co-op members from buying more organic food. Availability in other central city outlets, in particular supermarkets, would also lead to greater purchase of organic food.

Jim faced a dilemma. There appeared to be a hard core of people very committed to the principles behind SBOF. They were prepared to go out of their way to obtain organic products and were not averse to paying more for them. They appeared to be well educated and many worked within the university system. However, they constituted a small market, and bigger markets of potential buyers, such as mothers with young and teenage children, while having seemingly strong favourable attitudes about the environment and chemical-free foods, were more strongly influenced by the convenience of supermarket shopping and the price of conventional produce. Because many shopped to a budget, they felt they were not in a position to buy more expensive organic products.

QUESTIONS

1. What do you consider are the *key factors* if Jim is successfully to develop SBOF? Prepare a SWOT analysis that summarises the current situation for SBOF.

2. What market do you consider Jim should target based on the information provided by his research, and why?

3. Do you think Jim should relocate his retail outlet? Should he seek to sell organic produce and products through supermarkets?

4. Prepare a promotional strategy for SBOF that is targeted at shoppers similar to those interviewed during the focus groups.

5. What do you consider would be necessary to change attitudes about organic foods and to influence shopping behaviour more strongly?

This case study was prepared by Dr J. Cossens, Department of Marketing, University of Otago, New Zealand.

CONSUMER DECISION PROCESSES

CHAPTER 13

PROBLEM RECOGNITION

LEARNING OBJECTIVES

AFTER STUDYING THIS CHAPTER YOU SHOULD UNDERSTAND:

→ the various decision points faced by consumers;

→ the nature of consumer decision making as a process;

→ the various purchase situations within which decision making occurs, and how the decision process may vary for each;

→ the steps leading to problem recognition;

→ the various types of problem recognition and what outcomes may result from problem recognition;

→ how the marketer may use an understanding of the problem-recognition process to help in developing effective marketing programs.

To most marketers, a consumer decision marks the 'moment of truth'. Will consumers decide that they need the product we are selling? Will they decide to purchase our brand or a competitor's? Will they decide to purchase it from our store? These consumer decisions spell success or failure for marketers, making the study of the consumer decision-making process an extremely important one.

Our organising model of consumer behaviour (see Fig. 1.1) illustrates the central role played by the decision process. All other aspects of consumer behaviour are depicted as making up a circle, with the consumer decision process at the centre. By understanding, and responding to, the elements of consumer behaviour depicted on the outer ring, marketers are better able to develop a marketing program attractive to consumers; that is, a marketing program likely to result in a favourable consumer decision.

In this chapter we shall set the stage for Part 3 of the book by examining the decision process in some detail. First, the various decision points faced by consumers will be reviewed, and then the basic four-step decision process will be considered. Next, we shall consider some evidence that questions whether consumers typically go through a true decision process at all for most product purchases. After considering how the basic decision-making process might apply in various purchase situations, we shall begin a more thorough examination of the individual steps in the process, starting with problem recognition. Later chapters in this section will deal with the succeeding steps: information search and evaluation, purchasing processes and postpurchase behaviour.

CONSUMER DECISION POINTS

The general term 'the consumer decision-making process' is typically used to refer to some sequence of events and activities starting with the recognition of some unfulfilled need or want by the consumer, and proceeding through to the purchase and subsequent use of the product deemed most satisfactorily to fulfil the original need or want. However, as noted in the introduction to this chapter, consumers face many individual decision points within this overall process.

Perhaps the first decision point is at the *product category* level, when the decision is made to commit resources to the purchase of some product category (say, golf clubs) in preference to another (perhaps a washing machine). Marketers have traditionally glossed over this decision point, implicitly assuming that once a need or want has been identified, the consumer automatically begins moving toward a purchase. Other than in the purchase of daily-living requirements, this 'I need, therefore I buy' approach seems somewhat inconsistent with the situation of the average householder, who has recognised many needs, but has also recognised the financial constraints making it impossible to fulfil them all instantaneously. For many consumers, this first decision point is probably the most crucial: to which of my many needs will I allocate my limited resources?

A related decision point is the *price* to be paid. Many product categories span an enormous price range. And, of course, a consumer cannot consider price without simultaneously deciding on the *product features* required. The *quantity* to be purchased is another decision point that may or may not be important in a particular purchase decision. The *timing* of the purchase is influenced by such factors as urgency of the need and availability of the chosen item. Other elements such as store opening times, periods of sales and clearances, availability of transportation and freedom of family members to shop all have a bearing on when a consumer purchases.

While there is no disputing the importance of these decision points, consumer researchers have focused their greatest efforts on a single decision point: the *brand* decision. This preoccupation with brand probably relates to the needs of marketing practitioners, who have tended to focus on market share (i.e. how much of a particular brand consumers are buying relative to the other brands) as the key measure of success. A number of authors have recently recognised the need for marketers to broaden their consumer-decision research to encompass decision points beyond the brand decision, if a full picture of consumer decision-making is to be revealed.[1]

Another determination to be reached by the consumer involves *where* the selected product or service will be purchased. Convenience, after-sale service, selection or simply store atmosphere are factors consumers may consider in store choice. From the consumer's perspective, store features may well be part of the augmented product. Consider a stereo system you've seen at a store offering free delivery, the security of dealing with a local store and the quiet ambience of a well-laid-out showroom, versus the same system at the noisy, no-frills discount store on the other side of the city. Each product will probably be evaluated quite differently, on the basis of where you have seen it.

While we may wish to separate these decision points for ease of study, it should be obvious that in reality all are to some extent interrelated—except for the case of simple habitual purchases, it is difficult to conceive of a situation where a consumer could consider these individual decision points in isolation. Similarly, there does not appear to be any consistent ordering to these decision points, with the decision sequence varying across products and within products across individuals. For example, one research study found that the most common sequence in choosing a suit was store type, store, brand and area choice, while for 35 mm cameras it was brand, store type, store and area choice.[2]

In the following section we shall outline the main steps in the overall consumer decision-making process; that is, the sequence of events and activities leading from the recognition of an unfulfilled need or want through to the purchase and subsequent use of some product.

THE FOUR-STEP DECISION-PROCESS MODEL

The most widely-held view of consumer decision making treats consumers as reasonably rational beings going through a series of logical steps aimed at producing the best possible decision under the prevailing circumstances:

1. *Problem (or need) recognition.* The consumer recognises some need or want, and determines that it is of high-enough priority to warrant further attention.

2. *Information search and evaluation.* The various means by which the need/want might be satisfied are identified, information is gathered on the attributes of each alternative, and each 'package of attributes' is evaluated to determine the preferred alternative.

3. *Purchase.* Based on the evaluation just conducted and any intervening factors, a purchase decision is made and implemented.

4. *Postpurchase.* The consumer uses the product, and through this experience evaluates the decision made, storing this evaluation in memory for use in related or repeat purchases.

Importantly for marketers, each of these four steps represents both a threat and an opportunity. At any one of these steps, a consumer may eliminate a particular alternative from further consideration. Consumer failure to recognise a product as a means of fulfilling a particular need, poor access to product information, limited product distribution and no after-sales service can all result in a negative outcome to the decision process. Conversely, keeping the consumer aware of the product, ensuring the availability of relevant information, carefully matching distribution-channel design to consumer requirements, and providing customer-service facilities are just some of the opportunities available for marketers seeking to positively influence the decision process.

These steps may all occur in a short period of time but, particularly in the case of major purchases, substantial delays may occur. In an exploratory study of reasons consumers delay making decisions for major purchases, it was found that respondents spent an average of 12.1 weeks after they recognised the need for the product but before they began searching for information, 8.9 weeks searching for information and evaluating alternatives, and 7.7 weeks between choosing an alternative and actual purchase.[3]

The individual steps in the decision process will be examined in detail: problem recognition later in this chapter, and information search and evaluation, purchase and postpurchase in subsequent chapters.

ALTERNATIVE EXPLANATIONS OF CONSUMER DECISIONS

Before moving on to a more detailed examination of this process, it is useful to consider just how widely this generic decision-process model can be applied. As noted earlier, the four-step process was developed from a perspective of consumers as rational, thoughtful beings seeking to make good decisions. While this perspective and the basic model have broad popular support, many authors have presented cases in which consumer decision behaviour does not appear to fit this view.

Low-involvement purchases are frequently cited as possible exceptions.[4] In the purchase of staple food items, for example, problem recognition may not actually occur, as purchase is an automatic part of a fixed purchase routine. There may be no search for additional information (although some would argue that at a minimum consumers recall and process product-related information from memory) and only one product alternative may even be considered. There is mounting evidence to suggest that consumer involvement levels are low for many quite complex and expensive products, which have traditionally been considered to attract high involvement.[5]

Impulse purchases do not appear to fit the model particularly well either. An impulse purchase may be defined as one that is unplanned, is in response to some stimulus (e.g. seeing the item on display) and made 'on the spot'.[6] In such a purchase, problem recognition and the purchase decision occur essentially simultaneously, with no opportunity for any information search or evaluation.

Other purchases that may not fit well have been classified as *experiential purchases*, those that are acquired specifically for the feelings or emotions that are derived from acquisition.[7] The purchase of concert tickets or an expensive bottle of wine are clearly experiential. Even the purchase of everyday items may have an experiential component, as consumers may experiment with different brands and products in an effort to bring a little excitement into otherwise mundane aspects of their lives. This experimentation is known as *variety-seeking purchase behaviour*.

Are these examples sufficient for us to abandon the four stage decision-making model? Some prominent authors treat these situations as special cases of the basic model; that is, they argue that although in certain circumstances some of the steps may be very minimal, or simplified to the point of being virtually automatic, the basic model still holds.[8] For example, in the purchase of a tin of John West tuna, problem recognition may be simply the recognition that it's shopping day and tuna is always on the grocery list, information search may simply amount to recalling that John West is the brand you always buy and evaluation may be limited to the fact that there is no recall of any product dissatisfaction in the past. Thus, this very low involvement purchase can still be analysed using the four-step decision process. Similarly, an experiential purchase can be interpreted using the basic model, with the only adaptation being a recognition that the information sought and the evaluation criteria are based on feelings and emotions rather than more utilitarian aspects of product performance.

Other authors go further, and suggest that the decision-process model is inadequate to explain the full range of consumer-decision behaviour. In particular, some work has been done that suggests preferences can be formed and product decisions made with no processing of information at all (i.e. not even basic recall of product information from past experience).[9]

While it is important to recognise the value of these different perspectives, the four-step decision-process model remains an extremely useful approach for marketers (and aspiring marketers) seeking a broad understanding of consumer-decision behaviour. Therefore, when studying the decision-process model in more detail, we must be aware that in different types of decision situations, the different steps in the process may become more or less important. The next section examines these types of decision situations.

TYPES OF DECISION SITUATIONS

Figure 13.1 presents a typology of purchase-decision situations that accounts for many of the circumstances discussed in the preceding section. Decision situations are classified according to two criteria: does the consumer treat the purchase as *high involvement* or *low involvement*, and is the purchase decision *planned* or *on-the-spot*?

Extensive problem solving

In a high-involvement purchase situation, consumers are likely to expend considerable effort in making the 'right' decision. Alternate ways of fulfilling the need may be considered; substantial amounts of information may be sought from a variety of sources; and the various alternatives may be carefully evaluated over a period of time before a purchase is made. This well-planned approach to a high-involvement purchase is referred to as extensive problem solving, and fits quite well into the four-stage decision process. Typical examples might be the purchase of a car or a home computer.

	HIGH INVOLVEMENT	**LOW INVOLVEMENT**
PLANNED	Extensive Problem Solving (EPS) Brand Loyalty	Routine or Limited Problem Solving (RPS/LPS)
ON-THE-SPOT	High Involvement Impulse	Low Involvement Impulse Variety Seeking

FIG. 13.1 Types of purchase-decision situations

Brand loyalty

As the name suggests, extensive problem solving involves considerable time and effort on the part of the consumer. Once a high-involvement purchase has been made, and evaluated as satisfactory, consumers may decide to take a short cut the next time a similar purchase situation arises and simply buy the same brand again. The decision is still seen as high involvement, and there is still some preplanning, but the previous purchase experience allows the consumer to feel secure in following a much simpler decision path. The information search and evaluation and the purchase processes are thus likely to be quite restricted. An example may be a young person who at first agonises over the selection of appropriate peer-approved clothing (EPS), but after a few purchases comes to realise that buying accepted brands such as Hot Tuna or Country Road is a safe and simple approach.

High-involvement impulse

Not all high-involvement decisions are so well planned. Sometimes the way a product is displayed, the mood we are in or even seeing a product available at an irresistible price can stimulate a virtually instantaneous move from need recognition to the ultimate purchase decision. These on-the-spot impulse decisions may involve considerable financial and emotional involvement on the part of the consumer. Jewellery and fashion items are frequently used as examples of high-involvement impulse purchases.

Routine or limited problem solving

There are many products for which we tend to do some amount of purchase planning, but our lack of involvement restricts the effort put into the decision process.

Routine purchases such as tea bags or strawberry jam would elicit little decision effort, with the final purchase decision being largely a matter of product/brand familiarity and availability.

Some less frequently purchased products such as small appliances, clothing and perhaps car-repair services may be best described as limited problem solving. Such decisions may follow the four-step model, but a lack of involvement on the part of the consumer tends to keep the effort put into each step to a minimum. Research suggests that many purchases that have traditionally been assumed to be high involvement (VCRs, whitegoods, selection of a home builder) exhibit characteristics more in line with LPS decisions: very limited information search, consideration of only one or two alternatives, and the use of very simple decision rules for making the final choice.[10]

Low involvement impulse

Impulse purchases also occur in low-involvement situations. Seeing a bottle of tomato sauce on the shelf at Coles and suddenly remembering that the bottle at home is nearly empty, or driving by an automatic car wash and deciding to pull in are examples of this on-the-spot low-involvement type of decision. Studies have shown that up to 67 per cent of the purchases made in grocery stores are unplanned.[11]

Variety seeking

Closely related to impulse purchases are those classified in Figure 13.1 as variety-seeking decisions. This category includes all purchases made simply because the consumer feels like trying something a little different. Thus, buying Weet-Bix instead of the usual Corn Flakes, just for a change rather than as a result of any dissatisfaction with Corn Flakes, would be a variety-seeking decision. Again, information search and evaluation are limited, with the ultimate purchase likely to be the result of very simple impulses rather than a sophisticated assessment. While the product category element of the decision may well be planned, the ultimate purchase decision is the result of an on-the-spot desire for a change.

Table 13.1 outlines how the basic decision-making model may differ for each of the decision types just described.

It is important to note that although 'typical examples' were given for each of the decision situations described, the decision type is driven more by the consumer than the product. For example, while the purchase of a car might be an extensive problem-solving situation for many people, an impetuous person with some ready cash may well buy a car on impulse, while a very wealthy individual may even consider a car to be a low-involvement purchase. Thus, we can categorise products according to where they would typically appear in the matrix in Figure 13.1, but we need to be aware of individual consumer differences.

In the remainder of this chapter the first stage in our decision-making model will be further examined. Succeeding steps will be discussed in detail in the following chapters.

TABLE 13.1 The decision process for different types of decisions

	Problem Recognition	Information Search and Evaluation	Purchase Processes	Postpurchase Processes
EPS	Complex	Extensive	Wide ranging shopping around	Complex assessments important for future
Brand loyalty	Mixed	Limited	Limited	Limited unless expectations not met
High-involvement Impulse	On-the-spot response to stimulus	Nil	On-the spot	Complex
RPS	Simple, automatic	Very limited	Convenience, routine	Limited, although may form purchase habits
LPS	Mixed	Limited	Limited, mixed	Limited, some assessment for future
Low-Involvement Impulse	On-the-spot response to stimulus	Nil	On-the-spot	Limited, although may form purchase habits
Variety seeking	Mixed—automatic and on-the-spot	Limited—feelings rather than practical utility	Convenience, routine	Limited, although may form purchase habits

THE PROBLEM-RECOGNITION PROCESS

Problem recognition results when a consumer recognises a difference of sufficient magnitude between what is perceived as the desired state of affairs and what is the actual state of affairs, sufficient to arouse and activate the decision process.[12] For example, consider the case of a thirsty consumer going to the refrigerator on a hot summer day, expecting to find a cold bottle of XXXX light beer (desired state). Unfortunately, the refrigerator is empty (actual state), thus prompting problem (or need) recognition.

This process integrates many of the concepts that have been discussed in previous chapters. Figure 13.2 presents a view of the problem-recognition process and factors that influence it. For ease of study we can break the process into three stages: a preliminary stage, where we can consider the situations that may lead to problem recognition; an information-processing stage, in which the consumer actually recognises and defines the problem; and a results stage, where the consumer may or may not decide to take action.

An example of variety seeking   COURTESY OF SOUTHERN GAME MEAT PTY LTD

Situations leading to problem recognition

As shown in the top three blocks in Figure 13.2, consumers may have problem recognition triggered in three ways: by the actual state changing, by the desired state changing or by a combination of both changing. Under these headings there are innumerable specific situations that could lead to problem recognition; we will review only some of the more common examples.

CHANGES TO ACTUAL STATE

DEPLETED OR INADEQUATE STOCK OF GOODS Known more technically as *assortment deficiency*, this situation is probably the most common reason for

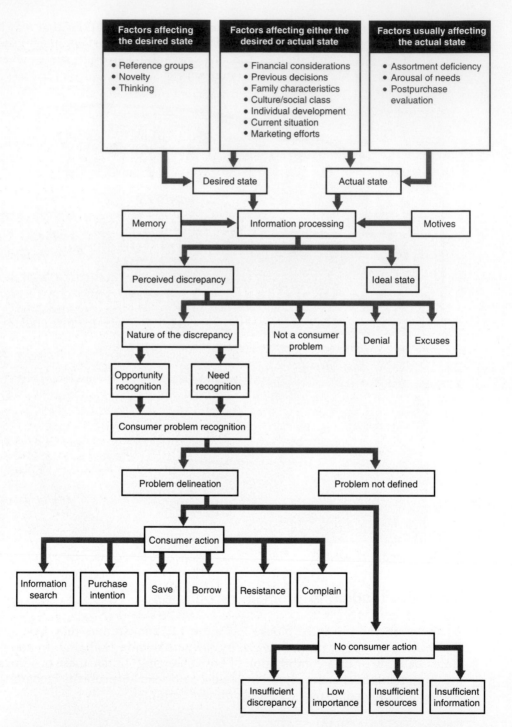

FIG. 13.2 The consumer problem-recognition process   Source: Gordon C. Bruner II and Richard J. Pornazal, 'Problem Recognition: The Crucial First Stage of the Consumer Decision Process', *Journal of Consumer Marketing* 5 (1) Winter 1988, p. 55.

consumers recognising problems. In the first situation, the consumer uses up an assortment of goods and must repurchase in order to replenish the supply. As long as there still is a basic need for the item, problem recognition should result from its consumption. The most obvious purchases that result from these circumstances are groceries, petrol, health and grooming aids, and other similar convenience goods.

AROUSAL OF BASIC NEEDS   Heavy work on a hot day will arouse a feeling of thirst; a new assignment at work may cause stress or exhaustion. The arousal of these needs (for a drink or for a rest) changes the consumer's actual state, and leads to problem recognition.

POSTPURCHASE EVALUATION   If a product purchased to fulfil a particular need is found to perform in a less than satisfactory manner, the problem originally identified remains. Thus, the consumer believed that his or her actual state had changed to match the desired state, but postpurchase evaluation of the product has proven otherwise.

An example of problem recognition   COURTESY OF GREENPEACE AUSTRALIA

CHANGES TO DESIRED STATE

REFERENCE GROUP CHANGES   Consumers' desired states may change if changes occur in the signals coming from their reference groups. For example, if a worker sees yet another workmate arrive at work in a new BMW, this may well stimulate changes in the desired state—a new, high-status vehicle is now the ideal, and the old Falcon, though still serviceable, just does not fit the new ideal. The cyclical changes in fashion also result in desired-state changes. Consumers may feel their clothing is no longer stylish, and they may desire to update their wardrobes. Even though the old clothes might be perfectly serviceable, they may be an embarrassment to wear.

THINKING   Sometimes in thinking about what we might like to do, how we might like to lead our lives, we reassess our desired, or ideal, state. For example, a consumer may become convinced of the desirability of owning a CD player simply by anticipating the pleasures resulting from ownership.

NOVELTY   Sometimes a consumer may just feel like a change. One research study on new-product adoption has shown that one-third of those switching to a new brand did so simply because they desired a change (desired state), not because they were dissatisfied with their present brand (actual state).[13]

CHANGES TO DESIRED AND/OR ACTUAL STATE

CHANGING FINANCIAL CIRCUMSTANCES   The financial status of the consumer has a very important relationship to problem recognition. The *actual* financial picture may trigger problem recognition as the consumer determines what purchases can be afforded. A consumer, for example, who inherits $50 000, or receives a $2000 salary increase may begin to consider new alternative ways of spending or saving the money. The person may also substantially alter his or her *desired* state in a positive direction based on a financial windfall.

PREVIOUS DECISIONS   Dissatisfaction with a present assortment of goods can also arise as the result of other decisions. For instance, consider the case of a family that remodels their 20-year-old home. After the work is completed, and the house looks new again, comes the letdown and dissatisfaction of having to move all the family's old and worn furniture into the newly decorated rooms. The previous decision (to remodel) has changed the actual state (the contrast between the decor and the furnishings) as well as the desired state (by drawing attention to the dilapidated state of the furniture).

CHANGING FAMILY CIRCUMSTANCES   Consumers sometimes encounter changes in their circumstances that lead to problem recognition, one of the most significant being the family's changing characteristics. As a family reaches different life-cycle stages, both the actual and desired states may change. A new baby, for example, brings a very definite change to the household (actual state), while also stimulating parents to consider a whole new dimension in desired states revolving around the addition to their family.

MARKETING ACTIVITIES The marketer frequently attempts to precipitate problem recognition through promotional efforts aimed at the consumer. With such efforts, the marketer seeks to influence the consumer's desired state by communicating the benefits of product ownership. Marketers may also attempt to change consumers' perceptions of their actual state. For example, Sony ads for its 8 mm camcorders emphasising small size and ease of recording by advertising may alert owners of older models to the bulkiness and awkward operation.

Research has suggested that as a consumer experiences problem recognition repeatedly over a period of time, a 'style' of recognising the need begins to develop. Thus, for some consumers, problem recognition is triggered mainly by a change in the desired state (we may call these consumers DS types). For others, a problem would rarely be recognised unless their actual state changed (AS types). These two types of problem-recognition styles may operate among consumers for numerous products, such as clothing, cologne, shampoo, home decorations, appliances and cars.[14] With some needs, however, almost all consumers may be AS types. For a light bulb purchase, nearly all buyers would only recognise the problem when a bulb burns out. In the opposite way we are almost all DS types when it comes to recorded music, because our motivation to purchase has more to do with novelty seeking than it does with replacing a lost or damaged record. Limited research also indicates that DS and AS types have different shopping orientations and information-source usages.[15] DS-type consumers are a similar group across related product categories, and seem to be an important group for the marketer to target. For example, problem recognition is more easily triggered for them, they have greater interest in the product and enjoy shopping for it, they are easier to reach using conventional communication channels and they perceive themselves as influential in others' shopping decisions.[16]

Information-processing stage in problem recognition

The situations discussed above lead to changes in the consumer's actual or desired states. For problem recognition actually to occur, consumers must then evaluate the situation through a processing of the information, as depicted in the middle section of Figure 13.2.

The first step in this information processing involves an assessment of the discrepancy between actual and desired states. If there is perceived to be no difference between actual and desired, an 'ideal state' exists, and no further action will be undertaken (see Fig. 13.2). If a discrepancy is perceived, the consumer becomes motivated to undertake further information processing.

The existence of a discrepancy between actual and desired states is not, however, sufficient to ensure any consumer action. As shown in Figure 13.2, a consumer may judge the discrepancy to be outside the realm of consumer activity (e.g. 'I'd like to see some better politicians in Canberra, but there's not much I can do about it'), or may choose to deny the discrepancy (e.g. 'the old car will last for a while yet') despite knowing it really exists.[17]

Assuming the consumer does choose to recognise the discrepancy, there is a distinction made between discrepancies leading to opportunities (typically resulting from changes to the desired state) and those to needs (resulting from actual state changes).[18]

Simply recognising the problem may still not result in consumer action unless the processing of information also results in the problem being sufficiently defined. For instance, the consumer who runs out of milk or bread has a clear definition of the problem. Other situations exist, however, in which consumers may not have such clear definitions of the problem. For example, we may feel that our clothing does not project quite the desired image, yet we are unable to define exactly what is wrong. In such cases, further information search may be engaged in to identify the problem more clearly. These cases of problem recognition and definition may often be complex. Of importance to marketers, this potentially complex process of problem definition may result in consumer delays, or perhaps even the abandonment of the decision process.

Consumer-action stage in problem recognition

Finally, at the lowest level of Figure 13.2, we reach the stage where the consumer is sufficiently aroused and activated to engage in some purposeful purchase-decision activity. In a high-involvement situation, a likely next step is the gathering of product-relevant information, progressing then to evaluation and purchase. For a low-involvement purchase process, the information search may be skipped, or at least minimised, and the consumer may move directly to forming a purchase intention. Planning for a future purchase may occur, with a consumer deciding to save up the required funds or approach a financial institution for a loan.

Even with a fully recognised and well-defined problem, consumers will not necessarily pursue these purchase-directed activities. Practical constraints such as lack of time, money or important information can delay consumer action (see next section for further discussion of delays), but consumers may simply lack the motivation to take action to resolve the identified problem. Motivation depends on two factors: the perceived magnitude of the discrepancy between the desired and actual states, and the importance of the problem to the particular consumer.[19] Consider again the thirsty consumer introduced at the beginning of our discussion of problem recognition. Although the desired state was to have a XXXX light beer, if the refrigerator had contained XXXX Gold, a mid-strength beer, it is likely that the discrepancy between desired and actual states would have been insufficient to motivate further effort—the Gold would probably be judged as acceptable. Finding only full-strength beer, on the other hand, may well have been perceived to be sufficiently removed from the desired state to motivate further action. The second factor determining motivation level is the perceived importance of the problem. Perhaps the consumer, on finding full-strength beer in the refrigerator, does recognise a significant difference between the desired and actual states, but does not judge the type of beer to be of sufficient importance to warrant going through the purchase decision-making process. Consumers cannot undertake purchase actions to resolve *all* of the discrepancies they perceive between their actual and desired states; they therefore attempt to address only the most significant problems as they perceive them (and not, incidentally, as an 'objective' outsider might view them).

Delays in the problem-recognition process

The above discussion of why consumers delay taking action focuses attention on the question of delays throughout the problem-recognition process. Delays can occur at many stages: in the recognition of changes to desired or actual states, in the clear definition of the problem or before any serious consumer action takes place.

One researcher found that in the case of VCR purchases, consumers spent anything from virtually no time at all up to a few years in a 'premarket' phase, where they had perceived a discrepancy between their desired and actual states, but were not yet ready to get serious about beginning a genuine information search. For most consumers this general interest phase (or delay) was considerably longer than the succeeding serious search phase.[20]

While some delays may reflect caution before committing resources to a high-involvement purchase, others may be due to the low priority placed on a particular problem, a lack of consumer resources, the need to convince other family members that the product is required, or uncertainty over the perceived benefits of purchase. Sometimes these delaying factors may be removed by precipitating circumstances, which act to stimulate a reassessment of the situation. In the case of the VCR research, typical precipitating circumstances were changed financial circumstances (inheritance, pay rise, extra cash from giving up smoking), changes in lifestyle and major price cuts.[21] Note that, in this case, these factors did not initiate problem recognition; rather, they acted to remove blocks in problem-recognition processes that were already well underway.

Delays may also occur when the problem occurrence is expected, but not until some point in the future. Thus problem recognition (or perhaps more correctly 'problem anticipation') has occurred, but an immediate solution is not necessary. For instance, a consumer who expects that the car will only last another year may begin to engage in window shopping, have discussions with friends about various brands and pay closer attention to car ads. Some product categories normally bought in anticipation of being used in the future might be termed 'preneed' goods and services.[22] Sometimes the ability to put off a purchase may lead to more complicated and difficult purchasing problems later, or even inability to purchase at all. For example, life insurance cannot be bought by someone diagnosed with terminal cancer. Examples of preneed services include insurance (life, auto, home, liability and health), prepaid legal services, extended automobile warranties, funeral services, prepaid college tuition, interval vacation ownership (time-sharing) and retirement plans. Because consumers may not seek out these services, marketers have developed strategies to target consumers before the need arises.

PROBLEM RECOGNITION FOR DIFFERENT PURCHASE SITUATIONS

As noted in Table 13.1, problem recognition differs between the different decision situations. Much of what we have discussed so far relates to high-involvement buying decisions, and extensive problem-solving situations (EPS) in particular. The model we have been discussing does, however, apply to other situations.

In routine problem-solving (RPS) situations, typical purchases are groceries and personal-care items. Problem recognition for such items is most likely to be stimulated by assortment deficiency—simply running low on current supplies. Because there is an established purchase routine for such purchases, there is minimal need for any further information processing or problem definition before moving on to the action phase. There are unlikely to be any delays in the process. Therefore the problem-recognition stage in this low-involvement situation can be described as simple or automatic (see Table 13.1).

Another low-involvement situation, variety seeking, also involves very simple problem recognition. Rather than being anything dramatic and highly goal-oriented, it is characterised more by point-of-purchase triggering or stimulation of problem recognition based on a likely familiarity with the brand, and the desire for a change. Relating this case to Figure 13.2, a desire for novelty (desired state) triggers problem recognition. Again, delays are unlikely, as problem recognition is largely emotive rather than the result of significant information processing.

Impulse purchases are, by definition, unplanned, on-the-spot and the result of exposure to a stimulus. Problem recognition therefore must be triggered by on-the-spot stimuli: marketing efforts and situational influences. Examples might be a particularly eye-catching window display, a special offer, the consumer's mood when shopping or even who the consumer is with at the time. The precise stimuli leading to problem recognition may be quite difficult to identify, even for the consumer. Perhaps a combination of circumstances leads to impulsive problem recognition. By definition, though, no delays can occur, making problem recognition a quick, though not necessarily simple, process.

MARKETING IMPLICATIONS OF PROBLEM RECOGNITION

Of course, our interest in the problem-recognition process relates to its utility to marketers: how can marketers use an understanding of problem recognition to aid in the development and implementation of superior marketing programs?

Activating problem recognition

By activating problem recognition, marketers are bringing consumers into the market. Activities may be focused on influencing the consumer's *desired state* and/or perceptions of the *actual state*, such that a difference of sufficient magnitude occurs between them. Promotion is probably the most common, but certainly not the only, tool used by marketers to stimulate problem recognition among potential customers.

INFLUENCING THE DESIRED STATE

Marketers often seek to influence consumers' desired states through advertising, stressing the desirability of product ownership. Sometimes these ads contain quite direct descriptions of the utilitarian benefits to be gained from the product, while others make much more subtle statements about the desirability of ownership. These ads serve different purposes and are directed at different stages of the overall purchase-decision process. At this early stage they may stimulate a change in the consumer's desired state; later in the purchase process consumers may use the ads as a source of information to aid in the evaluation of particular purchase alternatives.

Store merchandising may also be used to influence desired state. A particularly eye-catching display of fashion items, or perhaps jewellery, can lead a consumer to envision the benefits (utilitarian or emotional) of ownership. Also, a boutique approach is taken in some sections of many department stores. Products that may be used together are grouped together within the store, in the hope that after purchasing one item consumers will see related items and desire to own them also. For example, a travel boutique within a department store may contain a whole array of travel-related items that would traditionally be located in separate departments. Thus, coming to the store to purchase a suitcase, a consumer would also see such items as travel diaries, guidebooks, adaptors to allow use of Australasian electronic equipment overseas, and so on.

INFLUENCING PERCEPTIONS OF THE ACTUAL STATE

As noted earlier, in routine and limited problem-solving situations, problem recognition is virtually automatic, and triggers a routine purchase process where the buyer habitually purchases a brand without consideration of that brand's merits or of how alternative brands may be superior. Marketers may attempt to disrupt this rather automatic decision-making sequence by making the problem recognition *non*-automatic. One approach is to induce consumers to reassess their actual state. Advertising showing an attribute-by-attribute comparison of the marketer's brand versus the competitor's is one approach. Ansett recently used direct mail to target Qantas Club members, and explain to them the relative benefits of Ansett Golden Wings membership.

Comparison is not the only approach to influencing perceptions of the desired state. Heightening consumer awareness of the importance of particular product attributes may also lead to a reassessment of the current situation. Michelin ads stressing the safety aspect of their tyres and Yokohama ads focusing on the fuel economy of their tyres may lead consumers to reassess the attributes of their tyres.

Of course, one option open to marketers is to design new or modified products that solve previously unrecognised or recognised but unsolved problems. The Post-it note could be considered as an example here—no one really recognised a need for a memo pad with a weak strip of glue across one edge, but by producing such a product 3M essentially made people aware that they had a use for such a product.

REMOVING DELAYS IN THE PROBLEM-RECOGNITION PROCESS

As we saw earlier, there may be substantial delays between the initial recognition of a discrepancy between actual and desired states, and the serious commencement of consumer action. Marketers may attempt to provide the precipitating circumstances necessary to stimulate consumers to shift from this premarket 'just looking' state. The most common approaches involve price reductions and other special offers; consumers delaying because of uncertainty, risk aversion or insufficient resources may be stimulated to begin the purchase decision in earnest. Improved distribution is another tool that may remove some of the temporary blocking factors discussed earlier.

SUMMARY

This chapter initiated our discussion of consumer decision making which we described as the 'moment of truth' for marketers. First, various consumer decision points were described to indicate the diversity and complexity of the consumer purchase-decision process. The four-part consumer decision-process model was then introduced. While this model provides the framework for the discussion of consumer decision making over the next few chapters, we also looked briefly at some other views of consumer decision making. We concluded the first part of the chapter by examining different purchase situations, and looking at how the basic decision-making model might apply in each case.

The remainder of this chapter was devoted to examining the first stage of the decision process—problem recognition. Problem recognition occurs when the consumer recognises a difference of sufficient magnitude between what is perceived as the actual state and what is perceived as the desired state of affairs. A model of problem recognition was introduced, and each of the three basic phases in the model—situations stimulating problem recognition, consumer information processing and consumer action—were discussed. Consistent with the discussion in the first section of the chapter, we then examined how problem recognition might differ in various types of purchase situations. The chapter concluded with a discussion of applications of problem-recognition information to marketing analysis and decision making.

MANAGERIAL REFLECTIONS

For our product or service situation:

1. What types of problem-recognition situations typify our customers: routine, emergency, planning and/or evolving?

2. What situations appear to lead most frequently to problem recognition among buyers?

3. What factors typically constrain further purchasing process activity by the consumer, and how may we help the removal of such barriers?

4. What intentions to purchase do consumers express?

5. How may we help activate the consumers' problem-recognition process by emphasising their desired state, actual state or the level of discrepancy between the two?

6. How are consumers' predispositions to buy shifting over time? To what extent are favourable intentions being converted to purchase?

DISCUSSION TOPICS

1. Why is it important to understand consumer decision making?

2. Describe the general types of consumer decisions. Illustrate them with a recent decision of your own.

3. What is consumer problem recognition?

4. Describe from your own recent experience what factors led to problem recognition in at least three different product or service situations (not necessarily purchases). Explain the similarities or differences that exist in these situations.

5. Distinguish between problem recognition under conditions of low involvement and under conditions of high involvement. What implications might each of these situations have for promotional plans?

6. How can the marketer use purchase-intentions data?

REFERENCES

1. See, for example, William Wells, 'Discovery-oriented Consumer Research' *Journal of Consumer Research* 19, 1993, pp. 498–504; and Klaus Grunert, 'Research in Consumer Behaviour: Beyond Attitudes and Decision-making', *European Research*, August 1988, pp. 173–83.

2. Jeffrey J. Stoltman, James W. Gentry, Kenneth A. Anglin & Alvin C. Burns, 'Situational Influences on the Consumer Decision Sequence', *Journal of Business Research* 21, 1990, pp. 195–207.
3. Eric Greenleaf & Donald Lehmann, 'Causes of Delay in Consumer Decision Making: An Exploratory Study', in Rebecca H. Holman & Michael R. Solomon (eds), *Advances in Consumer Research*, vol. 18, Association for Consumer Research, Provo, UT, 1991, pp. 470–5.
4. Herbert Krugman, 'The Impact of Television in Advertising: Learning Without Involvement', *Public Opinion Quarterly* 30, 1965, pp. 349–56; also Stewart De Bruicker, 'An Appraisal of Low-involvement Consumer Information Processing', in John Maloney & Bernard Silverman (eds), *Attitude Research Plays for High Stakes*, American Marketing Association, Chicago, 1979, pp. 112–30.
5. See, for example, Keith Fletcher, 'An Investigation into the Nature of Problem Recognition and Deliberation in Buyer Behaviour', *European Journal of Marketing* 22 (5), 1988, pp. 58–66.
6. Frances Piron, 'Defining Impulse Purchase Behaviour', in *Advances in Consumer Research*.
7. John Mowen, 'Beyond Consumer Decision-making', *Journal of Consumer Marketing* 5, 1988, pp. 15–25.
8. James Engel, Roger Blackwell & Paul Miniard, *Consumer Behavior*, 6th edn, Dryden Press, Fort Worth, 1990; also Henry Assael, *Consumer Behavior and Marketing Action*, 4th edn, PWS Kent, Boston, 1992.
9. Kent Nakamoto, 'Alternatives to Information Processing in Consumer Research: New Perspectives on Old Controversies', *International Journal of Research in Marketing* 4, 1987, pp. 11–27; Richard W. Olshavsky & Donald H. Granbois, 'Consumer Decision Making: Fact or Fiction?', *Journal of Consumer Research* 6, September 1979, p. 93; and R. Zajonc & Hazel Markus, 'Affective and Cognitive Factors in Preference', *Journal of Consumer Research* 9, 1982, pp. 123–31.
10. Wilkie study, consulting project for WH by Paul Rainbird.
11. Mowen, op cit, Ref 7, pp. 15–25.
12. James F. Engel & Roger D. Blackwell, *Consumer Behavior*, 4th edn, Dryden Press, New York, 1982, p. 300.
13. Elihu Katz & Paul Lazarsfeld, *Personal Influence*, Free Press, New York, 1955.
14. Gordon C. Bruner II, 'Problem Recognition Style: Is It Need Specific or a Generalized Personality Trait?', *Journal of Consumer Studies and Home Economics* 14, 1990, pp. 29–40.
15. Gordon C. Bruner II, 'Problem Recognition Styles and Search Patterns: An Empirical Investigation', *Journal of Retailing* 62, 1986, pp. 281–97.
16. Gordon C. Bruner II, 'Profiling Desired State Type Problem Recognizers', *Journal of Business and Psychology* 4, Winter 1989, pp. 167–82.
17. Richard Pomazal, 'The Consumer Problem Recognition Process', *Proceedings of the Atlantic Marketing Association Conference*, American Marketing Association, Chicago, 1985, pp. 75–9.
18. M. Joseph Sirgy, *Social Cognition and Consumer Behavior*, Praeger Publishers, New York, 1983.
19. Del I. Hawkins, Kenneth A. Coney & Roger J. Best, *Consumer Behavior*, Business Publications Inc., Dallas, 1980, p. 388.
20. Keith Fletcher, 'An Investigation into the Nature of Problem Recognition and Deliberation in Buyer Behaviour', *European Journal of Marketing* 22 (5), 1988, pp. 58–66.
21. Ibid, pp. 58–66.
22. Myroslaw J. Kyj, C. Jayachandran & John L. Haverty, 'Expanding Marketing, Opportunities with Pre-need Services', *Journal of Services Marketing* 2, 1988, pp. 55–63; and C. Jayachandran & Myroslaw J. Kyj, 'Pre-need Purchasing Behavior: An Overlooked Dimension in Consumer Marketing', *Journal of Consumer Marketing*, 4, Summer 1987, pp. 59–66.

CHAPTER 14

SEARCH AND EVALUATION

LEARNING OBJECTIVES

AFTER STUDYING THIS CHAPTER YOU SHOULD UNDERSTAND:

➡ the major types of consumer information-seeking activities;

➡ the types and sources of information used by consumers;

➡ how much external search consumers engage in and what factors influence it;

➡ how consumers evaluate information obtained during search by establishing choice criteria, narrowing the range of brands considered and evaluating alternatives;

➡ what strategies marketers may use to influence the information search-and-evaluation process of consumers.

Once consumers have recognised the existence of a problem and are ready to move on in the purchase-decision process, they enter the information search-and-evaluation phase. There are many opportunities available to marketers who understand the nature of the information sought by consumers, and how they use it in making purchase decisions. Conversely, many dollars can be wasted providing inappropriate or untimely information.

In this chapter we shall first examine what the information-search process entails and the factors influencing it. Next, the process of evaluation will be discussed. Finally, some marketing implications will be presented to indicate how the marketer may seek to influence consumer search processes.

THE INFORMATION-SEARCH PROCESS

Types of consumer search activities

For our purposes here, *information* may be considered to be knowledge obtained about some fact or circumstance, and, in the context of this chapter, such knowledge is to be used in a consumer-behaviour situation. *Search* refers to mental as well as physical information-seeking and processing activities a consumer engages in to facilitate decision making regarding some goal-object in the marketplace.[1] Consequently, a consumer information search may be undertaken in order to find out about products, prices, stores and so on, related to the product.

Search may be categorised as *prepurchase* or *ongoing* (based on the purpose of search), and as *internal* or *external* (based on its source).

PRE-PURCHASE VERSUS ONGOING SEARCH

PRE-PURCHASE SEARCH Prepurchase search is the form of search we normally associate with the purchase decision. The consumer has recognised a problem, and therefore seeks information to assist in some element of the decision process.

ONGOING SEARCH Consumers also engage in information-search activities not directly related to specific needs or decisions, but simply because of an ongoing interest in the product category. Thus, an audiophile will keep informed of the latest developments in audio technology, a fashion-conscious person will want to be up with current styles, and a dog breeder will naturally be up-to-date with information on dog food, supplements and medication.

Such ongoing search activities may involve regular reading of specialist magazines, visits to relevant retailers, discussions with other interested consumers or simply paying particular attention to advertising for the category of interest. Notice that the same search activities could also be associated with prepurchase search (described previously): the difference here is that the activities are ongoing rather than limited to a particular problem. To an observer, however, the two forms of search may be difficult to distinguish.

Table 14.1 offers a summary of the similarities and differences between these two types of search in terms of determinants, motives and outcomes.

INTERNAL VERSUS EXTERNAL SEARCH

INTERNAL SEARCH The first stage to occur after the consumer experiences problem recognition is a mental process of recalling and reviewing any information stored in memory that may relate to the purchase situation. Consider the case of a consumer who has identified a need for a mountain bike. The consumer may recall that a friend made very negative comments about a particular brand of bike several months ago. Perhaps the consumer also recalls seeing a good display of

TABLE 14.1 A framework for consumer information search

	Prepurchase search	Ongoing search
Determinants	Involvement in the purchase Market environment Situational factors	Involvement with the product Market environment Situational factors
Motives	To make better purchases decisions	Build a bank of information for future use Experience fun and pleasure
Outcomes	Increased product and market knowledge Better purchase decisions Increased satisfaction with the purchase outcome	Increased product and market knowledge leading to: • future buying efficiencies • personal influence Increased impulse buying Increased satisfaction from search, and other outcomes

Source: Peter H. Bloch, Daniel L. Sherrell & Nancy M. Ridgway, 'Consumer Search: An Extended Framework', *Journal of Consumer Research* 13, June 1986, p. 13. Copyright 1986 by *Journal of Consumer Research* Inc., 1986. All rights reserved. Published by the University of Chicago.

different models at a particular store, and knows from past experience that another store tends to be a bit overpriced. All of this information was stored in the consumer's memory and is recalled now when needed to assist in the purchase decision. The recall may be immediate or may occur slowly, as a conscious effort is made to bring the information to mind. Once recalled, the information may be used in the evaluation process as the consumer seeks to resolve the purchase decision.

Consumers do not just use this internal search as a preliminary step prior to a more exhaustive external search for relevant information. In many purchase decisions internal information already in memory is the sole (or major) information source utilised. In one study of supermarket shopping behaviour, about 42 per cent of shoppers spent five seconds or less at a display before making a selection. Similarly, only slightly over half the sample even checked the price of the item selected, and the most frequent reason given for checking prices was 'just habit' rather than to assist in the brand or purchase-quantity decisions.[2]

This heavy reliance on internal search is also evident in some consumers' store-choice strategies. For instance, one study showed that most shoppers rely heavily on experiential information sources in determining where to shop.[3] That is, they turn inward to their previous shopping experiences for information on where to shop. Only a limited number of people engage in any external information search (whether from family, friends or advertisements) prior to making a major shopping trip.

Marketers need to be aware of this heavy use of internal information. In many instances shoppers form their beliefs and attitudes over a period of time before actually entering the market, and are not seeking new information at the time of purchase. This situation makes it especially difficult to overcome a negative image or mistaken impression that people in the market may have of a particular brand or retail store.

In other instances it appears that consumers rely heavily on internal information to address some of the 'early' decision points in the decision process. The term 'presearch decision making' has been used to denote these decisions consumers may make before actively engaging in external search for information on later (often brand and store) alternatives. Because consumers have been exposed to advertising messages over a long period and have had previous purchase experience with a brand, there is likely to be considerable information stored in their memories. When the decision process is initiated, consumers will rely on this stored information to help them make a variety of decisions before engaging in external information seeking. Thus, a considerable amount of decision making may be done prior to external search. Note that consumers who have already made presearch decisions are ready to buy and may require a minimal amount of persuasive selling effort.

One study developed a profile of consumer characteristics according to the level of presearch decision making they had engaged in for new cars. Table 14.2 describes the segments. This type of information may be used by the manufacturer and retailer to develop effective promotional strategies such as deciding on the nature of point-of-purchase materials and the critical selling points to be covered by the salesperson.[4]

TABLE 14.2   Consumer segments classified by level of pre-search decision making for automobiles

1. No premade decision	Not confident of ability to judge product Little prior knowledge about product Not satisfied with previous product Owned many different brands No expertise in household Buying the product for a new use High educational level; moderately high income
2. Premade manufacturer decision	Low confidence in ability to judge product Low satisfaction with previous product Many decision makers in household Consumer-information user Low income; moderate educational level
3. Premade brand decision	Moderate confidence in ability to judge product Satisfied with previous brand Not many decision makers in household Moderately high level of expertise in household High income

continues

TABLE 14.2   Consumer segments classified by level of pre-search decision making for automobiles *continued*

4. Premade retailer decision	A lot of prior knowledge about product Very satisfied with previous brand Not a consumer-information user High income
5. Premade brand and retailer decision	High confidence in ability to judge product A lot of prior knowledge about product Owned few brands Not a consumer-information user Trades brands every few years Low educational level

Source: Girish Punj, 'Presearch Decision Making in Consumer Durable Purchases', *Journal of Consumer Marketing* 4 (1), Winter 1987, p. 80.

The result or outcome of internal search and alternative evaluation may be that a consumer:

1. makes a decision and proceeds to engage in purchase behaviour;

2. is constrained by certain environmental variables (such as a determination that his or her cheque account cannot stand the purchase); or

3. determines that insufficient or inadequate information exists in his memory to make a decision now, and so *external search* is undertaken.

EXTERNAL SEARCH   External search is simply the process of obtaining information from other sources in addition to that which can be recalled from memory. Some typical sources from which such information might be obtained are advertisements, friends, salespeople, store displays and product-testing magazines.

Types and sources of information

A great variety of information of potential interest to consumers exists in the external environment. Three general categories are:

1. information about the existence and availability of various product and service offerings;

2. information useful in forming evaluative criteria—the standards that are employed to evaluate alternatives;

3. information on the properties and characteristics of alternatives.

In general, it appears that the type of information sought depends upon what the consumer already knows. For example, consumers with little knowledge about available offerings tend to focus their search efforts on learning about the existence of alternatives and forming appropriate evaluative criteria. When they feel sufficiently informed in these areas, they are likely to redirect their search toward learning more about the characteristics of available offerings in order to evaluate them.[5]

Consumers gain information from three major areas: marketer-dominated sources, personal sources, and neutral sources.

Information in *marketer-dominated channels* stems from advertising, salespeople, packaging, in-store signage and so on. Clearly, this information is provided by the marketer for commercial reasons; however, it may still form a vital information source for the consumer. There is some evidence to suggest that as consumers become more confident in their product knowledge, they tend to rely less on the evaluative information supplied by marketers.[6]

A consumer's *personal sources* include friends, family and others perceived to have some expertise in the product category of interest. Thus, friends might be consulted about the choice of a restaurant for a romantic evening, or a fellow student known to be a good tennis player may be asked for advice on how to choose an appropriate racket. This information often has a high level of perceived source credibility, but it typically requires greater effort on the part of the consumer to access these interpersonal sources.

Neutral sources include portions of the mass media, government reports and publications from independent product-testing agencies. Mass-media sources include both general sources, such as daily newspapers, news magazines, and regular radio and television programming, and more specialised sources, particularly the wide variety of specialist magazines dealing with virtually every interest imaginable. Unfortunately, the neutrality of some of these media sources is open to question. Can travel writers provide a truly neutral view when their travel and accommodation has been paid for by the very companies whose products are being reviewed? Can a specialist computer magazine be completely neutral in assessing the latest product of one of its largest advertisers? New-product news releases written by the marketer and the dreaded 'infomercials' now appearing on late-night television are more obvious cases of superficial neutrality.

One widely used neutral source within Australia is *Choice* magazine, a publication of the Australian Consumers Association. In an effort to avoid any doubts as to its neutrality, *Choice* has a policy of not accepting any advertising, product donations or manufacturers' news releases. Scrupulous attention to maintaining a neutral stance ensures credibility and therefore a ready market for *Choice*.

It appears that although marketer-dominated sources may be extensively used in the early stages of product awareness and initial interest, personal sources enjoy the most use in latter stages of the decision process.[7] The perceived trustworthiness of personal sources is usually cited as a reason for this finding.

Amount of external-search activity

Many studies have examined the amount of external search that consumers undertake. Most of these have used only one measure of total search activity.[8] However, when viewed together they paint a rather consistent and somewhat surprising picture of consumers' external-search behaviour. The following are representative of the general findings:

1. Research suggests that consumers typically consult few information sources (friends, articles, advertisements and so on) before making a purchase. For example, one study showed that, prior to purchase, 15 per cent of major-appliance and car buyers consulted no information sources, while 30 per cent consulted only one, and 26 per cent consulted two.[9]

2. Most shoppers visit a very limited number of stores before making a purchase. Various studies suggest that approximately 40–60 per cent of shoppers visit only a single store. This finding appears to hold across both durable and non-durable goods.[10]

3. Evidence regarding the number of alternatives buyers consider again suggests limited search. On average, less than 12 seconds elapse between the time grocery shoppers arrive and depart from a product display, leaving scant time for an extensive information search. Forty-two per cent of shoppers spend five seconds or less. The same research project found that for 85 per cent of the purchases only the chosen brand was handled, and 90 per cent of the shoppers physically inspected only one size.[11]

4. It is not just low-involvement products for which minimal information is sought on alternatives. For example, one study reported that 41 per cent of refrigerator shoppers considered only one brand, while 61 and 71 per cent considered only one brand of washing machine and vacuum cleaner, respectively.[12]

5. Research into information search and evaluation for consumer services suggests that the number of alternatives considered is even smaller than is the case for goods, with no more than two service providers typically being considered.[13]

Because they are based only on single measures of behaviour, each of the above studies provides an incomplete picture of consumers' external-search activity.[14] However, taken together these results strongly suggest that the majority of consumers actually engage in quite limited amounts of external search. Also, other studies have used composite indices of search by combining several measures together.[15] These studies confirm that many consumers, perhaps even the majority, engage in little external search for information. Additional evidence suggests that consumers can be categorised according to their general tendency to engage in external search. For example, one investigation identified three different groups among car buyers: low searchers, high searchers and selective searchers.[16] The latter group used intensively only certain sources of information (media, friends) and tended to ignore others.[17] Finally, a number of findings suggest that those people who typically engage in considerable external-search activity—the information seekers—are identified by a higher demographic profile (higher educational levels, income, occupational standing and so on) than are low searchers.[18]

FACTORS INFLUENCING EXTERNAL SEARCH ACTIVITY

The amount of external search that consumers engage in varies considerably across individuals and different purchase situations. Although a number of explanations have been offered for this variability, the cost/benefit view appears to be the most popular.[19] This explanation holds that external search will be undertaken and will continue as long as the consumer perceives the benefits of search to be greater than the costs involved. Included among the potential benefits of external search are:

1. a more comfortable feeling about making an 'informed' purchase;

2. an increase in the chances of making a choice that leads to greater satisfaction;

3. the positive feelings derived from being generally knowledgeable about products and services;

4. the pleasure that can result from engaging in shopping activities;

5. the high potential monetary pay-offs to search.

Potential costs of external search include the commitment of time, forgoing other pleasant activities, and the frustrations or tensions involved, as well as any actual monetary expenditures (such as petrol and parking costs).[20] It is important to appreciate that the costs and benefits involved are those that are perceived by the consumer, even if they do not correspond perfectly with reality.

Table 14.3 summarises many of the factors that can influence the amount of external search, either by directly affecting the consumer's cost/benefit perceptions or by indirectly acting as constraints on the process. Several of these categories are discussed further in the following section.[21]

TABLE 14.3 Determinants of the extent of external-information search

Increasing the following determinants will generally cause external search to:
+ = increase / − = decrease

Market environment	Knowledge and experience
+ Number of alternatives	− Stored knowledge
+ Complexity of alternatives	− Usage rate of product
+ Marketing mix of alternatives	− Previous information
− New alternatives on the market	− Brand satisfaction, loyalty and
+ Information availability	preference
+ Market-area size	

continues

TABLE 14.3 Determinants of the extent of external-information search *continued*

Increasing the following determinants will generally cause external search to:
+ = increase /– = decrease

Situational variables
– Time pressure
+ Social pressure (family, peer, boss)
+ Financial pressure
+ Organisational procedures
+ Physical and mental condition
+ Ease of access to information
  sources

Potential pay-off/product importance
+ Price
+ Social visibility
+ Perceived risk
+ Differences among alternatives
+ Number of important attributes
+ Product-class importance
+ Status of decision-making activities
  (in family, organisation, society)
+ Length of commitment

Retail variables
– Crowded store conditions
– Distance between stores
– Similarity among stores
– Store satisfaction, loyalty and
  preference

Individual differences
+ Ability to process information
+ Training
+ Enjoyment of shopping
+ Involvement
  Demographics
– Age
+ Income
+ Education
+ White-collar occupation
  Personality/lifestyle
+ Self-confidence
+ Open-mindedness
+ Need for stimulation/variety

Source: Adapted from Sharon E. Beatty & Scott M. Smith, 'External Search Effort: An Investigation Across Several Product Categories', *Journal of Consumer Research* 14, June 1987, pp. 86–7; and William L. Moore & Donald R. Lehman, 'Individual Differences in Search Behaviour for a Non-durable', *Journal of Consumer Research* 7, December 1980. Copyright 1980, 1987 by *Journal of Consumer Research* Inc. All rights reserved. Published by The University of Chicago. Reprinted with permission.

MARKET CONDITIONS Characteristics of the marketplace can have a significant effect on external-search behaviour. Availability of information, the number of alternatives to consider and the location of outlets are among the influencing factors. Also, certain market conditions lead consumers to attach more importance to the purchase situation and therefore engage in greater external-search activity. To illustrate, among the conclusions drawn from various studies are that external search is greater when:

1. prices are higher,[22] and price differences between brands are greater;[23]

2. style and appearance are perceived to be quite important;[24]

3. it is suspected that substantial differences may exist between product alternatives.[25]

BUYING STRATEGIES   Consumers often adopt various strategies that reduce the amount of external search. For example, patterns of brand and store loyalty can develop through purchase experience over time. Also, evidence suggests that when the purchase decision is complex or when the available information is difficult to process, consumers tend to adopt simple choice rules (such as 'pick the middle-priced one') and thereby significantly curtail their external search.[26]

INDIVIDUAL FACTORS   Of course, many of the consumer's own characteristics influence the degree of external-search activity. The following generalisations illustrate the variety of relevant findings:

1. Open-mindedness and self-confidence of consumers have been found to be positively related to greater search activity.[27]

2. Socioeconomic characteristics have been related to search. For example, higher educational levels and income have been associated with greater search, while a reduction in activity is related to increasing age.[28]

3. Some evidence suggests that consumers differ in their ability to process information, and if their processing limits are reached, the effect may be to decrease the extent of external search.[29]

4. As mentioned in Chapter 10, higher levels of consumer involvement with a product appear to be associated with a greater degree of external search.

5. Chapter 10 also suggested that consumers appear to require an optimum level of stimulation from their environment. When stimulation is sufficiently below this level, external search for novel and exciting stimuli is likely. Conversely, when stimulation is much greater than optimum, external search will tend to be toward less novel stimuli. This phenomenon will help the consumer return to the optimum stimulation level.[30]

Notice that this process may be occurring quite independently of any specific purchase problem the consumer may be facing at the time.

MARKET BELIEFS   Many consumers tend to hold a set of common, simple beliefs relating to different aspects of the marketplace. Consumer market beliefs are important because they serve to simplify consumer decision making by directing search-and-evaluation activities. These generalised associations between, say, objects (e.g. buyers, products, vendors), attributes (e.g. price, quality) or functions (e.g. marketplace competition) allow consumers to reduce their decision complexity and to make quicker judgments with less cognitive effort than if a more thorough analysis were undertaken. Table 14.4 illustrates a variety of market beliefs. It is easy to see how these could have a strong influence on the extent and nature of consumers' search-and-evaluation processes.

TABLE 14.4   Selected market beliefs

Brand

All brands are basically the same
Generic products are just name brand sold under a different label at a lower price
A brand's quality is the most important determinant of its success; bad brands just don't survive
The best brands are the ones that are purchased the most
When in doubt, a national brand is always a safe bet
In established product categories, brands that have been around the longest are the most dependable

---

Store

Specialty stores are a great place to familiarise yourself with the best brands; but once you figure out what you want, it's cheaper to buy it at a discount outlet
A store's character is reflected in its window displays
Salespeople in specialty stores are more knowledgeable than other sales personnel
Larger stores offer better prices than small stores
Stores that sell on a volume basis can afford to charge less for their merchandise
Locally owned stores give the best service
A store that offers a good value on one of its products probably offers good values on all of its items
Credit and return policies are most lenient at large department stores
Stores that have just opened usually charge attractive prices

---

Sales Personnel

In my experience, salespeople who work during the day are more knowledgeable than those who work in the evenings
Customers should always listen to sales personnel with real scepticism
A good way to judge brands is if salespeople in different stores have the same opinion
Older salespeople know more about the products they sell
The more salespeople there are in a store, the more expensive are its products
Salespeople are instructed to push brands that make the store most profit

---

Advertising and sales promotion

I associate 'hard-sell' advertising with low-quality products
The most heavily advertised brands are normally among the best brands
Stores that advertise a lot have overpriced merchandise
Items tied to 'giveaways' are not a good value (even with the freebie)
Coupons represent real savings for customers because they are not offered by the store
When you buy heavily advertised products, you are paying for the label, not higher quality

continues

TABLE 14.4   Selected market beliefs *continued*

Ability as a shopper

I can make pretty good decisions without a lot of running around (search)

One of the best ways to know which brand to select is to look at what everybody else is buying

Electronic products are changing so fast that I usually have to start all over again in figuring out which brand to buy

I have a very good idea of what is a fair price for most products

---

Source: Calvin P. Duncan, 'Consumer Market Beliefs: A Review of the Literature and an Agenda for Future Research', in Marvin E. Goldberg, Gerald Gorn & Richard W. Polloy (eds), *Advances in Consumer Research*, vol. 17, Association for Consumer Research, Provo, UT, 1990, pp. 733–4.

'All brands are basically the same' is a common consumer belief, but not usually with beer   COURTESY OF TOOHEYS LIMITED

KNOWLEDGE AND EXPERIENCE   Some researchers have postulated a negative relationship between amount of knowledge and extent of information search (see Table 14.3), based on the premises that knowledgeable consumers are more efficient searchers, and that they have more internal information already available to use in their product evaluations.[31] Other researchers support an opposing view, suggesting that added knowledge translates to the confidence and the ability to seek out *more* information.[32] One recent research project has gone some way toward reconciling these views, finding that in complex purchase decisions only, greater knowledge allows a consumer to limit the amount of inappropriate searching (i.e. reduce overall amount of search), and is also positively related to the number of product attributes examined (i.e. increase amount of search). The result is a more efficient, focused search than less knowledgeable consumers are able to undertake, but not necessarily a 'larger' or 'smaller' search. In simple purchase decisions, no such relationships were found.[33]

PERCEIVED RISK   Risk or uncertainty regarding the most appropriate purchase decision or the consequences of the decision is a significant variable influencing the total amount of information gathered by consumers.

It is important to recognise that risk is subjective. That is, the risk involved in a purchase decision is *perceived* by the consumer and may or may not bear a strong relationship to the risk that actually exists. For example, even the choice of a leg of lamb may involve considerable risk in terms of the impression a person wishes to make when purchasing it for a dinner party involving his or her boss.

There are several situations that influence the consumer's perception of uncertainty or consequences and, thus, the perception of risk:

1. *Uncertainty regarding buying goals.* For example, should a new shirt be purchased for dressy occasions or for very informal barbecues?

2. *Uncertainty regarding which alternative (such as product, brand, or model) will best match or satisfy the purchase goals.* That is, if private transportation to school is desired, what should be purchased: car or motorcycle; Ford Festiva or Holden Barina; two-door or four-door?

3. *Perceived possible undesirable consequences if the purchase is made (or not made) and the result is failure to satisfy buying goals.*[34]

If any of these situations is sensed by the consumer, he or she is said to perceive risk in the situation and is therefore likely to seek more information before making a decision.

PRODUCT FORM   One risk-related situation of particular interest to marketers is the marketing of services as opposed to goods. The intangibility and non-standardisation of services make it difficult for consumers to assess which alternative is most likely to match purchase goals (i.e. situation 2 above).[35] Some consumers adopt interesting information-search strategies in an effort to reduce the higher perceived risk in service decisions; others do not appear to make any special effort to reduce risk at all. Various research studies have found that:

1. consumers tend to rely on personal information sources more for services decisions than for product decisions;[36]

2. when making decisions related to purchase of a service, consumers who have prior experience with the service category tend to rely more heavily on internal information search than would be the case in a product decision;[37]

3. when selecting a service supplier, consumers on average consider only half the number of alternatives typically considered for a product decision, and on average consider only about three different purchase criteria;[38]

4. Even in the selection of professional services that would typically be considered to be subject to higher than average levels of physical

and/or financial risk, consumers consider very few information sources. New residents in an area were found to consult only a single source of information 38 per cent, 67 per cent and 55 per cent of the time in the selection of medical, legal and dental service suppliers, respectively.[39]

THE INFORMATION-EVALUATION PROCESS

Within our model of the decision process, evaluation, or choice, refers to the selection of a preferred alternative from among several available decision alternatives. During the search process the consumer has determined what the alternatives are and has collected relevant information about the alternatives; in the evaluation process the consumer compares these alternatives, using available information, so the consumer is ready to make a choice.

Early attempts by marketers to understand consumer evaluation processes were based on the classical economic perspective of individuals as rational decision makers attempting to *maximise the utility* they expect to gain from their choices. Utility theory explains the evaluation of product alternatives as a process whereby individuals attempt to maximise the total utility that can be gained within particular expenditure constraints. The utility of any acquisition is defined as a measure of the satisfaction or usefulness derived from it by some individual. When forced by budget constraints to choose between products, therefore, people are assumed to select the product that will provide the greatest satisfaction or usefulness.[40]

This intuitively simple process becomes quite complex when there are several decision alternatives available, full information is not readily available, each alternative may vary on several dimensions, or attributes, and the benefits of each attribute are typically uncertain.[41] Utility maximisation in such a situation becomes a prodigious information-processing effort for the average individual; therefore, actual choice behaviour frequently varies from an idealised situation where all alternatives are carefully weighed and the 'best' one chosen.

Recognising the above constraints, consumer researchers have adopted a theory of *bounded rationality* in choice, where individuals respond to the limitations of information availability, processing capacity, and time and cost constraints by 'satisficing' rather than 'optimising' in their choices.[42]

> *Most human decision making, whether individual or organisational, is concerned with the discovery and selection of* satisfactory *alternatives; only in exceptional cases is it concerned with the discovery and selection of* optimal *alternatives' [italics inserted].*

The satisficing decision maker is viewed as an information processor gathering data on the various attributes (and associated benefits) of each alternative, and then using some simplifying decision strategy, or heuristic, to make a choice.

Evaluative or choice criteria

As explained previously, consumers use the attributes of each alternative and the benefits associated with each attribute as the criteria by which they evaluate product alternatives. These criteria can be both objective (e.g. the fuel-economy rating of a particular car) and subjective (e.g. the status perceived to be associated with ownership of a particular car).[43]

Of course, each consumer has his or her own set of evaluative criteria for any particular decision. For example, when purchasing a pair of sports shoes, one buyer may be most concerned about arch support, weight and devices for cushioning impact. Another shopper, with other needs, may use quite a different set of evaluative criteria, including colour, style and perhaps price. Another shopper may use brand name as the only evaluative criterion.

The number and type of evaluative criteria may vary by product. Consumers generally use few evaluative criteria in low-involvement situations; for example, when purchasing most grocery items. However, when purchasing a home, car or other major durable item, a consumer would typically use more evaluative criteria in the evaluation process. Generally, however, the number of determinant evaluative criteria used in a consumer decision is six or fewer, although there is some evidence that the number may be as high as nine.[44]

Evaluative criteria may also change over time. As consumers gain new experiences and information, their evaluative criteria may shift. When innovations appear with previously unknown features, consumers may begin to incorporate these features into their evaluative criteria. As they learn from marketers or friends what features they should look for in a particular product purchase, consumers may change their evaluative criteria. Of course, this learning process has important implications for marketers who seek to influence the evaluative criteria favourably toward their particular brands. As will be mentioned later, however, it is often difficult to change such ingrained decision factors.

No matter how many criteria are evaluated by the consumer, they are likely to differ in their importance, often with one or two criteria being more important than others. Thus, while several evaluative criteria are *salient* (important) to the consumer, some are *determinant* (they are most important and are also perceived to differ significantly among the alternatives). A determinant attribute that meets both of these conditions for a particular consumer is sometimes called a *critical* attribute. That is, a critical attribute is the most determinant attribute for that consumer.

The marketer should note, however, that determinance requires two conditions: a criterion may be judged as very important by a consumer, but unless the consumer also perceives significant differences to exist between the alternatives on this particular criterion, it is not determinant. For instance, a recent study asked various groups to identify the top five criteria they used for choosing an airline for business and non-business travel.[45] Departure and arrival times, fares and itinerary routing were rated as very important for both types of travel, but consumers perceive that airlines exhibit very few differences on these factors. Consequently, these factors are not determinant attributes for most passengers. Marketers must determine whether to spend money trying to convince consumers that their airline is actually superior on one of these important attributes (i.e make one of the attributes determinant), or whether to promote a less important attribute in which differences are already perceived to exist. Determinance should be viewed as a dynamic concept, and marketers should conduct longitudinal research to stay informed of possible shifts in attitudes related to buying behaviour.[46]

Reducing the range of alternatives

The range of alternatives available to a consumer in any particular decision may be quite extensive, but the average consumer is unable to assess all of them adequately. Thus a filtering process must occur.

Consider the store-choice decision of a consumer seeking to purchase a pair of sports shoes. Alternatives include all local sports stores, specialist sports shoe stores, department stores, and perhaps even general shoe stores and discount stores. Similarly, the brand and model decisions also offer hundreds of alternatives. No consumer is likely even to be aware of all store and brand alternatives, much less give them all serious consideration. Thus, the range of alternatives available for consideration is initially limited to the consumer's *awareness set*.

Even within the awareness set, however, are some alternatives that the consumer will not seriously evaluate, for one or more of several reasons. These include:

1. financial considerations;

2. not perceiving the alternative as adequate given needs;

3. having insufficient information on which to evaluate them;

4. having tried them before and rejected them;

5. being satisfied with alternative currently favoured;

6. having received negative word-of-mouth communication.[47]

Alternatives that are automatically rejected for these and other reasons fall into one of two categories.[48] The *inert set* consists of those alternatives that the consumer has failed to perceive any advantage in buying; that is, they are seen neither positively nor negatively. Perhaps the consumer has insufficient information on which to evaluate them, or he or she simply may not perceive them as better than the alternatives already favoured. The *inept set* is made up of alternatives that have been rejected outright because of an unpleasant experience or negative feedback from others. Thus, the alternatives in this set are evaluated negatively by the consumer and will not be considered at all in their present form.

What we are left with is the *evoked set* (or consideration set), which consists of those few select alternatives that the consumer evaluates positively (are worthy of consideration). Ultimately, of course, the consumer must continue this elimination process until only the single preferred alternative remains.

Figure 14.1 diagrams the elimination process leading to the selection of a particular brand/model of four-wheel-drive vehicle. One interesting research finding is that consumers may not use the same variables for both evoked-set formation and purchase. Perhaps extrinsic factors (e.g. unavailability due to lack of dealership in the region) are used to eliminate many brands early in the purchase deliberation; then factors intrinsic to the product itself (e.g. power, price, comfort) may be used in the final evaluation. Thus, brands may need to possess acceptable levels across both rejection and purchase variables.[49]

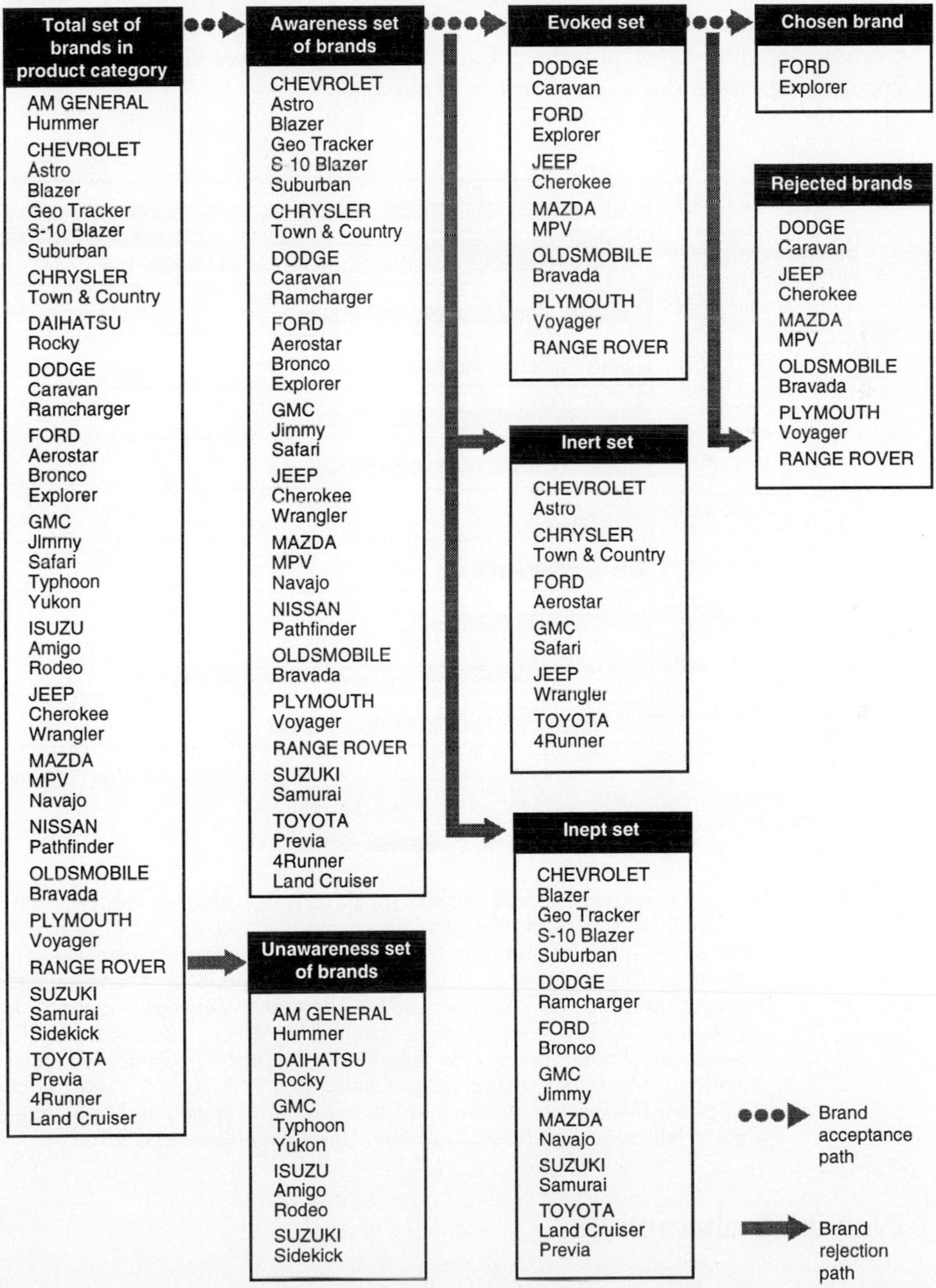

Total set of brands in product category

AM GENERAL
Hummer
CHEVROLET
Astro
Blazer
Geo Tracker
S-10 Blazer
Suburban
CHRYSLER
Town & Country
DAIHATSU
Rocky
DODGE
Caravan
Ramcharger
FORD
Aerostar
Bronco
Explorer
GMC
JImmy
Safari
Typhoon
Yukon
ISUZU
Amigo
Rodeo
JEEP
Cherokee
Wrangler
MAZDA
MPV
Navajo
NISSAN
Pathfinder
OLDSMOBILE
Bravada
PLYMOUTH
Voyager
RANGE ROVER
SUZUKI
Samurai
Sidekick
TOYOTA
Previa
4Runner
Land Cruiser

Awareness set of brands

CHEVROLET
Astro
Blazer
Geo Tracker
S 10 Blazer
Suburban
CHRYSLER
Town & Country
DODGE
Caravan
Ramcharger
FORD
Aerostar
Bronco
Explorer
GMC
Jimmy
Safari
JEEP
Cherokee
Wrangler
MAZDA
MPV
Navajo
NISSAN
Pathfinder
OLDSMOBILE
Bravada
PLYMOUTH
Voyager
RANGE ROVER
SUZUKI
Samurai
TOYOTA
Previa
4Runner
Land Cruiser

Evoked set

DODGE
Caravan
FORD
Explorer
JEEP
Cherokee
MAZDA
MPV
OLDSMOBILE
Bravada
PLYMOUTH
Voyager
RANGE ROVER

Chosen brand

FORD
Explorer

Rejected brands

DODGE
Caravan
JEEP
Cherokee
MAZDA
MPV
OLDSMOBILE
Bravada
PLYMOUTH
Voyager
RANGE ROVER

Inert set

CHEVROLET
Astro
CHRYSLER
Town & Country
FORD
Aerostar
GMC
Safari
JEEP
Wrangler
TOYOTA
4Runner

Inept set

CHEVROLET
Blazer
Geo Tracker
S-10 Blazer
Suburban
DODGE
Ramcharger
FORD
Bronco
GMC
Jimmy
MAZDA
Navajo
SUZUKI
Samurai
TOYOTA
Land Cruiser
Previa

Unawareness set of brands

AM GENERAL
Hummer
DAIHATSU
Rocky
GMC
Typhoon
Yukon
ISUZU
Amigo
Rodeo
SUZUKI
Sidekick

●●●▶ Brand acceptance path

▶ Brand rejection path

FIG. 14.1 Brand elimination process for four-wheel-drive vehicles

Figure 14.2 illustrates the size of the awareness and evoked sets of brands for a range of products. Notice that those favourably evaluated within the known brand alternatives are generally only one-third to one-half of the awareness brand set. Thus, knowledge of consumers' awareness sets of brands is valuable to marketers because they are interested in moving their items into their evoked set.[50] Only if consumers are aware of the brand and have evaluated it positively will it even be considered for purchase. Later in this chapter we will discuss alternatives for moving a brand into consumers' evoked sets.

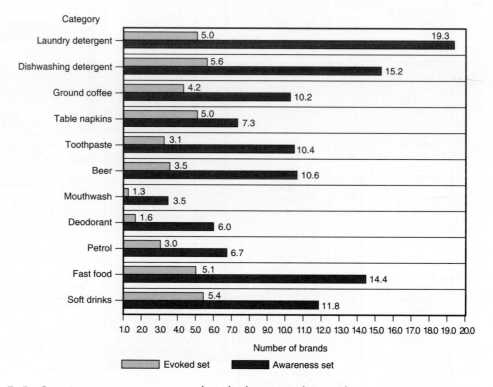

FIG. 14.2 Average awareness and evoked-set sizes by product category   Source: J. J. Brown & A. R. Wildt, 'Factors Influencing Evoked Set Size', *Working Paper 034–87*, College of Business and Public Administration, University of Missouri-Columbia, Columbia, MO, 1987; C. L. Narayana & R. J. Markin, 'Consumer Behavior and Product Performance: An Alternative Conceptualization', *Journal of Marketing* 39, 1975, pp. 1–6; L. Jarvis & J. Wilcox, 'Evoked Set Size: Some Theoretical Foundations and Empirical Evidence', *Combined Proceedings* American Marketing Association, Chicago, 1973, pp. 236–40; and B. M. Campbell, The Existence of Evoked Set and Determinants of Its Magnitude in Brand Choice Behavior, PhD thesis, Columbia University, New York, 1969.

Evaluating alternatives

Having discussed the process of reducing the number of decision alternatives in general terms, we must now focus on exactly how consumers use the information they have gathered to evaluate each alternative and ultimately select the preferred option. As explained earlier, the evaluation process involves some assessment on the part of the consumer as to how well the particular attributes and benefits of each alternative match up with the needs that the consumer is trying to satisfy (i.e. the evaluative criteria). Lack of time, interest, information and processing capacity make it difficult for consumers to undertake a detailed, attribute-by-attribute assessment of each alternative. Of particular interest to marketers, therefore, is the range of satisficing strategies that consumers use to select a preferred alternative.

Following are descriptions of some common evaluation strategies. To aid understanding, each strategy is discussed using the decision situation outlined in Table 14.5 as an example. This example involves a consumer trying to decide which calculator to purchase. The consumer has an evoked set of four models (listed down the side of Table 14.5) and six evaluative criteria (listed across the top). Additionally, this consumer has certain standards that the preferred alternative is expected to meet (listed in the bottom row in Table 14.5). The consumer's personal assessments of each model on each of the evaluative criteria appear in the body of the table. Keep in mind that these evaluations are the individual consumer's *perceived* assessments. A truly objective product evaluation might arrive at quite different results.

TABLE 14.5

	Evaluative criteria					
Brand	Price	Ease of use	Readability of display	Warranty	Features	Battery life
	$					
KMC 3000	9	Very good	Very good	90 days	Fair	Good
TI 1001	7	Very good	Fair	1 years	Good	Fair
Royal LC-80	13.75	Fair	Very good	6 months	Very good	Very good
Canon LC-20	7.50	Very good	Very good	1 years	Good	Very good
Acceptable level	Under $12	Good	Good	6 months	Good	Good

COMPENSATORY EVALUATION STRATEGY

Consumers using a compensatory strategy evaluate each alternative on all evaluative criteria. Thus, favourable perceptions of one attribute may offset negative perceptions of another. To illustrate, the KMC 3000 calculator would be evaluated quite well overall, with the good ratings for ease of use and readability compensating, to some extent, for the poor rating on functions. In a weighted compensatory model, each criterion would be assigned a weighting reflecting its perceived importance, and the product-attribute ratings would be expressed quantitatively.

The overall evaluation for each model would then be the sum of the six (attribute rating × attribute importance) scores. You have no doubt noted the similarity between this model and the multiattribute model of attitude formation discussed in an earlier chapter. Both are modelling the same basic phenomenon—the overall evaluation of a product.

A compensatory strategy is very demanding in terms of time, amount of information required and processing effort. Although consumers do not actually go through a process of computing scores for each alternative, just going through the basic process of an attribute-by-attribute, brand-by-brand trade-off in an attempt to find the best alternative would be very taxing. Thus, compensatory strategies are uncommon other than in high-involvement decisions relating to such products as cars, homes and computers. Even in these situations, simpler decision strategies are frequently adopted.

We trimmed the excess. Not the technology.

Shaped-up. And slimmed down. Yet filled with the latest innovations. That's the new Olympus Superzoom 110.

Designed to fit in the palm of your hand, the Olympus Superzoom 110 weighs less than 500 grams, so it can go wherever you go. Without weighing you down.

And its sleek shape hides the fact that it contains a powerful 38mm – 110mm zoom lens. With a 460-step multi-beam autofocus system that lets you zoom in on your subjects accurately, in seconds.

With the Olympus Superzoom 110 you also get a fully automatic state-of-the-art 35mm zoom camera with advanced features and functions. Designed to improve your photography at the touch of a button. And the Olympus exclusive "Thinking Flash System" and spot metering capabilities bring professional results within your reach.

To top it off, the Olympus Superzoom 110 is weatherproof – so a little water, dust or bad weather won't harm it. Or the film.

So try the Olympus Superzoom 110 on for size. Once you do you'll see the difference. It's a heavy hitter. Not a heavy weight. SUPERZOOM 110

OLYMPUS OPTICAL CO. LTD. Tokyo, New York, Hamburg, London

Camera manufacturers help consumers by providing information to suit many different decision strategies
COURTESY OF OLYMPUS

NON-COMPENSATORY EVALUATION STRATEGIES

Decision strategies are said to be non-compensatory when good performance on one evaluative criterion does not offset or compensate for poor performance on another criterion. There are several varieties of non-compensatory rules used by consumers.

CONJUNCTIVE STRATEGY   The conjunctive strategy requires the consumer to establish minimum levels of acceptability for each evaluative criterion (as in the far-right column in Table 14.5). Each alternative is then assessed against these standards, and rejected if it fails to meet all of them. Based on the conjunctive strategy, every alternative except the Canon LC-20 would be discarded from further consideration because each has one or more unacceptable attribute levels. For example, while the KMC 3000 has an acceptable price level and is rated as easy to use, it has a less attractive warranty and does not offer as complete a range of functions/features as desired by this shopper. Thus, the Canon LC-20 would be the chosen brand if this buyer followed a conjunctive decision strategy. Conjunctive strategies are often used as a first step, to reduce the number of alternatives being considered down to a manageable group. Actual choice of a single preferred alternative may then be made using a different approach, perhaps a simplified compensatory strategy.

DISJUNCTIVE STRATEGY   This strategy also requires the consumer to establish some performance standard for each of the evaluative criteria. An alternative will be deemed 'acceptable' if it exceeds the minimum standard on *any* single criterion. Unlike the case with the conjunctive strategy, the performance standards in a disjunctive strategy would typically be set quite high. Thus, to be acceptable, an alternative needs to have at least one really outstanding feature. An example might be a young person looking for a car. The overall list of evaluative criteria might include low price, sportiness, speed and fuel economy. Using the disjunctive strategy, alternatives rating 'average' on all criteria would not be evaluated highly, but an exceptionally cheap car or a very fast one would be acceptable, regardless of the other criteria. In such a situation, the disjunctive strategy is likely to be used to limit the number of alternatives, with the final evaluation of the remaining alternatives employing a different strategy. Only in low-involvement situations would a disjunctive strategy be likely to be used independently. An example may be evaluating restaurants on the basis of low price, convenient location and food quality, then choosing a restaurant because its great steaks give it an exceptionally high rating on food quality, while the other alternatives lack any outstanding characteristics.

LEXICOGRAPHIC STRATEGY   This strategy requires consumers to rank their evaluative criteria in order of importance, and then simply select the alternative that rates most highly on the most important criterion. If two alternatives are rated equally on the most important attribute, the second most important attribute is used to determine the preferred alternative. For instance, assume that the consumer's hierarchy of importance for the evaluative criteria presented in Table 14.5 were as follows: ease of use, features, price, warranty, readability of display and battery life. Using a lexicographic approach, all brands would be first evaluated on the most important dimension—in this case, ease of use. A tie exists between the KMC 3000, TI 1001 and Canon LC-20, which are all rated as very good. Discarded from any further consideration would be the Royal LC-80 (even though it ranks highest on the next most important dimension). The three remaining brands are then assessed on the evaluative criterion of features, and the KMC 3000 would be dropped from further evaluation. The TI 1001 and the Canon LC-20 are evaluated equally on this dimension, so an additional criterion must be assessed. On the next most important attribute, price, the TI 1001 as the lowest priced brand would be the chosen alternative. Of course, each consumer may have a different hierarchy of importance for these criteria, which would result in other brands being selected by these shoppers.

ELIMINATION BY ASPECTS   This strategy is very similar to the lexicographic approach. The consumer again begins by ranking all the key decision criteria, but then continues and sets minimum standards for each criterion. Then, starting with the most important criterion, alternatives are eliminated if they fail to meet the minimum standards. If our calculator shopper rated price as the most important criterion, followed by readability, warranty, ease of use, features and battery life, the first step would be to eliminate the LC-80, as it does not meet the minimum standard. The three remaining brands are still under consideration, having met the standard—note that a lexicographic approach would have eliminated all but the TI 1001 at this first step. Next, readability is evaluated, and the TI 1001 (the top-ranking alternative on the first criterion) is eliminated as it does not meet the minimum standard on this aspect, or attribute. Warranty is assessed next, and the KMC 3000 is eliminated because it does not meet the minimum acceptable warranty requirement of six months. Therefore, the Canon LC-20 would be the brand chosen for purchase using the elimination-by-aspects strategy.

Evaluation shortcuts

While some of the evaluation strategies just discussed obviously involve less time and effort than others, all require at least some assessment of the characteristics of each alternative against the consumer's evaluative criteria. Particularly in low-involvement situations, but also in some situations normally viewed as high involvement, consumers take evaluation shortcuts that do not consider evaluative criteria at all.

BRAND LOYALTY

One common short cut is *brand loyalty*. The brand-loyal consumer does not attempt any kind of attribute evaluation, but simply chooses the familiar brand on the basis of some overall positive feelings towards it. This overall positive evaluation typically stems from past experience with the particular brand under consideration. Thus, in selecting a calculator, a consumer may select the LC-20 because previous experience with Canon copiers, cameras or perhaps (but not necessarily) calculators has been positive, leading to an overall positive evaluation of the brand. Brand-loyal choices are a quick and easy way for a consumer to make a relatively safe, satisfactory choice—a more involved evaluation may lead to a superior decision, but the extra time and effort involved are not deemed to be justified.

CUES

Another short cut involves the use of simple *cues* as indicators of more detailed and difficult to evaluate criteria. Thus, price may be used as a cue for quality, the tidiness of an accountant's office as an indicator of accounting diligence and accuracy, the smile on a teller's face as an indicator of good service. One cue relates to the frequency of exposure to an item. A widely distributed, heavily promoted product may become so familiar to us that we unintentionally take this familiarity as a cue for liking. Another interesting cue is country (not state!) of origin. Some countries are associated with particular product attributes, particularly in some product categories. For example, country of origin could be used as a simple evaluative cue when trying to assess suits from Italy, Bulgaria and China. While trying to assess style, cut, finish and quality of material could be very difficult, simply recognising that Italy is known for design flair and fashion leadership, Bulgaria is still closely associated with inefficient state-run industry, and China is known more for cheap labour than high quality or style makes the evaluation quite easy. Again, the decision may not be the best, and the perceptions attached to country of origin may be quite unfair, but the result is a satisfactory outcome given the time and effort put into the decision.

MARKET BELIEFS

Finally, consumers can use their market beliefs to provide evaluative short cuts. Just as the beliefs outlined in Table 14.4 can influence the amount of external search, they can also influence the effort put into evaluation. Belief in a price/quality relationship may lead consumers to use price as a cue for other important attributes. A belief that generic store brands are simply name-brand products at a lower price could encourage consumers to dispense with any attribute evaluation at all, and simply use the decision rule 'always buy store brands when available'.

The impact of perceived risk on evaluation

If a particular decision is perceived to involve some element of risk, it stands to reason that consumers will adopt more careful evaluative strategies. There are several kinds of risks that consumers may perceive in a purchase situation.

1. *Monetary or financial risk.* The consumer may lose money if the brand chosen doesn't work at all or costs more than it should to maintain. Products and services that are very expensive are most subject to this form of risk.

2. *Functional or performance risk.* The product may not work properly or may fail completely, leaving the consumer with no alternative or backup. The consumer wastes time and effort getting the product adjusted, repaired or replaced. An expensive ride-on mower is an example of a product subject to functional risk.

3. *Physical risk.* The brand may be or become harmful or injurious to one's health. Food and beverages, mechanical and electrical items, firearms, drugs, medical services and flammable products are highly susceptible to this type of risk.

4. *Social risk.* The product purchased may negatively affect the way others think of the consumer. Houses, cars, clothes, jewellery, and recreational equipment are product purchases that are subject to social risk.

5. *Psychological risk.* The brand may not fit in well with the consumer's self-image or self-concept, making him or her feel guilty, self-indulgent or stupid for purchasing. Products that are high priced, luxurious and long lasting engender the most risk of this type. Cosmetic surgery is a service example that has a high potential for this form of risk.[51]

Consumers develop various evaluation strategies to relieve perceived risk of the types described above, including the following:

1. Choose the brand whose advertising has endorsements or testimonials from typical consumers, a celebrity or an expert on the product.

2. Choose the brand that the consumer has used before and found satisfactory.

3. Choose a major, well-known brand, and rely on its reputation.

4. Choose the brand that has been tested and approved by a private testing company.

5. Choose the brand offering a money-back guarantee with the product.

6. Choose the brand that has been tested and approved by a branch of the government.

7. Choose the most expensive and elaborate model of the product.[52]

These and other strategies are embodied in Figure 14.3, illustrating how each type of risk may be reduced.

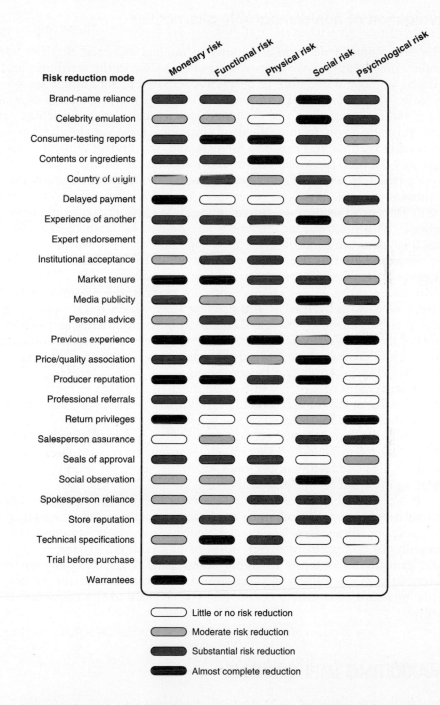

FIG. 14.3   Purchase risk types and reduction modes   Source: Robert B. Settle & Pamela L. Alreck, 'Reducing Buyers' Sense of Risk', *Marketing Communications*, January 1989, p. 35.

Evaluation of non-comparable alternatives

The discussion of decision situations so far has assumed that the alternatives under consideration were more-or-less comparable in the attributes and benefits offered, and could therefore be assessed/compared using a single set of evaluative criteria. Thus, because all electronic calculators are reasonably comparable in form and features, all can be evaluated on evaluative criteria such as readability, warranty, and so on. In some decision situations, however, the alternatives are not so readily compared. Consider, for example, the budget-allocation or product-category decision mentioned in the previous chapter, where consumers are trying to determine to which of their many needs and wants they should allocate their limited resources. How can consumers evaluate a holiday versus new lounge-room furniture, or an investment property versus sending a child to a private school? With no apparent attributes in common between the alternatives, how can a single set of decision criteria be applied?

Research in this area suggests that, despite the difficulty, consumers do attempt to find some common level of comparison, but perhaps at a more abstract level. The easiest comparisons are made at the most concrete level—the actual physical *attributes* of the product (e.g. which microwave oven has the largest cubic capacity?). Next in difficulty come comparisons at the more abstract level of the *benefits* that are derived from the attributes. Two dissimilar products, such as a microwave oven and a dishwasher, may not share many concrete attributes, but they probably can be compared at the benefit level (e.g. which will be more convenient or which will free up more of my time to spend with my family?). Finally, at the most abstract level, comparisons may be made of the *personal values* that are being satisfied by the benefits of product ownership (e.g. which is more important to me—the security and feeling of personal worth [personal values] I feel from having an investment property, or the strengthening of family relationships and feeling of personal worth [personal values] that will result from sending my child to a private school?).

It appears that in attempting to evaluate non-comparable alternatives, consumers first try to find some level of abstraction at which comparisons can be made. In some cases, however, the consumer may be unable to identify any meaningful comparisons at any level of abstraction. At that point it appears that consumers attempt to apply some overall measure of worth to each altern-ative (i.e. a holistic evaluation rather than a comparison on key critria).[53] This 'measure of worth' is conceptually very close to the economic concept of utility.

MARKETING IMPLICATIONS

There are a number of marketing implications that flow from this exposition of search and alternative-evaluation processes. In this section we shall examine some of the significant ramifications of this process for the marketer's task.

In order for marketers to influence the process of search and alternative evaluation, they first must have information about how consumers in the various market segments undertake these tasks. There are several pieces of the information-processing puzzle that marketers should seek to fill in (assuming that search activity is engaged in by significant segments of their markets). First, they need to determine what sources of information are used by consumers. Next, they must determine the key influences on each source.

Determining sources of information

There are several useful approaches by which data may be gathered on information-source effectiveness. The following two research activities probably represent the easiest and most widely used approaches to date.

WARRANTY CARDS

Where appropriate, many marketers use warranty registration cards to gather data on the information-search activities of their customers. These questionnaires enable the respondent to check the source of information as well as the place of purchase for a product. However, these cards are often so small, in order to be machine-processed, that the amount of information that can be written on them is rather limited. Thus, such questions as where the consumer shopped (as opposed to purchased) and which information source was the most important are usually left for the company to speculate about. As a result, this type of research approach, although useful, leaves many unanswered questions for the marketer attempting to make distribution or promotion decisions.

IN-DEPTH RESEARCH

Marketers may also utilise cross-sectional or longitudinal research approaches to obtain information on consumer search processes. While cross-sectional approaches may be acceptable for products with relatively short decision times, longitudinal studies may be more useful when the decision time for a product is long.

When formulating questionnaires to be used in such studies, it is suggested that the influence of information sources can be obtained by asking several types of questions:

1. *specific influence* questions about the decision process itself (rather than specific sources), such as 'How did you learn about this new product?' or 'Why did you decide to buy this brand?';

2. questions *assessing overall influence*, such as, 'Overall, what was the most important thing that caused you to purchase this product?';

3. questions about *exposure* to various sources of information, such as the checklists used on warranty cards.[54]

Determining influence of particular sources

One area of great interest to marketers is the influence of particular information sources on brand-purchase intentions and fulfilment. One typology that has been suggested for comparing various information sources categorises each one according to the following dimensions:

1. *Decisive effectiveness.* The consumer evaluates this source as having a major or dominant impact on the decision process.

2. *Contributory effectiveness.* The consumer evaluates this source as playing a specific role in the decision process, although it is not among the most important sources.

3. *Ineffective.* This source is rated as having no particular role in the decision process, even though exposure to it did occur.[55]

Several other facets of analysis would be helpful in isolating the problem. For example, analysis of information-source effectiveness by type of customer (demographic or psychographic bases) would help to determine which consumers are being effectively or ineffectively influenced. Of course, once the weak link in the information search-and-evaluation process is known (such as poor word-of-mouth advertising), the reasons for the poor performance must still be determined and corrected.

Influencing the consumer's evoked set

It is also beneficial for marketers to determine whether brands are perceived as being in their particular consumers' evoked, inert or inept sets.[56] A marketer can conduct research among a sample of consumers to determine all the brands they are aware of, the brand names that they do and do not consider buying, and reasons for their particular brand attitudes. Using this approach, the marketer can learn what percentage are aware of a particular brand and into which awareness set it primarily falls. From such a study, the marketer is likely to find that although consumers are aware of many brands in a product category they generally hold only a few brands in their evoked and inept sets. If the marketer determines that a large share of the market is unaware of his or her brand, it would indicate the need for an intensified advertising campaign. Reasons for a brand's position within consumers' awareness sets may also be learned by assessing information on their evaluative beliefs regarding the brand. This information may help explain why certain brands are in the evoked set while others are in the inept set. For instance, it may be learned that many consumers reject the marketer's brand because of its physical characteristics, dislike of the brand's advertising or lack of adequate information with which to evaluate the brand. Thus, the marketer might rectify these problems by modifying the physical features of the brand, changing the advertising copy, or utilising comparative advertising and free samples. As a result of such strategies, a brand currently in consumers' inept sets may move into their inert or evoked sets.

Measuring consumers' evaluative criteria

In order for the marketer to develop a successful marketing mix, there must be an understanding of :

1. what criteria are used by consumers in making a purchase decision for this product;

2. how important each criterion is;

3. how the consumer rates each brand on the various criteria.

Following is a discussion of each of these topics.

1. *Determining which criteria are used by consumers*. The marketer will first need to determine which evaluative criteria are used by consumers in a purchase decision. This task may be accomplished by *directly asking* consumers what factors they consider when they compare alternatives for purchase. It might be done in a survey questionnaire format, or perhaps through a focus-group meeting. Table 14.6 presents findings from an exploratory survey and illustrates evaluative criteria used by consumers in selecting four different types of service. The greatest drawback to this approach is that it assumes that consumers *know* why they buy or prefer one product to another, and also that they are willing to provide the requested information. In reality consumers may at times be unwilling or unable to answer such questions accurately. For example, they may provide the researcher with 'socially acceptable' responses rather than their true feelings, or they may have forgotten what the most important criterion was in a recent purchase. In order to secure valid data using this approach, the marketer should seek to develop questioning or measuring approaches that very carefully obtain the desired information.

If the marketer believes that consumers cannot or will not directly reveal their evaluative criteria, then an *indirect* approach may be utilised. In this situation, the marketer may, for instance, ask consumers what evaluative criteria they think 'someone else' would use. This type of projective questioning (allowing respondents to *project* their responses through the 'someone else') allows consumers to reveal what may be very private or socially unacceptable attitudes, without actually admitting ownership.

Still another technique for determining evaluative criteria is *perceptual mapping*, through techniques such as multidimensional scaling (MDS). MDS requires consumers to rate brand alternatives, two at a time, along a scale ranging from similar to dissimilar. The responses are processed by a computer, and a graphic output (usually called a spatial map) is produced in which brands judged by consumers to be similar are clustered closer together, while those alternatives judged to be dissimilar are further apart. The axes of such a map are therefore assumed to be the evaluative criteria by which consumers made their judgments of similarity/dissimilarity;

TABLE 14.6   Share-of-mind evaluative criteria in service selection

Criteria	Percentage mentioning criteria[a]			
	Doctor %	Bank %	Hairstylist %	Dentist %
Courtesy	27	13	23	28
Competence	31	2	22	28
Reputation	10	<1	5	6
Interpersonal skills	8	0	<1	4
Access/Availability	12	56	15	14
Security	0	<1	0	0
Reliability	<1	<1	1	<1
Physical facilities	2	<1	2	2
Personal appearance	<1	0	2	<1
Sex	3	0	0	<1
Age	2	0	0	<1
Responsive service	2	21	4	3
Price	1	6	25	15
N = 100				

(a) May not sum to 100% due to rounding
Source: F. G. Crane & T. K. Clarke, 'The Identification of Evaluative Criteria and Cues Used in Selecting Services', *Journal of Services Marketing* 2 (2), Spring 1986, p. 55. Reprinted with permission.

there is nothing in the analysis that allows for a definition of exactly what evaluative criteria the axes represent. This task is left to the intuition and informed judgment of the researcher, a situation that introduces subjectivity and considerable opportunity for error.

2. *Determining the importance of criteria used by consumers.* Once the evaluative criteria are known, a second measure that the marketer will find useful is the relative importance consumers place on these criteria. A direct method for researching this measure could involve the use of a *rating scale*, whereby consumers would be asked to evaluate the importance of each criterion on a 6-point scale. Another approach would be to use a *semantic differential scale*, with pairs of criterion descriptors such as 'high price' and 'low price' marking each end of the

scale. Another possibility is a *constant sum scale*, in which respondents typically allocate a fixed total of 100 points across the evaluative criteria, according to their judgment of the importance of each. For example, in assessing the criteria used in determining which hotel to stay in on a business trip, a respondent might allocate the 100 points as follows:

	points
convenient location	40
good restaurant	25
availability of meeting room	15
quiet	10
limo service to airport	10
	100

Which criteria does this advertisement for professional services address?
NORMAN NICHOLLS

Merely asking consumers which attributes are important in choosing a product may not be sufficiently meaningful to allow the focus to be narrowed to attributes that truly determine consumer behaviour. Thus, a dual-questioning approach may be much more useful. In this approach, consumers are first asked what factors they consider important in a purchasing decision. Next, they are asked how they perceive these factors as differing among the various brands. This approach is illustrated in Table 14.7 (A, B and C), which was developed from a survey of new depositors, attitudes toward banks.

These results illustrate that while some items (such as hours of operation) rank high in importance (part A), they are not thought to differ much among the various banks (part B). Therefore, these attributes are not the most determinant (part C), even though they are rated as being among the most important. Conversely, some elements differ greatly among the various banks (such as overdraft privileges on cheque accounts) but have relatively little influence in determining the choice of a bank. Additionally, some attributes are viewed as being very important, and a large percentage of those responding said that there is a big difference (and a small percentage said there is no difference) between banks. Thus, such features as friendly attitude of personnel and availability of credit may be relatively determinant attributes.

TABLE 14.7   Understanding the determinance ranking of evaluative criteria used by bank customers

A. Importance rating of bank characteristics	
Attribute	Average rating [a]
Speed/efficiency of service	4.44
Friendly attitude of personnel	4.39
Availability of credit	4.07
Hours of operation	4.06
Full service offering	3.96
Service charges on cheque accounts	3.86
Locations convenient to work/school	3.76
Overdraft privileges on cheque accounts	3.42
Recommendation by friends/relatives	3.26
Twenty-four-hour automated tellers	3.09
Convenience of parking	3.09
Charge cards available	2.61

(a) Scale ranges from 1 = not important at all, to 5 = extremely important.

continues

TABLE 14.7 Understanding the determinance ranking of evaluative criteria used by bank customers *continued*

B. Difference rating of bank characteristics

Attribute	Average rating [b]
Recommendation by friends/relatives	2.66
Friendly attitude of personnel	2.54
Overdraft privileges on cheque accounts	2.43
Availability of credit	2.40
Twenty-four-hour automated tellers	2.37
Service charges on cheque accounts	2.36
Convenience of parking	2.36
Speed/efficiency of service	2.34
Locations convenient to work/school	2.27
Full service offering	2.17
Charge cards available	2.10
Hours of operation	1.91

(b) Scale ranges from 1 = very similar, to 4 = very different.

C. Determinance ranking of bank characteristics

Attribute	Determinance score [c]
Friendly attitude of personnel	11.15
Speed/efficiency of service	10.39
Availability of credit	9.77
Service charges on cheque accounts	9.11
Recommendation by friends/relatives	8.67
Full service offering	8.59
Locations convenient to work/school	8.54
Overdraft privileges on cheque accounts	8.31
Hours of operation	7.75
Twenty-four-hour automated tellers	7.32
Convenience of parking	7.29
Charge cards available	5.48

(c) Determinance score = average importance rating x average difference rating.

Source: Adapted from R. Wayne Coleman, 'Determinance versus Importance in the Bank Selection Process', in Michael H. Morris (ed.), *Atlantic Marketing Association Proceedings*, vol. 5, Orlando, FL, 1989, pp. 323–6.

3. *Determining consumers' brand evaluations*. Having identified the criteria, and assessed the importance placed by the consumer on each criterion, the final step requires marketers to determine how consumers perceive each brand to rate on each of the criteria. This step is typically accomplished by simply asking respondents to evaluate, using scales similar in form to those described in point 2 above, particular brands on particular characteristics. A summary of the individual respondents' ratings would then be compiled. Such information allows the marketer to judge better the strengths and weaknesses of a brand on dimensions of importance to consumers.

Having now fully investigated the evaluative criteria on the three dimensions identified, the marketer is now in a position to understand, predict and even begin to influence the choices made by consumers.

Determining consumers' cue usage

Consumer use of cues as short cuts in the evaluation process was discussed earlier in this chapter. Because cues are used by consumers in place of other evaluative criteria, it is important to identify them. Table 14.8 illustrates the type and ranking of cues used by consumers when selecting four services. It is important to note that some cues have the potential to be adapted by marketers so that consumers develop the appropriate perception of their evaluative criteria as desired by marketers. For example, the evaluative criterion of bank security might be assessed by consumers on the basis of such cues as physical appearance of the building, including design, location, furniture and colours. Thus, control of these cues could lead to an enhanced perception of security.

TABLE 14.8   Cues relied on by individual service (rank order)

	Doctor	Bank	Hairstylist	Dentist
Most relied on	Personal referral	Physical location	Personal referral	Personal referral
	Physical facilities	Personal referral	Price	Demeanour
	Demeanour	Demeanour	Demeanour	Physical facilities
	Others present	Advertising	Physical facilities	Physical location
	Physical location	Physical facilities	Others present	Price
	Dress	Others present	Advertising	Others present
Least relied on	Price	Price	Physical location	Dress
	Advertising	Dress	Dress	Advertising

Source: F. G. Crane & T. K. Clarke, 'The Identification of Evaluative Criteria and Cues Used in Selecting Services', *Journal of Services Marketing* 2 (2) Spring 1986, p. 57.

Changing the characteristics of a dominant cue can have a dramatic effect on the product image. This effect is particularly important in the many cases where brands are perceived to be very similar. A marketer may be able to move a brand from the inert or inept set into the consumer's evoked set by a very minor change in a cue (e.g. making an electric food processor slightly noisier so that it seems more powerful to consumers). A 'just noticeable difference' between brands can be accomplished by emphasising a minor (but easy to evaluate with high confidence) difference in product, price or package. One regional bank in Australia has adopted a policy of requiring all frontline staff to use a customer's name at least twice during any dealings—using the name is intended to act as a cue for 'friendly personalised service'. Such subtle changes may be more effective than claiming a large and nearly unbelievable (i.e. difficult to evaluate with confidence) brand difference.

SUMMARY

This chapter expanded our discussion of consumer decision processes by examining search and alternative evaluation. First, the meaning of information search was discussed, and it was found that consumers may engage in prepurchase or ongoing, and internal- or external-search activities.

The information-seeking process was then described. Although consumers do not appear to rely to any great extent on marketer-dominated sources of information, the true extent of search activity is not well known. The amount of information-seeking activity was seen to be determined by a number of factors. The types of information sought and the major sources of consumer information were also discussed.

Consumer evaluation was extensively discussed and various evaluation strategies used by consumers were considered. Finally, several marketing implications of search-and-evaluation activities were presented.

MANAGERIAL REFLECTIONS

For our product or service situation:

1. What are the various types of search typically undertaken by our consumers?

2. What types of information are sought by buyers during the search process? How influential are these sources?

3. How much external search is generally made by consumers and what factors influence its extensiveness?

4. What evaluative or choice criteria have consumers established in their purchase? Which are salient, determinant and critical?

5. To what extent is the brand perceived to be a member of consumers' evoked, inert or inept sets? How may negative images be overcome and the brand moved into their evoked set?

6. Which decision rule is generally invoked for the purchase?

7. What types and amounts of information should be provided to buyers to help them make better decisions?

DISCUSSION TOPICS

1. Distinguish between prepurchase and ongoing, internal and external search.

2. 'Consumers should read more advertisements and visit more retail stores during the information-gathering stage of the decision process.' Evaluate this statement.

3. What are the benefits and costs of search activity?

4. What types of risk might consumers perceive in a purchase situation? How might consumers deal with these risks? How could the marketer seek to minimise each type?

5. Read several recent product-rating reports contained in *Choice* and evaluate the rating system used. What other information would you find helpful?

6. Choose a product category and develop a table similar to Table 14.5. Show what decision each evaluation method discussed in the text would yield.

REFERENCES

1. Robert F. Kelly, 'The Search Component of the Consumer Decision Process: A Theoretic Examination', in Robert L. King (ed.), *Marketing and the New Science of Planning*, American Marketing Association, Chicago, IL, 1968, p. 273.
2. Peter Dickson & Alan Sawyer, 'The Price Knowledge and Search of Supermarket Shoppers', *Journal of Marketing* 54, July 1990, pp. 42–53.
3. Elizabeth C. Hirschman & Michael K. Mills, 'Sources Shoppers Use to Pick Stores', *Journal of Advertising Research* 20, February 1980, pp. 47–51.
4. Girish Punj, 'Presearch Decision Making in Consumer Durable Purchases', *Journal of Consumer Marketing* 4, Winter 1987, pp. 71–82.
5. See John A. Howard & Jagdish N. Sheth, *The Theory of Buyer Behavior*, Wiley, New York, 1969, pp. 26–27, 46–47.
7. See Everett M. Rogers, *Diffusion of Innovations*, Free Press, New York, 1962; and Carol Kohn Berning & Jacob Jacoby, 'Patterns of Information Acquisition in New Product Purchases', *Journal of Consumer Research* 1, September 1974, pp. 18–22.

8. For an excellent and more extensive review of this subject see Joseph W. Newman, 'Consumer External Search: Amount and Determinants', in Arch G. Woodside, Jagdish N. Sheth & Peter D. Bennett (eds), *Consumer and Industrial Buying Behavior*, North-Holland, New York, 1977, pp. 86–92, upon which much of this section is based.

9. Joseph Newman & Richard Staelin, 'Prepurchase Information Seeking for New Cars and Major Household Appliances', *Journal of Marketing Research* 9, August 1972, pp. 249–57.

10. Newman, ibid, pp. 86–92.

11. Dickson & Sawyer, op cit, Ref 2, pp. 42–53.

12. William P. Dommermuth, 'The Shopping Matrix and Marketing Strategy', *Journal of Marketing Research* 2, May 1965, p. 130.

14. Jeff Blodgett & Donna Hill, 'An Exploratory Study Comparing Amount-of-search Measures to Consumers' Reliance on Each Source of information', in Rebecca H. Holman & Michael R. Solomon (eds), *Advances in Consumer Research*, vol. 18, Association for Consumer Research, Provo, UT, 1991, pp. 773–9.

15. George Katona & Eva Mueller, 'A Study of Purchasing Decisions', in Lincoln H. Clark (ed.), *Consumer Behavior: The Dynamics of Consumer Reaction*, New York University Press, New York, 1955; Newman & Staelin, *Journal of Marketing Research*, pp. 249–57; John D. Claxton, Joseph N. Fry & Bernard Portis, 'A Taxonomy of Prepurchase Information Gathering Patterns', *Journal of Consumer Research* 1, December 1974, pp. 35–42; and Geoffrey C. Kiel & Roger A. Layton, 'Dimensions of Consumer Information Seeking Behavior', *Journal of Marketing Research* 18, May 1981, pp. 233–9.

16. Kiel & Layton, ibid, pp. 233–9.

17. See Robert A. Westbrook & Claes Fornell, 'Patterns of Information Source Usage Among Durable Goods Buyers', *Journal of Marketing Research* 16, August 1979, pp. 303–12, for a typology of selective search based on different research evidence.

18. See Westbrook & Fornell, *Journal of Marketing Research*, pp. 303–12; Katona & Mueller, *Consumer Behavior*; Newman & Staelin, *Journal of Marketing Research*, pp. 249–57; Hans B. Thorelli, 'Concentrations of Information Power Among Consumers', *Journal of Marketing Research* 8, November 1971, pp. 427–32; Hans B. Thorelli, Helmut Becker & Jack Engledow, *The Information Seekers*, Ballinger, Cambridge, MA, 1975; and Kiel & Layton, *Journal of Marketing Research*, pp. 233–9, for representative findings.

19. See George Katona, *The Powerful Consumer*, McGraw-Hill, New York, 1960; Louis P. Bucklin, 'Testing Propensities to Shop', *Journal of Marketing* 30, January 1966, pp. 22–7; and Allen Newell & Herbert Simon, *Human Problem Solving*, Prentice-Hall, Englewood Cliffs, NJ, 1972, for alternative perspectives.

20. See Wesley C. Bender, 'Consumer Purchase Costs—Do Retailers Recognize Them?', *Journal of Retailing* 40 (52), Spring 1964, pp. 1–8; and Thorelli, Becker & Engledow, p. 16.

21. See Newman, op cit, Ref 10, pp. 86–92; and James R. Bettman, *An Information Processing Theory of Consumer Choice*, Addison-Wesley, Reading, MA, 1979, pp. 123–31, upon which much of this discussion is based.

22. Newman & Staelin, op cit, Ref 15, pp. 249–57.

23. Louis P. Bucklin, 'Consumer Search, Role Enactment and Market Efficiency', *Journal of Business* 42, 1969, pp. 416–38.

24. Claxton, Fry & Portis, op cit, Ref 15, pp. 35–42.

25. Claxton, Fry & Portis, op cit, Ref 15, pp. 35–42.

26. Edward J. Russo, 'The Value of Unit Price Information', *Journal of Marketing Research* 14, May 1977, pp. 193–201.

27. William B. Locander & Peter W. Hermann, 'The Effect of Self-confidence and Anxiety on Information Seeking in Consumer Risk Reduction', *Journal of Marketing Research* 16, May 1979, pp. 268–74; and Paul Green, 'Consumer Use of Information', in Joseph W. Newman (ed.), *On Knowing the Consumer*, Wiley, New York, 1966,

pp. 67–80. For a recent contradictory finding, see Kiel & Layton, *Journal of Marketing Research*, pp. 233–9.

28. See Thorelli, Becker & Engledow, *The Information Seekers*; Noel Capon & Marian Burke, 'Individual, Product Class, and Task-related Factors in Consumer Information Processing', *Journal of Consumer Research* 7, December 1980, pp. 314–26; Donald J. Hempel, 'Search Behavior and Information Utilization in the Home Buying Process', in P. Macdonald (ed.), *Marketing Involvement in Society and the Economy*, American Marketing Association, Chicago, 1969; and Newman & Staelin, *Journal of Marketing Research*, pp. 249–59. See also Kiel & Layton, *Journal of Marketing Research*, pp. 233–9, for both supporting and divergent findings.

29. See Jacob Jacoby, Donald Speller & Carol Kohn Berning, 'Brand Choice Behavior as a Function of Information Load: Replication and Extension', *Journal of Consumer Research* 1, June 1974, pp. 33–42; John T. Lanyetta & Vera T. Kanareff, 'Information Cost, Amount of Payoff and Level of Aspiration as Determinants of Information Seeking in Decision Making', *Behavioral Science* 7, 1962, pp. 459–73; and J. Edward Russo, 'More Information Is Better: A Re-evaluation of Jacoby, Speller and Kohn', *Journal of Consumer Research* 1, December 1974, pp. 68–72, for information related to this topic.

30. See P. S. Raju, 'Theories of Exploratory Behavior: Review and Consumer Research Implications', in Jagdish N. Sheth (ed.), *Research in Marketing*, vol. 4, JAI Press, Greenwich, CT, 1981, pp. 223–49.

34. Donald F. Cox (ed.), *Risk Taking and Information Handling in Consumer Behavior*, Division of Research, Graduate School of Business, Harvard University, Boston, 1967, pp. 5–6.

43. John A. Howard, *Consumer Behavior: Application of Theory*, McGraw-Hill, New York, 1977, p. 29.

44. James F. Engel & Roger D. Blackwell, *Consumer Behavior*, 4th edn, Dryden Press, New York, 1982, p. 418.

45. Cyndee Miller, 'Airline Safety Seen as New Marketing Issue', *Marketing News*, 8 July 1991, p. 1.

46. James Myers & Mark Alpert, 'Determinant Buying Attitudes: Meaning and Measurement', *Journal of Marketing* 32, October 1968, p. 14.

47. Chem L. Narayana & Rom J. Markin, 'Consumer Behavior and Product Performance: An Alternative Conceptualization', *Journal of Marketing* 39, October 1975, p. 2.

48. Narayana & Markin, ibid, p. 2.

49. Naeim H. Abougomaah, John L. Schlacter & William Gaidis, 'Elimination and Choice Phases in Evoked Set Formation', *The Journal of Consumer Marketing* 4 (4), Fall 1987, pp. 67–73.

50. Michel Laroche, Jerry A. Rosenblatt & Jacques E. Brisoux, 'Consumer Brand Categorization: Basic Framework and Managerial Implications', *Marketing Intelligence Planning* 4, 1986, pp. 460–74.

51. See Robert B. Settle & Pamela L. Alreck, 'Reducing Buyers' Sense of Risk', *Marketing Communications*, January 1989, pp. 34–40; Jacob Jacoby & Leon Kaplan, 'The Components of Perceived Risk', in M. Venkatesan (ed.), *Proceedings of the Third Annual Conference of the Association for Consumer Research*, Association for Consumer Research, Chicago, 1972, pp. 382–93; and Ted Roselius, 'Consumer Rankings of Risk Reduction Methods', *Journal of Marketing* 35, January 1971, pp. 56–61.

52. Roselius, *Journal of Marketing*, pp. 57–58.

54. Engel & Blackwell, op cit, Ref 44, p. 335.

55. Engel & Blackwell, op cit, Ref 44, p. 334.

56. Narayana & Markin, op cit, Ref 47, p. 2.

Note: References 6, 13, 31–3, 35–42 and 53 were not completed by Paul Rainbird before his untimely death.

CHAPTER 15

PURCHASING PROCESSES

LEARNING OBJECTIVES

AFTER STUDYING THIS CHAPTER YOU SHOULD UNDERSTAND:

➡ what motivates people to shop;

➡ how consumers choose a store and the factors that influence the process;

➡ how various merchandising techniques and personal-selling efforts affect in-store purchasing behaviour;

➡ that consumer purchasing processes are heavily influenced by the situation surrounding the decision;

➡ the nature of non-store purchasing processes of consumers;

➡ why store and brand loyalty are important to marketers;

➡ the implications of consumer impulse purchasing.

In this chapter we shall be looking at the actual shopping behaviour of consumers and seeking to build a better understanding of how consumers make their purchases. The shopping script shown in Table 15.1 provides information about the types of possible events and activities most consumers would share in a shopping trip. The script was used to understand differences in the frequency and importance of events/actions for different product purchases in grocery and department stores.

Purchasing processes involve not only the purchase decision, but also activities directly associated with the purchase. The purchase-decision stage itself involves selecting a course of action based on the preceding evaluation process. Some of the elements of the purchasing-process stage, such as choosing a store, may actually be viewed as part of search-and-evaluation activities. However, because they are more directly connected with making a purchase, they are best discussed at this point. Thus, we are considering in this chapter the various facets of the consumer purchase environment of which the marketer should be aware in order to attract the chosen segments successfully.

The first topics to be discussed in this chapter will be the motives consumers have for shopping and the matter of consumer store choice. This will be followed by a presentation of research findings regarding both in-store and out-of-store purchasing behaviour. Finally, we shall examine some repeat purchasing patterns and how consumers pay for purchases.

TABLE 15.1 A typical consumer shopping script

Action/event items	
Look at window displays	Put item(s) in cart
Enter store	Find/Select items—other areas
Get cart	Look at displays for ideas
Consult shopping list	Look—future purchase needs
Look at store directory	Find matching accessories
Go to appropriate department	Return previous purchase
Walk up and down the aisles	Talk with shopping companions
Browse	Go to checkout area
Find salespeople	Select fastest line
Avoid salespeople	Wait in a queue
Examine sales—needed items	Unload the cart
Examine sales—not needed	Watch cashier ring up sale
Look at/Inspect items	Give coupons to cashier
Compare items on price	Consider payment options
Compare on non-price basis	Pay for items
Select item(s) for purchase	Personally bag items
(*continued in next column*)	Leave store

Source: Jeffrey J. Stoltman, Shelley R. Tapp & Richard S. Lapidus, 'An Examination of Shopping Scripts', in Thomas K. Srull (ed.), *Advances in Consumer Research*, vol. 16, Association for Consumer Research, Provo, UT, 1989, p. 387.

WHY DO PEOPLE SHOP?

Before discussing the subject of why consumers shop where they do, a more basic question might be asked: why do people shop? The obvious answer that 'they need to purchase something' may not reflect the consumer's actual motivation in each circumstance. It has been suggested that both personal and social motives influence consumer shopping activities. The list in Table 15.2 has been suggested from exploratory research by means of individual in-depth interviews with men and women.

TABLE 15.2   Why people shop

Personal motives

---

1. *Role playing*. Shopping activities are learned behaviour and are expected or accepted as part of one's position or role.
2. *Diversion*. Shopping can offer a diversion from the routine of daily life and is a form of recreation.
3. *Self-gratification*. Shopping may be motivated not by the expected utility of consuming, but by the utility of the buying process itself. Thus, emotional states or moods may explain why (and when) someone goes shopping.
4. *Learning about new trends*. Shopping provides consumers with information about trends and movements and product symbols reflecting attitudes and lifestyles.
5. *Physical activity*. Shopping can provide a considerable amount of exercise.
6. *Sensory stimulation*. Shopping can provide sensory benefits such as looking at and handling merchandise, listening to the sounds (e.g. noise, silence, soft background music) and smelling the scents.

Social motives

---

1. *Social experience outside the home*. Shopping can provide opportunities for seeking new acquaintances, encounters with friends or just 'people watching'.
2. *Communication*. Shopping often affords an opportunity to interact with customers or salespeople having similar interests.
3. *Peer-group attraction*. Certain stores provide a meeting place where members of a peer group may gather.
4. *Status and authority*. Shopping may provide an opportunity to attain a feeling of status and power by being waited on.
5. *Pleasure of bargaining*. Shopping may offer the enjoyment of gaining a lower price through bargaining, companion shopping, or visiting special sales.

Source: Adapted from Edward M. Tauber, 'Why Do People Shop?', *Journal of Marketing* 36, October 1972, pp. 47–8, published by the American Marketing Association.

The recreational or hedonic aspects of shopping are important to many Australian and New Zealand consumers. Hedonic consumption involves those facets of consumer behaviour that relate to the multisensory, fantasy and emotive aspects of our experience with products.[1] Shoppers' attention is focused on the fun, emotional, sensory stimulation, fantasy and amusement elements as well as on the goods they buy for consumption. And the shopping centre is one of the central elements of our society. Consumers shop for experiential and emotional reasons as well as for goods, services and information. In fact, for some people the purchase of goods may be incidental to the experience of shopping. It could be argued that some people buy so that they can shop, not shop so that they can buy.[2] A 1991 New Zealand study by the Hillary Commission reported that over one-half of adult New Zealanders used shopping centres as leisure facilities, and 8 per cent of all New Zealanders over the age of 15 gave visiting shops as their favourite leisure activity.[3]

Responses to shopping vary over time and seem to swing with variations in the general economic and social mood of the country, and it seems as if Australia and New Zealand may be moving to a period when the hedonic aspects of shopping are not so important. The Australian Social Monitor has noted that consumers in the 1990s spend less time shopping than they did in the 1980s, and visit fewer stores to do their purchasing. However, their overall expenditure has increased together with the overall buyer-conversion percentage (the number of store visits that result in purchases).[4] The interpretation of this is that consumers are becoming more focused and that their motivations for shopping are less concerned with the hedonic aspects of shopping for its own sake and more with the functional aspects of shopping as a means to an end in acquiring products. A report based on repeat surveys of consumers in Sydney and Melbourne found significant changes in attitudes to shopping over as little as an eight-month period between August 1992 and April 1993. Further, there were significant differences in responses according to the age of consumers (see Table 15.3).[5]

TABLE 15.3   Australian attitudes to shopping

Age	'I enjoy going shopping': Percentage of people who agree	
	August 1992	April 1993
	%	%
18–24	79	57
25–34	63	66
35–44	55	49
45–54	54	34
55+	58	56

Age	'Shopping has become a real chore': Percentage of people who agree	
	August 1992	April 1993
	%	%
18–24	21	32
25–34	34	32
35–44	37	46
45–54	46	55
55+	34	38

Source: Adapted from Neil Shoebridge, 'The News Retailers Didn't Want to Hear', *Business Review Weekly*, 13 August 1993, pp. 65–6.

This report emphasises that people are becoming more adversarial in their shopping. They are now willing to haggle over price and quality of goods and they are much more cautious before buying. These changes were seen as responses to the effects of economic recession, but even so it is clear that a majority of consumers still profess to enjoy the experience of shopping.

It should be noted that the relationship between economic recession and shopping enjoyment is not a simple one. Research in both the United Kingdom and the United States has shown that shopping is used as a behaviour for mood repair.[6] Individual unemployed people, for example, may go shopping as a way to compensate for depressed moods induced by their position.

In the United States it is recognised that *antishoppers* constitute about 15–25 per cent of consumers. Antishoppers are known to make fewer store visits and fewer purchases per visit than the average retail customer. They apparently are relatively unattracted to advertising, price deals, personal-selling efforts, and product package or store modifications.[7]

Apathetic consumers, or antishoppers, shop only because they 'have' to. Table 15.4 illustrates how stressful shopping is perceived to be by American married couples. Shopping is viewed as an onerous task and one to be completed quickly. Consequently, they will shop at stores where they can get in and out quickly. Convenience of location is their crucial store-selection criterion and, as they are not interested in shopping, they minimise their expenditure of effort in purchasing products. In addition to coping with children on shopping trips, married couples often have greater pressure on their time and other activities may take priority over shopping for recreation.

TABLE 15.4 Shopping for stress—married-couple households with children, by number of earners in household

	Percentage agreeing with statement	
Statement	Dual earner	Single earner
	%	%
Shopping requires weekend time	71	39
I'm glad there are supermarkets that are open 24 hours a day	70	63
We have less time to shop than we did five years ago	66	42
I wish there were ways to reduce shopping time	58	35
Shopping and services tasks add stress to my life	50	35
Shopping becomes more of a chore each year	45	35
Shopping requires weekday evenings	38	27
Some stores are too big/I waste too much time shopping	36	24
Shopping interferes with quality time for our children	30	14

Source: Eugene H. Fram & Joel Axelrod, 'The Distressed Shopper', *American Demographics*, October 1990, p. 45. Reprinted with permission © *American Demographics*, 1990.

Thus, consumers' motives for shopping are a function of many variables, some of which are unrelated to the actual buying of products. Consequently, retailers need to understand the variety of shopping motives that may be present and incorporate this information into retailing strategy. Marketers need to understand that many buyers perceive shopping as a hassle and a chore. They will seek out ways to cope with the stress of shopping. Successful marketers should design in ways that facilitate shopping, not only to attract antishoppers but also to make the shopping experience more appealing to other shoppers. They should determine how much their stores are inconveniencing customers by reviewing all customer systems and selling-contact points. Procedures can be changed and personnel retrained to save customers' time.

CHOOSING A STORE

We all like to think of ourselves as intelligent shoppers. But how do we actually make store-choice decisions? Basically, consumers compare certain established evaluative store criteria with their perceptions of a store's characteristics. As a result of this process, stores are categorised as either acceptable or unacceptable and, hence, will be patronised on that basis. If the resulting shopping experience is favourable, consumers are reinforced in their learning experiences and the matter of store choice will become largely routinised over a period of time.

It is clear from this description that consumers engage in a decision-process approach for store choice as well as for product and brand choices. Thus, much of what we have already said regarding choice processes applies here also. For example, consumers may face complex store-choice decisions (LPS or EPS), or they may be able to routinise their store decisions (RPS). A couple new to an area may face a complex decision process as new store-patronage patterns are being developed, particularly for clothing or durables. However, a long-time resident or one facing a convenience-good purchase will probably have the decision process refined to more of a habitual or routinised response.

A summary model of the store-choice process is presented in Figure 15.1. This flow chart depicts the relative directions of influences among variables involved in store-choice behaviour. The model indicates that demographic, lifestyle and other buyer characteristics lead to general opinions and activities concerning shopping and search behaviour. These consumer characteristics also affect the importance a consumer places on store attributes as he or she evaluates store alternatives, and the consumer's store perception, or store image. The consumer's store attitudes then influence store choice and, ultimately, the product- and brand-choice decision. Satisfaction with the process will lead through feedback to a reinforcement in the store's image, which will then increase the likelihood of continued patronage; that is, greater store loyalty.[8]

In selecting a store in which to shop, just as in selecting products and brands within stores, the consumer makes use of certain information sources. One American research study that assessed the source shoppers use to pick stores found that previous shopping was more important than advertising. Table 15.5 illustrates, for two cities, the information sources consumers used for their last

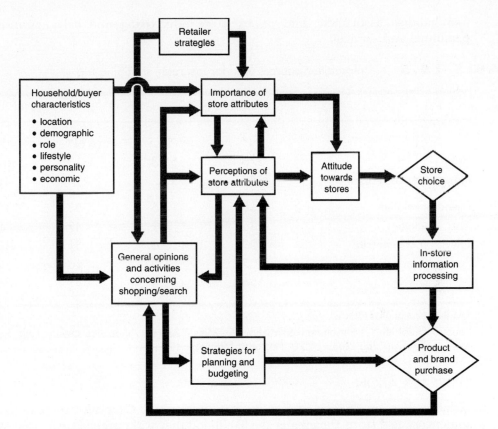

FIG. 15.1 The sequence of effects in store choice   Source: Kent B. Monroe & Joseph P. Guiltinan, 'A Path Analytic Exploration of Retail Patronage Influences', *Journal of Consumer Research* 2, June 1975, p. 21. Reprinted with permission © Journal of Consumer Research Inc., 1975. All rights reserved. Published by the University of Chicago.

retail shopping trip. This finding suggests that only a limited number of consumers—generally less than half—engage in active external information search when making retail trips. Thus, most consumers appear to be using a routinised behaviour pattern, which is consistent with the often-repeated nature of much shopping behaviour. One consequence is that the potential effectiveness of much retail advertising may be limited to less than half of the target population.[9]

Factors determining store choice

Several important factors influence consumer store-choice behaviour. Although the influence of these elements differs, depending on such variables as the type of product purchased, the type of store (discount, department, other) and the type of consumer, the factors discussed in this section have been found to exert general influence on store choice. They include store location, design and facilities, merchandise assortment and prices, store advertising and sales promotion, personnel and services.

TABLE 15.5 Information sources used for last retail shopping trip

	City A		City B	
	N*	%	N*	%
Habit	276	55.3	313	62.6
Newspaper advertisement	172	34.7	214	42.8
Friend or relative	38	7.6	51	10.2
Mail brochure	36	7.2	42	8.4
Television commercial	28	5.6	51	10.2
Radio commercial	5	1.0	10	2.0
	556	111.4	681	136.0

* Multiple responses allowed.
Source: Elizabeth C. Hirschman & Michael K. Mills, 'Sources Shoppers Use to Pick Stores', *Journal of Advertising Research* 20, February 1980, p. 49.

STORE LOCATION

Location has an obvious impact on store patronage. Generally, the closer consumers are to a store, the greater the likelihood they will purchase from that store. The farther away consumers are from a store, the greater the number of intervening alternatives, and thus the lower the likelihood they will patronise that store. Research on the influence of location on store choice has taken several directions.[10]

INTERCITY CHOICE   Marketers have long been interested in the factors that cause consumers outside metropolitan areas to choose city A rather than city B in which to shop. Research has been conducted on the drawing power of urban areas on consumers located near these cities. Believing that population and distance were not the causes of consumer store choice but could be used as good substitute variables for all the factors influencing consumers, one researcher developed the 'law of retail gravitation' to explain the strength of one city's attraction on consumers living near it.[11] In effect, this law states that two cities attract retail trade from an intermediate city or town in the vicinity of the breaking point (i.e. where 50 per cent of the trade is attracted to each city) approximately in direct proportion to their population and in inverse proportion to the square of the distances from these two cities to the intermediate town. This concept was tested by computing the breaking point between 30 pairs of cities. The predictions were very close to results of actual field studies in which the breaking point was measured.

In applying the laws of retail gravitation it should be kept in mind that they were meant to apply only to two large cities. In addition, the laws apply only to the division of shopping-goods trade, and particularly to fashion goods (often referred to as style or specialty goods), because a large part of convenience and bulk goods is purchased locally.[12] Although the work on retail gravitation has helped marketers to conceptualise intermarket behaviour, it is incomplete as an explanation for store-choice behaviour because it ignores such factors as income levels, the character of retailing in the two cities and consumer preferences.

While the above approach has taken a macro orientation to the examination of intermarket patronage, others have taken a micro approach, which rests on the assumption that consumers have different characteristics and therefore have a differential predisposition to forgo secondary costs such as time, money and effort in selecting one trade area over another. Studies have found that consumers frequently shop out-of-area (outshoppers), and they can be distinguished from non-outshoppers by certain demographic and psychographic characteristics.[13]

INTRACITY CHOICE   As shopping centres developed during the period since 1950 researchers began to investigate their influence on the shopping behaviour of consumers. These suburban alternatives to the central downtown shopping district introduced new wrinkles in explaining store choice.

To determine the factors that influence store choice within urban areas, some studies have examined the role of driving time on shopping-centre preference. In the United States, travel times longer than 15 minutes appear to be a barrier to many shopping-centre patrons.[14] Those who are willing to drive longer times seem to be attracted by the size of the shopping centre.[15] Another study indicates, however, that location of the shopping centre is not nearly as important as other variables, such as price, value, variety of product and store, store quality and cleanliness, and friendly sales personnel.[16] This result is contrary to the emphasis placed on distance measures in most site-location models.

Other work in the area of shopping-centre preference has involved development of a model to determine the retail trade area for a shopping centre.[17] The model estimates the probability that shoppers in homogeneous geographical segments (such as census tracts or neighbourhoods) will visit a particular shopping centre for a particular type of product purchase. The two fundamental variables associated with probability of patronage are square metres of floor space in the shopping centre and travel time to the centre. These variables substitute for population and distance used in the intercity model. Both square metres of floor space and population are indicators of size and attraction, while time and distance are deterrence measures. The probability of choosing a city or a centre for shopping is recognised as being a compromise between the attractiveness of the different options and the difficulty of access.

Although this shopping-centre model achieves a higher level of sophistication than the intercity model, it nevertheless fails adequately to incorporate variables that may influence consumer store preferences.[18] Travel time and shopping-centre size, although important, are not the only factors that influence store choice. However, newer models have refinements that offer substantial increases in performance.[19] One researcher has developed a model of patronage behaviour that incorporates key concepts from geography, social psychology and economics, and it appears to offer a more complete explanation of shopping behaviour.[20] Other models add such factors as shopping-centre descriptors (including centre design and operating hours) and transportation conditions (such as cost, performance and safety).[21] In addition, shopping-centre attractiveness has been studied on the basis of expected population changes, expected store characteristics and the evolving transportation networks.[22]

Ultimately, marketers must develop theories to explain how consumers make choices between the many types of shopping options available to them. For example, why would a consumer select a mall over options such as the central business district, a strip shopping centre, a freestanding store or direct marketing (such as catalogues)? Further, if several malls are available, why does the consumer select a particular one? Clearly, there are many important questions still to be answered.[23]

INTERSTORE CHOICE   Store location can also be very influential in shopper choice among competing stores, especially through its effect on store image. For example, stores in attractive surroundings are more likely to be patronised than are those in unattractive surroundings.

The remainder of this section looks at other components of a store's image and the way in which these factors affect store choice.

STORE DESIGN AND PHYSICAL FACILITIES

As we noted in Chapter 10, the design characteristics of a store visibly reflect its image and can dramatically influence patronage.[24] Many consumers appear to 'size up' a store's architecture and signs, and are either drawn to the store or repelled by it, based on their perception of whether this store looks 'right' for them. Interior design continues the image-fostering process. Such design features as store layout, aisle placement and width, carpeting and architecture, as well as physical facilities in a store, including elevators, lighting, air-conditioning and washrooms, influence store assessment by consumers.[25]

Quality of the store surroundings, or ecological design, may affect the consumer's mood state at the point of purchase, which, in turn, may influence purchase behaviour, brand evaluation and information acquisition.[26] The importance of atmospherics, defined as the conscious designing of buying environments to produce specific emotional effects in buyers that enhance their purchase probability, was illustrated effectively by the example in Chapter 4 which showed how the design and atmosphere of different stores in Roselands was adjusted to different social classes.

Not only are the non-person atmospheric elements (such as shelf space, in-store point-of-purchase promotion, lighting, noise, aisle design and square measure) of the retail store important, but also important are the atmospherics created by shoppers within the retail store.[27] One of the intended or unintended products of various current merchandising emphases is retail crowding. This store-atmosphere consequence is a result of high-density shopping environments, such as regional malls and superstores, as well as population shifts and concentrated shopping hours for working families. Such perceived crowding systematically affects shopping behaviour and consumer feelings about retail outlets and shopping trips.[28]

This supermarket display conveys a modern, hygienic and well-organised image
COURTESY OF COLES SUPERMARKETS AUSTRALIA PTY LTD

Another illustration of the significance of atmospherics and consumer mood is found in the use of in-store music. Research indicates that if retailers can positively affect their customer's mood at the point of purchase, the customer may be more responsive to in-store merchandising programs.[29] Positive mood also increases the time spent in a store and the customer's willingness to interact with salespeople.[30] Music can play an important part in a store's atmospherics by perhaps gaining customer attention, conveying a certain image or establishing a particular emotion that increases the likelihood of purchase.[31] Research on the benefits of in-store music shows that it can have a positive impact on a customer's predisposition to buy, the amount of time a shopper spends in the retail environment, the amount spent by the customer when purchasing and the consumer's perception of the quality of the shopping experience.[32]

MERCHANDISE

This image element has to do with the goods and services offered by a retail outlet. There are five attributes considered to be important here: quality, selection or assortment, styling or fashion, guarantees and pricing. For example, the product variety and assortment of a store have been found to influence store choice. Consumers prefer stores that offer either a wide variety of product lines, brands and prices, or substantial depth to their assortment, such as in sizes, colours and styles, over stores with only medium depth or breadth of assortment.[33]

With the trend in retailing toward much of the same merchandise being sold in a variety of mass outlets, the products purchased no longer determine where the buyer shops. For example, grocery and household products were once the province of supermarkets but are now bought in many outlets, ranging from petrol stations to discount stores. For this reason price, convenience and demographics are now strong determinants of store choice.[34]

ADVERTISING AND SALES PROMOTION

Within this category, such influences as advertising, sales promotion, displays, trading stamps, and even symbols and colours are considered important. Retail advertising does not have a consistent impact but instead appears to vary in influence, depending on product and store type. Nevertheless, it is certainly true that retail advertising can be important in fulfilling any of its three goals:

1. to inform consumers, such as for a new store opening;
2. to persuade consumers that they should patronise a certain store or buy a particular brand;
3. to remind customers of the store that they are appreciated.

As we also have learned, advertising can be highly influential in cultivating a store image in consumers' minds.

PERSONNEL

Employees of a retailer also are instrumental in influencing the store's image. Consumers generally desire to trade where store personnel, particularly salespeople, are perceived as helpful, friendly and courteous.[35] That shopping-centre preference is strongly influenced by such factors was demonstrated in one survey of five large metropolitan areas, which found salesperson knowledge/ability and helpfulness to be important elements in the choice of store for more than 75 per cent of people questioned.[36]

CUSTOMER SERVICES

Retail stores may offer numerous services in order to attract customers. One scheme classifies services according to those which:

1. increase product satisfaction (such as credit, alterations, installation and shopper information);
2. increase convenience (such as delivery, telephone ordering and parking);
3. provide special benefits (such as gift wrapping, product returns and complaint offices).[37]

Relationship retailing or merchandising focuses on converting customers into clients through providing better services to existing shoppers, thereby encouraging them to concentrate their purchases with the retailer.[37] This individual attention at the store level is expected to be a strong element in retailer survival and growth, as stores combine credit, point-of-sale and geodemographic data to establish ongoing personal relationships with their regular customers.

CLIENTELE

As we learned earlier, consumers' store choices have much to do with their social-class membership. Consumers will tend to patronise those stores where persons similar to themselves are perceived to be shopping. Thus, an important matching process occurs between the consumer's self-image and the store's image, with consumers choosing stores that possess images similar to the images the consumers have of themselves.[39]

The importance of store attributes

How important is each of these attributes when customers make store-choice decisions? It depends on the store type. Department-store shoppers seem to be concerned about the quality of the store's merchandise, the degree of ease of the shopping process and post-transaction satisfaction. Grocery shoppers are concerned about the store's merchandise mix, ease of the shopping process and cleanliness of the store.

The effect of store image

As indicated in Chapter 10, store image is a complex of tangible, or functional, factors and intangible, or psychological, factors that a consumer perceives to be present in a store. It is the way in which the store is defined in the consumer's mind.[40] The various determinants of store choice just discussed are intimately related to a store's image, and influence its attracting power. Consequently, retailers need to understand what evaluative criteria consumers use in store choice, how important each criterion is, what image consumers have of the retailer's store, and how this image compares to an ideal image and to competitors' images. Store management must determine the unique market segments they want to attract and then develop a store image useful in influencing patronage by those segments.[41] There is also a need periodically to review desired market segments and the consistency of store image to those segments. Such activities should prove useful in satisfying consumer needs and in maintaining the vitality of the organisation.

General shopper profiles

It has been found that consumers tend to shop at different stores, depending partly on their demographic characteristics and their attitudes toward shopping. Table 15.6 presents a categorisation of shopper types from a recent survey of American consumers. The results of this study are presented at a general level but it is obvious that such typologies will be relevant to describing the clientele of many individual stores or chains of stores. This is only one of the several different taxonomies that have been developed to profile shoppers. Other consumer taxonomies have also been developed on the basis of shopping orientations, and research is continuing in this field.[42]

TABLE 15.6 Shopping behaviour characteristics of six shopper typologies

	Yesteryears	Power purchasers	Fashion forgoers	Social strivers	Dutifuls	Progressive patrons
Percentage of population	17%	15%	16%	20%	16%	16%
Psychographics	Insecure; conservative; somewhat antisocial; resists change; risk avoider	Self-indulgent; variety seeking; spender; risktaking	Fashion laggard; unconcerned with image; mundane; antisocial	Style conscious; fashion experimenter; image conscious; social; likes shopping; brand conscious	Sacrificial; practical routine/mundane; risk avoider, conservative; comparison shopper	Self-confident; artistic; variety seeking; open-minded; risktaking; innovative; imaginative
Demographics	Typically female; concentrated in Older Households life-stage, but also found in Middle Market Younger Parents and Down-market Mid-life Families and Households; median income $19 600	Male or female; Up-market Young Singles to Mid-life Households; Middle Market Young Singles to Young Parents; median income $31 650	Tend to be male; no consistent life-stage or income group pattern; often single/alone; median income $25 350	Typically female; tendency toward Down Market; often young; median income $21 500	Male or female; Down-market Mid-life Families and Households; Down-/Middle-market Older Households; median income $17 800	Often male; young singles; young couples; Middle- and Up-market Mid-life Families; median income $28 650
Key differentiating patronage factors	Personal Clothing: low price; ease of finding merchandise; guarantees; convenient location Electronics: low price, ease of finding merchandise; speed of service	Personal Clothing: ease of finding merchandise; friendly sales; wide selection; high quality; speed of service Electronics: high quality; good sales; specific preferred brands	Personal Clothing: low price; ease of finding merchandise; convenient location Electronics: low price; wide selection	Personal Clothing: guarantees; friendly sales; wide selection Electronics: high quality; friendly sales; wide selection	Personal Clothing: low price; guarantees; ease of finding merchandise; convenient location Electronics: friendly sales; ease of finding merchandise; speed of service	Personal Clothing; ease of finding merchandise; high quality Electronics: high quality; wide selection; specific preferred brands
General consumption	Light	Very heavy	Light except for electronics and building materials	Heavy	Light	Very heavy
Store patronage	When shops, most often national mass merchandise chains or discount stores	Frequent department store and national chain store and fairly frequent specialty store usage	Below-average shopping frequency except for home centres	Shops every possible type of outlet frequently, with the exception of home centres	Below-average shopping frequency for all store types except for warehouse grocery	Tends to shop specialty stores with average frequency, frequent use of home centres, catalogue showrooms, and convenience stores

Source: S. Amanda Putnam, William R. Davidson & Ken Martell, *The Management Horizons' Six Shopper Typologies*, Management Horizons, Division of Price Waterhouse, Columbus, OH, © 1987, p. 45.

Store loyalty

The term 'store loyalty' refers to the consumer's inclination to patronise a given store during a specific period of time. Because consumer patronage results in revenue, store loyalty can be a very important factor influencing the company's profits. One Australian retailing chain has recently indicated that increasing customer retention levels by 5 per cent in the early 1990s resulted in a 50 per cent increase in profitability. Over time loyal customers will not only tend to concentrate their purchases in the store and thus increase their spending but also contribute to a retailer's performance in other ways. The costs of servicing loyal consumers are typically lower, especially because widespread advertising or costly sales promotions may not be needed to the same extent. Loyal customers bring further business to the store by word-of-mouth referral and they are also regarded as being less price sensitive than switchers; therefore, it may be possible to sustain a premium price. All these factors mean that store-loyal customers may represent a very profitable market segment if they can be readily identified.

The focus that encourages retailers to develop programs encouraging store loyalty has become known as 'Relationship Marketing'. This produces a longer term orientation, based on the realisation that higher profits tend to eventuate over time from loyal customers.[43] Store loyalty among consumers can be measured and it may vary by store type as well as by consumer type. For example, some evidence in the United States indicates that loyalty may be higher for supermarkets than for department stores, but other work from the United Kingdom suggests that it is very similar across food and mixed retailing sectors. However, all studies seem to suggest that store loyalty appears to be diminishing and that consumers are becoming more 'fickle and promiscuous'.[44]

Studies examining the demographic, socioeconomic and psychographic characteristics of store-loyal shoppers have found that there are patterns of personal characteristics.[45] In the United States, the generally store-loyal consumer tends to be older and have a lower educational attainment and a lower family income than the store switcher. Psychographically, this shopper tends not to be a fashion opinion leader, style conscious, venturesome in trying new products, urban-oriented, gregarious or a credit user. However, he or she does tend to be time-conscious, and a radio and television user. Thus, the store-loyal's profile is one of a relatively conservative, inactive, time-conscious, home-town oriented person. He or she expresses a positive attitude toward local shopping conditions but negative attitudes toward shopping in the nearest large city.[46] Another study finds that highly store-loyal shoppers engage in less comparison search among stores before purchasing, know about the existence of and have visited fewer stores, and concentrate their purchases in a smaller subset of stores than do other consumers.[47]

Research by the Cranfield Centre for Marketing Relationships in the United Kingdom produced many similar patterns.[48] Loyal shoppers tend to have the following characteristics:

1. They are single people rather than married couples or partners living together.

2. They tend not to be people who follow a 'live life to the full' philosophy.

3. They have a tendency to shop late afternoons, evenings and Saturdays.

4. They are of lower socioeconomic standing.

5. They have smaller monthly budgets.

6. They hold full-time jobs rather than do no work outside the home or do part-time work.

7. They have no or many children in the house rather than one or two.

8. They are men rather than women.

These results are similar to earlier findings from research in the 1970s and indicate a lot of stability in this aspect of shopping behaviour. At that time the non-loyal consumer was summarised as the full-time housewife with a strong interest in cooking and shopping, while the loyal consumer was typically working to help support a family. In this context, store loyalty is seen as a negative attribute, which households possess from necessity rather than choice, and chiefly as the result of constraints on time and a conservative approach to shopping. While the Cranfield study suggests that loyal shoppers may have lower budgets than non-loyal shoppers, it is quite clear that the available budget is allocated differently and that it is of considerable benefit to the retailer to be the first-choice store. 'Promiscuous', or non-loyal, shoppers only spent an average of 37 per cent of their budget at first-choice stores, while 'average' shoppers spent 61 per cent and 'loyal' shoppers spent 90 per cent.

Obviously, the financial benefit to the retailer of pursuing the store-loyal consumer may be very significant. The marketer should seek to understand the store-loyalty characteristics and patterns not only of customers but also of competitors' customers. Generally, it is important to learn as much as possible about why these families buy where they do. One element of the research should involve measuring the store's image in relation to the images of competitors. As a result of this kind of research, the marketer will be able to identify specific marketing programs to attract more store-loyal shoppers. An example of such a program is a scheme developed by Kmart in New Zealand in 1993, which is under consideration for extension to Australia. Kmart's program, entitled Kmart Plus, aims to build profiles of 100 000 loyal shoppers throughout the country. Personalised plastic cards are issued to members who can then earn discount points for every dollar spent and subsequently redeem vouchers in Kmart stores. Members receive monthly statements from Kmart and staff also seek to give members special attention in store. Kmart believe the success of the scheme comes from adding value for the frequent shopper, and when the full database is developed with personal information and data on buying patterns, they believe the store will have information on loyal shoppers that will provide a significant competitive advantage.[49] A further illustration of a scheme designed to promote store loyalty is that operated by the Morgan family supermarkets in Melbourne. They have developed a club for customers that offers discounts on over a thousand items as well as volume based

Christmas and birthday vouchers. They see the scheme as a big contributor to recent growth and a more cost-effective approach than general media advertising.[50]

IN-STORE PURCHASING BEHAVIOUR

Once consumers have selected the store they will patronise, they must then proceed to consummate the purchase. A number of factors influence consumers' behaviour within the store environment. In this section we shall examine some of the important variables affecting consumer shopping activities within stores.

Merchandising techniques

Merchandising techniques have an important influence on consumer shopping behaviour.[51] This is particularly true for low-involvement purchase decisions. For example, nearly two out of three supermarket purchase decisions are not specifically planned.[52] Because there is generally little consideration of such purchases until the point of sale, merchandising techniques affecting the consumer in the store are often of great significance in securing a purchase. A number of topics are discussed under the umbrella of merchandising techniques, including store layout, displays, product shelving, pricing strategies, branding and promotional deals.

STORE LAYOUT AND TRAFFIC PATTERNS

A store's interior is organised in such a manner as to accomplish the firm's merchandising strategy.[53] Traffic pattern studies are very popular with retailers in order to determine where good or bad sales areas are within the store. Supermarkets conduct such research in order to determine optimum layout and placement of goods. Shopper activity is diagrammed on these layouts for both density and main direction of traffic for each aisle, and for passing and buying rates within the aisles. These statistics show that customers shop a store in different ways. There are also differences in the times spent in the store among different patrons. Consequently, depending on the type of shopper and the length of time spent shopping, different expenditures result.[54]

Although use of passing and buying ratios can be helpful in visualising *what* consumers do, they fail to explain *why* these patterns exist. Thus, further research would need to be conducted by the retailer to understand why such passing and buying ratios exist and how a change in store layout could alter these patterns. Now stores are able to obtain customer-movement information electronically. In the United States, for example, Kmart has used a system of ceiling sensors in order to monitor how many people come and go, the direction in which the individual shopper walks, and how fast people are moving through the store or specific department.[55]

POINT-OF-PURCHASE MEDIA

With more than 80 per cent of supermarket shoppers making their final buying decisions in the store, point-of-purchase activities by marketers assume an important role.[56] An effective combination of good store layout and attractive displays can change a humdrum retail environment into one that not only is more exciting but also produces more sales. Special displays are used in stores in order to attract shopper attention to one or more products.

The bulk of published research on the effectiveness of displays has been conducted in American supermarkets and drugstores. Numerous examples of the effectiveness of displays in attracting consumer attention could be cited. The following are representative of the findings:

1. Of 2473 supermarket shoppers interviewed, 38 per cent had purchased at least one brand or item they had never before bought. The reason cited most frequently (25 per cent) for a first-time purchase was that it had been displayed.[57]

2. A study of 5215 customers in supermarkets, variety stores, drugstores, hardware stores, liquor stores and service stations found that one-third had purchased at least one of the displayed items.[58]

3. Kmart discovered a 251 per cent sales increase for sports products featured on continuous-loop film in point-of-purchase audiovisual displays.[59]

It is clear from these results that displays are effective in increasing sales.[60] In fact, the greatest gains can be realised generally by tying a price reduction to a display, as illustrated in Figure 15.2, which summarises data for a large number of markets in the United States. A legitimate question may be whether the display takes sales away from ordinary shelf sales. It has been found that displays do tend to reduce normal shelf sales. However, net sales of display and shelf combined are usually so far above normal that use of displays appears to be strongly substantiated. Moreover, tests show that there is a rapid return to normal shelf sales once the item is removed from display. This would indicate that customers are not simply stocking up on the item but are actually consuming more. Thus, there is much evidence to support the continued strong usage of displays as a merchandising tool.

In-store merchandising is continually changing as marketers seek to discover new ways of reaching consumers with their promotional messages close to the point of purchase. In-store promotion is not only growing rapidly but also becoming electronic, as marketers place messages on everything from shopping carts to store directories and shelves.[61]

PRODUCT SHELVING

Product shelving has an important influence on consumer behaviour. Both the height at which products are displayed and the number of rows presented (facings) can influence sales of products. In addition, the use of shelf signs and extenders can affect sales.

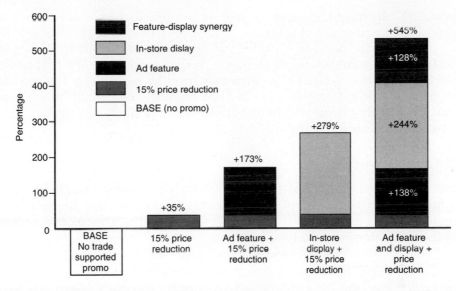

FIG. 15.2 Results of four promotion strategies Source: Data from 1989 Topical Marketing Report, Information Resources Inc., Chicago. From 'What Pittsburgh Can Teach the Rest of the Country', *P-O-P Times* 3, March/April 1990, p. 40.

SHELF HEIGHT Because the average shopper selects only 35 of the available 7000 or more grocery products during the average 27-minute shopping trip, it is easy to see why manufacturers clamour for the most visible eye-level shelf position. Tests conducted by *Progressive Grocer* indicate that the most favourable shelf position is generally at eye level, followed in effectiveness by waist level, and then by knee or ankle level. It has been calculated from *Progressive Grocer* data that sales from waist-level shelves were only 74 per cent as great and sales from floor-level shelves were only 57 per cent as great as sales from equivalent space allocations on eye-level shelves.[62]

Beyond the physical impossibility of stocking all products at eye level, some products are better placed on lower shelves. The shelf height dictated for an item is a function of its package size, its normal movement, whether or not it is being advertised and its market target.

SHELF SPACE It is crucial for a product to be given enough shelf space to attract the buyer's attention. In order to help ensure this, the science and industry of packaging has mushroomed. Yet, all of the manufacturer's careful packaging efforts can be counteracted by an insufficient amount of shelf space in the store. Without adequate shelf facings, the item will be lost in the mass of 22 000 other multiple facings lining the average supermarket's shelves.

There have been a number of experiments on *shelf-space elasticity*; that is, the ratio of relative changes in unit sales to relative changes in shelf space. The result of these experiments is that there is a small positive relationship between shelf space and unit sales. However, the relationship is not uniform among products or across stores or intrastore locations.[63] Supermarket tests have concluded that products can have too many as well as too few facings, with both situations resulting in wrong use of space.

An adequate number of facings is especially important for new products. Tests show that doubling shelf facings on new items during their first two to three weeks in stores produced sales increases from 85 per cent to 160 per cent over stores that stocked the items but did not make any facing adjustments. In addition, fast-moving items tend to react much more dramatically to changes in shelf space than do slow-moving products.

PRICING STRATEGIES

We have already discussed the way in which consumers' perceptual processes influence their evaluation of prices (Ch. 11). There are other elements of pricing that can affect consumers in their shopping activities. This section presents two of these influencing strategies.

PRICE AWARENESS   Although consumers have a critical attitude toward the general price level and supermarket prices in particular, they apparently have difficulty recalling the actual price paid for a previously purchased product. For example, only about one shopper in 12 can name the exact price of even one out of a broad range of common food-store items.[64] However, there has been some criticism of the method of such studies,[65] and recent research using a different approach suggests that shoppers are more knowledgeable about prices than earlier studies indicated.[66] Nevertheless, it is surprising just how imperfect information attention and retention are even at the point of purchase. Less than half the grocery shoppers in one study gave the correct price of the item they had just placed in their shopping cart; one in five had no idea what the item cost; less than half were aware that a selected item was selling at a reduced price; and those who gave incorrect answers were off by 30c on a $2 item.[67]

Even though consumers may not know the exact price of the items they purchase, they are often unwilling to pay full price. In fact, shopping on sale has become a way of life, as indicated by Figure 15.3. While single people are more likely to pay full price than are married people, there are few other differences by sex, age or income. Because price is one of the most critical criteria in store choice, it is often important for store operations to achieve a low-price image. This is often accomplished by the use of *loss leaders*—products that are heavily advertised and sold at slightly above cost to draw traffic into the store and create an impression of low prices.

PROMOTIONAL PRICING   One form of promotional pricing involves multiple pricing, the technique by which retailers price items in multiple quantities, such as 2 for $1.25, 3 for $1.99 and so on. The basic idea of multiple pricing is to offer the customer a lower price on a quantity purchase. However, the technique has long been complained about by some consumerists as a device that confuses customers more than it saves them money, and one that causes them to buy more than they had planned. Nevertheless, in the United States 74 per cent of supermarket customers usually buy items priced in multiple units.[68]

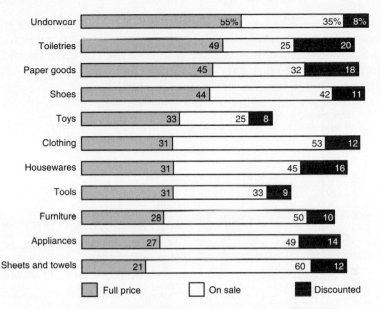

Underwear	55%	35%	8%
Toiletries	49	25	20
Paper goods	45	32	18
Shoes	44	42	11
Toys	33	25	8
Clothing	31	53	12
Housewares	31	45	16
Tools	31	33	9
Furniture	28	50	10
Appliances	27	49	14
Sheets and towels	21	60	12

 Full price   ☐ On sale   ■ Discounted

FIG. 15.3   How people buy; poll reveals pervasive 'on sale' mentality   Source: Kevin Kerr, 'Consumers Are Confused by Sears' New Policy', *Adweek's Marketing Week*, 12 June 1989, p. 31.

In addition to multiple pricing, there are other pricing approaches in which the marketer merely cuts the price of an item, offers a 'cents-off' special or provides some sort of rebate on the product as a way of stimulating sales. One consideration in all such approaches, however, is the effectiveness of the price deal for accomplishing marketing objectives.[69] For example, it appears that price promotions can induce brand switching in favour of the promoted brand. One study of regular ground coffee found that more than 84 per cent of the sales increase due to price promotion came from brand switching, while purchase acceleration in time accounted for less than 14 per cent and stockpiling for less than 2 per cent.[70] A related factor of importance to retailers is that shoppers may change stores to make their purchases, particularly as a result of price promotion.[71] It is not clear, however, that consumers remain with the brand once the deal is withdrawn (and, hence, the price is raised).[72] Thus, the marketer may not achieve lasting impact with price deals.

Can the 'deal-prone' consumer be identified and segmented? That is, do certain consumers react more favourably than others to deals? Although research results are inconsistent,[73] recent studies indicate that for certain frequently purchased goods, deal-prone households can be identified, and that the key variables are household resource variables (such as home and car ownership). Buyers with higher incomes, and owners of cars and homes are more deal prone.[74]

COUPONING   This is a form of price dealing in which a cents-off coupon is redeemed during purchase, thus reducing the product's price. Coupon distribution has had a sharp, continuing growth in the United States over the past few years. In 1990 an estimated 280 billion coupons (over 3000 per household) were distributed by companies in the United States. The face value of these coupons averaged almost 50c, representing potential consumer savings of \$136.7 billion. However, redemption rates are quite low (7.1 billion coupons for a total savings of \$3.5 billion) although they have begun to rise. Coupons appear to have a significant impact on consumer purchase behaviour, as indicated in Figure 15.4, which compares four sales-promotion devices.

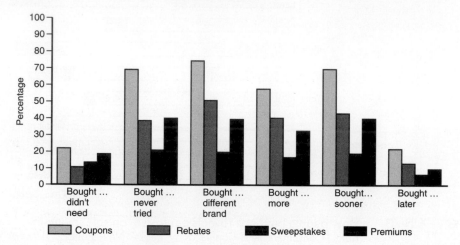

FIG. 15.4 Can promotions change consumer behaviour? Source: Data from United Marketing Services. From 'Study: Some Promotions Change Consumer Behaviour', *Marketing News*, 15 October 1990, p. 12.

Cents-off coupons have been criticised on several bases:

1. They discriminate against low-income and minority consumers and shoppers with high time costs.

2. They slow the checkout process.

3. They force food retailers to stock slow-moving items.

4. They impose costs on the food system by generating demand surges.

5. They distort consumer choices between advertised and private labels.[75]

In spite of these criticisms, the practice of couponing continues to grow. It has been estimated that 97 per cent of all households use coupons in a given month.[76] A consumer's decision to redeem a coupon is based on coupon characteristics, characteristics of the purchase, brand loyalty, the present promotional conditions and past coupon-usage behaviour.[77] Consumers attempt to strike a balance between their needs for economising and reducing shopping time and effort.[78]

Although coupons are generally claimed to influence consumers to try new products or improve the position of older products, it is hoped they will result in long-term loyalty once trial occurs.[79] However, most coupons have been shown to result in short-term sales gains only,[80] although such gains may be impressive.[81]

Who uses coupons? Coupon-responsive behaviour appears to be a manifestation of two psychological constructs: coupon proneness (a propensity to respond to a purchase offer because the coupon form of the purchase offer positively affects purchase evaluations) and value consciousness (a concern for paying low prices, subject to some quality constraint).[82] Coupon usage is greater among middle- and upper-income groups, those with higher educational levels, and those who are urban, less brand loyal and less store loyal. Such refunds also attract larger and older families.[83] Market mavens are particularly heavy coupon users and are active in providing coupons to others.[84]

PACKAGING

One of the most important point-of-sale influences is the package. This includes graphics, product information contained on the package and the physical design of the package. In addition, the package can be extremely instrumental in the success of store displays. Thus, it is a basic ingredient in attracting the shopper's attention while in the store—the marketer's 'silent salesperson'.

BRAND CHOICE: NATIONAL VERSUS PRIVATE

For a number of years, there has been a 'battle' between manufacturers' national brands and distributors' private brands for brand predominance in certain product categories. To the winner go greater product sales and profits. Owning strong brands allows companies to price them at a premium but for retailers such as Coles Myer the estimate is that private brands are 10 per cent to 15 per cent more profitable. But familiar national brands may be losing their punch as companies are forced by retailers to divert dollars from advertising for their products into expensive trade promotions and price discounts.[85]

Since the 1970s the Marlboro Man has been referred to as one of the classic success stories in branding. When private-label cigarettes first entered the market in the United States in the early 1980s it was assumed that the strength of the brand image for Marlboro would keep smokers loyal to the product. Instead the market shares of private-label cigarettes have gradually increased and they now take over 30 per cent of the American market. After trying for a number of years to maintain profits through price increases and maintaining a premium position for the brand, Philip Morris bowed to the inevitable in 1993 and cut the price of the Marlboro brand by 40c a packet—acknowledging that the price cut had compromised the position of the brand.

Philip Morris were not alone in this kind of dilemma. The day before the Marlboro price cut, Proctor & Gamble had slashed 16 per cent off the price of their disposable nappies in order to match the cheap prices of supermarket brands. What was also significant was the reaction of Wall Street. Philip Morris stock dropped 26 per cent in value following the price cut and knock-on effects were also felt by other consumer-goods companies with major brands, including Kellogg, Heinz and Quaker Oats. A financial analyst believes that since the recession in the United States many consumers have tried cheaper brands and found that Brand X is really not much different from the ones advertised heavily on television. Names such as Kraft, Kellogg and Listerine no longer have the same cachet, and consumers find it really hard to tell the difference between a 'Corn Flake' and a cornflake. Only truly good companies with unique products will survive. Good brands in that position may come out of the fight even stronger but the number 3 and 4 brands in the marketplace will get murdered.[86]

POSITION OF PRIVATE BRANDS   The competitive position of private brands differs from industry to industry. In both Australia and New Zealand it is most developed in the grocery sector, where distribution and retailing are controlled by either two or three major companies. From 1989 to 1993 the housebrand and generic range of Coles Myer's Bi-Lo chain has increased from 230 lines to 850 lines, and Woolworths have increased the number of products under their Home Brand label from 170 items in 1987 to 800 in 1993. A further indicator of the switch to housebrands and retailer power is the advertising spent by different companies. Six of the top 20 advertising spenders in New Zealand in 1993 were retailers, including The Warehouse, New World, Farmers, Noel Leeming, Deka and Mitre 10. Overall, housebrands take about 12 per cent of the grocery market in Australia, 17 per cent in New Zealand, 18 per cent in the United States and 32 per cent in Great Britain. Indeed, the Sainsbury chain in Britain draws over 50 per cent of its sales from housebrands that are no longer positioned on price but on the quality of the Sainsbury name. Indeed, research in Australia and the United States has also shown that perceived quality is one of the reasons for housebrand growth. For example, 38 per cent of Australians and 55 per cent of Americans surveyed agreed or strongly agreed that retail brands were as good or better than national brands in at least some product areas.[87] In Australia housebrands have been shown to do best in categories where there is little product differentiation and consumers perceive the item as a commodity. A strong housebrand presence in the marketplace is characteristic of a situation where there may be excess manufacturing capacity or low technical barriers to entry. In the latter case, it is relatively easy for new manufacturers to start up production to supply the housebrands. Both features make it easier for retailers to ensure a continuous and cheap supply of their own labelled products. Products with a high penetration of housebrand sales are ice-cream (28 per cent), potato crisps (20 per cent), facial tissues (19 per cent), bread (18 per cent), canned catfood (17 per cent) and cooking oil (16 per cent). Low share of sales includes yoghurt, breakfast cereals, toilet soap, toothpaste and shampoo; all around 2 per cent.[88]

A variation on the housebrand is the generic 'brand'. Generic, or 'no-name' brands, were pioneered by the French supermarket chain Carrefour. These products are easily distinguishable due to their plain packaging characteristics coupled with the attribute of primary emphasis on the contents of the package rather than on brand name. Early introductions were often marketed in stark white packages with bold black content labelling. This approach contrasts with private-label merchandise, which more closely resembles manufacturers' brands in that a brand name is stressed in the primary labelling with secondary emphasis given to content.[89]

Purchase of housebrands and generics is almost universal in Australian and New Zealand households—98 per cent of all households purchase them at some time. The biggest buyers are women aged under 44 with children under 15 years old. Low prices are the nominated reason for 73 per cent of housebrand and generic purchases, but there is also a significant perception that the quality and value of many products are high. The age and family characteristics noted above, together with the low-price motivations, fit well with family life-cycle theory. Those demographics place the high purchasers of housebrands and generics into the Full Nest I and Full Nest II stages of the family life cycle—typically periods where discretionary income is lower and more price-sensitive behaviour may be expected. These findings are compatible with American research on the purchasing of generics.[90]

Personal selling effects

We have been primarily discussing in-store purchasing behaviour for items that are sold via self-service. However, there are also many product-purchase situations in which customers interact with salespeople.

The influence of a personal sales representative may be very strong, as seen in our earlier discussion of interpersonal influence and social-group behaviour. From a consumer-behaviour viewpoint, however, little is known about what factors make this process a success. Studies of salespeople have generally sought to learn what main characteristics lead to success, and have assumed homogeneity among prospects. Usually, researchers point to a bundle of personality variables as predictors of good sales performance. More recently, however, researchers have begun to view selling as dyadic interaction in terms of the characteristics not only of the salesperson but also of the buyer, and how the two parties react to each other.[91]

As this recent research suggests, it appears that rather than focusing merely on the salesperson's traits, the marketer would do well also to consider the customer's traits. Careful research into market-segment characteristics and needs may result in more effective sales management. By hiring salespeople who more closely match desired customers and preparing them better to perform effectively in the dyadic interaction process, the firm may achieve more success in the market.[92]

THE SITUATIONAL NATURE OF CONSUMER DECISIONS

One of the most important factors influencing the choice and purchasing process is the situation surrounding the consumer's decision. Depending on the set of circumstances faced by the consumer in making a purchase, including the particular benefits sought in that instance, behaviour may take any number of directions. For example, the type of car the consumer may purchase for commuting might well differ from the type of car bought for holidaying. The brand of wine bought to serve at a dinner party for one's boss may be different from the brand bought for everyday consumption.

In these and countless other decisions, consumers may base their purchase acts on the situation attached to those acts. A *situation*, therefore, may be viewed as comprising all of those factors particular to a time and place of observation that do not follow from a knowledge of personal (intra-individual) and stimulus (choice alternative) attributes, and which have a demonstrable and systematic effect on current behaviour.[93]

Based upon this definition, five groups of situational characteristics may be identified:

1. *Physical surroundings*. The most readily apparent features of a situation, these include geographical and institutional location, decor, sounds, aromas, lighting, weather, and visible configurations of merchandise or other materials surrounding the stimulus object.

2. *Social surroundings*. These include such factors as other persons present, their characteristics and apparent roles, and interpersonal interactions.

3. *Temporal perspective*. This dimension of situations may be specified in units ranging from time of day to season of the year. Time may also be measured relative to a past or future event for the situational participant, such as time since the last purchase.

4. *Task definition*. This includes an intent or requirement to select, shop for or obtain information about a general or specific purchase. It may also reflect different buyer and user roles anticipated by the individual. For example, a consumer shopping for a small appliance as a wedding gift for a friend is in a different situation from one in which he or she is shopping for a small appliance for personal use.

5. *Antecedent states*. These are momentary moods (such as acute anxiety, contentment, hostility or excitation) or momentary conditions (such as cash on hand, fatigue or illness) rather than chronic individual traits, and they are immediately antecedent to the current consumer situation.[94]

Patterns have been found among consumer segments in the types of products bought for certain situations, ranging across snack foods, beverages, leisure activities, fast foods and many other items.[95]

The consumer decision sequence also depends on the situation. The consumer's needs for shopping (e.g. to buy, to obtain information by searching, to socialise or to satisfy other personal requirements) affects the order of the decision hierarchy related to product and outlet choice. For example, consider the following hypothetical shopping situations: a consumer making a weekly grocery-shopping trip; a recreational shopper with no pressing need for merchandise or information; a camera shopper desiring to compare several preselected brands; and a consumer concerned with quality and fashion criteria purchasing a business suit. Each purchasing situation may exhibit a different decision sequence.[96] Perhaps the shopping area or centre is chosen first, followed by storechoice; or perhaps the product or brand is chosen first, followed by selection of appropriate stores or areas. Thus, situational factors influence the consumer's decision hierarchy.[97]

Although the situation is an important influence in the purchase and consumption decision, it may frequently be overridden by product considerations. For example, the degree of brand loyalty a consumer exhibits may be very influential in purchase decisions. A highly brand-loyal consumer will tend to purchase a favourite brand time after time no matter what the variation in the consumption situation. Thus, strong brand loyalty results in weaker situational influence.

Another factor tempering situational influence is product involvement. Research indicates that when product involvement is low, the situation tends to determine behaviour; however, in high-product-involvement cases, situational factors are not as important.[98]

NON-STORE PURCHASING PROCESSES

Although the vast bulk of consumer purchasing processes now take place in shops, there is a growing amount of in-home shopping. It includes ordering via direct-response television, automatic vending machines, catalogues, party and club plans, door-to-door selling, video cassettes, Teletext, direct mail and other developing electronic technologies. Marketers usually refer to telephone and mail-order selling as direct marketing, while in-home selling is termed direct selling. Unfortunately, it is not possible to give accurate estimates of the value of non-store shopping in Australia and New Zealand because they are not identifiable in official statistics, but non-store retailing is known to be growing significantly. The same problem exists in the United States where estimates variously put it at between 2 per cent and 12 per cent of retail sales. Some figures are available from the Quantum Australian Social Monitor (based on the long-running Yankelovich Social Monitor in the United States), which show that 63 per cent of Australians are using at least one non-store channel from the list investigated.[99]

Avon have successfully used in-home selling methods for many years   COURTESY OF
AVON PRODUCTS PTY LTD

TABLE 15.7 Use of non-store retailing

| | Percentage of consumers | | | |
| | Australia | | United States | |
Non-store channel	1993	1992	1992	1991
	%	%	%	%
Store catalogue	37	33	36	44
Salesperson at the door	13	14	7	9
Party plan	12	13	16	15
Mail-order club (e.g. books, records)	12	8	13	13
Catalogue from mail-order company	10	11	31	32
Merchandise offerings in the mail	6	6	13	13
Ordered from TV advertisement	5	4	10	12
Classified ads in newspapers	19	17	n/a	n/a
Ordered from cable TV shopping channel	n/a	n/a	6	6
Percentage using at least one channel	63	58	n/a	n/a

Source: Don Porritt, 'What Retail Revolution?', *Australian Professional Marketing*, November 1993, pp. 23, 32.

> *Michael Schulhof is chairman of Sony Music Entertainment and, if he has his way, you will never look at your car radio the same way again. Say you hear a new song by Michael Jackson as you are driving along. It sounds good, so you take out a pocket-sized computer and quickly call up a database that lists all Jackson tunes. You then find the one you have just heard and order the album it is on by tapping the screen of your computer. The purchase is charged to your credit card and a retailer delivers it to your home overnight.*[100]

This example illustrates the potential impact of new technologies on retailing. Before such computers as described in the quote become widespread, the major impact is forecast to be made by home shopping via television. Television shopping networks have been part of the American industry since the mid-1980s, but are only now regarded as developing from fringe methods of retailing. In Australia both the Nine and Ten networks launched schemes in 1987 and both failed within six months, but evidence suggests that consumers may be more prepared to adopt non-store shopping methods in the 1990s. For example, Demtel, which promote their products only by television commercials designed to achieve a direct telephone response from consumers, recorded sales growth of 52 per cent in 1990/91, 54 per cent in 1991/92, 41 per cent in 1992/93 and forecast further growth of 38 per cent in 1993/94, to give total sales of approximately $28 million in Australia.[101] Home shopping by television will be further boosted by the adoption of interactive television through the rest of the 1990s. Adoption of this technology is forecast to be rapid in Australia and New Zealand, as it will also allow for features such as audience participation in games shows. It will enable consumers to make immediate responses to advertising (e.g. ordering a brochure) without leaving their armchairs. Requests are forwarded to a company via a mainframe computer, which sorts and analyses all consumer responses.[102]

Other technologies that will impact on conventional retailing are based around the personal computer. Consumers will be able to access information about products through CD-ROM and eventually purchase as more interactive CD systems are developed. IBM has already developed machines that could make conventional record stores redundant. A blank CD is fed into the machine, which downloads any one of the 30 000 CDs it has stored in memory. In the future that album may well be received directly into the home over the telephone cables. In France more than 5 million homes already have access to vast amounts of product information on electronic yellow pages, and social e-mail networks are also extensive. For example, the French may investigate buying a car and receive animated, detailed on-line brochures regarding all the models they wish to consider. Subsequently they may arrange a test drive, order the required model with customised extras and even complete the loan application without talking personally to a dealer.[103]

From the consumer perspective, this change toward telecommunication-based merchandising has taken place and will continue to grow for several reasons:

➡ an increased emphasis on consumer self-identity, with individuality expressed through goods and services, which leads to a desire to consider more items than a store can display;

➡ a higher proportion of working women who have less time to shop;

➡ demand from rural centres without convenient access to the comprehensive facilities of large shopping centres;

➡ the convenience of searching for information and shopping at times outside normal shopping hours;

➡ increased leisure-time pursuits of self-development and creative expression, which allow less time to shop from store to store;

➡ greater demand for specialty products and services that are difficult to get in most shopping centres;

➡ rapid acceptance of new technology such as VCRs, home computers and automatic teller machines, which means that more consumers are becoming technologically competent for new merchandising approaches;

➡ increased popularity of such recent non-store innovations as pay-by-phone, special-interest mail-order catalogues and televised direct marketing, resulting in consumers who are becoming psychologically prepared for new shopping forms.[104]

However, in spite of these favourable conditions leading to a receptive environment for new video-based marketing approaches, the situation is not all positive.[105] A survey by Benton & Bowles Inc. in the United States indicated that only 10 per cent of consumers were very interested in shopping at home via two-way television. The major reasons consumers express in opposition to more active involvement in new video technologies are:

1. they like to see products 'in person' before they buy;

2. they 'just don't need it';

3. they like to 'go out' to shop;

4. they want to relax while watching television and don't want to push buttons;

5. they feel they might be tempted to buy products they don't really need;

6. they fear that being 'hooked up' to a computer would invade their privacy.[106]

Perhaps when 'virtual reality' technology is perfected, probably sometime after 2010, even these consumers will enjoy shopping in-home. This technology will allow consumers to make a simulated shopping trip in their homes. They will be able to do virtually everything they can now do in a store—such as turning a jar around to read the label of ingredients—but from their own television set.[107]

Factors influencing in-home shopping

Because of the variety of approaches embraced by non-store shopping, it is difficult to generalise about either the characteristics or the motives of consumers who utilise these methods. The limited amount of work that has been done in the United States shows that such consumers tend to be from higher socioeconomic households, and that non-store shopping is also utilised more frequently by shoppers from rural areas. However, other expected relationships such as in-home shopping being used more by working women have not been consistently supported. It seems that two main factors may dominate: convenience and risk.

CONVENIENCE

Shopping convenience is probably the most important motivator in consumer decisions to shop at home, and is the one so often stressed by the industry. There are several different types of convenience that in-home shopping potentially offers: it can reduce the total amount of time spent on shopping; provide more flexibility in the timing of shopping; save physical effort; save aggravation; and provide the opportunity to buy on impulse. High-convenience orientation does explain some but not all in-home shopping motivation. For example, phone shoppers seem especially convenience-oriented, while catalogue buyers not only want shopping convenience, but also want merchandise assortment and uniqueness, competitive prices and useful descriptive shopping information. Mail order's strength today seems to lie less in its shopping convenience than in its ability to offer new, unique, personalised products.

THE RISK OF BUYING

In spite of the obvious advantages of shopping at home, the higher perceived risk that may be associated with buying by description partially explains why many consumers are hesitant to use this particular technique. Research on telephone, direct selling and mail-order shopping supports this hypothesis.[108] Personality characteristics found among in-home shoppers indicate that they tend to be more self-assured, venturesome and cosmopolitan in outlook and in shopping behaviour.

The results of one advertising agency's analysis of direct-response purchasers confirm these two features. They found that those characterised as 'impulse' buyers, where by definition a large element of risk is not assessed, and those who found it 'difficult to get to the store' were the most attractive prospects.[109] For example, of the 15 product categories in which direct-response sales are significant, the 'impulse' shopper ranks above average in nine of them.

Overall, active in-home buyers seem to be more cosmopolitan, style- and value-conscious, and convenience-oriented, and generally are more demanding shoppers than are other consumers. They are more flexible in shopping style, visit stores more frequently, and view shopping and shopping risk more positively. As we saw in our review of social class earlier, these were all characteristics that tended to be associated with higher socioeconomic groupings. In-home buying is usually discretionary, and often impulse- or convenience-oriented, and people who use it are prepared to use a variety of in-home buying methods and sources.

PURCHASING PATTERNS

This section focuses on two important purchasing patterns: the extent to which consumers develop repeat purchasing patterns and the extent to which purchases are unplanned. These subjects will be discussed in the context of brand loyalty and impulse purchasing.

Brand loyalty

Brand loyalty is a topic of much concern to all marketers.[110] Every company seeks to have a steady group of unwavering customers for its product or service. Because research suggests that an increase in market share is related to improved brand loyalty, marketers are understandably concerned with this element. Thus brands that seek to improve their market positions have to be successful both in getting brand users and in increasing their loyalty.[111] The significance of brand loyalty is illustrated in the following examples:

> *In the cereal market, people switch brands as often as 10 times a year, and a new brand has only six months to establish itself before losing out to a more popular competitor. Consequently, cereal brands scrap hard for shelf space and advertise loudly to catch consumer attention to be the one in three new brands that survives.[112]*

> *Brand loyalty in big-ticket durable purchases is relatively low (only one out of three repurchases the same brand in a particular product category), although category repurchases comprise two of every three sales in a product category, on average.[113]*

Thus, brand loyalty is a challenging goal each marketer seeks to attain, but marketers also recognise an apparent decrease in brand loyalty since the 1970s. This is attributed to several factors:

➡ sophisticated advertising appeals and heavy media support

➡ 'parity' of products in form, content, and communication

➡ price competition from private and generic labels

➡ sales promotion tactics of mass displays, coupons and price specials that appeal to consumer impulse buying

➡ general fickleness of consumers in buying behaviour

➡ high inflation of the 1970s and 1980s and a new mood of realism in shopping in the 1990s

➡ growth of new products competing for shelf space and consumer attention

Comparisons between Australia and the United States show that Australian consumers are likely to be less loyal and more likely to switch, though not so keen to shop for specials.[114] Comparison across the statements in Table 15.8 also reveals what appears to be a paradox, with most people claiming that they don't unthinkingly buy the same brand repeatedly, while at the same time a majority claim that it is difficult to shift them from a brand they really like. These results indicate how complex attitudes to brand loyalty are, and they also emphasise that loyalty, as measured in such surveys and by actual patterns of items purchased over time, covers a variety of consumer responses according to the involvement. True brand loyalty is likely to be a function of high involvement, whereas repeated purchasing of the same brand in a low-involvement situation is a feature of inertia.

TABLE 15.8   Attitudes to brand loyalty

Statement	Percentage agreeing with statement	
	Australia 1992	United States 1991
	%	%
I tend to buy the same brand over and over again without really thinking about it	42	69
I usually buy brands that are on special	52	73
Everything being equal, I prefer to buy products made by well-established companies	72	78
Once I find a brand I like, it is very difficult to get me to change brands	69	73
There is usually not much difference between competing brands; they are all about the same	65	60
It is risky to buy a brand with which you are not familiar	60	58

Source: Paul Leinberger, 'Make Way for the New Realists', *Australian Professional Marketing*, December/January 1992/93, p. 47.

Involvement also helps to explain why some products may show higher levels of loyalty than others. An American study of consumer loyalty to brands in 80 product categories asked people whether they would switch for a 50 per cent discount. Some products with high loyalty were cigarettes, laxatives, cold remedies, 35 mm film and toothpaste. Products having medium loyalty included colas, margarine, shampoo, hand lotion and furniture polish. Low-loyalty items included paper towels, crackers, scouring powder, plastic garbage bags and facial tissues. The study also showed that the leader in market share did not necessarily have the most loyal following.[115]

THE NATURE OF BRAND LOYALTY

Patterns of repeat purchasing can be classified into one of four forms, as follows:

1. *Undivided loyalty* is exhibited by families purchasing brand A in the following sequence: A A A A A A.

2. *Divided loyalty* is exhibited by the family purchasing brands A and B in the following sequence: A B A B A B.

3. *Unstable loyalty* is shown by the family buying brands A and B in the following sequence: A A A B B B.

4. *No loyalty* is shown by families buying brands A, B, C, D, E and F in the following sequence: A B C D E F.[116]

The majority of consumers seem to purchase a favourite brand or set of brands and the no-loyalty situation is comparatively rare. As one would expect, loyalty appears to be higher for well-established products in which little or no changes have occurred, and much lower in markets where product entries are frequent.

Various other studies have used these and other measures of brand loyalty, and have generally concluded that brand loyalty exists and is a relatively widespread phenomenon.[117] Most studies, however, suffer from a lack of comparability because of differing conceptions of brand loyalty. Until consumer-behaviour researchers agree on a common definition, there will continue to be difficulty synthesising results. Some researchers have suggested a useful definition of brand loyalty that recognises that true brand-loyal consumers should exhibit not only a high degree of repeat purchasing but also a favourable attitude toward the purchased brand. Perhaps the most complete definition recognising this position describes brand loyalty as (1) the biased (non-random) (2) behavioural response (purchase) (3) expressed over time (4) by a decision-making unit (5) with respect to one or more alternative brands out of a set of such brands, and is (6) a function of psychological (decision-making, evaluative) processes.[118]

FACTORS EXPLAINING BRAND LOYALTY

Although numerous studies attempting to explain brand loyalty have been largely inconclusive on this point, the following results appear to be indicated:

1. Some socioeconomic, demographic and psychological variables are related to brand loyalty (when extended definitions are used), but tend to be product-specific rather than general across products.

2. Loyalty behaviour of an informal-group leader influences the behaviour of other group members.

3. Some consumer characteristics are related to store loyalty, which, in turn is related to brand loyalty.

4. Brand loyalty is positively related to perceived risk and market-structure variables such as the extensiveness of distribution and market share of the dominant brand, but it is inversely related to the number of stores shopped.[119]

MARKETING IMPLICATIONS OF BRAND LOYALTY

Several marketing implications flow from our discussion of brand loyalty. The first question for the marketer attempting to attract more brand-loyal customers is the feasibility of segmenting this group. That is, are these consumers identifiable? As we have just seen from the correlates of brand loyalty, brand-loyal customers generally do not appear to differ significantly from other customers on most segmentation bases. The marketer may be more successful, however, in discerning unique characteristics of customers loyal to his or her particular brand or product. The results of such an analysis may provide useful insights for developing attractive marketing strategies.

Wind has proposed the matrix, presented in Figure 15.5, incorporating attitudes and behaviour by which the marketer may assess the brand's vulnerability. It provides some indication of the magnitude of exposure. In the first two rows, the more the brand is disliked, the greater its vulnerability. In the third row, the greater the brand is liked, the more vulnerable are customers to competitive brands. Of course, the marketer would need to identify the relevant reasons for consumers liking or disliking the brand. With such information, insights may be gained into not only the size of the loyal and vulnerable segments but also the magnitude and nature of customers' vulnerability. Marketing programs may then be developed aimed at reducing buyers' vulnerability while attracting customers of competing brands.[120]

<table>
<tr><td colspan="2"></td><th colspan="3">Attitude toward this brand</th></tr>
<tr><td colspan="2"></td><td>'Like' it</td><td>'Indifferent' to it and others</td><td>'Dislike' it</td></tr>
<tr><th rowspan="3">Purchase pattern with respect to this brand</th><td>Buy it regularly</td><td>'Loyal' to it
1</td><td colspan="2">Customers of this brand who are vulnerable to competitors
2 3</td></tr>
<tr><td>Buy it occasionally</td><td colspan="3">Customers of this brand who are vulnerable to competitors
4 5 6</td></tr>
<tr><td>Do not buy it</td><td colspan="2">Customers of this brand who are vulnerable to competitors.
7 8</td><td>Unlikely target for this brand
9</td></tr>
</table>

FIG. 15.5 The vulnerability matrix Source: Adapted from Yoram Wind, 'Brand Loyalty and Vulnerability', in Arch G. Woodside, Jagdish N. Sheth & Peter D. Bennett (eds), *Consumer and Industrial Buying Behaviour,* North-Holland, New York, 1977, p. 314.

These various goals of the marketer may necessitate different marketing strategies. For instance, increasing brand loyalty of present customers may necessitate better after-sale service, while attracting new customers to become steady users may require certain inducements such as price discounts. Thus, the varying ranges of brand loyalty that the marketer faces point to different competitive actions. For less highly committed consumers, a catchy advertising message, coupon offer, free sample, point-of-purchase display or attractive package could cause a switch to the marketer's brand. This is the reason we see so much of these sorts of activities and resultant brand switching in certain product groups (such as foods, soaps and detergents). The packaged-consumer-goods field can generally be considered highly dynamic in this regard.

In order to induce brand switching among customers who are more loyal, the marketer is likely to require more fundamental changes in consumer perceptions and attitudes. Therefore, significant revisions in product image are often necessary, and are frequently accomplished through revamped promotional programs.

Advertising decisions are usually geared to the loyalty situation that confronts the brand. It is suggested that if brand loyalty is high, the advertiser has a good case for 'investment' expenditures where large amounts are expended over short periods of time to attract new users, because continued purchases after the advertising has been curtailed will 'amortise' the advertising investment. Where a low degree of brand loyalty exists in the product class, advertising expenditures should be made at a fairly steady rate on a pay-as-you-go basis, with demonstrated returns in extra sales equal to or greater than the extra advertising costs.[121]

Frequency marketing approaches seek to increase the yield from the organisation's best customers by developing a long-term, interactive value-added relationship.[122] By concentrating on loyal customers, treating them as individuals and providing them with discounts, free products or services, or simply information (e.g. a newsletter), the firm can solidify the relationship between its brand and these customers.

Finally, it is clear that both retailers and manufacturers need to strive to avoid out-of-stock conditions, which might lead not only to reduced sales but also to less store and brand loyalty.

Impulse purchasing

Impulse buying—or as some marketers prefer to call it, unplanned purchasing—is another consumer purchasing pattern. As the term implies, the purchase was not specifically planned. In this section we will find that the process is rather widespread and may have significant implications for the marketer.

THE NATURE OF IMPULSE PURCHASING

It is difficult for marketers to agree on a definition of impulse buying. Four types of impulse purchases have been cited:

1. *Pure impulse*. A shopper makes a novelty or escape purchase that breaks a normal buying pattern.

2. *Suggestion impulse*. A shopper having no previous knowledge of a product sees the item for the first time and visualises a need for it.

3. *Reminder impulse*. A shopper sees an item and is reminded that the stock at home needs replenishing, or recalls an advertisement or other information about the item and a previous decision to purchase.

4. *Planned impulse*. A shopper enters the store with the expectation and intention of making some purchases on the basis of price specials, coupons and the like.[123]

While most marketing researchers have treated impulse purchasing simply as 'unplanned', some maintain that it is an irrational process in which the urge to gratify an impulse triumphs over the rational parts of the mind.[124] In this view, five critical elements seem to distinguish impulsive from non-impulsive consumer behaviour. First, the consumer has a sudden and spontaneous desire to act, involving a marked divergence from previous behaviour. Secondly, this sudden desire to buy puts the consumer in a state of psychological disequilibrium, where he or she feels temporarily out of control. Thirdly, the consumer may experience psychological conflict and struggle, weighing the immediate satisfaction against the long-term consequences of the purchase. Fourthly, consumers reduce their cognitive evaluation of product features. And, finally, consumers often buy impulsively without any regard for future consequences.

It has been suggested that the explanations of why consumers engage in such impulsive buying are that they do not realise the consequences of their behaviour; that they are compelled by some force to buy even though they realise the dire consequences; and that in spite of the ultimate problems of buying, they are more intent on fulfilling present satisfaction.[125]

How do consumers feel after impulse purchasing? One study indicates that impulse buying is an effective tactic for breaking out of an undesirable mood state such as depression, frustration or boredom. Ninety per cent of respondents felt 'somewhat' to 'extremely' happy after such purchases, indicating a pervasive immediate gratification from it. There was some ambivalence, however, with almost 40 per cent feeling 'somewhat' to 'extremely' guilty over their most recent impulse purchase.[126]

THE EXTENT OF IMPULSE BUYING

Several American studies have indicated the significant and growing trend toward unplanned purchasing. Here are some of the conclusions on the extent of impulse buying:

➡ More than 33 per cent of all purchases in variety stores and drugstores are unplanned.[127]

➡ One-half of buying decisions in supermarkets are unplanned.[128]

➡ Thirty-nine per cent of all department-store shoppers and 62 per cent of all discount-store shoppers purchased at least one item on an unplanned basis.[129]

These statements are somewhat deceiving in that no distinction is made between the various kinds of impulse purchases possible for consumers. Although many consumers may not use a shopping list, their product and brand purchases are certainly rational (as we have defined rationality), and most probably fit into the reminder and planned impulse categories rather than the pure and suggestion impulse types.

The important point for marketers is that there is a large amount of decision making occurring at the point of purchase. Thus, as far as the retail decision maker is concerned, impulse buying can be pragmatically defined as purchasing resulting from a decision to buy after the shopper has entered the store (or perhaps simply turned on their television at home to shop via cable).[130]

FACTORS INFLUENCING IMPULSE PURCHASING

The rather limited amount of research on unplanned purchases indicates that there are several product, marketing and consumer characteristics that appear to be related to the process.

A product that is low in price, fulfils a marginal need, has a short product life, is small in size or light in weight, and is easy to store may be subject to greater impulse purchasing.

Marketing factors influencing impulse purchasing include mass distribution in self-service outlets with mass advertising and point-of-sale materials, and prominent display position and store location.[131]

Few consumer personality, demographic or socioeconomic characteristics have been shown to be related to the rate of impulse buying. However, the percentage of unplanned supermarket purchases appears to increase with: size of the grocery bills; number of products purchased; major shopping trips; frequency of product purchase; absence of a shopping list; and number of years married.[132] Among department store shoppers, age and race may influence the amount of impulse purchasing.[133]

MARKETING IMPLICATIONS

The unplanned nature of much purchasing behaviour today places a greater burden on manufacturers and retailers. The extent to which shoppers buy on impulse and without written lists puts a strong emphasis on the various kinds of in-store merchandising and personal-selling stimuli that the marketer may use.

Managers of retail outlets need to understand the types and extent of occurrence of impulse purchases in order to better plan store layout, merchandise and display location and allocation, and so on. Manufacturers also could benefit from an improved understanding of impulse purchasing by determining how much in-store product information it may be necessary to provide on or with their products.

PAYING FOR THE PURCHASE

There has been a revolution in the way in which people pay for their purchases in the last 20 years. Though cash and personal cheques are still popular, four recent developments have been identified that are linked with the trend to what is termed the 'cashless society'.[134] The automatic teller machine (ATM), electronic funds transfer at point of sale (EFTPOS), telephone banking and prepaid payments cards have joined credit cards to change radically the way we purchase. In 1988 Australian consumers held over 10 million credit and charge cards between them, and by 1993 this had risen to 17 million debt cards on issue, including 3 million Visa cards and 2.8 million Mastercards. Rough figures indicate that by the early 1990s there were approximately 4000 ATM and 10 500 EFTPOS terminals in Australia, together with over 300 different kinds of plastic cards. It is estimated that by the year 2000 approximately 70 per cent of retail transactions will be made by EFTPOS.[135]

Though cash, EFTPOS and cheques predominate, our society is increasingly run on credit. The real growth in the provision of consumer credit has been the introduction of credit cards. The system originated in the United States with companies such as American Express and Diners Club. The original focus was the elimination of bad cheques, security in place of carrying cash and to help with foreign exchange for tourists. In this case, access to credit was limited, as the whole amount had to be repaid at the end of the monthly period. The arrival of revolving credit, with only a minimum payment required each period, changed the access and use of credit dramatically. Credit cards were first introduced to Australia in 1974 when the Australian banks established their own Bankcard system. Since then all major credit cards have become available, and this credit form is also served by building societies, credit unions and retail companies. Chief among the retail companies involved are department stores, petrol companies, automobile clubs and hotel companies. Indeed, in 1989 Coles Myer were the number 2 credit-card provider in Australia. While the trend over the last 20 years has been for a proliferation of different kinds of cards, the forecast is for a rationalisation so that consumers use one multipurpose card for all transactions. The Maestro card launched by Mastercard in 1993 is a development in this direction. The period from 1976 to 1988 saw the proportion of consumer debt increase from 8.5 per cent to 14.1 per cent of household disposable income, and debt per person rise from $807 to $1350. Since then it seems to have remained at a fairly constant plateau, but it is difficult to interpret official figures, which separate housing loans from other personal borrowing. In recent years many banks have developed a single loan facility that allows purchase of major items such as cars and boats on the standard mortgage.[136]

Obviously, marketers must make the arrangement of payment as easy as possible. Retailers have moved to ease the payment decision in numerous ways. For instance, making store checkouts easier facilitates the consumer's payment process. The use of electronic scanners at the point of checkout combined with compatible credit cards should also make the payment decision process easier and quicker. Moreover, retailers generally offer numerous payment alternatives in order to meet consumers' needs. However, care must be exercised with the provision of credit, which is subject to statutory control. This will be discussed further in Chapter 18.

SUMMARY

This chapter began with an explanation of the nature of shopper motives and of the purchasing process, which was found to involve not only the purchase decision but also activities directly associated with the purchase. We then examined the influence of various factors on consumer's store-choice decisions. Factors such as location, store design, merchandise assortment, prices, advertising and sales promotion, personnel and services are all very important influencing variables. Taken together, these and other elements form a store's image to the consumer that is of fundamental importance in store-selection decisions. We also profiled various types of shoppers and discussed the significance and implications of store loyalty.

In-store purchasing behaviour was described in detail. Merchandising techniques and personal-selling efforts were discussed to provide a better understanding of effective techniques that the marketer might utilise.

The situational nature of consumer choice and purchasing decisions was examined. Five situational characteristics surrounding the consumer decision process were described: physical, social, temporal, task and antecedent elements.

Non-store consumer purchasing processes were also discussed. This growing market is expected to have much significance for the marketer as we progress in the electronic era.

Next, we examined two often-used purchasing approaches: brand loyalty and impulse purchases. Both of these have important implications to the marketer and several strategies were suggested.

Finally, the decision of mode of payment was described and seen to be an important part of the purchasing process.

MANAGERIAL REFLECTIONS

For our product or service situation:

1. What personal and social motives seem to be relevant in our consumers' shopping activities?

2. What factors are most important to buyers' store-choice decisions and patronage behaviour?

3. Are we utilising the most effective in-store merchandising techniques to inform and attract shoppers?

4. Are personal-selling efforts carefully planned to succeed with our chosen market target?

5. What circumstances (situational conditions) surrounding the buying decision have a systematic influence on consumers' purchasing process and choice behaviour?

6. What is the nature of non-store purchasing activities among our customers?

7. To what extent have we achieved brand loyalty among buyers, and what is our degree of vulnerability on this dimension?

8. Have we considered consumers' shopping environment for opportunities to influence impulse purchasing?

DISCUSSION TOPICS

1. Describe the types of personal and social motives consumers may have for shopping.

2. How does store image influence consumer purchasing?

3. What implications do the factors of store layout, displays and product shelving have for customer shopping?

4. How may pricing strategies affect consumer purchases?

5. Describe the generic-brand buyer.

6. Describe the five situational characteristics surrounding consumer-behaviour decisions.

7. What do we know about the characteristics and motivations of in-home shoppers?

8. What is the nature and significance of brand loyalty to the marketer?

9. Keep a record of your product purchases for a period of time. How brand loyal are you? What factors seem to explain your degree of brand loyalty? How does your pattern and explanation differ from the patterns and explanations of other students in the class?

REFERENCES

1. Morris B. Holbrook & Elizabeth C. Hirschman, 'The Experiential Aspects of Consumption: Consumer Fantasies, Feelings, and Fun', *Journal of Consumer Research* 9, September 1982, pp. 132–40.
2. Frederick W. Langrehr, 'Retail Shopping Mall Semiotics and Hedonic Consumption', in Rebecca H. Holman & Michael R. Solomon (eds), *Advances in*

Consumer Research, vol. 18, Association for Consumer Research, Provo, UT, 1991, p. 428.

3. Hillary Commission, *'Life in New Zealand Survey'*, Wellington, June 1991.
4. Paul Leinberger, 'Shop-till-you-drops Drop Shopping', *Australian Professional Marketing*, June 1993, p. 42.
5. Neil Shoebridge, 'The News Retailers Didn't Want to Hear', *Business Review Weekly*, 13 August 1993, pp. 65–6.
6. Richard Elliott, 'Shopping Addiction and Mood Repair', in M. Davis (ed.), *Emergency Issues in Marketing*, vol. 1, Proceedings of the 1993 Annual Conference of the Marketing Educators Group, Loughborough University Business School, 1993, pp. 287–96.
7. James U. McNeal & Daryl McKee, 'The Case of Antishoppers', in Robert F. Lusch et al. (eds), *AMA Educators Proceedings*, American Marketing Association, Chicago, 1985, pp. 65–8.
8. Kent B. Monroe & Joseph B. Guiltinan, 'A Path Analytic Exploration of Retail Patronage Influences', *Journal of Consumer Research* 2, June 1975, pp. 19–28.
9. Elizabeth C. Hirschman & Michael K. Mills, 'Sources Shoppers Use to Pick Stores', *Journal of Advertising Research* 20, February 1980, pp. 47–51.
10. C. Samuel Craig, Avijit Ghosh & Sara McLafferty, 'Models of the Retail Location Process: A Review', *Journal of Retailing* 60, Spring 1984, pp. 5–36.
11. William J. Reilly, *Methods for the Study of Retail Relationships*, Research Monograph, no. 4, University of Texas, Bureau of Business Research, Austin, TX, 1929.
12. Paul D. Converse, 'New Laws of Retail Gravitation', *Journal of Marketing* 14, October 1949, pp. 379–84.
13. See, for example, Robert O. Herrmann & Leland L. Beik, 'Shoppers' Movements Outside Their Local Retail Area', *Journal of Marketing* 23, October 1968, pp. 49–51; John R. Thompson, 'Characteristics and Behavior of Outshopping Consumers', *Journal of Retailing* 47, Spring 1971, pp. 70–80; and Fred D. Reynolds & William R. Darden, 'Intermarket Patronage: A Psychographic Study of Consumer Outshoppers', *Journal of Marketing* 36, October 1972, pp. 50–4.
14. See, for example, James R. Lumpkin, Jon M. Hawes & William R. Darden, 'Shopping Patterns of the Rural Consumer: Exploring the Relationship between Shopping Orientations and Outshopping', *Journal of Business Research* 14, 1986, pp. 63–81; and James A. Brunner & John L. Mason, 'The Influence of Driving Time upon Shopping Center Preference', *Journal of Marketing* 31, April 1968, pp. 57–61.
15. William E. Cox Jr & Ernest F. Cooke, 'Other Dimensions Involved in Shopping Center Preference', *Journal of Marketing* 34, October 1970, pp. 12–17.
16. James W. Gentry & Alvin C. Burns, 'How Important Are Evaluative Criteria in Shopping Center Patronage?', *Journal of Retailing* 53, Winter 1977–78, p. 77.
17. David L. Huff, 'A Probabilistic Analysis of Consumer Spatial Behavior', in William S. Decker (ed.), *Emerging Concepts in Marketing*, American Marketing Association, Chicago, 1962, pp. 443–61. See also Art Palmer, 'Survey Discloses Shifts in Shopping Center Choices', *Chain Store Age Executive*, May 1985, pp. 68–78; Art Palmer, 'Retail Image Dimensions and Consumer Preferences', in Naresh K. Malhotra (ed.), *Proceedings*, Academy of Marketing Science, Miami Beach, FL, 1985, pp. 11–15.
18. For a discussion of problem areas in the Huff model, see David L. Huff & Richard R. Batsell, 'Conceptual and Operational Problems with Market Share Models of Consumer Spatial Behavior', in Mary Jane Schlinger (ed.), *Advances in Consumer Research*, vol. 2, Association for Consumer Research, Chicago, 1975, pp. 165–72; and Louis P. Buchin, 'The Concept of Mass in Intra-urban Shopping', *Journal of Marketing* 31, January–February 1958, pp. 37–42.
19. Chow Hou Wee & Michael R. Pearle, 'Patronage Behavior Toward Shopping Areas: A Proposed Model Based on Huff's Model of Retail Gravitation', in E. Hirschman &

M. Holbrook (eds), *Advances in Consumer Research*, vol. 12, Association for Consumer Research, Provo, UT, 1985, pp. 592–7.

20. Robert F. Lusch, 'Integration of Economic Geography and Social Psychological Models of Patronage Behavior', in Kent B. Monroe (ed.), *Advances in Consumer Research*, vol. 8, Association for Consumer Research, Ann Arbor, MI, 1981, pp. 644–7.

21. David A. Gautschi, 'Specification of Patronage Models for Retail Center Choice', *Journal of Marketing Research* 18, May 1981, pp. 162–74.

22. Glen E. Weisbrod, Robert J. Parcells & Clifford Kern, 'A Disaggregate Model for Predicting Shopping Area Market Attraction', *Journal of Retailing*, 60, Spring 1984, pp. 65–83.

23. Jeffrey J. Stoltman, James W. Gentry & Kenneth A. Anglin, 'Shopping Choices: The Case of Mall Choice', in Rebecca H. Holman & Michael R. Solomon (eds), *Advances in Consumer Research*, vol. 18, Association for Consumer Research, Provo, UT, 1991, pp. 434–40.

24. See Pierre Martineau, 'The Personality of the Retail Store', *Harvard Business Review* 36, January–February 1958, pp. 47–55.

25. Jay D. Lindquist, 'Meaning of Image', *Journal of Retailing* 50, Winter 1974–75, p. 31.

26. Meryl Paula Gardner, 'Mood States and Consumer Behavior: A Critical Review', *Journal of Consumer Research* 12, December 1985, pp. 292–3.

27. Robert J. Donovan & John R. Rossiter, 'Store Atmosphere: An Environmental Psychology Approach', *Journal of Retailing* 58, Spring 1982, pp. 34–57.

28. Sevgin A. Eroglu & Karen A. Machleit, 'An Empirical Study of Retail Crowding: Antecedents and Consequences', *Journal of Retailing* 66, Summer 1990, pp. 201–21; A. Eroglu & G. D. Harrell, 'Retail Crowding: Theoretical and Strategic Implications', *Journal of Retailing* 62, Winter 1986, pp. 347–63; and Gilbert D. Harrell, Michael D. Hutt & James C. Anderson, 'Path Analysis of Buyer Behavior under Conditions of Crowding', *Journal of Marketing Research* 17, February 1980, pp. 45–51.

29. Meryl P. Gardner & Ronald P. Hill, 'Consumers Mood States: Antecedents and Consequences of Experiential versus Informational Strategies for Brand Choice', *Psychology and Marketing* 5 (2), 1988, pp. 169–82.

30. Robert J. Donovan & James R. Rossiter, 'Store Atmosphere: An Environmental Psychology Approach', *Journal of Retailing* 58, Spring 1982 pp. 43–57.

31. Ronald E. Miniman, 'Using Music as an Atmospheric Variable to Affect the Behavior of Consumers in Various Retail Environments', in Robert L. King (ed.), *Marketing: Toward the Twenty-first Century*, Southern Marketing Association, Richmond, VA, 1991, pp. 345–50.

32. Cyndee Miller, 'The Right Song in the Air Can Boost Retail Sales', *Marketing News*, 14 February 1991, p. 2; Muzak Limited Partnership, 'Business Music: A Merchandising Tool for the Retail Industry', special report, 1989; and Richard Yalch, 'Effects of Store Music on Shopping Behavior', *Journal of Services Marketing* 4, Winter 1990, pp. 31–9.

33. Wroe Alderson & Robert Sessions, 'Basic Research on Consumer Behavior: Report on a Study of Shopping Behavior and Methods for Its Investigation', in Ronald E. Frank, Alfred A. Kuehn & William F. Massy (eds), *Quantitative Techniques in Marketing Analysis*, Irwin, Homewood, IL, 1962, pp. 129–45.

34. 'Products No Longer Determine the Selection of Retail Outlet', *Marketing News*, 1 April 1991, p. 9.

35. Stuart U. Rich & Bernard D. Portis, 'The "Imageries" of Department Stores', *Journal of Marketing* 28, April 1964, pp. 10–15; and David J. Rachman & Linda J. Kemp, 'Profile of the Discount House Customer', *Journal of Retailing* 39, Summer 1963, pp. 1–8.

36.' Why They Shop Some Centers', *Chain Store Age Executive*, May 1978, pp. 31–5.

37. C. Glenn Walters, *Consumer Behavior: Theory and Practice*, rev. edn, Irwin, Homewood, IL, 1974, p. 425.

38. Leonard L. Berry & Larry G. Gresham, 'Relationship Retailing: Transforming Customers into Clients', *Business Horizons*, November–December 1986, pp. 43–7.

39. Bruce L. Stern, Ronald F. Bush & Joseph F. Hair Jr, 'The Self-image/Store Image Matching Process: An Empirical Test', *Journal of Business* 50, January 1977, pp. 63–9.

40. Martineau, op cit, Ref 24, p. 47.

41. Leonard L. Berry, 'The Components of Department Store Image: A Theoretical and Empirical Analysis', *Journal of Retailing* 45, Spring 1969, p. 89.

42. Gregory P. Stone, 'City Shoppers and Urban Identification: Observations on the Social Psychology of City Life', *American Journal of Sociology* 60, 1954, pp. 36–45. See also William R. Darden & Fred D. Reynolds, 'Shopping Orientations and Product Usage Rates', *Journal of Marketing Research* 8, November 1971, pp. 505–8; Louis E. Boone et al., 'City Shoppers and Urban Identification Revisited', *Journal of Marketing* 38, July 1974, pp. 67–9; P. Ronald Stephenson & Ronald P. Willett, 'Analysis of Consumers' Retail Patronage Strategies', in Philip R. Macdonald (ed.), *Marketing Involvement in Society and the Economy*, American Marketing Association, Chicago, 1969, pp. 316–22; William R. Darden & Dub Ashton, 'Psychographic Profiles of Patronage Preference Groups', *Journal of Retailing* 50, Winter 1974–75, pp. 99–112; and George P. Moschis, 'Shopping Orientations and Consumer Use of Information', *Journal of Retailing* 52 (93), Summer 1976, pp. 61–70.

43. Michael Kieley, 'Relationship Marketing—Buzz Term or Marketing Zen', *Marketing*, March 1994, pp. 25–7; and David James, 'Why One Good Customer Can be Worth Five More', *Business Review Weekly*, 4 June 1993, pp. 85–6.

44. Robert F. Dietrich, 'Know Thy Consumer: A Quiz That Shows How Well You Do', *Progressive Grocer*, March 1975, p. 55; and Michael Kieley, 'Promiscuous Shoppers Aren't Worth Chatting Up', *Marketing*, February 1993, pp. 23–5.

45. Ben M. Enis & Gordon W. Paul, 'Store Loyalty as a Basis for Market Segmentation', *Journal of Retailing* 46, Fall 1970, pp. 42–56; and Fred D. Reynolds, William R. Darden & Warren S. Martin, 'Developing an Image of the Store-loyal Customer', *Journal of Retailing* 50, Winter 1974–75, p. 79.

46. Reynolds, Darden & Martin, ibid, p. 79.

47. Arieh Goldman, 'The Shopping Style Explanation for Store Loyalty', *Journal of Retailing* 53 (94), Winter 1977–78, pp. 33–46.

48. Kiely, op cit, Ref 43, pp. 23–5.

49. Helen Matterson, 'Mass Merchandiser Seeks the Frequent Shopper', *Marketing Magazine*, November 1993.

50. Tony Thomas, 'Grocers Promote Friendly Extras', *Business Review Weekly*, 10 December 1993, p. 48.

51. Francis Buttle, 'Merchandising', *European Journal of Marketing* 18 (6/7), 1984, pp. 104–23.

52. Louis J. Haugh, 'Buying Habits Study Update', *Advertising Age*, 27 June 1977, p. 58.

53. 'Prototypes: A Step Beyond Whimsy', *Chain Store Age Executive*, February 1985, pp. 22–7; and Kevin T. Higgins, 'Supermarket Designs Escape the Straight and Narrow', *Marketing News*, 6 June 1986, pp. 1, 18.

54. 'Consumer Behavior in the Super Market—Part I', *Progressive Grocer*, October 1975, p. 40.

55. Francine Schwadel, 'Kmart Testing "Radar" to Track Shopper Traffic', *Wall Street Journal*, 24 September 1991, pp. B1, B3.

56. POPAI Supermarket Consumer Buying Habits Study, Point-of-purchase Advertising Institute Inc., Fort Lee, NJ, 1987.

57. Howard Stumpf, 'P-O-P State-of-the-art Review', *Marketing Communications*, September 1976, p. 75.

58. 'Awareness, Decision, Purchase, Point-of-Purchase Advertising Institute', New York, 1961, p. 14.

59. 'POP-AV Displays Boost Retail Sales', *Marketing News*, 27 November 1981, pp. 2, 18.
60. Mark Gaynor, 'Displays Alone Increase Sales: Nielsen Data', *P-O-P Times*, November/December 1989, p. 38; and Jean Paul Gagnon & Jane T. Osterhaus, 'Effectiveness of Floor Displays on the Sales of Retail Products', *Journal of Retailing*, Spring 1985, pp. 104–16.
61. 'Agency Forecasts 21st Century In-store Media', *P-O-P Times*, March 1991, p. 32.
62. Ronald C. Curhan, 'Shelf Space Allocation and Profit Maximization in Mass Retailing', *Journal of Marketing* 37, July 1973, p. 56.
63. Curhan, ibid, p. 56.
64. Jo-Ann Zbytniewski, 'Shoppers Cry "Remember the Price"—But Do They Practice What They Screech?', *Progressive Grocer* 59, November 1980, pp. 119–22.
65. Kent Monroe, Christine Powell & Pravat Choudhury, 'Recall Versus Recognition as a Measure of Price Awareness', in R. Lutz (ed.), *Advances in Consumer Research*, vol. 13, Association for Consumer Research, Provo, UT, 1986, pp. 594–9.
66. Jerry Conover, 'The Accuracy of Price Knowledge: Issues in Research Methodology', in R. Lutz (ed.), *Advances in Consumer Research*, vol. 13, Association for Consumer Research, Provo, UT, 1986, pp. 589–93.
67. Peter R. Dickson & Alan G. Sawyer, 'The Price Knowledge and Search of Supermarket Shoppers', *Journal of Marketing* 54, July 1990, pp. 42–53.
68. 'Multiple-pricing Makes the Most of the Moment of Purchase', *Progressive Grocer*, March 1964, p. 128; and 'How Multiple-Unit Pricing Helps...and Hurts', *Progressive Grocer*, June 1971, pp. 52–8.
69. David Litvak, Roger Calantone & Paul Warshaw, 'An Examination of Short-term Retail Grocery Price Effects', *Journal of Retailing* 61, Fall 1985, pp. 9–25.
70. Sunil Gupta, 'Impact of Sales Promotion on When What and How Much to Buy', *Journal of Marketing Research* 25, November 1988, pp. 342–55.
71. V. Kumar & Robert P. Leone, 'Measuring the Effect of Retail Store Promotions on Brand and Store Substitution', *Journal of Marketing Research* 25, May 1988, pp. 178–85.
72. Robert W. Shoemaker, 'An Analysis of Consumer Reactions to Product Promotions', in Neil Beckwith (ed.), *1979 Educator's Conference Proceedings*, American Marketing Association, Chicago, 1979, pp. 244–8; Robert G. Brown, 'Sales Response to Promotions and Advertising', *Journal of Advertising Research* 14, August 1974, pp. 33–9; B. G. Cotton & Emerson M. Babb, 'Consumer Response to Promotional Deals', *Journal of Marketing* 42, July 1978, pp. 109–13; J. A. Dodson, Alice M. Tybout & Brian Sternthal, 'Impact of Deals and Deal Retraction on Brand Switching', *Journal of Marketing Research* 15, February 1978, pp. 72–81; Anthony N. Doob, J. Merall Carlsmith, Jonathan L. Freedman, Thomas K. Landayer & Tom Soleng Jr, 'Effects of Initial Selling Pace on Subsequent Sales', *Journal of Personality and Social Psychology* 11 (4), 1979, pp. 345–50; and Carol A. Scott, 'The Effects of Trial and Incentives on Repeat Purchase Behavior', *Journal of Marketing Research* 13, August 1976, pp. 263–9.
73. William F. Massy & Ronald E. Frank, 'Short-term Pace and Dealing Effects in Selected Market Segments', *Journal of Marketing Research* 2, May 1965, pp. 171–85; Frederick E. Webster Jr, 'The Deal Prone Consumer', *Journal of Marketing Research* 2, May 1965, pp. 186–9; and David B. Montgomery, *Consumer Characteristics and 'Deal' Purchasing*, Marketing Science Institute, Cambridge, MA, 1970.
74. Marvin A. Jolson, Joshua L. Wiener & Richard B. Rosecky, 'Correlates of Rebate Proneness', *Journal of Advertising Research* 27, February–March 1987, pp. 33–43; and Robert C. Blattberg, Thomas Buesing, Peter Peacock & Subrata Sen, 'Identifying the Deal Prone Segment', *Journal of Marketing Research* 15, August 1978, pp. 369–77.
75. J. N. Uhl, 'Cents-off Coupons: Boon or Boondoggle for Consumers?', *The Journal of Consumer Affairs* 16, Summer 1982, p. 162.

76. I. Teinowitz, 'Coupons Gain Favor With US Shoppers', *Advertising Age*, 14 November 1988, p. 64.
77. Richard P. Bagozzi, Hans Baumgartner & Youjae Yi, 'Coupon Usage and the Theory of Reasoned Action', in Rebecca H. Holman & Michael R. Solomon (eds), *Advances in Consumer Research*, vol. 18, Association for Consumer Research, Provo, UT, 1991, pp. 24–7.
78. Caroline Henderson, 'Modeling the Coupon Redemption Decision', in E. Hirschman & M. Holbrook (eds.), *Advances in Consumer Research*, vol. 12, Association for Consumer Research, Provo, UT, 1985, pp. 138–43.
79. 'Promotions in Advertising Contribute to Brand Identity', *Marketing News*, 7 June 1985, p. 16.
80. K. C. Blair, 'Coupon Design, Delivery Vehicle, Target Market Affect Conversion Rate: Research', *Marketing News*, 28 May 1982, pp. 1–2.
81. Kapil Bawa & Robert W. Shoemaker, 'Analyzing Incremental Sales from a Direct Mail Coupon Promotion', *Journal of Marketing* 53, July 1989, pp. 66–78; and 'How Coupon Promotions Can Affect Sales', *Wall Street Journal*, 25 September 1980, p. 31.
82. Donald R. Lichtenstein, Richard G. Netemeyer & Scot Burton, 'Distinguishing Coupon Proneness from Value Consciousness: An Acquisition-Transaction Utility Theory Perspective', *Journal of Marketing* 54, July 1990, pp. 54–67.
83. Louis J. Haugh, 'How Coupons Measure Up', *Advertising Age*, 8 June 1981, p. 58.
84. Linda L. Pace, Lawrence F. Feick & Audrey Guskey-Federouch, 'Couponing Behaviors of the Market Maven: Profile of a Super Couponer', in Michael J. Houston (ed.), *Advances in Consumer Research*, vol. 15, Association for Consumer Research, Provo, UT, 1988, pp. 354–9.
85. Mark Landler, 'What Happened to Advertising', *Business Weekly*, 23 September 1991, pp. 66–72.
86. Adapted from Richard Guillat, 'Marlboro Man Loses His Swagger', *Business Review Weekly*, 23 April 1993, p. 52.
87. Chip Walker, 'What's in a Name?', *American Demographics*, February 1991, pp. 54–7; Joseph A. Bellizzi, Harry F. Krueckeberg, John R. Hamilton & Warren S. Martin, 'Consumer Perceptions of National, Private, and Generic Brands', *Journal of Retailing* 57, Winter 1981, pp. 56–70; Dennis Rosen, 'Consumer Perceptions of Quality for Generic Grocery Products: A comparison across Product categories', *Journal of Retailing* 60, Winter 1984, pp. 64–80; and Amy Dunkin, 'No-Frills Products: An Idea Whose Time Has Gone', *Business Week*, 17 June 1985, pp. 64–5.
88. Neil Shoebridge, 'House Brands Make Themselves a Name', *Business Review Weekly*, 14 May 1993, pp. 72–73.
89. Jim L. Parks, 'Generics', in *Supermarkets*, A. C. Nielsen Company, Northbrook, IL, 1980, p. 2.
90. David M. Szymansh & Paul S. Busch, 'Identifying the Generics-prone Consumer: A Meta-analysis', *Journal of Marketing Research* 24, November 1987, pp. 425–31; Neil Shoebridge, *Business Review Weekly*, pp. 72–3; T. J. Sullivan, 'Generic Products in Supermarkets', *The Melsen Researcher* (3), 1979, p. 3; Roger A. Strang, Brian F. Harris & Allan L. Hernandez, 'Consumer Trial of Generic Products in Supermarkets: An Exploratory Study', in Neil Beckwith (ed.), *1979 Educators Conference Proceedings*, American Marketing Association, Chicago, 1979, pp. 386–8; Dub Ashton & Larry Anvik, 'Generic Product Purchasers: A Discriminant Analysis', in Robert S. Franz, Robert M. Hopkins & Alfred G. Toma (eds), *Proceedings: Southern Marketing Association 1979 Conference*, Southern Marketing Association, Lafayette, LA, 1979, pp. 234–7; Kent L. Granzin, 'An Investigation of the Market for Generic Products', *Journal of Retailing* 57, Winter 1981, pp. 39–55.
91. Irene Thorelli, 'Dyadic Interaction: A Theory of Interpersonal Compatibility', in P. Thistlethwaite, D. Billingsly & J. Berens (eds), *Proceedings*, Midwest Marketing Association, Macomb, IL, 1985, pp. 249–54; and Franklin B. Evans, *Dyadic*

Interaction in Selling: A New Approach, Graduate School of Business, University of Chicago, Chicago, IL, 1964 p. 25.

92. Michael Solomon, Carol Surprenant, John Czepiel & Evelyn Gutman, 'A Role Theory Perspective on Dyadic Interactions: The Service Encounter', *Journal of Marketing* 49, Winter 1985, pp. 99–111.

93. Russell W. Belk, 'Situational Variables and Consumer Behavior', *Journal of Consumer Research* 2, December 1975, p. 158.

94. Belk, *Journal of Consumer Research*, p. 149.

95. For a summary of these research efforts, see James H. Leigh & Claude R. Martin Jr, 'A Review of Situational Influence Paradigms and Research', in Ben M. Enis & Kenneth J. Roering (eds), *Review of Marketing, 1981*, American Marketing Association, Chicago, 1981, pp. 57–74.

96. Edgar A. Pessemier, 'Pretesting New Merchandising Strategies', in William R. Darden & Robert F. Lusch (eds), *Patronage Behavior and Retail Management*, North-Holland, New York, 1983, pp. 129–40.

97. Jeffrey J. Stoltman, James W. Gentry, Kenneth A. Anglin & Alvin C. Burns, 'Situational Influences on the Consumer Decision Sequence', *Journal of Business Research* 21, 1990, pp. 195–207.

98. Keith Clarke & Russell W. Belk, 'The Effects of Product Involvement and Task Definition on Anticipated Consumer Effort', in William L. Wilhe (ed.), *Advances in Consumer Research*, vol. 6, Association for Consumer Research, Ann Arbor, MI, 1979, pp. 313–18.

99. Don Porritt, 'What Retail Revolution?', *Australian Professional Marketing*, November 1993, pp. 23, 32.

100. Neil Shoebridge, 'Sony Lays Foundations for a Brave New World', *Business Review Weekly*, 16 April 1993, pp. 66–9;

101. Neil Shoebridge, 'Small Operator Plans a Home-shopping Empire', *Business Review Weekly*, 8 October 1993, pp. 68–70.

102. Neil Shoebridge, 'The Idiot Box Gets Smart', *Business Review Weekly*, 22 October 1993, pp. 24–30.

103. Richard Guilliatt, 'Future Shock Hits the Music Store', *Business Review Weekly*, 15 October 1993, pp. 68–70; and Tony Crease, 'New Consumers Welcome Brave New Techno-world', *Marketing*, April 1993, pp. 26–9.

104. Larly J. Rosenberg & Elizabeth C. Hirschman, 'Retailing without Stores', *Harvard Business Review* 58, July/August 1980, p. 105.

105. George Moschis, Jac Goldstucker & Thomas Stanley, 'At Home Shopping: Will Consumers Let Their Computers Do the Walking?', *Business Horizons* 28, March–April 1985, pp. 22–9.

106. 'Research on New Video Technologies', *Marketing News*, 29 May 1981, p. 1, published by the American Marketing Association.

107. 'Paper Foresees Radical Changes in Stores after 2000', *P-O-P Times*, May 1991, p. 59.

108. Robert A. Peterson, Gerald Albaum & Nancy M. Ridgway, 'Consumers Who Buy from Direct Sales Companies', *Journal of Retailing* 65, Summer 1989, pp. 273–86.

109. *A Look Before We Leap into the 1980s*, Ogilvy & Mather, Direct Response Inc., New York, 1979, p. 28.

110. Thomas Exter, 'Looking for Brand Loyalty', *American Demographics*, April 1986, pp. 32–3, 52–6.

111. S. P. Raj, 'Striking a Balance between Brand "Popularity" and Brand Loyalty', *Journal of Marketing* 49, Winter 1985, pp. 53–9.

112. 'Food in the AM', *Time*, 31 March 1980, p. 53.

113. 'Big Ticket Buyers Seek Fulfilment Not Utility', *Advertising Age* 4 July 1977, p. 3.

114. Paul Leinberger, 'Make Way for the New Realists', *Australian Professional Marketing*, December/January 1992/93, p. 47.

115. Anne B. Fisher, 'Coke's Brand-loyalty Lesson', *Fortune*, 5 August 1985, p. 46.
116. George H. Brown, 'Brand Loyalty—Fact or Fiction?', *Advertising Age*, 26 January 1953, p. 75.
117. See, for example, Ross M. Cunningham, 'Brand Loyalty—What, Where, How Much?', *Harvard Business Review* 34, January–February 1956, pp. 116–28; Lester Guest, 'A Study of Brand Loyalty', *Journal of Applied Psychology* 28, 1944, pp. 16–27; Lester Guest, 'Brand Loyalty—Twelve Years Later', *Journal of Applied Psychology* 39, 1955, pp. 405–8; and Lester Guest, 'Brand Loyalty Revisited: A Twenty-year Report', *Journal of Applied Psychology* 48, 1964, pp. 93–7.
118. Jacob Jacoby & Robert W. Chestnut, *Brand Loyalty: Measurement and Management*, Wiley, New York, 1978, pp. 80–1.
119. James F. Engel & Roger D. Blackwell, *Consumer Behavior*, 4th edn, The Dryden Press, New York, 1982, pp. 577–8.
120. Yoram Wind, 'Brand Loyalty and Vulnerability', in Arch G. Woodside, Jagdish N. Sheth & Peter D. Bennett (eds), *Consumer and Industrial Buying Behavior*, North-Holland, New York, 1977, pp. 313–19.
121. Brown, op cit, Ref 116, p. 76.
122. Richard Barlow, *Colloquy*, July 1990, p. 2.
123. Hawkins Stern, 'The Significance of Impulse Buying Today', *Journal of Marketing* 26, April 1962, pp. 59–60.
124. Dennis W. Rook, 'The Buying Impulse', *Journal of Consumer Research* 14, September 1987, pp. 189–99.
125. Dennis W. Rook & Stephen J. Hoch, 'Consuming Impulses', in E. Hirschman & M. Holbrook (eds), *Advances in Consumer Research*, vol. 12, Association for Consumer Research, Provo, UT, 1985, pp. 23–7; and Vic Pollard, '"Impulse Shoppers" Say Shoes, Candy Call Out to Them', *News Star World*, 27 April 1986, p. 20.
126. Meryl P. Gardner & Dennis Rook, 'Effects of Impulse Purchase on Consumers' Affective States', in Michael J. Houston (ed.), *Advances in Consumer Research*, vol. 15, Association for Consumer Research, Provo, UT, 1988, pp. 127–30.
127. Vernon T. Clover, 'Relative Importance of Impulse Buying in Retail Stores', *Journal of Marketing* 15, July 1950, pp. 66–70.
128. *Consumer Buying Habits Studies*, E. I. Du Pont de Nemours and Co., Wilmington, DE, 1965.
129. V. Kanti Prasad, 'Unplanned Buying in Two Retail Settings', *Journal of Retailing* 51, Fall 1975, pp. 3–12.
130. Frances Piron, 'Defining Impulse Purchasing', in Rebecca H. Holman & Michael R. Solomon (eds), *Advances in Consumer Research*, vol. 18, Association for Consumer Research, Provo, UT, 1991, pp. 509–14; and Danny N. Bellenger, Dan H. Robertson & Elizabeth C. Hirschman, 'Impulse Buying Varies by Product', *Journal of Advertising Research* 18, December 1978, p. 17.
131. Stern, op cit, Ref 123, pp. 61–2.
132. David T. Kollat, 'A Decision-process Approach to Impulse Purchasing', in Raymond M. Haas (ed.), *Science, Technology, and Marketing*, American Marketing Association, Chicago, 1966, pp. 626–39.
133. Bellenger, Robertson & Hirschman, *Journal of Advertising Research*, pp. 15–18.
134. Wolfgang C. Fischer & Andrew Massey, *Consumer Credit in North Queensland*, Department of Economics Research Monograph, James Cook University, Townsville, 1994, pp. 96–9.
135. Margaret Roberts, *The Credit Trap, Help for the Financially Overcommitted*, Netley, 1991; and Neil Shoebridge, 'Plastic Money War Extends its Front', *Business Review Weekly*, 2 April 1993, pp. 74–6.
136. Fischer & Massey, op cit, Ref 134, pp. 42–52.

CHAPTER 16

POSTPURCHASE BEHAVIOUR

LEARNING OBJECTIVES

AFTER STUDYING THIS CHAPTER YOU SHOULD UNDERSTAND:

➡ what additional behaviour by consumers may occur beyond the purchase decision;

➡ the nature of consumers' postpurchase evaluation process;

➡ the factors influencing consumers' decisions to dispose of products.

Marketers must recognise that consumer decisions do not end with the act of purchase, but continue as the consumer uses the product and evaluates his or her purchase decision and experience with the item, and possibly makes related purchases. In this chapter we shall examine the nature of consumer postpurchase behaviour. We will first discuss the types of behaviour that may be exhibited as a result of, and related to, the purchase. Next, the concept of postpurchase evaluation and the significant implications it holds for marketing strategy will be examined. Finally, the topic of consumer product disposition is discussed along with marketing implications.

BEHAVIOUR RELATED TO THE PURCHASE

Once the consumer makes a decision to purchase a product, there can be several types of additional behaviour associated with that decision. Two activities are of primary importance: decisions on the product's installation and use; and decisions on products or services related to the item purchased.

Decisions on product set-up and use

All consumers who have purchased consumer durables are familiar with the need to have their product set up or installed ready for use. Many durables, such as televisions, stereos, furniture, washing machines and air-conditioners, necessitate some set-up in order for them to be properly used. Even apparently simple products can be very complicated and frustrating in their set-up processes. For example, many parents can tell Christmas Eve horror stories about all-night exercises in 'simple assembly' of products for their children.

Of course, another element of product set-up and use concerns instructions given to the buyer for assembly and operation of the item. Products such as cars, calculators and microwave ovens may require detailed explanations as to methods of operation. In order to ensure buyer satisfaction such brochures (even books for some products) must be carefully developed to provide sufficient instructions. Finally, warranty information covering buyer protection in case of product failure should be provided to purchasers. This is an increasingly significant element in today's high-tech environment.

Decisions on related products or services

It often happens that a buyer of one item becomes a candidate for all sorts of options and related products or services. For example, Ford's Extended Service Plan, which is a service contract, is promoted to new-car buyers. As another illustration, consider a 35-mm-camera buyer who may become interested in numerous optional lenses, a camera bag, dust brush, filters, a slide projector and trays, photo-developing equipment, and even photography lessons. In fact, many retailers have learned that the big profits are often in the optional extras that a consumer purchases, rather than in the original product itself. As a result, for example, many camera retailers sell 35 mm cameras close to cost or as a loss leader in order to draw customers into the store and sell accessories on which the mark-up runs much higher. Similarly, a camping enthusiast may begin with a tent and buy a wide range of related products such as a stove, lantern, sleeping bag and backpack.

Marketing implications

Some very important marketing implications flow from these consumer postpurchase decisions.

PRODUCT SET-UP AND USE

One set of implications flows from decisions on product set-up and use. Three topics are relevant here: providing information and assistance; understanding the user's consumption system; and decisions about warranties.

PROVIDING INFORMATION AND ASSISTANCE   If the consumer purchases a major durable good such as a large-screen television, stove or washing machine from a full-service retailer, the store would ordinarily be required to carefully install or set up the product and explain its operation to the user. If the purchase is made in a self-service or warehouse environment, the consumer might assume the delivery and installation function. Nevertheless, there might still be an important need for the store to explain to the customer proper installation and operation of the product. Unless such activities are conscientiously undertaken, consumer dis-satisfaction is likely to result, and the consequence of consumer dissatisfaction, as we have seen in Chapter 8, is likely to be poor word-of-mouth communications about the product, the retailer or both. Thus, manufacturers need to select retail-ers carefully as members of their distribution team who will provide the kind of quality after-sale installation or warranty service that will enhance the manufac-turer's image. The retailer needs to have regard for after-sale service for the same reasons—it can be an important factor in generating a favourable image and repeat customers.

The importance of information on product set-up and use becomes even more critical in today's self-service economy. Consumers are buying many complicated products from self-service discount outlets, which may offer very little product knowledge or installation assistance. As a result, they must rely almost exclusively on whatever literature comes with the product. Such a situation provides an added impetus for manufacturers to assess their product literature and make sure it is readable and understandable. Consumers who fail to follow instructions with their microwave ovens are likely to blame the manufacturer rather than themselves.

UNDERSTANDING THE USER'S CONSUMPTION SYSTEM   Even more fundamental than the provision of information to consumers is the marketer's need to under-stand how his or her product is used by the consumer, not only to make improvements in its quality and functions, but also to suggest new uses for it. If marketers were to research more thoroughly the use-environment and behav-iour of their products prior to full-scale launching, we would undoubtedly see products more carefully attuned to consumers' lifestyles, and therefore fewer failures.

It is also important for the marketer to understand the user's consumption system; that is, the manner in which consumers perform the total task of what-ever they are trying to accomplish when using the product, whether it is washing clothes or cooking a meal.[1] By understanding how this product (let's say a wash-ing machine) fits in with other products (such as an iron and detergents) in terms of consumption behaviour, the marketer may be able to identify new marketing opportunities. Once a manufacturer understands how consumers use their prod-uct, they can then use the information to promote the product further, as in the Golden Circle advertisement.

DECISIONS ABOUT WARRANTIES   A related factor concerning product set-up and use has to do with the product or service warranty, which is a promise by the manufacturer or seller that the product or service is free from defects in

materials and workmanship, and that problems will be corrected if failure occurs during the warranty period. An effective warranty can offer several consumer benefits, including the following:

1. assurance of product service quality and value;

2. increased self-confidence about correctness of product/service choice;

3. Reduced feelings of risk of ownership because of return or refund privileges;

4. Reduced dissonance because of warranty assurance of quality.[2]

Today marketers are using warranties more as a competitive offensive weapon than as a defensive tool. Table 16.1 shows how the two approaches differ in thrust.

TABLE 16.1   Designing a warranty program: two approaches

Strategy	Offensive: maximise profits	Defensive: limit liability and costs
Warranty type	Replacement/repair	Pro rata
Warranty length	Long	Short
Warranty breadth	Broad	Narrow
Product scope	Holds true for all items	Only for some items in the product line
Market scope	Worldwide	Limited by country, state and channel
Coverage	Parts, labour, and some consequential damages	Parts only
Conditions	Loose	Strict

Source: Melvyn A. J. Menezes & John A. Quelch, 'Leverage Your Warranty Program', *Sloan Management Review* 31, Summer 1990, p. 73.

A properly administered warranty program should:

1. use simple, clear and easy-to-understand warranty wording;

2. encourage customers to use the warranty;

3. clarify who will execute the program and what standards must be met;

4. handle claims expeditiously and flexibly;

5. collect, analyse and use warranty information;

6. constantly monitor consumer and dealer response to invoking warranty;

7. promptly reimburse dealers or agents for warranty work;

8. monitor and control costs.[3]

Warranties have the potential to influence consumers significantly. For example, when launching a new high-performance brand, a strong warranty can have a positive effect on product evaluations.[4] When competition is tough, guarantees can be a powerful marketing tool to differentiate a company. Numerous companies have taken to heart the idea that they have to stand behind their products and services. Guarantees of satisfaction are being combined with the growing use of toll-free and FreeCall numbers by companies such as Demtel in Australia. One study found that a high percentage of consumers associate the availability of a toll-free number with quality products. Moreover, use of toll-free numbers to register complaints can boost consumer loyalty, and this loyalty is increased dramatically when consumers' complaints are addressed. A customer who complains and is satisfied will tell eight people; but if the experience is negative, the customer will tell twice as many people.[5]

If warranties or guarantees are used, they will be most potent when the following conditions exist for a product or service:

1. The price of the product or service is high.

2. Customers' egos are heavily involved.

3. Customers' expertise is low.

4. The negative consequences of failure are great.

5. The industry has a bad image for quality.

6. The company depends on frequent customer repurchases.

7. The company's business is strongly affected by word-of-mouth.[6]

RELATED PRODUCTS AND SERVICES

A second factor for the marketer to consider with regard to postpurchase activities concerns buyers' interests in related products and services. This is another area of potential profit that should be actively cultivated. An example of successful product linking is illustrated by a major oil company that, when replacing a customer's stolen credit card, distributes a flier offering a 'pick-pocket-proof wallet' for sale.

Because buyers may become interested in related items, they need to be made aware of the potential products that exist. Thus, literature enclosed with a product could present other products in the line. Camera manufacturers do an excellent job of presenting their full line of attachments and accessories in this way. Also, appliance manufacturers frequently feature a number of their major appliances in one advertisement, because the buyer who purchases a washing machine may soon be interested in a matching clothes drier. It is known, for instance, that there is an underlying common order of acquisition for many durables. Thus, marketers of these as well as non-durable goods might cultivate the potential products that exist by linking products together.[7] Another example of this practice in Australia is the packing of Finish automatic dishwashing rinse in certain makes of automatic dishwashers. Buyers of these appliances may be very susceptible to brand switching at this time. Consequently, new customers may be gained through such sampling.

In order to capitalise on the sales potential of related items, many marketers have diversified their operations. In Australia, for example, Gillette sell razors, shaving cream, hair spray and deodorants; while petrol companies now stock much more than petrol in their service stations. Thus, the marketer's task is to determine what product mix is most appropriate to the firm. This is largely a function of applying the marketing concept to identify products that may be related in nature and can be effectively marketed.

POSTPURCHASE EVALUATION

In addition to the overt types of behaviour that result from purchase, the consumer also engages in an evaluation of the purchase decision. Because consumers are uncertain of the wisdom of their decisions, they rethink their decisions in the postpurchase stage. This stage serves several functions. First, it serves to broaden the consumer's set of experiences stored in memory. Secondly, it provides a check on how well the consumer is doing in selecting products, stores and so on. Thirdly, the feedback received from this stage helps the consumer to make adjustments in future purchasing strategies.

Consumer satisfaction/dissatisfaction

Satisfaction is an important element in the evaluation stage. *Satisfaction* refers to the buyer's state of being adequately rewarded in a buying situation for the sacrifice he or she has made. *Adequacy* of satisfaction is a result of matching actual past purchase and consumption experience with the expected reward from the brand in terms of its anticipated potential to satisfy the consumer's motives.[8] Figure 16.1 presents a diagram of the process.

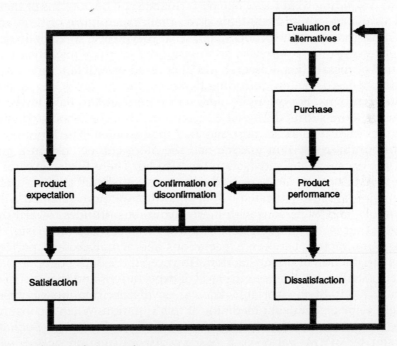

FIG. 16.1   The purchase evaluation process

The concept of satisfaction is one about which there are presently few agreed-upon definitions or approaches to measurement.[9] Nevertheless, Hunt has summarised the concept in the following statement:

*Satisfaction is a kind of stepping away from an experience and evaluating it ...
One could have a pleasurable experience that caused dissatisfaction because
even though pleasurable, it wasn't as pleasurable as it was supposed or
expected to be. So satisfaction/dissatisfaction isn't an emotion, it's the
evaluation of an emotion.*[10]

Consumers form certain expectations prior to the purchase. These expectations may be about:

1. the nature and performance of the product or service (i.e. the anticipated benefits to be derived directly from the item);

2. the cost and effort to be expended before obtaining the direct product or service benefits;

3. the social benefit or cost accruing to the consumer as a result of the purchase (i.e. the anticipated impact of the purchase on significant others).[11]

Advertising may often be an important factor influencing these expectations, as we shall see later. Consumers may have a variety of product-performance expectations, including what they hope performance will be in terms of their ideal level, what would be fair and equitable given their expenditure of time and money in obtaining and using the product, and what they expect to actually occur.

Once consumers purchase and use a product, they may then become either satisfied or dissatisfied. Research has uncovered several determinants that appear to influence satisfaction, including demographic variables, personality variables and expectations. For example, older consumers tend to have lower expectations and to be more satisfied. Higher education tends to be associated with lower satisfaction. Men tend to be more satisfied than women. The more confidence one has in purchase decision making and the more competence in a given product area, the greater one's satisfaction tends to be. There is also greater satisfaction when relevant others are perceived to be more satisfied.[12] Higher levels of product satisfaction are also indicated by persons who are more satisfied with their lives as a whole, and by persons with more favourable attitudes toward the consumer domain; that is, the marketplace, business firms and consumerism.[13]

The interaction between expectations and actual product performance produces satisfaction or dissatisfaction. However, there does not appear to be merely a direct relationship between the level of expectations and the level of satisfaction. Instead, a modifying variable known as 'disconfirmation of expectations' is thought to be a significant mediator of this situation. When a consumer does not get what is expected, the situation is one of disconfirmation. Such disconfirmation can be of two varieties: a *positive* disconfirmation occurs when what is received is better than expected; and a *negative* disconfirmation occurs when things turn out worse than anticipated. Thus, any situation in which the consumer's judgment is proven wrong is a disconfirmation.[14] Confirmation occurs if the expectations of performance are met. Consumers' expectations from a product, as well as whether those expectations are met, are strong determinants, then, of satisfaction. Although the cognitive dimension of postpurchase evaluation has been stressed here, it is important to recognise that consumers' emotional experiences in connection with product ownership and usage are also important. These positive affective responses need to be stimulated by marketers in the postpurchase period in order to enhance consumers' satisfaction and possibly favourable word-of-mouth communication.[15]

The emotional context in which product failure occurs may affect consumers' subsequent information processing. Research on the satisfaction/ dissatisfaction process has led to the proposition that disconfirmation is mediated by attributional processing in which consumers seek to understand why products fail.[16] Consumers seek to know three features about the causes of a problem:

1. stability (i.e. is it temporary or permanent?);

2. locus (i.e. is the problem with the consumer or the company?);

3. controllability (i.e. is the problem within or outside the control of someone?).[17]

Research also indicates that attributions can lead to specific types of emotional reactions.[18] For instance, if consumers felt a product problem were preventable by the company, they might be expected to be rather angry. It also appears that the consumer's mood prior to product failure can influence later cognitive and affective reactions.[19] For example, if a consumer is in an angry mood because of the day's events prior to ordering a meal in a restaurant, he or she is liable to engage in greater attribution processing over a poor meal being served than if he or she were not in a bad mood. Emotional context, therefore, interacts with disconfirmation to affect attribution, which results in certain emotions influencing satisfaction or dissatisfaction.

The result of satisfaction to the consumer from the purchase of a product or service is that more-favourable postpurchase attitudes, higher purchase intentions and brand loyalty are likely to be exhibited. That is, the same behaviour is likely to be exhibited in a similar purchasing situation. Thus, as long as positive reinforcement takes place, the consumer will tend to continue to purchase the same brand. It is true, however, that consumers will sometimes not follow these established patterns but will purchase differently simply for the sake of novelty.[20] For example, research in both the United States and New Zealand shows how only 40 per cent of new-car buyers who profess themselves satisfied actually repurchase the same model of car.

Consumer complaint behaviour

What happens when consumers experience dissatisfaction? There are several negative outcomes possible.[21] Consumers may exhibit unfavourable word-of-mouth communication; that is, they tell others about their problem. In fact, studies show that customers tell twice as many people about bad experiences as they tell about good ones. Such behaviour can severely damage a company's image.

Consumers may also not repurchase the brand. Those who are not fully satisfied with a brand are less likely to repurchase it than are satisfied buyers. Another course of action for the consumer is to complain. A summary of research on dissatisfied consumers in New Zealand across a wide variety of products and services, except fast-moving packaged goods, gave the following results:

➡ 48 per cent of people complain;

➡ the average person tells nine others about a negative experience;

➡ 7 per cent of dissatisfied people tell over 20 other people;

➡ 53 per cent of complainants make a point of taking their business elsewhere;

➡ 27 per cent just quietly switch.[22]

Such statistics emphasise three important points. First, organisations cannot rely on simply measuring complaints in order to monitor dissatisfaction. Secondly, they emphasise how people are likely to change suppliers and, finally, they demonstrate the pervasive nature of negative word-of-mouth.

Being prepared to complain is something that has come to Australian and New Zealand consumers in the last few years. Previously they were fairly docile compared with their counterparts in Europe and North America, and were prepared to put up with wide variations in the quality of products and services. The *1993 Australian Social Monitor* shows that 72 per cent of Australians now believe consumers should not hesitate to complain to retailers or to manufacturers, and that most people believe they will get some worthwhile response from making a complaint. The number of people who believe that it is a waste of time complaining in terms of a positive result fell from 51 per cent in 1992 to 41 per cent in 1993. The *Australian Professional Marketer*, April 1994, shows several generalisations exist from research on consumer complaining:

1. Complainers tend to be members of more up-scale socioeconomic groups than do non-complainers.

2. The severity of the dissatisfaction or problems is positively related to complaint behaviour.

3. Complaining is more likely when there is a more positive perception of retailer responsiveness to customer complaints.[23]

A model of consumer complaining behaviour (CCB) is shown in Figure 16.2. It illustrates the variety of actions possible. For instance, consumers may complain, not to the seller, but to some formal third parties such as the Department of Consumer Affairs, a newspaper or the legal system. Or they may engage in private CCB actions, such as telling friends and relatives about the bad experience and changing their own patronage behaviour. Alternatively, they may voice their complaints to the manufacturer or retailer involved, or they may take no action even when dissatisfied if they are loyal to the seller or believe complaining is pointless.

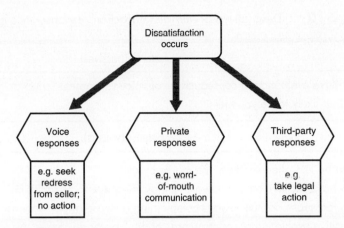

FIG. 16.2   Possible CCB responses   Source: Jagdip Singh, 'Consumer Complaint Intentions and Behavior: Definitional and Taxonomical Issues', *Journal of Marketing* 52, January 1988, p. 101, published by the American Marketing Association.

Along similar lines, one researcher classified dissatisfied consumers into four groupings based on the way they communicate their dissatisfaction: passives, voicers, irates and activists. The choice of a response style exhibited by consumers is determined by episode-specific variables (such as the probability of obtaining redress, the costs and benefits from complaint actions, and the nature of dissatisfying service) and personality variables (such as prior experiences, alienation and attitudes toward complaining). It could be that a consumer may consistently use the same response style in different dissatisfaction contexts over time.[24] Table 16.2 presents characteristics of individuals for the four response styles. These style differences imply that retailers could:

1. assess the distribution of the four groups among their customers over time to see how they are doing;

2. institute programs so as to make the voicer style a more attractive option, compared with other styles;

3. focus on corrective strategies for customer alienation because it undermines retailer loyalty and tends to lead to irates and activists.

TABLE 16.2   Descriptions of four dissatisfaction-response-style groups

Cluster 1 (passives)
Likely to be less alienated from the marketplace
Tend to have less positive attitude toward complaining due to its social benefits
Tend to feel less positive toward complaining because of personal norms
Less positive evaluation of consequences of third-party responses
Less positive evaluation of consequences of private responses

continues

TABLE 16.2 Descriptions of four dissatisfaction-response-style groups *continued*

Cluster 1 (passives)

Less positive evaluation of consequences of voice responses
Somewhat likely to be younger

Cluster 2 (voicers)

Likely to be less alienated from the marketplace
Tend to have positive attitude toward complaining due to its social benefits
Tend to feel more positive toward complaining because of personal norms
Less positive evaluation of consequences of third-party responses
Less positive evaluation of consequences of private responses
Very positive evaluation of consequences of voice responses
Somewhat likely to be older

Cluster 3 (irates)

Likely to be more alienated from the marketplace
Tend to have positive attitude toward complaining due to its social benefits
Tend to feel more positive toward complaining because of personal norms
Less positive evaluation of consequences of third-party responses
Very positive evaluation of consequences of private responses
Somewhat positive evaluation of voice consequences
Somewhat likely to be older

Cluster 4 (activists)

Likely to be more alienated from the marketplace
Tend to have very positive attitude toward complaining due to its social benefits
Tend to feel very positive toward complaining because of personal norms
Very positive evaluation of consequences of third-party responses
Very positive evaluation of consequences of private responses
Very positive evaluation of voice consequences
Somewhat likely to be younger

Source: Jagdip Singh, 'A Typology of Consumer Dissatisfaction Response Styles', *Journal of Retailing*, Spring 1990, p. 88.

It is important for marketers to realise that complaints are actually opportunities.[25] Simply listening to complaints tremendously boosts brand loyalty. The key is getting buyers to complain to the company rather than telling the typical nine or 10 people about their problem. But for everyone who complains, there are 26 others who feel the same way but do not voice a complaint.

Two factors deter consumers from complaining to the company. First, it is hard because our culture does not encourage being a whiner. Secondly, employees don't encourage it because they view it as a personal attack on their self-esteem. Nevertheless, when companies invest money on units that handle complaints and inquiries, the average return is over 100 per cent for makers of certain consumer durables. Thus, such companies as GE, Coca-Cola and British Airways are investing millions of dollars to improve complaint handling. Programs include toll-free and FreeCall number telephone systems, intensive staff training, liberal refund policies and even booths where irate customers can complain on videotape.[26]

Auto manufacturers are designing elaborate training procedures and operations manuals for dealership customer-service managers in an effort to help dealers win back dissatisfied customers. Nissan have found, for example, that as many as 20 per cent of customers said they would not buy from the same dealership after only six months of ownership. But when dissatisfied customers are allowed to complain to the dealer or manufacturer, nearly 20 per cent of them change their minds and buy from that dealership again. Another study found that 54 per cent of dissatisfied customers who feel that their complaints have been solved will buy from the offending dealer again.[27]

Postpurchase dissonance

As we learned in Chapter 12, consumers may become dissonant over a purchase decision. Cognitive dissonance occurs as a result of a discrepancy between a consumer's decision and the consumer's prior evaluation. Consider the illustration in Chapter 12 of the Nikon camera buyer who encounters some problems. This is a typical situation leading to postpurchase dissonance. Dissonance theory was derived from two basic principles: that dissonance is uncomfortable and will motivate the person to reduce it; and that individuals experiencing dissonance will avoid situations that produce more dissonance.

Let us examine this concept more closely to see what factors lead to dissonance, how the consumer deals with the conflict and what marketing implications are embodied in the concept.

CONDITIONS LEADING TO DISSONANCE

From a review of research findings on cognitive dissonance, it appears that dissonance is likely to occur under the following conditions:[28]

1. A minimum threshold of dissonance tolerance is passed. That is, consumers may tolerate a certain level of inconsistency in their lives until this point is reached.

2. The action is irrevocable. For instance, when a consumer purchases a new car, there is little likelihood of reversing this decision and getting the money back.

3. Unselected alternatives have desirable features. In our camera example earlier, the Pentax, Canon and Minolta (brands not selected) all had attractive features.

4. There are several desirable alternatives. Today's car buyer, for example, has an abundance of choices among similar attractive models. In fact, research indicates that those consumers who experience greater difficulty in making purchase decisions, or who consider a wider range of store and brand options, are more likely to experience greater magnitudes of postpurchase dissonance.[29]

5. Available alternatives are quite dissimilar in their qualities (there is little 'cognitive overlap'). For instance, although there are many automobile models, each one may have some unique characteristics.

6. The buyer is committed to a decision because it has psychological significance. A large and important living-room-furniture purchase is likely to have great psychological significance to the buyer because of its dramatic reflection of the buyer's decorating tastes, philosophy and lifestyle. Ego involvement will be quite high.

7. There is no pressure applied to the consumer to make the decision. If consumers *are* subjected to outside pressure, they will do what they are forced to do without letting their own viewpoints or preferences really be challenged. In other words, when pressure is applied, consumers will externalise the source of their dissatisfaction rather than allowing any mental unease or discomfort regarding their own cognition.

DISSONANCE REDUCTION

There are several major ways in which consumers strive to reduce dissonance. They may change their evaluation of the alternative, seek new information to support their choice or change their attitude.

CHANGING PRODUCT EVALUATIONS   One of the ways consumers seek to reduce dissonance is to re-evaluate product alternatives. This is accomplished by the consumers' enhancing the attributes of the products selected while decreasing the importance of the unselected products' attributes. That is, consumers seek to polarise alternatives in order to reduce their dissonance.[30]

Another approach to reducing dissonance is for the consumer to re-evaluate product alternatives to view them as being more alike than was thought at the purchase stage; that is, to establish or imagine that cognitive overlap exists. If the alternatives are viewed as essentially the same, it makes little difference which one is chosen; hence, little dissonance would be experienced.

In addition, selective retention may operate to allow the consumer to forget positive features of the unselected alternative and negative features of the chosen product, while remembering negative attributes of the unchosen item along with favourable features of the chosen alternative.

SEEKING NEW INFORMATION   A second way consumers may reduce dissonance is by seeking additional information in order to confirm the wisdom of their product choice. For example, rural Australian consumers of agricultural chemicals experience a high level of dissonance due to a high level of involvement accompanied by a high level of product complexity and few detectable differences between brands. According to dissonance theory, dissonant individuals would be expected actively to avoid information that would tend to increase their dissonance and seek information supporting their decision. Resellers of agricultural chemicals, then, must provide this information to the rural consumers in order to decrease dissonance and guarantee repeat purchasing. However, the resellers find this difficult due to the lack of information (either good or bad) provided to them by the manufacturers. It seems reasonable to assume that consumers would seek out advertisements for products they have purchased and tend to avoid competing ads. Research on this topic, however, has failed to support this hypothesis. Although it is widely documented that consumers experiencing dissonance do seek additional information, there is no evidence to substantiate either a general preference by consumers for supportive over non-supportive information or a greater information-seeking/ avoidance tendency by high-dissonance consumers. Consumers sometimes seek consonant information to support their choice, sometimes seek discrepant information to refute it, and sometimes look merely for useful information, no matter what the content. It appears to depend on the amount of information gathered before the decision and whether consumers perceive that they have made a wise choice. Thus, if consumers gather much evidence before purchase to support their decision and if they strongly believe they made a wise selection, they will feel free to seek out exposure to discrepant as well as consonant information.[31]

This Qantas advertisement has an important role to play reassuring travellers, as well as convincing them to fly Qantas in the first place COURTESY OF QANTAS AIRWAYS

Unfortunately, the research findings in this area have numerous methodological problems, so at present it cannot be concluded that dissonance factors have any effect on the consumer's postpurchase information-seeking behaviour.[32] Nevertheless, the fact that individuals do engage in selective exposure to marketing information and may at the same time be experiencing dissonance does have some implications for the marketing manager; these will be examined shortly.

CHANGING ATTITUDES   As a result of dissonance, consumers may change their attitudes to make them consonant with their behaviour. For example, when the marketer secures a new-product trial among target customers who initially have an unfavourable attitude toward the item (let's say they purchased it because of a coupon offer, or were given a free sample), this situation is likely to produce dissonance. That is, unfavourable attitudes toward the product are inconsistent with the behaviour of product trial. Motivation to achieve consonance will likely take the form of attitude change, because that is easier than renouncing the purchase and returning the product. By re-evaluating the product and adopting a positive attitude toward it, attitudes and behaviour are now consistent and consonance is achieved.

MARKETING IMPLICATIONS

There are several marketing implications that arise from our discussion of cognitive dissonance. Most of these suggestions relate to the promotional variable.

CONFIRMING EXPECTATIONS   When the purchase confirms the consumer's expectations, reinforcement takes place. When expectations are not confirmed, however, cognitive inconsistency develops and the consumer will likely reduce the dissonance by evaluating the product (or store) somewhat negatively. Thus, where a product fails to measure up to the consumer's expectations or guidelines for evaluation, the result may be no initial sale no repeat sale or unfavourable word-of-mouth communication.[33]

It is important, therefore, for the product to confirm expectations. Similarly, it is imperative that the marketer not build up expectations unrealistically. Marketers should first design products that will fulfil consumers' expectations in so far as possible. As science and technology advance, people come to expect fewer technical deficiencies in products. These expectations may be set unrealistically high, with resultant dissatisfaction when they are not fulfilled, as when the product breaks down for some reason. In order to reduce this occurrence products should be carefully developed with the consumer in mind. A clear understanding of how the product will be used and how it fits into the consumer's lifestyle is necessary. Thus, to prevent cognitive dissonance from arising, marketers would be well advised not to create unrealistic expectations in the minds of consumers.

Much of the advertising done today may appear to be harmless exaggeration or puffery, but it may be contributing unwittingly to less satisfaction on the part of buyers. Promotions that promise more than products can possibly deliver may be destined for problems. As a result, disconfirmed customers can spread unfavourable word-of-mouth communications and refuse to purchase the item again.

How can the advertiser counter this potential problem? One way is to develop promotions that are consistent with what the product can reasonably deliver. Sometimes this may go as far as producing a two-sided appeal in which not only are positive product attributes mentioned, but also some of the brand's deficiencies are cited. In the early 1980s the New Zealand Kiwifruit Marketing Authority ran a successful campaign in Australia based around the line 'Ugly is only skin deep'. Research had indicated that some consumers found the fruit visually unappealing. The advertising did not attempt to change this perception, but acknowledged the fact and attempted to reduce its importance in relation to other attributes of kiwifruit.

Because customer satisfaction is one of the major indicators of excellent quality in companies, it is important that marketers conduct an audit or review of this component as well as the more traditional quality-control approaches conducted by production and operation experts. Unless companies know what their customers actually think about their efforts to please them, they will not be able to focus their efforts for best results. Thus, companies should take regular measurements of the quality of their products and services as perceived by customers. With services, for example, companies and institutions in Australia, such as accounting firms and hospitals, conduct research to find out the difference between customers' perceived quality of their products and their ideal product quality. Hospitals are using these results to improve the overall quality of their services and reduce costs that are ultimately passed on to the taxpayers. In New Zealand, each year since the mid 1980s the major car companies buy into a syndicated survey of new-car buyers. This survey asks people about their levels of satisfaction with different aspects of the car, the dealers and complete purchasing and usage of the vehicle. Such a large-scale survey focusing on satisfied as well as unsatisfied product users might yield several important types of information:

➡ areas for improvement of the physical product;

➡ ideas for promotional copy to create favourable attitudes toward the firm's brand;

➡ promotional copy illustrating why the firm's brand is better, based on competitive product failures;

➡ guidelines for developing warranties or other kinds of guarantees.[34]

A key feature emerging from studies is that the attributes that give rise to most satisfaction tend to be different in nature from those causing dissatisfaction. It has been proposed that a similar distinction arises with products, as Herzberg, Mauser and Snyderman first described in studies on the motivation to work. They proposed that two sets of factors existed: one, called *motivators*, actually encouraged people to work harder; and the others, termed *hygiene factors*, caused dissatisfaction if performance did not reach certain acceptable levels.[35] With products, these attributes have been termed *expressive* and *instrumental*. If we consider clothing as an example, it is argued that features that give increased satisfaction include fashion, styling and sex appeal, which all contribute towards the goals that individuals may have in enhancing their self-images. The instrumental characteristics, which are predominantly associated with dissatisfaction, are the functional aspects, such as washability, colour fastness or crease-resistance.[36] Analysis of overseas visitors to New Zealand in the 1980s showed a similar dichotomy. Responses to questions about what tourists like are dominated by attributes such as scenery and the people. These are the motivators, or the expressive attributes. Dissatisfaction was caused by instrumental features such as shop opening hours and the poor state of public conveniences.[37] The key factor is that such attributes perform up to the expectations of consumers in order to avoid dissatisfaction. Performance over and above expectations may not result in any extra satisfaction that is salient to consumers' overall evaluations of their consumption experiences. A consumer's real happiness comes when an organisation surpasses expectations on the expressive attributes of a product. A further consequence of these findings is that they emphasise the potential importance of non-compensatory decision rules as opposed to the compensatory approach, as discussed in Chapter 14.

INDUCING ATTITUDE CHANGE   We saw earlier that when attitudes are inconsistent with purchase behaviour, they are likely to change. Consequently, the marketer may seek to induce behaviour changes in consumers through various means. Promotional tools including free samples and cents-off coupons are frequently used by the marketer to accomplish this. By offering these deals, the marketer may entice consumers to try the item and as a result adopt the product or switch brands. However, the size and nature of the inducements should be carefully considered.

There is some evidence that the smaller the incentive, the greater the consumer's dissonance and the greater the attitude change.[38] That is, a small inducement may cause the consumer to reflect on all the aspects of the purchase decision, including any pre-existing preferences. A large inducement may not have the same effect, because the consumer will explain the change in behaviour more simply by referring to the size of the bribe. Therefore, a coupon worth 25c off on an item may produce more attitude change than one for 50c off.

In the case of free samples, however, acceptance of the brand may never take place because consumers could fail to expose themselves fully to attitude change from use of the sample. Thus, there may very well be an optimum value range over which promotional techniques produce the desired attitude and behaviour change; beyond that point (either too low or too high) they may be relatively ineffective.

REINFORCING BUYERS   Although it has not been proved that one reason consumers engage in postpurchase information-seeking behaviour is to reduce dissonance, it may nevertheless be the prudent marketing approach to proceed on this supposition. Such an approach may pay handsome dividends to the company undertaking some promotion aimed at new buyers. It could be especially important in the case of a company launching an innovation.

The marketer may not have to develop special ads aimed at new buyers. Much of the regular advertising may be sufficient to reinforce buyers about their decision. In Australia the Cold Power laundry detergent television commercial, where the man is attempting to fade his jeans by repeated washings, is an excellent illustration of this approach. The ad is innovative enough to interest new buyers, but also conveys a feeling of satisfaction among present Cold Power users. Nevertheless, if a sufficient advertising budget can be mustered, some ads specifically designed to reduce dissonance among buyers could be developed. Besides, the marketer may find that the kind of advertisement designed to attract customers may not be very effective in reducing dissonance among present buyers. Thus, ads more specifically tailored to reinforce recent buyers may be necessary. Ford, for instance, for this reason have aimed certain advertisements specifically at new buyers.[39]

There are many illustrations of marketing strategies that appear to be logical approaches to reducing dissonance, in spite of the lack of substantiation in the published literature. For example, the marketer should supply sufficient dealer literature, which could provide new buyers with reinforcement. Moreover, instruction manuals should not only tell how to install and operate the product properly but also seek to convince the buyer of the wisdom of the selection. Information about warranties, guarantees, and where and how to secure service should help reduce postpurchase dissonance. These materials should be packed with the product. In addition, some firms spend huge sums to promote the availability and quality of their after-sale service in order to forestall dissonance.

Manufacturers and retailers may inaugurate correspondence with the new buyer as part of a dissonance-reducing campaign. For instance, car companies publish magazines that are sent to new-car buyers, telling them how to gain more enjoyment from their purchase. Some car dealerships provide a postpurchase videotape that shows consumers how to use their new car, but also reassures them about their decision. One car manufacturer has found that personal contact from the dealership in the form of phone calls, letters, flowers and gifts can not only reduce dissonance, but also increase the probability of that customer's repeat purchase from that car dealer or manufacturer. Manufacturers have also discovered that the timing and type of dealer contact can be manipulated to increase the probability of repeat purchase even more. Retailers have also learned that postpurchase messages to buyers can be beneficial. One study found that individuals receiving post-transaction letters from a retailer reinforcing their purchase decision experienced less dissonance.[40] Another study found that automobile buyers who received favourable postpurchase reinforcement from car salespeople had significantly lower back-out or cancellation rates.[41] Thus, marketers may develop several effective informational programs aimed at reducing cognitive dissonance in buyers.

PRODUCT DISPOSITION

A final topic of interest concerns the disposition of what the consumer has purchased. Most of the consumer-behaviour literature has ignored this subject. However, it is important from a public policy perspective as well as from a marketing management orientation to better understand how consumers make disposition decisions for a product.

Disposition alternatives and determinants

There are various alternatives for disposing of a product. These are diagrammed in Figure 16.3. In addition, the method of disposition may vary considerably across products. For example, while bicycles tend to be given away, this is not true of phonograph records, which are usually thrown away or stored.

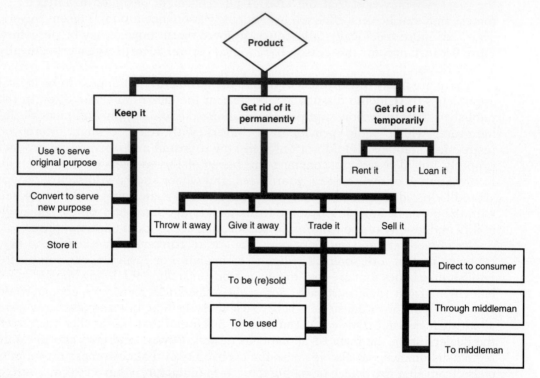

FIG. 16.3   Product-disposition alternatives   Source: Jacob Jacoby, Carol K. Berning & Thomas F. Dietvorst, 'What about Disposition?', *Journal of Marketing* 41, April 1977, p. 23, published by the American Marketing Association.

At present little is known about the factors that influence the disposition choice made by the consumer. The following categories of factors have been suggested, however:[42]

1. *Psychological characteristics of the decision maker.* Personality, attitudes, emotions, perception, learning, creativity, intelligence, social class, level of risk tolerance, peer pressure, social conscience and so on. Although consumer demographic variables have not proved to be very enlightening in understanding disposition behaviour, lifestyle factors have proved to be moderately useful.[43]

2. *Factors intrinsic to the product.* Condition, age, size, style, value, colour, power source of the product, technological innovations, adaptability, reliability, durability, initial cost, replacement cost and so on.[44]

3. *Situational factors extrinsic to the product*. Finances, storage space, urgency, fashion changes, circumstances of acquisition (gift versus purchase), functional use, economics (demand and supply), legal considerations (giving to avoid taxes) and so on.

Disposal of products often occurs in connection with the changing roles of consumers. As role transition occurs, consumers may dispose of their possessions in order to facilitate or validate both role and status changes, thus enhancing and solidifying their new self-concepts and social-role identities. Some of the role transitions consumers may encounter are leaving parents, graduating, taking a job, marrying, having children, moving, divorcing, changing jobs and retiring. These role transitions represent changes in the plays, parts, scripts and props in our lives. Disposal of products facilitates our movements to new plays, parts, scripts and props, and allows us to enact new roles.[45]

It has been suggested, too, that consumer product disposition is actually a process involving the steps of problem recognition, search and evaluation, disposition decision and postdisposition outcomes.[46]

It is interesting for the marketer to speculate, using these reference frames, on the various possibilities for consumer product disposition, as in the following situation:

Consider a wristwatch that still runs but is no longer stylish. The consumer is faced with a first-level decision: keep it, get rid of it permanently or get rid of it temporarily. Assume that he decides to keep it because of his thriftiness (psychological characteristic). He could also decide to keep it because, although it is not stylish, it is still very reliable (product characteristic) or because he has no money for another one (situational factor). At some later time the old watch is again brought to mind. He may decide to get rid of it permanently this time, because his status needs are no longer met by the watch (psychological characteristics), the band is worn (product characteristic), and/or he has too many old watches in his dresser drawer (situational factor). At the second level, he may decide to give it away to a charitable institution so that he can claim a tax deduction.[47]

Marketing implications

The implications of the consumer product-disposition process reflect on several areas of marketing. There are implications from a public-policy perspective as well as from a strategy perspective. The public-policy effects of disposition are many. For example, the effects of disposition choice on the environment include the long-run effects of a throwaway lifestyle, the resources wasted when an item is discarded and the resource depleted when it is replaced.[48] Thus, a study of the many problems of polluting and littering could be better addressed by considering consumer disposition.[49]

Habits of throwing away and littering might be changed by providing consumers with information about possible product uses or conversions (e.g. having an automobile-body shop inexpensively spraypaint a refrigerator so that it will fit in with new decor). In addition, inappropriate disposition decisions might be discouraged through educational activities designed to change basic attitudes and values. More recycling centres might be established and consumers made aware of the significance of these centres for their own well-being.

Consumer disposition can influence a company's marketing strategy in several dimensions. First, marketers may have to become more involved in facilitating consumers' disposition processes if buyers are not to become discouraged and withdraw from the purchasing process. For instance, old products must often be disposed of before new ones can be purchased. This might be due to the need for money with which to make a down payment on the new item, or it could be that a lack of storage space for both the old and new product dictates its disposal.

Secondly, forecasting sales of new products will have to take into account stocks of used goods that may also be on the market. For example, publishers and authors do not receive any income from college textbooks after the initial sale. The large used-book market for college texts, in which old books are bought and then resold, makes sales and income forecasting difficult for books in a publisher's line and substantially reduces the market for new titles.[50]

Thirdly, the marketer can effectively use information on consumer disposition decisions in developing promotion strategy. For example, the marketer may learn the reason that consumers acquire new products even though their old ones are still performing satisfactorily (such as the new product has better features or fits better with perceived self-images). Identification of reasons such as these and their relative incidence by product can provide marketing and advertising managers with information useful for developing promotional strategies.[51]

SUMMARY

This chapter examined the postpurchase stage of consumer behaviour. Postpurchase behaviour refers to those behaviours exhibited after the purchase decision. Consumers often make some important decisions related to the purchase, including installation and purchase of other related items.

We discussed the concepts of consumer expectations, satisfaction, postpurchase dissonance and the feedback mechanism in the postpurchase evaluation stage. Satisfaction was seen to be an essential ingredient of this stage and one that determines future purchasing behaviour.

Postpurchase or cognitive dissonance occurs as a result of a discrepancy between a consumer's decision and his or her prior evaluation. The conditions leading to dissonance were discussed, as well as ways in which consumers attempt to reduce dissonance. Because of methodological and conceptual limitations of dissonance research studies, definite statements about the applicability of dissonance theory to consumer behaviour are difficult to make. Nevertheless, the evidence is substantially in favour of it (except, as noted, with regard to postpurchase information-seeking behaviour). Marketing implications of cognitive dissonance were explored in order to suggest numerous ways in which promotional strategies could be used to offset dissonance and achieve a more favourable evaluation of the marketer's brand.

Product-disposition behaviour was seen to be an important element of the postpurchase process and yet one that is not well understood. A framework of disposition alternatives was described and several factors influencing it were discussed. Finally, marketing-strategy and public-policy implications of product disposition were cited.

MANAGERIAL REFLECTIONS

For our product or service situation:

1. What patterns of postpurchase behaviour are engaged in by our customers as they make decisions on such factors as product installation and use, and related items for purchase?

2. To what extent are our customers satisfied or dissatisfied?

3. How significant is postpurchase dissonance for our buyers and what strategies are in place for controlling it?

4. How do buyers dispose of the item and are there significant managerial or public-policy implications to such disposition?

DISCUSSION TOPICS

1. Why should the marketer be concerned with postpurchase behaviour?

2. Discuss the concept of satisfaction/dissatisfaction.

3. What is postpurchase dissonance, and what conditions lead to it?

4. How do consumers reduce cognitive dissonance?

5. Why should the marketer be concerned about consumer expectations in purchasing? What strategy implications are there in connection with expectation confirmation?

6. How can marketers reinforce buyers after the purchase?

7. Develop a questionnaire to measure consumer satisfaction/dissatisfaction with a durable good (such as a car, computer or stereo system) purchased

within the last year. Survey 10 students who bought that item and determine their level of satisfaction. What action was taken to resolve dissatisfaction? Discuss any marketing implications.

8. Select a consumer durable good and survey 10 people to determine their disposition behaviour. What is the significance of your findings to marketers of that product and to public-policy formulation?

REFERENCES

1. Harper W. Boyd Jr & Sidney J. Levy, 'New Dimension in Consumer Analysis', *Harvard Business Review* 41, November—December 1963, pp. 129–40.
2. James U. McNeal & Richard T. Hise, 'An Examination of the Absence of Written Warranties on Routinely Purchased Supermarket Items', *Akron Business and Economic Review*, Fall 1986, p. 21.
3. Mervyn A. J. Menezes & John A. Quelch, 'Leverage Your Warranty Program', *Sloan Management Review* 31, Summer 1990, pp. 77–9.
4. Daniel E. Innis & H. Rao Unnava, 'The Usefulness of Product Warranties for Reputable and New Brands', in Rebecca H. Holman & Michael R. Solomon (eds), *Advances in Consumer Research*, vol. 18, Association for Consumer Research, Provo, UT, 1991, pp. 317–22.
5. Karen Singer, 'Marketing's New Watchword: "Satisfaction Guaranteed"', *Adweek's Marketing Week*, 2 November 1987, p. 59.
6. Christopher W. L. Hart, 'The Power of Unconditional Service Guarantees', *Harvard Business Review*, July—August 1988, p. 60.
7. Jack Kasulis, Robert F. Lusch & Edward F. Stafford Jr, 'Consumer Acquisition Patterns for Durable Goods', *Journal of Consumer Research* 6, June 1979, pp. 47–57.
8. John A. Howard & Jagdish N. Sheth, *The Theory of Buyer Behavior*, Wiley, New York, 1969, p. 145.
9. Sunil Erevelles & Lawrence S. Lockshin, 'The Development of the Concept of Consumer Satisfaction in Marketing Thought', in Robert L. King (ed.), *Marketing: Toward the Twenty-First Century*, Southern Marketing Association, Richmond, VA, 1991, pp. 406–14.
10. H. Keith Hunt, 'CS/D—Overview and Future Research Directions', in H. Keith Hunt (ed.), *Conceptualization and Measurement of Consumer Satisfaction and Dissatisfaction*, Marketing Science Institute, Boston, 1977, pp. 459–60.
11. Ralph L. Day, 'Toward a Process Model of Consumer Satisfaction', in Hunt (ed.), pp. 163–7.
12. Gerald Linda, 'New Research Works on Consumer Satisfaction/Dissatisfaction Model', *Marketing News*, 21 September 1979, p. 8.
13. Robert A. Westbrook, 'Intrapersonal Affective Influences on Consumer Satisfaction with Products', *Journal of Consumer Research* 7, June 1980, pp. 49–54.
14. See the following for examples of research on disconfirmation: Richard L. Oliver & John E. Swan, 'Consumer Perceptions of Interpersonal Equity and Satisfaction in Transactions: A Field Survey Approach', *Journal of Marketing* 52, April 1989, pp. 21–35; Richard L. Oliver & Wayne S. DeSarbo, 'Response Determinants in Satisfaction Judgments', *Journal of Consumer Research* 14, March 1988, pp. 495–507; David K. Tse & Peter C. Wilton, 'Models of Consumer Satisfaction Formation: An Extension', *Journal of Marketing Research* 25, May 1988, pp. 204–12; Ernest R. Cadotte, Robert B. Woodruff & Roger L. Jenkins, 'Expectations and Norms in Models of Consumer Satisfaction', *Journal of Marketing Research* 24, August 1987,

pp. 305–14; Robert B. Woodruff, Ernest R. Cadotte & Roger L. Jenkins, 'Modeling Consumer Satisfaction Processes Using Experience-based Norms', *Journal of Marketing Research* 20, August 1983, pp. 296–304; Priscilla A. La Barbera & David Mazursky, 'A Longitudinal Assessment of Consumer Satisfaction/Dissatisfaction: The Dynamic Aspect of the Cognitive Process', *Journal of Marketing Research* 20, November 1983, pp. 393–404; William O. Bearden & Jesse E. Teele, 'Selected Determinants of Customer Satisfaction and Complaint Reports', *Journal of Marketing Research* 20, February 1983, pp. 21–8; Gilbert A. Churchill Jr & Carol Surprenant, 'An Investigation into the Determinants of Customer Satisfaction', *Journal of Marketing Research* 16, November 1982, pp. 491–504; Richard L. Oliver, 'A Cognitive Model of the Antecedents and Consequences of Satisfaction Decisions', *Journal of Marketing Research* 17, November 1980, pp. 460–9; Richard W. Olshavsky & John A. Miller, 'Consumer Expectations, Product Performance, and Perceived Product Quality', *Journal of Marketing Research* 9, February 1972, pp. 19–21; Rolph E. Anderson, 'Consumer Dissatisfaction: The Effect of Disconfirmed Expectancy on Perceived Product Performance', *Journal of Marketing Research* 10, February 1973, pp. 38–94; and Richard L. Oliver, 'Effect of Expectation and Disconfirmation on Postexposure Product Evaluations: An Alternative Interpretation', *Journal of Applied Psychology* 62, August 1977, pp. 480–6.

15. Robert A. Westbrook, 'Product/Consumption-based Affective Responses and Postpurchase Processes', *Journal of Marketing Research* 24, August 1987, pp. 258–70.
16. Jagdip Singh, 'Consumer Complaint Intentions and Behavior: Definitional and Taxonomical Issues', *Journal of Marketing* 52, January 1988, pp. 93–107.
17. Bernard Weiner, *Human Motivation*, Holt, Rinehart & Winston, New York, 1980.
18. Valerie S. Folkes, 'Consumer Reactions to Product Failure: An Attributional Approach', *Journal of Consumer Research* 10, March 1984, pp. 398–409.
19. Lalita A. Manrai & Meryl P. Gardner, 'The Influence of Affect on Attributions for Product Failure', in Rebecca H. Holman & Michael R. Solomon (eds), *Advances in Consumer Research*, vol. 18, Association for Consumer Research, Provo, UT, 1991, pp. 249–54.
20. M. Venkatesan, 'Cognitive Consistency and Novelty Seeking', in Scott Ward & Thomas S. Robertson (eds), *Consumer Behavior: Theoretical Sources*, Prentice-Hall, Englewood Cliffs, NJ, 1973, pp. 354–84.
21. Diane Halstead & Cornelia Droge, 'Consumer Attitudes toward Complaining and the Prediction of Multiple Complaint Responses', in Rebecca H. Holman & Michael R. Solomon (eds), *Advances in Consumer Research*, vol. 18, Association for Consumer Research, Provo, UT, 1991, pp. 210–16.
22. 'Tracking Customer Behaviour', *Marketing Magazine*, August 1993, p. 37; and Don Porritt, 'The Dynamics for Market Survival', *Australian Professional Marketing*, April 1994, pp. 34–5.
23. Marsha L. Richins, 'Negative Word-of-mouth by Dissatisfied Consumers: A Pilot Study', *Journal of Marketing* 47, Winter 1983, pp. 68–78.
24. Jagdip Singh, 'A Typology of Consumer Dissatisfaction Response Styles', *Journal of Retailing* 66, Spring 1990, pp. 57–99.
25. Jerry Plymire, 'Complaints as Opportunities', *Journal of Services Marketing* 5, Winter 1991, pp. 61–5.
26. Patricia Sellers, 'How to Handle Customers' Gripes', *Fortune*, 24 October 1988, p. 89.
27. Richard Thompson, 'The XYZs of CSI', *Automotive Executive*, November 1989, p. 32.
28. James F. Engel & Roger D. Blackwell, *Consumer Behavior*, 4th edn, The Dryden Press, New York, 1982.
29. Michael B. Menasco & Del I. Hawkins, 'A Field Test of the Relationship between Cognitive Dissonance and State Anxiety', *Journal of Marketing Research* 15, November 1978, pp. 650–5.
30. See William H. Cummings & M. Vankatesan, 'Cognitive Dissonance and Consumer

Behavior: A Review of the Evidence', in Mary Jane Schlinger (ed.), *Advances in Consumer Research*, 2nd edn, Association for Consumer Research, Chicago, 1975, pp. 21–31; and Leonard A. LoSciuto & Robert Perloff, 'Influence of Product Preference on Dissonance Reduction', *Journal of Marketing Research* 4, August 1967, pp. 286–90.

31. Engel & Blackwell, op cit, Ref 28, p. 507.
32. Cummings & Venkatesan, in *Advances in Consumer Research*, pp. 21–31. Also see William H. Cummings & M. Venkatesan, 'Cognitive Dissonance and Consumer Behavior: A Review of the Evidence', *Journal of Marketing Research* 13, August 1976, pp. 303–8, for a review of the methodological problems.
33. Richard N. Cardozo, 'An Experimental Study of Customer Effort, Expectation, and Satisfaction', *Journal of Marketing Research* 2, August 1965, pp. 244–9.
34. John E. Swan & Linda Jones Combs, 'Product Performance and Consumer Satisfaction: A New Concept, *Journal of Marketing* 40, April 1976, p. 33.
35. F. Herzberg, B. Mausner & B. Snyderman, *The Motivation to Work*, Wiley, 1959.
36. M. S. Ryan, *Clothing: A Study in Human Behaviour*, Holt, Rinehart and Winston, 1966.
37. Rob Lawson, 'Consumer Satisfaction: Motivation Factors and Hygiene Factors', *Marketing Discussion Papers*, No. 5, University of Otago, 1991.
38. Thomas S. Robertson, *Consumer Behavior*, Scott, Forestman; Glenview, IL, 1970, p. 58.
39. George H. Brown, 'The Automobile Buying Decision within the Family', in Nelson N. Foote (ed.), *Household Decision-making*, New York University Press, New York, 1961, pp. 193–9.
40. Shelby D. Hunt, 'Post-transaction Communications and Dissonance Reduction', *Journal of Marketing* 34, July 1970, pp. 46–51.
41. James H. Donnelly Jr & John M. Ivancevich, 'Post-purchase Reinforcement and Back-out Behavior', *Journal of Marketing Research* 7, August 1970, pp. 399–400.
42. Jacob Jacoby, Carol K. Berning & Thomas F. Dietvorst, 'What about Disposition?', *Journal of Marketing* 41, April 1977, p. 26.
43. Marian Burke, W. David Conn & Richard J. Lutz, 'Using Psychographic Variables to Investigate Product Disposition Behavior', in Subhash C. Jain (ed.), *Research Frontiers in Marketing: Dialogues and Directions*, American Marketing Association, Chicago, 1976, pp. 321–6.
44. M. DeBell & R. Dardis, 'Extending Product Life: Technology Isn't the Only Issue', in William Wilkie (ed.), *Advances in Consumer Research*, vol. 6. Association for Consumer Research, Ann Arbor, MI, 1979, pp. 381–5.
45. Melissa M. Young, 'Disposition of Possessions during Role Transitions', in Rebecca H. Holman & Michael R. Solomon (eds), *Advances in Consumer Research*, vol. 18, Association for Consumer Research, Provo, UT, 1991, pp. 33–9.
46. James W. Hanson, 'A Proposed Paradigm for Consumer Product Disposition Processes', *Journal of Consumer Affairs* 14, Summer 1980, pp. 49–67.
47. Jacoby, Berning & Dietvorst, op cit, Ref 42, pp. 26–7.
48. Burke, Conn & Lutz, op cit, Ref 43, p. 321.
49. Hanson, op cit, Ref 46, pp. 64–5.
50. Del I. Hawkins, Kenneth A. Coney & Roger J. Best, *Consumer Behavior: Implications for Marketing Strategy*, Business Publications Inc., Dallas, 1980, p. 503.
51. Jacoby, Berning & Dietvorst, op cit, Ref 42, p. 26.

CASE STUDIES

CASE 1   MOBIL OIL NEW ZEALAND

The last decade has seen a major change in the role of the service station in many countries. Whereas once the service station was where we got our mechanical repairs done and the petrol or diesel, the changing shopping patterns of consumers and competition between the oil companies have meant that consumers are demanding more, and consequently service stations are delivering more. Increasingly hectic lifestyles mean that consumers request more convenience in many different aspects of their lives.

In New Zealand Mobil were facing increasing competition from the other oil companies, who were gaining larger amounts of the market share. Mobil realised that if they didn't change their strategy, they were going to be left behind.

To counter these problems, Mobil set up a task force to prepare a strategy document. The first task was to undertake some market research: What did the customer want? What was the competition doing? What was happening in the environment? The major feedback from the consumers was that they wanted convenience, service, location and variety. They did not want to have to travel far to find a service station, the garage should be open when they needed it, the garage should stock a wide variety of products so that the customer could do one-stop shopping and the customers wanted quality service.

This, along with the changing environment of increased competition and rapidly developing technologies, meant that Mobil had to embark on a major overhaul of their marketing strategy. Mobil were already behind the competition in improving their marketing strategy, and so they had to move fast and make their service superior to that of the competition to try to regain lost market share.

First, many of the small local garages were closed down and replaced by large eight-to-15-pump stations. These service stations have easy access and parking for non-fuel customers, are easy to see in the distance (easy to locate) and very user friendly. The service stations now carry a wide range of food and consumer products along with the range of mechanical parts that is to be expected. Many of the service stations, especially those on main arterial routes and state highways, are open 24 hours. This means that the service stations attract not only fuel-seeking consumers but also those who want cash from an EFT-POS, or a snack late at night when dairies are closed. Corporate uniforms were introduced for staff along with higher quality training to improve the standard of service.

Now Mobil has equalled the competitions' standard and in many cases surpassed it. Regaining and maintaining market share is only possible, though, by continuing research so that improvements continue to happen.

QUESTIONS

1. Identify the major changes in consumer shopping behaviour revealed in this case.

2. What features should Mobil continue to track in the future in order to ensure that they maintain a competitive position?

This case study was prepared by Libby Benson, Department of Marketing, University of Otago, New Zealand.

| CASE 2 | A CONSUMER BEHAVIOUR PERSPECTIVE ON THE AUSTRALIAN FRESH PINEAPPLE INDUSTRY |

'To tell you the truth, pineapples don't have any sex appeal! Compare them with mangoes, other tropical fruit and some of the rare fruits. Even bananas and apples with their advertising campaigns have been made exciting. But a pineapple is just a pineapple at the moment. I don't know what can be done about it,' so complained a seasoned fruit merchant at the Flemington Central Markets in Sydney.

INTRODUCTION

During the 1994–1995 season, it was clear to most participants and informed observers of the Australian Fresh Pineapple Industry that all was not well. There was an oversupply of fruit on the market and quality levels and consistency issues were uncertain. Some wholesale merchants were predicting the demise or major 'downsizing' of the Central Markets as some of the major supermarket chains by-passed them and bought direct from growers. At the same time the Golden Circle Cannery reduced the quantities they wanted due to increased levels of imported canned pineapples, among other reasons, thereby forcing more cannery product onto the fresh market. Many in the fresh pineapple industry knew that they could all do much better, but it was not clear to all what needed to be done.[1]

THE PINEAPPLE BUSINESS

There is a difference of opinion as to whether fresh pineapples can be regarded as an all year round fruit or a summer fruit only. Related to this is the debate whether pineapples should be sold in winter as fresh fruit from anywhere south of the tropics. This dispute is also relevant because it has an impact on quality standards across the industry, and product image during winter consumption. There is very little branding at the retail level and thus fewer changes for end users to differentiate between product.

It is common for cannery growers to put their excess fruit onto the fresh fruit market, and also to use the fresh fruit market as cash flow while they wait for payment from the cannery.

Fresh food sales of all types have grown exponentially in recent times. For example, Woolworth's growth in this area is from $920 million in 1986–87 to $3.9 billion in 1993–94, and accounts for 40 per cent of turnover in their supermarkets. Other retailers report a 30–35 per cent of turnover level compared with less than 20 per cent five years ago. A CSIRO survey found that 45 per cent of men and 50 per cent of women had increased their consumption of fruit and vegetables since 1991 (Shoebridge 1994).

The so-called 'fresh-food revolution' that we are told started in the 1980s and accelerated into the 1990s, is attributed to a consumer search for healthy living, convenience needed due to the pace of modern life and more women in the workforce, an increased insistence on natural taste, and the ready availability of an abundance of fresh food through improved technologies and distribution.

COMPETITION

Price competition is generally strong, whether against other fresh produce, or the canned alternative. Wholesale agents must satisfy both growers and retailers, thereby adding competitive pressures.

Competition for the 'fresh-food' dollar is intense in terms of number of competitors, size and commitment of the competitors and budgets allocated. Pineapples would probably rank in the bottom quartile in terms of competitive muscle as an industry. At the same time the number of fresh food competitors is increasing. For example, Woolworths have

1.   (c) John Jackson. The author acknowledges with thanks the help of: RIRDC (The Rural Industry and Development Corporation) for funding and backing the project; the Faculty of Business, CQU; QFVG, Nick MacLeod, Paul Rainbird and all those many people in the Pineapple Industry who co-operated. Any errors are the author's own.

expanded their range of fruit and vegetable lines by 40 per cent since 1987 (Shoebridge 1994) and are still increasing. This puts pressure on shelf space and placings as well as the probability of consumers buying alternative discretionary foods.

Even less exciting foods are increasing their competitiveness. For example, in the U.S., the carrot industry is offering mini whole peeled carrots, carrot stick snack packs, microwaveable carrot packs, packs in resealable bags, and are developing hybrid carrot varieties, better flavours, better textures and increased carotene content. Consider also the case of apples. In 1992 about fifty different Australian entities exported 32,000 tonnes of apples while the New Zealand Apple and Pear Marketing Board exported 210,000 tonnes (and has invested in a major Chilean apple export company to provide access to low cost Chilean product).

BRANDING

At the consumer end, there is very little branding other than distinctive names, colours and designs on boxes. Most fresh pineapples are sold with no brand identification whatsoever. This is in contrast to the U.S. where 'Dole' and 'Del Monte' tend to have branding name stickers on each fruit. The size of the market is the main reason given for not doing the same in Australia.

At the retailer/merchant level, about 17 main brand names have been observed. These range from the main producers such as Tropical Pines and Talorb. Most brands have been neglected at the consumer level, though the main sheds have been recently working hard on this.

THE CANNED PINEAPPLE MARKET

Canned pineapple is available all year round and is supplied either by the Golden Circle cannery in Brisbane or as a generic brand by retailers sourcing mainly from Asian countries such as Thailand, Indonesia, Malaysia and the Philippines. Because of its ready availability, demand for the fresh alternative is relatively stable. Generally either a very well coloured or a less sweet fruit is used in the canning operation because sugars can be easily added in the process. The imported canned fruit varies enormously in quality.

The domestic market is very much influenced by the Golden Circle cannery in Brisbane. Most major growers have shares and a cannery quota, and only about 20 per cent of the pineapple crop goes to the fresh sector. However, there has been a general trend towards fresh product.

CUSTOMERS

Consumption is heavily weighted towards warm weather. Winter consumption is generally low. Practically all the fresh fruit, other than fruit salad and pineapple juice, is sold and consumed in a non value-added form. Most purchasers are families.

Generally consumer benefits sought are:

➡ consistent quality (sweetness, lack of disorders like black heart)

➡ versatility re use with other products (fruit, meat, pizza)

➡ attractive in a fruit bowl display (the more golden the better — though this can often result in an over-ripe eating experience when it is eventually cut).

Main consumer dislikes include sourness or tartness, black heart and other diseases, over-ripeness, and the fruit's lack of convenience in handling, preparation and eating. 'Customers are lazy; we need a pineapple with a zipper,' said one Brisbane pineapple floor manager at the central market. 'Speak to Bamix or some scientists about cheap and easy ways to cut,' suggested his business partners. Supermarkets and grocers report a lack of consumer confidence that each pineapple they get will be of a high enough quality. Consumers also have shown resistance to the 'talcum' powder put on some pineapples to reduce sunburn.

CUSTOMER EDUCATION

While some are reasonably well informed, it is clear that many customers (both retail and end-user) are fairly ignorant about pineapples. Many incorrectly believe, for example, that:

➡ a pineapple gets sweeter the longer you keep it

➡ the brighter the (golden) colour, the sweeter the fruit

➡ you can tell ripeness by how easily a leaf can be pulled out from the head

➡ a green coloured pineapple can never be sweet

➡ pineapples can be displayed for long periods and then still be eaten satisfactorily

➡ the fruit looks robust and thus can be roughly treated

The larger supermarket chains have urged growers to use both packaging and point of sale materials to educate consumers. One grower group has shown on its boxes for some time the best fruit colours to look for during each season. This has received compliments by others in the industry, but is very rarely seen at the retail store level where displays of pine-apples are very seldom put with the box illustrations.

Education of retailers is also important, especially in terms of handling, display, sales and advice to consumers. Several industry people state that they have been surprised by the lack of knowledge of retailers. 'Some will handle the pineapples very roughly and will buy once a week or fortnight, yet stock up on tomatoes three to four times a week,' said one experienced industry figure. 'And they will misinform consumers as well.'

MARKET RESEARCH—AN INTRODUCTION

Research is important to overcoming misunderstandings and misinformation. For example, paw paw research showed that many consumers wanted small 'breakfast' fruit whereas the wholesale merchants had been telling growers to grow only large paw paws for customer convenience.

A number of studies are worth examining for their marketing implications.

CSIRO Survey

This study, done in the early 1990s, found that 45 per cent of men and 50 per cent of women had increased their consumption of fruit and vegetables since 1991 (Shoebridge 1994).

QFVG 1992 Study

Their survey reported that consumers were significantly dissatisfied with fruit quality offered in terms of greenness, bruising, and going bad before ripening. Customers claim that modern fruit and vegetables lack taste, do not keep well and while often visually appealing, lack quality in eating. In particular cold storage and other artificial means of extending the life of produce is blamed. The finding prompted the QFVG General Manager to state that growers must realise that they grow for consumers and not for retailers or wholesalers (QFVG 1992).

Freshmark/Tropical Pines 1992 Study

This qualitative research by Marketshare Pty Ltd was into Tropical Pines pineapples (the brand name of the largest Cooperative packaging shed at the time) and modified atmosphere packaging (MAP) which was being considered as a ready-to-eat alternative. It involved focus group research with consumers and in-depth personal interviews with large fruit retailers in the greater Brisbane area.

The main findings of this study were:

(a) Generally pineapples are viewed positively, especially their versatile nutritional value and decorative effect in a fruit bowl. Fresh pineapple purchasers prefer the tangy taste over the canned alternative and strongly believe 'fresh is best'.

(b) Shortcomings concentrated on inconsistent quality, and the difficulty of knowing the quality before purchase. They are also seen as difficult to peel, carry, handle and store. Wastage and disposal problems were also cited.

(c) Respondents stated that fresh pineapple is mainly used as a fresh fruit snack and to accompany fruit salad, barbecues and ham steaks.

(d) There was an extremely low awareness of any brand names. Any guarantee offered by a branded pineapple would have a strong appeal, reported the study's respondents.

(e) MAP product, in taste test, was preferred by regular canned pineapple users. It was seen as benefiting from clear visibility, convenience and a longer shelf life than fresh pineapple. On the negative side, it could be viewed as 'not fresh', with preservatives added. The plastic packaging was seen by some as environmentally unsound, and by others as a real worry if it got pierced and the juice spilt out. Most respondents were prepared to try the product, and said they would pay a premium of about 50 per cent over fresh pineapple. Interestingly, fresh users saw MAP as a preferred substitute for canned pineapple, whereas canned users saw it as a substitute for fresh. Marketshare speculated that those consumers would be families living hectic lifestyles who wanted convenience and nutritional value, and thus MAP should be positioned as a lifestyle product. Of course, MAP fruit would require refrigeration both by retailer and consumers. Smaller packs of MAP pineapples were appealing to those who lived alone.

(f) The words mentioned by respondents as their top-of-the-mind associations with pineapples were 'juicy', 'fresh', 'tropical', 'inviting', 'difficult to peel', 'sunshine', 'summer', 'Queensland', 'fruit salad', 'prickly', 'golden' and 'Hawaii'.

(g) Uses of the product mentioned were 'for all sorts of cooking', 'sweet and sour', 'fruit salads', 'on the barbecue', 'crushed up in drinks', 'dessert with ice cream', 'on sandwiches', 'on pizza', 'on picnics', 'on a cheese platter', 'as a snack' and 'a fruit bowl centrepiece'.

(h) One interesting comment from both fresh and canned pineapple users was the necessity to buy canned, 'as most pineapple recipes require you to use canned pineapple'. Similarly, some respondents said that they 'wouldn't waste fresh pineapple in cooking or on pizzas'.

QFVG Market Research April 1994

This study, entitled 'Quantitative Research Report—Other Fruits', was conducted for the QFVG by Marketshare Pty Ltd. and involved 600 respondents in Sydney, Melbourne and Brisbane. As the title states, this research was not focused on pineapples and thus more detailed questioning and probing was not undertaken. Nevertheless, the key findings from the report are worth reporting.

➡ Overall, 16 per cent of respondents have purchased pineapple in the past week and a total of 37 per cent

in the last month. At the other end, 43 per cent say they 'rarely' or 'never' buy pineapple. Purchase of pineapple is similar in Brisbane and Sydney and between age groups. Respondents who bought higher numbers of different fruits on their last purchase occasion have a higher than average purchase of pineapple.

➡ Pineapples are bought less frequently than other fruits. Of those in the quota sub-sample, all of whom bought pineapples in the past month, only 13 per cent buy pineapples on every shopping occasion, 28 per cent on every second occasion, 35 per cent on one in three shopping occasions and 23 per cent less frequently than this.

➡ Pineapples are among the fruits with the highest numbers of respondents being prevented from purchasing in the retail situation. In all, 60 per cent of respondents have gone into a shop to buy pineapples and then decided not to purchase the fruit there.

➡ Overall, 33 per cent experience problems on half or more shopping occasions. This is in the average range for fruit included in this study.

➡ The factors which have prevented the purchase of pineapples are mainly concerned with the fruit not being ripe (52 per cent), a figure among the highest for the fruit considered in this research. Other factors include pineapples being too expensive (31 per cent), overripe (15 per cent), apparent poor quality or appearance (15 per cent) and too small (12 per cent).

➡ While pineapples are one of the fruits more commonly served at a particular time (35 per cent), like other fruits they are usually bought for family members to help themselves (56 per cent) or used for both purposes (10 per cent).

➡ In the serving situation, pineapples are offered most frequently at lunch and at dinner with dinner being the more frequent serving occasion.

➡ Pineapples are mainly served fresh, like other fruit. However, among the fruits considered, pineapples are one of the few more commonly cooked. Cooked fruit is only approximately a tenth of the serving occasions. Pineapples are served chopped or sliced. They are equally served on their own and with other fruits and the incidence of serving with a topping such as ice-cream or cream is relatively low. A minority of respondents use pineapple in a salad for the main course.

➡ Those respondents who have bought pineapple in the past month give as their particular family likes about pineapple, the sweet taste (42 per cent), the taste generally (20 per cent), the thirst quenching properties (35 per cent) and the juiciness (25 per cent). A further 11 per cent also mention the versatility of pineapple.

➡ When it comes to the dislikes a comparatively higher than average number of respondents (71 per cent) complain about pineapples. The main single complaint is the preparation which is given by 32 per cent of respondents, 21 per cent dislike fruit when it is sour or bitter and eight per cent dislike the fruit when it is bad inside.

➡ Respondents who have not bought pineapples in the past month give as their main reasons dislike of the taste (12 per cent), a dislike of the quality available (12 per cent), health or diet reasons (15 per cent) and the mess of preparation (11 per cent). A further 14 per cent say they prefer canned pineapple and 12 per cent that they only use pineapple occasionally.

PRODUCT

There are two main varieties, the more common smooth-leaf (all year, but best November to February) and the less common rough-leaf (October to January), with some trial

plantations of a 'Hawaiian' variety. The rough-leaf has increased in popularity due to its more reliable sweetness, but they only grow well in the far north and are still a difficult crop to grow consistently well. Pineapples are high in vitamin C and potassium, and are reported to help some hayfever sufferers in tests.

Each plant has a major crop, followed fifteen months later by 'ratoons' (a smaller size). Pineapples come in several sizes. Large fruit are often bought for display purposes. Unfortunately, these are often eaten too late, resulting in a dissatisfied eating experience. The purchase of pineapples, popular in fruit salads and barbecues, is clearly down during periods of rainy and cold weather.

Unlike many other fruits, pineapples are generally not 'user-friendly' and have to be carefully cut rather than spontaneously eaten. Although pineapples look very strong and 'armour-plated', they are in fact delicate fruit that can be bruised easily in transport and handling.

No commercial operation of dried pineapple pieces is widely available. In Asia, several brands made in Thailand and the Philippines are commonly offered for sale.

As regards cut-and-cored chilled pineapple slugs and pieces, one Wamuran grower has been offering these for a few years now, but sales rates have been modest (reportedly due to both high price and also poor fruit quality and presentation). The Golden Circle Cannery also has launched a new offering in margarine-style containers, but it is too early to comment on consumer uptake. Both Woolworths and Coles are trialling these options in both diced and sliced.

A further product modification is MAP (modified atmosphere processing) pineapple pieces that can increase shelf life by between 100 per cent and 500 per cent (Shoebridge 1994). Quality and taste are still too unpredictable. Companies are also experimenting with microbe-controlling coatings in some other food sectors. Some industry players say that Australians are conservative and prefer their fruit intact. Others say this has changed.

A major limiting factor with regard to new varieties, new product forms and other new ventures is the lack of corporate funds, expertise and drive that are not possible from a wide range of individual and small-group growers. Nevertheless, if the pineapple industry wishes to get into the rapidly growing and profitable convenience sector, what the

Americans are calling 'now food', the product will have to be looked at differently.

PRICING

Price competition is strong because of the over-supply of growers and fruit and also price pressures from supermarket, retail and end-use customers. In addition, the ready availability of inexpensive canned product also puts pressure on the prices achievable. Furthermore, when fresh prices have been good, cannery growers frequently switch into the fresh market thereby increasing supply.

Despite the distance, the Perth market consistently achieves the best prices (+/-$14–19 per carton), whereas other markets average in the $6–14 range and can readily go down to $6–8 (where money is not made by the growers).

Most industry participants see an opportunity for a premium quality product and a premium price at the consumer level. At this time such an offering is practically seldom done as there is no new variety or major differential in quality and presentation among end consumers.

Retail prices for pineapples vary enormously: from 10–20 cents in season at flea markets within growing areas, to $3.50 in some corner stores and greengrocers. A more typical retail price average is 99 cents in grower areas, $1.50–1.99 in most areas, and $2.99 elsewhere. Relative to other fruits it is not seen as an inexpensive fruit, and receives consumer hostility at these prices when the fruit has black heart, is over-ripe, or is under-ripe and tarty.

Pineapples sales do not respond well to price wars. As one wholesaler put it, 'you'd need to have one hell of a large family'. With the social trend towards both smaller families and single person households, the typical whole fresh pineapple is too big and over priced per edible amount for many consumers. Conversely this could constitute an enormous opportunity for the smaller sizes.

PROMOTION

Fruit displays, both at retail outlets and in the home, are an integral part of our culture and also a source of competitive edge. Pineapples are usually a feature in both locations.

Pineapples are included in full colour general fresh fruit posters and advertisements. In addition, some attractive full colour recipe cards and sheets featuring pineapples have been produced, though their distribution and volumes have been small. The major supermarket chains have run successful price and other promotions featuring pineapples according to their own requirements.

A video has been produced showing the harvesting and grading of pineapples and the cutting of the fruit. This has been used, along with taste tests, in supermarket promotions. These have generally been successful, but there is neither the staff nor the money to do the promotions regularly and widely.

Budgets for promotional campaigns have been minuscule compared to most food competitors and even very low compared to banana and apple multi-media campaigns. The QFVG has a general levy on pineapple growers of approximately 1.75 cents (1992/93), of which 1 cent (of every one dollar gross amount realised on sales) is for sales promotions. Only $4.5 million was spent promoting all Queensland fruit and vegetable products during 1992/93, with only $34,000 on pineapples. Some individual growers and small-group packaging sheds have done limited promotion for their brands.

Pineapples are sometimes merchandised in such a way that the artistic display would be disturbed by an inconsiderate consumer who might select one.

Except for price deals, fresh pineapples are very seldom part of salad promotions. Similarly they are not, to any noticeable extent, participating or benefiting from the growth of direct marketing.

CONCLUDING COMMENT

Industry figures are understandably unhappy. On the one hand, the industry faces all sorts of problems—profitability, politics, quality, consumer confusion, a lack of resources and so on. On the other hand, they know they have a popular, versatile product in a massively attractive general fresh foods market that is the envy of most outsiders. Is there a psychology or sociology of pineapple consumption and can we tap into them to breathe new life and 'sex appeal' into the product and industry?

BIBLIOGRAPHY

R. Armstrong, QFVG Chairman's Report, QFVG 1994 Conference, Townsville, 1994.
Horticultural Policy Council, 'The Way Forward—Future Direction for Horticulture', 1992.

D. Kingston, 'Horticulture industries will thrive in '94', *Townsville Bulletin*, 25 March 1994, p. 5.

Marketshare Pty. Ltd, USA Qualitative Research Report—Exploratory Investigation into Tropical Pines pineapples and MAP packaging', prepared for Freshmark and Tropical Pines, April 1992, Brisbane.

Marketshare Pty. Ltd., 'USA Quantitative Research Report—Other Fruits', prepared for QFVG, April 1994, Brisbane.

S. Newett, 'Pineman A comparative Analysis Service for Pineapple Growers', QDPI, 1994.

Queensland Fruit and Vegetable Growers, 'QFVG Research finds most consumers unhappy with quality of fresh produce', QFVG News, 22 October 1992, p. 1.

Queensland Govt, 'Exporting Queensland Primary Products', 1994.

N. Shoebridge, 'Fresh food boom demands quick action', *Business Review Weekly*, 18 July 1994, pp. 40–4.

QUESTIONS

1. Comment upon the case in terms of the following consumer behaviour concepts: perceived risk; perceived quality; brand loyalty and brand switching; high and low involvement; necessary vs discretionary (fruit) purchases; opinion leaders and reference groups; and the group dynamics of pineapple purchasing and consumption.

2. Identify three of the main steps you would take to change attitudes about pineapples.

This case study was prepared by John Jackson, Senior Lecturer, Central Queensland University, Rockhampton.

PART 5

ADDITIONAL DIMENSIONS

CHAPTER 17

MODELLING AND RESEARCHING CONSUMER BEHAVIOUR

LEARNING OBJECTIVES

AFTER STUDYING THIS CHAPTER YOU SHOULD UNDERSTAND:

➡ how useful contributions from related areas have been in our efforts to understand consumers;

➡ how theories and models are useful in understanding consumers;

➡ the nature and significance of consumer research;

➡ the role of different consumer-research strategies;

➡ different methods of gathering consumer information;

➡ how researchers measure various consumer characteristics.

As should be evident from the discussion so far, marketers are frequently uncertain about the variables that are affecting consumers. Sometimes this occurs because they do not clearly understand the extent of variables that might be having an influence. Many of these variables, such as personality or attitudes, are internal to the consumer (and not directly observable) and a variety of others, such as the economic climate, are external. In other cases the variables may be known by marketers but the exact nature and relative strength of their influence are not clear. In any of these circumstances it is useful to refer to some type of model of how consumers operate in order to organise and structure what is understood about consumers.

This chapter begins by discussing the nature of models for consumer behaviour. When considering this material, the reader may find it useful to reflect on the section 'Studying consumer behaviour' from Chapter 1. Two approaches to modelling consumer behaviour are then considered. First, we reflect on some basic perspectives from economics. Then we offer an illustration of the types of comprehensive models of consumer behaviour first developed by researchers in the late 1960s and 1970s, when the subject really grew up and developed as an area for study in its own right. Finally, discussion turns to some of the issues confronted when attempting to research consumers and their behaviour.

MODELLING BEHAVIOUR

As just mentioned, studying consumer behaviour can be quite complex, especially because of the many variables involved and their tendency to interact. Models of consumer behaviour have been developed in an effort to overcome these difficulties.

Definition of a model

A *model* can be defined as a simplified representation of reality. It simplifies by incorporating only those aspects of reality that interest the model builder. Other aspects that are not of interest only add to the complexity of the situation and can be ignored. Thus an architect's model of a building may not show furniture arrangement if that is not important to the building's design. Similarly, in modelling consumers we should feel free to exclude any aspects that are not relevant to their behaviour. Because we have defined consumer behaviour as involving a decision process, models that focus on this process will be of considerable interest to us.

Types of models

Any given property or process can be modelled in a variety of ways. We could model something by verbally describing it, by representing it with diagrams or mathematical symbols, or by characterising it with some physical process such as electrical current. The most common consumer-behaviour models are verbal, often supported by a schematic drawing.

Consumer-behaviour models can also be classified in terms of scope. Some are designed to represent a very specific aspect of behaviour, such as consumers' repetitive purchasing of the same brand over a period of time. Others are much more comprehensive because they attempt to include a great variety of consumer behaviours. These comprehensive models are less detailed in nature so that they can represent many diverse situations.

Uses of models

Models are devised for a variety of reasons, but the two purposes for developing most consumer models are:

1. to assist in constructing a theory that guides research on consumer behaviour;

2. to facilitate learning what is presently known about consumer behaviour.

In both cases the model serves to structure systematic and logical thinking about consumers. This entails identifying the relevant variables, indicating their characteristics, and specifying their interrelationships; that is, how they influence each other.

DEVELOPING THEORY

A *theory* is an interrelated set of concepts, definitions and propositions that presents a systematic view of some phenomenon. It presents a logical viewpoint that is useful in understanding some process or activity. More specifically, a theory has four major functions: description, prediction, explanation and control. The *descriptive* function involves characterising the nature of something, such as the steps consumers go through while deciding on a purchase. In its *predictive* role, a theory is used to foretell future events, as when learning theory is used to predict what brand names will be easier for consumers to remember. Theory can be used for *explanation* in order to learn the underlying causes of some event or activity. This would occur when we want to understand why a consumer regularly purchases the same brand of soup. Is it because of habit or loyalty to the brand? Although it is possible to predict events without understanding their causes, knowing why something happens greatly enhances our ability to predict its occurrence. *Control* is the ability to influence or regulate future events. This has been extremely difficult in the behavioural sciences due to the many variables involved and our lack of knowledge about them. Therefore, although marketers and others can sometimes influence consumers, we will find ample evidence that strict control of consumer behaviour is well outside our present capabilities.

A useful relationship exists between models and theories, because models can assist theory development by clearly delineating the relevant variables and their influence on each other. That is, models can be used to depict or express a theory. In this way, models can present a unified view of what is known about consumer behaviour and help to identify what remains to be explored. This allows researchers to advance knowledge by selecting the most important aspects of consumer behaviour for analysis and testing.

FACILITATING LEARNING

Another primary motivation for using models is to serve as a learning aid. In this role, models provide a structure helpful for organising knowledge about consumer behaviour into a logical pattern that is easier to comprehend. They also remind us of the interrelationships between relevant variables. Therefore, as we concentrate on one particular variable, reference to the model will remind us to consider how it interacts with other variables to influence behaviour.

MODELS OF CONSUMER BEHAVIOUR

Comprehensive verbal models have been employed most often in the study of consumer behaviour. A variety of such models exist, each taking a somewhat different view of consumers. Those chosen for presentation here are well known and represent a broad perspective.

Economic models of consumers

The earliest comprehensive consumer models were devised by economists seeking to understand economic systems. Economics involves the study of how scarce resources are allocated among unlimited wants and needs.[1] Its two major disciplines—macroeconomics and microeconomics—have each developed alternative views of consumers. Partially because they have undergone some modernisation, these models still influence contemporary views of consumers.

MICROECONOMIC MODEL

The classical microeconomic approach, developed early in the 19th century, focused on the pattern of goods and prices in the entire economy. It involved making a series of assumptions about the nature of the 'average' consumer, and then developing a theory useful in explaining the workings of an economy made up of many such people. Focus was placed on the consumer's act of purchase, which, of course, is only a portion of what we have defined as consumer behaviour. Thus, microeconomists concentrated on explaining what consumers would purchase and in what quantities these purchases would be made. The tastes and preferences leading to these purchases were assumed to be known already. Therefore, microeconomists chose to ignore why consumers develop various needs and preferences and how consumers rank these needs and preferences.

The resulting theory was based on a number of assumptions about consumers. Primary among these were the following:

1. Consumers' wants and needs are, in total, *unlimited* and therefore cannot be fully satisfied.

2. Given a limited budget, consumers' goals are to allocate available purchasing dollars in a way that *maximises* satisfaction of their wants and needs.

3. Consumers *independently* develop their own preferences, without the influence of others, and these preferences are consistent over time.

4. Consumers have *perfect knowledge* of the utility of an item; that is, they know exactly how much satisfaction the product can give them.

5. As additional units of a given product or service are acquired, the *marginal* (additional) satisfaction or utility provided by the *next* unit will be less than the marginal satisfaction or utility provided by previously purchased units. This is referred to as the *law of diminishing marginal utility*.

6. Consumers use the *price* of a good as the sole measure of the sacrifice involved in obtaining it. Price plays no other role in the purchase decision.

7. Consumers are *perfectly rational* in that, given their subjective preferences, they will always act in a deliberate manner to maximise their satisfaction.

Given these assumptions, economists argued that perfectly rational consumers will always purchase the good that provides them with the highest ratio of additional benefit to cost. For any given good, this benefit/cost ratio can be expressed as a ratio of its marginal utility to price (MU/P). Therefore, it can be shown that the consumer would seek to achieve a situation where the following expression holds for any number (n) of goods:

$$\frac{MU_1}{P_1} = \frac{MU_2}{P_2} = \frac{MU_3}{P_3} = \cdot \cdot \cdot = \frac{MU_n}{P_n}$$

If any one product's ratio is greater than the others, the consumer can achieve greater satisfaction per dollar from it and will immediately purchase more of it. Provided there is an adequate budget, the consumer will continue purchasing until the product's declining marginal utility reduces its MU/P ratio to a position equal to all other ratios. Additional purchasing *of that good* will then stop.

Although the microeconomic model has had an important influence on our understanding of consumers, it provides a severely limited explanation of consumer behaviour, with a major deficiency being its highly unrealistic assumptions. For example, consumers frequently strive for acceptable and not maximum levels of satisfaction.[2] In addition, consumers lack perfect knowledge regarding products, and they often influence each other's preferences.[3] Also, they appear to use many variables in addition to price to assess a product's cost, and may frequently use price as a measure of product quality as well as cost.[4] Finally, consumers simply do not appear to be perfectly rational in all their purchase decisions. These unrealistic assumptions may not have hindered the usefulness of this model in explaining the behaviour of an entire economic system, but they certainly are not as useful in understanding how actual consumers behave in specific purchase situations of concern to marketers and others.

An additional shortcoming of the microeconomic scheme occurs as a result of its focus on the specific act of purchase. Much consumer behaviour occurs before and after this act. Considerable decision making and search for information can precede it, and purchase evaluation as well as additional purchases can follow it. As the model does not address these activities, we cannot accept it as a comprehensive representation of consumer behaviour.

Even with its limitations, the microeconomic model has been useful. It provides a perspective from which to better appreciate contemporary models of consumer behaviour. In addition, we should now be more sensitive to the critical way in which the usefulness of a consumer model depends on its assumptions, and we should be ready to evaluate other models in terms of their dependence on stated or implied assumptions. Finally, because economists have modernised certain aspects of the microeconomic model, it continues to have an important influence on contemporary thinking regarding consumer behaviour.

MACROECONOMIC VIEWPOINTS

Macroeconomics focuses on aggregate flows in the economy—the monetary value of goods and resources, where they are directed and how they change over time.[5] From such a focus, the macroeconomist draws conclusions about the behaviour of consumers who influence these flows. Although the discipline has not generated a full unified model of consumers, it does offer a number of insights into their behaviour.

One interest centres on how consumers divide their income between consumption and savings. This deals with two economic facts of life: higher income families spend a smaller proportion of their disposable income than do lower income families, but as economic progress raises all income levels over time these proportions do not seem to change. That is, lower income groups do not significantly change the proportion of income devoted to spending as economic progress results in an increase in their income. The *relative-income hypothesis* explains this apparent contradiction by arguing that people's consumption standards are mainly influenced by their peers and social groups rather than by their absolute income levels.[6] Therefore, the *proportion* of a family's income devoted to consumption is expected to change only when an income change places the family in a different social setting. This will not happen when all income levels are rising at the same time.

Another macroeconomic proposition, the *permanent-income hypothesis*, explains why specific individuals are slow to change their consumption patterns even when their incomes do suddenly change. It proposes that consumers do not use *actual* income in any period to determine the amount of their consumption expenditures, but instead are influenced by their estimate of some *average*, long-term amount that can be consumed without reducing their accumulated wealth.[7] Sudden increases or decreases in income are viewed by the consumer as temporary and therefore are expected to have little influence on consumption activity. The permanent-income hypothesis is also linked conceptually to the family life cycle. For example, the amount of debt that a family is prepared to service when starting out, particularly mortgages and car loans, is determined by a long-term view of their income matched with expectations of their needs through different stages of the family life cycle.

A variety of other variables have been suggested by macroeconomists as influencing consumption patterns. Included are consumers' previous income experiences, accumulated liquid assets, and variations in taxes or credits. Although useful, these suggestions represent rather traditional approaches to studying consumers, stressing economic variables while tending to ignore the influence of psychological factors.

Behavioural economics

As mentioned earlier, traditional economics focused on the *results* of economic behaviour (supply, quantity demanded, prices and the like) rather than the actual behaviour of consumers themselves. Behavioural influences on consumers were viewed as complicating factors that could be assumed to cancel each other out.

George Katona found this approach lacking and argued that an appreciation of how psychological variables influence consumers could lead to a deeper understanding of the behaviour of economic agents.[8] Katona's viewpoint, now known as *behavioural economics*, was fostered by important changes that occurred in our economy, especially after World War II. Rising income levels gave a large number of consumers significant discretionary income—spending power available after necessities had been purchased. In short, our economy changed from one characterised as 'much for a few' to one described as 'more for many'.[9]

What made discretionary income so interesting to Katona and others is that it has become a very important component of our economic system, as a healthy portion of it is devoted to the purchase of durable goods such as cars, stereos, washing machines and CD players. Because the cost of these items is usually high, consumers will tend to purchase them when they perceive the general economic climate and their personal situations as being favourable. Therefore, this important influence on our economy is somewhat volatile and is affected by consumers' perceptions and economic expectations.

A very simplified representation of Katona's viewpoint appears in Figure 17.1. As in traditional economic models, actual economic conditions are shown as influencing consumers. These economic conditions include the rates of interest, inflation and unemployment, the level of the GNP, as well as more personal economic situations such as the household's current status regarding taxes, income and debt. However, as the diagram shows with a modulating arrow, rather than directly influencing the consumer, these actual economic conditions are modified by psychological factors, which include consumers' motivations, knowledge, perceptions and attitudes.

The diagram shows that consumer sentiment results from psychological processes modifying the effect of actual economic conditions on the consumer. *Consumer sentiment* may be thought of as the consumer's level of confidence about current economic conditions, and his or her expectations about the status of economic conditions in the future. This consumer sentiment, in turn, is a deciding factor in the amount of discretionary spending that the consumer will engage in at any given point in time. For example, even when current economic conditions are quite acceptable, if the consumer expects that an economic downturn with possibilities of unemployment will occur in the near future, he or she might postpone the purchase of a new car until confident of being able to handle future monthly payments. Katona argued that when many people in the economy share a similar view, a large number of consumers will hold back on discretionary spending, and this is likely to lead to an economic downturn.

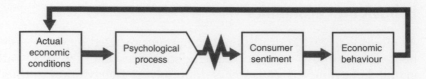

FIG. 17.1   A simplified representation of Katona's behavioural economics perspective

In order to test his arguments, in the early 1950s Katona began conducting surveys of consumers, and used their responses to a series of economic and personal finance questions to develop the *Index of Consumer Sentiment (ICS)*, which is published on a regular basis. This index is claimed to represent the confidence consumers have in the economy.

Was Katona justified in proposing that psychological variables are needed to understand better the spending behaviour of consumers and their effect on the economy? Does the ICS act as a good predictor of changes in the economy? Figure 17.2(a) shows a graph of the ICS for the United States from 1960 through 1992. Also shown on the graph are times that have been officially identified by the United States government as recessionary periods. The graph rather clearly shows that the ICS has declined prior to recessionary periods and, therefore, seems to be a predictor of their occurrence.

Figure 17.2(b) shows a time-series graph of the ICS plotted against actual light-vehicle sales in the United States during the period from 1970 to 1991. Here, again, we see that car purchases clearly follow trends in the ICS. In fact, when the ICS was used as an explanatory variable in a regression analysis of new-car sales, predictive power doubled when compared with using only income as an explanatory variable.[10] It appears quite reasonable for us to conclude that behavioural economics can contribute considerably to our understanding of aggregate behaviour in a given economic system.

In Australia and New Zealand a major consumer confidence index is run by the Roy Morgan Research Centre and published in association with *Time* magazine. The index is based on people's assessment of recent and future changes in their personal economic situation and their assessment of future general economic trends. The Australian index was started in March 1973 and the New Zealand index in August 1990. Figure 17.3(a) shows the trends in both the country indices since 1990 and how consumer confidence has grown as the countries have moved out of recession. Figure 17.3(b) shows how support for the incumbent government in Australia has varied in relation to the index since 1974. Even though the horizontal scale in the figure is somewhat compressed, there is a clear association between the two. In contrast with the light-vehicle sales in the United States, where there is easily discernible and reasonably constant lagged effect, voting intentions seem to turn fairly instantaneously with consumer confidence. This makes it more difficult for the marketers of the political parties to use the index to forecast trends than it does for the marketers of consumer items that require a longer term financial perspective.

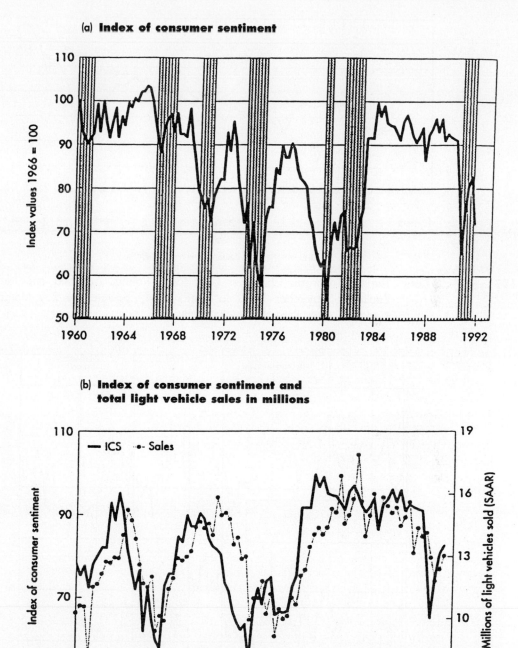

(a) Index of consumer sentiment

(b) Index of consumer sentiment and total light vehicle sales in millions

FIG. 17.2   Association of the Index of Consumer Sentiment (ICS) with measures of aggregate economic activity   Source: Courtesy of Surveys of Consumers, Survey Research Centre, University of Michigan.

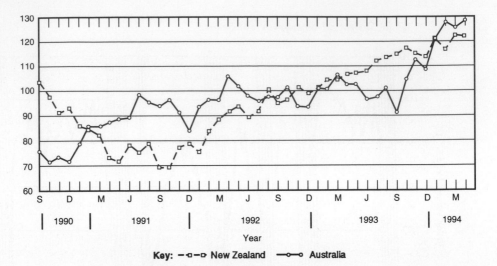

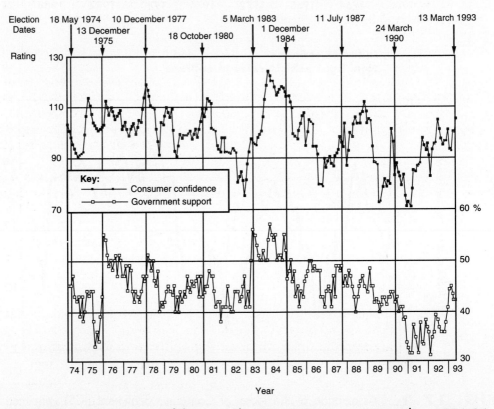

FIG. 17.3(a) The Roy Morgan Consumer Confidence Rating: Australia and New Zealand, September 1990 to April 1994   Source: The Roy Morgan Research Centre. Reproduced with permission.

FIG. 17.3(b) Consumer confidence and voting intentions in Australia, 1974–94 Source: The Roy Morgan Research Centre. Reproduced with permission.

Complex-decision models

As the study of consumer behaviour evolved into a distinct discipline, newer approaches were offered to describe and explain what influenced consumer behaviour. These contemporary views are quite different from previous models because of their concentration on the *decision process* that consumers engage in when deliberating about products and services. Therefore, contrary to the economic models, emphasis is placed on the mental activity that occurs before, during and after purchases are made.

A second distinguishing characteristic of complex-decision models is their extensive borrowing from material developed in the behavioural sciences. In fact, most of the variables discussed in these models were originally identified in the fields of psychology and sociology.

A large number of complex-decision consumer models have been developed, varying considerably in terms of their sophistication, precision, domain and scope. A complete evaluation of all the different approaches is not possible within the confines of this book and consequently we have chosen one example to illustrate the area. The model reproduced below was first developed by Howard and Sheth in 1969.[11] Together with that first generated by Engel, Kollatt and Blackwell in 1968,[12] it is regarded as one of the two most important and influential complex-decision models in consumer behaviour.[13]

HOWARD-SHETH MODEL

The Howard-Sheth model, depicted in Figure 17.4, serves as an integrating framework for a very sophisticated comprehensive theory of consumer behaviour. It should be noted that the authors use the term 'buyer' in their model to refer to industrial purchases as well as ultimate consumers. Thus, it can be seen that their interest was to develop a unified theory useful for understanding a great variety of behaviours.

The model attempts to depict rational brand-choice behaviour by buyers under conditions of incomplete information and limited abilities. It distinguishes three levels of decision making:

1. *Extensive problem solving.* In the early stages of decision making buyers have little information about brands and have not yet developed well-defined and structured criteria by which to choose among products (choice criteria).

2. *Limited problem solving.* In this more advanced stage choice criteria are well defined but buyers are still undecided about which set of brands will best serve them. Thus, the consumer still experiences uncertainty about which brand is 'best'.

3. *Routinised response behaviour.* Buyers have well-defined choice criteria and also have strong predispositions toward one brand. Little confusion exists in the consumer's mind and he or she is ready to purchase a particular brand with little evaluation of alternatives.

The model borrows from learning-theory concepts to explain brand-choice behaviour over time as learning takes place and the buyer moves from extensive to routinised problem-solving behaviour. Four major components are involved: input variables, output variables, hypothetical constructs and exogenous variables.

INPUT VARIABLES Input variables are depicted in the left portion of the model as stimuli in the environment. *Significative* stimuli are actual elements of brands that the buyer confronts, while *symbolic* stimuli are generated by producers representing their products in symbolic form, such as in advertisements. *Social* stimuli are generated by the social environment including family and groups.

OUTPUT VARIABLES The five output variables in the right-hand portion of the model are the buyer's observable responses to stimulus inputs. They are arranged in order from attention to actual purchase, and are defined as follows:

1. *Attention*. The magnitude of the buyer's information intake.

2. *Comprehension*. The buyer's store of information about a brand.

3. *Attitude*. The buyer's evaluation of a particular brand's potential to satisfy his or her motives.

4. *Intention*. The buyer's forecast of which brand he or she will buy.

5. *Purchase behaviour*. The actual purchase act, which reflects the buyer's predisposition to buy as modified by any inhibitors.

HYPOTHETICAL CONSTRUCTS A number of intervening variables are proposed, represented by hypothetical constructs in the large rectangular central 'black box' shown in Figure 17.4. They are categorised into two major groups: perceptual constructs dealing with information processing and learning constructs dealing with the buyer's formation of concepts.

The three *perceptual constructs* of the model can be described as follows:

1. *Sensitivity to information*. The degree to which the buyer regulates the stimulus information flow.

2. *Perceptual bias*. Distorting or altering information.

3. *Search for information*. Active seeking of information about brands or their characteristics.

The buyer's six *learning constructs* are defined as:

1. *Motive*. General or specific goals impelling action.

2. *Brand potential of the evoked set*. The buyer's perception of the ability of brands in his or her evoked set (those that are actively considered) to satisfy his or her goals.

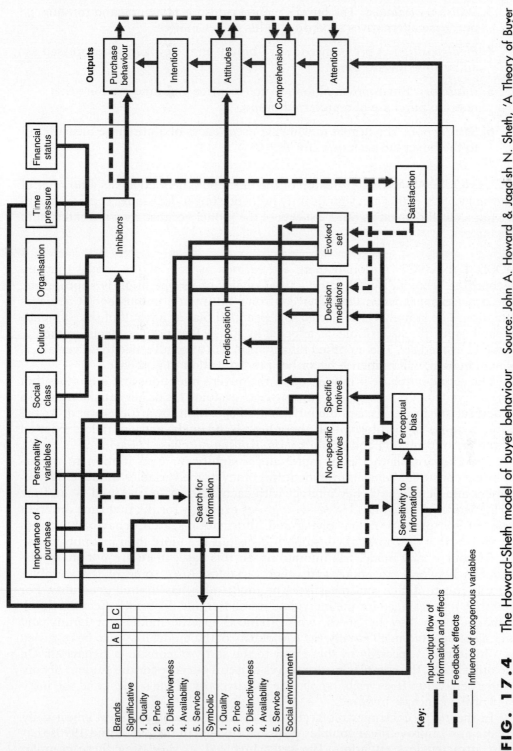

FIG. 17.4 The Howard-Sheth model of buyer behaviour Source: John A. Howard & Jagdish N. Sheth, 'A Theory of Buyer Behavior', in Harold H. Kassarjian & Thomas S. Robertson (eds), *Perspectives in Consumer Behavior*, rev. edn, Scott Foresman, Glenview, IL, 1973, p. 523.

3. *Decision mediators*. The buyer's mental rules for matching and ranking purchase alternatives according to his or her motives.

4. *Predisposition*. A preference toward brands in the evoked set expressed as an attitude toward them.

5. *Inhibitors*. Environmental forces such as price and time pressure that restrain purchase of a preferred brand.

6. *Satisfaction*. The degree to which consequences of a purchase measure up to the buyer's expectations for it.

EXOGENOUS VARIABLES At the top of the black box the model lists a number of external variables that can significantly influence buyer decisions. These variables are not as well defined as other aspects of the model because they are external to the buyer.

MODEL DYNAMICS Although there are various aspects of the model that are beyond the scope of this chapter, a brief review of its operation is appropriate. The process starts when the buyer confronts an input stimulus and it achieves attention. The stimulus is subjected to perceptual bias as a result of the influence of the buyer's predispositions as affected by his or her motives, decision mediators and evoked set. The modified information will also influence these variables, which, in turn, will influence his or her predisposition to purchase.

The actual purchase is influenced by the buyer's intentions and inhibitors that are confronted. A purchase leads the buyer to evaluate his or her satisfaction with it, and satisfaction increases the buyer's predisposition toward the brand. As the buyer acquires more information about brands, he or she engages in less external search for information and exhibits more routine purchase behaviour.

The Howard-Sheth model represents a significant contribution to understanding consumer behaviour. It identifies many of the variables influencing consumers and details how they interact with each other. Also, the model—and the earlier work on which it is based—recognises explicitly for the first time different types of consumer problem-solving and information-search behaviours. It also recognises that outcomes of consumers' decisions are more than just purchases.

Of course, any model has limitations. In this case, there are not sharp distinctions between exogenous and other variables. Also, some of the variables are difficult to define and measure. The model also has limited generality. For example, it is designed for the individual purchaser and does not reflect the developments made later by Sheth, who produced specific models for family and organisational buying.[14] Finally, the complexity of the model may also be regarded as a limitation, especially by those new to the study of consumer behaviour. On the other hand, the complexity also serves a useful purpose for the student of consumer behaviour. It serves to emphasise the diversity of the subject and the intricacy of the concepts involved.

In the 1970s consumer researchers made many attempts to test empirically, update and improve these complex decision models. In the 1980s and 1990s they have attracted less attention. The tasks involved in validating these complex models have led many researchers to place them in the 'too hard basket'. Also, there are divisions of opinion about how well they are able to reflect both low involvement and high involvement.[15] Complex-decision models are seen to reflect only part of one approach to consumer behaviour associated with cognitive psychology. The period since 1980 has seen an enormous diversification in the theoretical approaches used to study consumer behaviour, and these models are seen not to fit behaviourist or postmodernist approaches, for example.

The preceding sections have presented a considerable amount of information. It should be apparent to the reader that models are very useful in providing a framework for organising and understanding what has been learned about the behaviour of consumers. However, evidence about consumers continues to accumulate through new research studies. Therefore, it seems appropriate to briefly review some of the research approaches and methods that are used to develop knowledge about consumers and their behaviour. It is impossible to convey the breadth and depth of this subject in a portion of a single chapter. Consequently, no attempt is made to train the reader in research methods but merely to give a brief exposure to a sample of important consumer-research concepts.

CONSUMER-RESEARCH STRATEGIES

Many strategies are available in the process of researching consumers. For example, studies may differ according to the goal of the research, the type of data used and the time frame of the investigation. Each of these approaches will be discussed in this section.

Goals of consumer research

Two major strategies of consumer research, classified according to their goals, are exploratory and conclusive studies.

EXPLORATORY RESEARCH

Exploratory research is used to identify variables influencing consumers and discover how consumers may tend to react to these factors. This research occurs in situations where there is not enough known about consumers to draw conclusions about what variables are influencing their behaviour. Two significant methods used in exploratory research are consumer suggestions and focus groups.

CONSUMER SUGGESTIONS   In the business world, many influences and problems encountered by consumers are discovered through the spontaneous suggestions of consumers themselves. For example, many retailers conduct an informal type of research similar to the familiar 'suggestion box'. In this way, customers with complaints or new ideas are able to express them in a timely fashion. The more recent use of '008' toll-free telephone numbers (now '1800' numbers) for consumer questions, complaints and suggestions is yet another example.

Packages and products should be tested before they are offered to the market place
COURTESY OF CADBURY SCHWEPPES PTY LIMITED

FOCUS GROUPS Another popular technique for exploratory research is the focus-group interview. Focus groups generally bring together in a casual setting eight to 10 people with similar backgrounds to apply the principles of group dynamics and free association to a marketing problem. A moderator guides the discussion but allows consumers to interact with each other. The sessions, which last about two hours, are usually videotaped.

Focus groups can be helpful in specific ways to:

➡ generate hypotheses about consumers and market situations;

➡ suggest fresh and revitalised ideas;

➡ check an advertisement, package or product concept to determine if anything about it is confusing, misleading or negative;

➡ understand consumers' language and motivations;

➡ understand consumers' lifestyles and personalities;

➡ explore a new area as a prelude to a quantitative study;

➡ do a post-mortem on a failed product.[16]

It is important to appreciate that the primary objective of exploratory research such as focus-group interviewing is hypothesis formulation; that is, forming a conjectural statement about the relationship between two or more variables.

CONCLUSIVE RESEARCH

Conclusive research builds upon exploratory research. Specifically, the major goals of conclusive research are to describe consumers' behaviour and to offer explanations for its causes. In addition, the prediction of consumers' behaviour and methods of influencing it can be suggested by conclusive research.

Types of data used

Two basic sources of data can be used in consumer research: primary and secondary data. *Primary data* are those the researcher gathers first-hand for the specific problem being investigated. However, there is a vast amount of information about consumers that is already compiled and readily accessible to the researcher who knows how to find and use it. Such data that have been collected for a purpose other than the research project at hand are termed *secondary data*. Before gathering primary data the researcher should search through secondary sources to determine if any are applicable to the problem at hand. Because the types of secondary data are too numerous to describe here, an interested reader should refer to other sources for further information.[17] Our focus in this chapter will be on primary data and the methods used to gather them.

Research time frame

Generally speaking, in consumer-research studies primary data can be collected either at one time or over a period of time. We refer to these research designs as cross-sectional and longitudinal, respectively. These two approaches have different purposes. As its name implies, the *cross-sectional* design is used to study behaviour at any one point in time. For example, such a study may seek to determine the knowledge various consumers have about a particular brand right after an advertisement has been run for it.

Interest can also focus on how some aspect of consumer behaviour occurs or changes over time. For example, marketers know that overall sales, as well as brand shares, can undergo striking variations across weekly time periods. These situations are best studied by using a *longitudinal* design, which involves data gathering and analysis over a period of time. One popular type of longitudinal study is the continuous *consumer panel*. Consumers who are deemed representative of a particular group are chosen for inclusion and this fixed sample can be repeatedly studied. By asking the same questions of panel members over a period of time, changes in their behaviour, as well as reasons for these changes, can be determined. Panel members generally maintain a continuous record or diary of their consumption activities, such as shopping, purchase, use and product/brand decisions, as well as demographic and attitudinal characteristics.

METHODS OF GATHERING CONSUMER INFORMATION

In both cross-sectional and longitudinal designs, there are two general ways of collecting consumer-behaviour data: observation and communication. These two basic approaches can be further divided into three information-gathering methods: observation, experiments and surveys.

Observation

One way to study consumers is to observe their overt behaviour. In some cases, this alternative may be better than asking consumers how they act, because frequently discrepancies exist between how consumers say they behave and what they actually do. For example, soap makers have never been sure what to do about the colour pink. Whenever they put different-coloured bars of soap in front of us, we always point to the pink one as our favourite. But observation of store sales reveals that pink soaps are rarely among the best-sellers.[18]

Another benefit of the observation method is that it frequently can be accomplished subtly so that consumers do not realise that they are subjects and then change their normal behaviour. Therefore, this method may be quite successful in obtaining certain types of behavioural information. For example, hidden cameras are sometimes used to observe shoppers' behaviours in a retail-store environment. Because subjects are unaware that they are being observed, such cameras have the potential of recording true activities of consumers.

Other illustrations of this observation technique in consumer research often involve mechanical means of observation. For example, the A. C. Nielsen company gathers television-viewing data from a selected group of families by means of an electromechanical device that automatically records the times and channels of television viewing in a given household. Other forms of observation are the use of specially designed cameras to record eye movements and pupil dilation. Eye-movement tracking is able to document what aspects of an advertisement attract consumers' attention. Also, by measuring pupil dilation with another device, the emotionally arousing aspects of advertisements, packages and products can be documented by the extent the pupil dilates when observing the stimulus.

Another observation technique that has already revealed great benefits for certain marketers and researchers is the use of automatic scanning devices in retail stores. When a product bearing a universal product code (UPC) containing information related to the brand is passed over an automated scanner at the checkout counter, the scanner translates the UPC. In addition to recording the sale, output from the system creates an opportunity to expand our knowledge of the sales effects of advertising, sales promotions and other marketing stimuli. Such systems have the ability to segregate purchases electronically, as opposed to relying on consumers to record what they actually did. Scanning procedures will have a tremendous impact on the collection of data from consumer panels. Traditionally, these have been run by research houses in order to monitor spending and have involved consumers completing written diaries of expenditures. If personal electronic codes identifying individual panel members are incorporated into the scanning system, purchasing behaviour can be monitored instantaneously. This would offer other advantages for research. Scanner technology could be used in conjunction with advanced cable television systems to evaluate advertising effectiveness. For example, if 2500 panel-member homes in Brisbane were linked to cable television, half might receive the same commercials being shown to the general public and half could receive a set of test commercials. Purchase response at the store level would then show up via electronic scanning to indicate a measure of that test advertisement's effectiveness.

Experiments

In experimental investigations the researcher selects consumers, stores and so on (known as test units) and seeks to measure the effect of specific situations or conditions (known as experimental treatments) on a particular dependent variable such as consumers' attitudes or purchase behaviour. In this process, an attempt is made to control or hold constant the effects of other extraneous variables so that they will not influence the results. For example, if we wanted to determine whether the size of a magazine advertisement affects readers' attention, then the size might be varied, while such extraneous variables as the message or appeal used, and the colour of the ad were held constant so that they would not influence the results and confuse the issue.

Consumer researchers may conduct experiments in the 'field' (i.e. the actual setting of the marketplace), or they may test hypotheses under 'laboratory' conditions (which include any environment simulating real or actual conditions).

Field experiments provide a natural setting for research in order to overcome the problems of artificiality sometimes found in the laboratory. However, gaining realism from the marketplace environment can come at the cost of losing some control over the experimental situation.

Test marketing is one business equivalent of the scientist's field experiment. In the market test, different marketing variables (such as prices and advertisements) are tried in several market areas to determine which receives the most favourable consumer response. New-product introductions may be tested for approximately six months to two years or more, during which time the product is promoted and treated as if it were on the market in a full-scale way.[19]

Unfortunately, the expense of many field experiments can be prohibitive, and the length of time involved also makes this type of research inappropriate for some studies. The fact that the field experiment is conducted in the marketplace, however, can enhance the credibility of the results.[20]

Laboratory experiments are useful because they typically allow greater control over extraneous variables than is possible in the real world. Also, the investigator may be better able to manipulate experimental treatments in the controlled environment of the laboratory. However, a potential problem with such experiments is that they can sometimes become too artificial, thereby insufficiently representing the real world. An example of a laboratory experiment could be to discover consumer taste preferences regarding Fosters, Castlemaine XXXX and Swan beers. The laboratory situation allows control over extraneous variables such as temperature of the samples, types of containers, prices and brand names. Thus, rather than using the products' bottles or cans, drinks could be presented to subjects in glasses of the same size and colour with no brand name or price information on them.

Surveys

In the survey method of gathering data, consumers not only are aware of the fact that they are being studied, but also actively participate. There are three survey data-collection techniques: personal interviews, telephone surveys and mail surveys. Surveys have become very common in recent years. Research by Brennan in New Zealand has shown that possibly as many as 60 per cent of the adult population are exposed to at least one survey each year, while 14 per cent may be exposed to four or more surveys. With such high levels of surveying there is increased concern from market researchers about increased numbers of refusals to participate. Brennan shows that people are most likely to refuse if approached in shops and least likely if approached at home but the main reasons for non-participation are simply lack of interest and inconvenience rather than hostility to giving information.[21]

PERSONAL INTERVIEWS

Direct face-to-face interaction between the interviewer and the respondent is perhaps the personal interview's greatest advantage over other types of surveys. A large amount of information can be obtained with a relatively high degree of accuracy by this approach. Flexibility is a further advantage, as questions can be modified to suit the situation or clarification can be provided if necessary. A major disadvantage of this approach, however, is its high cost. Personal interviews often occur in shopping malls because of the relative ease of obtaining a representative group of respondents. These are known as *mall-intercept* interviews.

TELEPHONE SURVEYS

The telephone survey can be a useful alternative to the personal interview because it provides for interviewer-respondent interaction and is quicker and less expensive to conduct than are personal interviews. Telephone surveys work well when the objective is to measure certain behaviour at the time of the interview or immediately prior to the interview, such as radio listening or television viewing. It is also easier to reach subjects by telephone, and many people who would not consent to a personal interview are willing to participate over the phone. These surveys generally achieve higher response rates than do mail surveys or personal interviews.

A great deal of marketing research information is collected through personal interviews with shoppers NORMAN NICHOLLS

Telephone surveys have some basic limitations, however. First, the amount of information that can be obtained is limited because of difficulty in keeping respondents on the phone and interested for any extended period. Secondly, the type of information obtainable is limited. For example, measuring the intensity of consumers' feelings is difficult, and questions containing numerous response options are cumbersome.

MAIL SURVEYS

Although sometimes underestimated by market researchers, this approach has been successfully used by many companies. Mail-questionnaire surveys have long been used by researchers because of their low potential cost per respondent, their ability to reach widely dispersed consumers, and their ability to obtain large amounts of data and allow more sophisticated questioning techniques, such as measuring scales.

In this approach consumers receive a questionnaire in the mail, complete it at their leisure and return it, usually in a post-paid envelope. As respondents are seldom asked to identify themselves, a mail survey can reduce their reluctance to reveal sensitive information. Of course, there are also disadvantages to this type of survey. Mail interviews can result in a small number of responses, with many questionnaires ending up in wastebaskets. Another problem concerns the long time it may take for respondents to return the questionnaire. Follow-up letters to remind consumers of their delay can increase response rates but also boost costs.

Also, as there is no interviewer–respondent interaction, questions must be worded carefully to avoid ambiguity and the questionnaire should be carefully pretested to detect any deficiencies.

No matter which survey method is used, the researcher must be concerned about *non-response error*—error introduced when those who are not reached or refuse to co-operate are different in important ways from those who do respond. For this reason, researchers try to increase participation by such means as notifying the individual that a questionnaire is on its way, offering inducements to participate (such as prize draws) and making call-backs for not-at-homes.

MEASURING CONSUMER CHARACTERISTICS

Consumer research may also be classified according to whether demographic, activity or cognitive information is sought. The following discussion will focus primarily on cognitive research approaches.

Demographic measures

Demographic research is concerned with gathering vital statistics about consumers—such characteristics as their age, income, sex, occupation, location, race, marital status and education. Notice that as these characteristics are easily quantifiable, they enable the marketer to describe accurately and specifically and to understand better certain consumer characteristics.

Much of the demographic data on consumer markets is a product of federal, state and local government sources. The most important sources are the Australian Bureau of Statistics and Statistics New Zealand. Population statistics and other official information are easily obtained and can be useful, even vital, for small businesses that cannot afford expensive marketing research.

Consumer activity measures

Often the researcher seeks to understand various aspects of consumers' activities. For example, questions such as the following may be of interest: When do consumers buy this item? Which stores do they choose? How do they shop in these stores? How often do they shop or buy? How 'loyal' are consumers to certain brands? Which information sources do they utilise in making a decision on which brand to purchase?

Cognitive measures

Consumer researchers who desire to know more about their market than just demographic characteristics or activity patterns may attempt to collect cognitive information; that is, information about consumers' knowledge, attitudes, motivations, perceptions and information processing. Merely observing consumers cannot fully explain why they behave as they do, and questioning often does not provide reliable answers because of consumers' inability or reluctance to reveal true feelings to an interviewer. Thus, researchers attempt to utilise other techniques to explore intervening variables potentially useful in explaining consumer behaviour.

This section describes associative and projective techniques that are used in consumer research to help explain the why of consumer behaviour. Also, the depth interview is discussed because of its primary use in uncovering motives. Finally, attitudinal research approaches incorporating rating scales are presented.

MOTIVATION RESEARCH

During the 1950s companies became increasingly concerned with *why* consumers bought one product or brand instead of another. With the growth in income levels, particularly discretionary income, and as products became more alike, it grew even more important that marketers determine the attitudes, motives, values, perceptions and images that might govern consumers' product-brand selections. To provide such answers a group of investigators, termed 'motivation researchers', came to the forefront of marketing studies using 'qualitative' rather than 'quantitative' research approaches.[22]

A set of projective techniques that had originally been developed by clinical psychologists was adapted and began to be used in consumer research along with various notions from the field of psychoanalysis. These techniques and notions became known by the general term of *motivation research*, or in its abbreviated form simply *MR*. It must be emphasised that these techniques are not used exclusively for studying consumers' motivations, nor do they include all the tools available for such study. Actually, motivation research shares many techniques with other areas of consumer research that are seeking to understand consumers. Several of these projective techniques are briefly characterised below.

WORD-ASSOCIATION TESTS   Word association is a relatively old and simple technique used by researchers. Respondents are read a list of words, one at a time, and asked to answer quickly with the first thing that comes into their minds after hearing each one. By answering rapidly, respondents presumably indicate what they associate most closely with the word offered, and they thereby reveal their true inner feelings.

The *sentence-completion* test is an adaptation of the word-association test in which the interviewer begins a sentence and the respondent finishes it. For example, in conducting a study for a radio station, the interviewer might use the following: '93FM plays music that appeals to . . .' The *story-completion* test is yet another expanded word-association test in which the respondent is told part of a story and is instructed to complete it in his or her own words. This technique can be useful in uncovering the images consumers have about stores and products, and information that is generated can be applied in advertising and promotional themes.

PROJECTIVE TESTS   Projective tests call for the respondent to decide what another person would do in a certain situation. People may be reluctant to admit certain weaknesses or desires, but when they are asked to describe a neighbour or another person, they usually respond without hesitation. Thus, projective techniques are based on the assumption that respondents express their own attitudes or motives as they infer the attitudes or motives of someone else.

A classic motivation research study regarding consumer attitudes toward instant coffee and based on this theory was conducted in 1950 by Mason Haire.[23] Direct-question interviews revealed a dislike of instant coffee because of the taste, but this was believed to be a stereotyped response rather than the true reason. In an effort to discover other reasons for this negative attitude, an indirect approach was used. Respondents were shown one of two identical grocery shopping lists, varying only in the brand and type of coffee. One list contained 'Nescafé Instant Coffee' and the other, 'Maxwell House Coffee (drip ground)'. They were then asked to characterise the woman who purchased the groceries. Descriptions indicated that, compared with the drip-ground buyer, the instant-coffee purchaser was thought to be lazy, a spendthrift, not a good wife, and one who failed to plan household purchases and schedules well. Although these findings are probably not true today, they were initially useful in better understanding consumer motivations. They indicated that respondents were not really dissatisfied with the taste of instant coffee, but rather the idea of using it was unacceptable. Respondents were projecting their own feelings about instant coffee onto the descriptions of the woman who purchased it.

Another form of projective test makes use of pictures as stimuli. One example is the *Thematic Apperception Test (TAT)*, in which respondents are shown ambiguous pictures concerning the product or topic under study and asked to describe what is happening in the picture. Because the pictures are so vague, it is believed that the respondents will actually reveal their own personalities, motivations and inner feelings about the situation.

DEPTH INTERVIEWS As are the focus-group interviews, depth interviews are unstructured and informal. General questions are usually asked, followed by more specific questions that probe for needs, desires, motives and emotions of the consumer. Also, the questioning is sometimes indirect, such as, 'Why do you think your friends wear Reeboks?' as opposed to the direct question, 'Why do you prefer Reeboks?'. Again, this method attempts to circumvent inhibitions the respondent may have about revealing inner feelings. By carefully following cues given by the respondent, an interviewer can ask a series of questions that probe for underlying motivations.

The key factor with depth interviewing (as well as focus-group interviewing) is the interviewer's skill, which calls for imagination and thoroughness in probing consumer leads while not influencing the respondent's answers. Because of their very nature, interview results are interpreted subjectively rather than quantitatively. Thus, there is a great possibility for bias. An additional source of error from depth and focus-group interviews may arise with the use of small samples, which may not be representative of the entire population.

ATTITUDE-MEASUREMENT SCALES

Significant strides have been made in the area of measuring consumers' attitudes, resulting in the development of various self-reporting attitude-rating scales. The scales are termed 'self-reporting' because consumers express their own evaluation of their attitudes by responding to the scale in the way they think most appropriate.

The many scales available differ mainly in their structure and in the degree to which they actually measure attitudes. This section presents two of the more widely used scales in consumer research: the Likert scale and the semantic differential.

LIKERT (SUMMATED) SCALES   Use of this approach involves compiling a list of statements relevant to the attitudes under investigation with agreement–disagreement response scales ranging, for example, from 'strongly agree' to 'strongly disagree'. Each location on the scale carries a point value. Consumers indicate which response most nearly expresses their attitude about the statement. The following is an example of an individual's response to a Likert scale, where scale values range from 1 to 5:

	Strongly agree 5	Agree 4	Undecided 3	Disagree 2	Strongly disagree 1
Myer is generally a progressive store		X			
Myer stores are generally well stocked	X				
Myer merchandise is generally low-priced			X		

Often an individual's responses are summed to produce a total, or *summated*, score. Thus, we can see that this consumer would have a summated score of 12, which indicates a favourable attitude toward Myer. A lower score, such as 6, would be interpreted as revealing a rather unfavourable attitude toward Myer.

SEMANTIC DIFFERENTIAL   The semantic differential consists of pairs of bipolar adjectives or antonym phrases as ends of a continuum with response options spaced in between. This technique can be used in marketing to rate the psychological meaning of concepts, products, companies or people.[24]

Typically, a seven-position scale is utilised between the adjectives with the middle value being neutral. A consumer is asked to mark the position that most closely corresponds to his or her attitude toward the subject being studied. Responses can be tabulated and profiled, a procedure that dramatically illustrates consumer attitudes.

Figure 17.5 is a sample set of semantic differential scales (with only a few adjectives shown) that might be used to have consumers express their attitudes toward three brands of bread. A profile of consumers' responses is also drawn in.

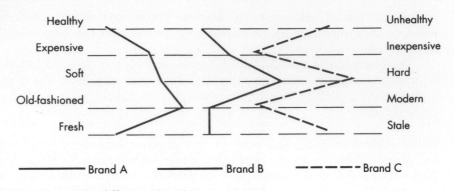

FIG. 17.5 Semantic differential scales

Notice that consumers have a favourable attitude toward Brand A, while Brand B is viewed somewhat neutrally and attitudes toward C are quite negative. Such a finding would be of value to Brand C and could help guide the company in making strategy decisions to overcome this unfavourable image.

As in all of the approaches that have been discussed, the decision to use a specific method or scaling technique must depend on the type of information being sought by the researcher as well as the way in which the data are to be applied.[25]

This brief review of research methods frequently used to learn more about consumers was certainly not designed to be comprehensive or even fully descriptive of each of the techniques chosen for review. However, it is hoped that what has been provided will give the reader a modest appreciation of some of the ways to discover more about consumers and their behaviour. This, coupled with the discussion of consumer-behaviour models, should be helpful in appreciating the complex but exciting nature of discovering how and why consumers act in certain ways.

SUMMARY

The purpose of this chapter was to introduce the concept of consumer-behaviour models, indicate their characteristics and review the usefulness of several specific consumer-behaviour models. In addition, the goals of consumer research and a variety of consumer-research methods were reviewed.

After an introductory example, models were defined and characterised. Their contribution to developing theories of consumer behaviour was also discussed. Attention then turned to a focus on several specific consumer-behaviour models. The microeconomic model was shown to be logically sophisticated but dependent on a number of restrictive assumptions about the nature of consumers. It has significantly influenced much thought about how consumers behave. The macroeconomic viewpoint was treated next, with several contributors being reviewed. Behavioural economics was then offered as a fresh contribution to traditional macro-economic viewpoints by introducing psychological concepts into economic explanations of consumers' behaviour.

An example of a complex-decision model was then reviewed. The Howard-Sheth model made an important contribution in distinguishing three levels of consumer decision making about products and services: extensive problem solving, limited problem solving and routinised response behaviour.

The chapter then turned to research strategies useful in testing these models and providing information about consumer behaviour to marketing managers. Exploratory and conclusive research were characterised and cross-sectional ('snapshot') research approaches were compared with longitudinal approaches, which are designed to collect data on consumers over an extended period of time. The research approaches of observation, experiment and surveys were then reviewed, with examples provided for each. The chapter concluded by discussing a variety of measuring devices used to research aspects of consumer behaviour ranging from consumers' activities and motivations to their attitudes about products, services and companies.

MANAGERIAL REFLECTIONS

For our product or service situation:

1. What are the various consumer response variables that are of interest?

2. What models or theories have we informally used when thinking about consumers?

3. What consumer motivations and problem-recognition situations may serve as sources for new product or service ideas?

4. What evaluative criteria do consumers appear to have for our products or services, and how are they developed?

5. What postpurchase processes are important?

6. What research studies have been conducted regarding our consumers? What still needs to be studied?

7. Will cross-sectional or longitudinal data-gathering activities be most appropriate for the questions about consumers that we are asking?

8. How will the information be gathered—by observation, survey, experiments or by some other means?

DISCUSSION TOPICS

1. What is a model? How can our study of consumer behaviour benefit from using models?

2. A hard-nosed marketing manager was heard to remark, 'All this talk about consumers' decision process still just boils down to the same old fact—it's what the consumer buys, and how much of it, that's really important to the practising marketer'. What is your reaction to this statement?

3. What major contributions do contemporary models of consumer behaviour make compared with traditional models?

4. How might producers of stereo equipment use Katona's model to understand better the consumers of their products? How might producers of chewing gum do the same?

5. Relate one of your experiences where postpurchase outcomes significantly influenced your future purchase behaviour.

6. Discuss the significance of consumer research to marketers, consumers and the economy.

7. Recommend a design for the following types of consumer research on a subject of your choice:
    (a) observation
    (b) survey
    (c) experiment

8. Design your own flow chart/verbal model of consumer behaviour. Feel free to borrow useful aspects of models presented in the chapter, but also offer your original contributions.

9. Conduct an in-class focus-group interview, using students in the class as subjects. Select one student to be moderator. Suggested topics include:
    (a) ways to improve the campus book store;
    (b) opinions and attitudes toward a new product (bring in an advertisement);
    (c) potential for opening a new restaurant near campus.

    The session should be videotaped if possible. Discuss how a researcher might use this information.

REFERENCES

1. Paul A. Samuelson & William D. Nordhaus, *Economics*, 12th edn, McGraw-Hill, New York, 1985, p. 5.
2. See James G. March & Herbert A. Simon, *Organizations*, Wiley, New York, 1958, for evidence of this in executive behaviour.
3. Thomas S. Robertson, *Innovative Behavior and Communication*, Holt, New York, 1971.

4. Kent B. Monroe & Susan M. Petroshius, 'Buyers' Perceptions of Price: An Update of the Evidence', in Harold H. Kassarjian & Thomas S. Robertson (eds), *Perspectives in Consumer Behavior*, 3rd edn, Scott, Foresman, Glenview, IL, 1981, pp. 43–55; and Werner W. Pommerehne, Freidrich Schneider & Peter Zweifel, 'Economic Theory of Choice and the Preference Reversal Phenomenon: A Reexamination', *American Economic Review* 72, June 1982, pp. 569–74.
5. Richard H. Leftwich, *The Price System and Resource Allocation*, 3rd edn, Holt, New York, 1966, p. 8.
6. J. S. Duesenberry, *Income, Saving, and the Theory of Consumer Behavior*, Harvard University Press, Cambridge, MA, 1949.
7. Milton Friedman, *A Theory of the Consumption Function*, Princeton University Press, Princeton, NJ, 1957; and J. William Levedahl, 'The Impact of Permanent and Transitory Income on Household Automobile Expenditures', *Journal of Consumer Research* 7, June 1980, pp. 55–66.
8. George Katona, 'The Relationship between Psychology and Economics', in S. Koch (ed.), *Psychology: A Study of a Science*, McGraw-Hill, New York, 1963.
9. George Katona, *Essay on Behavioral Economics*, University of Michigan, Ann Arbor, 1980, p. 6.
10. Richard T. Curtin, 'Indicators of Consumer Behavior: The University of Michigan Surveys of Consumers', *Public Opinion Quarterly* 46, 1982, pp. 340–52.
11. John A. Howard & Jagdish N. Sheth, *The Theory of Buyer Behavior*, Wiley, New York, 1969.
12. James F. Engel, David T. Kollat & Roger D. Blackwell, *Consumer Behavior*, Holt, Rinehart & Winston, New York, 1968.
13. For a review of a number of consumer behaviour models heavily based on behavioural science contributions, see Francesco M. Nicosia & Yoram Wind, *Behavioral Models for Market Analysis: Foundations for Marketing Action*, Dryden, Hindsdale, IL, 1977; Gerald Zaltman & Melanie Wallendorf, *Consumer Behavior: Basic Findings and Management Implications*, Wiley, New York, 1979, pp. 515–42; Charles D. Schewe, 'Selected Social Psychological Models for Analyzing Buyers', *Journal of Marketing* 37, July 1973, pp. 31–9; Philip Kotler, 'Behavioral Models for Analyzing Buyers', *Journal of Marketing* 29, October 1965, pp. 37–45; Howard & Sheth, *The Theory of Buyer Behavior*; and Jagdish N. Sheth, *Models of Buyer Behavior: Conceptual, Quantitative & Empirical*, Harper & Row, New York, 1974.
14. Jagdish N. Sheth, ibid.
15. For a more extensive review of these trends, see Rob W. Lawson, 'Consumer Behaviour', in M. Baker (ed.), *The Encyclopedia of Marketing*, Routledge, London, forthcoming 1995/6.
16. Roger E. Bengston, 'Despite Controversy, Focus Groups Are Used to Examine a Wide Range of Marketing Questions', *Marketing News*, 19 September 1980, p. 25; and Yolanda Brugaletta, 'Gives Guidelines to Set Up, Use, and Analyze Focus Groups', *Marketing News*, 24 October 1975, p. 1.
17. See Thomas C. Kinnear, James R. Taylor, Lester Johnson & Robert Armstrong, *Australian Market Research*, McGraw-Hill, Sydney, 1993, Ch. 6.
18. John Koten, 'You Aren't Paranoid If You Feel Someone Eyes You Constantly', *Wall Street Journal*, 29 March 1985, p. 22.
19. See, for example, Jennifer Alter, 'Test Marketing: No Shelving the Future', *Advertising Age*, 9 February 1981, pp. S-l, S-26; Carol Galginaitis, 'What's Beneath a Test Market?', *Advertising Age*, 9 February 1981, pp. S-2–S-28; Mary McCabc English, 'Marketers: Better Than a Coin Flip', *Advertising Age*, 9 February 1981, pp. S-14–S-16; Dylan Landis, 'Durable Goods, Good for a Test?', *Advertising Age*, 9 February 1981, pp. S-18–S-20; and 'Testing, Testing, Testing . . .', *Marketing & Media Decisions*, January 1981, pp. 60–1, 112.
20. For a more complete presentation of the experimental approach, see Keith Cox &

Ben M. Enis, *Experimentation for Marketing Decisions*, International Textbook, Scranton, PA, 1969; and M. Venkatesan & Robert J. Holloway, *An Introduction to Marketing Experimentation*, Free Press, New York, 1971.

21. M. Brennan, 'Survey Participation and Attitudes towards Surveys in New Zealand', *New Zealand Journal of Business* 13, 1991, pp. 72–96.

22. 'Qualitative Research—A Summary of the Concepts Involved', *Journal of the Market Research Society* 21, April 1979, pp. 107–24.

23. Mason Haire, 'Projective Techniques in Marketing Research', *Journal of Marketing* 14, April 1950, pp. 649–56.

24. William A. Mindak, 'Fitting the Semantic Differential to the Marketing Problem', *Journal of Marketing* 25, April 1961, pp. 28–33.

25. For a more complete presentation of cognitive research techniques, see Kinnear, Taylor, Johnson Armstrong, Ch. 6.

CHAPTER 18

CONSUMERISM

LEARNING OBJECTIVES

AFTER STUDYING THIS CHAPTER YOU SHOULD UNDERSTAND:

➡ the nature of consumerism and the consumer's bill of rights;

➡ the nature of laws affecting consumers;

➡ what ethical and social responsibility to consumers involves;

➡ the responses of the advertising and media industries to protect consumers;

➡ the responsibilities of consumers.

Australian consumers have been troubled for years by a brand of cooling fan that caught alight. Between 1976 and 1990, there were 106 reported fires involving the fans, one of which caused the deaths of two children. The fan in question is an Australian-made Mistral Gyro Aire. Because the manufacturer used a non-flame-retardant plastic, fire sometimes broke out when a component failed.

Electric spa pool heaters continue to burn. Since February 1991 the Fire Service has dealt with eight fires caused by spa pool heaters catching alight. And for every fire it attends, we are told there may be another 20 or 30 unreported cases where spa heater units have suffered 'meltdown'— dangerously overheating with the risk of causing a fire.

There are more than 50 000 electrically heated spa pools in New Zealand. Many have heating units that are not properly protected should a fault occur. If you have a spa heater bought before 1990, you must make sure that it is properly protected.

Both the quotations above are from the November 1992 issue of *Consumer*, published by the New Zealand Consumers Institute.[1] They illustrate just one issue, safety, among the many problems encountered by consumers in today's society. Although the nature of the problems varies, the fundamental issues are the same: consumer dissatisfaction with, or need for protection regarding, some aspect of their position as consumers.

The position of consumers in the marketplace and the status of consumerism are very similar on both sides of the Tasman and they have been brought even closer in recent years by the development of ANZCERTA (Australia New Zealand Closer Economic Relations Trade Agreement). Free trade in goods between the two countries was achieved ahead of schedule in July 1990, and in consequence many safety, labelling and other trade-practice issues have been standardised between Australia and New Zealand. Indeed many companies have moved ahead of and more responsibly than legislation in bringing uniform standards to the marketplace.

Consumerism is one of the most popular social issues and is becoming increasingly publicised as time passes. The scope of the movement is so extensive that it draws attention from a variety of disciplines. Thus, an appropriate conclusion for our study of consumer behaviour, before looking at organisational buying, is an understanding of the consumer's position in society. Knowledge of the problems faced by consumers in the marketplace and the reality of their experiences is useful for interpreting many other topics that have been discussed. The consumer of the future will be increasingly demanding, sceptical and critical. Neil Shoebridge said in January 1993 about Australian consumers:

> *Consumers this year are informed, anxious, sceptical, conservative and stressed. They want marketers to provide them with information, facts and tangible reasons to buy a product or service. Chastened by the recession and excesses of the now discredited 1980s, consumers have become tougher, noisier, more demanding and more discerning. They have higher expectations and greater freedom of choice. They are ready to complain if treated badly by a company or a product. They are increasingly aware of their rights as consumers and increasingly willing to exercise those rights. They will shift brand loyalties in an instant if they are offended or short-changed.*[2]

Marketers who fail to understand the changes that are occurring in consumer behaviour in today's marketplace are doomed to be less successful than they otherwise might be. Thus, the topic of consumerism is of prime importance for the marketer because it holds an important key to present and future success. Understanding consumers and being able to adapt to their changing demands will reward the innovative marketer.

The major issues discussed in this chapter are the development of consumerism in Australia and New Zealand; consumers' rights and legislative response; business's ethical and social responsibility with a focus on the codes of practice developed by the advertising industry; and the responsibilities of consumers.

THE DEVELOPMENT OF CONSUMERISM

The word 'consumerism' has many connotations, depending on who is using the term. Business, government, consumer groups and academic researchers have each developed their own definition of the term. These definitions span the gamut from challenging society's goals for material goods to reflecting people's desire for better values. One succinct definition is that 'Consumerism is a social movement of citizens and government to enhance the rights and powers of buyers in relation to sellers'.[3] Other authors have broadened this definition, stating that consumerism:

> . . . encompasses the evolving set of activities of government, business, and independent organisations that are designed to protect the rights of consumers . . . Consumerism is concerned with protecting consumers from all organisations with which there is an exchange relationship. There are consumer problems associated with hospitals, libraries, schools, police forces, and various government agencies, as well as with business firms.[4]

This broader definition will be used to reflect the many facets of the concept. Many organisations—business, government, consumer groups and non-profit groups—are concerned with ensuring consumers receive fair treatment in the exchange process.

There are numerous underlying roots of consumerism. The enduring problems that underlie the movement have been summarised as follows:[5]

1. *Disillusionment with the system.* All of our institutions have been subjected to increasing public scrutiny, scepticism and loss of esteem. Over 40 per cent of Australians profess to have no confidence at all in either federal or state government and over 50 per cent believe companies say untrue things just to sell goods. Many consumers think they get a worse deal in the marketplace than they used to. Thus, there is dissatisfaction with their bargaining position.

2. *The performance gap.* Many consumers express broad dissatisfaction with the goods they buy. Their expectations of product performance and reliability have risen (often because of advertising touting the new improvements). Yet the increased product complexity brings about new possibilities for malfunction and a perception by consumers that the promise–performance gap is widening. This trend has been identified across a range of services and products including banking, department stores, health insurance, clothing, newspapers and television. In every instance, more consumers see quality as worsening rather than improving.

3. *The consumer information gap.* Amateur buyers lacking the time, interest or capacity to process information adequately in order to make optimum marketplace decisions face literally thousands of complex products requiring evaluations along many dimensions relating to performance convenience, or even social concerns.

4. *Antagonism toward advertising.* Segments of the population are very sceptical of the usefulness and truthfulness of advertising information. Over 40 per cent of Australians profess to have no confidence in advertising and 72 per cent believe there is a need for new regulation to cover truth in advertising. In addition, it is criticised for its intrusiveness and clutter, irritation factor, stereotyped role portrayals, and promotion of unrealistic or insupportable expectations. Telemarketing calls are a related annoyance as is the quantity of 'junk' mail that now fills most domestic letterboxes.

5. *Impersonal and unresponsive marketing institutions.* Such marketing factors as the rise of self-service retailing, reduced knowledge of sales employees, computerisation leading to impersonal atmospheres, and bureaucratic structures are contributors to a feeling that no marketer is listening. In 1991, over 50 per cent of Australians did not feel it was worthwhile complaining when dissatisfied because no one would listen. This figure fell to 41 per cent in 1992, but it still represents a large alienated group of consumers.

6. *Intrusions of privacy.* Development of the many consumer-information databases made possible under our increasingly computerised society has caused concern over the access to and use of such data and has led to attempts to protect the consumer's privacy. New Zealand has responded to this with privacy legislation, which is hailed as a world leader, but which is seen as having important consequences for marketing practices as it is implemented over the next few years. Ninety per cent of Australians are seen to support similar legislation to safeguard privacy.

7. *Declining living standards.* Recent reductions in real discretionary incomes for many consumers and the widening gap between the rich and the poor have led to pessimism and disenchantment with the economic system and attempts to deal with the situation. Both Australia and New Zealand have experienced long periods of economic depression in the last two decades, and even in the brief periods of intermission real incomes have generally failed to rise and unemployment has failed to ameliorate.

8. *Special problems of the disadvantaged.* The young, the old and the poor are even more vulnerable than most other groups in society and face great difficulties coping in the marketplace, especially if problems are compounded by unemployment or sickness. Research into personal debt has shown how not just the very poor but even low- and middle-range-income people are under pressure to consume, which often places them in credit difficulty.[6] A typical example of consumer-debt problems given by the Western Australian Financial Counsellors Association shows a couple with three children, assets of $12 000, liabilities of $26 800 and the only current income as a Job Search Allowance. An analysis of consumer bankrupts in Melbourne also produced a very similar profile.[7] The mentally ill and physically disabled also face particularly difficult consumer problems. These range from simple access problems for the

physically disabled to problems of aid for mentally disadvantaged persons. The problems of the latter have been exacerbated in recent years by policies of returning previously institutionalised patients to live in the community without adequate support from social services.

9. *Different views of the marketplace.* Business people and their critics have radically different perceptions of the nature of the marketplace. As an example, the *Financial Counsellors Casework Manual (Western Australia)* argues that 'Increasing sophistication in marketing techniques and the inherent inequality between the consumer and the trader (or government department) create a need for the provision of support and advocacy for the individual or family which experiences consequent financial problems'.[8] Such a view is well away from ideals on consumer sovereignty, which underpin the way many marketers and business people view the marketplace.

Such elements as these have fostered the rise of the consumer movement in developed countries all over the world. The marketer of the future faces consumers who are better educated and informed, more militant than previous generations were and under great economic pressure. Additionally, professional consumer organisations are now well established and are able to obtain publicity and lobby effectively on behalf of a wider population who might not always be fully informed of all issues.

HISTORY OF CONSUMERISM IN AUSTRALIA AND NEW ZEALAND

Consumerism is not new. Even in the Middle Ages, religious leaders such as Martin Luther and John Calvin attacked deceptive selling practices of business and advanced the concept of a just price rather than what the market would bear. In the United States three eras of consumerism have been identified corresponding with the early 1900s, the 1930s and a continuing modern era that had its beginning in the 1950s.[9] In Australia and New Zealand the history of the consumer movement very much relates to this last period. At this time books such as Vance Packard's *The Hidden Persuaders* and publicity over experiments in subliminal advertising caused worldwide controversy. Also instrumental to the international development of consumerism at this time was John F. Kennedy's speech to the United States Congress in which he identified what has been referred to as the *Consumer's Bill of Rights*. In 1962 Kennedy presented in a message to Congress the following four fundamental rights:

1. The *right to safety*. To be protected against the marketing of goods that are hazardous to health or life.

2. The *right to be informed*. To be protected against fraudulent, deceitful or grossly misleading information, advertising, labelling or other practices, and to be given the facts needed to make an informed choice.

3. The *right to choose*. To be assured, wherever possible, access to a variety of products and services at competitive prices; and in those industries in which competition is not workable and government regulation is substituted, an assurance of satisfactory quality and service at fair prices.

4. The *right to be heard*. To be assured that consumer interest will receive full and sympathetic consideration in the formulation of government policy, and fair and expeditious treatment in its administrative tribunals.[10]

The International Organisation of Consumer Unions, of which both the Australian and New Zealand consumer organisations are members, subsequently added four further rights to those identified by Kennedy: the rights to have *basic needs met*, to have means to *redress*, to have *education*, and the right to a *healthy environment*. Together, these eight rights were adopted by the United Nations General Assembly in 1985 as international guidelines for the formulation of consumer protection policies. Since 1983 the International Organisation of Consumer Unions has marked March 15 as World Consumer Rights Day, and they use the day to publicise international developments.

In Australia, there are several organisations that have a role to play in representing the consumer interest.[11] An important non-government body is the Australian Consumers Association. The association is a member of the Australian Federation of Consumer Organisations, which includes various local and state organisations across a wide section of the community, and it is also affiliated to the International Organisation of Consumer Unions. The Australian Consumers Association was formed in 1959 and was the first consumer organisation to be formed outside the United States. It was conceived with the objective of offering 'independent and technically based guidance on an increasing variety of goods and services offered to consumers, to campaign against dishonesty in selling unsafe and deceptively labelled goods'. The main publication produced by the association is *Choice* magazine, which has been published since April 1960 and provides most of the revenue for the association through its subscriptions. Additionally, the Australian Consumers Associations produces a specialist travel magazine developed from a publication by the UK Consumers Association and a more general quarterly magazine entitled *Consuming Interest*. This is reformist in aim and designed to stimulate debate about a wide range of social, legal, government and environmental issues. The association also helps with individual problems and complaints, gives advice on improvements in legislation and participates in committees on Australian Standards, and develops material for consumer education. The status of *Choice* is seen by the fact that 45 per cent of Australians say they have great confidence in the recommendations made by the magazine. This is twice the rate attributed to other independent sources, such as television or newspaper reports, and confidence in commercial sources of information, including advertising, varies between 1 and 9 per cent.[12] The National Consumer Affairs Advisory Council is a semi-government but independent authority that was established in 1977 to advise the Commonwealth Minister for Consumer Affairs. The council currently has a membership of 17 individuals with a broad range of expertise in consumer issues including commerce and industry, marketing, standards, journalism, trade unions, conservation, tourism, law and government.[13] In government there are two national bodies that operate Australia-wide on consumer affairs. These are the Federal Bureau of Consumer Affairs and the Trade Practices Commission. The bureau is a division of the Attorney-General's Department in the portfolio of the Minister for Consumer Affairs, while the commission is responsible to the attorney-general for the promotion of the *Trade Practices Act 1974*. Each state government also has its own department responsible for administering consumer affairs and fair trading at that level.

Organised consumerism in New Zealand has been in existence an almost identical length of time as in Australia. The Consumers Institute in New Zealand and the Consumer Council were set up in 1959 as part of the Department of Industries and Commerce. Early appraisals of the Consumer Council suggested that it was a largely ineffective arm of 'government bureaucracy', and in 1966 it was reconstituted as an independent body with 12 regional members and the heads of the government departments of Education, Health, Trade and Industry, and the Department of Scientific and Industrial Research. At the same time the Consumers Institute became an independent statutory body under the *Consumer Council Act 1966*. The New Zealand Labour government appointed the first Minister for Consumer Affairs in 1984 and, subsequently, abolished the Consumer Council in 1988 and reformed the Consumers Institute as a private incorporated society in 1989. In consequence, the Consumers Institute no longer draws any funding from the government but relies solely on membership fees and subscriptions to its publications. Its principal aim is 'to collect and disseminate information of benefit to consumers; and in so doing to advance the interests of its subscribing members and those of consumers generally'. The institute has two main magazine publications: *Consumer* and *Consumer Home and Garden*. The former has been published monthly since the earliest days of the institute, and 80 000 members subscribed to the magazine at the end of 1993. *Consumer Home and Garden* is a specialised quarterly publication with 27 000 subscriptions as at the end of 1993.

CONSUMER RIGHTS AND CONSUMER PROTECTION

This section will review the consumer rights most relevant to marketing and where consumer-protection legislation influences marketing practices. Issues relating to rights to basic needs and education may be viewed more as matters of general public policy than specifically as marketing concerns. There are several pieces of legislation in both Australia and New Zealand that deal with different aspects of consumer protection. Additionally, Australia has variations according to state laws. A full review of all this material is a subject for study within its own right and in this section we offer only a brief overview of important aspects.[14] The two most important areas of legislation are sale of goods and trade practices. In Australia each state has its own relevant legislation governing the sale of goods and in New Zealand this is now covered by the *Consumer Guarantees Act 1993*. Trade practices are most importantly covered by the *Australian Trade Practices Act 1974* and its New Zealand counterpart, the *Fair*

Trading Act 1986. Both Australian and New Zealand sale of goods legislation was originally based on British legislation from 1893 and the Australian Trade Practices Act was used as a framework for the New Zealand legislation in that area. Hence, both countries follow very similar sets of principles, and the legislation has many parallel clauses and provides the basis for maintenance of consumer rights with respect to safety, choice, redress and information.

CONSUMER SAFETY

Consumer safety is the oldest and least controversial of the consumer's rights and generally one on which both business people and consumerists agree. In March 1994 five consumers in New Zealand found fragments of glass in pickles manufactured by Cerebos Greggs. The company established that this was due to a fault with machinery in their bottling plant and within 24 hours they had withdrawn all their pickles from shops throughout the country. Despite the immediate loss of sales as consumers stock up with competitors' products, such expedient action is recognised as being not only in the consumers' best interest regarding safety, but also in the best long-term interests of the company if consumers are going to retain confidence in their goods and services. Both the Australian Trade Practices Act and the Fair Trading Act have clauses precluding the supply of unsafe products and establish liability for traders who do so. In some cases where extra protection is warranted, particular safety standards can be imposed, for example, in the areas of children's nightwear, toys aimed at children under three years, bicycles and furniture flammability. It is characteristic of such standards that they tend to be developed for products aimed at recognisably vulnerable groups of consumers, such as children, where additional responsibility to cope for the consequences of misuse might be required. In reality, the major issues in consumer safety arise from three sources:

1. *Misuse of products by consumers.* One example is the excessive consumption of alcohol by individuals. The social issues related to excessive consumption such as violence and car accidents involving drunken drivers are well documented, as are the health aspects such as liver disorders. These are not problems for many consumers and other research actually suggests that small amounts of alcohol can have a beneficial effect on health for some people. There is an obvious dilemma for society in deciding what, if any, controls it wishes to impose, and what are the responsibilities of marketers and salespeople who are keen to encourage consumption of their products.

2. *The side-effects of products.* Examples include lead in petrol or the side-effects of drugs. The latter are individual in nature and are normally dealt with by redress through the legal system. Examples such as lead in petrol represent more difficult issues, as they operate at a societal level and are typical of the problems consumers face under the *right to a healthy environment.*

3. *The consumption of dangerous products.* Of their own free will some consumers choose to partake of a range of products that may damage their health. Some of these are banned by law, including many drugs, but others including tobacco have been well-established consumption symbols in our societies for hundreds of years. A further illustration is the recent growth in adventure tourism where thrill and an element of risk may be essential attributes of the product. Providing there are no side-effects that impact on the rights of other consumers, this issue resolves itself into an ethical debate about the individual's right to choose and how far the responsibilities of the marketing manager go regarding consumer information and product standards.

In the United States the Consumer Product Safety Commission has collected information about the most hazardous household products. The CPSC discovered that each year an estimated 20 million Americans are injured, with 30 000 of these victims killed and 110 000 permanently disabled, from 10 000 products under the commission's jurisdiction.[15] (Their jurisdiction actually excludes such potentially lethal products as motor vehicles, aeroplanes, boats, firearms, foods, drugs, cosmetics, medical services and pesticides!) Among the most hazardous products are sports and recreation equipment, home structures, home furnishings, housewares and personal-use items.[16]

THE MITSUBISHI VERADA.   WITH ABS FOR A START.

Mitsubishi Motors appeal on the basis of product safety COURTESY OF MITSUBISHI MOTORS

CONSUMER INFORMATION

Consumer rights with regard to information relate to the marketer's provision of adequate information that neither deceives nor misleads.

Deception of consumers

Both Australia and New Zealand have the same basic provisions under their respective Trade Practices Act and Fair Trading Act. Section 52 of the former states that a 'corporation shall not, in trade or commerce, engage in conduct that is misleading or deceptive or is likely to mislead or deceive'. Other clauses in either or both Acts extend specifically to goods, services, property and employment. Note that the way the legislation is phrased, it is not necessary that deception actually occurs in an advertisement, but merely that the advertisement has the *capacity* and is likely to deceive. It should also be noted that the advertiser cannot escape liability simply because he or she did not know that the ad's claim was false.

Advertisements have long been designed on the basis of the accepted approach of puffery; that is, the use of exaggerated praise for an advertised item. The most difficult question to resolve, however, is the point at which puffery becomes deception. In reality, very few cases are actually brought under legislation in this area and most complaints are reconciled by the industry-funded bodies responsible for regulating advertising standards. The basic distinction between puffery and misleading or deceptive claims that has been established is that puffery is recognisable by reasonable consumers and cannot lead to deception, because it is not believed. However, studies in the United States consistently produce a different conclusion, showing that puffed claims are frequently believed by consumers to be true.[17] A useful definition by which deception in advertising may be evaluated is as follows:

> If an advertisement (or advertising campaign) leaves the consumer with an impression(s) and/or belief(s) different from what would normally be expected if the consumer had reasonable knowledge, and that impression(s) and/or belief(s) is factually untrue or potentially misleading, then deception is said to exist.[18]

On the basis of such a definition, three types of deceptive advertising have been identified. First, the outright *lie* occurs where a claim is made that is completely false, even from an objective viewpoint. That is, it is impossible for consumers to achieve the claimed benefit. A claim that a juice is 100 per cent pure juice when it has water and sugar added would be such an example.[19] This is the easiest deception to deal with and the one that most involves the authorities. Secondly, the advertiser may be guilty of *claim–fact discrepancy,* in which a claimed benefit of the advertised product must be qualified in some way for it to be correctly understood and evaluated (but this is not done in the ad). A common example for this is the type of claim for a price discount that advertises '10 per cent off recommended retail price'. The term 'recommended retail price' may imply to the consumer that it is the normal price but in fact usual selling prices may be below the RRP because the product is used as a 'loss leader' or is frequently subject to discounts at different stores. For example, an advertisement may claim that 60 per cent of doctors recommend 'X'. If the consumer knew what types of doctors, how many were surveyed and what questions were asked, this claim could be more accurately evaluated. Thirdly, the advertiser may deceive on the basis of *claim–fact interaction*. That is, the advertisement's claim (while being neither explicitly nor implicitly deceptive) interacts with the accumulated beliefs and attitudes held by consumers in such a way that they are misled or deceived by it. In the United States, for example, Robert Young, an actor who played a medical doctor on the long-running television series 'Marcus Welby' may have been perceived by many consumers as acting in the role of a physician or recommending the product on the basis of medical knowledge when he appeared as a spokesperson in advertisements for Sanka-brand decaffeinated coffee. Even though no mention is made of the fact, for some consumers such a recommendation may interact deceptively with their beliefs. This is not an unlikely situation. Hugh Mackay points out viewers have blurred distinctions between soap operas and current affairs. Programs such as 'A Country Practice' and 'Neighbours' may provide as helpful a social commentary as more serious documentary-style discussion. Escape and information are not always distinguishable and in such situations claim–fact interaction is a distinctly possible effect.[20]

AFFIRMATIVE DISCLOSURE

Affirmative disclosure is designed to eliminate the potential for deception in promotional material by providing consumer information on negative attributes of some products and services. Affirmative disclosure specifically requires a company to disclose in its advertising or labelling the deficiencies or limitations of its product or service. The warning notices in cigarette advertising are an example of affirmative disclosure as is the provision of effective annual interest rates for consumer credit.

The assumption being made with affirmative disclosure is that such information will affect consumers' attitudes or purchase behaviour. This puts the consumer in a position of having both positive and negative information before making a purchase decision.

Availability of sufficient information

It is felt by many economists and by people in legislative, regulative and judicial circles that the consumer does not have adequate information on which to base decisions. Fischer states the case forcibly:

> *Certainly we can question the concept of consumer sovereignty. In short, the role of consumers is to lead the economy to the production of goods and services that they want by casting money votes [But this] cannot be declared as a dominating explanation of the reality in an economy, nor the real*

*consumer behaviour be explained in a highly sophisticated consumer theory
with a 'black box' assumption. The market failure with the lack of sufficient
information about price, quality, durability, availability, time and
environmental performance of consumer goods and services is indisputable.*[21]

Critics of current marketing practices claim that much factual information
relevant to consumer choice is simply unavailable and that this results in higher
prices, 'artificial' brand differences and a stress on frills that represent no real
value to consumers. Such commentators illustrate their arguments by reference to
products such as cheese, coffee and sachets of powdered drink, where the same
physical product from the same production line may be sold under different manufacturer and retail brand names at different prices in the same shop. Marketers,
on the other hand, rebut these claims by noting that in many of the cases in which
product promotions contained numerous facts, there has been little positive effect
on sales. In addition, marketers feel that if consumers really wanted and would
use more product information, our system of competition would provide it—
always allowing for the fact that many major sectors in the economies of the two
countries are effectively controlled by one or two major companies and that
effective levels of competition are restricted.

In any event, there is growing pressure for businesses to provide more and
better quality information so that more 'rational' or better decisions can be
made by consumers. A result of this belief has led to a number of consumer
information programs.

UNIT PRICING

Unit pricing means that the retailer not only displays the total price of the item,
but also displays the price per relevant unit of the product (such as dollars per
kilogram, dollars per litre and so forth). The basis for this program arose from
consumerists who alleged that consumers could not identify the most economical
item in a product class because of the large variety of brands, package sizes and
quantity sizes (such as jumbo, super, giant, large economy size and so on), and
the poor presentation of quantity information on packages. Even better educated
shoppers sometimes find it difficult to identify the most economical items.

The results of studies on usage of unit pricing have not been consistent, however. Most have found higher usage of unit-price information among higher
socioeconomic categories rather than among the lower-income groups who might
appear to benefit most from them. Research generally indicates a high awareness
among consumers of unit pricing, but much variability with regard to claimed
usage and effectiveness.[22] There are several possible reasons for such findings.
First, even with access to unit-price information, consumers may not necessarily
buy the most economical item because of such factors as brand quality differences and the convenience of smaller but more expensive sizes (such as to a single elderly buyer). Secondly, the method of unit-price information presentation
varies considerably and is not always easy to interpret. Thirdly, use of unit-price
information requires effort by consumers at the point of sale which they are not
always willing to make. In New Zealand one study found that the incidence of

'quantity surcharging', the term applied to the situation where a larger pack size carries a higher unit price than a smaller pack size, was almost 30 per cent of prepackaged grocery items. Interestingly, it was the same in supermarkets that provided unit-price information and those that did not. It is fair to assume that if its provision had any widespread effect on the behaviour of consumers, the stores providing the information would have a lower incidence of quantity surcharging.[23]

NUTRITIONAL INFORMATION AND FOOD LABELLING

With the growing concern over dietary deficiencies among the public (particularly among young people) and the increasing demand to know what really goes into the foods we eat, manufacturers have been under pressure to increase their nutritional labelling. Manufacturers in Australia and New Zealand have also been forced to be more proactive in providing nutritional information because of the more stringent requirements of many overseas countries. For example, in the United States the Nutritional Labelling and Education Act 1990 makes labelling mandatory for all processed foods, and voluntary for seafood and commonly consumed fruits and vegetables; and requires definitions for such nutritional terms as 'light', 'low fat', and 'reduced calories'. In Europe the European Commission has been working for a very long time towards standardisation of labelling and has developed an extensive number-labelling system to cover colouring agents, emulsifiers, preservatives and other additives to food. This system is increasingly being adopted in other parts of the world and is now regularly seen as information for Australian and New Zealand consumers.

Research in the United States has shown that the extent to which consumers are able to understand and thus use nutritional information is problematic. Findings of studies have not always produced consistent results, but there are clear indications that more consumers are demanding and using information in Australia in the 1990s than was evident in the United States in the 1970s when many of the benchmark studies in the area were carried out.[24] Part of the interest in nutritional information is attributed to the ageing population. Older people are becoming more concerned about their health and see a good diet as a key preventive issue. As a result, consumers are taking greater personal responsibility for their health and are actively searching for information on diet and nutrition. A focus-group survey of 406 people in Sydney and Melbourne in 1993 indicated that 44 per cent of people were reading the labels of packaged food for information and 64 per cent read labels for over-the-counter pharmaceuticals. The study also showed that consumers are obtaining information on diet and nutrition from a vast array of other sources not recorded in previous surveys, including television (44 per cent), magazines (44 per cent), newspapers (35 per cent), radio programs (22 per cent) and books (9 per cent). These figures are indicative of the serious interest Australians are taking in health issues. Indications are that consumers are moving past the stage of being satisfied with generalities such as 'rich in iron' or 'high fibre', and are wanting more specific information about the particular benefits of particular ingredients. Over 60 per cent of the people in the Sydney and Melbourne study claimed to have changed their diet in recent years, and among people who read labels the most sought after information is sugar content. This is followed (in order) by fat content, artificial colourings, salt content, preservatives and artificial flavourings. Over half the study was also concerned about the use of chemicals and additives in food, including residues in fresh food.[25] This is all specific information and supports the thesis that consumers of the 1990s are becoming more educated and informed than the consumers portrayed in earlier research results.

Even so, most consumers are still amateurs at interpreting nutritional information and one major difficulty for consumers is coming to grips with the often contradictory results reported from medical studies and the simplistic way in which they can be reported in the general media. Consumers are often genuinely confused about what constitutes a good diet and if, for example, they should take more or less fat, and they should be concerned about whether it is saturated or not. With these points in mind, it is difficult to know how marketers should respond to consumers' wishes for nutritional information in both the detail of the information and the method by which it is presented. One study in the United States showed that consumers preferred labels with moderate levels of nutritional information, compared with those with either the least or the most information.[26] Another American study utilising point-of-purchase nutrition signing in supermarkets found that the point-of-purchase signs had no effect on the in-store purchase behaviour of customers, but significantly enhanced the image of the shops.[27]

As with research on unit pricing, most studies on nutrient labelling have found that consumers in lower socioeconomic categories are less likely to use such information. In some respects, the discussion about who uses nutritional information is not important. Individual people often require particular information to contend with medical conditions such as diabetes, high blood pressure or hyperactivity in children, and their needs for information are critical. In New Zealand it is also possible for individuals to apply for the release of information under the *Official Information Act 1987*. This legislation includes universities and state-owned enterprises as well as traditional government departments. Information may be withheld for trade or commercial reasons but these are quite specific.

OPEN DATING

This is the practice whereby dates are printed on packaged food products to inform consumers of their freshness. It is normal to provide a 'use by' or 'best by' date, and consumers seem to make frequent use of this information for particular categories of products such as meat and dairy foods.

TRUTH-IN-LENDING

Truth-in-lending refers to information regarding credit arrangements offered to consumers. In the United States research has shown that the effects of providing such information as annual rates of interest are unclear. One study showed that although the practice of making such information available apparently improves consumer knowledge of credit rates and charges, it has been found to do little to change credit behaviour, because of the importance of the retailer in the credit decision. Moreover, it was shown that most consumers (particularly those with lower incomes and education) remained uninformed about interest rates; many did not even understand the concept of interest, nor could they calculate it in dollars. Thus, this study concluded that consumers should not only be provided with information but also be taught to understand it and use it.[28] In Australia the situation is similar. The calculations required to calculate effective annual interest rates under the Australian standards are extremely complex and well beyond the capabilities of many consumers.[29] Legal controls on truth-in-lending in Australia are chiefly effected by different state statutes. The main recent development in this area is the formulation of the Code of Banking Practice (1993) for Australia, which seeks to:

1. establish minimum standards of good practice that customers are entitled to receive;

2. promote more transparent and fairer relationships through the disclosure of information, including documentation in plain English;

3. define principles for establishing fair and efficient processes for the resolution of disputes (i.e. provide consumers with an effective means of redress).

The requirements of the Code of Banking Practice have now exceeded much of the protection previously offered by state legislation on consumer credit with the result that legislation is being revised to uniform standards and may be superseded by federal legislation.

In New Zealand truth-in-lending is controlled by the *Credit Contracts Act 1981*. The relevant clauses of this Act are also incorporated into the Code for Financial Advertising, which is promulgated by the New Zealand Advertising Standards Authority and gives the consumer an additional form of protection against receiving false information. Particular consumer safeguards required include the provision of the cash price if deferred payments are offered, information on interest rates and the components of the credit, and a three-day 'cooling off' period during which the consumer may cancel credit agreements controlled under the Act.

Information overload?

Many of the foregoing research studies on consumer-information programs indicated that consumers do not heavily use them. What causes this lack of use? Some researchers suggest that the problem may be the result of information overload. That is, there are limits to the amount of information that consumers can process; hence, too much information can lead to dysfunctional processing.[30]

In the first systematic study of information overload, subjects were asked to make decisions on product brands with varying quantities of information.[31] The researchers concluded that as the amount of information increased, consumers were less able to select the brand best for them. Yet, the information had beneficial effects on the consumer's degree of satisfaction, certainty and confusion regarding his or her selection. That is, subjects appeared to feel better with more information while actually making worse purchase decisions! This result was taken to mean that an information-overload phenomenon had been identified. Similar results were found in a succeeding study, in which information overload was observed to be related to an increase in the number of brands. It was found, however, that increased information per brand resulted in better decisions.[32]

Critics of these two studies raised a number of conceptual and methodological issues. Moreover, reanalysis of the data obtained in these research projects, with a more powerful analytical procedure, suggested that information overload may not have occurred in the experiments.[33] However, additional research studies have again led to findings of information overload.[34] Thus, additional replication is desirable across other decision-making situations in order to understand the nature and extent of information overload.

How do consumers cope with information overload? They may employ several strategies to reduce the amount of information used in purchase decision making so as not to be overwhelmed by the great amount available. It has been suggested that consumers base their decisions on the most important three to five product-attribute dimensions rather than on all of the information available.[35] Further, it should be re-emphasised that some of the decision rules discussed in Chapter 14 are very simple and suggest that the consumer may choose to concentrate on very limited amounts of information. Another suggestion is that consumers organise and integrate the separate information bits into larger information 'chunks', as described in Chapter 11. For example, a brand name may serve as the consumer's basic device for summarising the impressions and comparisons that exist among brand alternatives in the marketplace.[36] Also, we are aware that prior knowledge and the ability and motivation to process information will affect how much information search is completed by consumers.

Although few definitive statements can yet be made, the concept of information overload may become an extremely important issue among marketers, consumerists, legislators, regulators and others who seek to provide even more information to the consumer. The 'more information is better' argument, however, may result in shoppers feeling better but not necessarily making better purchase decisions.

CONSUMER CHOICE

With the array of products available for purchase, it would seem that Australian and New Zealand consumers have very little restriction in choice within the marketplace. However, some consumer activists argue that the consumer actually has less choice than might be possible and desirable, because of the economies of scale necessary in order to enter and compete effectively in certain industries. For example, in the breakfast-cereal market it is claimed that a small new producer of cereal would find it virtually impossible to enter and be successful because of the scale of production, distribution and marketing support that would be necessary. Costs of advertising alone are a major barrier to entry when supermarkets will demand at least six-figure advertising support for a new product before they will agree to stock it. The Trade Practices Act and the Fair Trading Act are both designed to prevent the development of monopoly conditions in markets and hence avoid situations where the consumer has no effective choice. As such they impose controls on takeovers and mergers to prevent the dominance of particular industries.

In reality, the situation is rather more complex than this simple principle. Decisions on market dominance are taken on the basis of the 'public good', which encompasses more than just what is good for the consumer and may involve considerations such as local employment or the protection of industries from overseas competition. In a small economy such as New Zealand these features become especially clear. In order to support companies of a size capable of competing in global markets it is often necessary to allow them to develop dominance within the domestic marketplace. Sometimes this is even endorsed by statute. For example, until 1994 the New Zealand Apple and Pear Marketing Board controlled the supply of all apples and pears in New Zealand because of the opinion that competition between New Zealand producers in overseas markets would be destructive to the New Zealand industry. As a result, the New Zealand consumer had no freedom of choice but to purchase the Board's produce. A further interesting example of the complexities of issues involved in consumer choice, and where it is not placed as the pre-eminent issue, is provided in the case below:

Fisher & Paykel dominate the whitegoods market in New Zealand with over 80 per cent of market share. This was a position they established before import controls were lifted in 1987 and duties particularly to Australian manufacturers were reduced under ANZCERTA. Fisher & Paykel responded to this situation by signing a series of exclusive dealing arrangements with their distributors—in essence, they would refuse to supply Fisher & Paykel goods to any dealer stocking other manufacturers' products. This arrangement was condemned by the Commerce Commission in 1989, as it reduced competition and restricted consumer choice. Fisher & Paykel appealed this decision to the Court of Appeal and the appeal was consolidated with a case brought by the Australian company Email/Simpson, who saw the arrangement as restricting their access to the New Zealand market. The Fisher & Paykel appeal was successful and they have managed to retain effective control of distribution channels in New Zealand and restricted widespread consumer access to Simpson products. Critical to the court's judgment was the relative global sizes of the two companies. While Fisher & Paykel are dominant in New Zealand, they are small in comparison with their competitors and only able to make small penetration into the Australian market. The court allowed that the exclusive dealing arrangements allowed Fisher & Paykel to generate other benefits, such as savings in costs, that were to the public good and that there would be probable loss of employment in New Zealand, both in manufacturing and distribution, if the agreements ceased.[37]

The findings in this case proved quite controversial and they are difficult to reconcile in terms of ANZCERTA. However, they show very effectively how issues of consumer choice tend to be lost among other issues relating to the public good. Conventional economic arguments would hold that by ensuring consumers had a legitimate choice, other benefits, such as reduced costs, would follow from the competition.

Other consumer-choice issues are those also related to 'freedom of rights'. Many of these issues overlap with our earlier discussion on consumer safety and relate to situations where choice is removed from consumers in order to protect them from their own actions or to reduce costs to society as a whole. An example is the recent removal of choice regarding cycle safety helmets. Realistically, few people argue with such developments and accept that official restrictions are sometimes necessary in order to persuade people to do what is best for them and society.

THE CONSUMER'S VOICE AND CONSUMER REDRESS

The consumer has the right to be listened to in the marketplace. That is, consumer input as a means of setting government policies should be available, and consumer complaints directed to businesses should be facilitated and, more importantly, responded to in an equitable way.

There are numerous ways in which consumers can make themselves heard, including complaints, boycotts and legal redress. Undoubtedly among the most organised and significant actions are those representations made by consumer organisations and television programs such as 'Consumer Watch' and 'Fair Go'. The remedies sought by consumers normally just involve restitution of goods and/or money, but they can also involve punitive actions. The best way for marketers to be protected from consumer redress is to *prevent* problems from occurring.[38] Adequate market research and the monitoring of customer satisfaction will go a long way to preventing problems. Also, marketers can establish codes of conduct, make better disclosures of information and substantiate claims in order to forestall problems. Indeed, many codes of conduct established for industry sectors such as advertising, banking and insurance also include specific methods for complaint and redress for consumers.

In both Australia and New Zealand the most effective way in which consumers can seek legal redress is through the Small Claims Tribunal and the Disputes Tribunal, respectively. Claims may be brought for sums up to $5000 in an informal environment, which actually discourages the use of lawyers and where there is no provision to award costs against the loser. These provisions make it an inexpensive and low-risk option for consumers to pursue in order to win redress. There is some evidence that knowledge among consumers of formal methods of redress is very slight. One study of a sample of complainants to the Ministry of Consumer Affairs in Perth in 1991 showed that only 26 per cent of those people were aware of the Small Claims Tribunal as a possible method of resolving disputes.[39] Further, the same study showed unprompted awareness of other possible agencies to help with redress, such as community organisations (e.g. the Citizens Advice Bureau) and industry associations, was typically less than 1–2 per cent. As members of this group were in the position of already having taken a complaint to a third party, it would be reasonable to expect them to be more knowledgeable about options for redress than average consumers. The most important source of information about the Ministry of Consumer Affairs itself was word of mouth from friends and relatives (37 per cent).

ENVIRONMENTAL CONCERNS

A consumer right, not enumerated by Kennedy but now viewed as increasingly important, is the right to a *clean environment*—to be assured that the environment the consumer lives in is free from pollution. Widespread and large-scale pollution seems to be a by-product of an economically developed society, but it is also an area of great concern for many consumers who are demanding information about the environmental impacts of different products and the right to choose products regarded as environmentally safe.

Significance of environmentalism

The 1990s are anticipated to be the decade of the environment. The 'green' movement—the term is borrowed from the name given to Germany's radical environmentalists—is growing significantly and marketers are seeking to cash in on an environmental awakening. 'Green' may be to consumers in the 1990s what 'light' was to them in the 1980s, with products clamouring to show how they are environmentally sensitive. Consider just a few dimensions of the environmental crisis:[40]

➡ The world's forests are being destroyed at the rate of one football-field-sized area each second.

➡ Plant and animal species are becoming extinct at the rate of 17 per hour.

➡ Australia produces the equivalent of 680 kilograms of rubbish per year for every person—enough to keep the family home knee-deep in garbage. This figure is second only to the United States and just ahead of New Zealand. Despite the small populations of Australia and New Zealand, they both face disposal and landfill problems. The problems are concentrated especially because of the heavily urbanised nature of both populations.[41]

➡ Eighty-five per cent of New Zealanders believe that environmental protection is an urgent and immediate problem. Only 2 per cent do not believe it is a problem at all.[42]

➡ Over 80 per cent of Australians believe that there is a need for new regulations on business with respect to water pollution, air pollution and toxic waste. This is a higher percentage than support regulation on any other issue.[43]

Loudon and Della Bitta show how environmentalism is changing in the United States and how it is affecting consumer behaviour. For example, they quote evidence to show that some people avoid particular types of packaging or agree to pay more for environmentally friendly products. They also explain how the United States seems to be five to seven years behind Europe and Canada in its understanding and approach to environmental issues.[44]

Equivalent research has not been completed in Australia and New Zealand, but it would seem that the situation is perhaps more complex and such generalisations may not be appropriate. The two countries are at the forefront of fighting some environmental problems such as ozone depletion and wildlife protection (e.g. driftnet fishing), but are regarded as laggards in other areas such as controls on the use of herbicides and pesticides and disposal of effluent. One international study of attitudes to the environment found five different groups of countries, which were positioned on two dimensions as shown in Figure 18.1. In this analysis New Zealanders are portrayed as negotiators along with Great Britain, France, Belgium and Japan. These countries show a fairly high degree of concern for the environment but trade ecological benefits with other elements of the product. Therefore, behavioural change only occurs when it involves limited disruption to everyday life and the ecological benefits do not involve significant compromises on quality, performance and price premiums. Australia is positioned with Spain, Greece, Italy, Argentina and Portugal as 'Lip Service Environmentalists'. In this group the environmental concern is lower and the predisposition to trade off benefits is even less.[45]

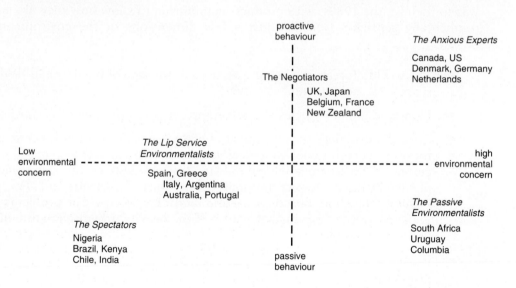

FIG. 18.1   Environmental concern and behavioural change   Source: Janet Brocklesby, 'The Truth about Environmental Concerns', *Marketing*, February 1994, p. 52.

Academics have discussed the need for marketers to become environmentally aware since they first talked about the broadening of the marketing concept to societal aspects in the 1970s. Fortunately, it seems that the lesson is at last being learned by businesses in the 1990s. The emergence of segments such as the 'Educated Greens', who were discussed in Chapter 3, together with other examples such as the growth of ecotourism, has provided the economic stimulus for manufacturers to take environmental issues seriously. A 1991 study in New Zealand showed that significant numbers of consumers had changed some aspect of their buying behaviour in response to environmental concerns:[46]

➡ 38.4 per cent claimed to use 'environmentally friendly' products generally;

➡ 34.6 per cent changed to using ozone-safe sprays;

➡ 26.9 per cent changed brands of cleaning products;

➡ 23.0 per cent changed from plastics to alternative products;

➡ 21.5 per cent changed to unbleached paper products;

➡ 13.0 per cent changed to using biodegradable alternatives;

➡ 12.3 per cent changed from paper to alternative packagings;

➡ 10.0 per cent changed from glass to alternative packagings.

Work by Suchard, Polansky and Chan showed that in considering information prior to purchase, Australians ranked the following impacts in order of importance:

1. dangers to health

2. biodegradability

3. general environmental friendliness

4. recyclability

5. harm to animals

6. harm to the environment in manufacture and disposal

7. consumption of energy in use or disposal

8. adverse environmental effects on other countries

The amount of consideration given to environmental aspects also varied according to products. Most thought was given to environmental concerns in purchasing aerosols and pesticides while little consideration was given in the purchasing of wood (for building), cosmetics, petrol, power and paper products.[47] One major problem is the complexity of many environmental issues, which means that it is very difficult for the environmentally concerned consumer to decide on the best alternative behaviour. As an example, research studies on packaging materials simply fail to agree on the best environmental alternative. Glass may be reusable and recyclable but it is not biodegradable and has very high energy requirements in manufacture. Paper and board may use renewable resources and be biodegradable, but the manufacturing process is not a friendly affair and is notorious for its effects on waterways. Are some plastics genuinely biodegradable or do they simply break down to dust that will contaminate soils for thousands of years? While experts cannot reconcile these issues consumer activity and choice will be confused. As about 60 per cent of aluminium cans are recycled in Australia, and over 70 per cent in New Zealand, it would seem that consumers have got some messages such as recycling, but research has shown that there is genuine confusion over many concepts such as renewable resources and biodegradability.[48]

Environmental consumer types

Ecologically concerned consumers generally belong to the upper class.[49] They tend to be older, better educated and earn higher incomes. In New Zealand one study has looked at environmental attitudes among consumers in some depth.[50] This study segmented consumers on the basis of general lifestyles and found six segments showing many similarities with those in the New Zealand research discussed in Chapter 3. Table 18.1 gives specific information on the attitudes of these groups towards environmental issues.

1. *Classic Kiwis (32.4 per cent of the sample)*. Very representative of the average in education, income, social status and age. Share many characteristics with the popular conception of a typical New Zealand person—a love of sports, New Zealand, their family and the company of other people. This group is concerned about the environment and occasionally acts in accordance with these concerns. They feel that insufficient information is given to consumers on environmental aspects of consumption.

2. *Nostalgic Older Persons (9.6 per cent)*. Mainly over 60, retired, with the lowest education and income levels. Old-fashioned and conservative, they have a narrow set of interests based around their day-to-day lives. They are concerned with personal safety and tend to feel somewhat alienated from many modern trends. Nostalgic Older People express concern for the environment but have not acted upon it, believing that it is the responsibility of government and industry to control environmental damage. Concerns such as the environmental impacts of packaging were viewed by this group as a passing fad.

3. *Career-driven Individuals (17.2 per cent)*. A young group (mainly 18–34) in full-time work and roughly half without children. This is the highest educated group and has the highest income. These are strongly career-orientated individuals, who see themselves as leaders in society and are very interested in health and fitness. They express concern about the environment and express a willingness to pay more for environmentally friendly products.

4. *Apathetic Mid-lifers (8.0 per cent)*. Younger and older singles and couples without families but in full-time work. Even so, incomes are not high and socioeconomic status is below average. Members of this group prefer to follow rather than lead and are not gregarious. They appear uninterested in environmental issues. Very few Apathetic Mid-lifers have ever taken any action themselves to change their behaviour for environmental reasons, and they feel plenty of information exists for the individual who wants to understand more on environmental issues.

5. *Lifestyle Greens (13.2 per cent)*. Primarily aged 35–59, this is a group associated with families and children. There are more females than males in this group, and it is the second most affluent and educated group after

the Career-driven Individuals. Members of this group have four key priorities: family, health, the environment and their careers. They show active concern for the environment and are pro legislation. However, they also accept responsibility as individuals to change their behaviour and indicate a willingness to pay more for environmentally friendly products. Lifestyle Greens are attracted by simplicity and natural living and are concerned with eating unprocessed food.

6. *Young Working-class Families (19.6 per cent).* Members of this group have lower education levels and incomes than average and see themselves as conservative. They are not interested in following fashions and are the least concerned with health and safety. Environmental issues are not a priority for these people, who seem to have more pressing needs competing for their dollars.

TABLE 18.1 Environmental attitudes of New Zealand consumers[a]

Attitude/behaviour statement	Classic Kiwis	Nostalgic Older Persons	Career-driven Individuals	Apathetic Mid-lifers	Lifestyle Greens	Young Working-class Families
I'm actively concerned about the environment	2.41	1.96	2.12	3.50	2.12	3.98
I think that controlling for environmental damage is the task of the government	4.62	2.88	4.58	5.15	5.21	4.37
I separate out my rubbish for special collections	2.41	2.38	3.14	3.65	2.88	5.31
I am attracted by simplicity and natural living	2.86	1.79	3.02	4.05	2.48	3.24
I don't worry about environmental issues as I can't do anything	5.52	4.00	6.40	4.90	5.70	4.00
People shouldn't be expected to recycle without incentives	5.84	3.42	6.37	5.75	6.45	5.06
I make a special effort to eat raw and unprocessed food	3.89	3.63	3.84	4.15	2.67	4.81
I go out of my way to recycle anything I can	3.05	3.17	3.17	3.95	2.36	5.14
I think the government should legislate to prevent environmental damage occurring	2.21	1.63	2.23	2.55	1.45	2.55

continues

TABLE 18.1 Environmental attitudes of New Zealand consumers [a] continued

Attitude/behaviour statement	Classic Kiwis	Nostalgic Older Persons	Carees-driven Individuals	Apathetic Mid-lifers	Lifestyle Greens	Young Working-class Families
Ads should be forced to mention ecological disadvantages of products	2.83	2.13	2.56	3.45	1.67	2.65
I worry about additives in food harming my health	2.50	2.38	2.86	3.85	1.79	3.32
I always try to buy goods in environmentally friendly packaging	2.74	2.21	2.51	3.15	2.79	3.88
I try to consider how my use of products will affect the environment	3.21	3.17	2.58	4.50	2.79	4.29
I never read the information on the pack that tells you how to dispose of it	4.11	2.96	4.16	4.00	4.82	3.04

(a) Based on a 7-point rating scale, with 1 indicating agreement with the statement.
Source: Suzannah Wall, *Packaging and the Environment—Perceptions of the New Zealand Consumer*, Department of Marketing, University of Otago, Dunedin, 1991, pp. 103–12.

CONSUMER PRIVACY[51]

A further consumer right that has now been established relates to privacy, information, databases and similar emerging issues. Consumer information, collected, merged and exchanged through computer and communication technologies, has become the main resource that business and government use to facilitate the millions of daily transactions engaged in by consumers. Timely, accurate and complete consumer information is needed by a variety of organisations such as banks, retailers, commercial lenders, mortgage lenders, financial service organisations, direct-response marketers, advertising agencies, insurance companies and public utilities. Consumer information may be used for such things as approving or denying credit, issuing credit cards, writing insurance policies, selecting people for direct-mail solicitation, preventing fraud, determining eligibility for government aid, investigating and law enforcement purposes, and many other activities.

The United States moved to introduce principles controlling the disclosure of personal information as long ago as the 1970s, and the topic has emerged as a hot issue again in the 1990s.[52] However, the most stringent legislation in the world controlling the privacy rights of consumers is regarded as the *Privacy Commissioner Act 1991* introduced in New Zealand from 1 July 1993. Twelve principles are established in law that govern the collection, storage, identification and disclosure of personal information. In particular, they emphasise that information collected for one purpose cannot be used for any other purposes and that agencies holding information cannot, with very limited exceptions, disclose it to anyone else. The principles do not generally affect the market-research industry, as bona fide operators conform to rigorous standards applied by an industry code of practice, but they will have a significant impact on the direct-marketing business. The New Zealand Direct Marketing Association has negotiated an exclusion to principle 11 in the Act regarding disclosure until 1996 to allow for existing arrangements on things such as the purchase and exchange of mailing lists to be phased out. After that date it will be much more difficult for marketers to access personal information on consumers. The Australian direct-marketing industry is looking apprehensively at the New Zealand situation and fears similar controls may be enacted that will impact on its operations. In 1992 the AMR/Quantum Social Monitor indicated that 90 per cent of Australians believed that it was too easy for businesses to find out about spending and saving behaviour and that legislation was needed to safeguard privacy.[53]

BUSINESS RESPONSES TO SOCIAL AND ETHICAL ISSUES

The social and ethical responsibilities of business have become topics of much public debate. Many corporations have responded to their critics. These responses have three characteristics: changes in boards of directors, more emphasis on ethics and use of social-performance disclosures, sometimes called social audits. Some boards of directors now include outside directors, such as influential academic, minority and religious leaders, who give 'society's' view during decision making.[54] As marketing is usually the most visible activity of an organisation, it must assume responsibility for developing useful products, fair pricing of products and services, and promoting them in an accurate manner.

Social responsibility and profits often complement each other. Some of the most profitable companies are often named as being the most socially responsible. In the United States the *Business and Society Review*, which specialises in social responsibility issues, gives annual awards to the most socially responsible companies. Some of the recent recipients have been Mobil Oil, IBM, Bank of America and Honeywell, which are also very profitable companies.

Corporate ethics are difficult to define and discuss because they are related to individual philosophies and values. Nevertheless, there must be an ethical base for making marketing decisions.[55] The problem comes from determining which base or reference point to use. While a variety of theories are relevant to marketing and consumer behaviour,[56] we can examine two basic approaches to use in deciding the morality of a particular decision or action.

One approach uses *relative standards* (also known as situation ethics, or speculative philosophy) in which the correctness of an action depends on the specific circumstances involved. In this view, ethics are subjective, situational, culturally determined and autonomous; they are developed by people on the basis of human experience. There are two approaches to considering situation ethics: *utilitarianism*, which looks at the consequences of an act to decide whether it is morally right;

and *intuitionism*, which uses an individual's conscience to decide whether an act is ethical. The first approach strives to achieve the most good for the greatest number of people; the second, to satisfy the individual's own feelings about right and wrong. The problem with these approaches is that there may be little agreement among people as to what is the morally correct thing to do—decisions may appear to be arbitrary due to different situations. Moreover, there is uncertainty about the moral correctness of decisions because values change over time.

A second approach uses *absolute standards* (also known as moral idealism, or moral revelation), in which the correctness of an action depends on permanent, rigid, universal rules or moral ideas, which are to be applied whatever the circumstances. The Bible provides the basis for the Judeo-Christian values by which most people in Australia and New Zealand resolve moral dilemmas in using absolute standards. This is the approach recommended by many moral philosophers today.[57] It is upon such universals that a business's, marketer's and consumer's ethical philosophy must be built. The code of ethics reproduced in Figure 18.2 was developed by the Australian Marketing Institute.

Advertising regulation in Australia and New Zealand[58]

Ethical standards are a key dimension to codes of practice developed by industries and professions to regulate the behaviour of their members and afford protection to the consumer. Two important codes that impact on marketers in Australia and New Zealand are the codes of practice developed by the advertising industries of both countries. The first industry code of practice for advertising was developed in Great Britain in the early 1960s. Both the Australian and New Zealand codes have many shared principles with that system but also some important differences. Both the Australian Advertising Standards Council and the New Zealand Advertising Standards Authority were formed in the early 1970s. They are both funded by levies on the advertising industry, though these are operated in slightly different ways and are sometimes referred to as examples of self-regulation by industries. The term 'self-regulatory' is not ideal in their situation. Both have constitutions designed to ensure that they operate as independent and autonomous identities despite the source of their funding. For example, the Australian Advertising Standards Council has 16 members and two alternate public members. Ten of the 16 members represent the public interest, including the chair and the two deputy chairs. The alternate members are eminent Australians unconnected with the advertising industry and nominated by the chair. The other six representatives are nominated by the advertising industry. The current chair is the Hon. Paul Toose, a former judge, and he is responsible for the appointment of public members. The charter of the AASC is quite explicit in requiring the council to appoint its public members with regard to 'the diversity of Australian society in matters of age, sex, background, ethnic origin, colour, regionalism and any other considerations deemed relevant by the chairman'. This constitution is markedly different from those of other self-regulatory systems that typically oversee services such as police and health throughout different countries. The Advertising Standards Complaints Board in New Zealand has eight members, four of whom are public members, including the chair. In this case, the public

Australian Marketing Institute
Code of
Professional Conduct

1. Members shall conduct their professional activities with respect for the public interest.

2. Members shall at all times act with integrity in dealings with clients or employees, past and present, with their fellow members and with the general public.

3. Members shall not intentionally disseminate false or misleading information, whether written, spoken or implied nor conceal any relevant fact. They have a duty to maintain truth, accuracy and good taste in advertising, sales promotion and all other aspects of marketing.

4. Members shall not represent conflicting or competing interests except with the express consent of those concerned given only after full disclosure of the facts to all interested parties.

5. Members in performing services for a client or employer, shall not accept fees, commissions or any other valuable consideration in connection with those services from any one other than their client or employer except with the consent (express or implied) of both.

6. Members shall refrain from knowingly associating with any enterprise which uses improper or illegal methods in obtaining business.

7. Members shall not intentionally injure the professional reputation or practice of another member.

8. If a member has evidence that another member has been guilty of unethical practices it shall be their duty to inform the Institute.

9. Members have a responsibility to continue the acquisitions of professional skills in marketing and to encourage the development of these skills in those who are desirous of entry into, or continuing in, the profession of marketing management.

10. Members shall help to improve the body of knowledge of the profession by exchanging information and experience with fellow members and by applying their special skill and training for the benefit of others.

11. Members shall refrain from using their relationship with the Institute in such a manner as to state or imply an official accreditation or approval beyond the scope of membership of the Institute and its aims, rules and policies.

12. The use of the Institute's distinguishing letters must lie confined to Institute activities, or the statement of name and business address on a card, letterhead and published articles.

13. Members shall co-operate with fellow members in upholding and enforcing this code.

FIG. 18.2 Australian Marketing Institute Code of Ethics Source: Australian Marketing Institute

does not have an inbuilt majority, as in Australia, but neither does industry; and as the proportion of complaints upheld in both countries is similar, it does not appear to affect independence. In New Zealand the latest figures available show that the board upheld 30.5 per cent of complaints in 1991 and 43.7 per cent in 1992, while in 1993 the Australian council upheld 32.9 per cent of complaints processed (398 upheld and 813 not upheld).

Both the Australian and New Zealand systems are based upon a general code of ethics (see Table 18.2), which is then supplemented by specific codes for certain situations or industries. The Media Council of Australia, which administers and enforces the codes of practice on which the Advertising Standards Council makes judgments, has tried to limit the number of special codes it has formulated and currently lists codes for therapeutic goods advertising, slimming goods advertising, cigarette advertising and alcoholic beverages advertising. New Zealand has been more prepared to develop special codes for different situations and has specific regulations for the following:

➡ liquor advertising

➡ cigarette advertising

➡ baldness or hair loss

➡ driving and petrol consumption claims

➡ financial advertising

➡ the way people are portrayed in advertising

➡ slimming or weight loss

➡ the reproduction of banknote images

➡ farm safety

➡ advertising for children

➡ environmental claims

➡ comparative advertising

In 1993 the Australian Advertising Standards Council received a total of 1300 complaints, 1036 coming from individual members of the public as opposed to competitors, interest groups or government agencies. This level of complaints was almost double that of the previous year when 691 complaints were forwarded. In New Zealand the trends are the same, though obviously the total numbers are fewer. In 1989, 24 complaints were received. In 1990 this rose to 34 and since then growth has been spectacular—160 in 1991, 225 in 1992 and 320 in 1993. A small part of the New Zealand trend is explained by the authority taking over some work previously handled by the Broadcasting Standards Authority on television and radio advertising following the 1993 amendment to the *Broadcasting Act 1989*. This is interpreted as reflecting government confidence in the speed and quality of complaint handling within the 'self-regulatory' system and should be seen as a positive development in supporting ethical programs by industries. Overall, the growth in complaints received by the two authorities is largely seen as a response to the efforts they have made to increase awareness of their role over the past few years, but it is also seen as reflecting the continued growth of consumerism in the two countries.

TABLE 18.2 The Media Council of Australia Advertising Code of Ethics (incorporating amendments to 1st October 1993)

The object of this Code is the regulation of advertising in its broadest sense. However, it applies only to the content of advertisements submitted for publication or broadcast by constituent members of the Media Council of Australia and members of constituent and associate organisations of the Media Council of Australia.

In this code the term 'advertisement' shall mean matter which is published for payment or other valuable consideration and which draws the attention of the public, or a segment thereof, to a product, service, person, organisation or line of conduct in a manner calculated to promote or oppose directly or indirectly that product, service, person, organisation or line of conduct.

This Code has been adopted by the Media Council of Australia to be applied within the advertising self-regulation system.

The provisions of this Code are recommended to those advertisers, advertising agencies and media outside the Media Council advertising self-regulation system.

The Advertising Standards Council shall, in matters placed before it, be responsible for (a) the interpretation of the code and (b) the determination of whether breaches of the Code have occurred.

This Preface forms part of the Code.

The Code

1. The conformity of an advertisement with this Code will be assessed in terms of its probable impact, taking its content as a whole, upon a reasonable person within the class of those to whom the advertisement is directed and also taking into account its probable impact on persons within other classes to whom it is likely to be communicated.

2. Advertisements shall comply with Commonwealth law and the law of the relevant State or Territory.

3. Advertisements shall not encourage breaches of Commonwealth law or the law of the relevant State or Territory.

4. Advertisements shall not encourage dangerous behaviour and shall not encourage illegal or unsafe road-usage practices.

5. Advertisements shall not engage in unlawful discrimination and shall not demean the dignity of men, women or children.

6. Advertisements shall not contain anything which in the light of generally prevailing community standards is likely to cause serious offence to the community or a significant section of the community.

continues

TABLE 18.2 The Media Council of Australia Advertising Code of Ethics (incorporating amendments to 1st October 1993) *continued*

7. Advertisements shall be truthful and shall not be misleading or deceptive.

8. Advertisements shall be clearly distinguishable as such.

9. Advertisements of a controversial nature shall disclose their source.

10. Advertisements shall not exploit the superstitious nor unduly play on fear.

11. Advertisements shall not disparage identifiable products, services or competitors in an unfair or misleading way.

12. Advertisements for any product which is meant to be used by or purchased by children shall not contain anything including dangerous practices which would result in their physical, mental or moral harm. Advertisements shall not directly urge children to put pressure on their parents to purchase the product advertised.

13. Scientific, statistical or other research data quoted in advertisements shall be neither misleading nor irrelevant.

14. Testimonials used in advertisements shall honestly reflect the sentiments of the individuals represented. Claims in testimonials are subject to the same rules as other advertising.

15. All guarantees or warranties referred to in advertisements shall comply with the provisions laid down by Commonwealth law and the law of the relevant State or Territory.

Source: Media Council of Australia, 'Australian Advertising Co-regulation; Procedures, Structures and Codes'.
Note: The Media Council of Australia has disbanded the current system of Advertising Codes with effect from 31st December 1996. During the period immediately after that date individual media organisations will continue to subject advertising to a test of suitability for publication until a new structure can be developed.

CONSUMERS' RESPONSIBILITIES

While the consumer's rights have been discussed in this chapter, nothing has been said about the obligations that accompany these rights. It has been suggested that consumer rights can only be achieved when accompanied by consumer responsibilities. Thus, consumers have the obligation to choose wisely, keep informed, put safety first and help protect their environment.[59] In other words, the original notion of *caveat emptor* (let the buyer beware), by which markets have operated for thousands of years, is not totally outmoded. Much consumer behaviour is freely chosen, and primary obligations and duties still lie with the consumer to behave in a socially responsible and ethically defensible way.

Consumers must establish an appropriate ethical framework in which to handle decisions that confront them. One issue that consistently presents some consumers with ethical decisions is the problem of buying imported goods. For instance, when buying a luxury imported car, an Australian consumer may invoke decisions about what is 'right', 'correct', or 'moral'. On the one hand, the purchase may result in obtaining a car that will convey high status and offer quality, trouble-free transportation. On the other hand, its purchase could contribute to the Australian trade deficit and, by not supporting local industry, put domestic workers out of their jobs. Thus, the consumer who has strong personal values on each of these issues will face an important moral dilemma in which satisfying his or her own desires is contrary to the interests of others. 'Buy Australian' and 'Buy New Zealand' campaigns, which have run extensively in both countries, work by making choice an ethical problem and suggesting to consumers that there is a *right* thing to do. A recent Australian survey showed that 73 per cent of people agreed with the sentence 'To improve our economy we will have to buy only Australian-made products in future'. Also, a substantial number of people appear to be prepared to pay up to 10 per cent more to obtain Australian products instead of imported goods. Results showed a range from 52 per cent of the sample prepared to pay extra for food items to 26 per cent for cars. The variations in these figures for different product classes reflect perceptions of the differing quality of Australian goods vis-a-vis imported ones.[60] Another example that forces consumers to introduce an ethical dimension into their purchasing is the way in which marketers may link the purchase of their product to a charitable donation. This is an increasingly common form of sales promotion and has produced some spectacular results for both the companies and charities involved. Two very successful examples are the support by PAL dog food in New Zealand for rescue dogs and Mainland Cheese's repeatedly successful Australasian promotion to support the yellow-eyed penguin, the world's rarest penguin.

Research indicates that consumers can identify purchase situations in which they have faced an ethical dilemma. Moreover, those who choose alternatives they perceive as unethical use a somewhat different decision process from that used by those choosing neutral or ethical alternatives. Finally, consumers selecting unethical alternatives reported feeling significantly more anxious, guilty, nervous, remorseful, embarrassed, shameful and unethical than those making an ethical selection.[61]

In the United States ethical dilemmas are being brought increasingly to shoppers' attention. For instance, the non-profit Council on Economic Priorities publishes a supermarket shopping guide rating 168 companies, 1800 brands and 20 supermarkets on the following social responsibility criteria: charitable contributions, women's and minorities' advancement, military contracts, animal testing, information disclosure, community outreach, nuclear power and family benefits. Apparently, the guide is impacting on buyer behaviour. Almost 80 per cent of readers switched brands based on the book's ratings.[62]

Deviant consumer behaviour

Most consumer-behaviour research has concentrated on improving marketing or consumer effectiveness in the marketplace. Very little attention has been devoted to consumer behaviour that has negative consequences for marketers or consumers themselves. These 'deviant' consumer behaviours include negligent and fraudulent behaviours.[63]

NEGLIGENT-CONSUMER BEHAVIOUR: COMPULSIVE BUYING

Most consumers engage in buying as a normal and routine part of their everyday lives. But buying may become compulsive under two situations: when the product itself is addictive (e.g. tobacco), and when the *act* of buying becomes compulsive. In the latter case, the goal shifts from obtaining utility from the purchased item to achieving gratification from the purchasing process itself. Compulsive buying is chronic, repetitive purchasing that becomes a primary response to negative events or feelings. It is essentially seen as a method of mood repair.[64] Compulsive buying becomes very difficult to stop and ultimately results in harmful consequences to the individual and the rest of the family, such as amassing huge amounts of debt that are difficult to retire, and feelings of remorse, lowered self-esteem and weakened interpersonal relationships.[65] 'Shopaholics' are addicted to purchasing and use it as a fix to offset emotional deprivation.[66] And when they are confronted over their spending habits, they will often switch to another type of chronic destructive habit such as overeating, workaholism or overexercising.[67]

The extent of compulsive buying should not be underestimated. It is a pervasive phenomenon and is particularly prevalent among adult females. Studies show that perhaps as much as 10 per cent of the American population can be classified as 'hard-core shoppers' who shop for shopping's sake rather than to fill real needs.[68] One factor facilitating the process is the easy availability of credit cards. It is probably no coincidence that there has been a rapid growth in bank and retail cards issued during the rise in the problem of compulsive consumption. The result of easy credit can be staggering debt, and specialist organisations such as the Financial Counsellors Association in Australia have been developed to help with advice in such situations.

FRAUDULENT CONSUMER BEHAVIOUR: SHOPLIFTING

Shoplifting is an example of a fraudulent or criminal type of deviant consumer behaviour that involves the theft of retail merchandise during store hours by someone who is shopping or pretending to shop. The extent of shoplifting in Australia and New Zealand is unknown. Recent evidence from Australia suggests that much 'shrinkage' (the term retailers use to describe material lost from inventory before it is sold) is actually due to staff theft rather than customers. Estimates for shrinkage across the Australian retail sector vary from $1 billion, approximately 2 per cent of retail sales, to $3.8 billion, or 4 per cent of retail sales. Shrinkage rates vary by type of stores, with chainstores and clothing stores typically experiencing 6 per cent. Security consultants now attribute approximately 50 per cent of shrinkage to theft by staff and about 30 per cent to shoplifting by consumers. Figures for recorded shop thefts for Western Australia show trends that are typical of other states, with numbers having risen from 12 658 to 17 184 over the three-year period from 1990 to 1992.[69]

These figures place shoplifting in Australia at similar proportions to the United States, where it is estimated that shoplifting equals about 2 per cent of all retail sales excluding petrol and car purchases. Each American family pays an extra $150 per year in increased prices to cover the cost of thefts. Other American shoplifting statistics suggest that:[70]

➡ Perhaps 60 per cent of consumers have shoplifted at some time.

➡ About 200 million shoplifting incidents occur yearly.

➡ About 20 million Americans steal from a store at least once a year.

➡ Shoplifters are caught only about one in 50 times.

➡ About 40 per cent of apprehended shoplifters are adolescents.

➡ From 1.5 to 3 per cent of all shoppers may attempt to shoplift, but the rate is about 6 percent in department-store costume-jewellery sections.

➡ Only 4 per cent of shoplifters are true kleptomaniacs with an obsessive desire to steal.

➡ Most shoplifters in one study were women, mainly in their teens or 20s. Divorced, separated or widowed women were most likely to shoplift.

Though no comparable studies have been completed by consumer researchers in Australia and New Zealand, it is evident from the Australian figures that shoplifting is a major problem. More study of the problem, its causes and marketing solutions is needed to reduce this form of fraudulent/criminal consumer behaviour.

Thus, it must be emphasised that consumers, just as business and other organisations, have an obligation to act responsibly in the marketplace in exchange relationships.

SUMMARY

This chapter discussed the underlying causes of the consumer movement in Australia and New Zealand and briefly described its evolution. The movement is based around the establishment of a series of consumer rights, and the presentation of the material in the chapter was arranged around the six rights most relevant to marketing issues. First, consumers have the right to product safety. Although safety is of paramount importance and widely supported, cases still occur of unsafe products. Secondly, consumers have the right to be provided with adequate information that protects them from fraud and deceit. Unit pricing, nutritional labelling, open dating and truth-in-lending were cited as areas where specific developments have taken place to provide consumers with more useful information. However, consumers may be overloaded with such information, leading them to make worse decisions. Thirdly, consumers have the right to choose, and several dimensions of this were discussed that explain how the issue is related to other matters of public good. Fourthly, consumers have the right to be heard and to obtain redress. Prevention, restitution and punishment were cited as remedies to consumer problems. Fifthly, consumers have the right to a clean environment. Sixthly, consumers have the right to privacy.

In discussing this material we drew attention to some of the important legislative responses to consumer-protection issues, and also showed how marketing and industry people can make effective responses through the operation of codes of practice, which provide guidance to help prevent problems and may provide a mechanism for complaint and redress. Finally, some of the responsibilities of consumers were explored in order to emphasise that both parties in a purchase transaction have obligations to behave in a socially responsible way.

MANAGERIAL REFLECTIONS

For our product or service situation:

1. Is the product or service safe for the consumer?
2. What information is being provided to the consumer and how can this process be improved?
3. Are there any parts of the marketing program that might be deceptive?
4. Are there environmental or pollution aspects of the product or service that need to be addressed?
5. Are the concerns of consumers fully understood by our personnel?
6. Has a system been established to respond effectively to consumerism issues?

DISCUSSION TOPICS

1. What is meant by the term 'consumerism'?
2. Discuss the history of consumerism as it relates to current marketing practices.
3. Which of the consumer's rights are of most concern to you? Why?
4. What does the term 'deceptive advertising' mean?
5. Find an ad you feel to be deceptive for a product or service, and explain how it should be altered to alleviate the deception.
6. Explain how consumer complaints can be a useful asset to a company.

7. Why is it important for an organisation to be responsive to consumers and how is the responsiveness of firms to consumer problems related to consumer legislation?

8. Visit a supermarket and select one aisle of products to obtain the following information:
   (a) number of products
   (b) number of brands
   (c) number of sizes in each brand.

   On the basis of this experience, do you think there is information overload? Why or why not?

9. Choose an example of consumer-protection legislation, or of a regulation designed to protect consumers. Indicate where knowledge of consumers would be helpful to possible revision of that legislation or regulation.

REFERENCES

1. 'Fans on fire' and 'Spa pool fires', *Consumer*, November 1992, pp. 3, 25.
2. Neil Shoebridge, 'Shoebridge', *Business Review Weekly*, 15 January 1993, p. 53.
3. Philip Kotler, *Marketing Management*, 5th edn, Prentice-Hall, Englewood Cliffs, NJ, 1984, p. 85.
4. David A. Aaker & George S. Day, 'A Guide to Consumerism', in David A. Aaker & George S. Day (eds), *Consumerism: Search for the Consumer Interest*, 4th edn, Free Press, New York, 1982, pp. 8–15.
5. David A. Aaker & George S. Day, *Consumerism: Search for the Consumer Interest*, 2nd edn, Free Press, New York, 1974, p. xvii. Figures in this section are taken from the Quantum Australian Social Monitor, published in *Australian Professional Marketing*, April 1993, p. 35, and in *Australian Professional Marketing*, April 1994, pp. 34–5.
6. Wolfgang C. Fischer & Andrew Massey, *Consumer Credit in North Queensland*, Department of Economics Research Monograph, James Cook University, Townsville, 1994, pp. 90–9; and Jacinta Wigham, *Financial Counsellors Resource Project*, Perth, 1994.
7. Martin Ryan, 'Consumer Bankrupts in Melbourne', *Australian Journal of Social Issues* (1), 1993, pp. 34–49.
8. *Financial Counsellors Casework Manual (Western Australia)*, Financial Counsellors Association of Western Australia, 1990, p. 15.
9. Robert O. Herrmann, 'Consumerism: Its Goals, Organizations, and Future', *Journal of Marketing* 34, October 1970, p. 56.
10. United States, House of Representatives, *Message from the President of the United States Relative to Consumers Protection and Interest Program*, Document No. 364, 87th Congress, 2nd session, 15 March 1962.
11. The material in this section is largely drawn from information supplied by the Australian Consumers Association, Sydney, NSW, and the New Zealand Consumers Institute, Wellington.
12. Paul Leinberger, 'Consumers seek out "C" solutions', *Australian Professional Marketing*, April 1993, pp. 34–5.
13. National Consumer Affairs Advisory Council (NCAAC), *Consumer Affairs Administration in Australia*, Canberra, 1991.
14. The most comprehensive review of this subject suitable for non-law students is provided by J. Collinge & B. R. Clarke, *The Law of Marketing in Australia and New*

Zealand, Butterworths, Sydney, 1989. However, students should also be aware that significant changes have taken place since publication of that book; for example, the *New Zealand Consumer Guarantees Act 1993* and work in Australian on the harmonisation and strengthening of consumer credit legislation.

15. 'Coming: A Rush of New Consumer-safety Rules', *US News & World Report*, 18 July, 1977, p. 61.

16. *Consumer Product Safety Commission Annual Report*, 1 July 1982–30 June 1983, US Government Printing Office, Washington, DC, 1983.

17. Michael A. Kamins & Lawrence J. Marks, 'Advertising Puffery: The Impact of Using Two-sided Claims on Product Attitude and Purchase Intention', *Journal of Advertising* 16 (4), 1987, pp. 6–15.

18. David M. Gardner, 'Deception in Advertising: A Conceptual Approach', *Journal of Marketing* 39, January 1975, p. 42.

19. 'The Big Squeeze', *Consumer*, November 1992, pp. 4–6.

20. Hugh Mackay, *Reinventing Australia*, Angus & Robertson, Sydney, 1993, p. 219.

21. Fischer & Massey, op cit, Ref 6, p. 88.

22. Kent B. Monroe & Peter J. La Placa, 'What Are the Benefits of Unit Pricing?', *Journal of Marketing* 36, July 1972, pp. 16–32; and Monroe P. Friedman, 'Consumer Responses to Unit Pricing, Open Dating, and Nutrient Labeling', in M. Venkatesan (ed.), *Proceedings of the Third Annual Conference of the Association for Consumer Research*, Association for Consumer Research, Chicago, 1972, pp. 361–9.

23. James Henry & Rob Lawson, Unit Pricing in Dunedin Supermarkets, unpublished Preliminary Study for the New Zealand Consumers Association, University of Otago, 1993.

24. Warren A. French & Hiram C. Barksdale, 'Food Labeling Regulations: Efforts toward Full Disclosure', *Journal of Marketing* 38, July 1974, pp. 14–19; and Raymond C. Stokes, 'The Consumer Research Institute's Nutrient Labeling Research Program', *Food, Drug, and Cosmetic Law Journal* 27, May 1972, pp. 263–70.

25. Neil Shoebridge, 'Health Becomes a Holistic Market', *Business Review Weekly*, 10 December 1993, pp. 67–8.

26. Edward H. Asam & Louis P. Bucklin, 'Nutrition Labeling for Canned Foods: A Study of Consumer Response', *Journal of Marketing* 37, April 1973, pp. 32–7.

27. Dale D. Achabal, Shelby H. McIntyre, Cherryl H. Bell & Nancy Tucker, 'The Effect of Nutrition P-O-P Signs on Consumer Attitudes and Behavior', *Journal of Retailing* 63, Spring 1987, pp. 9–24.

28. George S. Day & William K. Branditt, 'Consumer Research and the Evaluation of Information Disclosure Requirements: The Case of Truth in Lending', *Journal of Consumer Research* 1, June 1974, pp. 21–32.

29. Fischer & Massey, op cit, Ref 6, pp. 96–9.

30. G. A. Miller, 'The Magical Number Seven, Plus or Minus Two: Some Limits on Our Capacity for Processing Information', *Psychological Review* 63, 1956, pp. 31–97; and Richard N. Cardozo, 'Customer Satisfaction: Laboratory Study and Marketing Action', in L. George Smith (ed.), *Reflections on Progress in Marketing*, American Marketing Association, Chicago, 1964, pp. 283–9.

31. Jacob Jacoby, Donald E. Speller & Carol A. Kohn, 'Brand Choice Behavior as a Function of Information Load', *Journal of Marketing Research* 11, February 1974, pp. 63–9.

32. Jacob Jacoby, Donald E. Speller & Carol Kohn Berning, 'Brand Choice Behavior as a Function of Information Load—Replication and Extension', *Journal of Consumer Research* 1, June 1974, pp. 33–42.

33. J. Edward Russo, 'More Information Is Better: A Revaluation of Jacoby, Speller and Kohn', *Journal of Consumer Research* 1, December 1974, pp. 68–72; John O. Summers, 'Less Information Is Better?', *Journal of Marketing Research* 11, November 1974, pp. 467–8; and William L. Wilkie, 'Analysis of Effects of Information Load', *Journal of Marketing Research* 11, November 1974, pp. 462–6; Naresh K. Malhotra,

Arun K. Jain & Stephen W. Lagakos, 'The Information Overload Controversy: An Alternative Viewpoint', *Journal of Marketing* 46, Spring 1982, pp. 27–37.

34. Kevin Lane Keller & Richard Staelin, 'Effects of Quality and Quantity of Information on Decision Effectiveness', *Journal of Consumer Research* 14, September 1987, pp. 200–13.

35. Fleming Hansen, 'Consumer Choice Behavior: An Experimental Approach', *Journal of Marketing Research* 6, November 1969, pp. 436–43; and Jerry Olson & Jacob Jacoby, 'Cue Utilization in the Quality Perception Process', in M. Venkatesan (ed.), *Proceedings of the Third Annual Conference of the Association for Consumer Research*, Association for Consumer Research, Chicago, 1972, pp. 167–79.

36. Jacoby, Speller & Berning, ibid, pp. 33–42.

37. *Fisher & Paykel Ltd v. Commerce Commission*, High Court (Commercial List), Auckland, 12, 13, 14, 15, 16, 20, 21, 22, 23, 26, 28, 29 March; 27 April 1990; and *Fisher & Paykel v. Commerce Commission*, Court of Appeal, Wellington, 11, 21 December 1990.

38. Dorothy Cohen, 'Remedies for Consumer Protection: Prevention, Restitution, or Punishment', *Journal of Marketing* 39, October 1975, pp. 24–31.

39. Natalie Dall, *A Study of the Pathways Used by Consumers Who Contact the Ministry of Consumer Affairs for Assistance*, Edith Cowan University, Perth, 1991, pp. 58–68.

40. Walter Coddington, 'It's No Fad: Environmentalism Is Now a Fact of Corporate Life', *Marketing News*, 10 October 1990, p. 7; Joe Schwartz, 'Earth Day Today', *American Demographics*, April 1990, pp. 40–1; and 'Get Ready for the Green Wave: The Environmental Sell', *Scan*, January/February 1990, p. 3–4.

41. Barbara Lord & Peter Allan, *Recycling Made Easy*, Wilkinson Books, 1994.

42. Hyam Gold & Alan Webster, *New Zealand Values Today*, Alpha Publications, Palmerston North, 1990, pp. 42–4.

43. Don Porritt, 'The Dynamics of Marketing Survival', *Australian Professional Marketing*, April 1994, pp. 34–5.

44. David L. Loudon & Albert J. Della Bitta, *Consumer Behavior*, McGraw-Hill, New York, 1993, pp. 637–40.

45. Janet Brocklesby, 'The Truth about Environmental Concerns', *Marketing*, February 1994, p. 52.

46. Suzannah Wall, *Packaging and the Environment—Perceptions of the New Zealand Consumer*, Masters Thesis, Department of Marketing, University of Otago, Dunedin, 1991.

47. Hazel T. Suchard, Michael J. Polansky & Ricky Yee-Kwong Chan, 'Factors Influencing Environmental Buyer Behaviour', *Proceedings of the International Marketing Educators Conference, 14–16 April 1993*, Edith Cowan University, Perth, 1993, pp. 505–28.

48. Rob Lawson & Suzannah Wall, 'Consumer Perceptions of Packaging Materials', in J. Saunders et al., *Proceedings of the MEG Annual Conference*, University of Loughborough, 1993, pp. 592–601.

49. Ingo Balderjahn, 'Personality Variables and Environmental Attitudes as Predictors of Ecologically Responsible Consumption Patterns', *Journal of Business Research* 17, August 1988, pp. 51–6.

50. Wall, op cit, Ref 46.

51. This section is adapted from *The Equifax Report on Consumers in the Information Age*, Equifax Inc., 1600 Peachtree Street, Atlanta, GA 30302, copyright 1990.

52. Martha F. Riche, 'The Rising Tide of Privacy Laws', *American Demographics*, March 1990, p. 24; and Dan Fost, 'Privacy Concerns Threaten Database Marketing', *American Demographics*, May 1990, pp. 18–21.

53. John Swan & Andrew Stewart, 'Marketing Law: Data Privacy', *Marketing*, May 1993, p. 54; and Paul Leinberger, 'Consumers Seek "C" Solutions', *Australian Professional Marketing*, April 1993, pp. 54–5.

54. Patrick E. Murphy, 'An Evolution: Corporate Social Responsiveness', *Michigan Business Review*, November, 1978, pp. 19–25.
55. The remainder of this section is adapted from Geoffrey A. Lantos, 'An Ethical Base for Marketing Decision Making', *Journal of Consumer Marketing* 3, Fall 1986, pp. 5–10.
56. R. Eric Reidenbach, Donald P. Robin & Lyndon Dawson, 'An Application and Extension of a Multi Dimensional Ethics Scale to Selected Marketing Practices and Marketing Groups', *Journal of the Academy of Marketing Science* 19, Spring 1991, pp. 90–1.
57. Donald P. Robin & R. Eric Reidenbach, 'Social Responsibility, Ethics, and Marketing Strategy: Closing the Gap between Concept and Application', *Journal of Marketing* 51, January 1987, p. 46.
58. This section is based on information supplied by Colin Harcourt (Australian Advertising Standards Council, Sydney) and Glen Wiggs (New Zealand Advertising Standards Complaints Board, Wellington).
59. Hans Thorelli, 'Consumer Rights and Consumer Policy: Setting the Stage', *Journal of Contemporary Business* 7, Autumn 1978, pp. 3–16.
60. Don Porritt, 'Buying into Australian Made', *Australian Professional Marketing*, December 1993/January 1994, pp. 29–30.
61. Lawrence J. Marks & Michael A. Mayo, 'An Empirical Test of a Model of Consumer Ethical Dilemmas', in Rebecca H. Holman & Michael R. Solomon (eds), *Advances in Consumer Research*, vol. 18, Association for Consumer Research, Provo, UT, 1991, pp. 720–8.
62. Cathy Freeman, 'Some Firms Get Poor Environmental Rating in New Shopper's Guide', *Marketing News*, 19 March 1990, p. 19; and Joe Queenan, 'Ethical Shopping', *Forbes*, 17 April 1989, p. 80.
63. George P. Moschis & Dena Cox, 'Deviant Consumer Behavior', in Thomas K. Srull (ed.), *Advances in Consumer Research*, vol. 16, Association for Consumer Research, Provo, UT, 1989, pp. 732–7.
64. Richard Elliott, 'Shopping Addiction and Mood Repair', in J. Saunders et al., *Proceedings of the MEG Annual Conference*, University of Loughborough, 1993, pp. 287–97.
65. Thomas C. O'Guinn & Ronald J. Faber, 'Compulsive Buying: A Phenomenological Explanation', *Journal of Consumer Research* 16, September 1989, p. 155.
66. Betsy Morris, 'As a Favored Pastime, Shopping Ranks High with Most Americans', *Wall Street Journal*, 30 July 1987, pp. 1, 13.
67. Carol Gentry, 'No Joy in Store for "Shopaholics"', *Morning Advocate*, 25 August 1991, p. 7E.
68. Patrick McDonnell, 'Shop Until You Drop?', *Forbes*, 11 January 1988, p. 40.
69. Ali Cromie, 'How Retail Crime Pinches Profits', *Business Review Weekly*, 4 June 1993, pp. 50–5; also statistics obtained courtesy of the Crime Research Centre, University of Western Australia.
70. Dena Cox, Anthony D. Cox & George P. Moschis, 'When Consumer Behavior Goes Bad: An Investigation of Adolescent Shoplifting', *Journal of Consumer Research* 17, September 1990, p. 149; and 'War on Shoplifting Using New Tactics', *News Star*, 4 February 1990, p. 9A.

CHAPTER 19

ORGANISATIONAL-BUYER BEHAVIOUR

LEARNING OBJECTIVES

AFTER STUDYING THIS CHAPTER YOU SHOULD UNDERSTAND:

➡ the nature of organisational buying;

➡ how and why organisational-buyer behaviour differs from final-consumer purchasing;

➡ the nature of the different variables influencing the organisational buyer's behaviour;

➡ the types of decision situations confronting organisational buyers;

➡ how organisational buyers make decisions on purchases of goods and services.

In Chapter 1 we discussed the fact that the marketplace may be divided into two groups: final consumers and organisational buyers. The behaviour of final consumers—those who purchase for their personal or household use—was the subject up to this point. Now it is behaviour within the organisational buying context that we will examine in this chapter. Although there are many similarities between organisational and consumer buying, there are also some substantial differences and because of this, *organisational marketing*—that is, marketing to organisational buyers—can be quite different from consumer marketing.

THE NATURE OF ORGANISATIONAL BUYING

Organisational buying is in some ways similar to consumer buying, as it is not organisations making the buying decisions but people within organisations. But there are significant differences that must be understood by marketers in order to succeed in the organisational market. These points of variance are addressed in this section. It is also relevant to note that this chapter also concentrates on one particular context of organisational buying that is also the closest parallel to the consumer situation. Table 19.1 lays out the different approaches to investigating organisational buying behaviour.

TABLE 19.1   Approaches to organisational buying

		Organisational focus	
		Intra	Inter
Decision process focus	Within a decision	A decision within the buying organisation	A discrete buyer/seller transaction
	Over a series of decisions	A series of related decisions in a buying organisation	Long-term buyer/seller relationships

Source: D. W. Barclay, 'Organisational Buying Outcomes and Their Effects on Subsequent Decisions', *European Journal of Marketing* 26 (4), pp. 48–64.

Most research on organisational buying has focused on single decisions within organisations. It is this approach that brings organisational buying closest to studies of consumer behaviour, especially those relating to the family. The right-hand column in Table 19.1 recognises the importance of relationships and networking between companies, and the interdependence of many of these relationships. The bottom row of the table emphasises the longer term nature of many interactions between many organisational buyers and sellers.[1] Realising that organisational buying has these additional dimensions is very important and makes it a worthwhile subject for study in its own right.

Purpose of organisational buying

Organisational buyers make purchase decisions in order to satisfy their goals, as do final consumers. But the goals differ. Organisations have the goals of producing a good, providing a service or reselling an item, and therefore buy products and services that will allow them to engage effectively in these activities. Thus, these buyers may manufacture products (GM, Ford and Toyota); provide services (AMP Society, Hertz, Ansett Airlines and Australian Department of Defence); or resell items (Myer, Mitre 10 and Woolworths). Buyers may be for-profit operations or not-for-profit, product- or service-orientated, governmental or private. In all cases, organisational buying takes place in order to produce a product, provide a service or engage in resale.

Organisational buying, then, is the decision-making process by which organisations establish the need for purchased products and services, and identify, evaluate, and choose among alternative brands and suppliers.[2]

Since World War II organisational buying activities have evolved significantly in most companies. Shifting from very unsophisticated operations in which clerks with little expertise or specialisation in purchasing did most of the buying, companies today with as few as 20 employees may have a purchasing specialist; and various competing factions such as engineering, quality control, the user and senior management all exert influence on the purchase. Organisational buying has received special emphasis over the last decade as companies in Australia and New Zealand have struggled to cope with economic recession. As organisations have struggled to control costs their buying processes have come under special scrutiny. In New Zealand the search for improved ways of purchasing health services and pharmaceuticals led to a whole restructuring of the public health sector in the early 1990s. In this current complicated environment, the purchasing specialist attempts to satisfy the corporation's product or service needs in a complex process requiring balancing of relations with suppliers, colleagues and superiors, product specifications, trade regulations, his or her personal reputation, price and other factors.[3] The average purchasing professional is a well-qualified person who works hard at a complex job handling large-dollar amounts of business.

Organisational buyers versus final consumers

The same consumer-behaviour concepts discussed earlier in the text cannot simply be applied to individuals engaging in purchasing behaviour as part of their job in the organisation, because the context is different. There are several major ways in which organisational markets and their buying behaviour differ from consumer markets and their buying behaviour.[4] The major variations are in market structure and demand, buyer characteristics, and decision processes and buying patterns.

MARKET STRUCTURE AND DEMAND

The organisational marketer should recognise that several factors related to market structure and demand distinguish these buyers.

GEOGRAPHICAL CONCENTRATION Buyers are more concentrated than in consumer markets. For example, in New Zealand 33 per cent of all businesses are located in the Auckland area with 28 per cent of the population. If specific industries, and therefore specific organisational markets, are considered, this situation is compounded. Auckland has over 40 per cent of manufacturing companies and nearly 50 per cent of business and financial services. In Australia the same patterns are found in Sydney and Melbourne.

FEWER, LARGER BUYERS Buyers are also concentrated by size in the organisational market. Unlike consumer markets where demand is spread across many household units of similar sizes, organisational markets tend to be characterised by concentration of demand into a few large companies, so the focus of marketers is often to maintain a few good large customers, and segmentation by sales volume is important. For example, the tyre companies have completely different marketing problems in dealing with the few large car, truck and tractor makers who comprise their organisational markets, compared with dealing with the consumer market through a widespread dealer network.

VERTICAL OR HORIZONTAL MARKETS Organisational-buyer markets may be either vertical or horizontal. In a *vertical* market, the product or service would be sold to virtually all organisations in perhaps one or two industries. Certain drilling bits are intended only for use in the oil exploration industry. Downturns in the target industry may hit vertical marketers extremely hard. *Horizontal* markets are those that are very broad, and in which the product or service is sold to a wide spectrum of industries. Computer and cleaning services, office supplies and small motors are used by many industries, and so are not as radically affected by shifts in any one industry, as effort will be focused on other industries not affected by changing technology or tastes.

DERIVED DEMAND Organisational demand is derived from consumer demand. For example, in part, a company manufacturing window blinds has demand for metal, cords and parts to produce the blinds because of the demand consumers have for blinds in new and remodelled homes. If the housing industry slumps, the company and many other suppliers face reduced demand for their products. In order to avoid the general decline, the window-blind company must look to increase its share of the overall market by manipulating the elements of its marketing mix effectively (e.g. heavy advertising or sales promotions).

INELASTIC DEMAND Total industry demand for industrial goods is relatively unaffected by changes in price in the short run, compared with the price influence on demand in consumer markets. If all tyre manufacturers were to raise their tyre prices by $3 to car manufacturers, this would have little effect on demand. Car manufacturers would continue to purchase roughly the same amount, as tyres represent such a small price in the overall cost of the finished car, and a $15 increase in car price will have no perceptible effect on the consumer. Similarly, an overall increase in the price of computer chips will have little overall effect on the price of the finished computer, and therefore little, if any, impact on total computer demand. While this situation is true for industry demand, an individual firm's demand may be strongly affected by a price change. For example, if a single computer chip maker raised its price, it would likely find significantly reduced demand for its chips with orders flowing to lower priced competing producers. In other words, the demand schedules for total industries tend to be relatively inelastic but for any one firm it may be elastic.

FLUCTUATING DEMAND Organisational demand is characterised by much greater fluctuation than that of consumer markets. Generally, organisational buying is closely related to the economic cycle. When demand for consumer goods is up, demand for industrial goods is also up, and organisational buyers may build large inventories of raw materials and component parts, and may add office equipment and other items to their plant and factories. When the economy slows down or reverses, manufacturers, wholesalers and retailers may use up existing inventories and postpone purchases of supplies, equipment and so forth. The recent development of more flexible manufacturing systems has meant that organisations are now able to carry lower inventories than in the past, which tends to emphasise this aspect even further and it can be important that suppliers can respond to orders within a matter of hours.

BUYER CHARACTERISTICS

There are several important organisational-buyer characteristics typically cited that differentiate them from final consumers.[5]

GROUP INVOLVEMENT Because products purchased by organisational buyers are often costly and complex, a group of individuals may be involved in the decision. People from engineering, production, finance, purchasing and even top management could participate in a large packaging-machinery purchase decision.

TECHNICAL KNOWLEDGE Professional buyers, generally quite knowledgeable about the products or services being bought, make the purchase decision or may be directed by other technically competent individuals (such as engineers) to the appropriate purchase decision based on a group decision. These buyers are known as *purchasing agents* in industrial, governmental and institutional organisations. In resellers, such as discount houses, these people are known as *buyers*, and they are in charge of purchasing the line of merchandise to be resold.

RATIONAL MOTIVATIONS As indicated by the skilled, technical nature of purchasers, organisational buyers are often strongly directed by rational motivations. Such motivations are generally economically based and can be translated into dollars and cents so that costs and benefits may be carefully weighed. For example, product-quality specifications and consistency, prompt delivery assurance, price, credit terms, warranty and service are all rather objective elements influencing buyers in their selection of a vendor.

In addition to such rational considerations, though, buyers are also influenced by emotional motivations, and these are often difficult for a vendor to assess.[6] For example, buyers are human in their likes or dislikes for vendor salespeople, concern for their own job security, need to be respected in their job, willingness to take risks and so on. Purchasing agents are confronted with a variety of stresses in their work, and their responses are influenced by the reward structures and cultures in place in their organisations. The perceived risk connected with making buying decisions is one of the most significant stresses they face. In one study, purchasers were presented with a hypothetical buying situation that would provide buyer autonomy while generating considerable perceived personal risk to themselves. Respondents were asked to indicate the certainty and seriousness of a series of potential negative personal consequences if the chosen supplier failed to satisfactorily perform the required tasks. In addition, respondents rated the importance of nine risk-handling tactics that might be used before selecting a new vendor for that type of purchasing situation.[7] Table 19.2 presents the perceived risk scores and the tactics to handle prepurchase stress.

ONE OF THE ABOVE COULD GET YOU IN VERY HOT WATER

Can you tell which? It's not easy is it?
But the pack on the left could well fail to comply with the Fair Trading Act. Not by much — but by enough. Because the claim may be misleading or deceptive.
The pack on the right, however, is unlikely to contravene the Act since the product claim is a self-evident exaggeration which is not capable of objective proof.
In other words, mere puffery is all right. It's not capable of misleading the ordinary person.
Now all this might seem very simple — but it's not. The Fair Trading Act is complex and requires a legal mind to steer you clear of its pitfalls.
What's it for, you might well ask?
Well, in a nutshell, the Fair Trading Act has been introduced to bring New Zealand trading practices into line with other Western countries in terms of consumer protection.
Now the Act is not a pair of handcuffs that will restrict your business. It's there to promote competition and fair play.
What the Act is very hot on is conduct which is misleading, or deceptive or is likely to mislead or deceive.
Hence the need to be particularly careful in what you do or say. Or omit to do or say.
So if you're dealing with publicity — whether television, radio, press, direct mail or any other media — we suggest you cut the risks and talk to Brandon Brookfield. We'll tell you just what will and what won't wash.

Auckland: (09) 799-350, Wellington: (04) 726-904.

BRANDON · BROOKFIELD
BARRISTERS · SOLICITORS · NOTARIES

This advertisement combines concern and rational arguments to motivate organisations to buy legal advice COURTESY OF BROOKFIELDS

TABLE 19.2   How purchasing agents handle personal risk

A. Magnitude of various components of perceived personal risk		
Component	Average risk [a]	Rank
You will feel personal dissatisfaction	6.32	1
Your relations with the users of the purchased product will be strained	5.13	2
The status of the purchasing department will decrease	3.59	3
Your next performance review will be less favourable	3.41	4
You will have less chance for promotion	2.92	5
Your next raise will be smaller	2.71	6
You will lose status among your peers	2.68	7
You will lose your job	2.25	8
Your personal popularity will diminish	1.78	9

(a) Where risk is computed as the product of seriousness (1 = annoying but not serious, 2 = somewhat serious, 3 = very serious) and probability (1 = not probable, 2 = somewhat probable, 3 = very probable).

B. The importance of various tactics for handling perceived personal risk		
Tactic	Average importance [b]	Rank
Visit the operations of the potential vendor to observe its viability first-hand	4.46	1
Question present customers of the vendor concerning their experience with the vendor's performance	3.61	2
Multisource the order to ensure a backup source of supply	3.57	3
Obtain contract of penalty clause provisions from the potential vendor	3.48	4
Obtain the opinion of colleagues concerning the potential vendor	3.23	5
In choosing a vendor, favour firms that your company has done business with in the past	2.98	6
Confirm that members of your upper management are in favour of using the supplier as a vendor	2.75	7
Limit the search and ultimate choice of a potential vendor to well-known vendors	2.53	8
Obtain the opinion of a majority of your co-workers that the chosen vendor is satisfactory	2.16	9

(b) Where the importance scale ranged from 1 = not important to 5 = very important.

Source: Jon M. Hawes & Scott H. Barnhouse, 'How Purchasing Agents Handle Personal Risk', *Industrial Marketing Management* 1, November 1987, pp. 290–1.

Many personal and individual factors may play a significant—but difficult to calculate—role in purchasing behaviour. A buyer who enjoys being entertained, for instance, may direct a greater share of purchases to a supplier who, with an equal product, 'treats the buyer better'. Nevertheless, the days of 'personality selling' are over in business-to-business relationships. Today there is more interest in what salespeople have to sell, and less interest in the personality of the individual salesperson. Specific actions purchasers have adopted to redefine their supplier relationships on a more rational basis include:

➡ reducing the supplier base to only a few key suppliers of a component or service;

➡ basing procurement on long-term cost per unit, not simply price per unit, as a way of recognising quality and service differences and costs;

➡ thoroughly analysing supplier companies, using teams with members from various functions within the purchasing company;

➡ instituting supplier 'partnering', such as early involvement in new-product-development projects.[8]

Handling objections and closing sales are out of place in today's business environment, if practised in a manner other than presenting solutions to customers' problems. The focus must be on understanding customer needs and meeting them, not just getting a sale. Consequently, selling to the 'new breed' of purchasers may involve:

➡ educating salespeople more thoroughly on all aspects of company products in order for them to function on customer problem-solving teams;

➡ using in-depth selling to relate to everyone in the customer's organisation;

➡ practising patience in case another supplier already has the contract—the salesperson can build toward the next contract award.[9]

DECISION PROCESS AND BUYING PATTERNS

Organisational buying patterns are characterised by a number of differences from the buying patterns of final consumers in their decision process and purchase patterns.

FORMALITY   Much organisational-buyer behaviour is typified by greater formality than that of final consumers. Often proposals, quotation requests and purchase contracts are involved, which lend to the formality. Consumers may sometimes obtain written price and product quotes and specifications, but this is rare, in contrast with the normally precise and formal processes used among organisational buyers, particularly in large organisations, which generally have elaborate procedures and policies for purchasing.

COMPLEXITY This is a prime cause of the formality necessary in purchasing. Because organisational-buyer behaviour is so much more complicated than consumer behaviour, products and services are more technically complex, and the financial risks are generally much higher than those faced by consumers, greater formality in decision making requires the conscious consideration of the large number of factors involved in the decision.

LENGTHY NEGOTIATION Much organisational buying requires more extensive negotiation over a longer time period than typically occurs among final consumers. Some of the reasons for this situation are:

1. the size of the order is large and the purchase price is very important;

2. a large number of people are involved in the decision;

3. the product is complex and specifications must be carefully agreed to.

MULTIPLE SUPPLIERS Organisational buyers hesitate to limit their buying of an item to a single source, because their supply could be jeopardised by unforeseen circumstances such as strikes or fires. Company policies, therefore, may not allow a single vendor to supply more than a certain percentage of the company's requirements. Instead, buyers source the same product from two or more suppliers in order to be assured a steady supply of the item. This competition between vendors also can be a healthy lever for buyers to use in obtaining attractive terms and effective service from suppliers.

LARGE ORDERS The typical organisational purchase is much larger than that made by final consumers. For example, Qantas may purchase a fleet of 20 new jets from Boeing to be delivered over a two-year period at a cost of several hundred million dollars. Resellers also purchase in large quantities, break into smaller lots, and sell to other organisational buyers or final consumers. This has become increasingly important in Australia and New Zealand in recent years as retail power has concentrated into a very small number of companies. For example, three companies now control most of the grocery sector on both sides of the Tasman.

INFREQUENT PURCHASE Obviously, very large scale and costly items (such as buildings and large computers) would be only infrequently purchased by organisations. But even smaller, less expensive products may be bought on a contract basis, which is renewed only yearly. In addition, such items as office supplies may be bought only every one to three months. The organisational marketer must, therefore, be vigilant about selling opportunities because they may arise only infrequently.

DIRECT BUYING Although marketing directly from producer to final consumer is growing, such a pattern has long been quite common in the organisational market. Because of order size, product complexity and bulk, technical assistance prior to and after the sale, and geographic proximity of customers, a direct relationship between producers and buyers has been widely adopted for many organisational purchasing situations.

RECIPROCITY   Reciprocity occurs when two organisations agree to purchase from each other, and is found more frequently in industries where products are homogeneous with little price sensitivity. Chemical, paint, steel, rubber and paper industries have exhibited a history of reciprocity; for example, an auto company may buy steel from one supplier, which, in turn, buys trucks from the automotive firm. It must be noted that the systematic use of reciprocity may infringe provisions of the *Australian Trade Practices Act 1974* and the New Zealand *Fair Trading Act 1986*, which both have provisions regarding items such as exclusive dealing arrangements because of their potentially anti-competitive nature. There is still informal and 'innocent' reciprocity among firms, but it should always be justifiable on the basis of gaining a competitive quality product, price, delivery, terms and service from suppliers; otherwise, it makes poor economic sense and is a source of frustration for professional buyers. An important dimension of reciprocity is the use of 'contradeals' for promotion purposes. These are a particularly important way for manufacturers to motivate and influence members of the distribution channel. A typical example is the provision of prizes by companies for television game shows, the deal being negotiated on the basis of the publicity provided to the supplier.

IMPORTANCE OF SERVICE   Organisational buyers, more so than final consumers, require service because it has such a direct bearing on their costs, sales and profits. Companies known for their exceptional service tend to be the ones who excel in an industry, and it is of particular importance to those firms who are unable to stand out otherwise in markets with homogeneous products and prices. Buyers can be effectively marketed to with an edge in such service areas as on-time delivery, credit, repair, market information and inventory maintenance.

INFLUENCES ON ORGANISATIONAL-BUYER BEHAVIOUR

There are four broad categories of factors that influence organisational-buyer behaviour: environmental, organisational, interpersonal and individual.[10] Understanding these factors is critical to the marketer in preparing an effective marketing strategy.

Environmental factors

Seven environmental factors influence organisational buyers: physical, technological, economic, political, legal, ethical and cultural.

PHYSICAL

The physical environment includes such factors as the climate and geographical location of the organisation, and can affect the behaviour of organisational members and determine the constraints and options for the buying organisation. A supplier's geographical location, for example, is an important consideration in whether it is chosen or not. Many firms prefer local suppliers, and in the international sphere many buyers prefer to use domestic suppliers where possible. Climate and geography also determine the availability of raw materials from forests, farms or mines for the organisation, as well as its location decision based on such things as these raw materials, labour availability and transportation systems.

TECHNOLOGICAL

The level of technological development defines what types of goods and services are available to the organisational buyer. In addition, it influences the quality of the buying process itself through development of improved purchasing technology using more sophisticated equipment such as computers to facilitate complex purchasing and inventory control decisions.

ECONOMIC

The economic environment for the buying organisation is affected by price and wage conditions, money and credit availability, consumer demand and levels of inventory in key industry sectors. These sorts of factors will determine the availability of goods and services, ability of buyers to finance purchases and what prices will be paid. Just as for final consumers, the economic environment will influence organisational buyers' optimism or pessimism and, consequently, their buying behaviour.

POLITICAL

Political influence could include such factors as country trade agreements, tariff barriers, lobbying activities, defence spending, government assistance to certain industries or companies, and government attitude toward business generally.

LEGAL

State and federal legal and regulatory environments have an influence on buying activities. Government regulation sets standards for what must be bought in order to be included on products (e.g. auto and lawn-mower safety equipment). Terms of sale and conditions of competition are also enforced by legal means on organisational buyers.

ETHICAL

The ethical environment is of major importance in the buyer–salesperson relationship. Buyers and salespeople must exhibit ethical behaviour if they are to be accepted as professionals. Consequently, each group needs to know what is considered to be ethical and unethical behaviour. Unfortunately, little research has been conducted on how purchasing agents view the ethics of particular salesperson behaviours. However, when selling activities are perceived as unethical by purchasers, they may negatively affect choice of supplier as well as hurt the purchaser's career.[11]

CULTURAL

As discussed in Chapter 3, culture establishes values that are shared by members and which influence them in their buying behaviour. Large organisations, too, have developed their own *corporate cultures* which differ in their values, norms, habits, traditions and customs. The nature of these differing values, styles and behaviours may be evident in an organisation's buying behaviour. For example, companies such as 3M and Hewlett-Packard emphasise technological expertise and would look for this quality in suppliers.

These environmental influences may be exerted through a number of different types of organisations including business firms (suppliers, customers and competitors), government, labour unions, trade and professional organisations, and other social institutions such as religious and educational organisations. How do these various institutions exert their influence on the buying decision process? In several ways. First, they determine the availability of goods and services to the organisational buyer. Secondly, they define the general business conditions in which the firm operates. Thirdly, they define the values and norms guiding buying actions.

Organisational factors

Because organisational buying occurs within the framework of a formal organisation, the organisation's objectives, policies, procedures, structure and systems of rewards, authority, status and communication will all have an important influence on every part of the buying decision process. The marketer must understand four aspects of the organisational buying process in order to design an effective strategy to influence that process. These four sets of interacting organisational variables have to do with the tasks, structure, technology and people involved with buying.

TASKS

The buying task is performed by the organisation in order to accomplish its objectives. These tasks may be classified in different ways such as by purpose, level of expenditure, type of good or service purchased, extent to which the process is routine or not, and extent to which responsibility for purchasing is centralised or decentralised. For example, buying tasks and decisions reflect the type of organisation doing the buying, or its purpose. Manufacturers and retailers have characteristic buying tasks that differ significantly from each other, and these two differ considerably from a third organisation, such as a prison, although they all share some types of buying tasks.

The organisation's goals will influence its purchasing objectives and behaviour. For instance, in companies that strive to be technological leaders in their industry, buying tasks will be performed in a more scientific, high-quality, engineering-oriented way in order to assure this technological leadership.

STRUCTURE

The buying structure of the organisation has an effect on the purchasing process.[12] An organisation has a formal and an informal structure. The organisational chart illustrates the formal relationships between people in the organisation. Informal relationships and communication patterns may be quite different, however, from the formal structure. Marketers must understand both the formal and informal organisation in order to sell effectively to a buyer.

Several dimensions of the organisational structure are influential in its buying processes. The degree of centralisation is a significant factor. A centralised organisation will retain purchasing authority in the hands of a relative few who are typically highly placed in the organisation. When power is concentrated in this fashion, there may be only a few individuals who must be contacted as either influencers or decision makers. However, they may be difficult to gain direct access to because of their high position.

The organisation's degree of formalisation is a second factor. Individuals within a very formalised organisation adhere strictly to stated policies and procedures. This greater formality generally results in more people in more organisational units participating in the buying decision. The decision process is also likely to be quite structured and to follow written guidelines. For example, in the United States the purchasing manual of IBM lists over seventy items under the topic of 'purchasing regulations', and provides strict guidelines for purchasing managers to follow in any corporate purchases. When organisations are highly formal, marketers may find them difficult to sell to because the inertia of established patterns may inhibit new ideas and approaches from gaining a foothold.

An organisation's specialisation is also influential in its buying structure. Where the organisation is divided into numerous departments according to functional specialisation, more people are likely to be involved in the purchasing decision. The marketer's challenge is to determine which influential people must be reached with the sales message.

TECHNOLOGY

Technology may influence not only what is bought but also the buying decision process itself. For instance, some organisations have implemented sophisticated management-science techniques in the buying process, including models for inventory control and price forecasting, purchase scheduling charts, and computer routines for determining optimum order quantities and for company buying alternatives. While manual systems for directing and controlling the buying process are widespread in industry, computerisation is rapidly taking over. Marketing success requires an understanding of the organisation's technology so that any new product or service fits into the system that is already in place.

PEOPLE

The people in the organisation who are involved in the purchasing situation will be a major determinant of the organisational buying process. These people are interdependent and interact with each other to influence members' buying behaviour. The marketer's task is to identify those within the organisation with responsibility and authority for buying decisions in order to persuade them to purchase. Therefore, it is important to know which people are involved with the decision. Their interaction is an important topic that should also be understood.

Interpersonal factors

The interaction between only two people or a larger number is a significant influence on organisational buying decisions. As people involved in a purchasing decision interact they may provide information to each other as well as attempt to influence the purchasing outcome for their benefit. This influence of one person on another is what we mean by interpersonal influence, and commonly occurs in organisational purchasing within the context of a group known as the buying centre.

THE BUYING CENTRE

The buying centre comprises those people in the organisation who interact during the buying decision process. This decision-making unit may vary in size based on how novel, complex and important the purchase decision is; and how centralised, formalised and specialised the organisation is. Rather few organisational buying decisions are made by only one person.[13] Most are made through the interaction of a buying centre. Frequently, purchases entail much lateral and vertical communication and involvement.[14] For example, the purchase of intensive-care monitoring systems by a hospital would likely involve physicians, nurses, administrators, engineers and purchasing people. Consequently, marketers must understand which organisational members are participating in a decision, and what their functions, interests, and degrees of influence are likely to be.[15] For instance, in the hospital equipment purchase just mentioned, not all members of the buying centre are likely to be highly involved or to be involved equally throughout the buying process. As Table 19.3 indicates, their level of involvement would vary across buying-centre participants and over the course of the purchase decision. Even within the context of hospital purchasing it is important to realise the variations that may occur for similar types of equipment. For example, surgical equipment for use in theatres, including basic items such as scissors, has a much larger input from physicians than equipment for ward use where volumes are higher, price more important and the purchasing officer has more influence at each stage.[16]

Most research studies have used the buying centre as the basic unit of analysis by focusing on a particular purchasing decision, the organisational members involved in the purchase, and their communication and influence flows during the decision process. Some have criticised the buying-centre approach to research as being based on concepts of a 'group', which may not be appropriate in the buying-centre context.[17] A feature of the term 'buying centre' is that it tends to emphasise a formal group, whereas this is often not the case. Consequently, another, less widely used research approach has focused on the *buying system* as the unit of analysis and examined the streams of behaviour that characterise ongoing organisational buying activities in the firm. The buying system includes

TABLE 19.3   Involvement of various hospital buying centres in the procurement process

Buying-centre participants	Identification of need	Establishment of objectives	Evaluation	Selection
Physicians	High	High	High	High
Nursing	Low	High	High	Low
Administration	Moderate	Moderate	Moderate	High
Engineering	Low	Moderate	Moderate	Low
Purchasing	Low	Low	Low	Low

Source: Gene R. Laczniak, 'An Empirical Study of Hospital Buying', *Industrial Marketing Management* 8, January 1979, p. 61. Copyright 1979 by Elsevier Science Publishing Co. Inc. Reprinted as adapted with permission of the publisher.

organisational members drawn from diverse functional areas representing different levels in the organisational hierarchy who participate in one or more of the purchasing-related flows. These members are connected by a work-flow and communication network reflecting formal and informal properties.[18]

BUYING-CENTRE ROLES

Like the members of a family, the members of a buying centre exhibit certain roles. These roles correspond precisely to those cited earlier for family members. In the context of organisational buying, a brief review of these roles will be useful.

INITIATORS These are the first to recognise a need for the product or service in the organisation. They perceive a discrepancy between desired goals and actual performance. For example, a company's computer systems director may first suggest a new computer acquisition.

USERS These are the people who will be using the organisational product or service purchased. They often initiate the buying process and may help develop product specifications. They will also typically provide feedback about product performance based on their use of it.

INFLUENCERS Influencers may directly or indirectly influence purchase decisions by supplying information for evaluating alternatives or by defining buying specifications related to design, quality, delivery and so on. In manufacturing companies, technical personnel are important influencers. For example, research and development, design engineering, production engineering and manufacturing personnel may all be instrumental in buying decisions for such companies.

Some individuals may often exert a powerful influence over the group's purchase decision when they act as advocates. These group members are leaders with high status who are more highly involved in group decisions. By virtue of their knowledge and expertise about an issue and the interaction they have with those outside the organisation, they are in a powerful position to influence purchase decisions. Consequently, vendors must seek to identify and enlist such advocates in the promotion process. A strong advocate in the buying organisation for the seller's product may be very influential in securing the sale.[19]

Organisation members who perform *linking-pin* roles are people in key positions of leadership within their own group who exert influence at higher organisational levels. For example, a study of the purchase of innovative hospital radiology equipment found that the chief radiologist in a hospital not only could greatly influence the radiology department but also may be influential with the hospital's financial management staff and top administrators. The interests of such linking-pin individuals and their domain of influence must be understood by marketers in order to target them effectively with marketing programs.[20]

BUYERS Buyers have the formal authority to select vendors and negotiate the terms of the purchase. Often purchasing managers or agents and buyers perform this function, but others such as the organisation's president may also assume this authority. Buyers may also participate in setting specifications for the purchase.

DECIDERS Deciders have either formal or informal authority to select suppliers and make the final buying decision. The buyer may often also be the decider, but it could be a separate individual. For example, if a design engineer were to set specifications for a product that could only be met by one supplier, the engineer is the decider while the purchasing agent may be the buyer. Deciders are often the most important members of the buying centre to a vendor organisation, but they may also be difficult to identify.

GATEKEEPERS These people control the various forms of information flowing into the buying centre. For example, purchasing agents and secretaries may determine whether important advertising and promotional material—and salespeople when they make their calls—will be directed to the appropriate parties in the buying centre such as influencers and deciders. Gatekeepers may significantly influence purchase decisions because they play a role in identifying the organisation's buying alternatives.

Table 19.4 illustrates how the different roles may be involved at the various buying-decision-process stages to be described later. The same individual may play all roles in small organisations, but in larger organisations the roles are generally performed by different individuals or groups. As a result, marketers must identify which organisational members are part of the buying centre and what responsibility and influence they have in the purchase decision for the company's product or service. Typically, the supplier's salesperson must first contact the purchasing department before approaching the other members of the buying centre. This underscores the gatekeeping power purchasing agents may wield.

TABLE 19.4   Decision stages and roles in the buying centre

	User	Influencer	Buyer	Decider	Gatekeeper
Identification of need	x	x			
Establishing specifications and scheduling the purchase	x	x	x	x	
Identifying buying alternatives	x	x	x		x
Evaluating alternative buying actions	x	x	x		
Selecting the suppliers	x	x	x	x	

Source: Frederick E. Webster Jr & Yoram Wind, *Organisational Buying Behaviour*, Prentice Hall, Englewood-Cliffs, NJ, 1972, p. 80.

CONFLICT WITHIN THE BUYING CENTRE

Because several members of the buying centre may be involved in a purchase, the opportunity for *conflict* to develop is an ever-present reality. Differences in perceptions by members of the buying centre as to their roles in the joint purchasing decision may lead to a destructive spiral if not managed effectively.[21]

Three types of conflicts may occur within the buying centre.[22] The first and most serious form of conflict can occur over differences in members' objectives, personalities and decision-making styles. This type of conflict may result in a lack of trust within the buying centre. Resolution could take several forms: group pressure on dissenters to conform; offering rewards to the buying group based on overall rather than individual performance; and removing the decision to a higher level organisation member.

A second type of conflict concerns disagreement between members over the criteria to be used in evaluating vendors and products. Resolution should be possible by persuading individual members to take a broader, corporate perspective rather than their narrow, functional or departmental view.

A third occasion for conflict develops when members of the buying centre dispute the capabilities of vendors to perform their obligations. Members should be able to resolve this type of conflict by gathering more relevant information about supplier attributes.

Buyers confronted with conflict situations are predisposed to utilise a collaborating (e.g. 'Maybe we can work this one out') or a compromising (e.g. 'Let's split the difference') approach. But buyers appear to favour different conflict-handling styles depending on the particular member of the buying centre involved and their role in the decision.[23] Table 19.5 identifies five possible conflict-handling styles among buyers.

TABLE 19.5 Five conflict-handling styles

1. *Competing.* 'Let's do it my way!': The desire to win one's own concerns at the other party's expense, i.e. the desire to dominate, to yield no quarter, to envision the interaction as a win–lose power struggle; assertive, unco-operative behaviours.

2. *Accommodating.* 'I see your point of view': The desire to satisfy others' concerns without attending to one's own concerns, i.e. peaceful coexistence, perhaps entertaining long-run motives; unassertive, co-operative behaviours.

3. *Collaborating.* 'Maybe we can work this one out': The desire to fully satisfy the concerns of both parties, i.e. sharing responsibility, problem solving, in-depth exploration of issues, reaching a mutually beneficial agreement; assertive, co-operative behaviours.

4. *Avoiding.* 'Better let the situation cool down before we act': Exerting an attitude of indifference to the concerns of either party, not immediately addressing the conflict, can take the form of diplomatically sidestepping an issue, postponing an issue until a more opportune time or withdrawing from a threatening situation; unassertive, unco-operative behaviours.

5. *Compromising.* 'Let's split the difference!': The desire to reach an expedient, mutually acceptable agreement, which is somewhere short of total satisfaction for either party, i.e. exchanging concessions or seeking a middle-ground solution; intermediate in both assertive and co-operative behaviours.

Source: Ralph L. Day, Ronald E. Michaels & Barbara C. Perdue, 'How Buyers Handle Conflicts', *Industrial Marketing Management* 17, May 1988, p. 155.

Among industrial buyers, *role stress* may be experienced when expectations about their roles are either unclear or in conflict with one another. Roles may be ambiguous in various ways; for example, when individuals lack information about how much authority they have in carrying out negotiations. Role conflict may also result from a variety of circumstances. For instance, expectations may be incongruent with the buyer's orientation or values, such as when an organisational norm of purchasing reciprocity conflicts with the buyer's view that it is unethical or illegal. Research suggests that salespeople need to understand the buyer's work environment so that they can be sensitive to those who are experiencing severe stress and not contribute to the problem.[24]

POWER RELATIONSHIPS

As one observer notes, 'Managers do not wear tags that say "decision maker" or "unimportant person".' It is, therefore, difficult to apply the buying-centre concept because of the often invisible nature (at least, to outside vendors) of power being wielded in the purchase decision within the organisation. Not even the organisational rank of an individual may be a good indicator of power exerted in the decision because, as we saw previously, secretaries may effectively screen out salespersons whom they may not like. Thus, lower level gatekeepers may have a much more significant influence than their corporate rank would indicate.

The marketer must be careful, however, to accurately assess the role and power relationships that may exist in a buying centre. For example, one study of joint purchase decisions in organisations found that participants generally exaggerated their roles in the process.[25] In addition, an earlier study found that purchasing agents perceived themselves to have a higher level of involvement in buying decisions than did other executives.[26] Therefore, the true locus of power in an organisational buying decision must be understood by the vendor.

In Chapter 5 we described the nature of social power exhibited in groups of consumers. These same concepts are also applicable to the organisational buying decision.[27] The marketer must understand and be able to identify the powerful influentials in the buying centre for a purchase decision. Their influence may be positive, negative or both. That is, they may act as a product or service champion, promoting its purchase, or they may hold veto power over the decision.

A recent study of 251 organisational purchase decisions found expert power to be the most important determinant of an individual's influence in a buying centre, followed by reinforcement (i.e. reward/coercive) power. The effectiveness of individual power bases was found to vary with buying-centre size, viscidity (i.e. the extent to which buying-centre members work together as a team, rather than being fragmented and hostile toward each other), time pressure and the strength of accompanying influence attempts. The research suggested that individuals who primarily had expert power tended to be more influential in committees that were large, viscid and not under time pressure, and when they did not make very strong attempts at influence. Individuals exhibiting primarily reinforcement power were more influential in small, viscid committees that were under time pressure, and where strong influence attempts were made.[28]

The marketer's challenge is to understand power relationships in a prospect's buying centre.[29] This involves knowing what approach appeals to key individuals. For example, a technical approach may work best on those who base their power on expertise, while a sales call by senior management may be productive for those who are most concerned with status power.

Individual factors

Participants in the organisational buying process bring to the situation their own individual thoughts, feelings and actions. These psychological factors are very relevant. For example, one author has suggested that sellers should determine psychological data about customers in order to develop an effective strategy. The types of important data needed by sales representatives include information about who the buying-centre members are, how powerful they are and what their positions are, what 'hot buttons' each has in terms of specific benefits they want, and how they perceive the vendor.[30] From such information more productive sales calls will result. Organisational-buyer behaviour is thus composed of individual behaviour in an organisational context. The same individual determinants of consumer behaviour discussed in Part 3 could be reviewed to understand their meaning in an organisational buying setting. However, only several of the more significant individual dimensions will be discussed here.

MOTIVATION

Motivations of buying-centre members are difficult to assess accurately. They have generally been categorised into task-related and non-task-related motives.[31] *Task-related* motives include such needs as product quality, price, service and delivery, or getting the 'right' product for the 'right' price at the 'right' time from the 'right' source. These pertain to the problem leading to the buying decision. *Non-task-related* motives include such variables as potential for promotion, salary increases, more job security and so forth. Generally, these pertain to the individual's personal advancement, recognition, and desire to reduce uncertainty or risk. Thus, the concept of reward is an important element of the organisational buying process.[32] The marketer must be prepared to show effectively how buying-centre members may achieve their goals.

A basic rule of motivation is that buyers act selfishly; that is, they try to maximise their gains and minimise their losses in a purchase. In doing so they seek to decompose a product or service into various benefits, which can be categorised as financial, product–service, social–political and personal. Not all buyers will be interested in the same benefits, however, so some represent a higher priority or what may be thought of as hot buttons. But because all buyers run a risk that the desired benefits will not be realised, they can only be persuaded if they are sufficiently confident that the seller will keep his or her promise.

PERCEPTION

As we learned earlier, individuals receive and interpret stimuli and organise them into a coherent picture of their world. Organisational buying-centre members' perceptions are important to marketers' development of effective strategies. Two dimensions of this element are significant: perceptions of the selling company's products and people, and perceptions of their own role in the buying-centre decision process.

Buyers will have some overall perception of the seller based on a number of factors. Often this perception, whether accurate or not, is highly instrumental in a seller's success.[33] For instance, companies that are large and well known, such as IBM, are generally perceived by buyers to be better able to keep their promises and, therefore, may frequently obtain sales over their lesser known rivals. Some computer buyers opt for 'Big Blue' because there is safety in IBM's image. After all, if product failure occurs, buyers can claim that it is not their fault because they went with the best.

Perception of company sales representatives is also highly influential in supplier choice. For example, Table 19.6 illustrates how industrial buyers perceive the most effective attributes of saleswomen to be empathy and expertise. There is no reason to believe this would be different for salesmen. In other studies it has similarly been learned that salespeople who understand the buyer's decision process and who are most like the buyer are most effective in obtaining the purchase. Obviously, marketers must understand what perceptions buyers have of sellers. This can be effectively obtained by asking sales administrators to periodically evaluate the way buying-centre members perceive the vendor's products and personnel. As buyers are much more likely to purchase from salespeople they like, the most marketing attention should be directed among buyers with positive attitudes toward the vendor, not among those who view the vendor quite negatively.

TABLE 19.6   Attributes that affect the perception of industrial salespeople

1. Understanding of other people
2. Willingness to go to bat for the buyer within the supplier firm
3. Knowing how to listen
4. Knowledge of firms selling to
5. Knowledge of buyer's product line
6. Imagination in applying supplier products to buyer's product line
7. Confidence
8. Self-reliance
9. Product knowledge
10. Preparation for sales presentations
11. Understanding of buyer's problems
12. Follow-through on deliveries
13. Regularity of sales calls
14. Having a personalised presentation for each buyer
15. Providing technical assistance
16. Presenting many new ideas to the buyer
17. Willingness to handle rush orders

Source: Adapted from John E. Swan, David R. Rink, G. E. Kiser & Warren S. Martin, 'Industrial Buyer Image of the Saleswoman', *Journal of Marketing* 48, Winter 1984, p. 111, published by the American Marketing Association.

A second area of interest in understanding the organisational buying decision process has to do with the individual's role perception within the buying centre. While each of us likes to believe that we are the centre of the universe, our importance is overrated. One study of the perceived responsibilities of a group of purchasing agents compared their responses with those of other executives in the same firm. The purchasing agents rated themselves as more important to the purchasing decision than other executives did. Thus, the marketer must be careful to obtain a reasonably objective view of each buying-centre member's actual influence in the decision process so as not to waste time and effort.

LEARNING

Learning is another variable strongly influencing the individual in the organisational buying process. Learning occurs as buyers make decisions that are satisfactory and this reinforcement increases their tendency to make the same decision in future similar situations. The continual reinforcement of a decision leads to a habit, which is a relatively automatic response. Just as for final consumers, much organisational buying becomes habitual, which helps to simplify the decision process. The development of a routine purchasing process results in increased reliance on known suppliers to meet the organisation's needs for present products and for information on new products. Such buying decisions help the organisation to reduce risk of failure by sticking with known sources.

ORGANISATIONAL BUYING DECISIONS

So far, the numerous elements influencing organisational buying decisions have been reviewed. We now link this information together to examine the types, nature and variations of the actual decision-making process among organisations.

Types of decision situations

As we learned in Chapter 13, final consumers have a continuum of buying-decision types, ranging from very habitual or routinised decisions, to those that entail limited decision making to those that involve extended decision-making processes. The organisational buying-decision process is analogous to that of final consumers, although different terms are generally used to define the stages of the continuum (see Fig. 19.1). These buying situations—part of a *buying* model—are sometimes referred to as *buy-classes* and vary depending on such factors as the newness of the problem, the extent to which new alternatives are considered and how much information is gathered to solve the problem. The three types of buying situations are termed new task, modified rebuy and straight rebuy.[34]

New task situations are those that are new to the organisation. These first-time or unique purchases require much gathering of information and careful establishment of the criteria on which to evaluate the product for purchase. The purchase of an extensive electronic security system for a plant is an example of such a purchase. Such purchases may represent the foundation for a strong and continuing profitable relationship between vendor and customer; therefore, they are very significant to marketers.

Modified rebuy situations occur when buyers re-evaluate and may make changes in their available purchase alternatives. For example, an auto manufacturer's robotised assembly system may be re-evaluated by the manufacturer when a competing supplier provides information on its newer, cheaper and more productive robot welders. Some organisational buying research indicates that new tasks and modified rebuys are rather similar, but straight rebuys are quite different.[35]

Straight rebuy situations are rather routine purchases usually under similar terms of sale to meet continuing or recurring requirements. Purchase of computer ribbons, floor wax, copy paper or delivery truck fuel are examples of routine replenishment from present suppliers as long as satisfaction exists with past products, terms and service.

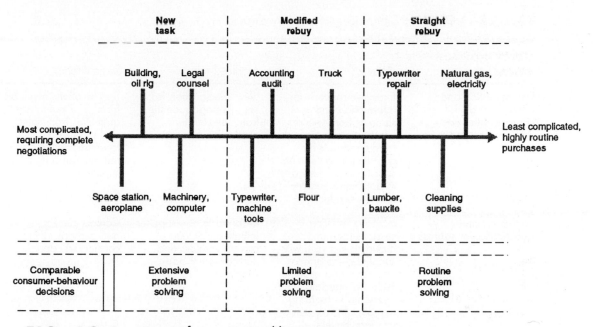

FIG. 19.1   Types of organisational buying situations

Although we can associate the purchase of particular goods and services with different *buy-classes* in the same way that we can associate particular goods and services with different levels of involvement for consumers, it is important to realise that some purchases may cover a wide variety of situations in this model. For example, research on how firms buy market research in New Zealand indicates a wide range of variation according to the task in hand. Purchase of a specialised survey of consumer satisfaction may be very different from a more routine evaluation of advertising.[36]

Table 19.7 provides a more complete summary of the differences between these buy-classes according to the different activities involved in the purchase process. Understanding these differences can help marketers develop more effective strategies depending on the buying situation.

It is also important to understand how buying influences may vary depending on product type in these buy-classes. For example, in the purchase of components, engineers are most influential in new task decisions, perhaps because of the need to determine product specifications and ascertain the seller's ability to meet these criteria. For modified and straight rebuy situations, however, purchasing agents exercise the most influence, perhaps because of the emphasis in these decisions on price and delivery considerations.[37]

The role of the various influences on organisational buying decisions discussed earlier also varies in these buy-classes. For instance, a survey of 200 organisational buyers found that organisational influences are more significant in new task situations (probably because of the economic scope of the decision), while the individual influence of the buyer is more significant in straight rebuy situations.[38]

TABLE 19.7   Differences among buy-classes

Activity in purchase process	New task	Modified rebuy	Straight rebuy
Determination and description of characteristics and quantity of items to be purchased	Extensive requests for information and samples from vendors, informally and through formal requests for quotation to determine specifications; forecasts to determine quantity for new product	New specification from engineering; quantities from sales and production forecasts	Specifications available from prior purchases; quantities from sales and production forecasts; negligible information sought from suppliers
Search for and qualification of sources	Intensive working sessions (perhaps including site visit) with suppliers who appear interested and capable. Technical specialists interested in reducing number of prospective vendors; buyers interested in increasing number	Respond to non-supplier initiative; contact current vendors and perhaps other non-suppliers	Contact current vendors and perhaps others considered capable
Acquisition and analysis of proposals	Obtain and analyse formal quotations, samples, results of tests; refine specifications	In some cases, seek new quotations from established suppliers; in others, seek new information only from non-supplier involved	For annual or continuing supply agreement, seek quotations from vendors who have qualified; for individual purchases, draw against supply agreement
Evaluation of offers, suppliers	Evaluation by technical personnel; senior management may add other considerations not directly related to value analysis	Technical evaluation of non-supplier's offering	Evaluate against preset criteria, price and delivery offered; some organisations maintain multiple sources
Negotiation	Much negotiation on specifications, performance and guarantee; some on delivery; little on price	Negotiations with emphasis on price and delivery	Minimum negotiation; emphasis on price, delivery and terms of sale
Selection of order routine and performance evaluation	Routine for new task varies by organisation; new vendors monitored closely at first	Similar to new task for new vendor; similar to straight rebuy for established supplier	Order routine specified in supply agreement; in addition to regular informal contact, evaluation through formal vendor rating system; exception reports from using department *continues*

TABLE 19.7 Differences among buy-classes *continued*

Activity in purchase process	New task	Modified rebuy	Straight rebuy
Length of process	7–60 months	7–60 months	1 week to 7 months
Source of problem/opportunity recognition	New-product development Analysis of operations Expansion of capacity	Change in specifications or process for existing product Expansion of operations New offer from non-supplier; dissatisfaction with current supplier (resembles straight rebuy except for seeking bids from non-suppliers)	Inventory control system Production schedule Sales forecast
Initiator of purchase	Senior management; marketing engineering or research	Engineering; purchasing	Purchasing or department using the product
Source of contact with supplier	Line managers, technical specialists	Manufacturing, engineering and/or purchasing	Purchasing
Membership in decision-making unit	Senior management; functional managers; technical specialists from marketing, engineering, manufacturing; purchasing specialist	Line managers, technical specialists, purchasing	Purchasing; engineering; manufacturing

Source: Richard N. Cardozo, 'Situational Segmentation in Industrial Markets', *European Journal of Marketing* 14, May–June 1980, pp. 266–7.

Although the buygrid framework has become a popular conception of the organisational buying process and a useful analytical tool, its simplicity has been its major weakness. Some studies have found that participation and influence do not vary according to the buy-classes.[39] Critics of the framework suggest that there is too much reliance on the newness of the task as a primary descriptor, and urge that such factors as the complexity and importance of the purchase situation be included.[40]

Research has found that the purchase-situation attributes of novelty (lack of buying experience within the organisation), complexity (amount of information needed to make an accurate evaluation) and importance (perceived impact on the firm) affect the participation and influence of buying-centre members in an industrial purchase decision. Such findings emphasised the necessary role of salespeople to discover and contact members of the buying centre beyond the purchasing group. Highly technical products representing a novel and important situation for buyers make it imperative that salespeople supply timely and accurate information showing how the product meets the needs of each individual buyer in order to reduce the perceived risk and differentiate the product from those offered by competitors. Aiming sales efforts at plant management and engineering groups will be worthwhile because these individuals have the greatest participation and influence throughout the process.[41]

The organisational buyer's decision process

The organisational buying process could be distilled to the same four steps that were described for final consumers; namely, problem recognition, information search and alternative evaluation, purchasing process and postpurchase processes. However, emphasising the formality of the organisational buying process, it is helpful if we subdivide these stages into greater detail to understand exactly what organisations do. Consequently, we will discuss an eight-step decision process.[42]

PROBLEM RECOGNITION

As with final consumers, problem recognition occurs when someone in the organisation perceives a difference of sufficient magnitude between the desired state and the actual state of affairs. Either external or internal stimuli may be the cause of problem recognition. For instance, an organisation may learn externally of new packaging equipment for its manufacturing operation through a visit to a trade show, an ad seen in an industry trade magazine or a sales call by a supplier's representative. Such information could cause the manufacturer to realise that increased speed, greater cost savings and less down time could result from purchasing the proposed equipment.

Internally the company could experience problem recognition by such means as having its packaging equipment break down, planning for the launch of a new product that needs different packaging equipment, or undergoing a series of bad experiences with outside service representatives from its current packaging-machinery supplier. Note that in all these instances, whether external or internal stimuli are involved, problem recognition occurs in order to solve problems or take advantage of new opportunities.

NEED DESCRIPTION

Once problem recognition occurs, the organisation must generally determine the quantity and describe the characteristics of the item needed. This is analogous to the final consumer determining how much of a certain type of product will fit his or her needs, but for the organisation the level of complexity may be much greater. Standard items such as office supplies are comparatively easy to describe by persons involved in the buying process, and they may be obtained from a wide array of roughly equal suppliers. A new weapon system for a branch of the armed services, however, is vastly different, involving perhaps hundreds of people in the general need-description stage to outline the qualities of the product and its required quantities.

PRODUCT SPECIFICATION

After the need has been recognised and described, detailed specifications of the product must be prepared by the using department to communicate precisely what is needed. Sellers have opportunities at this and the previous stage to assist the buyer in describing needs and writing specifications. These specifications may include detailed performance requirements, product attributes and service support needs. For complex products, using departments will typically be involved as well as engineering experts and financial executives.

Value analysis, or *value engineering*, is an analytical tool used to study systematically the costs and benefits of a material, component or machine. It asks what function the item performs and whether a better alternative may be available. The best purchase is a product that will satisfactorily perform this function at the lowest cost without loss of quality. A checklist of questions such as those in Table 19.8 may be used to analyse the item or component. When organisations apply value analysis to their purchasing, they become more aware of substitutability, consolidating, eliminating, simplification and standardisation. Such a buying orientation leads to a continuous search for new materials, processes and products to perform a task better and/or at less cost.

TABLE 19.8   Supplier value-analysis checklist

Name and number _____

Buyer _____

In order to assure the functional usefulness of the above part, we solicit your help through answers to the following questions:

Questions	Check		Suggestions
	Yes	No*	
1. Do you understand part function?			
2. Could costs be reduced by relaxing requirements: Tolerances? Finishes? Testing? By how much?			
3. Could costs be reduced through changes in: Material? Ordering quantities? The use of castings, forgings, stampings etc.? By how much?			

continues

TABLE 19.8   Supplier value-analysis checklist *continued*

Questions	Check		Suggestions
	Yes	No*	

4. Can you suggest any other changes that would:
    Reduce weight?
    Simplify the part?
    Reduce overall costs?
    By how much?			

5. Do you feel that any of the specifications are too stringent?			
6. How can we help alleviate your greatest element of cost in supplying this part?			

7. Do you have a standard item that could be substituted for this part?
    What is it?
    What does it cost?			

8. Other suggestions?			

Supplier _____   Address _____

Signature _____   Title _____   Date _____

*If 'No', functional information can be obtained from buyer involved.

Source: B. Charles Ames & James D. Hlavacek, *Managerial Marketing for Industrial Firms*, Random House, New York, 1984, p. 44.

VENDOR SEARCH

At this stage the organisation tries to identify companies who may be appropriate suppliers of the specified product. For many situations, this stage is closely linked with previous stages. In order for the organisation to write its specifications on complex products, it must start with what products and suppliers currently exist, moving from there to the next stage, which may involve decisions on the 'who' and 'how' of supply for an item that is presently unavailable in the marketplace. Sometimes a company will decide to make it rather than buy it.

Organisational buyers have a wide range of information sources to use in their assessment of products and supplies: visits by sales representatives from potential suppliers, trade shows, trade-publication articles and advertising, direct mailings, professional and technical conferences, Yellow Pages, trade directories and word-of-mouth, to name some of the more significant ones.

Trade exhibitions can be a powerful promotional tool   COURTESY OF EXHIBITIONS AND TRADE PAIRS
PTY LTD

The organisational buyer's evoked set of suppliers or brands will include those who are thought to be able to satisfactorily meet a buyer's requirements. Such suppliers may even be on a list of approved suppliers.[43] Vendors who are on this list or in the buyer's evoked set will face a different and far easier challenge than those who are off the list or outside the buyer's consideration.

The marketer must work to blend the correct promotion mix so that potential buyers are aware of the firm, have a favourable image of it and consider it as a supplier.

PROPOSAL REQUEST

Particularly with new task and modified rebuy situations, the company may next send a request for proposal to qualified vendors asking them to bid based on the product specifications. Suppliers who respond to the request will submit a proposal via perhaps a catalogue, a sales call, or a detailed written offer specifying product or service features, terms of supply and price. Large companies may establish an *approved vendor* list, which limits those who may submit bids on products to carefully chosen suppliers. For example, a fast-food operation may require its franchise outlets to obtain most supplies only from distributors who have been approved through an extensive evaluation process.

VENDOR SELECTION

The supplier/product choice decision is made by one or more members of the buying centre based on the proposals submitted. One conceptualisation of the vendor-selection decision-making process suggests two possible strategies a firm may pursue: simultaneous scanning or sequential evaluation. In simultaneous scanning, a company arrays and reviews potential suppliers at the same time, whereas in sequential evaluation the potential vendors are first ranked and then evaluated sequentially until one is found that satisfies purchase needs. Sequential evaluation would likely occur in the case of straight rebuys or when one supplier is clearly predominant in a market. Simultaneous scanning is likely in a new task buying situation or when several attractive potential vendors are available.[44] One research study discovered that buyers select a few qualified sellers on the basis of such criteria as dependability, reliability, and price, then choose a product from these vendors based on technical specifications.[45]

In addition, the selling firm must recognise that groups in the buying centre have different areas of dominance. For instance, one study learned that engineers and production managers have the greatest influence in the product-selection decision, while purchasing agents are most influential in the selection of a vendor.[46]

There are a number of evaluative criteria used in making the selection of a supplier.[47] Table 19.9 lists some typical attributes considered by the buying centre. Such characteristics may be rated for each supplier in order to select the best candidate. Generally, it appears that the criteria used by the buying centre range in order of importance as follows: product quality, product availability, service capability, vendor reputation, product warranty and price. However, these objective criteria may not always dominate decisions. Research indicates that previous relationships with a supplier and the existence of a well-known name by the vendor can sometimes be more important than such things as price and delivery.[48]

Negotiation with several alternative vendors may also occur at this stage in order to win concessions on price, terms and so on, and perhaps to secure multiple sources of supply. The negotiation process is an important part of industrial buyer and seller relationships that needs to be understood by participants.[49]

PURCHASE-ROUTINE SELECTION

This stage involves placing an order (specifying all terms of purchase) with a vendor who processes it and ships the product. It is then received and approved, and payment is made. Status reports within the company will let management know whether timetables are being met. Rather than writing a purchase order for each purchase in a straight rebuy situation, companies often negotiate a contract to cover purchases over a specific length of time.

POST-PURCHASE EVALUATION

The last step in the purchase decision process involves an evaluation of the supplier's performance by the buyer. This is an important stage in providing feedback so that the buyer and seller will be better able to work as a team. Management may periodically have several departments rate the supplier's performance on

TABLE 19.9 Attributes used to evaluate suppliers

---

1. Overall reputation of the supplier
2. Financing terms
3. Supplier's flexibility in adjusting to your company's needs
4. Experience with the supplier in analogous situations
5. Technical service offered
6. Confidence in the salespeople
7. Convenience of placing the order
8. Data on reliability of the product
9. Price
10. Technical specifications
11. Ease of operation or use
12. Preferences of principal user of the product
13. Training offered by the supplier
14. Training time required
15. Reliability of delivery date promised
16. Ease of maintenance
17. Sales service expected after date of purchase

Source: Donald R. Lehmann & John O'Shaughnessy, 'Difference in Attribute Importance for Different Industrial Products', *Journal of Marketing* 38, April 1974, p. 38, published by the American Marketing Association.

such criteria as product quality, delivery and postsale service. The overall rating developed is used by the buyer to make decisions about continuing to use the supplier or perhaps switching to an alternative source. Vendors may also receive the report so that they can modify their performance where necessary to better serve customers' needs.

SUMMARY

This final chapter departed from the subject of the text to this point by addressing organisational buying behaviour. Although there are commonalities with consumer behaviour, there are enough substantial differences to warrant a separate discussion of the topic. First, the nature of organisational buying was characterised to distinguish it from consumer buying. It differs by purpose (organisational buying is for production, servicing or reselling). We defined it as the decision-making process by which organisations establish the need for purchased products and services, and identify, evaluate, and choose among alternative brands and suppliers. Organisational markets and their buying behaviour were distinguished from consumer markets and their buying behaviour along three dimensions: market structure and demand, buyer characteristics, and decision and buying patterns.

Next, four influences on organisational buying behaviour were described: environmental, organisational, interpersonal and individual. Seven environmental factors were seen to influence organisational buyers: physical, technological, economic, political, legal, ethical and cultural. Four sets of organisational factors affect the buying process: tasks, structure, technology and people involved with buying. Interpersonal factors are very important in the buying decision process as individuals interact with each other in the buying centre. Within the buying centre members play various roles in the decision process, and are able to exert varying levels and types of power on decisions to be made. The last set of factors influencing organisational buying are those related to individuals, including motivation, perception and learning characteristics.

The final portion of this chapter discussed organisational buying decisions. First, types of decision situations were characterised, according to buy-classes, as new task, modified rebuy and straight rebuy. Next, an eight-step organisational buyer's decision process was described, which added greater detail to the four-step model described in earlier chapters for consumers. It included problem recognition, need description, product specification, vendor search, proposal request, vendor selection, purchase-routine selection and postpurchase evaluation.

MANAGERIAL REFLECTIONS

For our product or service situation:

1. How does the market's structure and demand pattern affect our marketing program?

2. Which buyer characteristics are most critical to marketing success?

3. What important decision process and buying pattern differences exist among our customers?

4. Which environmental factors specifically influence potential buyers and what are their effects?

5. How do customers' organisational factors affect their buying decision processes?

6. Who are members of our customers' buying centre and what roles are played?

7. What psychological factors are most relevant to potential organisational buyers?

8. What type of buying decision situation will generally be faced?

9. What decision process do potential buyers typically pursue and how can our marketing strategy successfully influence each step?

DISCUSSION TOPICS

1. How do organisational markets and their buying behaviour differ from those of final consumers? How should industrial vendors consider changing their marketing strategy as a result?

2. How may organisational factors influence industrial buyers?

3. How can the concept of the buying centre be used to better understand and market to organisational buyers?

4. What is the significance of customer hot buttons to the organisational marketer?

5. Characterise the types of organisational buying-decision situations known as buy-classes, and illustrate each with an example. How do these compare with final-consumer buying situations?

6. Describe the steps involved in the organisational buying-decision process.

REFERENCES

1. D. W. Barclay, 'Organisational Buying Outcomes and Their Effects on Subsequent Decisions', *European Journal of Marketing* 26 (4), 1992, pp. 48–64.
2. Frederick E. Webster Jr & Yoram Wind, *Organizational Buying Behavior*, Prentice-Hall, Englewood Cliffs, NJ, 1972, p. 2.
3. Dean S. Ammer, 'Top Management's View of the Purchasing Function', *Journal of Purchasing and Materials Management* 25, Spring 1989, pp. 16–21; and Gregory D. Upah & Monroe M. Bird, 'Changes in Industrial Buying: Implications for Industrial Marketers', *Industrial Marketing Management* 9, 1980, pp. 117–21.
4. Ernest F. Cooke, 'What Is Business and Industrial Marketing?', *Industrial Marketing Management* 1, Fall 1986, pp. 9–17.
5. See Edward F. Fern & James R. Brown, 'The Industrial/Consumer Marketing Dichotomy: A Case of Insufficient Justification', *Journal of Marketing* 48, Spring 1984, pp. 68–77, for a challenge to the industrial/consumer classification dichotomy.
6. W. S. Penn Jr & Mark Mougel, 'Industrial Marketing Myths', *Industrial Marketing Management* 7, 1978, pp. 133–4.
7. Jon M. Hawes & Scott H. Barnhouse, 'How Purchasing Agents Handle Personal Risk', *Industrial Marketing Management* 16, November 1987, pp. 287–93.
8. William Atkinson, 'Know Thy Customer: Purchasers Redefine Supplier Relationships', *Management Review*, August 1989, pp. 18–22.
9. Atkinson, ibid, pp. 18–22.
10. These categories were first suggested by Frederick E. Webster Jr & Yoram Wind, 'A General Model for Understanding Organizational Buying Behavior', *Journal of Marketing* 36, April 1972, pp. 12–19.
11. I. Frederick Trawick Jr, John E. Swan & David R. Rink, 'Back-door Selling: Violation of Cultural versus Professional Ethics by Salespeople and Purchaser Choice of the Supplier', *Journal of Business Research* 17, November 1988, pp. 299–309.
12. Robert E. Spekman & Louis W. Stern, 'Environmental Uncertainty and Buying Group Structure: An Empirical Investigation', *Journal of Marketing* 43, Spring 1979, pp. 54–64.
13. W. E. Patton III, Christopher P. Puto & Ronald H. King, 'Which Buying Decisions Are Made by Individuals and Not by Groups', *Industrial Marketing Management* 15, 1986, pp. 129–38.
14. Wesley J. Johnston & Thomas V. Bonoma, 'Purchase Process for Capital Equipment and Services', *Industrial Marketing Management* 10, 1981, pp. 253–64.
15. Melvin R. Mattson, 'How to Determine the Composition and Influence of a Buying Center', *Industrial Marketing Management* 17, 1988, pp. 205–14; and Joseph A. Bellizzi & C. K. Walter, 'Purchasing Agent's Influence in the Buying Process', *Industrial Marketing Management* 9, 1980, pp. 137–41.
16. R. W. Lawson & D. Taylor, 'George Hobson Ltd', in L. Moutinho (ed.), *Cases in Marketing*, Addison-Wesley, pp. 58–9.
17. Julia M. Bristor & Michael J. Ryan, 'The Buying Center Is Dead, Long Live the Buying Center', in Melanie Walendorf & Paul Anderson (eds), *Advances in Consumer Research*, vol. 14, Association for Consumer Research, Provo, UT, 1987, pp. 255–8; and Robert E. Spekman & Kjell Grønhaug, 'Conceptual and Methodological Issues in Buying Center Research', *European Journal of Marketing*, 7 November 1986, pp. 50–65.
18. John R. Ronchetto Jr, Michael D. Hutt & Peter H. Reingen, 'Embedded Influence Patterns in Organizational Buying Systems', *Journal of Marketing* 53, October 1989, pp. 51–62.
19. Robert E. Krapfel Jr, 'An Extended Interpersonal Influence Model of Organizational Buying Behaviour', *Journal of Business Research* 10, 1982, pp. 147–57.
20. Yoram Wind & Thomas S. Robertson, 'The Linking Pin Role in Organizational Buying Centers', *Journal of Business Research* 10, 1982, pp. 169–84.

21. Ronald H. Gorman, 'Role Conception and Purchasing Behavior', *Journal of Purchasing* 7, February 1971, pp. 57–61.
22. Jagdish N. Sheth, 'A Model of Industrial Buyer Behavior', *Journal of Marketing* 37, October 1973, p. 37.
23. Ralph L. Day, Ronald E. Michaels & Barbara C. Perdue, 'How Buyers Handle Conflicts', *Industrial Marketing Management* 17, May 1988, pp. 153–60.
24. Ronald E. Michaels, Ralph L. Day & Erich A. Joachimsthaler, 'Role Stress among Industrial Buyers: An Integrative Model', *Journal of Marketing* 51, April 1987, pp. 28–45.
25. John P. Grashof & Gloria P. Thomas, 'Industrial Buying Center Responsibilities: Self versus Other Member Evaluations of Importance', in Kenneth L. Bernhardt (ed.), *Proceedings*, American Marketing Association, Chicago, 1976, pp. 344–9.
26. Robert E. Weigand, 'Identifying Industrial Buying Responsibility', *Journal of Marketing Research* 3, February 1966, pp. 31–84.
27. Robert J. Thomas, 'Bases of Power in Organizational Buying Decisions', *Industrial Marketing Management* 13, 1984, pp. 209–17.
28. Ajay Kohli, 'Determinants of Influence in Organizational Buying: A Contingency Approach', *Journal of Marketing* 53, July 1989, pp. 50–65.
29. Thomas V. Bonoma & Wesley J. Johnston, 'The Social Psychology of Industrial Buying and Selling', *Industrial Marketing Management* 17, 1978, pp. 213–24.
30. Bonoma, ibid, p. 118.
31. Webster & Wind, op cit, Ref 2.
32. Paul F. Anderson & Terry M. Chambers, 'A Reward/Measurement Model of Organizational Buying Behavior', *Journal of Marketing* 49, Spring 1985, pp. 7–23.
33. H. Michael Hayes & Steven W. Hartley, 'How Buyers View Industrial Salespeople', *Industrial Marketing Management* 18, 1980, pp. 73–80.
34. Patrick J. Robinson, Charles W. Faris & Yoram Wind, *Industrial Buying and Creative Marketing*, Allyn & Bacon, Boston, 1967.
35. Peter Doyle, Arch G. Woodside & Paul Michell, 'Organizations Buying in New Task and Rebuy Situations', *Industrial Marketing Management* 8, 1979, pp. 7–11.
36. R. Roberts, The Organisational Purchase Decision for Market Research Services, Department of Marketing Research thesis, University of Otago, Dunedin, 1994.
37. Earl Naumann, Douglas J. Lincoln & Robert D. McWilliams, 'The Purchase of Components: Functional Areas of Influence', *Industrial Marketing Management* 13, 1984, pp. 113–22; and Jack Pingry, 'The Engineer and Purchasing Agent Compared', *Journal of Purchasing* 10, November 1974, pp. 33–45.
38. Lowell E. Crow & Jay D. Lindquist, 'Impact of Organizational and Buyer Characteristics on the Buying Center', *Industrial Marketing Management* 14, 1985, pp. 49–58.
39. Joseph Bellizzi & Phillip McVey, 'How Valid Is the Buygrid Model?', *Industrial Marketing Management* 12, February 1983, pp. 57–62; Wade Ferguson, 'An Evaluation of the Buygrid Framework', *Industrial Marketing Management* 8, January 1979, pp. 40–4; Donald W. Jackson Jr, Janet E. Keith & Richard K. Burdick, 'Purchasing Agents Perceptions of Industrial Buying Center Influence: A Situational Approach', *Journal of Marketing* 48, Fall 1984, pp. 78–83; and Wolfgang U. Mayer, 'Situational Variables and Industrial Buying', *Journal of Purchasing and Materials Management* 19, Winter 1983, pp. 21–5.
40. Erin Anderson, Wujin Chu & Barton Weitz, 'Industrial Purchasing: An Empirical Exploration of the Buyclass Framework', *Journal of Marketing* 51, July 1987, pp. 71–86; Alvin Silk & Manohar Kalwani, 'Measuring Influence in Organizational Purchase Decisions', *Journal of Marketing Research* 19, May 1982, pp. 165–81; and Wesley J. Johnston, 'Industrial Buying Behavior: A State-of-the-art Review', in Ben M. Enis & Kenneth J. Roering (eds), *Review of Marketing*, American Marketing Association, Chicago, 1981, pp. 75–88.

41. Daniel H. McQuiston, 'Novelty, Complexity, and Importance as Causal Determinants of Industrial Buyer Behavior', *Journal of Marketing* 53, April 1989, pp. 66–79; R. Roberts, The Organisational Purchase Decision for Market Research Services, Department of Marketing Research thesis, University of Otago, Dunedin, 1994.

42. See, for example, Robinson, Faris & Wind, *Industrial Buying and Creative Marketing*; and Yoram Wind & Robert J. Thomas, 'Conceptual and Methodological Issues in Organizational Buying Behavior', *European Journal of Marketing* 14, May–June 1989, pp. 239–63.

43. Ralph W. Jackson & William M. Pride, 'The Use of Approved Vendor Lists', *Industrial Marketing Management* 15, 1986, pp. 165–9.

44. Richard N. Cardozo, 'Segmenting the Industrial Market', in Robert L. King (ed.), *Proceedings*, American Marketing Association, Chicago, 1968; and Richard N. Cardozo & James W. Cagley, 'Experimental Study of Industrial Buying Behavior', *Journal of Marketing Research* 8, August 1971, pp. 329–34.

45. Lowell E. Crow, Richard W. Olshavsky & John O. Summers, 'Industrial Buyers Choice Strategies: A Protocol Analysis', *Journal of Marketing Research* 17, February 1980, pp. 34–44; and Niren Vyas & Arch G. Woodside, 'An Inductive Model of Industrial Supplier Choice Processes', *Journal of Marketing* 48, Winter 1984, pp. 30–45.

46. Jackson Jr, Keith & Burdick, op cit, Ref 39, pp. 75–83.

47. Christopher P. Puto, Wesley E. Patton III & Ronald H. King, 'Risk Handling Strategies in Industrial Vendor Selection Decisions', *Journal of Marketing* 49, Winter 1985, pp. 89–98.

48. Richard N. Cardozo & James W. Cagley, 'Experimental Study of Industrial Buyer Behavior', *Journal of Marketing Research* 8, August 1971, pp. 329–34; and Guy R. Banville & Ronald J. Dornoff, 'Industrial Source Selection Behavior—An Industry Study', *Industrial Marketing Management* 2, 1973, pp. 251–60.

49. Paul A. Dion & Peter M. Banting, 'Industrial Supplier–Buyer Negotiations', *Industrial Marketing Management* 17, February 1988, pp. 43–7.

CASE STUDIES

WHICH PHOTOCOPIER TO BUY?

Ted Bear is general manager of a small, financially sound light-engineering company. There are increasing demands for photocopying, and the present Canon machine is consistently requiring repair, which means that it is nearing the end of its economic life. Margaret, the office manager, has successfully argued the case for a replacement on the grounds of reliability, the type of work required and the speed with which it is required.

Drawing upon their own knowledge and the suggestions of the office secretary, who does a lot of the work, Ted and Margaret have drawn up the specifications. The machine must:

1. be capable of 60 copies per minute;
2. be able to handle A3 and A4 paper size;
3. have a sorter function;
4. be capable of printing on both sides automatically;
5. be able to be serviced locally;
6. hopefully cost around $15 000 or less.

All capital expenditure over $10 000 has to have board approval.

The organisation has a good relationship with the Canon people and the managers of both organisations know each other well. As the board is involved, the office manager has invited written quotations from a number of potential suppliers, including Minolta, Gestetner, Fuji and Xerox. All have been given the above specifications upon which to base their quotation.

All of the companies respond by first visiting the organisation to discuss the requirements with the office manager. Some such as Xerox and Fuji offer to have a trial machine installed, and talk to the office secretary. For some reason the secretary takes a dislike to the representative from Fuji. The office manager goes to all the suppliers to have a demonstration. The particular Xerox model is not yet available for demonstration.

All the quotations arrive on time apart from Xerox's, which requires a follow-up call, and can be classified according to Table 1 below:

Table 1   Summary of photocopier quotations from five companies

	Canon	Fuji	Gestetner	Minolta	Xerox
Speed (copies)	90/min	75/min	80/min	80/min	50/min
Meets other requirements	Yes	Yes	Yes	Yes	Yes
Service contract	1c/copy	1c/copy	1c/copy	1c/copy	1st year free 1c/copy
Local service	Yes	Yes	Yes	Yes	Yes
Guarantee	2 years	1 year	2 years	3 years	2 years
Delivery	Immediate	Immediate	1 week	Immediate	Next shipment
Price ($)	19 600	14 500	15 200	17 800	9 800
Other	Technically superior	Good support	Good demo	Excellent reputation	New model

After discussions with the general manager regarding the quotations, it is decided to call Canon and ask them to reconsider their offer in the light of there being such a significant difference in price between the various quotations. The Gestetner sales manager calls to discuss her company's quotation and offers to look at the margins when told who the competition are and that they are not the cheapest. Canon requote in the light of the information that they have received. Gestetner's requote is $14 800 and Canon's is $15 100. The sales manager from Xerox offers a free trial when a machine is available.

The Canon machine breaks down again and the secretary gets annoyed that she is being held up and that others are complaining about the lack of photocopying facilities. The office manager explains that an analysis has been done and that a decision will be made at the board meeting next week where the facts will be presented.

QUESTIONS

1. What is the buying centre for this purchase?

2. Summarise the buying decision process.

3. What is your recommendation for purchase, and why?

This case study was prepared by James Henry, Department of Marketing, University of Otago, New Zealand.

CASE 2 HAHN BEER ADVERTISING

In 1990 the Advertising Standards Council received a number of complaints regarding an outdoor advertisement in New South Wales for Hahn beer. The content of the advertisement is summarised in the following extract from one complainant's submission:

It portrays a male Negro with facial characteristics which happen to be part of his culture. On his extended lip is displayed a bottle of Hahn beer. The caption reads 'get your laughing gear around this'.

The complainant went on to argue that there were two things to laugh at in the implied message, and that it was demeaning using people from other cultures in that way.

The deputy leader of the Opposition in New South Wales also passed comment on the advertisement, saying:

The beer bottle placed on the top lip is in extremely bad taste, and would not be tolerated if it sent up rituals less foreign to our society. This sort of advertising draws on the same racial stereotyping that products such as 'nigger boy soap pads' and 'darkie toothpaste' once used. In a multiracial society I would have thought that we would have outgrown such paternalistic attitudes.

The chairman of the Ethnic Affairs Commission of New South Wales alleged that the advertisement:

. . . is a clear example of appealing to racist stereotypes. The image depicted . . . undermines the dignity of indigenous people and is therefore both racially offensive and insulting.

Other complainants said:

The man in the picture has ceased to be a human being; he is a prop, a mere support for the beer bottle.

To have a black face making googly eyes with beer perched in his lip plate is extremely insulting and silly . . . it reeks of entertainment for the white man and denotes a black servant mentality with the carrying of beer on the tray [lip plate].

In considering these complaints, the Advertising Standards Council took into account the following submission from the black talent appearing in the advertisement:

[Named complainant] has said that he feels the ads are racist, offensive and were making out that black people were less intelligent and dignified than others. It

seems to me that these feelings are not written into the ads but are read into them by people who are not quite in touch with their own feelings regarding racism. People such as [these] should explore their own feelings regarding different races and how they are treated. I will go further to say that I feel these people are grandstanding on a non-issue and believe that they would best serve our multiracial communities by standing up for and embracing some real racial issues which affect us directly every day.

[Named complainant] said that he believes everyone should be treated equally but by his actions is actually ensuring that people treat black people differently. He has singled out these advertisements and is treating black people as oversensitive and being unable to laugh at themselves.

The Hahn ad is clearly written to be humorous in a most straightforward manner. It cannot be considered offensive or racist because a black man (rather than a laid-back typical white Aussie) is making a humorous (and typically Australian) comment about Hahn beer.

I would consider that the job of the Advertising Standards Council is to ensure that the standards you set are applied to all ads equally . . . The beer ads should not be treated differently just because they involve black men as opposed to white Australians.

I feel that the few high-profile people who oppose these advertisements are being oversensitive and are themselves displaying a racist attitude by singling out these ads and trying to get them withdrawn. Surely they could easily be accused of inciting racial disharmony in this manner.

If these advertisements were withdrawn, you would not only be saying that black people should be treated differently, you would also be sending out a clear message to the advertising agencies that they could be risking many thousands of dollars if they were to use a black person in the ads because of possible racial implications.

QUESTIONS

1. Summarise the main issues that form this case.

2. What advice would you offer the Advertising Standards Council regarding the continuance or withdrawal of the Hahn advertising? What reasons would you give to support your advice?

This case study was adapted from the Advertising Standards Council Case Report, November & December, 1990.

INDEX